The Horseman's Companion

EDITED BY DORIAN WILLIAMS

The Horseman's Companion

ST. MARTIN'S PRESS
NEW YORK

LIBRARY OF CONGRESS
CATALOG CARD NO.: 80-52657

Williams, Dorian
   The Horseman's Companion.

New York : St. Martin's
290 p.
8103   800625

Contents

Part I
The Horse in History and Legend

Part II
Equestrian Lore

Part III

Famous Horses and Horsemen

Part IV

Great Races

Part V

Horse and Hound

8 CONTENTS

Part VI

The Horse in Fiction

Part VII

The Horse in Verse

Illustrations

Acknowledgements and thanks for permission to reproduce drawings are due to
the Trustees of the British Museum for 'Copenhagen' by James Ward, R.A. (published by R. Ackermann) and 'York Meeting' (published by R. Cribb, jr); to
Mr Charles Banks Wilson for 'Mustangs' from *The Mustangs* by J. Frank Dobie
(Hammond, Hammond, 1954); and to Mrs Lionel Edwards for 'Escaping fox' by
the late Lionel Edwards, R.I. from *More Shires and Provinces* by 'Sabretache' (Eyre
& Spottiswoode, 1928.)

'Przevalski's horse' is from *The Horse Through the Ages* by Cecil G. Trew (Methuen's
Outlines, reprinted 1963); 'Knights in combat' from *Lyfe of saynt George* by Baptista
Spagnuola (printed by Richard Pynson [1515?]); 'First day of the season' and 'A
horse with only one fault', both by John Leech, from *Handley Cross* by R. S. Surtees
(1854); 'The White Knight' by Sir John Tenniel from *Through the Looking-Glass and
What Alice Found There* by Lewis Carroll (1872); and 'Pageantry' from *Robert the
deuyll* (printed by Jan van Wynkyn de Worde, [1517?]).

Other decorations are from *Handbook of Early Advertising Art* by Clarence P.
Hornung (3rd ed., New York, Dover Publications; London, Constable, 1956);
A Source Book of French Advertising Art compiled by Irving Zucker (Faber, 1964);
and *1800 Woodcuts by Thomas Bewick and his School* (New York, Dover Publications,
1962; London, Constable).

The Horseman's Companion

Introduction to the Second Edition

There can be no doubt that the compiler of an anthology gets more pleasure from it than anyone else. Not only does he have the pleasure of reading and re-reading all the material that eventually constitutes the finished article, but in addition he gets almost equal pleasure from reading much that is regretfully discarded: pleasure that is only slightly tempered by the knowledge that almost certainly many people will be looking in vain for pieces that, in their opinion, could not possibly be omitted.

One hopes, of course, that such readers will be compensated by the rediscovery of something that they had forgotten, or by being introduced to something new.

In compiling this Companion I have attempted to include both the fairly – and rightly – obvious with the less well known, even the completely unknown. Obviously the browser must be able to turn at once to Trollope and Surtees, to Will Ogilvie and Whyte Melville, and to the pundits from Xenophon to Fillis and Wynmalen. But it may also be intriguing to discover the wit of 'Gambado' and Damon Runyon, the expert approach of D. H. Lawrence and Enid Bagnold, the eye for equine detail in Daphne du Maurier and the charming, unexpected versifying of Charles Kingsley.

Other names may be safely anticipated – George Borrow, Somerville and Ross, Rudyard Kipling, Nimrod, Nat Gould – but the chosen extracts from their works may be a little unexpected.

It is scarcely necessary to remind readers of the enormous amount of literature inspired by the horse and the various sports and activities associated with the horse. Apart from the fact that anyone who is anyone in the world of horses in our own century appears to feel it obligatory to put himself into print sooner or later, either with instruction or reminiscences, most writers of distinction in earlier days at one time or another wrote about horses because horses were a part of their lives.

Of the former, only those generally accepted as qualified to theorize and capable of writing as well as riding have been included. Of the latter, although literally hundreds of thousands of words have had to be consumed only to be discarded, the happy result is that one is in a position to quote passages, short or not so short, from authors whose names are household words but not usually connected with horses: Henry Fielding, Sir Walter Scott, Charles Dickens, Anthony Trollope, Lewis Carroll, R. D. Blackmore, Winston Churchill.

Although it has to be admitted that, except for the purely factual works of instruction, our own times are not so rich in good writing about horses as was the case in the past, yet we are fortunate in having a small number of exceptionally talented authors whose skill with their pen is equal to their skill in the saddle: notably John Lawrence, who writes as Audax in *Horse and Hound* and as Marlborough in the *Daily Telegraph* and who has brought a unique distinction to the art of racing journalism; Dick Francis, who was at one time not so long ago Champion National Hunt Jockey and immemorially associated with the Queen Mother's Devon Loch, also a journalist now, but more important a very successful and competent novelist.

With such an enormous amount of material available, obviously it must be sorted into parts. It would be possible, of course, to multiply the parts, and again one is necessarily forced to be somewhat arbitrary in one's arrangements, but on the whole the subject does generally allow it to be broken up into seven groups.

Firstly, there is *The Horse in History and Legend*. As the horse was taken for granted for so many centuries people did not habitually eulogize about their horses, and although it might be recorded that Alexander had a horse called Bucephalus, little is known of the horse itself. Fortunately, considerable research on the origins and development of the horse has been carried on in recent years, and it is possible therefore to include fascinating accounts of the early American horse, the Mustang, and the horse in Russia and Mongolia. In a more plebian manner it is possible, too, to read of the carriage horse and charger, their feats and their background.

Particularly charming are some of the legends concerned with the horse, two of the most enchanting coming not surprisingly from Ireland and Japan, though whether Corporal Ashihei Hino's touching little tale (included in Part III) is fact or fiction must be left to the opinion of each individual reader.

Secondly, what one might call *Equestrian Lore*. All down the ages horsemen have felt compelled to set down for the benefit of others their own ideas regarding almost every aspect of horses and horsemanship. What is so interesting is that one frequently finds that the theories of the very earliest writers – Xenophon, for instance – are still held and respected today. Again one finds theories dearly held and propounded with the utmost urgency in one generation totally discarded and discredited by the next generation.

This is in many ways the charm of equestrianism: even after many thousands of years of association with the horse, people, even the greatest experts, differ on the best ways of breaking, schooling and riding it. Names such as Rodzianko, Wynmalen and Fillis inevitably find a place in this section: also the mythical 'Gambado', who, of course, was freely quoted by Mr Jorrocks in Surtees' *Handley Cross*. Allegedly he was a great expert with, to put it mildly, the strangest ideas and theories. In fact, there was no such person. He was invented by an anonymous editor – Henry William Bunbury – in 1787 to pull the leg of those who, then as today, liked to set themselves up as authorities and expressed themselves at length in books and treatises.

He is described as equerry to the Doge of Venice, a position he never filled, being shipwrecked en route and drowned, having 'mounted himself on the largest saddle he could find, and taking a bridle in one hand and a paper case in the other, desired to be thrown into the sea'. This was complied with, but the informant adds that the boatswain being somewhat desirous to save his life likewise, 'hastily jumped up behind the unfortunate Gambado', and he apprehends that the saddle, though new and large, was not master of his additional weight, 'for it dropped with such precipitancy as to throw our author out of his seat, and his foot catching and hanging in the stirrup, soon put an end to this mortal'.

And it must be confessed that he made his exit 'en parfait cavalier', and 'an honour to his leather he was'. But not equerry to the Doge. Fortunately, however, his 'papers' were rescued and produced in two volumes, *An Academy for Grown Horsemen* (1787), and the *Annals of Horsemanship* (1791) – letters with extra-ordinary problems addressed to Gambado which he answers. It is all a brilliant and most amusing take-off of the so serious writers often associated with horses. For the same reason Colonel Lyon's return tilt at those who for so long have discussed the pros and cons of the forward seat finds a place.

Obviously there had to be parts for *The Horse in Fiction* and for *Famous Horses and Horsemen*. In the former an attempt has been made not only to cover short stories connected with horses, such as those classics by 'Saki', D. H. Lawrence and Rudyard Kipling, and extracts from larger fiction such as 'The First Ride' from *Lavengro*, and 'The Highwayman's Mare' from *Lorna Doone*; but also to give coverage to the whole range of taste from youth, even extreme youth, to maturity. Hence the thrilling fire scenes from *Black Beauty*; and, interestingly, an extract from a book about its author, Anna Sewell, *The Woman who wrote Black Beauty*. How that description of the fire kept me awake at night as a child of ten or so! Also a lovely story by Ernest Hemingway, 'War Cloud', and a little known story by Turgenev, 'Lebedyan'. There is also 'The White Knight', though this is as much included because of its in-comparable wit. Then there are the classics to which somewhat reluctantly one was introduced at school; and finally there are the modern novelists, all of whom represented can talk convincingly of horses and riders even if equestrianism plays only a small part in their respective books.

In *Famous Horses and Horsemen* my choice has been inevitably more contemporary, mainly because there is little factual writing about the legendary horses of the past. Fortunately, though, there is a good deal of material available concerning some of the legendary horsemen of previous ages and, particularly fascinating, on some of the great jockeys, Archer, Tod Sloan, Donoghue. And in view of the immense popularity of show jumping today, it seems right to include in this section some of the spate of writing about this sport and various events connected with it that has appeared during the last ten years, spotlighting as it does, so to speak, many of the personalities, equine and human, that have become household names: Alwin Schockemöhle and, in a rather different way, the legendary Colonel Sir Michael Ansell, who, though blind, for twenty-five years dominated the show-jumping scene.

Hunting and racing are such specialist aspects of horsemanship that each is entitled to its own section. Indeed, the Chase has inspired a unique literature all its own. Hunting people, it seems, were not always the illiterate morons that many today would have us believe.

I have already mentioned Trollope and Surtees, Whyte Melville, and Fielding. They are, as it were, universal. I have mentioned, too, Somerville and Ross. Their *Experiences of an Irish R.M.* is a classic; but an equally delightful tale of Irish hunting is Marigold Armitage's *A Long Way to Go*. The north country can enjoy fame for its incredible run described by Alfred Pease; while the Shires are well represented in the famous Frank Freeman story, in Squire Osbaldeston's long-distance feat and in the Pytchley 'Dream' with which Whyte Melville commences his great Civil War book, *Holmby House*.

Siegfried Sassoon brings great distinction to the hunting scene and the Weald of Kent with his *Memoirs of a Fox-Hunting Man*, and his 'first day' will, I hope, make an interesting contrast with my own description of a great professional huntsman's last day: Will Pope with the Grafton.

Racing on the whole does not appear to inspire or to lend itself to great writing. Neither Edgar Wallace nor Nat Gould quote well, but there is a wealth of first-class journalism that creates the very breath of the race course, none being superior to that of John Lawrence. Equally successful is the trainer turned journalist, Ivor Herbert. The extract from his book on Red Rum is particularly interesting in that it quotes verbatim from the television commentary on his great win in 1973. Chris Collins's brilliant account of the Pardubice is also a superb example of 'I was there' journalism.

The final section is verse. Many people will feel that verse connected with horses is more notable for quantity than for quality; and yet there is much that is attractive and full of feeling. Will H. Ogilvie, for instance, catches the very essence of horses and hunting. In the same way Lionel Edwards may not be a Munnings, but he portrays with accuracy and feeling the hunting field. Will Ogilvie is the Lionel Edwards of verse.

One's great hope in compiling an anthology is that one is giving people the opportunity of renewing acquaintances with old friends, at the same time making new ones. So often one borrows a book, or perhaps one is given one for Christmas, reads it and then discards it, intending to return to it later to enjoy again some passage that has particularly impressed one. Somehow one seldom does. An anthology of this sort should enable one to do just that, to return to passages that at some time in one's life have given one pleasure. One hopes, too, that an extract from a book that is new to one will prompt one to turn to the original, thus making a new friend.

Inevitably for every passage included in this book there will be a passage that someone will feel has wrongly been omitted. Such a book can but be a personal selection. As I said earlier, only the compiler will get complete satisfaction, but I hope that there is enough in *The Horseman's Companion*, and of sufficient variety, to ensure that most readers will find something to their satisfaction.

Foscote, 1978   DORIAN WILLIAMS

PART I

The Horse in History and Legend

Das Urwildpferd

[*A note on the behaviour of* Equus przevalskii przevalskii Poljakoff, *the prehistoric wild horse of Mongolia, found today in many zoological gardens, including Whipsnade. The brothers Gr. and M. Grim. Grshimailo, about 100 years ago, observed the wild horse in his haunts, the steppe near the Tachin-Shara-Nuru mountains. These horses have now been hunted to extinction.*]

It was interesting to watch the behaviour of the stallion. When he sensed danger he gave the herd a sign by snorting and at once the horses followed single file, a young stallion in the lead and the foals in the middle between the mares. As long as the herd was on the move and the hunters were on one side, the stallion remained on this side, driving the herd before him, first with his head, then by striking with his forelegs in the direction of the track that he wished them to follow. When the horses had broken through the chain of hunters and men were hunting them from behind, the stallion stood on guard in the way of those following.

It was funny to see how he tried to drive a tiny foal on that could not reach the others on its weak legs. When the foal really began to hang behind, the dam tried to encourage it by whinnying to it. When she saw that this did not help, she left the herd, obviously unwilling to leave her child behind. But the stallion refused to allow this sort of disorder and with two forceful strikes with his forelegs he made her gallop back to the herd and himself undertook the care of the foal. At first he pushed it along with his nose, then he seized it by the withers and pulled it along, and then he tried to animate it by seizing it and throwing it into the air.

Dr Erna Mohr

The Origin of the Horse

WALTER PRESCOTT WEBB

The origin of the horse, like most other origins, is lost in antiquity. Early cave men in France were familiar with him, as is shown by pictures etched in the rocks; but to these men the horse was merely game. Fossil remains indicate that horses roamed over both North America and South America, to disappear before Columbus came and probably before the Indians themselves arrived. These horses, in both France and America, belonged to the pre-domestic period and are of no interest to the historian. It is only when man and horse became associated that the horse has much interest for the anthropologist and the historian. That association seems to have originated in Asia and to have spread thence to Europe, Africa, and later to America.

The point of emphasis here is that the association of man and horse apparently arose in an environment very similar to the Great Plains of America; that is, in the steppes of Asia. Clark Wissler says in *Man and Culture*:

> Upon most maps of Asia will be found a region just east of the Caspian Sea labelled the Kirghiz Steppes. If the map also delineates the general topography, it will show a great stretch of plain which is in the main grass land, varying in fertility from arid spots in Turkestan, on the south, to rich open prairie-like lands in south-western Siberia. Somewhere in this great area, at some remote period, horse culture arose.

This description of the steppes of Asia would apply equally well to the Great Plains.

These wild horsemen of the steppes extended their forays in every direction. The Huns came west into Europe; other tribes passed eastwards into China, compelling the Chinese to erect the Great Wall on their northern border. Others harried Chaldea, and the wild Kassites introduced their horse culture into Babylon two thousand years before our era. After that time the use of the horse can be traced to Egypt, to Greece, and to the modern nations. Wissler says that horse culture was borrowed in practically every case as a military expedient which would enable the settled peoples to repel or contend with the mounted invaders.

In such a primitive society the mounted man had a great advantage in warfare, particularly in an open country. History relates that the Frankish kings took the Church treasures in order that they might be able to send horsemen to meet the Saracens from Spain. Chivalry itself was but the recognition of the value of horsemanship in war, but it was horsemanship in a country not primarily suited to horses; hence, perhaps, its artificial nature and its decline under peals of laughter aroused by the fine satire and broad burlesque of Cervantes. Wissler makes the further point:

> The horse was a different thing to the wild nomad, on the one hand, and the Egyptian (or the civilized man), on the other. To the Egyptian he was a mere fighting machine and so but a military incident in Egyptian life, but to the nomad, the horse was as much a part of individual life as his master's boots. From what glimpses we have of the ancient nomad life it seems that everybody rode at all times, in fact lived on horseback. Hence, for the nomad to fight as cavalry was the natural or only way, for the truth of the matter is that his whole life was adjusted to the horse rather than to fighting. When he moved about, he rode; when he indulged in sport, he also rode; and when he met with dangers, the chances are that he was mounted.

To put the matter briefly, there arose in Europe two traditions of horsemanship, or horse culture – the one that of a settled people with whom horses were but one of the incidents of life, and the other the tradition of the nomadic people to whom horses were vital. Both traditions found their way to America, and each found its appropriate environment. The 'civilized' culture came through Europe to England and found lodgment in the English colonies of the Atlantic coast; the nomadic horse culture came from the Asiatic steppes to the plains of Arabia, thence across northern Africa to Spain, and with the Spaniards to the pampas of South America and to the Plains of the United States. It would not be far wrong to name one the horse culture of the woodland, and the other that of the plains. Certain it is that a plains environment exists through much of Spain, North Africa, Arabia, and in the steppes of Asia where men and horses first became associated as masters and servants.

from THE GREAT PLAINS *1931*

Tarpán – A Mongolian Legend

JOSÉ ANTONIO BENTON

The Torguts belong to the Mongols. In the days of yore they roamed through the central Asia Steppe as nomads without any idea of time – men, women, camels, horses and cattle. You could find them in Tibet, Tangut and Turan. That is why they were then called Turagets: 'the people from Turan'. Sometimes they were called: Turscythians.

Their horses were medium-sized with neat heads, good shoulders, straight backs and hard legs. Their tails were plaited up with silken threads and that is how they were recognized.

They thought it humiliating to settle down in one place. Altogether they owned 180,000 tents, 1,000,000, camels, 4,000,000 horses and 15,000,000 cows, bullocks, oxen, sheep and goats. An incredibly dusty, tumultuous crowd. They possessed neither carts nor waggons.

When they were on the move or at rest, they were divided into *Ulus*, which means tribes. The tribe of Torgut owned 7,674 tents; Loosang 1,800; Jäldäng 3,785; Oooli 2,000. There were others as well which were called: Baaron, Jandyk, Menghön, Dipson, also Tugul, Usengut and Ulan. Much earlier all these tribes had been nations. But their legends say that they were all descended from Irgit, of whom no one can say whether she was mortal or the terrestrial Moon-goddess herself.

Their way lay across the Ula-nor lake and the Koko-nor, the Tibetan Blue Lake to the Ebi-nor. Then in half-circle westwards through the yellow sandy wastes as far as the river Sary-Su. They crossed the Irtysch on floating bridges and later the Jamba.

They were wonderfully rustic men, who liked work, with a great power of imagination, bow-legged and proud. Their riding-boots were made of red morocco leather and decorated with silver. Their trousers lay in a thousand folds – they were so wide, and they were held up with gold-embroidered girdles, hung with long cords and tassels, and rolls of tobacco for their pipes. They loved the taste of tobacco on their tongues.

Their long tunics were blue and made of silk and the Turkish-Mongolian broadsword hung nearly to their feet. Their high-boned faces were sun-burned, they wore moustaches with the points turned downward past their chins, twisted to a half-circle. On their heads they wore sheep-skin caps, set at an angle with the tip enclosed by a golden ring. Gold over red and blue – a brave, quaint rather barbaric sight.

At last in the year 1560, they arrived on the banks of the Jaïk, the river-frontier of the Urals, between Europe and Asia. The Ruler in Russia at this time was Iveen Wasilovviz, who called himself 'Gossudar' – the master, and whom people called 'Sudebnik', which means 'the law-book'.

The Torguts themselves maintain that Torgut means 'bred from a stallion'. Stallion is the same as Tarpán.

This Irgit then, of whom no one knows the origin, was the wife of the 'maimed Oerlik'. Oerlik's tribe was made up of oxen, bullocks, cows, silver, gold, young men and maidens, camels and donkeys. He owned no horses. Altogether he possessed 6,000 sheep; 7,000 head of cattle; 8,000 she-donkeys and 5,000 girls who were virgin. He was broad-shouldered, rather bent and dragged his right foot. He was also a man of few words and generally silent. He hunted with hounds and tried to forge black iron. Also he was unable to grow a beard.

One day Irgit and her shepherdesses went together to a lovely grove to talk. And there appeared three shining women with wings, flying over the clearing. Their breasts were bare, their bodies white and they were dressed in pure linen. They said to Irgit: 'We know how sad you are that you have no son. Go early tomorrow morning to the Lake called Ulan-or. There you will see a strong and spirited animal, a deer without horns. Go up to it. You will have a son.'

Irgit asked if these things were not forbidden. But the celestial women only laughed, instead of answering.

Irgit was quite a young woman and clearly a princess as well. Although small, she was strong with the little feet of a half-grown girl. She had lovely big eyes, with scarcely any lids. On her head she wore the golden coil decorated with turquoises. Her hair was combed out behind her ears and held in a clasp. The effect was almost like the horns of a mountain sheep.

Next day the air was warm and Irgit asked Oerlik if she should not go to the Lake Ulan-or? Oerlik lay in his tent on his cushions, with his hounds all round him. She said: 'I wish you would get up.' Oerlik replied: 'But I am very comfortable here.'

So she went slowly over the hills to the lake and called through her cupped hands. 'Oh, where are you, deer without horns?' Perhaps it would not come after all. But on the other side of the marsh, from a clump of birches she heard a loud whinny. The ground thundered and the stones shot fire under the powerful hooves as a magnificent stallion appeared – the leader Tarpán. His head was like that of a pike, the neck muscled under the shining coat. His eyes blazed but were unafraid. As soon as he perceived Irgit he stopped short, threw up his head and reared. His lips were open and he showed his teeth – he had forty. From his nostrils there came forth vapour. . . .

The plains were alight and flashes of fire illuminated the air like drops of water falling from an oar. A whiff of mist came up from the lake and seemed to cover the gleaming plain, and then Irgit, and then the spirited animal.

When the mist cleared, she was sitting on the stallion's back, like an Amazon gently carried.

Irgit's son was called Torgut. On the day of his birth there came from the north an endless procession of horses, stallions, mares and foals – all Tarpán's folk and he at their head. They joined Oerlik's tribe and paid him homage. Thus the human and the animal kingdom was created.

On his forelock, between his ears, Tarpán wore the nine-pointed silver crown. . . .

The Torguts cannot explain this legend. They accept it as true and they revel in their dreams. But in fact, this origin set them apart from all other peoples.

So they wandered, stopping and preparing themselves for their great expedition. A raid went over the Persian frontier to get fresh stallions for the mares. Torgut's tribe had discovered that the character and spirit of their herds was improved when stallions from the south covered the mares from the north. There were roughly seventeen mares to one stallion.

Almost before the foals could stand their nostrils were slit so that they could breathe more easily when galloping. The stallions were magnificent animals. They were the princes of the herds, the Adonis' and well they knew it. They galloped round their womenfolk – tails high – far out into the steppe and then thundered full gallop back to them.

Tarpán was away out ahead of them all, the silver crown on his forelock.

It came to a battle with the wolves in the valley where the seven rivers meet.

The army of wolves had come from the south-west, silently, creeping down-wind through the high grasses of early summer, driven on by a dreadful hunger. The old songs say that Tarpán was the first to smell them. He scarcely believed it. Then he pulled himself up to his full height, tail high, ears stiffly pricked whilst a shrill unnatural-warning threatening tone came from his throat to the skies – not a neigh, a blast. The effect of his warning was startling, catching, robbing the senses and a tremendous uproar broke out. The nearest stallions stood on guard, repeating the call again and again. All over the steppe, the cry of horses: 'Wo . . . Wo . . . Wolves are here. Hui . . . Huiii . . . Huidäch – däch'. Mothers called their foals who ran to hide themselves behind the older horses, which had pressed themselves into a tight mass with their hind-quarters and hooves outwards and so they formed themselves into a four-cornered closed rank – a moving, excited mass. At the same time, distant neighbouring and friendly herds came galloping from all sides. As if they had descended from the skies. With every newcomer the fury grew. The earth trembled. The plains were no longer meadows for grazing, but a huge arena. Every herd was led by a stallion, snorting and raging as if stung by wasps. Partridges and runners fluttered and flew away. Grasshoppers took to the air and departed chirping. Steppe hares tried to flee but tiring were destroyed under the threshing hooves.

Dust rose in great clouds over the land. The ground shook. The sun was nothing more than a flaming circle. Bridges of fire appeared to spring from cloud to cloud.

At last the entire huge army had formed. Full-blooded stallions with tossing manes and flowing tails circled ceaselessly around their mares, foals and yearlings and even the geldings; generals, standard-bearers and war-trumpeters at one and the same time. 10,000 stallions and more than a million other animals. Suddenly Tarpán let out another cry, not a warning this time, but an immediate attack. At this the mares and geldings turned their quarters and presented a front towards the oncoming enemy. From the centre the army began their attack. Tarpán at their head. And since he was first he saw the foremost wolf. Teeth against teeth, and with his teeth he galloped at them, at the grey shadow in front, forefeet threshing, flanks heaving, the stallion's teeth met in the stinking grizzled fur near the neck. Hurled into the air doubled up into a curve, the body of the wolf fell under the hooves of the oncoming mares and was trampled. Then the young stallion Kittasch went down, bitten through the throat. First one pack of wolves, then another, a third and a fourth hastened to counter-attack the on-rushing horses. Jabasch fell and Karaktasch. With them Temäne and Zuktor and Löktör. Wild cries of death could be heard and the howl of angry wolves.

But Tarpán was aware that Torgut was sitting on his back – Irgit's grandson. Without a saddle, his left hand clutching his mane and in his right on a cord the sceptre – a club of iron whose head was studded with iron nobs. 'Over there,' he heard a whisper: 'those eyes, Tarpán, those wicked, gleaming eyes belong to the King of the Wolves. Get close to him . . . nearer . . . now: I can't quite reach him . . . one more stride.' And right in the middle of his bound, out of the air, came the club crashing down, first the club, then the hooves. Even now, although badly wounded, the wicked brute was not finished. He somersaulted, angered by fear, with savage yellow eyes, once more he sprang against his mortal enemy. He fastened his teeth in the stallion's shoulder, blood spurted out, then for the second time a human hand dealt him his death blow. He crumpled to the ground. The hungry pack stared as if fascinated by this horrible spectacle. They began somewhat undecidedly with uneasy movements to circle back and forth. But then, quite suddenly in the distance, a mourning cry was uttered by an old wolf: 'The King is dead . . . our King is dead.' Then the great pack turned to flee, a disorganised, panic-stricken flight, broken up and hounded by the horses until nightfall.

The distant mountains looked terrible and pitiless. The sky was overcast. A flash of lightning tore the clouds and put a stop to the chase. 20,000 wolves lay crumpled on the field. During the night there was a great storm and the next day a rainbow spanned the mountains as far as the base of the north-western river.

Stepping proudly, with the silver crown on his forelock, Tarpán trotted across the battlefield.

It is obvious that an historical episode has been handed down as legendary biography.

from TARPÁN *1962*

The Legend of the Odd-Coloured Horses

ILSE MIRUS

In olden days, the worthy and holy St Nicholas wandered throughout great Russia. He roamed through towns and villages, through inpenetrable dark forests and pathless marshes, in all directions, in rain and snow, in frost and heat.

We always kept him fully occupied: softening the heart of a fearful despot, changing the mind of an unjust judge, reprimanding a greedy merchant, freeing an innocent prisoner from a damp and musty prison, begging mercy for a wrong death sentence, saving the drowning, giving courage to the desperate, comforting a widow or finding a home for an orphan with kind foster parents.

Our people are a rather ignorant people, weak and not very willing to learn. They are so wrapped up in sin, like an old stone covered in moss and dirt that has lain by the roadside for a long time. What can one do, when the need is great, in illness or in death and when everything is there for all to see? It is a long way to God and one lacks confidence. Anyway, one can scarcely bother the Heavenly Mediator if a peasant has caught the mange. And the rest of the Holy and Blessed Ones have their own business to attend to. They have no time. But Nicholas, he doesn't mind, he is one of us, always handy and anyone can talk to him. And it's not just those who believe who go to him with their troubles, but all the rest of them: the Mordwins, the Syrjans, the Wotjaks and the Tschermissen people – idolators those. Even the Tartars respect him. And the rogues and horse thieves to whom nothing comes amiss, they don't mind taking the trouble to say a short prayer.

So the holy Nicholas roamed throughout the vastness of old Russia, until one day a celestial messenger appeared: 'You've got yourself so lost in the wilderness, Holy Father, one has to go to great trouble to find you and you've neglected all your Church affairs. There's no doubt but that something awful is about to happen. The wicked giant Arius has angered the true believers. He takes no notice of all that the Church fathers have tried to teach, and jokes about the most sacred things. He boasts that he will destroy the true faith for all time on the first Sunday in Advent, in the Nikita Cathedral before the entire congregation. Come quickly and help us, Holy Nicholas, you're our only hope.' 'I'll come,' said the Holy Man.

'But dear man, don't delay! There's very little time left and you know how far it is.'

'I'll start today. Now you can fly off at peace. . . .'

The Holy man knew of a coachman called Wassilij. He was a man who lived in the fear of God and who had no equal amongst his familiars. There was not another coachman who could drive such a distance. The Holy man went to his yard. 'Get dressed, Wassilij. Water the horses. We're off.'

Wassilij did not ask how far it was. He knew that had the distance been short, the kindly Nicholas would have gone on foot, because he was always sorry for the horses. All he said was: 'At your service, Father. Wait in the cabin. I'll be ready in a second.' That winter the snow lay God knows how high, and few roads had been cleared. Wassilij put his three horses to in random – one behind the other. The leader was a small pony, really a very small pony, but she was pretty clever and could find her way in a remarkable manner. Then came a coal-black horse, who could gallop well, although he was lazy. One might say that he needed the whip just as much as he needed oats. Between the shafts he harnessed an active brown mare that he had bred himself. Her name was Mascha. Wassilij put an armful of straw on the sleigh, covered it with a sack, tucked it in at the sides and put the Holy Man on top. But he himself sat on the box like a coachman, one foot in the sleigh and one outside so that he could guide it better up hill. He had all six reins in one hand and two whips as well. One of them, the short one, was stuck in his boot, but the other, enormously long, hung by a cord from his wrist and the thong trailed along behind the sleigh and left marks in the snow.

Wassilij's sleigh is not very handsome, but there's no other equal to it. The first two horses have bells on their harness (the bells are tuned differently) and on the yoke over the third horse hangs a sweetly tuned bell from the Walda mountains. This music could be heard at least five versts away – there go honest people. If one saw them from a long way off, it looked as though the horses were only trotting along, but there's not a single famous race-horse could have kept pace with them – he'd have lost his wind.

The white pony had dropped her head to smell the snow, looking sharply to right and left. Even where there was a bend in the road one need not give the reins a tug; she sensed the right way.

Sometimes Wassilij dosed off on his box, but even in his sleep he was listening with one ear.

As soon as he heard that the bells were not ringing to tune, he woke up. For instance when one of the horses cheated by not pulling properly and let the other work, then he used his whip to bring it to attention. And if one of them tired then he held it together with the reins, so that soon everything was in order again.

The horses kept up a rhythmic gait, only occasionally they pricked their ears back. So on the long journey through the snow the bells jingled merrily.

From time to time they met thieves. Highwaymen crept out from under a bridge and stood like a turnpike on the road.

'Halt! Stop the horses, coachman! Where are you going? Is it a landowner with much land? Is it a merchant with bags of money or a well-provided priest? Say, your death or life!'

But Wassilij said only: 'Look inside, you idiots! Can't you see who it is?'

When the thieves had looked inside, they threw themselves to the ground.

'Forgive us ne'er do weels, O Holy Father! Now we've done it, fools that we are! Do please forgive us.'

'God forgive you,' replied Nicholas compassionately. 'But it would be better if you weren't so cruel, children. You'll have to pay a heavy account in the other world.'

'Oh dear, we really are bad, worthy Father, we're up to the ears in wickedness . . . please remember us in your prayers, merciful one! Peace be with you.'

'Peace be with you, too, you rascals!'

Many days and nights Wassilij drove the Holy Man. He stopped to fodder at coaching stations he knew. Everywhere he had good friends and intimates. They had already driven through the land of Saratov and passed the colonists on the Don, as far as Little Russia. After this there were strange countries.

In the meantime the giant Arius had descended from his high tower and had put an ear to the ground. He listened a long time, stood up, dark as a cloud and called his faithful servants.

'You are my servants, my sworn servants. From afar I have heard that the miracle-worker Nicholas is hurrying here from Russia. Wassilij the coachman from Kessem is driving him. If Nicholas arrives here before the first Sunday in Advent we'll all be destroyed like so much rubbish. Do what you like and as you will, but see that you hinder the Holy Man a day or two on the way. Otherwise I'll chop off your heads and not one of you will be spared. But the first of you to carry out my orders will be richly rewarded with gold and jewels. And I'll give you my daughter, the lovely Jeressja to wife.' The servants departed as if on wings.

Wassilij drove the Holy Man through strange lands. The people are all old, ugly and rude. And they can't speak Russian at all. On top they have black hair but are clean shaven. Their eyes squint and are wicked like those of a wolf.

The travellers had the last part only of their journey in front of them. They wanted to arrive the next day at the Nikita Cathedral in time for the midday Mass. They stopped for the night at a coaching house at the very end of the village. A morose man came towards them. He was rude and spoke little. They asked for some oats for the horses.

'There are no oats, they're all used.'

'It doesn't matter, Wassilij,' said Nicholas, 'pull out the sack from under the seat and shake it out over the manger.'

Wassilij did as he was told and out of the sack tumbled a stream of golden corn which filled the manger. Wassilij asked for something to eat. The man made a sign to him: 'No, I've nothing for your sort.'

'All right,' the Holy Man answered, 'if there's nothing, then even the Emperor can't demand it. You have some bread left over, Wassilij?'

'Yes, certainly, worthy Father, a small crust, but very dry.'

'It doesn't matter, we'll soak it in water and eat it like bread pudding.' They ate, prayed and lay down to sleep. Nicholas slept like a child. But Wassilij couldn't sleep, he felt very uneasy.

About midnight he got up and went to look at the horses. He went into the stable and returned immediately. He was chalk-white and shaking all over. He had had such a fright.

He woke the Holy Man. 'Father Nicholas, please get up a moment. Come with me to the stable and see what a terrible misfortune has befallen us.'

They went. They opened the stable door. The Holy Man looked and stared. The horses were lying all over the place, chopped up into pieces: there some legs, there the heads, somewhere else the necks and quarters . . . Wassilij began to cry. They had been such lovely horses.

The Holy Man spoke to him kindly. 'It's all right, Wassilij, it's all right. Don't grumble, don't worry yourself to death. We can do something about it. Come, put the horses together – so, just as they were.'

Wassilij obeyed. He put heads to necks, and necks to legs on to the quarters. Then he stood up to see what would happen.

Nicholas, the miracle-worker, said a short prayer and before one could count, all three horses sprang to their feet, as well and lively as if nothing had happened, shook their manes, danced around and nuzzled into their corn. Wassilij threw himself at Nicholas's feet.

Before sunrise they were on their way. It got lighter. In the distance they could see the Cross gleaming on the bell-tower of the Nikita Cathedral. But the Holy Nicholas noticed that Wassilij was always leaning forward on his box-seat – first right, then left – as if he were trying to make out something on the horses.

'What are you doing then, Wassilij?'

'Yes, Holy Father, I keep looking . . . it seems to me as if my horses had become different colours. Originally they were of plain colours but now they're chequered like calves. Surely in my hurry in the dark I didn't put the wrong pieces together? That would be awful.'

But the Holy Man answered: 'Don't worry and don't fiddle about. They can stay like that. But you, my good man, get on with the driving so that we don't arrive too late.'

In fact, they nearly did arrive too late.

The service in the Nikita Cathedral had already started. Arius stood on the steps leading to the altar. Huge as a mountain, in a brocade surplice with diamonds and the two-pointed mitre on his head. There he stood before the congregation and began to say the Creed backwards: 'I do not believe . . .' and so on, right through, and just as he came to the end, the big door opened and Nicholas hastened in.

He had jumped straight off the sleigh, had only just managed to cast aside his heavy coat and straw clung to his hair, his beard and his worn-out surplice.

The Holy Man went quickly to the altar steps. No! he did not hit him, he simply looked at Arius very angrily.

The powerful giant began to shake and would have fallen if his servant had not caught him. He was unable to finish his bad words. 'Take me out to the air – it's so close, I feel ill.'

They led him outside into the little garden. He crouched on the ground and then something quite awful happened – in a convulsive fit, he died without Confession.

Since then coachmen have always used odd-coloured horses – piebald or skewbald. And everyone knows quite well that such horses have the strongest lungs and that their legs are like iron.

Now it is winter. It is night. We have gone outside on to the road to see if the marks made by the thong of Wassilij's long whip are there in the snow, if the tinkle of the bells can be heard. Nothing to see. Nothing to hear.

Listen!

Was that it?

from HUFSCHLAG ERKLANG *1960*

Genghis Khan's Dispatch Service

KURT VON KNOBELSDORFF

Between 1215 and 1223, the Mongolian despot Genghis Khan ruled over Central and Eastern Asia, part of China and European Russia. Once he had united these lands into one great Empire and with a sure eye to the future and holding his Empire together, Genghis Khan organised a firstclass dispatch service.

This ensured that his orders were taken by the shortest routes to the farthermost posts of his domain. They were sometimes nearly 6,000 miles apart, but it ensured that his commanders received the latest news of what was happening in record time. Watch towers were erected every twelve miles between the most important places and were guarded day and night. Mounted couriers were ready at a moment's notice to spring to action.

The Mongolian ponies which had been crossed with Oriental, Tartar and Turkmene breeds were specially suited for this service. They were famed for their speed, stamina and hardiness. Noisy bells were hung around their necks so that they could be heard some distance away. Thus it was possible for a fresh relay rider to be ready mounted to take over the dispatches without delay. Loss of time meant death. Within 24 hours the ruler's orders could be carried nearly 600 miles. It mattered not if a horse died in the effort. But a dispatch that arrived too late cost the orderly his life or, worse still, terrible punishment that was, in fact, worse than death itself.

A quite remarkable order and peace reigned over this vast

domain, since under this system every princeling, provincial governor or official found himself under control. It was kept alive with great severity. It was made easier, however, by the fact that with the occupation of every new district, the intelligentsia together with the ruling princelings were, without exception, done away with.

This method of subjugation was different from that of Attila, King of the Huns, who formed a confederation with the conquered German and Scythian States between 434 and 453. After Attila's death, this fell apart, whereas the Mongol Empire held together until about 1480 and even enjoyed a fairly prosperous period between 1370 and 1405.

In 1239 Genghis Kkan's grandson, Batu, advanced as far as Silesia, where he was met near Liegnitz by Duke Henry of Breslau with 30,000 knights and men-at-arms. In spite of hard fighting Duke Henry fell with his entire army and the way was open for the Mongol hordes, to the heart of Germany.

By means of dispatches, Batu received orders to return home immediately. Ghenghis Khan had died and a new ruler had to be chosen. So Europe was saved and the attempt was not made again as the unity of the Asiatic empire was destroyed through quarrels among the descendants of its founder.

It is worth noting that especially valuable dispatches and orders were carried by a specially selected courier who was often more than fifty hours in the saddle. His whole body was bandaged, rather after the manner of that of an Egyptian mummy and in order that the best relay horses were ready and waiting for him the bells at his horse's throat were of unusual tone. He was thus recognised from far off as a Special Dispatch Rider.

Uncountable numbers of horses were used for the carrying of dispatches and in the armies of the Great Khan, and horses were indispensable in founding a vast empire – just as they have been indispensable in so many other ways throughout the history of civilization.

from SANKT GEORG *1-3-1965*

The General Tournament

SIR WALTER SCOTT

It was a goodly, and at the same time an anxious sight, to behold so many gallant champions, mounted bravely, and armed richly, stand ready prepared for an encounter so formidable, seated on their war-saddles like so many pillars of iron, and awaiting the signal of encounter with the same ardour as their generous steeds, which, by neighing and pawing the ground, gave signal of their impatience.

As yet the knights held their long lances upright, their bright points glancing to the sun, and the streamers with which they were decorated fluttering over the plumage of the helmets. Thus they remained while the marshals of the field surveyed their ranks with the utmost exactness, lest either party had more or fewer than the appointed number. The tale was found exactly complete. The marshals then withdrew from the lists, and William de Wyvil, with a voice of thunder, pronounced the signal words – *Laissez aller*! The trumpets sounded as he spoke; the spears of the champions were at once lowered and placed in the rests; the spurs were dashed into the flanks of the horses, and the two foremost ranks of either party rushed upon each other in full gallop, and met in the middle of the lists with a shock, the sound of which was heard at a mile's distance. The rear rank of each party advanced at a slower pace to sustain the defeated, and follow up the success of the victors of their party.

The consequences of the encounter were not instantly seen, for the dust raised by the trampling of so many steeds darkened the air, and it was a minute ere the anxious spectators could see the fate of the encounter. When the fight became visible, half the knights on each side were dismounted, some by the dexterity of their adversary's lance; some by the superior weight and strength of opponents, which had borne down both horse and man; some lay stretched on earth as if never more to rise; some had already gained their feet, and were closing hand to hand with those of their antagonists who were in the same predicament; and several on both sides, who had received wounds by which they were disabled, were stopping their blood by their scarfs, and endeavouring to extricate themselves from the tumult. The mounted knights, whose lances had been almost all broken by the fury of the encounter, were now closely engaged with their swords, shouting their war-cries, and exchanging buffets, as if honour and life depended on the issue of the combat.

The tumult was presently increased by the advance of the second rank on either side, which, acting as a reserve, now rushed on to aid their companions. The followers of Brian de Bois-Guilbert shouted – 'Ha! *Beau-séant! Beau-séant!* – For the Temple – For the Temple!' The opposite party shouted in answer – '*Desdichado! Desdichado!*' – which watchword they took from the motto upon their leader's shield.

The champions thus encountering each other with the utmost fury, and with alternate success, the tide of battle seemed to flow now towards the southern, now towards the northern extremity of the lists, as the one or the other party prevailed. Meantime the clang of the blows, and the shouts of the combatants, mixed fearfully with the sound of the trumpets, and drowned the groans of those who fell and lay rolling defenceless beneath the feet of the horses. The splendid armour of the combatants was now defaced with dust and blood, and gave way at every stroke of the sword and battle-axe. The gay plumage, shorn from the crests, drifted upon the breeze like snowflakes. All that was beautiful and graceful in the martial array had disappeared, and what was now visible was only calculated to awake terror or compassion. . . .

Amid the varied fortunes of the combat, the eyes of all endeavoured to discover the leaders of each band, who, mingling in the thick of the fight, encouraged their companions both by voice and example. Both displayed great feats of gallantry, nor did either Bois-Guilbert or the Dis-inherited Knight find in the ranks opposed to them a champion who could be termed their unquestioned match. They repeatedly endeavoured to single out each other, spurred by mutual animosity, and aware that the fall of either leader might be considered as decisive of victory. Such, however, was the crowd and confusion that, during the earlier part of the conflict, their efforts to meet were unavailing, and they were repeatedly separated by the eagerness of their followers, each of whom was anxious to win honour by measuring his strength against the leader of the opposite party.

But when the field became thin by the numbers on either side, who had yielded themselves vanquished, had been compelled to the extremity of the lists, or been otherwise rendered incapable of continuing the strife, the Templar and Dis-inherited Knight at length encountered hand to hand, with all the fury that mortal animosity, joined to rivalry of honour, could inspire. Such was the address of each in parrying and striking, that the spectators broke forth into a unanimous and involuntary shout, expressive of their delight and admiration.

But at this moment the party of the Dis-inherited Knight had the worst; the gigantic arm of Front-de-Bœuf on the one flank, and the ponderous strength of Athelstane on the other, bearing down and dispersing those immediately exposed to them. Finding themselves freed from their immediate antagonists, it seems to have occurred to both these knights at the same instant that they would render the most decisive advantage to their party by aiding the Templar in his contest with his rival. Turning their horses, therefore, at the same moment, the Norman spurred against the Dis-inherited Knight on the one side, and the Saxon on the other. It was utterly impossible that the object of this unequal and unexpected assault could have sustained it, had he not been warned by a general cry from the spectators, who could not but take interest in one exposed to such disadvantage.

'Beware! Beware! Sir Dis-inherited!' was shouted so universally, that the knight became aware of his danger, and, striking a full blow at the Templar, he reined back his steed in the same moment, so as to escape the charge of Athelstane and Front-de-Bœuf. These knights, therefore, their aim being thus eluded, rushed from opposite sides betwixt the object of their attack and the Templar, almost running their horses against each other ere they could stop their career. Recovering their horses, however, and wheeling them round, the whole three pursued their united purpose of bearing to earth the Dis-inherited Knight.

Nothing could have saved him, except the remarkable strength and activity of the noble horse which he had won on the preceding day.

This stood him in the more stead, as the horse of Bois-Guilbert was wounded, and those of Front-de-Bœuf and Athelstane were both tired with the weight of their gigantic masters, clad in complete armour, and with the preceding exertions of the day. The masterly horsemanship of the Dis-inherited Knight, and the activity of the noble animal which he mounted, enabled him for a few minutes to keep at sword's point his three antagonists, turning and wheeling with the agility of a hawk upon the wing, keeping his enemies as far separate as he could, and rushing now against the one, now against the other, dealing sweeping blows with his sword, without waiting to receive those which were aimed at him in return.

But although the lists rang with the applauses of his dexterity, it was evident that he must at last be overpowered; and the nobles around Prince John implored him with one voice to throw down his warder, and to save so brave a knight from the disgrace of being overcome by odds.

'Not I, by the light of heaven!' answered Prince John; 'this same springal, who conceals his name, and despises our proffered hospitality, hath already gained one prize, and may now afford to let others have their turn.' As he spoke thus, an unexpected incident changed the fortune of the day.

There was among the ranks of the Dis-inherited Knight a champion in black armour, mounted on a black horse, large of size, tall, and to all appearance powerful and strong, like the rider by whom he was mounted. This knight, who bore on his shield no device of any kind, had hitherto evinced very little interest in the event of the fight, beating off with seeming ease those combatants who attacked him, but neither pursuing his advantages nor himself assailing any one. In short, he had hitherto acted the part rather of a spectator than of a party in the tournament, a circumstance which procured him among the spectators the name of Le Noir Fainéant, or the Black Sluggard.

At once this knight seemed to throw aside his apathy, when he discovered the leader of his party so hard bestead; for, setting spurs to his horse, which was quite fresh, he came to his assistance like a thunderbolt, exclaiming, in a voice like a trumpet-call, 'Desdichado, to the rescue!' It was high time; for, while the Dis-inherited Knight was pressing upon the Templar, Front-de-Bœuf had got nigh to him with his uplifted sword; but ere the blow could descend, the Sable Knight dealt a stroke on his head, which, glancing from the polished helmet, lighted with violence scarcely abated on the chamfron of the steed, and Front-de-Bœuf rolled on the ground, both horse and man equally stunned by the fury of the blow. Le Noir Fainéant then turned his horse upon Athelstane of Coningsburgh; and his own sword having been broken in his encounter with Front-de-Bœuf, he wrenched from the hand of the bulky Saxon the battle-axe which he wielded, and, like one familiar with the use of the weapon, bestowed him such a blow upon the crest that Athelstane also lay senseless on the field. Having achieved this double feat, for which he was the more highly applauded that it was totally unexpected from him, the knight seemed to resume the sluggishness of his character, returning calmly to the northern extremity of the lists, leaving his leader to cope as he best could with Brian de Bois-Guilbert. This was no longer matter of so much difficulty as formerly. The Templar's horse had bled much, and gave way under the shock of the Dis-inherited Knight's charge. Brian de Bois-Guilbert rolled on the field, encumbered with the stirrup, from which he was unable to draw his foot. His antagonist sprang from horse-back, waved his fatal sword over the head of his adversary, and commanded him to yield himself; when Prince John, more moved by the Templar's dangerous situation than he had been by that of his rival, saved him the mortification of confessing himself vanquished by casting down his warder, and putting an end to the conflict.

from IVANHOE *1819*

Hanoverian Times

A. A. DENT and DAPHNE MACHIN GOODALL

Daniel Defoe's *Tour Through England and Wales*, mostly relating to the year 1722, contains a great deal of information about English farming and stockbreeding early in George I's reign, and much valuable matter about horse-breeding in particular, but its evidence concerning pony-breeding is completely negative by contrast to what he says about Galloway. He calls Exmoor 'a filthy, barren ground. It gives indeed, but a melancholy view, being a vast tract of barren and desolate lands'. Somerset, he says, exports 'Colts, bred in great numbers on the moors, and sold into the northern counties, where the horse copers, as they are called, in Staffordshire and Leicestershire, buy them again, and sell them for London for cart-horses and coach-horses, the breed being very large'. By the last four words we see that the old order of things, whereby draught-horses were invariably smaller than saddle-horses, had gone for ever – it had gone within the last sixty or seventy years. But how do we account for the large colts 'bred in the moors'? The fact is that to Defoe and contemporary Londoners 'moor' meant marsh or fen, not a heath. They thought of the swamp outside the old Moorgate. He speaks indeed of the 'moors or marsh grounds which extend themselves up the rivers Perrot and Ivill into the heart of the country'. As for London, we learn from him that West Smithfield horse market was still, after more than six hundred years, being held every Friday as in Fitzstephen's time; the number of animals turned over was very great but the class of horse more restricted, only the more expensive sorts being found there; Smithfield was no longer the place to go for a pack-horse, a plough-mare or a hackney.

He has a revealing remark about the standards of height prevalent in his day, when in the course of a report on the cloth towns of west Yorkshire he describes the horse he rode there as 'not a very small pad; of fourteen hands and a half high'. The pad is what the palfrey of earlier ages had now generally come to be called; it was the traveller's horse par excellence; as likely as not, it still paced where others trotted, since it often had to carry a

43

side-saddle or a pillion for feminine passengers; it was still predominantly of native stock; and the 'very small' ones would be around thirteen hands. We also see by his account of the West Riding that at that place and time the demand for pack-horses was greater than it had ever been or was ever to be again in England. The textile trade had expanded enormously in the last generation but it was in the hands of a multitude of small masters whose stock was not counted by the complete wagon-load. Moreover it was carded and spun and woven and waulked and bleached in different establishments: some of the processes were put out as piece-work in the workers' own homes, distributed in small parcels, and collected again, by pack-horses, a vast number of which threaded their way along the narrow tracks over the increasingly grimy moorlands and splashed across the increasingly polluted becks that ran into the Nidd and the Aire, the Wharfe and the Don. Of the descendants of Chaucer's Webber, Tapicer and Dyer Defoe says 'every clothier must keep a horse, perhaps two, to fetch and carry for the use of his manufacture'. There was still no local network of carriage roads to carry this great traffic of raw materials, part-finished cloth and piece-goods, and perforce it went by pack. Even if some wholesalers sent it to London or to the ports by wagon, many of them supplied pedlars whose stock was retailed from panniers carried on a pony. The same was true of the Sheffield cutlers not far away.

This is not the place to retail Defoe's illuminating remarks about the increasing trade in large coach-horses, or in 'galloping horses' in the Midlands and in north Yorkshire, except to note that in his time the majority of breeders did not record pedigrees 'for a succession of ages, as they say they do in Arabia and in Barbary . . . yet they will advance the price of a horse according to the reputation of the horse he came of'. That is to say, the price of young stock depended chiefly on the sire's performance (individual performance, not the known quality of his other progeny) and hardly at all on the dam or on the ancestry of the sire. It seems that the passion for genealogy of the Celts and of the early English had quite died out. No longer could a minstrel sit on the ale-bench interminably grinding out heroic pedigrees, while his spellbound audience was willing to stand him another horn of mead as often as he chose to pause and take breath between the stanzas in which

Sceaf begat Scyld and Scyld begat Seaxnot who begat Hengest who begat Oisc da capo; all of which Defoe would find just as boring as you and I would. And so it was in the horse world also, except in a very narrow circle centring on Newmarket Heath.

The landowning class of the eighteenth century, that age of agricultural improvement, lost all interest in the breeding of native ponies because they were bewitched by that most marvellous of all inventions before the railway – the wonderful galloping machine which we call the Thoroughbred. Who can blame them? What we find less easy to forgive is the itch of these people and their dependants to improve the past as well as the present. For more than two thousand years there had been a class of monument, peculiar, so far as is known, to the lowland zone of Britain, in honour of the equestrian gods and heroes of past ages; these were the White Horses carved on the chalk hills such as Uffington in Berkshire, originally part of the cults of Epona, Rudiobus, Magog, etc. Landlords had regarded it as a pious duty to pay for and otherwise encourage the cleaning and repair of these, our oldest equestrian pictures, as the old Berkshire ballad says:

> The owld White Horse wants zettin to rights
> And the Squire hev promised good cheer.
> Zo we'll gee'un a scrape to kip 'un in zhape,
> And A'll last for many a year.

Perhaps the finest of these monuments was that at Westbury in Wiltshire, which up to 1778 seems to have preserved the lineaments of an Iron Age horse as seen by an Iron Age artist. But in that year Lord Abingdon's steward, charged with the duty of repair, found that it resembled a cart-horse; as well it might, for the Wiltshire cart-horse of the 1770s probably did resemble pretty closely a warrior's horse of two thousand years ago. So he had the outline filled in and a new image cut, facing the other way, with a profile along the approved Newmarket lines of his own day. Eighty years later the memory of the original monument was still strong enough for the white horse to be remodelled again, this time facing the right way, but no one could remember what the outlines of the original had been, so that the work of that conscientious, meddlesome Philistine Mr Gee could not be quite undone, and is with us yet.

In speaking of various imported sires and their performance in competition with 'the gallopers of this country' – meaning Yorkshire – Defoe reveals two things. Firstly, like many people today, he believed in a 'native' English strain in the Thoroughbred, but, like the same people today, failed to realize that while this element undoubtedly existed in a sense, it owed its genetic, but not its environmental qualities, to a long series of imports stretching back with some interruptions to Roman times and perhaps earlier – all imports from the Near and Middle East, a very few direct but the most part via Italy and Spain. If we take his knowledge of horses to be that of the average well-informed Englishman of his day – and it was probably well above that average – we find that the distinction between the Spanish jennet proper, which was a pony from north-western Spain, and the Barb and the larger Andaluz had vanished from the English memory. Defoe runs them all together as the 'Barb or Spanish jennet from Cordova' – which is in the south.

The Welsh part of Defoe's *Tour* is nothing like so comprehensive as the English. Yet he does say, of Montgomeryshire, that 'This county is noted for an excellent breed of Welsh horses, which, though not very large, are exceeding valuable, and much esteem'd all over England'. As to his standards of 'exceeding value', we can only say that the biggest price he mentions as asked and given for a horse is 150 guineas (at Penkridge fair in Staffordshire, which he reckons the greatest horse mart, for quantity as for quality, in England). Farther north, in Teesdale, he notices that the exigencies of Queen Anne's wars had led to a demand for more substantial horses for senior officers' chargers at the expense of speed and 'fineness'. This does nothing to temper his admiration for the studs of north Yorkshire in general, but if the tendency he remarks was at all general it cannot but have had its effect on the type of Dales horses proper as well as on the 'gallopers' of Bedale and Northallerton.

from THE FOALS OF EPONA *1962*

The Mustang – Wild and Free

J. FRANK DOBIE

No one who conceives him as only a potential servant to man can apprehend the mustang. The true conceiver must be a true lover of freedom – a person who yearns to extend freedom to all life. Halted in animated expectancy or running in abandoned freedom, the mustang was the most beautiful, the most spirited and the most inspiriting creature ever to print foot on the grasses of America. When he stood trembling with fear before his captor, bruised from falls by the restrictive rope, made submissive by choking, clogs, cuts and starvation, he had lost what made him so beautiful and free. Illusion and reality had alike been destroyed. Only the spirited are beautiful. The antlered buck always appears nobler leaping the brush than he measures lifeless upon the ground. One out of every three mustangs captured in south west Texas was expected to die before they were tamed. The process of breaking often broke the spirits of the other two.

Out on the plains, Josiah Gregg relates, his party 'succeeded in separating a gay looking stallion from a herd of mesteñas, upon which he immediately joined our caballada and was lazoed by a Mexican. As he curvetted at the end of the rope or stopped and gazed majestically at his subjectors, his symmetrical proportions attracted the attention of all; jockeys at once valued him at five hundred dollars. It appeared that he had before been tamed, for he soon submitted to the saddle, and in a few days dwindled down to scarce a twenty-dollar hackney.'

The aesthetic value of the mustang topped all other values. The sight of wild horses streaming across the prairies made even the most hardened of professional mustangers regret putting an end to their liberty. The mustang was essentially a prairie animal, like the antelope, and like it would not go into a wooded bottom or a canyon except for water and shelter. Under the pursuit of man he took to the brush and to the roughest mountains, adapting himself like the coyote, but his nature was for prairies – the place for free running, free playing, free tossing of head and mane, free

47

vision. He relied upon motion, not covert, for the maintenance of liberty.

One early morning on the south plains of Texas, a surveying party saw a great troop of mustangs galloping towards them fully two miles away. Not a tree or a swag broke the grassed level, but from pure wantonness of vitality the oncoming line, following the leaders, deflected here and there into a sinuous curve. Coming nearer, the phalanx charged straight. A hundred and fifty yards away, it halted, with a front of about a hundred horses. Heads tossing high, nostrils dilated, the wild and free stood in arrested animation. The bright light of the rising sun brought out details of prominent eye, tapered nose, rounded breast, and slender legs on small feet. It glistened on sleek hairs of bay and sorrel, brown and grullo, roan, dun and gray, with here and there black, white and paint. Now with loud snorts, they wheeled and dashed away like a flight of sportive blackbirds, adding symmetry of speed to symmetry of form, contour of individual blending with contour of earth-skimming mass.

Only by blotting out the present can one now see those wild horses of the prairies. They have gone with the winds of vanished years. They carried away a life and a spirit that no pastoral prosperity could in coming times re-present.

from THE MUSTANGS *1954*

The Horse Culture amongst the American Indians

WALTER PRESCOTT WEBB

Then came the horse; and overnight, so to speak, the whole life and economy of the Plains Indians [of the United States] was changed. Steam and electricity have not wrought a greater revolution in the ways of civilized life than the horse did in the savage life of the Plains. So important was the horse in the Plains culture that the anthropologists have named the period extending from

1540 to 1880* the horse-culture period. Practically all that scholars know about the Plains Indians comes from this period. The pre-Columbian time is one of conjecture; the reservation period after 1880 is little else than a story of imprisonment. It has already been stated that the Plains Indians maintained their integrity against the white man much longer than any other group. It was the horse and the buffalo, but primarily the horse, that enabled them to hold out; without the horse they would have been easily disposed of, but in possession of this animal they were both uncontrollable and formidable. . . .

The introduction and spread of the horse over the Plains area and over all the West is a most interesting subject and one which throws much light on the white man's history in that region. It is a well-known fact that the Spanish explorers brought horses to America in considerable numbers. At the time of their coming no Spaniard would have thought of going on a warlike expedition without horses. Feudalism was then giving way to nationalism, chivalry was still in vogue, and the Spaniards had but recently expelled the Moors from Spain. Here were three good reasons, any one of which would have been sufficient to make horsemen of the Spaniards.

The student of social origins and institutions would like to put his finger on the exact spot where the Spanish explorer's horses (mares and stallions, for gelding was not then practised) broke

* Clark Wissler, *North American Indians of the Plains* (3rd edition, 1927), chapter VII.

their tethers and rushed away into the wild country. Perhaps the horses were stampeded by Indians or by herds of buffalo; but it is more than likely that some were set free because they became too poor or footsore or crippled to be of further use to their masters. It is not remarkable that horses escaped; but it is remarkable that they survived, multiplied, and spread over the region west of the Mississippi and Missouri rivers. Not only did they spread as beasts of burden for the Plains Indians, but they grew wild in vast herds, proving that they had found a natural home.* It is generally accepted by anthropologists that these herds originated from the horses lost or abandoned by De Soto about 1541. Whether they came from De Soto's horses, or from those of Coronado, or from other explorers is not material; we know that the Kiowa and Missouri Indians were mounted by 1682; the Pawnee by 1700; the Comanche by 1714; the Plains Cree and Arikara by 1738; the Assiniboin, Crow, Mandan, Snake and Teton by 1742; and the most northern tribe, the Sarsi, by 1784. How much earlier these Indians rode horses we do not know; but we can say that the dispersion of horses which began in 1541 was completed over the Plains area by 1784. This dispersion proceeded from south to north and occurred in the seventeenth and eighteenth centuries. At the same time, horse culture spread in the region east of the Mississippi and west of the Rocky Mountains, but in both cases it was restricted, never developing to any extent north of Virginia or the Ohio on the east, or north of California on the west.† In the spread of the horse and horse culture through the whole Plains area, as contrasted with its partial spread both to the east and to the west, we have another example of the cultural unity of the Plains.

It is desirable to dwell at some length on the horsemanship and the weapons of the Plains Indians. The Indian, the horse and the weapon formed a perfect unit. They were adapted to each other and, taken together, made a formidable fighting machine. Clark Wissler's characterization of the first nomads‡ would apply

* Clark Wissler, 'The Influence of the Horse in the Development of Plains Culture', *American Anthropologist* (N.S.), XVI ('1914), No. 1, 1–25. In his various books Wissler touches constantly on the horse in Plains culture, and the anthropological facts here stated are largely drawn from his researches.

† *Ibid.*, 9.   ‡ *See page* 24.

to the Plains Indians at any time in the later eighteenth and the early nineteenth century. The horse revolutionized transportation on the Plains and made the Indians out-wanderers, raiders and splendid thieves. By the time the whites came well into contact with them, the Indians counted their wealth in horses, paid their debts in horses, and bought their wives with horses. The horse was not only a source of wealth and a means of transportation but a supply of food, to be eaten on occasion. The Indian rode his commissary into battle, and though it was only when he could obtain no other food that he ate his horse, his willingness to do so made him more formidable.

The Indians had horses for all purposes. The buffalo horse was merely a trained cow pony; he bore a special mark or nick in his ear to distinguish him. He had to be alert, intelligent, willing to follow the game and press close to the side of the running animal, yet able to detect its intention and swerve from it so as not to become entangled, and all with no more guidance than the Indian exerted by pressure of his knees.* The war horse and the buffalo horse were renowned for their speed, intelligence, and endurance. They were prize possessions and were valued above all else.

The horse fitted in perfectly with the Plains Indian's scheme of life, with his penchant for war, and with his care for his own safety. The Indian's conception of valour and bravery differed from that of the white man. The Indian made war for the purpose of destroying his enemy and preserving himself. Of the two the latter was by far the more important consideration. Treachery, stealth, wariness, with boldness and cruelty in an advantage and readiness to flee if necessary, characterized his warfare.† The horse fitted into this complex, made the Indian bolder in advance, faster in pursuit, and fleet as the wind in retreat. Where all men were mounted, the Indian's courage depended almost solely on the speed of his horse. Clark says:

> In going to war on horseback, if they possess or can get them,

* Theodore R. Davis, 'The Buffalo Range,' *Harper's Magazine*, XXXVIII, 147 ff.
† In explanation of the Indian method Clark says (*The Indian Sign Language*, 131): 'Their education and training, their social laws and conditions of physical existence, demand a certain order of strategy; and the great vital principle of this is to do the greatest possible amount of damage to the enemy with the least possible loss. There is no pension list with them, and the widows and orphans are thrown upon the charity of their people.'

each Indian takes two ponies. The best and fleetest, or, as we have named it, 'war pony', is not ridden until an emergency arises. Indians keenly and thoroughly appreciate the value of a fresh animal, either for a dash and pursuit after their enemies, should they come suddenly upon them, or as a means of escape. An Indian mounted on an animal which he considers better than that of his enemies does not fear to penetrate into their very midst, and as a scout will be apt to do excellent service; but let him once feel that his mount is less fleet, less enduring, than are those of his enemy, and he is worthless, he will take no risks where a white man might be persuaded to at least do his best.*

Just as a good horse glorified the individual Indian, so did the possession of horses glorify the Plains tribes and lift them up to an eminence that they could not attain as footmen on the Plains. The horse fitted in excellently with the mode of life of the Plains Indian, who, before the horse came, might be called a dismounted nomad. The second point is that the horse practically revolution-ized the habits of the Indian by an intensification of his acquired traits.

The horsemanship of the Plains Indian aroused the wonder and admiration of all who observed it. The following account of the prairie warrior's equestrian skill is by Captain Marcy.

His only ambition consists in being able to cope successfully with his enemy in war and in managing his steed with unfailing adroitness. He is in the saddle from boyhood to old age, and his favourite horse is his constant companion. It is when mounted that the prairie warrior exhibits himself to the best advantage; here he is at home, and his skill in various manœuvres which he makes available in battle – such as throw-ing himself entirely upon one side of his horse and discharging his arrows with great rapidity towards the opposite side from beneath the animal's neck while he is at full speed – is truly astonishing. Many of the women are equally expert, as eques-trians, with the men. . . . Every warrior has his war-horse, which is the fleetest that can be obtained, and he prizes him more highly than anything else in his possession, and it is

* *The Indian Sign Language*, 233.

seldom that he can be induced to part with him at any price. He never mounts him except when going into battle, the buffalo chase, or upon state occasions.*

All the Plains Indians were good horsemen, but the Comanche Indians were certainly among the best, if not the very best of them all. Their position on the southern Plains made them among the first to come into possession of the Spanish horses as they came out from Mexico and drifted northwards. The climate of the southern Plains was the best climate for the horse. He could live and thrive there the year round. Since the south was the natural habitat of the wild horses, they soon became more numerous there than on the northern Plains, and therefore the Comanches had more horses than the northern tribes. The contact of the Comanches with Mexico made it possible for them to recruit their herds by theft from the Mexicans. They, in turn, supplied the neighbouring tribes, with the result that horses were constantly moving northwards.

The Comanches played such an important part in the history of the Plains that it is necessary to devote considerable attention to them here. Catlin says of the horses owned by the Comanches:

> The wild horse of these regions is a small, but very powerful animal; with an exceedingly prominent eye, sharp nose, high nostril, small foot and delicate leg; and undoubtedly [has] sprung from a stock introduced by the Spaniards, at the time of the invasion of Mexico. . . .
>
> These useful animals have been of great service to the Indians living on these vast plains, enabling them to take their game more easily, to carry their burthens, etc.; and no doubt, render them better and handier service than if they were of a larger and heavier breed. Vast numbers of them are also killed for food by the Indians, at seasons when buffaloes and other game are scarce.
>
> Whilst on our march we met with many droves of these beautiful animals, and several times had the opportunity of seeing the Indians pursue them, and take them with the lasso.†

Of the horsemanship of the Comanches, Catlin says:

* Randolph B. Marcy, *Thirty Years of Army Life on the Border*, 28–9.
† George Catlin, *North American Indians*, 486–7.

In their ball plays and some other games they are far behind the Sioux and others of the northern tribes; but in racing horses and riding they are not equalled by any other Indians on the continent. Racing horses, it would seem, is a constant and almost incessant exercise, and their principal mode of gambling. . . . The exercise of these people, in a country where horses are so abundant, and the country so fine for riding, is chiefly done on horseback; and it 'stands to reason' that such a people, who have been practising from their childhood, should become exceedingly expert in this wholesome and beautiful exercise.*

Some of the remarkable feats are thus described:

Amongst their feats of riding, there is one that has astonished me more than anything of the kind I have ever seen, or expect to see, in my life: a stratagem of war, learned and practised by every young man in the tribe; by which he is able to drop his body upon the side of his horse at the instant he is passing, effectually screened from his enemies' weapons as he [lies] in a horizontal position behind the body of his horse, with his heel hanging over the horse's back; by which he has the power of throwing himself up again, and changing to the other side of the horse if necessary. In this wonderful condition, he will hang whilst his horse is at fullest speed, carrying with him his bow and his shield, and also his long lance of fourteen feet in length, all or either of which he will wield upon his enemy as he passes; rising and throwing his arrows over the horse's back, or with ease and equal success under the horse's neck. . . .

This astonishing feat which the young men have been repeatedly playing off to our surprise as well as amusement, whilst they have been galloping about in front of our tents, completely puzzled the whole of us; and appeared to be the result of magic, rather than of skill acquired by practice.†

It should be pointed out here that Catlin was accompanied by a cavalry troop whose members should have been familiar with all the feats of horsemanship that are known to military science or to the people of the Eastern states. It was a case of the two horse cultures coming into contact in the West. Catlin declared the horsemanship of the Comanches the best.

* *North American Indians*, 495–6.   † *Loc. cit.*

A people who spend so very great a part of their lives actually on their horses' backs must needs become exceedingly expert in everything that pertains to riding – to war, or to the chase; and I am ready, without hesitation, to pronounce the Comanches the most extraordinary horsemen that I have seen yet in all my travels, and I doubt very much whether any people in the world can surpass them.*

He gives a vivid impression of the effect of the horse upon the Comanches:

The Comanches are in stature rather low, and in person often approaching to corpulency. In their movements they are heavy and ungraceful; and on their feet, one of the most unattractive and slovenly-looking races of Indians that I have ever seen; but the moment they mount their horses, they seem at once metamorphosed, and surprise the spectator with the ease and elegance of their movements. A Comanche on his feet is out of his element, and comparatively almost as awkward as a monkey on the ground, without a limb or a branch to cling to; but the moment he lays his hand upon his horse, his *face* even becomes handsome, and he gracefully flies away like a different being.†

In this connection it is worth noting that the Comanches were comparatively newcomers on the Plains; previously they had dwelt in the mountains to the west, had been a mountain tribe. Wissler shows that these Indians were the shortest in stature of any Plains Indians, having the stature of mountain Indians.‡ It is interesting to speculate on the reasons and conditions that made it possible for the short-legged mountain Indian to come into and take possession of the most desirable portion of the Great Plains, take it from the long-legged Indians who had for centuries been trekking across the vast distances. Is it not reasonable to assume that the Comanches found it necessary to become horsemen to compensate for their short legs? Being poor walkers they had to become good riders. They soon came to hate walking, just as the

---

* *Ibid.*, 496–7.   † *Ibid.*. 497. (Punctuation revised.)
‡ Wissler's figures (*The Indians of the Plains*, 149) for the height of the Indians in inches are as follows:

Cheyenne						68·7	Blackfoot				67·5
Crow						68·1	Kiowa				67·2
Arapaho						68·03	Dakota				67·09
Plains-Ojibway					67·8	Comanche				66·06

cowboys did later, and like the cowboys they looked – and were – awkward on the ground.

The ability of the Comanches as horse thieves bears on later historical problems and therefore is briefly discussed. Colonel Marcy says:

> The only property of these people, with the exception of a few articles belonging to their domestic economy, consists entirely in horses and mules, of which they possess great numbers. These are mostly pillaged from the Mexicans, as is evident from the brand which is found upon them. The most successfu! horse thieves among them own from fifty to two hundred animals.*

Old Is-sa-keep told Colonel Marcy that he had four sons and that they were a great source of comfort to him in his old age 'and could steal more horses than any young men in his band'.†

Colonel Dodge says, in speaking of the proclivity of these Indians for horse-thieving:

> Where all are such magnificent thieves, it is difficult to decide which of the plains tribes deserves the palm for stealing. The Indians themselves give it to the Comanches, whose designation in the sign language of the plains is a forward, wriggling motion of the fore-finger, signifying a snake, and indicating the silent stealth of that tribe. This is true of the Comanches, who for crawling into a camp, cutting hobbles and lariat ropes, and getting off with animals undiscovered, are unsurpassed and unsurpassable. . . . I have known a Comanche to crawl into a bivouac where a dozen men were sleeping, each with his horse tied to his wrist by the lariat, cut a rope within six feet of a sleeper's person, and get off with the horse without waking a soul.

Colonel Dodge gives other examples where horses were stolen under the most adverse conditions, oftentimes setting military expeditions afoot.‡ He is of the opinion that the Cheyennes excelled the Comanches in boldness and dash and that the Kiowas come next.

---

* *Thirty Years on the Border*, 22.   † *Ibid.*, 23.
‡ *The Hunting Grounds of the Great West*, 401 ff.

The Indian's weapons were remarkably well adapted for use on horseback. The warrior carried a small bow not over three feet long, and often only two and a half feet. It was made from ash or bois d'arc and sometimes, it is said, of bone. Experience had taught the Plains tribes to use a short bow because it was more effective on horseback. The arrows were carefully selected, and were tipped with points of bone, flint, or steel. In the buffalo arrows the barbs were fixed fast to the shaft, but in arrows meant for the enemy the barbs were so attached that they would come loose when the shaft was withdrawn, leaving the barb in the wound. The arrows were carried in a quiver slung over the shoulder corresponding to the hand that pulled the bowstring. To protect himself when in battle the Indian carried a shield, usually circular, made of the hide of the buffalo's neck smoked and hardened with glue from the hoofs.* This shield, or arrow-fender, was carried on his bow arm. If advancing, the Indian carried the shield in front; if retreating, he slung it over his back so as to cover his vital parts. The shield gained in effectiveness because it hung loosely, gave readily to the stroke of the arrow, and would deflect any missile, either arrow or bullet, that did not strike it at right angles. The Indian could further protect himself, as we have seen, by using his horse as a shield. Thus armed and mounted the Plains Indian was a formidable warrior in his country. To realize how formidable he was, we must bear in mind that he could carry a hundred arrows, and that he could shoot them from his running horse so rapidly as to keep one or more in the air all the time and with such force as to drive the shaft entirely through the body of the buffalo.† 'In this country of green fields,' says Catlin, 'all *ride* for their enemies, and also

---

* In speaking of the Indian shield Catlin says (*North American Indians*, 65): 'This shield or arrow-fender is, in my opinion, made of similar materials, and used in the same way, and for the same purpose, as was the clypeus or small shield in the Roman and Grecian cavalry. They were made in those days as a means of defence on horseback only – made small and light, of bulls' hides, sometimes single, sometimes double and tripled. Such was Hector's shield, and of most of the Homeric heroes of the Greek and Trojan wars. In those days [there] were also darts or javelins and lances; the same were also used by the ancient Britons; and such exactly are now in use amongst the Arabs and the North American Indians.'

† As an example of the skill of the Indians, Catlin relates seeing the Mandans practise 'the game of the arrows', each Indian undertaking to have the most arrows in the air at the same time. The Indian held eight or ten arrows in his left hand, shooting them from the bow with his right. He could have eight arrows up at once. (*Ibid.*, 230.)

for their game, which is almost invariably killed whilst their horses are at full speed.'* The Plains Indians used spears more frequently in the south, it seems, than in the north, though Catlin says they were found among all the Plains tribes. The spear was useful in chasing the buffalo or an enemy and enabled the savage to save his arrows and dispatch his game or dismount his adversary with one blow.

Thus armed, equipped and mounted the Plains Indians made both picturesque and dangerous warriors – the red knights of the prairie. They were far better equipped for successful warfare in their own country than the white men who came against them, and presented to the European or American conqueror problems different from those found elsewhere on the continent.

from THE GREAT PLAINS *1931*

The Open Road

NIMROD

May we be permitted . . . to make a little demand on our readers' fancy, and suppose it possible that a worthy old gentleman of this said year – 1742 – had fallen comfortably asleep à la Dodswell, and never awoke till Monday morning (1836) in Piccadilly? 'What coach, your honour?' says a ruffianly looking fellow, much like what he might have been had he lived a hundred years back. 'I wish to go home to Exeter,' replies the old gentleman, mildly. 'Just in time, your honour, here she comes – them there grey horses; where's your luggage?' 'Don't be in a hurry,' observes the stranger; 'that's a gentleman's carriage.' 'It ain't! I tell you,' says the cad; 'it's the Comet, and you must be as quick as lightning.' Nolens volens, the remonstrating old gentleman is shoved into the Comet, by a cad at each elbow, having been three times assured that his luggage is in the hind boot, and twice three times denied, having ocular demonstration of the fact.

* *North American Indians*, 361.

However, he is now seated; and 'What gentleman is going to drive us?' is his first question to his fellow passengers. 'He is no gentleman, sir,' says a person who sits opposite to him, and who happens to be a proprietor of the coach. 'He has been on the Comet ever since she started, and is a very steady young man.' 'Pardon my ignorance,' replies the regenerated; 'from the cleanliness of his person, the neatness of his apparel, and the language he made use of, I mistook him for some enthusiastic bachelor of arts, wishing to become a charioteer after the manner of the illustrious ancients.' 'You must have been long in foreign parts, sir,' observes the proprietor. In five minutes, or less, after this parley commenced, the wheels went round, and in another five the coach arrived at Hyde Park gate; but long before it got there, the worthy gentleman of 1742 (set down by his fellow-travellers for either a little cracked or an emigrant from the Backwoods of America) exclaimed, 'What! off the stones already?' 'You have never been on the stones,' observes his neighbour on his right; 'no stones in London now, sir.' 'Bless me!' quoth our friend, 'here's a noble house; to whom does it belong? But why those broken windows, those iron blinds, and strong barricade?' 'It is the Duke of Wellington's,' says the coach proprietor, 'the greatest captain since the days of Scipio. An ungrateful people made an attack upon his life, on the anniversary of the day upon which he won the most important battle ever fought in Europe.' Here a passenger in black threw out something about Alcibiades, which, however, the rattle made it impossible to understand. 'But we are going at a great rate,' exclaims again the stranger. 'Oh no, sir,' says the proprietor, 'we never go fast over this stage. We have time allowed in consequence of being subject to interruptions, and we make it up over the lower ground.' Five and thirty minutes, however, bring them to the noted town of Brentford. 'Hah!' says the old man, becoming young again; 'what! no improvement in this filthy place? Is old Brentford still here? A national disgrace! Pray, sir, who is your county member now?' 'His name is Hume, sir,' was the reply. 'The modern Hercules,' added the gentleman on the right; 'the real cleanser of the Augean stable.' 'A gentleman of large property in the county, I presume,' said the man of the last century. 'Not an acre,' replied the communicative proprietor: 'a Scotchman from the town of Montrose.' 'Ay, ay; nothing like the high road to London for those Scotchmen. A great city merchant, no doubt, worth a plum or two.' 'No such thing, sir,' quoth the other; 'the gentleman was a doctor, and made his fortune in the Indies.' 'No quack, I warrant you.' The proprietor was silent; but the clergyman in the corner again muttered something which was again lost, owing to the coach coming at the instant, at the rate of ten miles in the hour, upon the vile pavement of Brentford.

In five minutes under the hour the Comet arrives at Hounslow, to the great delight of our friend, who by this time waxed hungry, not having broken his fast before starting. 'Just fifty-five minutes and thirty-seven seconds,' says he, 'from the time we left London! – wonderful travelling, gentlemen, to be sure, but much too fast to be safe. However, thank heaven, we are arrived at a good-looking house; and now, waiter! I hope you have got breakf – .' Before the last syllable, however, of the word could be pronounced, the worthy old gentleman's head struck the back of the coach by a jerk, which he could not account for (the fact was, three of the four fresh horses were bolters), and the waiter, the inn, and indeed Hounslow itself ('terræque urbesque recedunt'), disappeared in the twinkling of an eye. Never did such a succession of doors, windows, and window-shutters pass so quickly in his review before – and he hoped they might never do so again. Recovering, however, a little from his surprise – 'My dear sir,' said he, 'you told me we were to change horses at Hounslow? Surely they are not so inhuman as to drive these poor animals another stage at this unmerciful rate!' 'Change horses, sir!' says the proprietor; 'why we changed them whilst you were putting on your spectacles, and looking at your watch. Only one minute allowed for it at Hounslow, and it is often done in fifty seconds by those nimble-fingered horse-keepers.' 'You astonish me – but really I do not like to go so fast.' 'Oh, sir! we always spring them over these six miles. It is what we call the hospital ground.' This alarming phrase is presently interpreted: it intimates that horses whose 'backs are getting down instead of up in their work' – some 'that won't hold an ounce down hill, or draw an ounce up' – others 'that kick over the pole one day and over the bars the next' – in short, all the reprobates, styled in the road slang bo-kickers, are sent to work these six miles, because here they have nothing to do but to gallop – not a pebble as big as a nutmeg on the road; and so even, that it would not disturb the equilibrium of a spirit-level.

The coach, however, goes faster and faster over the hospital ground, as the bo-kickers feel their legs, and the collars get warm to their shoulders; and having ten outsides, the luggage of the said ten, and a few extra packages besides on the roof, she rolls rather more than is pleasant, although the centre of gravity is pretty well kept down by four not slender insides, two well-laden boots, and three huge trunks in the slide. The gentleman of the last century, however, becomes alarmed – is sure the horses are running away with the coach – declares he perceives by the shadow that there is nobody on the box, and can see the reins dangling about the horses' heels. He attempts to look out of the window, but his fellow-traveller dissuades him from doing so: – 'You may get a shot in the eye from the wheel. Keep your head in the coach, it's all right, depend on't. We always spring 'em over this stage.' Persuasion is useless; for the horses increase their speed, and the worthy old gentleman looks out. But what does he see? Death and destruction before his eyes? – No: to his surprise he finds the coachman firm at his post, and in the act of taking a pinch of snuff from the gentleman who sits beside him on the bench, his horses going at the rate of a mile in three minutes at the time. 'But suppose anything should break, or a linchpin should give way and a wheel let loose?' is the next appeal to the communicative but not very consoling proprietor. 'Nothing can break, sir,' is the reply; 'all of the very best stuff; axle-trees of the best KQ iron, faggotted edgeways, well bedded in the timbers; and as for linchpins, we have not one about the coach. We use the best patent boxes that are manufactured. In short, sir, you are as safe in it as if you were in your bed.' 'Bless me,' exclaims the old man, 'what improvements! And the roads! ! !' 'They are at perfection, sir,' says the proprietor. 'No horse walks a yard in this coach between London and Exeter – all trotting ground now.' 'A little galloping ground, I fear,' whispers the senior to himself! 'But who has effected all this improvement in your paving?' 'An American of the name of M'Adam,' was the reply – 'but coachmen call him the Colossus of Roads.'

from THE CHASE, TURF AND THE ROAD *1840*

The Coach Horse

THOMAS BROWN

On the first introduction of coaches into Great Britain, the horses used were of the large heavy kind, as great speed was not regarded in those days; for, if travellers could be savely conveyed fifteen or twenty miles in a day, it was then considered a great feat. The coach horses were just such as are now used in the lighter kinds of wagons. Some notion may be formed of the tardiness of their action, when it is considered, that about sixty years ago, a journey betwixt London and Edinburgh occupied from a fortnight to three weeks, which is now performed in forty-three hours.

These heavy horses have now been given place to a lighter breed, much improved as respects speed, with a good deal of blood in them. Very compact and elegant in their figures, some of them, in appearance and qualities, are equal to hunters.

The better kind of coach horses owe their origin to the Cleveland bay, and are principally bred in Yorkshire, Durham, and the southern districts of Northumberland; and some few have been produced in Lincolnshire. The coach horse is propagated by a cross of the Cleveland mare with a three-fourth, or thoroughbred horse, which is possessed of a sufficient substance and height. The produce of these is a coach horse of the highest repute, and most likely to possess good action. His points are, substance well placed, with a deep and well proportioned body, strong and clean bone under the knee, and his feet open, sound, and tough. He possesses a fine knee action, lifts his feet high, which gives grandeur to his figure and paces; he carries his head well, and has an elevated crest. The full sized coach horse is, in fact, only an over-grown hunter, too large for that sport.

Some have supposed that, in Britain, the rage for breeding coach horses for so much speed, is a prostitution of the powers of the animal, and that it is barbarous to drive them at the great speed which is now the prevailing fashion. I do not see exactly that this is very blamable, as expedition is so desirable for the mercantile interests of the country; and if proper care is taken to shorten the stages, there can be little harm to the horses, travelling short distances at a pretty sharp rate. It is quite certain, that within the last few years, every means have been used to promote the establishing of post horse stations at very short distances.

I do not mean here to vindicate the cruel treatment to which this horse is but too frequently subjected on our public roads. Many of these are unable to throw all their natural weight and power into the collar, being frequently bought, at a low price, lame, or with such tender feet, that they cannot apply them to the hard roads. In this condition, however, they are wrought, and, with brutal chastisement, compelled to draw. Forced to proceed, by the smarting lash they acquire a peculiar mode of going, so as to save their lame limbs, by using the sound ones only; and in time they become as if sound on all fours. The torture the poor animal has endured rewards the inhuman perpetrator by the recovery of tolerably good movements; but this soon brings strains on the muscles, rapid exhaustion ensues, and death puts a period to his sufferings.

from BROWN'S ANECDOTES OF HORSES *1830*

Marengo and Copenhagen

STELLA A. WALKER

MARENGO – NAPOLEON'S CHARGER

Napoleon's spectacular successes on the field of battle were due, almost entirely, to the brilliant way in which he used his cavalry. He once wrote: 'Cavalry charges are equally effective at the beginning, in the middle and at the end of a battle'; but in fact his usual custom was to keep a cavalry force as a strong reserve to assure victory and to use it finally for the vigorous pursuit and annihilation of the enemy. In 1806 his cavalry numbered 65,000, but he later raised it to 100,000 with officers, men and horses carefully selected.

It is not surprising, therefore, to find that Napoleon himself was mounted on excellent chargers, all of them Arabs or Barbs, and nearly always grey or cream in colour. These horses were specially schooled at the Imperial Stud Farm at St Cloud. They were trained to remain steady and alert under gunfire, and to become easy-gaited for the long, weary marches of distant campaigns. To be one of Napoleon's chargers was a dangerous privilege, as he is supposed to have had eighteen horses killed under him in battle.

The most famous of these chargers was Marengo, a light grey or white Arab stallion imported from Egypt as a six-year-old in 1799 after the Battle of Aboukir. It is thought he was probably descended from the renowned El Naseri stud. The Emperor rode the horse at Marengo, and was wounded by cannon-shot which carried away a piece of his left boot. The engagement was saved from defeat only by the initiative of General Kellerman, who ordered a cavalry charge at the crucial moment, turning near disaster into brilliant victory. Napoleon was so impressed by the courage, speed and vitality of his new charger under fire, that he named him after the victorious battle.

Marengo stood only 14.1 hands high, but no horse was so long or so closely associated with Napoleon. This little Arab carried him at Austerlitz, Jena and Wagram. He survived the ill-fated Russian expedition of 1812, when it is said he stumbled on the icy roads and unhorsed his imperial rider. This mishap was regarded by the superstitious as an omen of the misfortunes that befell the brave and devoted French army, thousands of whom perished from famine and the bitter cold in the retreat from Moscow.

Marengo was not, apparently, among the horses sent to share the Emperor's exile in the Isle of Elba. The imperial stables suffered little change under the new régime and he is supposed to have been kept in his usual surroundings until Napoleon's re-entry into France.

The Emperor then took his old favourite to Waterloo, though Marengo at that date was twenty-two years old. The final and culminating defeat there was largely due to the failure of the newly re-organized French cavalry which lacked its former unity and co-ordination, and was thus unable to break through the British squares of mounted soldiers.

On the eve of the battle the Emperor's horses were stabled at La Ferme du Caillou. Three chargers were installed there, Désirée, Marie and Marengo, and it was the little Arab that carried Napoleon through the early part of the battle. According to one report he was slightly wounded in the left hip, his eighth wound in action. Later in the day Napoleon rode Marie and was hotly pursued by the English and Prussian cavalry. As he galloped by La Ferme du Caillou he stopped to change the tired Marie for a fresh horse. There was no time to saddle Marengo, and only an instant to take the first horse that stood ready, before the Emperor dashed away at full speed for Charleroi, where he picked up a carriage, and, travelling without pause, reached Paris in three days. Marengo, left in the stables at the farm, was captured by the British.

He was brought to England by Lord Petre, and there was some idea that he should be exhibited publicly as Napoleon's charger, but he was purchased by General J. J. Angerstein of the Grenadier Guards, who hoped to breed racehorses from him. He stood at New Barnes near Ely, and was well cared for and petted. He is advertised, in spite of his age, as late as 1820 at a fee of ten guineas, but his progeny achieved no success on the turf, which perhaps is not remarkable, as one contemporary description admits he was of bad conformation and ill-tempered, and, of course, his small size was not conducive to the production of racing stock. On the other hand, a different authority pronounces him faultless with all the finest eastern characteristics.

He died in 1831 at the great age of thirty-eight years, and his skeleton is preserved in the museum of the Royal United Services Institution. One of his hooves was made into a snuffbox and presented by General Angerstein to brother officers of the Brigade of Guards at St James's Palace.

There has been considerable controversy whether Marengo was a Barb or an Arabian, and whether he was light grey and only white in old age. The evidence is conflicting on both points, but in the many paintings of him he is depicted with the points and conformation of the typical Arab, and both artists Vernet and Meissonier show him as a white horse. In the familiar picture painted by James Ward, RA, in 1824, Marengo also appears as pure white, but as the horse was over thirty years old at the time it provides no real evidence.

COPENHAGEN – THE IRON DUKE'S CHARGER

Copenhagen, the famous charger of the Duke of Wellington, was almost as renowned as the Iron Duke himself. Contemporary diaries and letters are full of references to this stallion and anecdotes abound of his amazing stamina and personality.

Copenhagen's dam was Lady Catherine, the mare that carried General Grosvenor at the siege of Copenhagen. She embarked for England in foal to Meteor, second in the Derby of 1786, himself the son of the famous Eclipse; and in 1808 produced the bright chestnut foal that was named Copenhagen, after the campaign. Though he is referred to as a thoroughbred, he was not actually eligible for the General Stud Book as his grand-dam was a half-bred hunter mare. However, as he was well endowed with speed and good looks, General Grosvenor had him trained for the turf, but in his thirteen races in public he won only a match at Newmarket and a sweepstake at Huntingdon.

The Duke of Wellington bought him in 1812 from Sir Charles Stewart in Spain, where he was being used as a charger, and from that date he never changed hands again. The Duke rode him throughout the Peninsular Campaign and is supposed to have hunted him with the sixteen couple of hounds he brought over from England.

On active service the two were inseparable, and the spectacle of the stern, taciturn Duke galloping from one vantage point to another soon became a familiar and much-loved sight with the troops. Copenhagen's speed and agility made him an ideal ride, and the sudden dashing appearance of Wellington on his handsome chestnut at the crucial moment steadied many a wavering division and snatched victory when defeat was imminent.

The endurance of Copenhagen at the time of the Battle of Waterloo was tested to the utmost limits. On the day previous to the conflict, Wellington rode Copenhagen nearly sixty miles on visits to the headquarters of the Prussian troops and also to conferences with his own generals. The Duke wrote: 'On June 17th before 10 o'clock I got on Copenhagen's back – so much to do that neither he nor I were still for many minutes together. I never drew bit and he never had a morsel in his mouth till 8 pm. The poor beast I myself saw stabled and fed in the village of Waterloo.'

Seven hours later, at 3 am, Wellington rose and wrote important letters. As soon as it was light he mounted Copenhagen and rode him throughout the entire battle, a period in all of over seventeen hours. Undeterred by cannon shot, rainstorms and the devastating cavalry charges of General Ney, Wellington on Copenhagen calmly directed operations, reconnoitring and galloping from one viewpoint to another. The Duke personally launched the Household Cavalry against the French with the words, 'Now, gentlemen, for the honour of the Household Cavalry!' At the enemy's capture of La Haye Sainte he took command of the Brunswickers and saved the day. The Duke and his chestnut horse, both oblivious of danger, were everywhere. The final phase of the battle lasted from 7.30 pm until dark. Night had fallen when Wellington met Blucher at the farm La Belle Alliance, and the two men embraced each other in the hour of victory in the presence of the troops.

Wearily the Duke and Copenhagen returned to the village of Waterloo across the field of battle, where 45,000 dead and wounded lay in an area of three square miles. As Wellington and his charger picked their way along the muddy road in the bright moonlight, wounded men recognized the pair and roused from their pain and delirium to cheer the two as they passed. But the Duke was sunk in deep depression, worn out by sheer physical fatigue and devastated with grief at the appalling losses his victory had entailed. At last he reached his quarters and stiffly slid from the saddle, but Copenhagen, perhaps feeling that the hour of triumph merited some display of spirit, lashed out and only by inches missed killing his master.

The next day, when the Duke and Copenhagen were in Brussels, the horse once more kicked up his heels as his rider dismounted, and this time he broke loose and galloped half through the city before recapture. An animal of such indefatigable energy and verve deserves his place in the records of England's great victory.

In the years of peace that followed Copenhagen lived at the Duke's seat at Strathfield Saye. Both he and Wellington were much flattered and admired by the fair sex; and the Duke gave to a favoured few the privilege of a ride on Copenhagen, which proved, in some cases, an uncertain pleasure for the lady. Frances Lady Shelley writes in 1815 in her diary: 'I dined at three o'clock in order to ride with the Duke, who offered to mount me on Copenhagen. A charming ride of two hours. But I found Copenhagen the most difficult horse to sit of any I have ever ridden. If the Duke had not been there, I should have been frightened. He said, "I believe you think the glory greater than the pleasure in riding him!".'

Lady Georgiana Lennox also found him a trying mount: as always, at the sight of troops, he neighed loudly. When she was riding him he greeted in this way a bunch of soldiers who shouted at her: 'Take care of that 'ere horse, he kicks out; we knew him well in Spain'.

In later years he sired several good foals for the Duke. Mrs Arbuthnot, Wellington's great friend and confidante, relates how on July 16, 1826, she was taken to see a fine foal by Copenhagen 'which was the most beautiful creature I ever saw'.

For the last ten years of his life Copenhagen was not ridden, and he became accidentally blinded in one eye. The Duke's devotion to the horse never lessened, and when Copenhagen died in February 1836, he was buried with military honours at Strathfield Saye, where a headstone marks his grave, with this inscription:

> God's humble instrument, though meaner clay,
> Should share the glory of that glorious day.

There was universal grief at the passing of the famous old charger, which R. E. Egerton Warburton voiced in a poem entitled 'Epitaph'.

> With years o'er burdened, sunk the battle steed;
> War's funeral honours to his dust decreed;
> A foal when Cathcart overpower'd the Dane,
> And Gambier's fleet despoil'd the northern main,
> 'Twas his to tread the Belgian field, and bear
> A mightier chief to prouder triumphs there.
> Let Strathfield Saye to wondering patriots tell
> How Wellesley wept when Copenhagen fell.

Years later, in extreme old age, the Duke would still talk of his famous horse and relate endless stories of his fire and energy. He is recorded as saying: 'There may be faster horses, no doubt many handsomer, but for bottom and endurance I never saw his fellow.'

In London, opposite Apsley House, there is a fine bronze statue by Sir Joseph Edward Boehm of Wellington on Copenhagen. The most successful portrait is that by James Ward, which was painted as a companion picture to Napoleon on Marengo.

from HORSES OF RENOWN *1954*

To His Royal Highness Prince Albert, K.G.

'BLUE ROCK'

SIR – One so accustomed as Your Royal Highness to receive public marks of respect could not reasonably be expected to listen to the congratulations of an individual – now most respectfully offered to you on your auspicious marriage with the beloved Queen of our Isles – were they unaccompanied by matter of a nature permanently interesting, and deserving the serious consideration of those who desire to maintain our ancient pre-eminence in the breed of horses.

Whilst the attention of all around is more or less engaged in the public affairs of the nation, you may safely congratulate yourself that the force of circumstances has placed you beyond the turmoil of politics.

In your abundant leisure, therefore, it is natural to expect, and by thousands it will be ardently desired, that you may turn your attention to, and seek recreation and amusement from, our animating and diversified field sports, which the country of your adoption happily affords in a degree *unequalled* in any other part of Europe.

Considering Your Royal Highness in the light of a sportsman then, how much to be envied is your unrivalled ability to drain the cup of sylvan pleasures to its dregs! The opportunities which the Poet aspired to are yours, in possession, to the utmost extent:

> Give me to back the steed, and through the chase
> To wind my fearless way; to wield the gun
> On moor or mountain, or in the thorny depth
> Of forest intricate; nor less to seek,
> 'Mid slippery rocks and hoarse resounding floods,
> The noblest tenants of the stream. Then Health
> Shall brace my vig'rous frame and Cheerfulness,
> Health's handmaid, fill my soul with harmless joy.

Hoping, then, that we may see the sports of the field flourish under the revivifying patronage of your exalted station, I beg to draw the attention of Your Royal Highness to certain abuses which have crept into a leading branch of our national diversions, confidently expecting you will see the expediency of prevailing on Her Majesty to apply the axe, as Her Majesty has fully the power of doing, to the root of *one* evil at least.

In order that the subject may be clearly understood, it is necessary to explain, that down to the end of the last century, our ancestors, in breeding horses for the turf, were guided by principles involving the national advantage – their object being, not only to combine *speed* with *stoutness* to go a distance, but likewise *power* to carry high weight. The consequence was, that such horses as proved deficient in the first requisite were yet found immeasurably superior, as chargers, to the dragoon horses of any other country: in strength, bone, and substance they were equal to the best; whilst their courage and lasting powers, derived from their high blood, defied all foreign competition. The breeders of such horses deserved to be encouraged, and they were so, not only by the fostering care of the Crown, but by the patriotic munificence of individuals.

As far back as the reign of Queen Anne, a gentleman left a sum of money, the yearly interest of which, amounting to 1,300 guineas, he directed should be annually divided into thirteen Plates or Purses, to be run for *at such places as the Crown should appoint* (whence they are called the King's or Queen's Plates or Guineas), *upon condition that each horse, mare, or gelding should carry* TWELVE STONE, THE BEST OF THREE HEATS, OVER A FOUR-MILE COURSE.

This munificent bequest was made with the view and purpose of encouraging the breed of *a strong and generally useful* description of thorough-bred horse; and no question but the laudable intention of the donor was fully answered down to the end of the last century. About that period, however, unfortunately for the country, there existed a person who had acquired sufficient popularity on the turf to enable him to prevail on the public to patronise races for *short* distances, and *light* weights. Under the plea of 'humanity' to the horse, the late Sir Charles Bunbury established the practice of working foals – *yearlings*! – in the *severest* of all work, that of training, for the great Stakes. The consequence has been, that scarcely five animals in a hundred have stood training until they attained their full strength; and those

few which, *malgré* their owners' 'humanity', have attained a full
mouth without acquiring physical blemish, have unquestionably
been injured, more or less, constitutionally, by the *stimulating food*
given to excite unnatural precocity, and by the hard work –
sweating in a load of clothes – and strains of their early youth.

Another consequence of the establishment of short races and
early work not less lamentable and injurious, is, that a breed of
horses of a totally different character is encouraged, light in
substance and flashy in speed; horses that will live out the end of
their third year – for beyond that age there are now no great
Stakes to contend for – and then, as far as their owners care, for
all racing purposes they may descend to the tomb of the Capulets;
being really fitted in general for no more powerful work than
bearing a spinster through her constitutional airing on such fine
mornings as the sun happens to shine.

As to mounting our dragoons on the light ephemera of the turf
of the present day, the idea even has been lost sight of – has disappeared with the strength and substance produced by the
breeders of the last century; and such has been the infatuation of
the country in blindly following this destructive fashion, that even
the Crown suffered itself to be drawn into the vortex of folly,
having been prevailed on by the disciples of Sir Charles Bunbury –
himself one of the most implacable traducers of the late Prince of
Wales – to consent to the 'King's Plates' being run for at light
weights and for short distances! Shades of our ancestors! was
there ever heard of, since the goose with golden eggs, such
national folly and breach of trust combined!

This corruption and abuse, Your Royal Highness, cries aloud
for reformation. The trustee of the origination of 'Queen's Plates'
has the power of restoring his munificent gift to the patriotic
object he had in view. A few words from your lips will be
sufficient to convey to Her Majesty's ready apprehension the real
circumstances of the case; and when Your Royal Highness bears
in mind how much more *safely* and pleasantly the rider is carried
by a horse whose powers are two or three stone above the weight
he has to bear, the 'cherishing care of a husband' will doubtless
suggest an argument in favour of the utmost encouragement
being given to the breed of strong thorough-bred horses. – So
for this branch of my subject.

There is another of scarcely less importance, namely, the reckless and unchecked exportation of our half-bred mares.

During the last ten or twelve years our half-bred hunting mares have almost entirely disappeared from the country, the few that remain being luckily in the hands of those who cannot be tempted to sell them.

So long as stallions *alone* were exported, little injury was done; but the moment the foreign dealer cast a *sheep's eye* at our superior brood mares, the laws of the land, *and had they not been sufficient* the powers of Parliament, ought to have interposed by some such prompt measure as that lately passed by His Grace of Richmond – a measure, by the by, which, if really sound – and I am prepared with argument to question its being so – involves not one ten-thousandth part of the national interest and importance of the subject now commented upon.

'When the steed is stolen we lock the stable door,' says an old proverb: and the satire is but too applicable in this instance to the nation at large. When our brood-mares are gone not to return; when promising foals are not to be heard of, much less seen; *then* it is we begin to look about us, and inquire into the cause of the scarcity. After searching the country from end to end, making the most diligent inquiry, the mortifying truth forces itself upon us, that even were an entire stop *now* put to further exportation, a sufficient stock of *first-rate brood-mares* could not be replaced under the most favorable circumstances (a repeal of the corn laws, for instance, which would induce agriculturists to turn their chief attention to grazing) in less time than a quarter of a century! The Savage of the Desert, the unlettered Arab, retains more of Solomon's wisdom. *His mares cannot be purchased.* 'You are a rich Elchee' (Nobleman) 'I understand,' he replied to the late Sir John Malcolm, after coquetting about the price of a mare, enticing our countryman to double and treble his biddings: 'now, you want my mare, but you shall not have her for all you are worth, and all the money of your kindred into the bargain!'

Notwithstanding for so many years the exportation of our best horses has been suffered to obtain to so great an extent, there are laws in full force to be found in our Statute Books prohibiting under heavy penalties the exportation of mares above the value of *ten shillings*, unless a special licence be first had from the Crown under the Great or Privy Seal.

The validity of this assertion, involving a matter of such importance to the country as well as to its internal enemies, the exporters, can be ascertained by reference to the Statute 11 Hen. VII, c. 13, sec. 1 and 2; and 1 Edw. VI, c. 5, sec. 1; and the 1 Eliz., c. 6, sec. 9. Those Acts have never been repealed, though they were virtually suspended for a time by different Statutes which imposed a duty on the exportation of horses; viz., the 22 Cha. II, c. 12, sec. 8, and the 49 Geo. III, c. 52. But on the repeal of these two last-mentioned Statutes by the 59 Geo. III, c. 52, the aforesaid Acts of Henry, Edward, and Elizabeth resumed their original force and operation. Besides other penalties, one of those Statutes prohibits the exportation beyond sea or into Scotland (repealed as to Scotland by the Act of Union, Art. 18) of any 'horse, mare, or gelding', under pain of forfeiture of the same, besides a *penalty of £40 for each animal*, half to the informer, and last, though not least perhaps to some horse-jockeys, *one year's imprisonment of the offender*. Here it is obvious to remark, that had the *treadmill* been known in those days, the addition of its wholesome exercise might have had the desired effect of inculcating in the minds of our present dealers a proper notion of political economy.

As that is not the case, however, and as our common informers have lost sight of their vocation, it is highly necessary Her Majesty's Attorney General should be required to put a stop to the further progress of the great evil alluded to, by enforcing the laws as they exist in our Statute Books; or otherwise, if found to be insufficient, which I maintain they will not be, by submitting to Parliament a Bill that will give the necessary power to protect the country from so exhausting a drain as that which has been but too long suffered to exist – the *reckless* exportation of our brood-mares.

In conclusion, I would beg to call attention to the low price fixed for the maximum value of the mares which were suffered to be exported under the Statute of Elizabeth. What sort of animal would ten shillings command in the reign of that Queen?

If we allow the value of money to have increased by ten fold, and the value of horses after the same ratio, which is more than can be fairly demanded, we shall contemplate a mare worth *now* about ten pounds – an animal that no foreign dealer would accept the gift of were he compelled to take her out of the country!

It is clear, therefore, that if the policy which prohibited the exportation of mares above the value of ten shillings in Queen Elizabeth's reign was sound and good, as it is apprehended there can be no question it was, the wisdom of the present day ought no longer to countenance an evil which has progressed to a degree that a long course of years only can repair.

I have the honour to subscribe myself,

Your Royal Highness's most respectful

and most obedient servant,

BLUE ROCK

from THE SPORTING MAGAZINE *1840*

The Last Great Cavalry Charge

WINSTON S. CHURCHILL

We advanced at a walk in mass for about 300 yards. The scattered parties of Dervishes fell back and melted away, and only one straggling line of men in dark blue waited motionless a quarter of a mile to the left front. They were scarcely a hundred strong. The regiment formed into line of squadron columns, and continued at a walk until within 300 yards of this small body of Dervishes. There was complete silence, intensified by the recent tumult. Far beyond the thin blue row of Dervishes the fugitives were visible streaming into Omdurman. And should these few devoted men impede a regiment? Yet it were wiser to examine their position from the other flank before slipping a squadron at them. The heads of the squadron wheeled slowly to the left, and the Lancers, breaking into a trot, began to cross the Dervish front in column of troops. Thereupon and with one accord the blue-clad men dropped on their knees, and there burst out a loud crackling fire of musketry. It was hardly possible to miss such a target at such a range. Horses and men fell at once. The only course was plain and welcome to all. The Colonel, nearer than his regiment, already saw what lay behind the skirmishers. He ordered 'Right wheel into line' to be sounded. The trumpet jerked out a shrill note, heard faintly above the trampling of the horses and the noise of the rifles. On the instant all the sixteen troops swung round and locked up into a long galloping line, and the 21st Lancers were committed to their first charge in war.

Two hundred and fifty yards away the dark-blue men were firing madly in a thin film of light-blue smoke. Their bullets struck the hard gravel into the air, and the troopers, to shield their faces from the stinging dust, bowed their helmets forward, like the Cuirassiers at Waterloo. The pace was fast and the distance short. Yet, before it was half covered, the whole aspect of the affair changed. A deep crease in the ground – a dry water-course, a Khor – appeared where all had seemed smooth, level plain; and from it there sprang, with the suddenness of a panto-mime effect and a high-pitched yell, a dense white mass of men nearly as long as our front and about twelve deep. A score of horsemen and a dozen bright flags rose as if by magic from the earth. Eager warriors sprang forward to anticipate the shock. The rest stood firm to meet it. The Lancers acknowledged the appari-tion only by an increase of pace. Each man wanted sufficient momentum to drive through such a solid line. The flank troops, seeing that they overlapped, curved inwards like the horns of a moon. But the whole event was a matter of seconds. The riflemen, firing bravely to the last, were swept head over heels into the Khor, and jumping down with them, at full gallop and in the closest order, the British squadrons struck the fierce brigade with one loud furious shout. The collision was prodigious. Nearly thirty Lancers, men and horses, and at least two hundred Arabs were overthrown. The shock was stunning to both sides, and for perhaps ten wonderful seconds no man heeded his enemy. Terrified horses wedged in the crowd, bruised and shaken men, sprawling in heaps, struggled, dazed and stupid, to their feet, panted, and looked about them. Several fallen Lancers had even time to remount. Meanwhile the impetus of the cavalry carried them on.

Stubborn and unshaken infantry hardly ever meet stubborn and unshaken cavalry. Either the infantry run away and are cut down in flight, or they keep their heads and destroy nearly all the horsemen by their musketry. On this occasion two living walls had actually crashed together. The Dervishes fought manfully. They tried to hamstring the horses. They fired their rifles, pressing the muzzles into the very bodies of their opponents. They cut reins and stirrup-leathers. They flung their throwing-spears with great dexterity. They tried every device of cool, determined men practised in war and familiar with cavalry; and, besides, they swung sharp, heavy swords which bit deep. The hand-to-hand fighting on the further side of the Khor lasted for perhaps one minute. Then the horses got into their stride again, the pace increased, and the Lancers drew out from among their antagonists. Within two minutes of the collision every living man was clear of the Dervish mass. All who had fallen were cut at with swords till they stopped quivering.

Two hundred yards away the regiment halted, rallied, faced about, and in less than five minutes were re-formed and ready for a second charge. The men were anxious to cut their way back through their enemies. We were alone together – the cavalry regiment and the Dervish brigade. The ridge hung like a curtain between us and the army. The general battle was forgotten, as it was unseen. This was a private quarrel. The other might have been a massacre; but here the fight was fair, for we too fought with sword and spear. Indeed the advantage of ground and numbers lay with them. All prepared to settle the debate once and for ever. But some realisation of the cost of our wild ride began to come to those who were responsible. Riderless horses galloped across the plain. Men, clinging to their saddles, lurched helplessly about, covered with blood from perhaps a dozen wounds. Horses, streaming from tremendous gashes, limped and staggered with their riders. In 120 seconds five officers, 65 men, and 119 horses out of fewer than 400 had been killed or wounded.

The Dervish line, broken by the charge, began to re-form at once. They closed up, shook themselves together, and prepared with constancy and courage for another shock. But on military considerations it was desirable to turn them out of the Khor first and thus deprive them of their vantage-ground. The regiment again drawn up, three squadrons in line and the fourth in column, now wheeled to the right, and, galloping round the Dervish flank, dismounted and opened a heavy fire with their magazine carbines.

Under the pressure of this fire the enemy changed front to meet the new attack, so that both sides were formed at right angles to their original lines. When the Dervish change of front was completed, they began to advance against the dismounted men. But the fire was accurate, and there can be little doubt that the moral effect of the charge had been very great, and that these brave enemies were no longer unshaken. Be this as it may, the fact remains that they retreated swiftly, though in good order, towards the ridge of Surgham Hill, where the Khalifa's Black Flag still waved, and the 21st Lancers remained in possession of the ground – and of their dead.

Such is the true and literal account of the charge at Omdurman.

from THE RIVER WAR *1899*

Warrior's Great Adventure

LORD MOTTISTONE

I had stabled Warrior the night [of March 26, 1918] in the drawing-room of a little French villa which was still completely intact – so much so that I remember giving him his corn on a small ormolu table.

At dawn that next morning I stood in the square of the little village dictating orders to my brigade major, Connolly The Germans, who were not far off, perceived that the village was occupied, and opened fire with a big naval gun. Almost the first shell that came over our heads hit the little villa fair and square and exploded inside, knocking it completely down except for one corner.

I said to Connolly: 'I am afraid that is the end of Warrior'. But, no, there was his head poking out from the few bricks still standing, with the joist of the ceiling resting on his back.

We started to try to pull the bricks away, but before we had got very far with it, Warrior made a supreme effort and bounded out. As he emerged the joist fell, and the whole of the remaining corner of the house collapsed, in a heap.

Except for a little lameness from having carried most of the weight of the top storey, Warrior was none the worse, and I rode him all that day.

On the night of March 29 we camped at a little village called Boves near the main line from Paris to Amiens. Things looked very black then. I knew that if the Germans reached the ridge covering Amiens, the French and English armies had orders to fall back, the French on Paris, the English on the Channel Ports.

Next morning, early, General Pitman, who commanded our division, woke me where I was sleeping close to Warrior under a wall. He told me that the German advance had continued, that they had captured the vital Moreuil Ridge, but that our infantry were holding on, much reduced in numbers, to the left of the Moreuil village, which was for the moment held by the French. He directed me to take my brigade in that direction in order to help the infantry, and to cover their retirement when it became necessary. His last words were: 'Don't get too heavily involved; you will be badly needed later'. . . .

Although he must have been weary, Warrior put up a good gallop, and we clattered into the little village of Castel in fine style. There were a good many bullets flying down the road, but by turning to the right behind some houses we were in complete security.

By great good fortune I found the French divisional commander there. It seemed to me quite clear that unless we recaptured the Moreuil Ridge it was all over with Amiens, and probably with the Allied cause. I told the Frenchman this, and he agreed with me, but added that my little brigade could not possibly achieve it. In this he was wrong, as the event proved, but the main thing was that he sent orders to his men to hold on to the village of Moreuil on our right.

Sitting there on Warrior's back I decided to attempt the apparently impossible – to recapture the Moreuil Ridge.

Warrior was strangely excited, all trace of exhaustion had gone; he pawed the ground with impatience. In some strange way, without the least doubt, he knew that the crisis in his life had come.

At this moment the colonels of each of my regiments came galloping up as we had arranged. I dismounted and gave Warrior to Corporal King to hold. We consulted briefly, and I then ordered them to rejoin their regiments, the leading one, the Royal Canadian Dragoons, being only half a mile away.

The plan was that I should ride across the little river separating Castel from the Bois de Moreuil with my staff and my signal troop and, as the brigade advanced, should go forward with the signal troop and plant my little triangular red flag at the point of the wood. Our infantry were only some four hundred yards from this point, and were firing into the wood. It seemed clear to me that under cover of their fire I could do this vital thing, and establish the flag and headquarters at the point of the wood so that every man could see, as he passed our infantry front line, that the first phase of the battle had been won.

Now comes the wonderful part of the story as it concerns Warrior. As I have said elsewhere, after nearly four years of war Warrior had learnt to regard shell-fire as being part of ordinary war risks, but he had learnt to show great respect for rifle-fire, and would always try to swerve right or left in order, as he clearly understood, to reduce the danger from it. But this day all was changed.

I bade farewell to my French comrade, and mounted Warrior. As I rode round the corner of the little house behind which we had been consulting into the main road of Castel, Warrior took charge and galloped as hard as he could straight for the front line. At the bottom of the hill, where we were in dead ground, I induced him to slow down to a trot as we crossed the stream by a little half broken bridge. Then up to the opposing slant we went, still out of direct view of the enemy, and across a field of winter wheat. A hundred yards behind us was our own thin front line of infantry, lying down and returning the enemy fire.

There were about twenty of us all told when I halted Warrior for a moment and looked round to give final orders. I turned in my saddle and told my comrades that the faster we galloped the more certain we were of success, that I would tell the infantry to redouble their fire as we passed through them and that the day was as good as ours. But I could hardly finish my sentence before Warrior again took charge.

He was determined to go forward, and with a great leap started off. All sensation of fear had vanished from him as he galloped on at racing speed. He bounded into the air as he passed our infantry, and I remember shouting to a young infantry officer on my left: 'Fire as fast as you can.'

There was, of course, a hail of bullets from the enemy as we crossed the intervening space and mounted the hill, and perhaps half of us were hit, but Warrior cared for nothing. His one idea was to get at the enemy. He almost buried his head in brushwood when we reached the point of the wood at the chosen spot. We were greeted by twenty or thirty Germans, who fired a few shots before running, doubtless thinking there were thousands of us following.

Corporal King jammed his lance with the red flag into the ground, the survivors of my signal troop jumped off their horses and ran into the wood with their rifles, and the first phase of the battle was over. It was perhaps an odd way to use a signal troop, but it was the only thing to do.

But what I must record, and it is indeed the truth, is that so far as I am concerned the credit for this wild adventure, which succeeded in so miraculous a fashion, was due not to me, but to my horse Warrior. He it was who did not hesitate, and did not flinch, though he knew well the danger from those swift bullets which he had seen kill so many hundreds of men and horses all around him in the preceding years.

It was a wonderful day. The main attack swept up and the wood soon filled with galloping Canadian horsemen. Both sides, ours and the Germans', seemed to be filled with some extra-ordinary exaltation. Neither would surrender. Again and again these brave Bavarians and Saxons too, and men from every part of Germany, surrounded and wounded, would continue to fire out, but, on either side, not one man would hold up his hands and surrender. One determined Bavarian, with a sword thrust right through his neck, raised his rifle just level with Warrior's near shoulder, and had a last shot before he died.

Such was the spirit of the men who took part in this desperate action. So it was with the horses, and especially with Warrior, who, as all my surviving Canadian comrades will testify, was an outstanding example to all on that fateful day.

from MY HORSE, WARRIOR *1926*

The English Gentleman and his Horse

BARBARA W. TUCHMAN

The English gentleman was unthinkable without his horse. Ever since the first mounted man acquired extra stature and speed (and, with the invention of the stirrup, extra fighting thrust), the horse had distinguished the ruler from the ruled. The man on horseback was the symbol of dominance, and of no other class anywhere in the world was the horse so intrinsic a part as of the English aristocracy. He was the attribute of their power. When a contemporary writer wished to describe the point of view of the county oligarchy it was equestrian terms that he used: they saw society, he wrote, made up of 'a small select aristocracy born booted and spurred to ride and a large dim mass born saddled and bridled to be ridden'.

In 1895 the horse was still as inseparable from, and ubiquitous in upper-class life as the servant, though considerably more cherished. He provided locomotion, occupation and conversation: inspired love, bravery, poetry and physical prowess. He was the essential element in racing, the sport of Kings, as in cavalry, the élite of war. When an English patrician thought nostalgically of youth, it was as a time 'when I looked at life from the saddle and was as near heaven as it was possible to be'.

The gallery at Tattersall's on Sunday nights when Society gathered to look over the horses for the Monday sales was as fashionable as the opera. People did not simply go to the races at Newmarket; they owned or took houses in the neighbourhood and lived there during the meeting. Racing was ruled by the three Stewards of the Jockey Club from whose decision there was no appeal. Three Cabinet Ministers in Lord Salisbury's Government, Mr Henry Chaplin, the Earl of Cadogan and the Duke of Devonshire were at one time or another Stewards of the Jockey Club. Owning a stud and breeding racehorses required an ample fortune. When Lord Rosebery, having married a Rothschild, won the Derby while Prime Minister in 1894, he received a telegram from Chauncey Depew in America, 'Only heaven left'. Depew's telegram proved an understatement, for Rosebery won the Derby twice more, in 1895 and 1905. The Prince of Wales won it in 1896 with his great lengthy bay Persimmon, bred at his own stud, again in 1900 with Persimmon's brother Diamond Jubilee, and a third time, as King, in 1909 with Minoru. As the first such victory by a reigning monarch, it was Epsom's greatest day. When the purple, scarlet and gold of the royal colours came to the front at Tattenham Corner the crowd roared; when Minoru neck and neck with his rival battled it out at a furious pace along the rails they went mad with excitement and wept with delight when he won by a head. They broke through the ropes, patted the King on the back, wrung his hand, and 'even policemen were waving their helmets and cheering themselves hoarse'.

Distinction might also be won by a famous 'whip' like Lord Londesborough, president of the Four-in-Hand Club, who was known as a 'swell', the term for a person of extreme elegance and splendour, and was renowned for the smartness of his turnouts and the 'gloss, speed and style' of his carriage horses. The carriage horse was more than ornamental; he was essential for transportation and through this role his tyranny was exercised. When a niece of Charles Darwin was taken in 1900 to see Lord Roberts embark for South Africa, she saw the ship but not Lord Roberts 'because the carriage had to go home or the horses might have been tired'. When her Aunt Sara, Mrs William Darwin, went shopping in Cambridge, she always walked up the smallest hill behind her own carriage, and if her errands took her more than ten miles the carriage and horses were sent home and she finished her visits in a horsecab.

But the true passion of the horseman was expressed in the rider to hounds. To gallop over the downs with hounds and horsemen, wrote Wilfrid Scawen Blunt in a sonnet, was to feel 'my horse a thing of wings, myself a God'. The fox-hunting man never had enough of the thrills, the danger, and the beauty of the hunt; of the wail of the huntsman's horn, the excited yelping of the hounds, the streaming rush of red-coated riders and black-clad ladies on side-saddles, the flying leaps over banks, fences, stone walls and ditches, even the crashes, broken bones and the cold aching ride home in winter. If it was bliss in that time to be alive and of the leisured class, to hunt was a rapture. The devotee of the sport – man or woman – rode to hounds five and sometimes six days a

week. It was said of Mr Knox, private chaplain to the Duke of
Rutland, that he wore boots and spurs under his cassock and
surplice and 'thought of horses even in the pulpit'. The Duke's
family could always tell by the speed of morning prayers if Mr
Knox were hunting that day or not.

Mr Henry Chaplin, the popular 'Squire' in Lord Salisbury's
Cabinet, who was considered the archetype of the English country
gentleman and took himself very seriously as representative in
Parliament of the agricultural interest, took himself equally
seriously as Master of the Blankney Hounds and could not decide
which duty came first. During a debate or a Cabinet he would
draw little sketches of horses on official papers. When his presence
as a minister was required at question time he would have a
special train waiting to take him wherever the hunt was to meet
next morning. Somewhere between stations it would stop, Mr
Chaplin would emerge, in white breeches and scarlet coat, climb
the embankment, and find his groom and horses waiting. Weighing
250 lbs, he was constantly in search of horses big and strong
enough to carry him and frequently 'got to the bottom of several
in one day'. 'To see him thundering down at a fence on one of
his great horses was a fine sight.' On one occasion the only
opening out of a field was a break in a high hedge where a young
sapling had been planted surrounded by an iron cage 4 feet 6
inches high. 'There were shouts for a chopper or a knife when
down came the Squire, forty miles an hour, with his eyeglass in his
eye seeing nothing but the opening in the hedge. There was no stopping him; neither did the young tree do so, for his weight and that
of his horse broke it off as clean as you would break a thin stick
and away he went without an idea that the tree had ever been there'.

The cost of being a Master who, besides maintaining his own
stable, was responsible for the breeding and upkeep of the pack
was no small matter. So extravagant was Mr Chaplin's passion
that he at one time kept two packs, rode with two hunts and,
what with keeping a racing stud, a deer forest in Scotland and
entertaining that expensive friend, the Prince of Wales, he ultimately ruined himself and lost the family estates. On one of his
last hunts in 1911, when he was over seventy, he was thrown and
suffered two broken ribs and a pierced lung, but before being
carried home, insisted on stopping at the nearest village to

telegraph the Conservative Whip in the House of Commons that he would not be present to vote that evening.

George Wyndham, who was to acquire Cabinet rank as Chief Secretary for Ireland in 1902, was torn like Mr Chaplin between passion for the hunt and duty to politics. In Wyndham's case, the duty was untinged by ambition, since he had every intention of becoming Prime Minister. As he likewise wrote poetry and had leanings towards art and literature, life for him was full of difficult choices. A sporting friend advised him against 'sacrificing my life to politics and gave Harry Chaplin as a shocking example of whom better things were expected in his youth'. It was hard not to agree and prefer the carefree life when gentlemen came down to breakfast in their pink coats with an apron tied on to protect the chalked white of their breeches, or when on a Christmas night as Wyndham described it, 'we sat down thirty-nine to dinner' and thirty hunted next day. 'Today we are all out again. . . . Three of us sailed away (fifty lengths in front of the nearest followers). The rest were nowhere. We spreadeagled the field. The pace was too hot to choose your place by a yard. We just took everything as it came with hounds screaming by your side. Nobody could gain an inch. These are the moments . . . that are the joy of hunting. There is nothing like it.'

Older than fox-hunting, the oldest role of the horseman was in war. Cavalry officers considered themselves the cream of the Army and were indeed more notable for social prestige than for thought or imagination. They were 'sure of themselves', wrote a cavalry officer from a later vantage point, 'with the superb assurance that belonged to those who were young at this time and came of their class and country'. In their first years with the regiment they managed, by a daily routine of port and a weekly fall on the head from horseback, to remain in 'that state of chronic numb confusion which was the aim of every cavalry officer'. Polo, learned on its native ground by the regiments of India, was their passion and the cavalry charge the sum and acme of their strategy. It was from the Cavalry that the nation's military leaders were drawn. They believed in the cavalry charge as they believed in the Church of England. The classical cavalry officer was that magnificent and genial figure, a close friend of the Prince of Wales, 'distinguished at Court, in the Clubs, on the racecourse, in the hunting field . . .

one of the brightest military stars in London Society', Colonel
Brabazon of the 10th Hussars. Six feet tall with clean and symmetrical features, bright grey eyes and strong jaw, he had a
moustache the Kaiser would have envied, and ideas to match.
Testifying before the Committee of Imperial Defence in 1902 on
the lessons of the Boer War, in which he had commanded the
Imperial Yeomanry, General Brabazon (as he now was) 'electrified
the Commission by a recital of his personal experiences in hand
to hand fighting and his theories of the use of the Cavalry Arm
in war'. These included, as reported by Lord Esher to the King,
'life-long mistrust of the weapons supplied to the Cavalry and his
preference for shock tactics by men armed with a Tomahawk'.
Giving his evidence 'in a manner highly characteristic of that
gallant officer . . . he drew graphic pictures of a cavalry charge
under these conditions which proved paralysing to the imagination of the Commissioners'. They next heard Colonel Douglas
Haig, lately chief Staff Officer of the cavalry division in the South
African War, deplore the proposed abolition of the lance and
affirm his belief in the *arme blanche*, that is, the cavalry sabre, as an
effective weapon.

from THE PROUD TOWER *1966*

Envoi – The Salutation

WERNER BERGENGRUEN

Spring came, wild cherry trees blossomed in the bare woods and
in the Café Verbano they had already opened the windows. The
sky was blue and the morning sun shone. The captain and I sat
drinking our apéritifs. He had put his tobacco tin on the table
and was rolling cigarettes for us both.

Idly, or on business, people came and went, natives and
strangers, busy bell-ringing cyclists, men in Basque berets with
shopping carriers, occasionally a priest, elegant women in trousers
that were so cut that they looked as if they had been cast aside by

the old fishermen. Every few seconds a car tore, flew, or thundered past; they were either expensive, ostentatious, sporting, worn out, or vans carrying goods on four or two wheels. We sat and looked at them and were not ashamed to admit that we neither of us knew the first thing about motorcars, and that we had not the slightest wish ever to possess anything of the kind. We boasted that one still counted in horse power and not in abstract measures; and this, in spite of the fact that horse-power is an individual, flexible condition, and even children and motor mechanics know that a Shire or a Thoroughbred has more strength than a small pony.

'We're agreed then,' said the captain, 'that the horse is the real thing and that a car is simply an imitation. And like all imitations it is exaggerated.'

'Science has long since set up a memorial to its conquest,' I replied.

'Long isn't eternal. One shouldn't jump to conclusions. You see, in the second world war, that wasn't even my war, there were motorized captains, like tank captains. Well, why not? Of course, they weren't real captains, they were simply called like that. You know, rather as if I addressed my slippers as riding boots. Nothing against my slippers of course, without them I'd be lost, and they never even expect to be polished. But you must agree that they're not riding boots.'

'I? I'll tell you much more. I know that the horse has carried the pinnacles of our lives for centuries and that it has kept civilization on the right road. And what is it today? Doomed to extinction like the raven, beaver, golden eagle, wild-cat, and lynx. Of course, it will be kept for a while yet like some lovely old fashioned antique, like a plaything or a relic it will be kept artificially alive. Just the same, it will die out and when that happens, much of human character and perception will die out too.'

'And we shall die out with it,' said the captain, 'no one will put us into a Nature Reserve. Nature Reserves are a contradiction. There'll be quite different people about. Well! after all, the world doesn't stand still. Wait – what did I want to tell you – everything is not lost. Horses will come again and riders as well. Perhaps not for pleasure. Horses and riders stand at the bottom of all mortal things. Do you remember the Horsemen of the Apocalypse? One is riding a white horse, another a red, one is on a black and one on a dun. And that's not all. Riders and horses will have their hour again, a terrible hour. Turn over the pages of the Revelations of St John and when the trumpet blast sounds for the sixth time, hordes of horsemen pour over the earth, two hundred million of them. I don't know what sort of men will be able to sit on lion-headed, snake-tailed fire-and-sulphur breathing horses; it says that the riders will wear flame-coloured, blood-red sulphur-yellow cuirasses; not a particularly inviting troop it seems to me. For my part, I served once with the Dragoons, I shouldn't have liked to serve with the Apocalypse, they're not my type. God's Will be done. Probably there's time yet. Let's keep to horse-power.'

He raised his glass.

'You studied Latin. Did you know that in the Liturgy it says something about horsemanship? It is said at every Mass: *vere dignum et justum est, aequum et salutare* – in English: "In the spring it is proper and right to salute a horse". Don't you think that a remarkable translation? Truthfully the joke didn't come out of my fifth form, but from the Priest at Arceqno. Still, we won't be small-minded! Let's get used to the idea, not only in spring time when we're more than willing to do something unusual, but at any time of the year to salute every horse that we meet, whether it's the shabbiest old milk-horse between Vladivostok and Gibraltar. And not "as well as" but above all other creatures. How much longer shall we be able to do such a thing?'

'Spring is here,' I said, somewhat reservedly.

'Only the horse is missing,' the captain answered.

'Now listen, Captain. Here's a suggestion. We'll toss. Whichever of us loses has to go out and salute the next horse that comes down the street.'

'That's a sensible proposition,' the captain agreed. 'D'accord, then!'

We threw and I won.

'Good,' he said quietly and lighted his cigarette once more. 'It can't be helped, and even if the Emperor of China were watching, to say nothing of all the market people – I'll salute him.'

I heard something rumbling.

'Watch out,' I cried; 'There's a cart coming.'

The captain stood up, the cart was being pulled by two cows, the captain sat down again.

For a time only cyclists, motor-cyclists and cars passed.

I went out on to the street and walked a few paces, far enough so that I could see what was coming round the corner. Not far away was a two-wheeled cart, laden with faggots. Beside it walked a dirty, half-grown lad who was driving the horse which had become rather uneasy because of the traffic. It was a pitiable creature with a neglected ungroomed coat, its ribs sticking out and a melancholy drooping head. The scum and an outcast of the horse world.

'Get ready!' I called, returning, 'here comes the horse.'

The captain stood up. On one of the pegs was an expensive hat. Its owner had gone out for a moment. Besides ourselves the only other person in the room was the waitress, a pretty dark-haired girl from Wales. The captain took the hat and put it on his head although it did not fit and slipped backwards and forwards. He strode to the door, stopped suddenly before he reached it, as if he had forgotten something. Then he tidied himself by straightening his tie and smoothing his beard. When he had done this, he strode with his long, still elastic rider's legs into the street. The cart was just about to pass the Verbano.

The captain came to a halt and with great earnestness raised his hat; he was in no hurry. At the same time he bowed and clicked the heels of his unpolished shoes together, so that one could almost hear the sound of his spurs. But this did not satisfy him. Instead of raising his head, he bowed still deeper – and seriously, it was no longer an ordinary bow; unnoticeably his obeisance had become one with which a devout of the Greek Church shows his respect and reverence; the top and lower part of his body were at right angles. Then he slowly stood upright.

The lad took his cigarette from his mouth and started.

'Eh, il capitano,' he said, with a silly grin.

Hat in hand, the captain remained standing until the wretched equipage had gone. Slowly behind the cart, a saloon car of the newest type followed, impatiently blowing its horn. The occupants appeared to be rather taken aback that they were unable to overtake the farm cart because of the oncoming traffic. A young man in a canary shirt sat at the steering wheel. Also in the car were three carefully sunburned, good-looking and lightly clad ladies; one of them might have been a psychotherapist, at least as an amateur. They all stared at the captain as at a phenomenon. None of them realised that they had witnessed a sacred incident, none of them was aware that leave had been taken of centuries of human history, none of them understood that God in the image of his creature had been honoured.

The captain turned, without hurrying, into the café and put the hat back on its peg. The hat was still shaking slightly when its owner returned, but he did not notice it.

The waitress, who was used to the captain and his occasionally odd ways, had observed this disconcerting event, half startled, half amused.

Now she addressed him with a pretty, slightly surprised laugh: 'But Captain, sir, what are you doing now. . . ?'

'Ah, child,' he replied in a fatherly way. 'That was something important. Bring me another Campari.'

from DER LETZTE RITTMEISTER *1955*

PART II

Equestrian Lore

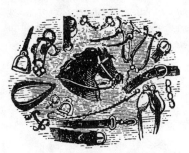

HARNESS-MAKER.

On Horsemanship

The one best precept – the golden rule in dealing with a horse – is never to approach him angrily. Anger is so devoid of forethought that it will often drive a man to do things which in a calmer mood he will regret. Thus, when a horse is shy of any object and refuses to approach it, you must teach him that there is nothing to be alarmed at, particularly if he be a plucky animal; or, failing that, touch the formidable object yourself, and then gently lead the horse up to it. The opposite plan of forcing the frightened creature by blows only intensifies its fear, the horse mentally associating the pain he suffers at such a moment with the object of suspicion which he naturally regards as its cause.

Xenophon 365 BC

Hints for the Rider

XENOPHON

As there will, doubtless, be times when the horse will need to race downhill and uphill and on sloping ground; times, also, when he will need to leap across an obstacle; or, take a flying leap from off a bank; or, jump down from a height, the rider must teach and train himself and his horse to meet all emergencies. In this way the two will have a chance of saving each the other, and may be expected to increase their usefulness.

And here, if any reader should accuse us of repeating ourselves, on the ground that we are only stating now what we said before on the same topics, we say that this is not mere repetition. In the former case we confined ourselves to advising the purchaser before he concluded his bargain to test whether the horse could do those particular things; what we are now maintaining is that the owner ought to teach his own horse, and we will explain how this teaching is to be done.

With a horse entirely ignorant of leaping, the best way is to take him by the leading-rein, which hangs loose, and to get across the trench yourself first, and then to pull tight on the leading-rein, to induce him to leap across. If he refuses, someone with a whip or switch should apply it smartly. The result will be that the horse will clear at a bound, not the distance merely, but a far larger space than requisite; and for the future there will be no need of an actual blow, the mere sight of someone coming up behind will suffice to make him leap. As soon as he is accustomed to leap in this way you may mount him and put him first at smaller and then at larger trenches. At the moment of the spring be ready to apply the spur; and so, too, when training him to leap up and leap down, you should touch him with the spur at the critical instant. In the effort to perform any of these actions with the whole body, the horse will certainly perform them with more safety to himself and to his rider than he will, if his hind-quarters lag, in taking a ditch or fence, or in making an upward spring or downward jump.

To face a steep incline, you must first teach him on soft ground, and finally, when he is accustomed to that, he will much prefer the downward to the upward slope for a fast pace. And as to the apprehension, which some people entertain, that a horse may dislocate the shoulder in galloping down an incline, it should encourage them to learn that the Persians and Odrysians all run races down precipitous slopes; and their horses are every bit as sound as our own.

Nor must we omit another topic; how the rider is to accommodate himself to these several movements. Thus, when the horse breaks off into a gallop, the rider ought to bend forward, since the horse will be less likely to slip from under; and so to pitch his rider off. So again in pulling him up short the rider should lean back; and thus escape a shock. In leaping a ditch or tearing up a steep incline, it is no bad plan to let go the reins and take hold of the mane, so that the animal may not feel the burthen of the bit in addition to that of the ground. In going down a steep incline the rider must throw himself right back and hold in the horse with the bit, to prevent being hurled headforemost down the slope himself, if not his horse.

It is a correct principle to vary these exercises, which should be gone through sometimes in one place and sometimes in another, and should sometimes be shorter and sometimes longer in duration. The horse will take much more kindly to them if you do not confine him to one place and one routine.

Since it is a matter of prime necessity that the rider should keep his seat, while galloping full speed on every sort of ground, and at the same time be able to use his weapons with effect on horseback, nothing could be better where the country suits and there are wild animals, than to practice horsemanship in combination with the chase. But when these resources fail a good exercise may be supplied in the combined efforts of two horsemen. One of them will play the part of fugitive, retreating helter-skelter over every sort of ground, with lance reversed and plying the butt end. The other pursues, with buttons on his javelins and his lance similarly handled. Whenever he comes within javelin range he lets fly at the retreating foeman with his blunted missiles; or whenever within spear-thrust he deals the overtaken combatant a blow. In coming to close quarters, it is a good plan first to drag the foeman towards oneself, and then on a sudden to thrust him off; that is a device to bring him to the ground. The correct plan for the man so dragged is to press his horse forward: by which action the man who is being dragged is more likely to unhorse his assailant than to be brought to the ground himself. . . .

In the Saddle

I shall next set down the method of riding which the horseman may find best for himself and his horse, when once he has received him for mounting. First, then, with the left hand he must take up lightly the halter which hangs from the chin-strap or the noseband, holding it so slack as not to check the horse, whether he intends to raise himself by laying hold of the mane about the ears, and to mount in that way, or whether he vaults on from his spear. With the right hand, he must then take the reins at the withers and also grasp the mane, so that he may not wrench the horse's mouth at all as he gets up. In springing to his place, he must draw up the body with the left hand, keeping his right stiff as he raises himself with it; for in mounting thus, he will not look ungraceful even from behind. The leg should be kept bent, the knee must not touch the horse's back, and the calf must be brought clean over to the off side. After having brought his foot completely round, he is then to settle down in his seat on the horse. I think it good that the horseman should practice springing up from the off side as well, on the chance that he may happen to be leading his horse with the left hand and holding his spear in his right. He has only to learn to do with the left what he did before with the right, and with the right what he did with the left. Another reason why I approve of the latter method of mounting is that the moment he is on horseback the rider would be completely ready, if he should have to engage the enemy all of a sudden.

When the rider takes his seat, whether bareback or on the cloth, I do not approve of a seat which is as though the man were on a chair, but rather as though he were standing upright with his legs apart. Thus he would get a better grip with his thighs on the horse, and, being upright, he could hurl his javelin more vigorously and strike a better blow from on horseback, if need be. His foot and leg from the knee down should hang loosely, for if he keeps his leg stiff and should strike it against something, he might get it broken; but a supple leg would yield, if it struck against anything, without at all disturbing the thigh. Then, too, the rider should accustom himself to keep his body above the hips as supple as possible; for this would give him greater power of action, and he would be less liable to a fall if somebody should try to pull or push him off. The horse should be taught to stand still when the rider is taking his seat, and until he has drawn his skirts from under him, if necessary, made the reins even, and taken the most convenient grasp of his spear. Let him then keep his left arm at his side; this will give the rider the tidiest look, and to his hand the greatest power. As for reins, I recommend such as are alike, not weak nor slippery and not thick either, so that if necessary the hand may hold the spear as well.

When the horse gets the signal to start, let him begin at a walk, for this frets him least. If the horse carries his head low, hold the reins with the hands a bit high; if he carries it somewhat high, then rather low; this would make the most graceful appearance. Next, by taking the true trot the horse would relax his body with the least discomfort, and come with the greatest ease into the hand gallop. And as leading with the left is the more approved way, this lead would best be reached if the signal to gallop should be given the horse at the moment when he is rising with his right in the trot; for, being about to raise his left foot next, he would lead with it and would begin the stride as he comes over to the left – for the horse instinctively leads with the right on turning to the right, and with the left on turning to the left.

I recommend the exercise known as the Volte, because it accustoms the horse to turn on either jaw. Changing the direction is also a good thing, that the jaws on either side may be equally suppled. But I recommend the Career with sharp turns at each end rather than the complete Volte; for the horse would like turning better after he has had enough of the straight course, and thus would be practising straight away running and turning at the same time. He must be collected at the turns, because it is not easy or safe for the horse to make short turns when he is at full speed, especially if the ground is uneven or slippery. When the rider collects him, he must not throw the horse aslant at all with the bit, nor sit at all aslant himself; else he must be well aware, that a slight matter will be enough to bring himself and his horse to the ground. The moment the horse faces the stretch after finishing the turn, the rider should push him on to go faster. In war, of course, turns are executed for the purpose of pursuing or retreating; hence it is well that he should be trained to speed after turning.

After the horse appears to have had enough exercise, it is well to give him a rest and then to urge him suddenly to the top of his speed, either away from other horses or towards them; then to quiet him down out of his speed by pulling him up very short, and again, after a halt, to turn him and push him on. It is very certain that there will come times when each of these manœuvres will be necessary. When the moment comes to dismount, neve do so among other horses, nor in a crowd of bystanders, nor outside of the riding-ground; but let the horse enjoy a season of rest in the very place where he is obliged to work.

from ON HORSEMANSHIP *365 BC*
translated by Maurice Morgan 1962

The Propertyes of a Good Horse

JOHN FITZHERBERT

And first though shalt knowe that a good horse hath l [i.e. 50] propertyes, that is to say ii of a man, ii of a badger, iv of a lyon, ix of an oxe, ix of a hare, ix of a foxe, viii of an asse, and vii of a woman.

Of a man: To have a proude hearte, and to be bold and hardy.

Of a badger: To have a whyte rase[1] or ball in the forehead and to have a white foot.

Of a lyon: To have a brode breste; to be styffe-docked; to be wylde in countenance; and to have foure good legges.

Of an oxe: to be brode rybbed; to be lowe brawned; to be short pasturned; to have greatte senewes; to be wide between the challes;[2] to have greatte nose thrylles; to be bygge on the chyne;[3] to be fatte and well fedde; and to be upryghte standyng.

Of an hare: To be styffe-eared; to have great eyen; round eyen; to have a lean heed; to have leane knees; to be wyght[4] on

---

[1] Mark   [2] Jaws   [3] Back   [4] Swift

the foot; to turne upon a lyttel grounde; to have short buttocks; and to have two good fyllettes.[5]

Of a foxe: To be prycke-eared; to be lyttell-eared; to have round syded; to be syde[6] tayled; to be shorte-legged; to be blacke-legged; to be shorte-trottynge; to be well coloured; and to have a lyttel head.

Of an asse: To be small-mouthed; to be longe-rayned; to be thyn-cressed; to be strayght-backed; to be lathe[7] legged; to be round-foted; to be holowe foted; and to have a tough hove.

Of a woman: To be mery of chere; to be well paced; to have a brode forehead; to be hard of warde;[8] to be good at a longe journeye; to be alwaye besye with the mouth; and ever to be chowynge on the brydell.

> *from* [Title] *Here begynneth a newe tract or treatyse*
> *moost profytable for all husbande men* [1523]
> *(i.e.* THE BOOK OF HUSBANDRY. *Anon. Often*
> *attributed to Sir Anthony Fitzherbert the*
> *law writer but really the work of John*
> *Fitzherbert author of the Book of Surveying.)*

The Errors of Horsemanship

M. BARET

For in the errors in Horsemanship [they] doe not alwaies proceede from the Horse, neither from that place (in the Horse) where it is first decerned, (as it is for the most part holden) but the cause of most errors (howsoever they are judged in the Horse) doe chiefly first proceede from the man, though unknowne unto him when it was committed: and although at the first it might seeme a very small escape, (yet being unreformed) by much use and practise, it will grow very grosse and palpable. . . .

Therefore the Horseman must (first) know himselfe to have an apt and able body, and also how to governe the same orderly

[5] Fore-parts of the shoulders   [6] Long   [7] Slender   [8] Hard to manage

and commendably, for the least disorder in the gesture of the man, causeth a greater in the horse, not onely in his teaching (the horse being governed chiefely by the motions therof) but also in the grace of his show, for the least error that a man doth commit in the government of himselfe, is encreased in the horse, in a double proportion. . . .

Also hee must carry his body upright, neither yeelding too farre backe (as if hee were pulling at a great tree), nor too forward as if he were asleep, for those two motions serve to other ends (as hereafter shalbe showne) neither to sit on one side, like a crab, or to hand his body over as if he were drunken, as I have seen some horsemen doe (which have carried good fame), for when they would have their horses go sidewise, they would hang their bodies so farre over the contrary side, as if they were to have fallen forth of the saddle, so that a man might safely perceive, what lesson they were teaching as farre as they could be seene, which is a very grosse error in a Horseman. Neither ought he to carry his legs so close to his horses sides, that hee cannot give any motion therewith, except hee first thrust them forth, for so, by continuall custome of his legs touching his side, he will be so careless that he will become very sadde, and have no quicke motions except the spurre be alwaies in his side, or (at least) he shall be driven to strike so hard with the calves of his legs, that the beholders may perceive him a good distance off, which thing also is an absurdity. Neither must he carry his legs (out) staring like stilts, (without joynts, as Saint George painted on horse-backe,) before his horses fore shoulder, or, (at the least) against his middle shoulder, for so hee cannot help, nor correct him, but the bringing in of his legs, wilbe very apparant to the beholders, and also if his horse should be any thing stirring, he cannot be able to keepe his seate truely, which wilbe held very ediculous in a horseman.

from AN HIPPOMONIE *1618*

Taming Vicious Horses

F. TAYLOR

How to Approach and Halter a very Vicious Horse
First provide yourself with a stout leathern halter, a strong iron staple and hammer, and a light timber hurdle about five feet long and four feet high, with some green boughs stuck in the top. Proceed to the stable alone, and in the cheek of the door of his box, or in the wall, drive your iron staple firmly, pass the rope part or shank of your halter once through the staple *downwards* – the shank of your halter should be about twelve feet long, and free from weak places. During these preliminaries be careful that the horse does not reach over the door of the box, and bite you. You must now place against the door of the box, *on the outside*, the hurdle, and on the most prominent twig hang the nose part of your halter, and now stand back and watch his movements. He will begin to smell and nibble at the boughs, which to him is a novelty, and his attention will be taken from you. Stand where you are for an hour, rather than hurry the business, during which time you may feed him with a piece of carrot or swede turnip. By this time you have established a sort of friendship between you, and the horse has become familiar with the halter, by coming frequently in contact with it during his examination of the boughs, and you may now attempt to place it on his head. If you should (by this) enrage him, you must wait for a second opportunity, and you will generally succeed (but it is important that you possess a good nerve), for if the horse finds out that you are afraid of him he will follow up the advantage. This class of animal is always very cunning, and attacks you instantly, and often without warning. Having haltered him, take hold of the end of your rope, and cautiously draw it through the staple without tugging at the horse, or letting him feel that he is fast, until you have his head in a favourable position, and as near as possible to the staple; then pass the end of your rope through the staple a *second* or *third* time, and secure the end, and you now have him fast and completely in your power. He will probably struggle fiercely to get loose. Stand quietly by, and, with hammer in hand, watch your staple,

and if by any chance his struggling and pulling should loosen it, hammer it up again, or fasten the rope end to some stronger pivot or fastening; a pulley firmly fastened to one of the rafters in the ceiling is not a bad thing. Keep him there some time, and he will give over struggling when he finds his efforts to release himself unavailing. The *first part of taming* the vicious horse is over, and you may now open the door of the box and dexterously fasten up his near foreleg. . . . Now place on his head a strong bridle, with a wooden bit about eight inches long and one inch and a half in diameter, with a cross at each end to prevent it slipping through his mouth, and this effectually prevents him from biting you. Put round his girth a circingle, and you may then slacken the rope, and he will probably hop about the box on three legs. If he stop, pull on the rope, and keep him moving from ten to twenty minutes, according to the degree of determination which he may exhibit. When he is thoroughly exhausted, place on him the strap No 2, and act as before directed, and you will find that he will succumb to you as soon and as easily as any other subject, for the previous arrangements have taken a considerable portion of his natural fierceness out of him, and he will lie quieter, and submit to more liberties being taken with him. Don't let him lie too long, or take the wooden bit out of his mouth, but take off the short strap from his near foreleg, and let him get up, by slapping him smartly with your hand on the ribs, and speaking the words 'get up', when he will rise to his legs, and shake himself, and stare around him in a vacant manner. The fierce, malignant expression has now partly disappeared and when he has been led round the box a few times, again place on him the short strap, to which he will submit, and repeat the treatment four or five times, and you may pull the bridle (with the wooden bit) off, and lead or ride him anywhere. He will obey *you*, but (for the present) *you alone*, in everything. If possible, let no other person be near him for a week, and when you leave him for the night, let the halter be on his head, and so contrived as to let the end be on the outside, and then you can draw him up anywhere when you again visit him. Sometimes the horse's head is tied to the rack on the *first* night, but I do not agree with that system; it is cruelty. Repeat the treatment two or three times a day for a week, and the savage is then thoroughly tamed. He will do anything for you. Let no other

person use him for three or four months, and occasionally practice
the art upon him, and, above all things, don't allow any one to
strike him or otherwise abuse him, and he will be *permanently*
cured, and remain docile; but if he change hands, and be again
ill-used, and challenged, as it were, to fight, it will again revive
his old hatred to mankind, and he will relapse, and be as bad or
worse than ever.

Adhere strictly to these instructions; be patient, persevering,
and courageous; and, above all, discard anything like harshness
from your breast, and you will succeed in taming horses like
'Cruiser' or the striped sleepy-looking animal called the 'Wild
Zebra of the African Desert', which will bring you into more
repute than professing to *tame* an animal, which can be led in and
out of a one-stalled portable stable designated a *cage*.

If your vicious horse be in a stall with his head tied to the rack,
speak sharply to him and go up boldly, and (without the least
hesitation) take hold of the halter close to his head, lead him out
of that stable into a building at least twenty-four feet square with
plenty of litter on the floor, and, if possible, let it be a building
where the horse has never been before. The examination of the
building will occupy his attention while you place the apparatus
on his legs.

The apparatus used in horse taming consists of a strap No 1,
thirty inches long, and about the strength and breadth of a common
stirrup leather, with a running loop and covered buckle. The
strap No 2, is about 14 feet long, and an inch broad, lighter than
strap No 1, and with a loop and ring, and a small strap attached
to the loop to buckle round the pattern joint. No whip, or spur,
or stick of any description, is used by Mr Telfer, either in taming
vicious horses, or first approaching colts. Mr Rarey, in his work
on *The Taming of Horses*, strongly recommends the use of 'a long
switch whip', as he describes it, 'a whalebone buggy whip, with
a good silk cracker, so as to CUT KEENLY and make a *sharp report*,
which [he goes on to say] if handled with dexterity and rightly
applied will be sufficient to enliven the spirit of any "horse" ', and
this treatment is recommended to all when they first approach the
colt. I leave it to my readers to say which of the two methods is
the best or most humane, that of Rarey or Telfer.

To subdue a very vicious horse is best performed by experienced persons, who have a thorough knowledge of the nature and disposition of the animal, and most essential recommendations being a good nerve, great patience, a quick eye, activity, and plenty of common sense. Amateurs should practise upon ordinary quiet animals before they attempt to subdue vicious horses.

Mouthing and Teaching a Colt his Paces

Having thoroughly established confidence between yourself and the colt, it is now time to mouth him and teach him his paces – walk, trot, canter and gallop. In saddling for the first time you may (after casting him as instructed), immediately on his rising up, place the saddle carefully on his back, and buckle the girths not too tightly at first; lead him round the riding-school, or paddock; and then carefully put your foot in the stirrup, and raise yourself gently from the ground, with your knees together, and pressed tightly on the skirt of the saddle, and your right hand resting on the back part (or cantle) of the saddle. Remain in that position a moment; and if it do not alarm him, which is of rare occurrence, you may gently raise your right leg, and pass it over his back; sit still a short time; pat him, and make much of him; and if he do not seem inclined to move which is sometimes the case, let some person lead him a few times round, until he will go on by himself, but let the man continue to walk by his side until he gets accustomed to his burden. Dismount and remount several times during the first lesson, which should not exceed an hour; treat him kindly, and avoid exciting him in any way. You may now take him on a quiet road, and commence your first instructions to him in walking, by keeping a steady feel of both reins on the bridle, which should be a plain snaffle only, and urging him gently on by a light pressure of both legs. If he be lazy, you may feel him very carefully with both spurs, behind the girth; and if he be inclined to get into a jog-trot, pull him back, by a steady, even pull of both reins, into a walk; and keep him at that pace until he performs it to your entire satisfaction. After this, commence teaching him to trot, by easing your hands on the reins, and a gentle, even pressure of both legs, and he will answer by trotting slowly on; and by an increased pressure of both legs, he will trot fast, or, as it is called in the army, 'trot out'. But be careful you do not let him mix these paces, but keep him to one kind, whatever that may be; and instruct him to change from one pace to the other without unseemly or awkward blundering. When you wish him to canter, start him neatly from the walk, and again bring him back from the canter to the walk without trotting between. In changing the paces, and when you require him to canter, ride him round in a circle, on soft ground, with his near side outwards; and with a light feel of the left rein and pressure of the right leg, bend his head a little to the left, and pull him lightly together, to collect him and bring his haunches under him. He will then canter with his right or proper leg foremost. And if you reverse the direction of his head in going round the circle, he will (by using his contrary leg or hand) canter on his other leg, or left leg foremost, which very rarely should be practised or encouraged, as it is considered the wrong way, and certainly looks ungainly for a lady, for whose riding this kind of pace is especially suited.

A clever horse-breaker will never practice a horse in the circle beyond a gentle pace; for, if he is urged to fast trotting, it teaches him an uneven, jogging style of going, the outer leg, having to step out longer than the inner one, sometimes appears lame; and when once young horses acquire bad habits, they are, like children, a long time in forgetting them. Heavy mouthing bits, crosses, and the multitude of tackle generally used, are not required in Telfer's system of training. A plain snaffle and easy-fitting saddle answer every practical purpose.

To Put a Colt in Harness the First Time

After casting him a few times and fondling with him, while he is on the ground, you may, without the slightest opposition on his part, proceed to harness him (having previously placed portions of the harness on his side, legs, and head, and rattled it about him), and having completed this, see that his knee-caps are properly on, and lead him about a little, or let him stand in the stable with harness on, until he seems at home with his gear. Now, get a well broken horse and carriage, or break, and let a man drive the horse about with your unbroken horse, not in a vehicle, but loose and free, keeping your hand on his near rein, close to his head, and walk him near to your horse in harness, with his head level, and body parallel with him, so that he can hear the rattle, and, having on no blinkers, partly see the carriage and driver while going; and, if he appears at all frightened stop the vehicle, and, turning his head round, let him examine everything carefully, by leading him gently around the vehicle; then start again, gradually increasing the pace to a slow trot, and when he moves along by the side of your other horse quietly, and without alarm, put him in the break, and run the other horse by his side, still leading him, and let the same man drive. Under no circumstances whatever, allow a whip to be used, nor should there be loud talking or shouting; if anything be said, speak out yourself distinctly, and accompany the word with a motion, to give the colt some idea of what you require him to do. Always be careful not to hurt your colt the first time you put him in harness, and examine him after you have taken the harness off carefully, to see that it has not chafed him, and especially remedy any unequal pressure of the collar. One hour is quite sufficient for a lesson. It will be necessary to repeat the casting for a few of the first lessons – say six; and he will then go through the exercise mechanically, and without opposition, because, in the first step, you have shown him that you are his superior, and that by proving your dominion over him you have been merciful, and that your intention is to instruct and not punish him.

Mr Telfer, has, by these means, thoroughly broken, to single and double harness, and saddle, seven horses in ten days, giving each horse a lesson daily. There are few broken by the old system in less than three weeks.

At Liverpool, in April last, Mr Telfer haltered a colt, tamed, put him in harness, and drove him through the public streets in an hour. He had never before had on a halter, and was an entire horse.

Very vicious horses may, after taming, be placed in harness, in some soft place, with the near leg strapped up, which sometimes has a very good effect; but if a horse begins to struggle or plunge, they are apt to come down and injure themselves. When you put a vicious horse in harness, be sure you put on the knee-caps, or a case of broken knees may follow. A very efficacious plan to adopt with vicious horses is to place them in a strong well-loaded cart; and, if they be confirmed kickers, place the ropes upon them and let them stand an hour or two; that will permanently cure them of kicking. You may now place them in a light carriage, starting from the same spot, and they will be glad to get away. Repeat this a few times, even after the horse is quiet. If he should stop on the road, instead of whipping and fighting with him (if it be convenient), let him stand still, and get some one to bring him his old torment – the loaded cart. Place him in it; and indulge his propensity to stop by staying with him an hour or two. Take him out, and he will start again very willingly, and, remembering the cart, will not attempt to stop again that day. As often as he stops repeat the treatment, and he beats himself. If you be in saddle, and your horse have the same fault, carry the small strap in your pocket, and immediately dismount, and strap up his near foreleg. Let him stand ten minutes. Take off the strap – mount; and he is glad to be off at any pace you please.

from TELFER'S SYSTEM OF HORSE TAMING *1858*

The Perfect Horse

GEOFFREY GAMBADO

To define a perfect horse is nearly impossible, and to tell you where to buy one, completely so. However, I shall endeavour to describe such outward beauties and active qualifications, as are requisite to the composition of one; and should such a phoenix fall in your way (and the taste of these times are so vilely perverted, I believe you have a better chance at present than you would have had some years back) I hope you will not let him slip through your fingers.

The heighth of a horse is perfectly immaterial, provided he is higher behind than before. Nothing is more pleasing to a traveller than the sensation of continually getting forward; whereas the riding a horse of a contrary make, is like swarming the bannisters of a stair-case, when, though perhaps you really advance, you feel as if you were going backwards.

Let him carry his head low, that he may have an eye to the ground, and see the better where he steps.

The less he lifts his fore legs, the easier he will move for his rider, and he will likewise brush all the stones out of his way, which might otherwise throw him down. If he turns out his toes as well as he should do, he will then disperse them to the right and the left, and not have the trouble of kicking the same stone a second time.

A bald face, wall eyes, and white legs (if your horse is not a grey one) is to be preferr'd; as, in the night, although you may ride against what you please, yourself, no one will ride against you.

His nose cannot project too much from his neck, for by keeping a constant tight rein on him, you will then sit as firm as if you were held on.

A horse's ears cannot well be too long: a judicious rider steers his course, by fixing his eyes between them. Were he cropt, and that as close as we sometimes see them now a days, in a dusky evening the rider might wander the lord knows where.

I have found many persons who have purchased horses of me, very inquisitive and troublesome about their eyes; indeed as much so, as if their eyes were any way concerned in the action of the animal. As I know they are not, I give myself very little trouble about them. If a rider is in full possession of his own, what his horse has, is perfectly immaterial; having probably a bridle in his mouth to direct him where to go, and to lift him up with again, if he tumbles down. Any gentleman chusing, indeed, to rise without a bridle, should look pretty sharp at a horse's eyes before he buys him: be well satisfied with his method of going, be very certain that he is docile, and will stop short with a 'Wohey',* and, after all, be rather scrupulous where he rides him. Let no man tell me that a blind horse is not a match for one with the best of eyes, when it is so dark that he cannot see: and when he can, it is to be supposed the gentleman upon his back can, as well as he; and then, if he rides with a bridle, what has he to fear? I flatter myself, I have proved as clear as day, that eyes are of little consequence; and as I am, no doubt, the first author that has made it known, my readers, if they lose no time, may mount themselves at Aldridge's, or the Rhedarium, as well, and for half the money they would have done, before I let them into this secret.

Be sure to buy a broken knee'd horse, whenever he falls in your way: the best bit of flesh that ever was crossed will certainly come down one day or another; whereas one that has fallen, (and sacrificed himself pretty much) never will again if he can help it.

Spavins, splints, corns, mallenders, sallenders, etc, etc, being all curable, are beneath your notice. A few of these little infirmities in your stable, is always a subject of conversation, and you may, perhaps, now and then want one; it will likewise justify you to your lady, in embellishing your bookcase with Bracken, Gibson, Bartlett, and Griffiths; excellent authors in their way, and extremely useful! for you will have no occasion to be sending for an apothecary upon every trifling ailment in your family, but will know yourself how to make up a good stout and effectual dose of physic for your wife or servants, in the gooseberry season, and at the fall of the leaf.

I would recommend a long tail, if it is to be had for love or money; if that is not to be got, buy a horse with a rat tail, if possible; though inferior in point of convenience to the former, there is a *je ne sçai quoi* of comicality about it, that inclines us to merriment whenever it makes its appearance. There is one inconvenience attending long tails in summer (when the poor animals

* I have searched Chambers and Johnson for this Wohey! but cannot find him. I do not recollect such a word in all Shakespeare, and he dealt at large in the language. Neither is it to be met with in Master Bailey's delicate Collection of Provincialisms. What is Wohey?

have most need of them); and that is, horses full of grass are very subject to scourings; in this case ride your horse with his tail in a bag, or else he may annoy you.

Having described for my reader a horse, and I hope he likes him, I would fain form as complete a horseman, and having done so, my ambition would be gratified, my end answered, and I would never ride again myself, as long as I liv'd.

from AN ACADEMY FOR GROWN HORSEMEN *1787*

The Runaway

GEOFFREY GAMBADO

When a man is once well run away with, the first thing that occurs to him, I imagine, is how to stop his horse; but men by no means agree in their modes of bringing this matter about. Some will run him at a ditch, which I allow to be a promising experiment, if he leaps ill, or not at all. Frenchmen (and the French are excellent horsemen) will ride against one another; no bad way either: and I have seen riders make directly for a stable (if a door happens to be open) and with good effect. How Julius Caesar stopped his horse, when he rode with his hands behind him, I am at a loss to divine.

I remember seeing an ingenious Frenchman make four experiments upon Newmarket Heath, in only one of which he succeeded. His horse made away with him whilst Gimcrack was running a match, and the Count's hopes of stopping him being but small, he contrived to turn him across the course, and rode slap-dash at Gimcrack, hoping to effect it by a broadside; but he was too quick for him, and he missed his aim. He then made full at Lord

March, but unluckily only took him slanting: baffled in this second attempt, he relied on the Devil's ditch, as a certain check to his career; but his horse carried him clean over, safe and well: and had not the rubbing-house presented itself to his view, he assured me, he believed he should have soon reached London; dashing at this, with a true French spirit, he produced the desired effect; his horse, not being able to proceed, stopped, and thus so suddenly, that the Earl of Pembroke himself would have been dislodged, and old Newcastle lain with his mother Earth. The Count, it is true, came off, but tolerably well; the horse broke his head, and the Count likewise; so that according to the ancient opinion of two negatives making an affirmative, little or no harm was done.

Having said thus much on the subject of being run away with, it is necessary I should decide, for the benefit of my readers, on the means I most approve of for putting a stop to such doings; and I am clearly for the stable door; if, entering it full speed, you should be afraid of your head, spread out your legs sufficiently, and your horse will go in without you.

from AN ACADEMY FOR GROWN HORSEMEN *1787*

Letters of Horsemanship

GEOFFREY GAMBADO

THE SIXTH LETTER

Sir,

Being informed that you are now at home, and desirous of giving every information in your power to those who may stand in need of it, respecting their Horses, I beg leave to submit my case to you; which, considering how fond I am of the chace, you must admit to be a lamentable one. Relying however, Sir, as I do, on your Philanthropy (I should more properly say Philipiggy), and that zeal in the cause which has so long characterised you, I make no doubt but the small difficulties I now labour under will be soon surmounted.

You must know, Sir, I am very fond of hunting, and live in as fine a scenting country as any in the kingdom. The soil is pretty stiff, the leaps large and frequent, and a great deal of timber to get over. Now, Sir, my brown horse is a very capital hunter; and though he is slow, and I cannot absolutely ride over the hounds (indeed the country is so enclosed, that I do not see so much of them as I could wish), yet, in the end, he generally brings me in before the huntsman goes home with the dogs; so, thus far, I have no reason to complain. Now, Sir, my brown horse is a noble leaper, and never gave me a fall in his life in that way; but he has got an awkward trick (though he clears everything with his fore legs in a capital stile), of leaving the other two on the wrong side of the fence; and if the gate or stile happens to be in a sound state, it is a work of time and trouble to get his hind legs over. He clears a ditch finely indeed, with two feet, but the others constantly fall in; that it gives me a strange pain in my back, very like what is called a Lumbago; and unless you kindly stand my friend, and instruct me how I am to bring these hind legs after me, I fear I shall never get rid of it. If you please, Sir, you may ride him a hunting yourself any day you will please to appoint, and you shall be heartily welcome. You will then be better enabled to give me your advice; you can't have a proper conception of the jerks he will give you, without trying him.

I am, Sir, humble Servant,

Nic. Nutmeg, Clerk.

Hinderclay, near Botesdale, Suffolk.

PS I hope what I have enclosed is genteel.
Mr Geoffrey Gambado.

The Answer

Reverend Sir,

Your brown horse being so good a hunter, and, as you observe, having so fine a notion of leaping, I should be happy if I could be of any service in assisting you to make his two hind legs follow the others; but, as you observe, they seem so very perverse and obstinate, that I cherish but small hopes of prevailing upon them.

I have look'd, and found many such cases, but no cure. However, in examining my papers, I have found out something that may prove of service to you, in your very lamentable case.

An Hostler (or Osteler, for so I believe it is usually written, though I find in the most learned Dictionary in our language, which explains some thousands of words more than Johnson, that it is vulgarly and improperly written Ostteler, for Otsteler, query Oat-stealer, and this, it must be allow'd, appears to be the true word), an Osteller has informed me, that it is a common trick play'd upon Bagsters, or London Riders, when they are not generous to the servants in the Inn, for a wicked boy or two to watch one of them, as he turns out of the gateway, and to pop a bush or stick under his horse's tail, which he instantly brings down upon the stick and holds it fast, kicking at the same time at such a rate as to dislodge the Bagman that bestrides him. Here, Sir, is a horse that lifts up his hind legs without moving his fore ones; and just the reverse, as I may say, of yours; and, perhaps, the hint may be acceptable. Suppose, then, when your horse has flown over a gate or a stile in his old way, with his fore legs only, you were to dismount, and clap your whip, or stick, properly under his tail, and then mount again; the putting him in a little motion will set him on his kicking principles in a hurry, and it's ten to one but, by this means, you get his hind legs to follow the others. You will be able, perhaps, to extricate your stick from its place of confinement, when you are up and over (if you an't down); but should you not, it is but sixpence gone. I send you this as a mere surmise; perhaps it may answer, perhaps not.

I thank you for your offer, which is a very kind one, but I beg to be excused accepting it; all my ambition being to add to the theory, with as little practice as possible.

I am, Rev. Sir, your most humble Servant.

G. Gambado.

Rev. Nic. Nutmeg, Hinderclay, Suffolk.

NB What you enclosed was perfectly genteel, and agreeable too.

THE SEVENTH LETTER

To G. Gambado, Esq.

Sir,

Hearing much of your knowledge in horses, I beg leave to ask your advice in a business wherein my delicacy as a Gentleman is deeply concern'd, and flatter myself that you will sensibly feel for my situation, my future fortune in life in a great measure depending on your decision. I have the happiness to be well received by a young Lady of fortune in this town, who rides out every morning, and has had the goodness to permit me to join her for some days past. I flatter myself I am belov'd; but, Sir, the horse I ride is my Father's, and he will not allow me to part with him: and this horse, Sir, has an infirmity of such an extreme indelicate nature, that our interviews are broke off every five minutes, and my dear Miss S—— will perhaps ride away with some other Gownsman who is more decently mounted.

I really, Sir, dare not mention, in plain terms, the shocking failure of my horse; but, perhaps, if you look into Bailey's Dictionary, you may find it out under the article of Wind. Be pleas'd, Sir, to send me a recipe for this horrid infirmity, or I may lose my dear girl for ever. I have tried several experiments, but all in vain; and unless you stand my friend, I shall go distracted.

   Infandum Regina junes renovare dolorem.
  I am, my dear sir,
    In a great fuss, Yours most truly,
      George Gillyflower.

St John's Coll. Cambridge.

PS Regina is not her name, don't imagine that. May I be allowed to say, I am very anxious for an immediate answer, as she rides out again on Friday next.

Memorandum

In consequence of the above, I sent the case to my farrier, who forwarded directly some powders to Mr Gillyflower with the following note. The efficacy being so certain, the trifling indelicacy of the prescription must be excused.

Honoured Sir,

By advice from Mr Gambado of your horse's complaint, I have sent you a powder so strong, that if administer'd night and morning in his corn, will be bold to say no horse in England shall ever fart again after Thursday next. Shall be very thankful for your Honour's custom in the same way in future, and your Lady's too, if agreeable; being,

Honoured Sir,

    Your Servant to command,
      Jo. Wood.

At my House at Chestnut every day. Horses shod agreeable to nature and according to art.

G. Gillyflower, Esq., St John's Coll. Cambridge.

Additional Memorandum

I thought it necessary to employ my Draughtsman, to delineate an interview, between a Gentleman and Lady enamour'd of each other, mounted on horses, labouring under the infirmity mentioned in the above letter. The attitude of the animals at these times, is admirably singular; and has such an effect on the Rider, as always to attract his eyes towards the tail, to see what is the matter. Indeed the back becomes somewhat like that of a camel, until all is ventilated. I have seen so many things of this kind, that I am concern'd for ·the young Lady's feelings, on this occasion, knowing they must be great. But still, those feelings, well delineated, might have as fine an effect as Le Brun's Passions. – I fear, however, my friend Wood, and his prescriptions, will be in disgrace; for a day or two ago, the learned Dr—— of St John's College (the same to which Mr Gillyflower belongs), call'd on me for an ointment to make the hair grow on his horse's tail; and talking about Mr Gillyflower's horse, he said he knew him; and that he had bought him out of the Duke of Norfolk's Stud. I then told the Doctor of the awkward infirmity he had; upon which, he said, he was not a bit surpriz'd, for the horse was got by Phlegon, and Phlegon was one of the Sun's horses he drove in his chariot; and that Phlegon and the other three were all got by the winds;* so that no Wood in the kingdom would be able to get his windy tricks out or him.

Mr Gillyflower being a scholar, might have known as much, methinks.

G. G.

from ANNALS OF ꓯORSEMANSHIP *1791*

* Naturum (observed the Doctor) expellas furea tamen usque recurret.

Helping a Lady how to Mount

A PUPIL

The man who is to mount the lady should advance facing her
and almost touching the horse' shoulder with his left arm. He
should stoop down a little away from the horse till his left
shoulder comes almost under the lady's right hand, which she now
advances and lays on it. At the same time he slides his left foot
forward between where she stands and the horse and makes a
cradle between his knees of his two hands. Into this she places
her left foot, and pressing a little on the saddle, and a good deal on
his shoulder, says 'Now', and gives a slight hop up. He straightens
his back and stands upright, raising the foot that is in his hands
steadily and rapidly up till he feels, by the sudden turn of it and
the relief of weight, that the lady is in the saddle. She is, however,
not really in a riding position at all, but only sits on her horse as
a man might sit on a gate with both feet at the same side of it.

He does not let go the lady's foot altogether, but keeps the
palm of his right hand under the sole of the boot, while, with the
left, he adjusts the folds of the habit so that all the loose part
hangs down in front and not a single fold is between the lady's
right knee and the saddle. As soon as this is done she turns a
little, as she sits, towards the horse's head and lifts her right knee
over the crutch. The habit fits it smoothly, and nothing remains
but for the man to fasten the strap that is beneath the skirt over
her left foot and put the toe in the stirrup. He should be able to
do this by feeling, without stooping himself or raising the skirt
to see what he is about.

printed in RIDING FOR PUPILS *1890*

Hard to Catch

R. S. SUMMERHAYS

Whether its cause is playful devilment or whether it is fear, there is no more exasperating habit in a horse than that of evading the man who wants to catch him – and, by the way, few things are more exhausting to the horseman. The dice are heavily loaded in favour of the horse, because few fields are so kindly devised as to contain a trap into which the unfortunate man can hope to drive the more fortunate horse. If such a convenient corner is to be found in the field, then the task is made comparatively easy, but what chance has one individual in an ordinary rectangular field of catching a horse which has just made up his mind for one reason or another not to be caught? It is easy enough to say that you should take a sieve of corn and the battle is more than half won, but countless people have tried this and have failed.

I do believe, however, that this trouble which I am now describing is overcome by the old idea of the master mind exerting itself over the subject horse. It may sound boastful to say that I rarely have any difficulty in catching a horse in a field, but I mention it because I try to approach the horse with a mixture, hard to define, of determination to accomplish what I set out to do, and outward calm and apparent indifference to the job and an appearance of time being no object. Such a mixture is just that which it is necessary to serve up to a horse in these circumstances. One needs a sieve of oats or oats and chaff with a hemp halter so placed (and more or less covered with the chaff) that it can be slipped easily over the horse's head when he drops his nose into the sieve. That sounds very nice and very easy, but I must admit you have got to get near enough to the horse for him to get his nose down; and for the purpose of being helpful I must assume that you just cannot get near him and none of the wiles or the chasings which you have tried are of any avail whatever.

You have, therefore, what we must admit is an impossible horse to catch, and what are you going to do about it? As so many people find it necessary to keep horses at grass, either for economy or perhaps because the horses are mountain- or moorland-bred and are better so, a way must be found to make this horse-catching a simple job. You must do one of two things: either hobble your horse or tether him. Of the two I prefer the latter. You must have a long rope attached to his head stall and a really strong iron spike driven heavily into the ground. But I am not suggesting that you should always tether him. Tether him only for the time being, and when you want to catch him in the morning go out with your sieve of oats or chaff; and the more attractive it is made by the addition of some sliced carrots or what you will, the better. Let him enjoy two or three minutes with his nose in the sieve and then untether him and lead him away for the ride, tethering him again after.

Repeat this a number of times, and unless I am much mistaken you will find that your horse associates your arrival in the field with something really good to eat. Next time turn him loose in his field when he will probably forget he is untethered and will either let you catch him or, what is more likely, will come to you. Like almost everything connected with horses this requires quite an amount of patience, and it may be much better to keep him tethered: this question of how soon he may be a free horse again will depend upon your horse's temperament, and you will be the best judge of that.

Alternatively, and if it is possible, make a pen in one corner of the field and always feed him there. Let him feed there a number of times before your first attempt to catch him.

Do not make the fatal mistake of walking the horse out of the field directly you have put the bridle on, when, perhaps, he has had only a mouthful out of the sieve. Play the game and give him a chance of eating up the lot. You will then find it much easier to catch him the next time.

from THE PROBLEM HORSE *1949*

Buying a Horse

JACK LEACH

The first item for the beginner to master is the sales catalogue. It never intentionally tells an untruth; but it gives what might be called a selection of facts. The dam 'Good Lady foaled in 1945', it says, 'is a daughter of Sharp Shooter who headed the list of winning sires six times'. Loosely translated this means that Good Lady, in six or seven years at stud hasn't produced anything that could keep itself warm.

Again, if you read that a yearling is the son of Trigger Happy, sire of winners of over £200,000 in stakes, it probably means that he is a damn bad specimen of a damn good breed. Here as elsewhere the way of a translator is hard.

In many cases the catalogue will tell you that the dam of a yearling never ran. You then go and ask the breeder why it never ran and the answer is almost invariably, 'Fastest filly Fred Darling ever trained and could stay for ever, but met with an accident the day after it was tried'. One owner, when asked why the dam of one of his very good two-year-olds never ran, said, 'Because it wasn't good enough to win a donkey race on New Brighton sands'. But then, he doesn't sell yearlings.

The next thing is to inspect the yearling. There are a few people who do this in ordinary clothes, but they are not considered quite the thing. Very old tweeds will do; in fact any garment will do as long as the wearer would be reluctant to be found dead in it anywhere except in the sale paddock.

A yearling must be approached from the left side in contrast to a cow which must be milked from the right. You must, however, refer to this as the 'near' side and the other as the 'off'.

You usually find yourself looking at someone who was there before you, but part of the pleasure of the sales is to exchange greetings with friends.

Next comes the front view in which you look, for instance, for splints and other bony enlargements. The man holding the yearling is generally in the way, having been well schooled by the breeder. The forelegs should be studied intently and if you are not afraid of horses it is as well to pass one hand slowly and carefully over the knees.

Naturally one side of a horse looks very much like the other, so it is not necessary to spend much time on the 'off' side – but the view from the rear is vitally important.

At this juncture you say to the groom, 'Does he always stand like that? Pull him up a step'. The yearling steps up, and if he is at all normal, comes to rest in the same position. Then the viewer grunts something and writes ZYX in the margin of the catalogue. This may not mean anything, but sometimes it does, especially if it is NBG.

The main thing is whether the animal looks like a race-horse. Has he got 'the look of an eagle in his eye' as the old man said in that very good racing film *Kentucky*? This may sound a bit funny to some dyed-in-the-wool experts, but I honestly believe there's a lot in it. Of course, soundness is really the main thing – a horse can't run unless he has feet and legs, and good ones at that; but naturally I am taking it that the trainer has sorted out only well-bred, sound animals to look at. Then, as I say, it's the way a horse carries himself and looks about him, whether he has that jaunty walk and the appearance of being able to lick creation – in other words, is he a racing machine? That's what counts. It is almost impossible to buy a perfect yearling, and so if one is struck by the overall appearance, the way the animal walks, etc., it is best to overlook a minor fault. I have bought what I thought to be a perfect yearling only once in my life. This was Delirium. I could not possibly fault him, he had everything right, and turned out a good one. On the other hand, another good one I bought, Figaro, was slightly back at the knee. The knees were slightly concave and looked to be tied in just underneath. This is considered quite a bad fault, as the animal is liable to 'jar' in training. (Being over at the knee, like an old cab horse, or like Brown Jack, is a good fault – they very seldom break down when they are like this.)

... There are some obvious faults one must look for. I have just mentioned back at the knee. Then there are splints – easily visible bony enlargements, generally on the side of the shin bones on the forelegs. They are serious only very occasionally, but they do show that there may be a certain weakness there. Nature has thrown out these extra protections, and as the animal gets stronger they will most probably disappear altogether. So I have often chanced a splint when everything else is all right.

The same goes for curbs, bony enlargements at the back of the hock. The jumping fraternity will not look at a horse with a curb because of the tremendous strain on hocks when jumping, but flat racers very seldom get any trouble from them for any length of time. A curb is another thing I should chance if the rest of the animal was OK.

Conformation is a great thing. Look for a good head, of course, but most important is an oblique shoulder, a deep girth (plenty of room for heart and lungs) and a wide behind. Watch the animal walk towards you and away from you. If it turns its feet out like Charlie Chaplin, go and look at another one, but if it toes in slightly it doesn't matter so much – in fact many judges say that this indicates speed. But the great thing is to keep a poker face; we are a babbling race greatly impressed by silence. If your opinion is asked, shake your head and mutter, 'Might be all right, but look at that', pointing vaguely in the direction of the animal's near fore. The next thing you know you'll be asked to judge at a yearling show.

from SODS I HAVE CUT ON THE TURF *1961*

The Psychology of the Horse

Lt-Col M. F. MACTAGGART

Before we start training a horse, it is very necessary to understand the mental attributes of the animal we wish to master.

Although horses are as different from each other as children in their personal character, there are nevertheless certain character-istics which are common to the genus horse, and which apply to all circumstances and all occasions.

The first of these is timidity. The horse's main defence is flight, and his very nature is to run from unexpected sights, and to fear unaccustomed situations. Being an animal of the prairie he dreads the bog more than anything else.

A second characteristic is that not only is he timid, but he is very sensitive to pain. Unfortunately for him, unlike the dog, he has slight facial expression, and we have to know horses well, before we realise how much they hate punishment. The dog, on the other hand, not being an animal of flight, has fangs to fight with, and can stand punishment far better than the horse. I do not think this point of view has been sufficiently realised.

A third outstanding trait in the horse's character is docility. He is most willing to do anything he is asked provided he understands what is required and he is ridden in the right way. Just as, in an ordinary ride, he will walk, trot, canter or gallop, turn to the right or left etc., at the will of his rider, so as his training progresses he will also perform more difficult tasks with the same willingness.

In fact, as Le Bon points out in his *L'Equitation Actuelle*, 'Horses in High School work will often try first one thing, and then another, in order to find out what definitely is wanted, and then when they have discovered it, they do it with evident pride and pleasure, as for example in the Spanish trot'.

A fourth characteristic is tranquillity. The natural condition of a horse is rather bovine. He would sooner eat grass, or doze in the shade, than do any other thing.

A fifth characteristic is a degree of laziness. Unlike the dog, who longs to go out, the horse's only desire is to go home.

A sixth is excitability. Even the most lethargic horse can become excited. When he is in this state his mental equilibrium seems to have become unbalanced, and he is ready to do almost anything, however foolish. He will hurl himself against a stone wall, or bang himself against a passing vehicle. His sense of self-preservation seems to vanish, and he becomes foolhardy and sometimes danger-ous. Consequently, in our schooling we must do everything we possibly can to prevent this characteristic displaying itself.

A seventh characteristic is courage.

This trait is a most perplexing one. On the one side we have a timidity which is sometimes ridiculous, and on the other we see a courage that may even be suicidal. But it can be explained, I think, by the docile trait, which makes the horse, placing obedience before self-preservation, throw himself into the task which is imposed upon him.

For example, let us take the instance of the horse being ridden at a muddy ditch. His instinct is to avoid it. He refuses. Perhaps he refuses again and again. But at last, ready to oblige he hurls himself over at top speed, with a courage and a sacrifice of self which commands our respect. But the underlying characteristic is fear, all through, and if we would be successful trainers we must keep this ever before us.

An eighth characteristic which must not be overlooked, is gregariousness, which can be made use of by jumping etc., towards other horses.

The ninth is the spirit of cooperation by which I mean the desire to learn, as distinguished from docility, a readiness to be taught.

A tenth is love of routine. Horses will usually do things, even those they naturally dislike, with readiness, provided they are accustomed to them, and if we train our horses on a strict curriculum, we shall attain much quicker results than if we keep changing the programme.

Training starts best in the stable, where perfect quietness should prevail. Even if grooms don't actually hit their horses, they can alarm them very much by shouting at them.

Horses should be so content in their stables, that they lie down a great deal even in the day time, and should be so confident of their groom that they don't get up even if they were to sit upon their backs. That is the standard we should always aim at.

With a quiet horse in the stable we have gone a long way to a quiet horse under saddle. But no horse will be really quiet if he is expecting the application of either whip or spur, so that is the next point to observe in our schooling.

But having said this, I feel it must be enlarged upon. Let us take the example of the refusing horse. Let us suppose that normal methods of patience have been exhausted, that the horse has often jumped that fence before, and still he refuses.

In the more general method of schooling the rider would bring out the whip, give the horse a good 'one, two', and it is possible the horse might go over. When this occurs we have to face the following statement:

'That's the way to train a horse. You have to show him you are master, and then he will jump all right.'

And the fact that the horse very often jumps after punishment, makes the practice difficult to dispute.

But that it is the wrong way, I hope to be able to prove. A sound horse refuses a fence because he is being badly ridden, or because he fears it. (He refuses sometimes because he is lazy, but that can be soon rectified.)

If we try to overcome his fear by punishment, his courage comes to his aid, he sets his jaw, and hurls himself over, and in that style he will jump that fence, and probably every other, for evermore.

To teach a horse to jump a fence artistically, we must eliminate excitement, rushing and jaw setting. We want to get him to canter up, in flexion, to the fence, as quietly as if it wasn't there, and then with a quickening stride to 'pop' him over, returning without excitement to his original quiet canter. This standard cannot be attained by punishment.

As I have said in a previous chapter, the best solution to the problem of a refusing horse is to lower the rail, but where this is impossible, our best results will be achieved by patience and determination.

It takes a bit longer than the other way, but those who are in a hurry should never school horses. We can undoubtedly get results of a sort, by exciting our animals, but the results are obtained by utilising the tranquil characteristic.

Our lessons will progress all the more quickly if we remember the lazy or the gregarious trait, and jump towards home, or towards other horses, in all the early stages.

So that if we keep in mind these ten characteristics, when handling our horses, and use them to the best advantage, we shall get not only excellent results, but ones which will surprise us.

The difficulty in studying the psychology of a horse is that, unlike the dog, whose mental attributes and reasoning powers are obvious, we cannot always fathom his thoughts and reasons for his actions.

Remember what the characteristics are:

FEAR, SENSITIVENESS, DOCILITY, TRANQUILLITY, LAZINESS, EXCITABILITY, COURAGE, GREGARIOUSNESS, ZEAL, LOVE OF ROUTINE.

So that our rule should be:

To suppress	FEAR, EXCITABILITY, LAZINESS
to develop	DOCILITY, TRANQUILLITY
and to utilise	GREGARIOUSNESS, SENSITIVENESS
	COOPERATION, LOVE OF ROUTINE

from HINTS ON HORSEMANSHIP *1919*

A Horse in Training

Colonel PAUL RODZIANKO

To understand the psychology of a horse, we must put ourselves in his position. Think how this animal must feel when he first comes into the hands of the trainer. Everything is strange for him, the kit that is put on seems uncomfortable and 'funny'. Before the training starts, he regards a human being as an object who looks after him and feeds him. When the trainer puts the tackle on his back or begins to lunge him and demand various actions, the animal obviously *feels* very strange and greatly surprised or frightened by these unexpected novelties.

Mentality

That is why the trainer must study and understand the mentality of his pupil. This mentality varies every time a new horse comes into his hands. It stands to reason that the trainer must educate his pupil.

The mentality of a horse varies as much as that of a human being.

Some horses are quicker than others in grasping the will of the trainer.

The horse pays attention to any movement of the trainer and every tone of his voice. If the trainer caresses the horse after each demand, the animal naturally gains confidence and becomes obedient. His mentality develops and he begins to understand what is required of him. If trained correctly he will work willingly, and good results will be obtained. The correct principles must be developed in the horse's mind.

We often hear the expression, 'a well-mannered horse', but manners are chiefly due to the good training the horse received at the beginning of his career.

Intelligence

Some people seem to find the horse an intelligent animal. In training however, intelligence seems to be an insignificant factor. The horse has an exceptional memory and this helps to obtain good results if the animal is properly instructed.

All the acts performed by the horse are learnt by constant practice and therefore are based more on memory than intelligence.

We see that it is really memory that makes the horse able to perform exercises. Of course, correct training helps to develop the horse's intelligence, however small it may be.

Voice of the Trainer

The tone of voice which the trainer uses is a most important aid and should constantly be made use of. A soft, low, soothing voice has a wonderfully calming effect. As it becomes familiar to the horse it will instil confidence and dispel fear. Tone acts on the horse more than anything else. A prolonged sound is likely to be satisfactory for decreasing speed and a sharper tone for increasing. The horse should be taught to respond to all the different tones and words used by the trainer.

The horse appreciates being talked to and it is extraordinary how quickly he begins to remember and understand the sound of the voice.

In cases of fear and shyness use a soothing tone of voice instead of roughness, spurs, whip, etc, which give unsatisfactory results. Mistakes of this kind are dangerous factors in training.

I am certain that it is partly through the medium of the voice that some trainers have a wonderful mesmeric influence over the minds of their animals.

'Making Much'

When the horse begins to respond to the will of the trainer it is most essential that he should be 'made much' of *immediately* he has performed an exercise in a satisfactory manner. If the reward is not given immediately it will be useless. By the expression 'making much' I mean caressing the horse and using a soothing tone of voice.

Tact

The trainer needs great tact and patience in the difficult and gentle work of training horses. He must not forget that the horse is sensitive and appreciates kindness and feels pain. A horse will not easily forget if he has been roughly treated.

A tremendous amount of tact must be used when dealing with horses. The trainer has to remember that in his work he has to deal with the horse's memory, sensitiveness, instincts, and mentality.

Punishment

There are certain times when punishment is inevitable, but great discretion, tact, and common sense must be used. The horse has a good memory, and it will take a long time to correct him if he has been unjustly punished. Any punishment is useless unless delivered immediately.

Sounds

Sounds have a very great effect on horses. For instance, when out hunting the sounds of the horn and hounds soon become familiar to the horse. On hearing them he gets excited and looks forward to the joy of the day.

Nerves

The more breeding a horse has the more highly strung he will be. During the training of a well-bred horse particular care must be taken, as, if wrongly managed, the animal will get more and more excited.

It is important that the nervous system of any horse should be carefully studied. A well-bred horse will usually respond most quickly to the will of the trainer.

A horse is very often shy when he thinks he may be hurt, when he sees a strange object, or hears a new sound for the first time. All this should be carefully taken into consideration during tuition, as it has a great effect on the nervous system of the horse.

If he is not dealt with in the correct way during his training, it may cause him to become obstinate, excited and disobedient. Firmness, tact, patience and kindness will produce confidence, calmness, and discipline.

Temper of the Trainer

The trainer or rider must keep his temper strictly under control. By losing his temper he may lose his battle.

During the training it is important that the work with the horse is not interrupted until the desired result has been obtained, as the horse will remember that the trainer gave in and will certainly be disobedient next day. Temper and tact have a great effect on the psychology of the horse.

from MODERN HORSEMANSHIP *1930*

The Horse's Nature and Mentality

HENRY WYNMALEN

Since our means of schooling the horse is to teach him the conventional language, which we call the aids, it follows that we shall not be able to claim success unless and until this language of ours be thoroughly understood and assimilated by our equine pupil.

It is well known and generally appreciated that to be a good teacher of children one requires a sound understanding of a child's mentality and sincere sympathy with its working. Unfortunately it seems less well known and not so generally appreciated that these same requirements apply *a fortiori* to the teacher of horses, since obviously there exists a much wider gap between the animal's mind and that of his human master than there is between the mind of a child and that of its grown-up teacher.

It is necessary to understand the horse before we can hope to make him understand us and the true art of schooling is to adapt our methods to his nature and to his intelligence.

Intelligence is mentioned purposely, since it seems to have become a fashion of late to pronounce the horse 'a stupid animal', devoid almost of this asset. I often wonder if the people, who so glibly make this statement, are qualified to express an opinion on so notably difficult a subject as 'intelligence in animals', which is, and has been for many years, a subject of intense study by eminent scientists and of acute controversy between different schools of animal psychology.

Intelligence is the capacity of the mind for knowng and understanding, and implies the faculty to make a reasoned use of physical and mental attributes, and of employing means to ends; if we accept this definition as correct then it is obvious that the horse has considerable intelligence.

The spending of a couple of hours in the saddle daily is no qualification to judge the horse's mind; if we have the gift of observation and sufficient interest to apply this to a constant study and understanding of the horse's ways in and out of the stable, whilst schooling, before, during and after rides, we are likely, at any rate, to come much nearer the truth.

The horse's principal mental attributes are observation, memory, the faculty to understand and to assimilate, reason, thought and imagination, and judgement.

His 'sense of observation' is exceedingly keen and little or nothing in his surroundings, or during a ride, escapes his attention.

His 'memory' is almost proverbial; he never forgets places where he has been, nor things that have happened to him; this memory is of great use for schooling purposes, if carried out on the right lines, but equally detrimental if the schooling has been done on the wrong lines.

It is on his 'faculty to understand and assimilate' that our whole system of schooling is based, since without this faculty no results would ever be possible.

His 'reason' is manifested when he refuses to go forward into a bog or to cross a bridge which he fears is not up to his weight, and manifested more strongly no doubt when, having learned to trust his rider, he will change his mind and go forward, notwithstanding his fear, because he reasons that where his master takes him, he will not come to harm.

'Thought and imagination' we will detect, when on a long ride the horse shows his inclination to enter into the gates of some drive, because he there imagines to find a warm bed, a full manger and a cooling drink. Or else when nearing a place where he has once been frightened, he will manifest his fear of the object that comes back to his mind, clearly depicted, which he 'imagines'.

His 'judgement' is apparent enough in the way wherein he quickly weighs up the capacity of a strange rider and determines his own conduct accordingly.

Though the horse thus has considerable 'intelligence' and possesses the 'faculty to employ means to ends', he does not possess much 'intellect', as that would imply the capacity to conceptual thinking. In other words his reasoning powers remain limited and his brain is incapable of connecting cause and effect otherwise than when observed simultaneously. It is consequently 'human stupidity' to punish the horse half an hour or half a minute 'after' he has done wrong, since he would no more be able to understand the reason of such punishment than he could grasp the feelings that might animate the human inflicting it.

Human 'intellect' enables us to try and imagine ourselves in the horse's place but the horse's intelligence does not enable him to imagine our mind. If, therefore, the horse does not understand, it is not his intelligence which deserves the blame but that of the man who has been unable to explain what he wanted, in a manner to help the horse!

The main peculiarities in the horse's mental make-up are, on the credit side, his extreme docility and readiness to do whatever is wanted of him, provided he has been made to understand it, and, on the debit side, his tendency to being easily, suddenly and throughly upset by things that frighten or hurt him or which he cannot understand.

Nature has made him an animal whose protection from danger lies in flight and his safety in speed. Hence his tendency to shy and swing round from objects that frighten him. He is gregarious and the company of others of this kind will raise his courage. Hence the presence of an older horse as 'schoolmaster' will quieten a frightened youngster, who in addition will carefully 'observe' the older horse and will generally follow confidently wherever the other one leads.

By cultivating the youngster's 'confidence in his master' we will be able to make him transfer his trust in the other horse to us, and we will find that gradually he begins to look to us for protection and guidance. His mind is much the weaker, and once we have established our 'mental' ascendancy, which to do is the true secret of human control over animals, the horse will 'like' this ascendancy more and more, since our moral mastery will both quieten and encourage him. In fact such a horse, when loose and in danger, will instinctively run up to his master for sense of protection.

And in this respect there is no happier horse than a really well-schooled one, whose instinct it will have become to act on his master's slightest wish, often without any need of actual indications or aids!

To deal successfully with horses and their schooling we need patience and sympathy, and no opportunity should be missed to increase, simultaneously with our own understanding of the horse, his understanding of us and the amount of his confidence. Anything that it is in our power to do in order to further the horse's comfort and contentment will tend to increase his 'intelligent understanding' and will materially assist in educating him into a lively and friendly creature who will be ready to give of his best, cheerfully and without constraint.

In this respect the everyday treatment of our charges in the meadow, in the stable and while at work, is of the utmost importance. While sentimentality is misplaced and must be avoided, we should treat our horses with unaltering friendliness, and above all, with quiet determination and complete fearlessness. In my experience no horse, once used to being treated on such lines, will ever bite, kick or otherwise try to injure its masters.

For the sake of comfort and contentment the horse should be stabled in a loose-box, be able to see other horses and to watch the goings and comings in the stable yard, wherein he will invariably take a keen interest. None of my horses is ever tied up, except for grooming when done outside; they are groomed, clipped, trimmed, saddled and bridled, and done everything to that may be required, while standing completely free. Such treatment inspires them with confidence and makes them easy to handle and manage under all circumstances.

It is never necessary to 'hit' a horse, it is a sin to do so in his stable, and it is quite unpardonable to do so at his head. A horse who is frightened of his head is difficult to bridle and it may be impossible to groom, trim or clip him about the ears without having to resort to that mediaeval instrument, the twitch. The defect is invariably caused by hitting at or in the direction of his head and whilst brought about in no time by injudicious handling it will take a very long time and immense patience to cure. In this connection attention must be drawn to an injurious practice almost invariably met with in dealers' stables and far too frequently in private stables, namely that of waving a hat or cap, or merely the arm, in the direction of a horse's head in order to make him stand back in his stable, so as to give a visiting customer or friend a better view. This, though it may seem 'horsey', is a most unhorsemanlike procedure, and should never be allowed; the proper way to show a horse is to put a halter or bridle on him and to take him outside his box. In his box we want to encourage him to come up to us confidently, and to give us a friendly nuzzle; under no circumstances should we frighten him or cause him to shy away from us.

The horse has very keen senses and is, by nature, very gentle. His hearing is wonderfully acute and it is consequently both useless and senseless to speak to him loudly, leave alone to shout at him! But he is very sensitive to the human voice, used quietly and softly, and it need be raised only slightly for the purpose of a reproof. No strength is required in handling him, since the biggest heavy-hunter can be made to move about his box, in whatever way required, by a mere pressure of the hand. He has the inborn disposition to 'fine aids' and if later on he can be made to 'pull like a train', or to acquire other 'rough aids', that will be his breaker's and not the horse's fault.

It does no end of good to visit a horse frequently, to speak to him, to give him a pat and sometimes a tit-bit, to straighten his mane or tail, to adjust his rug or inspect his feet, in other words to make him thoroughly familiar with and confident in our treatment. The horse enjoys these visits and will frequently show his pleasure in an unmistakable manner.

Horses out at grass, and especially youngsters, should be dealt with similarly, when they will soon come up to meet us or to answer our call; horses so treated will never acquire the habit of 'being difficult to catch', which is due to nothing else but unwise or indifferent treatment. Youngsters should be 'handled' as much as possible, when they will invariably become friendly, quiet and confident and it would be no exaggeration to say that a properly treated youngster is more than half broken, so much so, in fact, that the remaining half of that operation will cause little or no trouble.

Treatment makes the horse, since none was ever born vicious!

from EQUITATION *1930*

The Long and Short of it

W. E. LYON

It is curious how, in a world of journalism, some subjects seem to cling. They are to editors of magazines or daily newspapers what emergency rations are to a soldier – something only to be produced when *in extremis*. . . . In sporting periodicals which cater for the tastes of those whose lives are ruled by the horse, or are even remotely connected with the noble animal, there is one unfailing subject of controversy – the rider's seat.

This refers especially to what was at one time described as the Italian Seat, but now generally known as the Forward Seat. Whatever name is attached to it, it means the same thing in principle, that is, the placing of the weight of the human body equally over the centre of balance of the horse.

There is nothing very complicated about the theory, and perhaps we are all getting tired of a discussion where there is now little to discuss. If I were the editor of a weekly paper I should bar the subject altogether; yet, such is the inconstancy of the editorial mind, that here I am – at one time an editor – not only including an article on the much hackneyed discussion, but actually writing it myself.

My only excuse for rehashing the subject is that, after a certain amount of research, I have discovered that the theory of the Forward Seat was first tried out in competitive riding, not by Caprilli, who made a profound study of the subject in the early 1900s, nor by Tod Sloan, the American jockey who brought it on to the English racecourse in 1897; but earlier still by a humble Negro slave.

The story is not without interest, but in order to give it a background I must go back to those days when it was considered correct to ride a race with a long stirrup.

The greatest exponent in those days was the inimitable Fred Archer (1857–86), who, had he lived in these days, might have proved a redoubtable rival to Sir Gordon Richards, especially as regards his prestige amongst other jockeys. He, like Sir Gordon, was, in fact, the Head Prefect of the Race Riding School.

Being the Head Prefect in Archer's days carried with it more advantages than it does today, for in those days – to take one very piquant example – at the start of a race there was no drawing for places, consequently, as Archer was generally the first to be out of the paddock and canter up to the start, he always took the most advantageous position in the line-up. Even had he not been up there first, I doubt if any smaller fry would have had the temerity to challenge his right to the inside berth.

Fred Archer was the son of William Archer, a well-known steeplechase jockey who lived in Cheltenham, now the home of steeplechasing.

Fred was always highly strung, which accounted for his brilliance as a race rider, but I wonder if this story of him, as a boy, can be true? He had ridden a good enough race one day which ended in a dead-heat, but afterwards he was found sobbing silently to himself because *he had not ridden both horses.*

Fred Archer had a brain above average, his success being due mainly to his accurate judgement of pace and his astute appreciation of the merits of other horses in the race. As a contemporary of his once said of him: 'Archer had a brilliant brain, so much so, that had his education been profound enough, he would have made a better Prime Minister than some of those who have held that exalted position since his days.'

Fred Archer had one great rival in his day – George Fordham. Many said that he was the better jockey of the two, but, only going by hearsay, it looks as if honours were fairly divided. Archer certainly had terrific dash and an iron nerve, so he rode his races with a resolution bordering on recklessness. Poor Archer's handicap was his height and build; he was continually having to waste, by means both of starvation and drugs.

Eventually he contracted typhoid fever, and his brain being affected, he shot himself. So, at the early age of twenty-nine, Fred Archer, a great gentleman as well as an inspired jockey, met his tragic end.

I started by saying that in those days it was the fashion to ride a race with long stirrups, but also with a rigid horizontal back. Archer and Fordham, it would seem, were the first to break away from the mounted policeman position, and, by crouching, they adopted a more balanced and less wind-resisting seat. So perhaps we can say that this was the first short step towards the Forward Seat.

When Archer died in 1886, it was a case of 'exit Archer, enter Sloan', for it was in that year that Tod Sloan first made his appearance in the racing world, though he did not appear on an English racecourse until eleven or twelve years after Fred Archer had died. This made it almost impossible for Turf historians to compare the two men as jockeys, though contemporary writers are agreed that as judges of pace, quick thinking and fearless riding there was little to choose between them. There was a subtle difference, though, in their 'fearless riding'; Fred Archer knew exactly what risk he could take and get away with it; Tod Sloan's 'fearless riding' was, however, often interpreted by the Stewards as 'reckless riding'. It was this, combined with a low taste in companions, that eventually led to the American's downfall.

Tod Sloan, too, was as temperamental as a prima donna; when he was in good form and pleased with himself he could get the most unpromising horse past the post, but when he was low-spirited he was useless.

I remember the late George Lambton – that charming and most successful of trainers – telling me that on one occasion Tod Sloan came into the paddock to ride one of the horses in his stable. He had a tough race before on a great big lazy horse, and was most reluctant to ride, so he lay on his back in the paddock, repeating 'It's no use; I can't ride, I'm too tired'. Then, still on his back he glanced at the filly he was to ride, and liking the look of her, his whole attitude changed and, forgetting his fatigue, he got up and won his race.*

Of course, when Tod Sloan came to England and started riding with his leathers half a dozen or more holes shorter than anybody else's, he was ridiculed by even the most enlightened owners and trainers. It was not long, however, before Tod Sloan began to win races on the most unfancied horses, so in consequence there gradually developed a strong demand for his services, and, of course, the knowing ones always *had* known that the American Seat was the only seat that was any good. Other American jockeys

* See page 199 for Lambton's account.

came over and beat our jockeys, Danny Maher being one of the best exponents of the Forward Seat. To link up with contemporary times, Stephen ('Come on Steve') Donoghue was a disciple of the new school, though he does not go so far as to admit it.

It was just the same with the irresponsible Tod Sloan, who claimed to have invented the Forward Seat, but would he have ever practised this particularly ugly position in the saddle with such devastating success had it not been for Huggins, and would Huggins have been the architect of this curious design had it not been for this particular little nigger boy?

Huggins was a trainer of great repute in America, who later came over to England during the 'American Invasion' in the 1890s, when owners, trainers, and jockeys arrived and upset the form of the English Turf. Trainers from the USA were probably more up to date in their methods. Their jockeys made ours look ridiculous until they woke up to the idea of what was going on. The usual style of riding a race adopted by the old brigade in England, was not to exert yourself or your horse unduly until about two furlongs from home, and then ride like mad. When Tod Sloan and the others came on to the English racecourse they started riding their horses hard from the start, with the result that the English jockeys were so late getting on the move that they could never catch them.

J. Huggins was not only a first-class trainer, when in England, but also one jump ahead of the others in America, and this is where the Forward Seat originated. I will tell the story as Huggins told it to George Lambton.

In the more primitive parts of America, 'up-country', there were many rough and ready race meetings, but the horses, though rough, were not often ready, and the same applied to the jockeys; that does not mean, however, that there were not a few useful horses about. Huggins, appreciating the situation, used to pick out one of his horses that had a bit of form, and send it round the country meetings. Anything that beat this horse he would buy, bring it home and win races with it – so improved was it by his good systematic training. After a time in these 'up-country' meetings, owners took to putting up black boys on their horses, probably because they were cheaper than the white boys. Huggins discovered to his cost that those horses which had been ridden by black boys and won 'up-country' did not appear to make the same improvement as those he had bought in the old days.

This puzzled Huggins very much until one day, after he had bought a horse, the little black boy who had ridden him in his races asked Huggins to buy him as well so that he could look after him. This Huggins did, but in his first race his new purchase was defeated easily by the horse that had beaten him 'up-country', and the reason remained a mystery.

The 'darkie' then politely suggested that he should ride the horse in the next race, which he did, and won with some ease. This was no fluke, for almost anything he rode afterwards came past the post first.

Then at last the penny dropped, and this was the solution that came tumbling out of the slot. American jockeys in those early days were taught to ride in the approved fashion, with even longer stirrups and straighter backs than the English jockeys. The black boys, on the other hand, were never taught to ride at all nor were they allowed the luxury of saddles; so, with – at the most – a rug to sit on, they used to tuck their knees up and by means of crouching and hanging on to the horse's mane, managed to stay on top.

Huggins, shrewd observer that he was, saw that they 'had something there'. So this position, through the instrumentation of Huggins, became the craze.

Now this is where the sub-conscious mind comes into the picture.

I have, in my life, sometimes been struck by a brilliant idea which I truly believed at the time to have sprung from my own inventive brain, only to discover later that the germ had, unknowingly, been sown in my mind at some earlier date.

These experiences with their somewhat humiliating aftertastes must have happened to most of us, and moreover, I think that these delusions may be no fault of ours, rather let us blame them on our sub-conscious self.

Having delivered myself of this profound thought, let us now apply it to the Forward Seat.

Steve Donoghue, who started riding in 1905 with short stirrups, says in his memoirs: 'It has been said that I was one of the first to copy the *Tod Sloan crouch*. It is not so; the Forward Seat in the saddle came absolutely natural to me, and was always part and parcel of my riding. But I certainly always admired Sloan's riding; in fact, I consider he was a genius on horseback.' The italics are my own and speak for themselves.

Oddly enough, it was at this identical time that Captain Caprilli initiated the principle of the Forward Seat, and all honour to him, but we know that instantaneous photography was in a pretty advanced stage by then, so is it not possible that a picture of Tod Sloan was imprinted on his sub-conscious mind when he 'invented' the Forward Seat?

Then what are we to think about Tod Sloan, who was always boasting that his particular 'Monkey-up-a-Stick' seat – as it was called in those days – was entirely his own idea? When Sloan was riding in America, Huggins was training there, and it was then that the trainer cashed in on the secret of crouching seat suggested to him by the way his little nigger boy rode.

Might not such a revolutionary and successful style of riding have been in Tod Sloan's mind when he 'invented' the Forward Seat?

I feel sorry for that little 'coloured gentleman', because nobody has ever given *him* any credit for inventing the Forward Seat – but perhaps after all he was not the first in the field – maybe he saw a frightened little monkey sitting astride a branch in a high wind – a picture which may have imprinted itself on his sub-conscious mind!

Alas! We shall never know.

from THE HORSEMAN'S YEAR *1948*

Bitting and Collection

JAMES FILLIS

I have nothing particular to say about the snaffle, except that it ought to be rather thick, so as to reduce its severity, and that it should be placed at about an equal distance from the bit and the corners of the mouth.

The form of a curb bit and the position it is placed in the mouth are points of great importance. It is impossible to decide at first glance what kind of curb will suit a young horse best, and what position it should occupy in his mouth. Baucher says that he would use the same kind of bit for all kinds of horses, which statement is the consequence of his pet theory farther on, and I will here content myself with saying that even the most inexperienced horseman will state that horses go better in one bit than in another, and that certain animals will go kindly in a snaffle, but will resent the use of a rather severe curb. This is a generally accepted fact which has been amply proved. We can find the best curb for a horse only by trial. But there are always certain general principles to help us in making our experiments, which we may sum up as follows:

The curb which is used at the beginning of the breaking should have a thick mouth-piece, low port, and short cheek-pieces, so that it may be easy to the mouth. Its width should be proportionate to that of the mouth of the horse. If it is too narrow, the lips will be compressed by the cheek-pieces. If it is too wide, the horse, either in play or to relieve the bars of his mouth from pressure, will bring it too much over on one side of his mouth, so that a part of the port will rest on one of the bars, and consequently the mouth-piece will exert an uneven pressure, which will almost always cause the horse to carry his head sideways.

In order that the curb may fit properly, it should be wide enough for the cheeks to keep clear of the lips on each side. The mouth-piece should have an even feeling on both sides of the mouth, and should be mid-way between the tushes and the corners of the lips, and consequently it will be lower in the mouth than the snaffle in the case of a double bridle. Later on I shall point out some exceptions to this rule. The lower ends of the cheek-pieces, yielding to the pull of the reins, cause the upper ends to revolve forward, and thus to produce pressure on the bars of the mouth. The curb-chain which prevents the upper ends of the cheeks from revolving forward, increases the pressure on the bars proportionately to its shortness. Hence, the length of the curb-chain should be proportionate to the lightness of the horse's mouth, which we are unable to estimate in the case of a perfectly 'green' horse. With such an animal, we should at first leave the curb-chain very loose, as there will always be time to take it up. It would not, on the contrary, be right to say that there is always time to slacken a tight curb-chain, which causes pain that will continue to be felt by the horse after the curb-chain has been let out. If, however, we begin with a loose curb-chain, and gradually shorten it to the desired extent, we shall avoid hurting the bars of the mouth and irritating the horse to resistance, and we gain time. But if, at the beginning of the work, we hurt or even irritate the bars by undue pressure, we shall fail to obtain any of the required indications. By artificially increasing the sensitiveness of the bars, we fail to estimate it correctly, and work on a wrong method from the beginning. The bruising or even the mere irritation of the bars does not disappear as soon as the work is finished and the bridle taken off, but continues for a more or less long period. Consequently, when the next lesson is given, the bars are congested and painful. The rider will then be apt to form an opinion of the effects he produces on the mouth of the horse without taking into consideration that it is in an abnormal condition, and he will increase the evil which has been done, and he will become more and more unable to estimate correctly what is the natural condition of the mouth. In a word, he will do the very things he ought not to do. From the foregoing observations we can see that, at the beginning of the breaking, the curb-chain should be loose. In fact, it is better to take it off.

The knowledge of the mouth of a 'green' horse is an important and delicate manner. In order gently to feel the mouth without spoiling it, we must begin with great lightness of hand, and gradually increase the pressure up to the point of making the horse feel it, which sensitiveness varies in degree according to the animal. If a horse yields to the light pressure of a curb which has no curb-chain, of what use is the curb-chain, and what is the good of seeking for a more powerful means of restraint?

I have thoroughly broken horses, not only for the manège, but also for outdoor work, without using a curb-chain, which may remain hooked up on one of the curb-hooks, so that it can be instantly used in case of need. As a rule, it should not be employed unless the rider finds that he needs its help. When he uses it, he should never put more tension on it than is actually required; the proper maximum being when the curb-chain is tightened up, so that it makes an angle of 45° with the lower jaw.

As the tension of the curb-chain should be proportionate to the sensitiveness of the bars, so should the pressure caused by the pull of the reins be proportionate to the resistance. If this resistance is slight, the effort to overcome it should be light, and the point of its application should be high up on the jaw. If the resistance is great, the effort should be energetic, and it should be applied low down. Therefore, without greatly altering the middle position which the mouth-piece should occupy between the tushes and the corners of the lips, we may raise or lower the mouth-piece so that the horse may yield his jaw by, respectively, a light feeling of the reins, or by a strong pull on them. In other words, the softer the mouth is, the higher should be the mouth-piece; and the harder, the lower should it be placed. In no case, however, should it press on, or even touch, the corners of the lips or the tushes.

We learn from the foregoing remarks that the proper tension of the curb-chain and the right position of the mouth-piece in the mouth of a young horse can be found only from experience, which should be gained from very slight effects that can be gradually increased in severity as the case may demand.

Before going farther, we may recapitulate as follows the results we have obtained: the horse carries himself very freely forward on the legs being brought close to his sides; he correctly does the direct and lateral flexions on the jaw; is well in hand; yields immediately to the action of each leg; easily executes the respective rotations of the haunches and shoulders; and performs all the changes of direction with facility.

It must be well understood that during all the time my horse does these suppling exercises while I am on foot, I had also given him the same work mounted, and that I only seek by general effects to confirm and improve the results obtained on foot.

Respecting flexions and collection when mounted, I ought to remark that it is more easy to profit by acquired propulsion than to create it. By this I mean that, if I am at the walk, I have two things to do, namely, first to create impulsion by the legs; and, second, to make the horse do direct or lateral flexion. At the end of a turn at the trot and canter I am, on the contrary, full of impulsion, and to get the horse in hand I need only a fingering of the reins (in direct or lateral flexion), while keeping the legs close to the sides. Under these conditions there is no risk of the horse getting behind his bit, and then he comes most easily to hand.

Direct flexion should always be preceded, sustained, and completed by the action of the legs pressing the hind quarters on the forehand.

The legs ought to take and give like the hands, and with the hands, that is to say, simultaneously and in the same proportion. This constitutes general movement. If the hands give and the legs continue their action, the horse will be out of hand, because the propulsion developed by the legs will no longer be received by the hands. If the hands act without the legs sending them any impulsion, the horse will bring his chin into his breast or will get behind his bit; because his hocks have been left too far behind him. The expression 'take and give', as I have explained it when speaking of direct flexion, therefore applies as well to the action of the legs as to that of the hands. Legs and hands should always act in harmony, according to the desired result. We get the horse in hand by this combination of the alternate actions of the legs and hands acting on the whole.

Getting the horse in hand, which is an excellent term of the old school, is the result of equilibrium during propulsion, obtained and preserved by direct flexion, resulting from the action of the legs impelling the hind quarters on to the forehand. Here we are in the best conditions of good horsemanship. The hind legs, being well under the body, drive it forward and maintain equilibrium by the high position of the neck. The momentum of the mass ends at the bit, namely, at the end of the arm of the lever (of which the flexibility from front to rear increases from rear to front), whence the hand of the rider sends back, in its turn, the amount necessary to maintain equilibrium, towards the hindquarters, which by a fresh spring again impels all the mass forward; and so on. This horse is thus truly in hand. In my opinion, he ought at the same time to be on the hand. The horse is on the hand when, being in direct flexion, he closes his jaw on the bit from time to time, so as to remain in constant communication with the hand of the rider.

Finally, the horse comes up again on the hand when the impulsion communicated by the legs brings the hocks strongly under the animal's body and sends him freely on the bit, which is possible only when the horse is in hand to a maximum extent, which form of control is the rassembler. It is necessary that the tension of the reins is light enough to allow the propulsion to pass, but great enough to establish contact between the bit and the hand, and to give us the feeling that as the impulsion comes freely on the hand, we can dispose of it as we like.

As the neck in this case is necessarily high, and as the action of the horse is lofty, the meaning of the expression, 'the horse comes up to the hand', is perfectly clear.

We can now understand what is meant by the horse being between the hands and legs, both of which send back impulsion to each other, so as to preserve equilibrium while going forward.

from BREAKING AND RIDING *1902*

Dressage v. Uhlanage

JOHN PAGET

For years critics of the BHS three-day event training methods have been offering unrefuted and unrefutable evidence to prove that in combined training at international level the horses that do best on the first day are precisely those most likely to be defeated by a testing cross-country course. Indeed at Tokyo [1964] our team, that set out in the lead, was eliminated along with South Korea and Japan by a distinctly sub-Olympic course.

The BHS has been pleased to call this obsolete training system, about which such extravagant and unjustifiable claims are still being made, 'dressage', a misnomer if ever there was one. In fact it only means training.

Since the system of training sponsored by the BHS is in fact pre-war German Cavalry practice a less appropriate name than dressage would be hard to imagine.

The correct German usage is too much of a mouthful so it is proposed to coin a new term, namely, UHLANAGE.

In its defence I venture to refer the uhlans and their imitators to La Guerinière whose authority they are always invoking. For according to the super pundit of classical equitation the correct use of the equestrian terms is the basis of good riding.

Furthermore, it is respectfully submitted, if eliminating uhlanage has proved fatal to our three-day eventers, it is no more help to our Grand Prix competitors.

No Olympic discipline is more bedevilled by double-think than the FEI's Grand Prix de Dressage Artistiane. All use the same terms, but though they are adequately defined in the regulations, very different interpretations are given to them, and the judges continue to go along with the majority of competitors rather than insist on a rational interpretation of the rules.

Lightness, for example, means to the uhlans and their party what is meant by democracy behind the iron curtain – an abject and unquestioning obedience, however reluctant.

Their opponents, however, will settle for nothing less than our understanding of that term as free consent and intelligent co-operation.

The pundits writing in the French language magazines claim that 'uhlanage', as demonstrated by the German gold medallists at Tokyo, was in flagrant contradiction with the FEI definitions of 'dressage artistique'.

For, if the strong arm methods of the German team, to which the jury is alleged to have turned a blind eye, are to be regarded as a criterion of excellence, our ladies might just as well stay at home.

Since we have no male competitors, it stands to reason that the BHS have a vested interest in upholding the existing regulations and joining their author, Colonel Max Thommen (Switzerland), in condemning uhlanage and all its works, ungrateful as this may seem.

The snag to this obvious policy is, that it also entails condemning the riding and training of the Spanish Riding School, that the BHS has conditioned a whole generation of horsemen to regard as perfection itself. There are so many legitimate reasons for admiring the quadrille of the White Stallions in their splendid riding school that criticism, however justified, is invariably regarded as churlish and in the worst of taste.

James Fillis, who knew what he was talking about, and was certainly no sentimentalist where horses were concerned, called the training of the Lipizzaners he had witnessed in Vienna, the massacre of the innocents.

Without going into the rights and wrongs of Fillis's case against the Spanish Riding School, it must be recognized that the rittermeisters of Vienna have departed much further than, for example, the Lusitanian rejoneadores from a common tradition.

If the Portuguese can still fight bulls riding in the classic style of the 18th century, what possible excuse can there be for a conservatory of such riding like the Spanish School of Vienna, adopting the decadent cavalry practice of the mounted infantry and the mechanised cavalry of the present century.

In Colonel Podhajski's latest book there is a photo of the author riding into a stadium hat in hand, with his horse's head suspended on the snaffle reins. No portrait of any period of a charger going like this is known to me. Uhlanage is the only word to describe such riding.

The seat of the rittermeisters is also as unclassical as it is unlovely. But if common animal like a Lipizzaner is to stay on the bit, the strongest possible seat is required with the stirrups short enough to keep the spurs unobtrusively against the horse's flanks.

If period bits were used the whole quadrille would be stalled, because the bits in question were not designed to be leant on. Maddened by pain the poor horses would soon prop the long cheek pieces against their chests leaving their riders helpless. And yet competent cowboys of the Robert Taylor order can ride such horses in severe bits with the utmost distinction.

La Guerinière did not ride like Colonel Podhajski, any more than he talked about dressage; like the rest of his 18th century colleagues he rode in substantially the same manner as the rodeo champion or the hardy annual of the western films; but in Europe this sort of riding is a lost art. For a start it calls for a suppleness of the back and a hardness of thigh that the motorised horseman no longer possesses.

Colonel Podhajski is in no way to blame for this state of affairs. Uhlanage was in practice at the Spanish school before he took over. But regardless of overwhelming statistical evidence to the contrary, Colonel Podhajski continues to advocate uhlanage for general training purposes. He has, in consequence, no cause for complaint when he becomes the object of attacks of this nature delivered by critics who believe that he has, however unwittingly, done, and is doing, a great disservice to English horsemanship.

The case against uhlanage in England is not merely a question of riding and training *per se*, but of the difference in the nature of the horse population of the British Isles and Germany. It ruins most horses. For example look at Miss Jenny Bullen's horses before and after she took up advanced dressage.

The Germans would not ride and train their horses in the way they do unless it produced satisfactory results. Their horses are predominantly harness bred and in consequence slow and temperate animals of great substance and power. Because they have a virtual monopoly of this type of animal and the Olympic show jumping competition suits it perfectly, the German team wins far more of the right kind of medals than any other.

Show jumping is an increasingly artificial sport that lends itself, particularly in the case of this type of horse, to some of the worst excesses of uhlanage. For instance 'the running rein rubber ball' technique, that finally spurred even a 'laissez-faire' body like the FEI into taking drastic action, to stop such abuses.

The same is true of Grand Prix 'dressage'. For unhappily, with the exception of Filatov and Absent, the only horses that can do the test correctly are mechanised zombies, the product of uhlanage, as practised in Scandinavia and central Europe generally.

This is, of course, the fault of Saumur, although the failure of that famous school to produce Grand Prix horses in fact reflects no discredit upon its Cadre Noir.

For the last 150 years the French cavalry has set its face against a return to 18th century manège. It was rightly held that the best trained horse at a cavalry school must be the prototype of the officer's charger of the day.

Ever since Waterloo the Europeans in general and the French in particular wanted to ride like the Meltonians of our sporting prints, and this is precisely like the sort of riding taught by the famous Comte d'Aure at Saumur and elsewhere.

The horses that took part in the pre-war carrousel of the Cadre Noir, that so delighted the audiences at Olympia in 1935 and 1937, were expected to run in regimental races, military chases under rules, and take part in show jumping competitions, three-day events, etc.

It is possible to race and jump a perfectly trained school horse, for Captain Bendant actually did so successfully. Cadet Saint-Phalle, Fillis's only serious competitor, won all the phases of a

100 kilometre combined training event on a TB that could do every natural and artificial air in the book. But it was much too much to expect of officers doing a three-year course.

The result was that a very low standard of precision was required of the horses and difficult airs were kept down to a minimum in the carrousel.

When it came to the Olympic games of 1936, still French dominated FEI used coefficients in the Grand Prix de Dressage to increase the value of the easy airs and paces at the expense of the haute école movements required.

Nevertheless the ex-Kaiser's riding master, Loerke, produced a perfect automation in Cronos that could perform the Grand Prix ride perfectly with short reins. Indeed there is a film of him doing so.

The French were second, but this was the last time Saumur has fielded a serious contender. Colonel Jousséaume, whose Harpagon won a moral victory at Stockholm, was a free lance gunner in no way indebted to the Cadre Noir for his success.

Needless to say the countries whose cavalry training was inspired by Saumur fared no better, so after the war the exponents of uhlanage had it all their own way in competitions like the three-day event and the Grand Prix de Dressage.

However as the standard of performance went steadily down the FEI 'dressage' committee finally instructed Colonel Max Thommen, as reporter, to draw up a new set of definitions calculated to put a stop to the worst abuses of uhlanage and compel competitors to respect the classical traditions of their art.

Anyone who cares to read the Colonel's violent protest against the failure of the FEI judges to enforce the regulations, published in *Année Hippique* in 1960, and Cadet Saint-Fort Paillard's similar denunciation of the judging at Tokyo in the current issue of that magnificent publication, will see that uhlans are still driving a coach and four through the rules.

The only one of the Olympic games that is not uhlan dominated is the least artificial of the three, combined training. For over and over again under stiff cross country conditions a high degree uhlanage has proved too great a handicap to the horses.

After the war the BHS can hardly be blamed for promoting uhlanage in this country. Saumur had virtually ceased to exist, and the Spanish Riding School was the last bastion of the classical tradition. Two out of three of the Olympic competitors called for this sort of schooling in an elementary or an advanced form.

But today there are alternatives. The Irish with the help of Mr E. Schmit-Jeusen, a sound exponent of Fillis's method, and Colonel Hume Dudgeon's Riding Establishment, are demonstrating that uhlanage, so opposed to sound modern horsemanship, is no longer a must in the three-day event, for Major Boylan demonstrated at Badminton that it is perfectly feasible to ride in a consistent manner throughout all the phases of the competition.

The result is that their three-day teams now include genuine all rounders, who have distinguished themselves in all the disciplines that are simulated in the three-day event, which is precisely what the BHS has so signally failed to achieve thanks to its mistaken insistence upon uhlanage.

The report on our dressage team's performance at Aachen published in *Horse and Hound* made depressing reading.

All our riders were said to be hopelessly out-classed by the German men and most of them by the continental women as well.

After twenty years of concentrated effort by the BHS promoting uhlanage in this country, this is a disastrous result.

Fortunately there is an alternative. In his article, referred to above, Colonel Thommen found in favour of Princesse de la Tour d'Auvergne's interpretation of his definitions on Rath Patrick, and against Herr Bolt and Cadet St Cyr's.

The light handed riding of Miss Patricia Galvin, as she was then, is within the reach of our ladies and is also acceptable to our horses, Herr Bolt's is neither.

We have lost the art of fine riding, and the sooner we realise it the better. Indeed a survey of the equitation practised by the greatest cavalry nations of the past has left me in no doubt that uhlanage is nothing more or less than a decadent expedient of the 20th century motorist, whose incipient curvature of the spine and weak thighs prevent him riding properly.

In conclusion it behoves us to remember that under the present dispensation, and largely thanks to Colonel and Mrs V. D. S. Williams's efforts and generosity we did sit on the top of the tree in the three-day event for a number of years, no mean accomplishment in these days of fierce international competition.

They deserve our grateful thanks.

In retrospect it is easy enough to see that our decline as a force in the three-day event was due to our beating the uhlans at their own games, but who seriously expected first the Australians and then the Italians to make monkeys out of us and our Germanic riding masters at Rome and at Tokyo. We had been watching the wrong horses, it was a mistake that could have happened to anyone, including the critics; but let us all recognise uhlanage for what it has turned out to be, a snare and a delusion.

from THE HORSEMAN'S YEAR *1966*

The Make-up of a Racehorse

R. C. KIDD

It is always fascinating to visit a Thoroughbred stud and see the stallions and mares, many of whom have had distinguished careers on the Turf. If, however, the visitor is a breeder or has some knowledge of horses, interest may be accompanied by a little surprise that some of the mares should have been selected for stud.

Not all possess the physical conformation desirable for breeding, and a few may have such serious defects that they should be discarded instantly for such a purpose.

Studs which are run on commercial lines cannot, however, afford to refuse mares, nor will criticism prove very popular with the owners.

The very high price of a mare both beautiful and impeccably bred may preclude purchase by all but the very rich. Some owners who aspire to breed a winner may not themselves have much knowledge or experience of horses, and for these, and for those who must be content with a mare of more moderate price, it may be helpful to consider the general principles by which they should be guided.

Speed in the racehorse is dependent upon a combination of physical conformation and the energy transmitted to the muscles.

Of these two main factors, conformation can be seen and assessed by a practised eye, while the potential energy of a horse is hidden and is subject to a number of complicated processes, many of which are obscure. It is, however, useful to have a superficial knowledge of how this energy is produced.

It is customary to use the expression 'blood-strain' to denote the inherited characteristics which influence a horse's energy, although the word 'blood' in this connection is something of a misnomer.

While the number of red and white corpuscles may vary slightly, there is virtually no difference in the nature of the blood of any horse, whether he be Thoroughbred or a carthorse. The function of the blood is to provide a means of introducing and dispersing the necessary chemicals to the muscles through the circulatory system.

During violent exertion in a race, lactic acid is formed in the muscles in amounts far greater than can be disposed of contemporaneously. Unless counteracted, the muscles would then seize up, somewhat in the manner of an engine lacking oil, but this accumulation is rapidly removed in the presence of oxygen.

The oxygen carried in the blood performs this function while the venous blood returning to the heart removes the waste products.

In steady, prolonged exercise, fatigue is due to a number of ill-understood factors, but in the main it is attributed to changes in the brain resulting from slight loss of oxygen.

The phenomenon known as 'second wind' is familiar to athletes, but this again has not yet been satisfactorily explained. Does this ability to gain second wind affect the distance capacity of a horse?

Why can some horses expend a large amount of energy for a short period while others produce a smaller amount for a longer period and are thereby classified as sprinters or stayers? Science cannot provide a precise answer to these questions.

The exact part played by the nervous system in the production of energy is also uncertain. A runner will continue to run or an oar to row long after the chemical conditions required for the expansion and contraction of muscles have passed, and will automatically continue this exertion until unconsciousness supervenes.

In much the same way a courageous horse will refuse to accept defeat and will battle on with instinctive determination. The reason is not understood, but it will be noticed how every part of the body makes its contribution to the general effort.

The pulmonary 'bellows' supply the oxygen and the heart sends the blood mainly to the parts which need it. The efficiency with which the whole matter of this intricate system works depends upon the successful blending of inherited characteristics by matings to produce the ideal combination of speed, stamina and courage.

The possession of long and detailed records of breeding and performance renders the Thoroughbred horses a most fruitful field for the study of genetics. It is proof of the difficulties which beset research that, in spite of all the data available, only certain general principles have been evolved to assist the breeder.

Various methods have been devised, of which the Bruce Lowe evaluation system is one, but in the main all that has been established is that certain blood-strains are pre-eminent and that some will produce stamina and others speed. Such progress as has been made has been by dint of experience and has continued by trial and error.

That magnificent horse Irish Elegance was a champion sprinter of his day, but his pedigree was not above suspicion. When put to stud his progeny were virtually useless. The heart of Brown Jack, one of the most outstanding stayers of all time, is believed to have been abnormally large.

From such, and similar, instances a little more information has been gained. From all this uncertainty and scanty knowledge of how energy is produced only two helpful conclusions can be drawn. They are that oxygen is essential and that 'blood will tell'.

Happily it is a little easier to determine the physical conformation which is desirable. It is true that horses do win races in all shapes, but it is significant that, unlike some of the mares, the stallions are rarely seen to possess physical defects.

These horses have been sent to stud on account of their good breeding and notable achievements on the race-course, and it is not unreasonable to suppose that their conformation has made a considerable contribution to their success.

Oxygen is obtained from the air and it is obvious that the flow must not be impeded. A horse which develops ailments in the nerves and muscles of his throat is useless unless surgically treated. Similarly the lungs must have space to expand and the heart to work. The throat should be fine with unrestricted movement to the neck, the chest wide and the girth deep.

However brilliant, a horse that will not stand up to the rigours of training and racing will only prove a disappointment and expense.

Although the bone of a Thoroughbred horse is of finer texture than that of his humbler brother, the racehorse must possess limbs of reasonable substance, particularly below the knee.

A comparison of photographs of a horse when standing and galloping disclose that when fully extended in a gallop the fetlock joint is noticeably nearer the ground. This action of the pastern stretches the tendons of the leg, and the tension is accentuated if the pasterns are unduly long and sloping, the tendons becoming strained or 'bowed'.

While short, straight pasterns may lead to jarring of the leg, a suitable compromise between two extremes is required. A recession of the knee (back at the knee) will have similar effects.

Even abundant energy will not achieve its purpose unless provided with an efficient machine in which to work. The length and angle of the limbs must be suitable for propulsion. In this connection it is interesting to examine the conformation of other animals, such as the hare, the greyhound and the hunting leopard, which are noted for speed.

All have one characteristic in common. It is the exceptional length from the hip to the hock and from the shoulders to the knee, which increases the length of the natural stride. The racehorse should be built similarly, both knees and hocks being near the ground.

It has been said that 'a good big 'un is better than a good little 'un'. Hyperion, however, was a small horse, and within reasonable limits the actual height is probably not so important as correct proportion.

The stride of a horse is also governed to some extent by the length of the neck, since the forefeet cannot meet the ground beyond a vertical line dropped from the point of the nose. A short neck is therefore undesirable, since it will restrict this movement, apart from having other disadvantages.

The action of the gallop requires a great effort in propulsion. A long back or hind legs which are noticeably behind the body do not provide the most efficient system of leverage. It is preferable for the horse to be close-coupled, with hocks set within the quarters.

This brief attempt to analyse speed and stamina does not pretend to produce answers to the intricate problems of selection of lineage, which is in itself the study of a life-time. It is intended only to draw attention to certain aspects of breeding which are important to the avoidance of producing misfits and useless animals.

Inherited characteristics are no less persistent in the equine than in the human race. A Grecian profile, a Hapsburg lip, good looks and length of limb all have their counterparts in horses.

It is unwise to send a mare to stud merely because she is half-sister to a noted winner unless she herself possesses reasonable conformation, since it is probable she will transmit her defects to her offspring.

Neither perfect conformation nor impeccable breeding will necessarily achieve success. All that can be said is that, given similar blood, a well-proportioned horse is more likely to win races than one whose conformation is faulty. It is a consideration which does not always receive all the attention it deserves.

7 March 1969

from NINETY YEARS OF HORSE AND HOUND *1977*

Horse Faces

MICHAEL SCHAFER

As we have seen, horses have a whole range of vocal expressions at their disposal, although these sounds are by no means equal to the importance of their comprehensive 'facial language'. This ranges from relatively plain, very obvious signals to very slight changes of the face that are scarcely noticed by humans. They cannot knit their brows as we do, and the area between the bridge of the nose, eyes and ears is immobile, but, in spite of this the play of the features – the ears, nostrils and mouth – is full of meaning for those standing near enough.

Play of the Ears

Different moods are best recognized by the positions of a horse's ears, signals that play an important part in the language between animals. Although the ears of the various Equidæ, including domestic horses, vary in shape and size – from the tiny pricked ears of some pony breeds to the long ears of the ass and the spoon-shaped ears of the Grévy zebra – all signals of intention and mood given by the ears are understood equally well by all the Equidæ species. Thus, when a horse lays his ears back as a threat, it is understood by zebras or donkeys as a warning. If we put our hands on our cheeks and allow three fingers to show above our head, we can imitate ear signals to which they will react attentively and their mood can change, if for only a few moments, because of the movement backwards or forwards of our artificial ears. Not only the human lack of ear signals, which may possibly appear to a horse to be a constant threat, but also the different ways a dog uses its ears can be misinterpreted, for example, when a dog lets its ears go back and its face breaks into a friendly grin, showing all its teeth, horses do not necessarily interpret this as a happy greeting or a challenge to play and it is usually regarded as a terrible menace.

The ears can denote and emphasize a whole series of moods, from the forward pricked position, denoting vigilance or curiosity, to the various positions backwards, until, when really angry, they lie flat and almost invisible on the horse's neck. Apart from these different positions of the ears (moving in an arc, like a swinging barometer needle, going forwards or backwards), particular moods such as inferiority, tiredness or concentration not adjusted to an audible stimulus are often shown by the ears drooping sideways in varying degrees from vertical to horizontal. To these combinations of direction there is in addition the subtle moment of mutual understanding, when the opening of the ear is turned towards or away from the object. Depending on certain exterior stimuli or an automatic response, the ears turn more to the side or droop downwards.

Twitching of Nostrils and Muzzle

Besides the visible play of the ears, the twitching of the nostrils and muzzle is equally a form of expression. Although this is not so readily understood by humans, the slight nuances are both seen and interpreted by the horses themselves. The different degrees of expansion of the nostrils, the drawing back or curving forwards of the outer corners of the nose, the extension or retraction of the lips which is done passively or as an element of an active alteration of the lines of the mouth, the varying shapes of the corners of the mouth and the openness of the mouth, possibly showing the upper and/or the lower incisor teeth – these are all part of the in-audible language of horses when they are very close together.

Meaningful Eye Signals

Compared to other facial features, the eye holds far less mean-ing, since the value of its signals at a distance is nil. Apart from passively blinking, opening and closing the eyelid and the extent to which the eyeball is retracted in its socket, the only direct pos-sibility of expression is by rolling the eyes as a means of intimate understanding. There remain only the vague and emotional, from the kind and maternal to the wicked and mean, expressions in the eyes, which at least give humans some idea of the character, temperament and mood of the animals and their physical well-being or illness. Otherwise the eyes are never used for any kind of mutual understanding since, as we said before, the horse's bearing and other expressions are sufficient for the horses themselves, as well as for people who have learnt their language. None the less, a great deal of nonsense has been written about this particular organ. Some horse-lovers are quite unable to free themselves of ideas which they developed when young and they usually see only the reflection of an inner virtue in the 'dark, velvety, liquid eye' directed kindly in the direction of the human concerned! It is obvious that we, whose interest in the horse is just as great but rather more objective, should not attempt to humanize him by seeing all his virtues in his eyes, but should see him and all animals as harmonious entities, and we must look much more closely in order to interpret the expression of a large or small, a round or elliptic, equine eye.

Orientation

There are many different forms of expression that characterize the enormous complexity of orientation behaviour. Equidae are not just content, when grazing, to inform themselves about things concerned with eating and drinking; they try to satisfy their curiosity with all their senses and to safeguard themselves as far as possible against the unknown. Assessment over a distance, which is usually directed to moving objects, relies chiefly upon optical impressions, assisted by the sense of hearing as the interesting object comes closer, at which point the sense of smell comes into action as the third source of information in addition to seeing and hearing, whilst taste and sense of touch are of less importance.

Assessment by Sight and Sound

Hearing plays an important role in orientation, whether the object concerned is near or far away, and the attentive play of the horse's ears, even for an inexperienced observer, is very instructive. To establish the direction of a familiar noise it is usually sufficient to turn the ears towards the source, without having to use the eyes or the sense of smell. Horses demonstrate this most clearly out in the paddock, when they follow the progress of the approaching groom, although apparently they continue to graze contentedly. This behaviour will change according to interest or uneasiness, i.e. how near the object approaches, and the horses stop grazing, jerk their heads upwards, prick their ears and look directly at the disturbing object. With this typically attentive movement, the nostrils are partly open to take in the scent and, from the position of the head, the expert as well as the other horses can easily determine exactly where the enemy was spotted. The characteristic position of attention is not the only clear indication to the other members of the herd to be on their guard, but the clear silhouette of the horse's body also shows the direction and distance, though the exact position of the object is always a little further away than the horse's nose appears to indicate. The further the horse gazes into the distance, the higher the head is held; the nearer the source of disturbance, the lower the head will be bent.

It remains to be discovered, as far as the different Equidae are concerned, how far the shape of the skull, the position of the nostrils and the eyes, and their ability to focus, are decisive factors in the way the animal throws up its head. A larger skull with the eye in a higher position, like those of some heavy horses and wild Equidae, allows the head to be carried lower, whilst the smaller Arabian head, with its proportionally broader cranium, like that of the foal whose profile is somewhat convex above the eyes, results in the head being held higher and more horizontally.

The horse's face also expresses with varying intensity his degree of interest in the surroundings. As long as events are harmless there is almost no expression; participation is shown by a change of head and neck position, and by the position of the ears. In real or supposed danger the eye-lids are opened wider than usual, the nostrils more inflated and, above all, the general alertness of the horse gives the impression that he is really wide awake. Other Equidae are just as alert, but this fact is not so noticeable for anatomical reasons, and I do not think it is always correct to assume that such Equidae are less intelligent.

If the origin of a disturbance, a strange noise, sight, taste or smell cannot be explained clearly, horses wear a definitely puzzled expression, distinctly evident from the nervous movement of the ears from side to side, eventually turning in different positions. The play of the nostrils and the uneasy glance portray the great inner conflict of the horse – divided between irritation, indecision, aggression and fear. Very young foals often look like this, since on their first excursions they have to cope with a great number of new and foreign impressions.

Assessment by Smell

Horses have a wider range of vision than humans because their eyes are placed at the sides of their head, although immediately in front of the nose there is a small area where they see nothing at all. If they want to examine something lying very near them, they have to decide either to examine it optically or to use their sense of smell. Depending upon whether the object is recognized or is strange, horses approach with confidence or more carefully with the head lowered, nostrils opened, ears pricked and eyes wide open. Stallions, which are very exact when examining the dung or urine places left by their comrades, hold their nose immediately over the rising scent, whilst the ear-openings are turned sideways, so that, though concentrating on the sense of smell, they can still control possible danger beyond their range of vision. Their outline is different to that when grazing and, when they lift their head to flehm – as they always do when smelling these dunging places – the particular position of the head and neck seems to me to be the signal for all the other male members of the herd to become interested too.

One rarely sees horses trying to catch a distant scent; if they do smell something carried on the wind, they toss their heads high, sniffing with wide nostrils. It is clear that in this case the nose plays a larger role in orientation than the eyes and ears. One of the most impressive gestures of all horses of all age groups and both sexes is the so-called flehm. When horses flehm after smelling something interesting or strange to them, they turn their top lip so far upwards that their nostrils are closed completely. If at the same time the bottom lip hangs down, the closed incisors can be seen in all their glory. They gradually lift their head upwards, often until it is almost vertical, move it to left and right, and shut or roll their eyes in full enjoyment, whilst their ears turn in all directions. The reason for this remarkable action, when the air is held and the nose blocked, is the position of the Jacobson organ at the base of the nose. This organ is a mucuous-covered tube composed of cartilege and filled with a vital liquid. As far as I am aware it is not known what special odour it is which causes such an intensive olfactory examination. Stallions always flehm after smelling the sexual organs of mares which are in season; mares, on the other hand, flehm considerably less.

Assessment by Taste and Touch

As soon as their interest has been awoken, Equidae seek to inform themselves with all their senses. Foals, especially, possess a marked curiosity and always investigate strange objects with their muzzles, nostrils and tongues, whilst the long hairs on the muzzle and chin, which have nerve cells at the end, help too. Some foals and even fully-grown horses examine objects with their forefeet. Perhaps they hope by this means to 'loosen' the object in order to be able to smell it better. It can also be a gesture of impatience. Horses have an excellent sense of taste and with their tongues can separate anything foreign in their food, for instance, when grazing, an unwanted weed or stone is carefully allowed to drop out of the mouth. Even small weed heads, tiny pieces of paper, straw, etc., are carefully sorted from the oats which they are in the process of eating.

from THE LANGUAGE OF THE HORSE *1974*

Horse Coping

JOHN SKEAPING

The first thing I did on arriving in Dublin was to go to see a horse coper I knew in Ballsbridge to seek his advice about the purchase of a horse. We went to a pub and over a few draughts of porter discussed the matter at great length. He was a fairly honest man as horse copers go, but he trusted nobody, not even me. His advice was to keep away from horse dealers and racing people and go wandering around the farms and out into the bog. 'Take your time,' he said. 'Take your time' was music to me for I was in no hurry to go back.

We decided that the best thing for me to do was to hire a pony and trap from him and drive across the bog in a westerly direction. I was to pay him fifty pounds for the hire, and on returning the pony and trap to him in good condition, he would give me back forty pounds. Back again in the yard, he showed me a smart black Connemara mare and a nice, well-sprung trap. 'Come back after you've had a bite to eat and a pint and I'll have her ready for you.'

I went off and did as I was bid. I got together a few necessities for my journey, which included a second-hand fly rod with which to do a little poaching en route. When I returned the pony was already harnessed up and in the trap. A bale of hay was roped on to the rail-board and a small sack of oats placed under the seat. I gave him the fifty pounds in cash, for which he gave me a receipt, and a sixpenny piece for luck. 'She'll trot until the cows come home,' he said, adding, 'Be lucky.'

Out of the yard I turned towards the west and away we went at a beautiful trot. Don't ask me what time it was for this was of no consequence to me once I had set foot on the Emerald Isle. Even the date didn't matter and I couldn't tell you that either. I was on the 'pig's back' as the Irish say. All I know is that as the sun settled down into the horizon I was well out into the country and travelling on a lovely peat track. The pony had been trotting all the time and we must have covered some forty miles or so. It was time to call it a day and find somewhere to spend the night.

It was nearly dark and time for the 'little people' to come out, when I came up to a hovel, the only building of any kind I had seen for miles. It didn't look very promising, but having no choice in the matter I stopped, threw the reins over the pony's back and got down. There was no fear of her going off as she, like myself, was dead tired.

I tapped on the door – there was no answer. I tapped louder and heard some movement inside, then the clanging of chains and bolts groaning like a rheumaticky old man. The door opened about three inches and a hand appeared holding a candle which was thrust into my face. A soft voice said, 'What do you want?' 'A night's rest for myself and a bait for my pony,' I answered. 'Fine for the pony,' she said, 'but yourself?'

Having thoroughly scrutinized me through the chink of the open door, she came out with the candle in her hand, shutting the door behind her, and went straight over to the pony.

'It's a nice mare you have there.'

'It is,' I said, 'and she's trotted all the way here from Dublin today.'

'Is she yours?'

'No,' said I, 'I hired her from Mr Hogan at Ballsbridge this morning.'

'Ah! You did, did you?'

Then she started to take the pony out of the shafts and tie it up in a 'lean-to' at the side of the hovel, throwing down on the ground an armful of hay.

She then returned to me and the questions continued. 'Who are you?' 'What are you doing here?' 'Where are you going?' 'And for why?' I did my best to satisfy her on these points.

This over, she asked me if I would be wanting a cup of tea.

Would I indeed! I was invited in at last, and was seated on a wooden box in front of a peat fire above which hung an iron kettle. In the dim light I could see no furniture or any other sign of habitation, but I did see in one dark corner of the room something that looked like a donkey. Closer inspection showed me that the donkey was leaning up against a straw-filled wooden bunk.

The woman pointed at the bunk saying: 'You can sleep there.' 'What about the donkey?' I asked her. 'Where will he sleep?'

'Sometimes he stays where he is now and sometimes he goes outside,' she replied.

Pushing the donkey to the side I climbed into the bunk. Despite the donkey leaning up against me all night and snoring, I slept like a log.

Very early the following morning the woman gave me a lovely cup of tea and some soda bread. She had already been out to feed my pony and her donkey. When I was ready to take my leave I asked her how much I owed her. 'Nothing at all, at all,' she said, 'and I hope you'll be after having a good night.'

Harnessed up and away we did not stop until eleven o'clock when we came upon a ford crossing a small river, where I gave the mare a drink. So far the only animals I'd seen were a few sheep, one or two donkeys and the odd heron or crow. Life was so blissful that I had forgotten everything of my past life; I had almost forgotten what I had come to Ireland to look for.

It was not until I got into the region of Ballinasloe that I saw some horses. Apparently they were collecting in the district for the famous annual horse fair which opened on 4 October and lasted for several days. I decided to go into the town and spend a few days there, looking around and asking questions. This would also give my mare a few days' much needed rest. There was only one hotel as far as I can remember and I was lucky enough to get the last room. I had still over two hundred pounds left and could well afford this luxury.

The gypsies and the tinkers started arriving and camping on the common. They brought their horses with them and soon there were more horses in Ballinasloe than there were people. On the first morning, by nine o'clock, the bar was packed with buyers and sellers. Aided by a Guinness or two I rather unwisely divulged the reason for my coming to Ireland. From then on I was struck by the great generosity of my companions who kept standing up pints for me on the counter. They, of course, were the 'sellers' who were hoping to get me into a spending mood. With slightly dimmed vision I would be less likely to see any defects that their wares might have.

When they thought I was 'ripe', one of them moved in on me and said he had a real bargain, a chance of a lifetime. For me, as I was such a nice fellow, he would make a special price. Grabbing me by the arm he pushed me through the jostling, singing, happy crowd, out of the smoke-filled bar and into the fresh air of the entrance hall. There, tied to the hat-stand, were two ponies – were there two, or was I seeing double? Twin greys, two-year-olds, as alike as peas in a pod. 'They're beautiful,' I said. 'How much are you asking for them?' 'To anyone else I would be after asking one hundred pounds, but for you I will take half that amount – fifty pounds only.' Struck by his generosity I handed him over the money, we slapped hands and he gave me back the customary six-pence for luck.

The next thing I knew was the hotel proprietor was asking me to remove my purchases before the bar closed down for the night and at the same time to clear up the large heap of manure which they had deposited on the flag stones during the long day.

Shocked and faced with reality I started to come to my senses. What had I done?! These two animals had only been handled but not broken. What was more, where could I take them to at that time of night and what use could they be to me? I finally decided that there was only one solution – take them out and let them go on the common. They might stay out there along with the others and that would give me time to work things out overnight.

I untied these two youngsters who were by now raring to go and took them outside. Before I had a chance to remove their halters they had pulled themselves free of me, galloped away towards the common and disappeared in the darkness.

All night long I lay in bed afraid to move, for every time I did so it felt as though my head would come off, roll off the pillow and under the bed. Next morning I had a cup of tea, so strong that the spoon would nearly stand up in it without touching the side of the cup. Then into the bar for a brandy and a chat with the proprietor. 'What had happened yesterday?' I wanted to know.

'Well,' he said. 'Those ponies you bought won't be out there now, for they will have galloped straight back to the gypo you bought them from and he'll be on his way to the next fair where he'll find another sucker like yourself. That's the third time he's sold them to my knowledge and he'll do it yet again. They're worth a fortune to him.'

Taking pity on me, he put me on to a farmer friend of his who was there at the time. He told me he had a five-year-old for sale. I wasted no further time and went out with this man to see his horse. It was out in the field and, as far as I could see, a bay. It was so covered in mud that I could hardly tell what colour it was.

Having a real good look at it, I could see that it had good bone, stood about sixteen hands and appeared to have nothing wrong with it. I asked the farmer how much he wanted for it and why he was selling it? Twenty-five pounds was the price, cheap enough in all conscience. He told me his reason for selling it was merely that he wanted to make room for other horses. He had had it in training with Mr Mullins last year when it ran two or three times in one-and-a-half-mile hurdle races. It had jumped well and had been close up in all three events.

The long and short of it was that I bought it. I went with him to see this Mullins and arranged with him to take the horse and get it going again during the winter. The horse's name was Cnàmh (Fishbone).

The meeting was successful and I think the fee for training was three pounds per week, two months payable in advance. I could see my way to managing this, or at least took the risk, thinking that I might win a race, which would pay all my expenses. Mullins was to let me know when Cnàmh was ready, enter him somewhere, and I could come over again and have a ride. I then drove back to Dublin, returned the pony and trap and regretfully left for England.

from DRAWN FROM LIFE *1977*

PART III

Famous Horses and Horsemen

And to create the mare, God spoke to the South Wind:
'I will create from you a being which will be a happiness
to the good and a misfortune to the bad. Happiness shall be on
its forehead, bounty on its back and joy in the possessor.'
                                          from THE KORAN

The Godolphin Arabian

THE SPORTING MAGAZINE

In compliance with the request of *Stud* we have procured M. Eugene Sue's *History of the Godolphin Arabian*, which runs through twelve numbers of *La Presse*, the substance of which, however, may be summed up in a much smaller compass; for M. Sue has indulged his fancy in extending the 'Life, character, and behaviour' of this celebrated Father of the English Turf into a romantic legend, founded (as he says) 'on the English and French Racing Calendars, THE SPORTING MAGAZINE, and the portrait of the animal in the Library at Gogmagog': including the extraordinary attachment between the horse and his Moorish groom, Agba, a mute, who follows him through all his vicissitudes, resolved on seeing the accomplishment of his destiny, inasmuch as, according with the practice of the Moors and Arabs, the 'nativity' of the animal had been cast, and his horoscope presented one portion of his life to be the most miserable, and another the most glorious. A cat is also introduced, for which the horse had formed a most ardent affection; and in Stubbs's portrait of the Arabian Godolphin at Gogmagog Hall, a cat is introduced, the ground-work, no doubt, on which M. Sue has sketched his imaginative biography.

The story opens with an English philanthropic Quaker, on a professional visit to Paris in 1732, receiving letters from home announcing that his only daughter had gratified his fondest hopes in making him a grandfather, and, according with the custom of his sect, he resolved on evincing his gratitude to the Giver of all good for the fortuitous event by performing some charitable action. In his progress on this work of mercy – it was a dreadful cold night in the latter part of January – he saw a great crowd at the foot of the Pont Neuf, and a horse, in a heavy cart loaded with wood, attempting in vain to draw his burthen up the ascent, whilst the carter was urging him on with brutal severity. All the efforts of the animal to move forward were ineffectual, and, driven to desperation by the lashings of his hard task-master, he plunged with so much violence, the ground being extremely slippery, that he fell on his knees and was unable to rise. The carter renewed his blows, and with horrid imprecations seized the bit of his bridle, attempting to force him up, but with such violence that the mouth of the poor animal was filled with blood. With violent efforts he at length got on his legs, but only to fall again, when, turning on his side, he lay trembling covered with sweat, and his eye reproachfully fixed on his inhuman tyrant, who, unmoved by his piteous groans, kicked him repeatedly on his streaming nostrils, till every one cried 'Shame!' but all were too much afraid of his known brutality further to interfere. Their horror was increased when the fellow, going to the tail of his cart, took out a handful of straw, and, twisting it into the form of a torch, and lighting it, was in the act of applying the brand to the poor animal's foot, when the compassionate Friend interfered, arrested his arm, and exhibited fifteen Louis-d'or spread on the palm of his hand, offering the whole as the price of his purchase. Although he had treated the execrations of the multitude with contempt, the 'timber-merchant' was not proof against the glittering coin, and crushed the torch under his foot. The purchase was agreed upon, the horse disengaged, and the parties proceeded to the driver's stable to complete the contract.

The carter, mollified by receiving the money, so far beyond his estimation of the value of the animal, said he ought in justice to tell the purchaser that the horse was the most malignant and ungovernable brute he had ever met with, and so dangerous to approach that he was obliged to put his corn into the manger before he entered his stable; that, from his vicious habits, he had bought him for a mere trifle, having given only twenty crowns for him; that 'the beggar' when in the humor, would draw well, but whenever he had a heavier load than usual, he would play him the same trick he had done that day, and nothing but extreme severity would induce him to do his work. He was also so cunning as to utter groans on the lightest punishment, and then he would put on the appearance of submission till he released him from the vehicle, when he would kick and run at him with open mouth in the most savage manner. The only way he could subdue him was to keep him constantly in the shafts, so that he could not lie down either by night or by day, and he placed both horse and cart under a shed for protection from the weather, the only sleep he got being as he stood. Once a week (on Sunday) he permitted the Moor to release him, and then the three – Agba, Scham (for such was his Moorish appellation), and the cat – seemed in a state of extacy.

The carter goes on to state, that an uncommon attachment subsisted between the three; that the Moor doated on the horse, having accompanied him to Paris from Barbary, and that the cat would jump on his back, purring continually, the horse whinnying in evident gratification at his presence. He then proceeds to say, that he had purchased the animal from one of the Royal cooks; and on the Quaker expressing his astonishment that an animal so meagre should ever have belonged to the King, the woodman proceeded to state how he came into his possession.

Scham was employed in the most menial capacity, drawing a covered wagon from the Paris *cuisine* to that of Versailles but he was so vicious and so savage with other horses, especially if any mares were in sight, that they could do nothing with him, and the Comptroller ordered him to be sold. No one, however, would purchase him, not only from his known character, but that he consumed more food than he was worth, and he was at length given to one of the cooks, to get rid of him, on condition that he would find him sustenance. It appeared, however, that his new master kept him on short commons, for he actually attempted to make a meal of the cook, having seized him with his teeth, and bitten a large piece of flesh through his clothes. This was enough for the *cuisinier*, who determined to get rid of the vicious brute. He accordingly sent for the wood-merchant, and offered to sell him for thirty crowns, but eventually parted with him for twenty.

M. Sue then proceeds. The driver spoke truly: the horse so lately put to the drudgery of the wood-merchant's heavy cart was one of the eight Barbary steeds which the Bey of Tunis had sent as a present to Louis XV in 1731, in consequence of having concluded a treaty of commerce, which was effected in His Majesty's name by M. the Viscount de Manly, a Commander in the King's Navy. On the arrival of these animals in Paris, they for a short time attracted the attention, or rather the curiosity of the King and his Court; but from their wild appearance, their restless and haughty deportment, their lean and angular forms, rendered more so by the fatigue of the voyage, they were received in the Royal stables with perfect indifference, and subsequently with contempt. M. Sue accounts for this from the prevailing fancy of His Majesty to the great Norman horses, both for war and the chase, and more especially for those bred in Suffolk – short in the loins, well knit together, going close to the ground, and termed *thick-set*. As the King's name is a tower of strength in war, so in fashion his taste is paramount, and these Barbary horses excited the greatest raillery and scorn – their deep chests, their small mouths, their beautiful nervous and bony forms, so typical of the character of this precious race, and so religiously preserved pure in the East, were all lost on King, courtiers, equerries, and grooms.

Of the eight Tunisian slaves sent from Africa by the Bey, Agba alone remained, the other seven having returned to their native country. The poor mute was so attached to Scham, that even the natural affection for home was disregarded, and, though excluded from the Royal stables, he hovered about their precincts for the purpose of seeing his favourite whenever he was suffered to pass the door, living on the charity of those who pitied his unhappy condition. Since he had become the property of the wood-carrier, the Moor had taken up his quarters in the shed for the sole purpose of enjoying the society of the Barb, and obtained his food by begging, for he (the carter) refused to encourage him, believing that his witchcraft rendered the horse so vicious. He suffered him to remain in the shed, as he was much amused to see the evident affection subsisting between the mute, the horse, and the cat. On his return home, Agba and Grimalkin were always in waiting, the former squatting down disconsolately, with the cat curled up by his side. On permitting him to give the horse his food, the Moor would rise up in extacy, embrace the animal, take his head between his hands, jump on his back, then dismount, and creep under him; to all of which endearments the horse seemed as gratified as himself: he would whinny, and appear to talk to him, as if rejoiced to see him. On the other hand, if the Moor was not in the shed, he became furious, stamped with his feet, laid back his ears, and attempted to attack the carter. On one occasion, the Moor was not in the shed, but returned when he was chastising the horse, and was so exasperated that he seemed inclined to attack him, but he shewed him his shoulder-of-mutton fist, and the demonstration was sufficient.

When the Quaker, who had been struck with their mutual attachment, told the Moor that he had purchased the horse, and that both should accompany him to England, the poor fellow shewed the most extravagant joy, threw himself on his knees at the feet of the Englishman, and placed his foot on his head in token of submission, and shewing that he would be his slave for life. He removed the cumbrous harness with which he was caparisoned in a sort of frenzy, believing that the malign influence had departed from his companion. The hard-stuffed collar covered with blue sheepskin, and rusty haimes, the ponderous wooden saddle, and the thick bridle, were all dashed to the ground in the greatest indignation: then, drawing from one of the pockets of his cloak a horse-hair glove, he began to rub down Scham after the manner of the Moors of Tunis (who never use a currycomb) the friction of which soon renders glossy the handsome and fine skin of the horses of the pure race. Scham, thus harnessed, could be better examined by the Quaker. He was a brown bay, about fifteen hands high, with a white spot on the off-hind leg. He was terribly thin: his sharp bones seemed to pierce through his skin, naturally so fine and delicate, and he was covered with wounds by the friction of the heavy collar and the shafts of the cart. The dust and dirt which covered the poor animal rendered his coat quite dull and rough, formerly so bright and smooth, and his mane was matted with filth. Notwithstanding his distressing and miserable appearance, a judge of horseflesh would still have admired his bony frame; and on seeing his deep chest – sure indication of capacious lungs and strength of wind – it was evident that Scham could perform without the slightest difficulty a lengthened course. Judging also from the construction and strength of his well-proportioned limbs, his speed must be prodigious; and his large hams, flat and so singularly tapering off, seemed steel springs to his iron frame – these, added to his uncommon beauty, and his graceful tail, flowing like a plume of silk, proved him to be an illustrious descendant from the purest *caste*.

The Quaker shortly after returned home, accompanied by his purchase, his mute attendant, and the faithful cat.

Arrived in England, Scham is located at Bury Hall, the residence of the Quaker, situate about fifteen miles from London on the bank of the Thames; and in a short time, through the care of Agba and plenty of nutritious food, he recovered his pristine form, so that no one could have believed him to have been the miserable object so cruelly treated at the foot of the Pont Neuf. Agba was feared and despised by the other domestics, for they had not the Quaker's tolerance, but they respected him for his attachment to the horse and devotion to his master.

A cloud, however, soon lowered on the destiny of Scham: his vicious disposition began to shew itself, and he would suffer no one to ride him but Agba. He had defeated all the attempts of one Tom Stag, a rough rider, to reduce him to obedience, and had put him on one occasion in peril of his life by almost crushing his leg against a wall: he had also thrown his master's son-in-law, Dr Harrison, and this was deemed the climax of ingratitude by the benevolent Quaker, who in consequence determined to part with him. Scham was then sold to one Rogers, landlord of the Royal Lion, a large inn near Charing Cross, to whose stables he was forthwith transferred, the Quaker making Agba the offer of remaining in his service or giving him a sum of money. The mute, determined not to lose sight of his companions, accepted the latter, and, accompanied by the cat, followed Scham to London, and took an obscure lodging as near the inn as possible; for Rogers, having the same impression as the Paris carter, that the devilries of the horse were owing to the malignant influence of the Moor, had rejected all further intercourse. Every attempt to enter the stable was indignantly resented, not only by Rogers, but by all the subordinates in his employ; and Agba had the satisfaction of seeing two of them brought out on shutters, and carried to the Hospital, from the wounds received from the 'born-devil', the appellation Scham had obtained from his new masters. Agba, refused all admission to the stables, was almost in despair from being unable to obtain a sight of his favourite, and, determined at all hazards to accomplish his purpose, he scaled the walls which environed the stables, and, being caught by Rogers, was committed to Newgate on a charge of attempted burglary. Here, unable to express his innocence, he sank into despair, although his mild demeanor had excited the pity of his gaolers. The Quaker's housekeeper being called to the prison by a relative, who had come under the ban of the law, and learning the cause of the poor Moor's incarceration, proclaimed her conviction of his innocence, and gave so much of the history of Scham, and Agba, and his cat, as to produce the greatest commiseration for the unfortunate mute. His case coming to the ears of the young Lord Godolphin, who was struck with the attachment of 'the horse and rider', he interested himself in his behalf, had an interview with the Quaker, learnt his history, purchased the horse from Rogers, who withdrew his prosecution, and poor Agba and Scham were sent off to Gogmagog Hall, there to be treated with the same indifference and contempt as Scham had experienced in the Royal Stables of Louis XV.

Hobgoblin was then the Lord of the Ascendant in the seraglio of Gogmagog, and so cruelly, in Agba's opinion, was Scham neglected, that he often wished the Barb again enclosed within the den of Rogers, where death might have relieved him from his misery. The progeny of Hobgoblin had been hitherto successful above all their competitors, and Lord Godolphin having purchased Roxana, by Flying Childers out of Monica, for 600 guineas – a great price at that period – he resolved to found a new dynasty in the future generation of Roxana and Hobgoblin.

M. Sue then gives the *liaisons* of Roxana and Scham – how that Roxana refused the caresses of Hobgoblin, and when she neighed indignantly at the approach of the Lord of the Harem, she was answered by one so loud and shrill that the hill re-echoed the sound – that Roxana recognising the impassioned cry, expressed the most vivid astonishment and delight, and at the moment Hobgoblin was brought into the paddock, Agba opened the door of the stable, and Scham rushed in frantic energy on his rival. A tremendous battle ensued, Hobgoblin being eventually driven from the field, and Scham triumphed both in love and victory. Lord Godolphin, exasperated at the defeat of his project, immediately ordered the culprit off to a stud-farm at a distance of sixty miles, where he was turned out to seek his food on an almost barren common.

Two years had elapsed, when Agba was roused from the most painful reflections by approaching sounds, and was no less surprised than gratified by a courier announcing his Lord's commands to return to Gogmagog: and in less than an hour, Agba, Scham and the cat were on their way to the Hall.

The cause of this recall is explained in few words. Lath, the produce of Scham and Roxana, shewing some fine racing points, the prejudices of Lord Godolphin and his stud-groom began to subside: with a force and a vigor beyond his years, he excelled all his rivals in their exercises; and the progeny of the Darley Arabian, brought from Aleppo in 1717, having proved successful in all their contests with the indigenous breed, people began to wonder that they had so long neglected the source of so much beauty and purity of blood. In addition, Lath had beaten all the descendants from the hitherto-renowned Hobgoblin.

The author then jumps over four years, and in 1738, three sons of Scham, who had beaten everything opposed to them, were engaged in influential Stakes at Newmarket – Lath, in one for five-, Cade in one for four-, and Regulus in one for three-year-olds. Lord Godolphin, partaking of the now generally-prevailing opinion in favor of the Arabian blood, which in every instance had defeated all competitors, felt so confident that the three descendants of Scham would carry off the respective Stakes, that he resolved that the sire should partake of the triumph of his sons, and the formerly-despised Barb was led on the Heath, arrayed in purple, and mounted by Agba in magnificent Oriental costume, two grooms on each side (for safety) holding him by silken cords attached to his golden bridle. On his appearance the air resounded with acclamations. The predictions of Lord Godolphin were realised, and each of his horses having won the prizes for which they contended, the spectators appeared in a state of extacy, and cheered with renewed applause, which Scham appeared to receive with dignified composure, as if conscious of his claims to distinction. As to Agba he was in a state of absolute hallucination – the malign star had disappeared, and the glory of his horse was established. They returned to Gogmagog in triumph; and to prove his admiration of the wondrous powers of the Barb, Hobgoblin's splendid stable was appropriated to Scham, and the words GODOLPHIN ARABIAN, which the Noble Lord had given to Scham, engraved in letters of gold on its marble pediment.

This celebrated horse died at Gogmagog, in 1753, aged 29. Grimalkin had preceded him to the tomb, and Agba did not long survive him. – And thus ends M. Eugene Sue's biography.

Eclipse

STELLA A. WALKER

The arrival of a colt foal in 1764 to Spiletta, a mare belonging to the Duke of Cumberland, third son of George II, would hardly have aroused much interest. The dam was of little value, having raced once only and been beaten, and the sire of the foal, Marske, was a stallion considered at that time of such small merit that at the Duke's death the following year he was sold for a mere trifle. The foaling, however, coincided with the great eclipse of the sun, and as this was thought an augury of some importance by the superstitious, the colt was named Eclipse. No one realised that this bright chestnut foal with the white blaze and sock on his off hind leg and black spots on his quarters would prove to be the greatest horse of his century. Yet in the pedigree of Eclipse were the elements of distinction, for his great-grandsire was the Godolphin Arabian and he was also a great-great-grandson of the Darley Arabian.

As a yearling Eclipse was big and leggy, already measuring 15.2 hands high, but he developed into a tall horse of great beauty, though his conformation was unusual. The pictures of him by Stubbs and Sartorious show him lengthy in body and large in limb, rising very little at the withers, and higher behind than before; in fact the critical could have called him roach-backed. But his shoulders had great size, and his quarters were ample and finely proportioned. He was said to have resembled a sixteen-stone hunter. His head was small and Arabian in character, bearing striking testimony to his eastern forbears. A curious fact about him was that, though perfectly sound, he was thick-winded and puffed and roared audibly.

After the Duke's death in 1765 his stud was put up for sale, and it was the intention of Mr Wildman, a Smithfield salesman, who kept a string of racehorses at Mickleham, near Epsom, to purchase the yearling Eclipse. But before his arrival the horse had been put up and knocked down for seventy guineas. Looking at his watch, Wildman found the sale had commenced before the time advertised. He insisted that all the lots should be re-sold, and he then bought Eclipse for seventy-five guineas.

Unfortunately the temper of Eclipse proved so unstable that it was found impossible to train him for racing. Eventually, Mr Wildman placed the horse in the hands of a roughrider near Epsom, who almost worked the rebel to a standstill, riding him on his business by day and often keeping him out all night on poaching expeditions. Gradually Eclipse became tractable and his education for the racecourse began. Immense time and patience were spent in training Eclipse. Wildman allowed the colt to mature fully before he raced him, with great benefit to his stamina and ultimate success. Much trouble was also taken in finding a suitable jockey who would understand the horse's difficult temperament. Finally it was decided that he should have his first race at the Epsom May meeting, ridden by John Oakley.

Rumours of the horse's phenomenal speed had already reached the public, and he had been freely backed. This excited the curiosity of some of the heavy betters of the day, who failed in their attempts to watch Eclipse's final trial. They received information, however, from an old countrywoman who said: 'I saw a horse with a white leg running away at a monstrous rate, with another horse a great way behind trying to run after him; but I am sure it will never catch the white-legged horse even if it runs right on to the world's end.'

And so Eclipse, a five-year-old, made his *début* carrying eight stones in the Fifty Guineas Plate of four-mile heats for horses that had never won a race of the value of £30, on May 3, 1769, on the Epsom racecourse. He won the first heat, beating Mr Fortescue's Gower, Mr Castle's Cade, Mr Jenning's Trial and Mr Quick's Plume – and all his jockey had to do was to sit still. It was then that Colonel O'Kelly made his famous wager that he would place the horses in the next heat – 'Eclipse first, and the rest nowhere'. His words were proved. Eclipse out-distanced all the others with ease, and in the last mile practically ran away with Oakley. Immediately after the race Wildman sought out the Dorset farmer who had purchased, for the sum of £20, Eclipse's sire, Marske, bought the stallion, and eventually resold him for a thousand guineas to Lord Abingdon, in whose stud he remained until his death in 1779. Soon after this victory at Epsom, O'Kelly bought a half share in Eclipse from Wildman for six hundred and fifty guineas, and by the end of the year he became the sole owner of the horse at the cost of a further one thousand one hundred guineas. And never was a better bargain struck!

Throughout his racing career Eclipse was never beaten. No horse could match his huge stride, amazing pace and stamina. He was nearly always ridden by John Oakley, who sat quietly and never attempted to hold him, never touched him with whip or spur, but let him have his head and go as he pleased. The only time he was even partially extended was in a match against Bucephalus who ran like 'a good and true son of Regulus; but never afterwards regained his form, so severe and heart-breaking were the efforts he made'.

Eclipse's ability to carry weight over long distances was prodigious. He won the King's Plate for six-year-olds at Winchester, carrying twelve stones, and his powers of endurance were never thoroughly tested, for their limit was never reached. His career on the turf lasted only one year and five months as no horses could be found to race against him, but he won all the twenty-six races and matches in which he ran, including eighteen King's Plates, and amassed for his owner over £25,000 in stakes.

His success at stud was no less spectacular. He stood at Clay Hall, near Epsom. He sired 344 winners of over £158,000 in stakes, and over a hundred of his descendants have won the Derby. About 1781, by some strange neglect with an animal of such value, Eclipse's forefeet became dropped in the hoof and foundered, and he was eventually taken from Epsom to Colonel O'Kelly's home, Canons, Stanmore, travelling in a wheeled carriage drawn by two horses, accompanied by the devoted Oakley. Here Eclipse lived until his twenty-sixth year when he died on February 27, 1789, from violent colic. He was given a fine funeral, mourned by a large assembly, who were regaled with cakes and ale.

Always of uncertain temper, Eclipse was more capricious than vicious, and in his later days showed a marked affection for his groom, with whom he was always gentle and friendly.

Professor Charles Vial de Saint Bel of the Royal Veterinary College, London, made a special study of Eclipse's measurements during life, and of his skeleton after death, to try to establish the mechanical reason for the horse's speed and great stride. He proved that Eclipse could cover twenty-five feet at each complete action and make two and two-third such actions in a second.

He also found that his heart weighed fourteen pounds, and to this fact he attributed his great stamina.

There are several skeletons claiming to be that of Eclipse, but the true remains of the horse are supposed to be those in the Natural History Museum, London, on permanent loan from the Royal Veterinary College. One of his hooves, mounted in the middle of a gold salver and presented by William IV to the Jockey Club in May 1832, is in the Rooms at Newmarket, and the Rosebery family has a portion of his hide. His birthplace at Cranbourne Tower, Windsor Park, is recorded by a tablet made for Prince Christian by a Windsor tradesman, and set up in March 1879.

These mementoes have a certain historical value, but Eclipse is sure of everlasting glory as a sire whose stamina and speed still persist in the thoroughbred of the twentieth century, and as one of the greatest racehorses in the history of the English turf.

from HORSES OF RENOWN *1954*

Phenomena, the Trotting Mare

THOMAS BROWN

1800. This celebrated and matchless mare, for years the admiration of the sporting world, was bred by Sir Edward Astley, Bart, at his seat, Melton-Constable, in the country of Norfolk. She was foaled in May 1788; her dam was a half bred mare. As Phenomena's very extraordinary properties are not generally known, we subjoin some of her performances. In May 1800, then twelve years old, she was matched by her proprietor, Mr Joseph Robson, of Little Britain, to trot seventeen miles within one hour, which she performed in July following, on the road between Cambridge and Huntingdon, in fifty-six minutes, carrying a feather; beating against her, eighty pounds to twenty pounds – a feat unheard of in the annals of trotting. The fairness of the trotting was doubted by many, and very large bets were offered, that she did not do the same distance in the same time. Mr Robson accepted the challenge;

and, within a month after her former amazing performance, she again trotted the seventeen miles, to the astonishment of the assembled spectators, a few seconds under fifty-three minutes! This was for a bet of four hundred pounds to one hundred pounds.

Prior to her last performance, she was matched to trot nineteen miles within the hour, for a bet of two hundred guineas to one hundred; but, on her winning the match with such ease, the opposite party thought proper to forfeit.

Mr Robson then offered to trot her, at high odds, nineteen and a half in one hour; but everybody refused to make stakes to that match, in consequence of its being proved, by several stop watches, that, during her last match, she did four miles in under eleven minutes. This alarmed the sportsmen, who one and all declared that she literally flew, and were of the opinion that she could trot twenty miles within the hour! observing they would have nothing more to do with her.

From hard labour, and other causes, this most appropriately named mare became so reduced, in every respect, that, in 1810, she was actually offered for sale at the low price of seven pounds!

In February 1811, when twenty-three years old, this valuable animal trotted nine miles in twenty-eight minutes and thirty seconds. Within six months after this event, being then in the possession of Mr Boswell, she won four extraordinary matches in one day. After performing such Herculean tasks, in her twenty-sixth year, she became the property of the late Sir R. C. Daniel, who, to his credit be it spoken, succeeded in bringing her into such high condition, within a few months, notwithstanding the hardships to which this prodigy had been subjected, that she still retained her beautiful symmetry, and appeared fresh and clean on her legs; convincing proofs of an equally excellent stamina, strong constitution, and good nursing.

This wonderful mare was about fourteen hands three inches high; colour, dark brown, and her near fetlock joint white.

from BROWN'S ANECDOTES OF HORSES *1830*

Remarkable Equestrian Feats of the 19th Century

THOMAS BROWN

1825. In the first week of December 1825, a blood mare, fifteen hands one inch high, with the rider, who stood five feet three inches high, belonging to J. Wright, Esq., was frightened and ran away, full speed, from the Sand-hills into Parliament Street, and, in the attempt to guide her towards the forest, a cart being in the way, the animal dashed into the passage of the Peach Tree public house, the entrance door to which is six feet eight inches high, and two feet eight inches wide, the passage is eighteen feet long, and three feet ten inches wide, and in it were three barrels, three feet high, and other brewing vessels, which the mare leaped over; and across the centre of it, a beam eight feet from the floor; and in front, twelve feet from the last door, is the wall of a court to the left, twenty feet long, so full of brewing utensils, etc, that the mare had just room to stand between them; yet, strange to tell, the animal did not fall, or receive the slightest injury, or do the least damage of any kind. The rider sat till the mare stopped; he was only very slightly grazed on the back of the head, and on one knee, which, all the circumstances considered, is one of the most extraordinary feats and hair-breadth escapes ever recorded.

1793. On the 21st November, 1793, a young gentleman, an inhabitant of Lancashire, riding in the afternoon, on the road between Ravenglass and Whitehaven, on a very high spirited blood horse, not far distant from Egremont, passed by a single horse chaise, which occasioned the animal to be very unruly; thinking to pacify him, by passing the chaise, he cantered forwards; but the horse no longer restrained, bolted off at a full gallop, and coming upon Egremont Bridge (the middle of the battlements of which presents nearly a right angle to the entrance upon it), was going with such fury, that, unable to retrieve himself, he leaped along upon the battlements, which are upwards of four feet high. The rider, finding it impossible to recover the horse, and seeing the improbability of saving either of their lives, had he floundered over head-foremost, just as the horse was falling headlong down, had instantaneous presence of mind to strike him on both sides with his spurs, and force him to take a clear leap. Owing to this precaution he alighted upon his feet, and the rider firmly keeping his seat, held up the horse, till, reaching the bottom, he leaped off. When we consider the height of the bridge, which has been accurately ascertained to be upwards of twenty feet and a half of perpendicular height from the top of the battlements, and that there was not one foot depth of water in the bed of the river where they alighted, it is really miraculous that they were not both struck dead on the spot.

The gentleman travelled with his accustomed vigour from Egremont to Whitehaven, a distance of five miles. The only injury he received, was a slight sprain in one foot, which confined him three days at the King's Arms Inn, at Whitehaven. He remained there three days longer, waiting the recovery of his horse, who had a slight wound in the stifle joint. Both, however, were perfectly well after that time. The horse's foot had struck one of the parapet stones of the bridge with such violence as to throw it four inches out of its situation.

1819. Mr William Hutchinson, horse-dealer, on the 6th May, undertook, for a wager of six hundred guineas, to ride from Canterbury to London Bridge in three successive hours. He started from the Falstaff Inn, St Dunstan's, at half past three o'clock, and accomplished his task in two hours and twenty-five minutes, being more than thirty-four minutes within the allotted time, without any accident or inconvenience. After taking refreshment in town, he returned by the Wellington Coach, and arrived at Canterbury at a quarter before three, to dine with the respective parties concerned in the bet, at the Rose Inn, where the greatest harmony prevailed. The company unanimously voted that the freedom of the city of Canterbury should be purchased, and presented to Mr Hutchinson, in consideration of the extraordinary feat he had performed, with a faithfulness as honourable to himself as it was satisfactory to every individual concerned. At the end of each stage Mr Hutchinson dismounted by himself, but was assisted at remounting; this he calculated occupied rather more than half a minute at each stage. The horse he rode from Boughton Hill to Beacon Hill ran out of the road at Preston Lane; that also which he rode from Moor Street to Chatham Hill made a bolt at Rainham; the horse he rode from Welling to Blackheath bolted twice going down Shooter's Hill, and again upon Blackheath. The horses rode upon this occasion were his own property, and that of his particular friends, and some of them were selected from the stud of the Wellington Coach; they all performed their journey apparently with as much ease as their rider, who considered that he could have returned to Canterbury the same day in three hours, without inconvenience.

The following are the places at which he changed horses, and the time in which each stage was performed, viz.:

From Canterbury to Boughton Hill	Miles $4\frac{3}{4}$ in Min. 12 Sec. 45
Boughton Hill to Beacon Hill	$5\frac{1}{2}$ 14 20
Beacon Hill to Sittingbourne	5 12 40
Sittingbourne to Moor Street	5 12 50
Moor Street to Chatham Hill	4 10 30
Chatham Hill to Day's Hill	$4\frac{1}{4}$ 12 9
Day's Hill to Northfleet	$6\frac{1}{2}$ 17 0
Northfleet to Dartford	$5\frac{1}{2}$ 14 18
Dartford to Welling	5 13 4
Welling to the Great Mart, Blackheath	5 13 7
Blackheath to London Bridge	5 13 8

$55\frac{1}{2}$ miles

Total time, 2 hours, 25 minutes, 51 seconds.

1822. On Monday August 12, 1822, a race of a very novel nature, attended with almost unparalleled brutality, was betted upon between two notorious characters of Burford, in Oxfordshire. They agreed to run their hacks against each other, and ride themselves, for twenty guineas aside, from Burford to Gloucester and back, being a distance of sixty-two miles. One of the parties, weighing upwards of thirteen stone, his horse strong and bony, between fifteen and sixteen hands high; the other a slender man, weighing little more than nine stone, and waging his stakes on the well known bottom of his pony, but little exceeding twelve hands high. It was agreed, that if either of the riders dismounted from the commencement to the termination of the race, he should lose it, and umpires attended to observe the performance of such agreement. On Tuesday they started at score, digging and flanking, as if only a mile heat, and continued in that manner for two miles, when their nags were nearly winded, each calculating thereby to ensure success; however it did not prove so, and they thought proper to pull up into a more regular and lasting pace; they then continued passing and repassing each other until they had advanced many miles on the road, when they agreed to keep together in a friendly manner till within a certain distance from home, and then indulge the persons who would be waiting their arrival with some good sport, by making the best play they could to win the race. They arrived at Gloucester, and both men and horses would fain have halted for repose and refreshment, but this was not permitted by the umpires. They proceeded on their return, but not with a shadow of alacrity with which they had started; however they travelled until their high-mettled racers were within three miles of the place of destination, and almost reduced to a standstill; the best speed they could make being a walking pace, and that not exceeding two and a half miles an hour, and at such they from necessity continued. When the pony came within thirty yards of the winning post, his rider perceived his adversary fifty yards behind at a dead stand, and apparently unable to move a step farther. As a number of spectators were waiting their arrival, and as much betting had taken place in favour of the pony, it may be easily imagined what a lively sense of gratification pervaded the backers of the latter. Bursts of applause greeted him, and great odds were offered, but not taken, it being deemed a sure thing. But, lo! to the astonishment and consternation of hundreds the poor pony, all of a sudden, à la donkey, made a dead stand, placed his muzzle to the ground, and could not be prevailed upon to budge another inch. All heads were now at work to manage the remaining ground. They got in a body behind him, and endeavoured to push him onwards; they turned him round, they pushed his hindquarters foremost, and put in practice every device and experiment that avarice or momentary frenzy could suggest, but all would not do. In the interim the hindmost made a move, and hobbled on till he came neck to neck, and then passed his antagonist; a sudden thought now shot across the bewildered brain of the pony's jockey, and, pursuing the momentary impulse, he instantly alighted, and pulled the bridle, and by doing so lost the race. The horse had now nothing to do but make good his ground. In the midst of acclamations, the horse advanced within ten yards of the post, when he shook his head, and to the terror of his rider, seemed to imitate the example of his fellow sufferer. The jockey, strongly advised, pulled up and took wind for nearly a quarter of an hour; bets looked alive, and some few took place; the horse at last walked in, and won the twenty guineas amidst loud huzzaing. This race, from beginning to end, created as much interest as any we ever heard of; but the day's diversion received a check, which must inevitably have destroyed all gratification in the minds of the feeling part of the spectators; for no sooner had the winning horse got into the town, than he fell down dead from the excessive fatigue occasioned by his brutal master; and the poor pony, when persuaded to go home, as soon as he reached home, also fell down, and experienced a similar fate. The time taken to complete the race was seven hours.

from BROWN'S ANECDOTES OF HORSES *1830*

Frank Buckle

NIMROD

Of course we must go to Newmarket for the élite of this fraternity; and this reminds us that Francis Buckle is not there. He is in his grave; but he has left behind him not merely an example for all young jockeys to follow, but proof that honesty is the best policy; for he died in the esteem of all the racing world, and in the possession of a comfortable independence, acquired by his profession. What the Greeks said of Fabricius might be said of him – that it would have been as difficult to have turned the sun from its course, as to have turned him from his duty; and, having said this, we should like to say a little more of him. He was the son of a saddler, at Newmarket – no wonder he was so good on the saddle – and commenced in the late Honourable Richard Vernon's stables at a very early age. He rode the winners of five Derbys, seven Oaks, and two St Leger stakes, besides, to use his own words, 'most of the good things at Newmarket', in his time; but it was in 1802 that he so greatly distinguished himself at Epsom, by taking long odds that he won both Derby and Oaks, on what were considered very unlikely horses to win either. His Derby horse was the Duke of Grafton's Tyrant, with seven to one against him, beating Mr Wilson's Young Eclipse, considered the best horse of his year. Young Eclipse made the play, and was opposed by Sir Charles Bunbury's Orlando, who contested every inch of ground with him for the first mile. From Buckle's fine judgment of pace, he was convinced they must both stop; so, following, and watching them with Tyrant, he came up and won, to the surprise of all who saw him, with one of the worst horses that ever won a Derby. The following year, Young Eclipse beat Tyrant, giving him four pounds. Buckle, having made one of his two events safe, had then a fancy that Mr Wastell's Scotia could win the Oaks, if he were on her back; and he got permission to ride her. She was beaten three times between Tattenham's Corner and home; but he got her up again in front, and won the race by a head. The Newmarket people declared they had never seen such a race before, snatched out of the fire, as it were, by fine riding. In another place (Lewes), he won an extraordinary race against a horse of the late Mr Durand's, on which he had a considerable sum of money depending; thus winning his race, but losing his money. He rode Sancho, for Mr Mellish, in his great match with Pavilion, and was winning it when his horse broke down. He also won the Doncaster St Leger with Sancho.

Buckle, as we have already said, commenced riding exercise at a very early age; but his first appearance in public was on Mr Vernon's bay colt, Wolf, in 1783, when he rode one pound short of four stone, with his saddle. He soon entered the service of the late Earl Grosvenor, with whom he remained to his, the earl's death. His weight was favourable, being seldom called upon to reduce himself, as he could ride seven stone eleven pounds with ease. He continued riding in public until past his sixty-fifth year, and his nerve was good even to the last, although, as might be

expected, he was latterly shy of a crowd; and generally cast an eye
to the state of the legs and feet, when asked to ride a horse he did
not know. His jockeying Green Mantle, however, for Lord
Exeter, in the second October Meeting, 1828, and winning with
her, after the tricks she played him before starting, showed that
even then his courage was unshaken. But it is not only in public,
but in private life, that Buckle stood well. He was a kind father
and husband, and a good master; and his acts of charity were
conspicuous for a person in his situation of life, who might be
said to have gotten all he possessed, first by the sweat of his brow,
and then at the risk of his life. In a short biographical sketch of
him, his little peculiarities are noticed in rather an amusing style.
'He was', says his biographer, 'a great patron of the sock and
buskin and often bespoke plays for the night in country towns.
He was a master of hounds, a breeder of greyhounds, fighting-
cocks, and bull-dogs (proh pudor!) and always celebrated for his
hacks. In the language of the stud-book, his first wife had no
produce, but out of the second he had several children. We may
suppose he chose her as he would a race-horse, for she was not
only very handsome, but very good.' He left three sons, who are
comfortably and respectably settled in life – one a solicitor, one a
druggist, and the other a brewer. 'Young Buckle' is his nephew,
and considered a fair jockey, though he does not ride so often as
his uncle was called upon to do. But Frank Buckles are scarce.

from THE CHASE, TURF AND THE ROAD *1840*

John Mytton

NIMROD

As a horseman I need say little of Mr Mytton, his merits having
been proclaimed in every country in which he had hunted. In fact,
taking him at everything, he had not many equals, and very few
superiors in the saddle, for he could ride over a course as well as
a country. His prodigious strength was of great service to his
horses, in proof of which they seldom tired with him; and, making

allowance for the seemingly impracticable fences he would ride at, he got but few falls. Considering his hard usage of them also, he was fortunate in his stud, several of his horses lasting many seasons; and his famous little horse, Baronet, carried him nine seasons with hounds, after he had used him as a charger in the Hussars! He had his portrait painted on the horse, having his horn in his hand, and the hound Hudibras at his side. Baronet was a mean looking horse with only one eye; but Nature had made amends for that in giving him more than one life, or he would never have survived the last seven years that he was in Mr Mytton's possession. He may be said to have been as stout as steel; and if there was rank amongst brutes, this Baronet should have been raised to the peerage. Having, however, mentioned this gallant animal in connexion with his hard riding master in my *Crack Riders of England*, I will quote here what I there said of both. In speaking of the master, I say, 'There is no man better entitled to a place amongst hard – ay, desperate – riders to hounds than Mr Mytton is, and a welter weight too. But how is it that he can come under the latter denomination who, ten or twelve years back, was riding amongst the gentleman jockeys under twelve stone? The question is best answered by the fact of his having been, by the aid of excess in good living, upwards of fifteen, with his saddle for some years past; and I think Sir Bellingham Graham will confirm the truth of my assertion, that he was nothing short of that weight, on his capital Hit-or-Miss mare, when he so distinguished himself in that famous run with his (Sir Bellingham's) hounds, of an hour and forty minutes, from Babinswood, in Shropshire. But it has not been in this run, or that run, in one country or in another country, that Mytton has made himself signal; and yet I might hazard an imputation on my veracity were I to recount all the extraordinary deeds of this most extraordinary man in various situations with hounds. Indeed, adding the hazards for his neck that he has encountered in the field to those to which he has subjected himself elsewhere, the most extraordinary thing after all is, that he is at this moment in existence. However, confining my remarks to his riding, I am bound to pronounce him one of the most daring horsemen that ever came under my eye; and I must likewise add, that, all things considered, he has had fewer falls, and tired fewer horses in chase, than his larking and desperate system of crossing countries could warrant him the expectation of. But this has been attributable to the immense muscular powers of the man; to a short iron grasp by which he holds his horses in his hands at all times, and upon all occasions, which, let your slack rein gentlemen say what they may, is no small support to a horse by going his (Mytton's) pace over a country, and particularly over the uneven surface, the deep ditches, and blind grips of the country, Shropshire. Indeed, when I last met him, I asked him whether it had ever been his fate so to tire a hunter as not to be able to ride it home, when he declared he never recollected having done so. As to the height and width of fences which have been ridden over by him, I repeat, I am afraid to recapitulate them; but I have very respectable attestation to my once having measured a brook that he rode Baronet over, in cold blood, in my presence, on our way home from hunting, and found it exceed, by some inches, nine yards from hind foot to hind foot! He afterwards backed Baronet to clear nine yards over hurdles placed at some distance from each other; but he performed the task with him before the appointed time, that the horse refused it, and lost his master's money. In Lord Bradford's park he cleared one of his Lordship's deer hurdles, upwards of six feet high; and, what is more surprising, he covered the space of eight yards in length at the same time. This was accomplished on a horse called the Hero, which he purchased of me for 500 gns, and was the same that leaped the gate with him in Mr Jellicoe's grounds in Shropshire, the height of which was seven feet. But far from pleasing reflections are the result of looking back on these brilliant feats of horsemanship, rarely excelled by anyone. On the contrary, we cannot help lamenting that a person gifted to shine in the field, as Mr Mytton proved himself to be, should not have taken more care to preserve, unimpaired, the almost unequalled natural powers which he possessed – so essential to the figure he made. . . .'

In 1829, having been disappointed by a blank day with Sir Edmund Edward Smythe's hounds, which then hunted the Shrewsbury country, he was determined upon a lark when he got home. He accordingly ordered some draft hounds, which he had in his kennels at Halston, together with all the terriers and bull-dogs about the house, to be taken to a certain place, where he also ordered to be assembled all the servants of his establishment, mounted on whatever they could catch – such as ponies, donkeys or mules – and a fox to be turned before them. The scene was, as may be supposed, a most ludicrous one. . . . But Mytton was often in the habit of mounting his servants with his hounds when he turned out bag foxes, merely for the sake of witnessing the falls they got, from their want of skill in horsemanship. And he was equally fond of creating amusement even at the expense of his own person.

In speaking of Mr Mytton as a horseman, I have stated the singular fact of his never having so completely tired his horses in the field as to have been obliged to walk home, which I in great attribute to his strength of hand in assisting them in their work. It is true he rode excellent horses, for bad ones were useless to him; but he really appeared to have a sort of magic influence over their tempers – at all events it seemed as if they sympathised with him, and would do anything he required them to do.

from THE LIFE AND DEATH OF JOHN MYTTON *1850*

Kincsem – the Wonder Mare

PHILIPP ALLES

International Turf History has known many famous Thoroughbred mares: Pretty Polly, Sceptre, La Flèche, Formosa, Corida, Astronomie, Plucky Liège, Aveole, Nereide, Schwarzgold and Bella Paola and Prince Aly Khan's favourite grey mare Petite Etoile. None of the stars of today bear comparison to the Hungarian-bred Kincsem. She was unbeaten in five countries and in 54 races. When one realises the difficulties of transport in those days, her achievement is all the more remarkable.

Kincsem won the Grand Prix of Baden 1877, 1878 and 1879, and was later called 'the horse of the 19th Century'. Her portrait hangs in the International Club in Baden. On the same day as the 'Grand Prix' the Kincsem race is run. In addition there is the Kincsem Fountain in Baden-Baden and thereby hangs a tale, as will be told later. At the Röttgen Stud, Cologne, one can see

Kincsem's descendants – all the horses of the famous W family (Wacholdis, Wicht, Waldcanter) have Kincsem blood.

Kincsem's origin was accidental, she was born on March 17th 1874, at the Hungarian National Stud Kisbér. She was not the result of a selected mating. Her dam Water Nymph was to have been partnered by the Stallion Buccaneer, but instead, through a misunderstanding, she was taken to Cambuscan. And in Kincsem's pedigree there is nothing to show how she could have come by her exceptional ability – how this 'chance event' could have become a 'racing machine'.

Fate played its part for a second time. Kincsem's breeder, Herr von Blascovitch, always sold his yearlings off *en bloc*. In 1875 he had two colts and five fillies. Baron Orczy offered 7,000 florins for all seven. But he refused to accept two of the fillies 'because they looked so common'. Later the name Orczy became famous as the creator of *The Scarlet Pimpernel*. It could have been famous forty years earlier. One of the unwanted fillies was Kincsem.

In those days, race horses had to travel days and weeks on end in extremely uncomfortable railway waggons which today would be regarded as very primitive. It is really rather remarkable that Kincsem was travelling constantly for over two years. (Even today any owner or trainer would think twice whether to let a young race horse travel from Dortmund to München or Ostend.) Kincsem did not win her first race at Budapest, but at Berlin-Hoppegarten [in] 1876, June 26th. From then until the end of August she won all six two-year-old races in Germany including Hanover, Hamburg, Bad Doberan, Frankfurt and Baden-Baden. In addition she won in Budapest, Sopron and Vienna and Prague.

Kincsem always had her jockeys guessing at the starting post because she would stand quietly grazing, especially on her favourite daisies as if she had no part whatever in the proceedings. She almost always missed the start and then in easy swinging strides which covered the ground, she overtook her opponents – with the exception of the Grand Prix of Baden-Baden in 1878. Her jockey, E. Madden, made a mistake during the race and the result was a dead heat with Prince Giles. The rules of those days demanded a re-trial, and Kincsem won easily by 5 lengths.

After every win this 'ladylike mare' was extremely pleased with herself, and her breeder Von Blascovitch always presented her with a bouquet of flowers that had to be fastened to her bridle. Once he forgot the flowers and they had to be hurriedly bought because Kincsem refused to let herself be unsaddled until they came.

The mare loved travelling, but refused to eat strange oats or to drink strange water. Both of these had to be taken with her from her home stud in great quantities – a great nuisance. One day in Baden-Baden the water had run out and for several days Kincsem drank nothing. Luckily on the third day water was found with the same earthy taste as that of her home spring. And to this day it is called the 'Kincsem Fountain'.

Everyone knows that some horses get very excited when they are travelling (today we can make use of tranquillizers). But a good many races have been lost by bad travellers. However, Kincsem did not belong to this group. On the contrary, she thoroughly enjoyed travelling by rail all over the countryside. As soon as she spotted her waggon she would neigh, then she entered it slowly and carefully, after a few moments she would lie down but not before her two best friends were also inside – a cat and Frankie her groom: the inseparable trio.

When Kincsem returned victoriously after winning the Goodwood Cup, for the first time in her life, she refused to go into the waggon at Deauville. Her beloved cat had disappeared. Probably it was hunting rats in the ship. For two hours the mare waited on the quayside neighing the while. Suddenly the cat appeared in a terrible hurry, sprang up on to her back and they both entered the waggon.

She also had a very warm friendship with her groom Frankie. No one ever knew his surname and he always signed himself Frankie Kincsem. He served in the Army under this name and was later so buried, not long after the death of his beloved mare. Kincsem won 19,705 Gulden in her 54 races – an enormous sum for those days.

During Kincsem's short life at stud she produced three daughters and two sons. The most famous of them was the mare Budagyönye. When she was born on Budapest Station on January 1st, 1882, Herr von Blascovitch bet 10,000 marks at 100–1 that the daughter of such a famous mother would win the German Derby.

On the evening of Derby Day 1885, the Bookmaker Lehmann had to pay out one million golden marks.

None of Kincsem's descendants achieved as much as their famous ancestress. They won 41 classic races in Austria-Hungary, Germany, Italy, Rumania, Poland and France. Kincsem's blood has lost itself all over the world, but it is highly valued in the W family in the Röttgen Stud near Cologne.

Kincsem entered the horses' Heaven on her 13th birthday, March 17th, 1887.

from SANKT GEORG *15-3-1964*

The Pacing Mustang

ERNEST THOMPSON SETON

There are several ways of capturing wild horses. One is by creasing – that is, grazing the animal's nape with a rifle-ball so that he is stunned long enough for hobbling.

'Yes! I seen about a hundred necks broke trying it, but I never seen a mustang creased yet,' was Wild Jo's critical remark.

Sometimes, if the shape of the country abets it, the herd can be driven into a corral; sometimes with extra fine mounts they can be run down, but by far the commonest way, paradoxical as it may seem, is to walk them down.

The fame of the Stallion that never was known to gallop was spreading. Extraordinary stories were told of his gait, his speed, and his wind, and when old Montgomery of the 'triangle-bar' outfit came out plump at Well's Hotel in Clayton, and in presence of witnesses said he'd give $1,000 cash for him safe in a box-car, providing the stories were true, a dozen young cow-punchers were eager to cut loose and win the purse, as soon as present engagements were up. But Wild Jo had had his eye on this very deal for quite a while; there was no time to lose, so ignoring present contracts he rustled all night to raise the necessary equipment for the game.

By straining his already overstrained credit, and taking the already overtaxed generosity of his friends, he got together an expedition consisting of twenty good saddle-horses, a mess-waggon, and a fortnight's stuff for three men – himself, his 'pard' Charley, and the cook.

Then they set out from Clayton, with the avowed intention of walking down the wonderfully swift wild horse. The third day they arrived at Antelope Springs, and as it was about noon they were not surprised to see the black Pacer marching down to drink with all his band behind him. Jo kept out of sight until the wild horses each and all had drunk their fill, for a thirsty animal always travels better than one laden with water.

Jo then rode quietly forward. The Pacer took alarm at half a mile, and led his band away out of sight on the soapweed mesa to the south-east. Jo followed at a gallop till he once more sighted them, then came back and instructed the cook, who was also teamster, to make for Alamosa Arroyo in the south. Then away to the south east he went after the mustangs. After a mile or two he once more sighted them, and walked his horse quietly till so near that they again took alarm and circled away to the south. An hour's trot, not on the trail, but cutting across to where they ought to go, brought Jo again in close sight. Again he walked quietly toward the herd, and again there was the alarm and flight. And so they passed the afternoon, but circled ever more and more to the south, so that when the sun was low they were, as Jo had expected, not far from Alamosa Arroyo. The band was again close at hand, and Jo, after starting them off, rode to the wagon, while his pard, who had been taking it easy, took up the slow chase on a fresh horse.

After supper the wagon moved on to the upper ford of the Alamosa, as arranged, and there camped for the night.

Meanwhile, Charley followed the herd. They had not run so far as at first, for their pursuer made no sign of attack, and they were getting used to his company. They were more easily found, as the shadows fell, on account of a snow-white mare that was in the bunch. A young moon in the sky now gave some help, and relying on his horse to choose the path, Charley kept him quietly walking after the herd, represented by that ghost-white mare, till they were lost in the night. He then got off, unsaddled and picketed his horse, and in his blanket quickly went to sleep. At the first streak of dawn he was up, and within a short half-mile, thanks to the snowy mare, he found the band. At his approach, the shrill neigh of the Pacer bugled his troop into a flying squad. But on the first mesa they stopped, and faced about to see what this persistent follower was, and what he wanted. For a moment or so they stood against the sky to gaze, and then deciding that he knew him as well as he wished to, that black meteor flung his mane on the wind, and led off at his tireless, even swing, while the mares came streaming after.

Away they went, circling now to the west, and after several repetitions of this same play, flying, following, and overtaking, and flying again, they passed, near noon, the old Apache look-out, Buffalo Bluff. And here, on watch, was Jo. A long thin column of smoke told Charley to come to camp, and with a flashing pocket-mirror he made response.

Jo, freshly mounted, rode across, and again took up the chase, and back came Charley to camp to eat and rest, and then move on up stream.

All that day Jo followed, and managed, when it was needed, that the herd should keep the great circle, of which the wagon cut a small chord. At sundown he came to Verde Crossing, and there was Charley with a fresh horse and food, and Jo went on in the same calm, dogged way. All the evening he followed, and far into the night, for the wild herd was now getting somewhat used to the presence of the harmless strangers, and were more easily followed; moreover, they were tiring out with perpetual travelling. They were no longer in the good grass country, they were not grain-fed like the horses on their track, and above all, the slight but continuous nervous tension was surely telling. It spoiled their appetites, but made them very thirsty. They were allowed, and as far as possible encouraged, to drink deeply at every chance. The effect of large quantities of water on a running animal is well known; it tends to stiffen the limbs and spoil the wind. Jo carefully guarded his own horse against such excess, and both he and his horse were fresh when they camped that night on the trail of the jaded mustangs.

At dawn he found them easily close at hand, and though they ran at first they did not go far before they dropped into a walk.

The battle seemed nearly won now, for the chief difficulty in the 'walk-down' is to keep track of the herd the first two or three days when they are fresh.

All that morning Jo kept in sight, generally in close sight, of the band. About ten o'clock, Charley relieved him near José Peak and that day the mustangs walked only a quarter of a mile ahead with much less spirit than the day before and circled now more north again. At night Charley was supplied with a fresh horse and followed as before.

Next day the mustangs walked with heads held low, and in spite of the efforts of the black Pacer at times they were less than a hundred yards ahead of their pursuer.

The fourth and fifth days passed the same way, and now the herd was nearly back to Antelope Springs. So far all had come out as expected. The chase had been in a great circle with the wagon following a lesser circle. The wild herd was back to its starting-point, worn out; and the hunters were back, fresh and on fresh horses. The herd was kept from drinking till late in the afternoon and then driven to the Springs to swell themselves with a perfect water gorge. Now was the chance for the skilful ropers on the grain-fed horses to close in, for the sudden heavy drink was ruination, almost paralysis, of wind and limb, and it would be easy to rope and hobble them one by one.

There was only one weak spot in the programme, the Black Stallion, the cause of the hunt, seemed made of iron, that ceaseless swinging pace seemed as swift and vigorous now as on the morning when the chase began. Up and down he went rounding up the herd and urging them on by voice and example to escape. But they were played out. The old white mare that had been such help in sighting them at night had dropped out hours ago, dead beat. The half-bloods seemed to be losing all fear of the horsemen, the band was clearly in Jo's power. But the one who was the prize of all the hunt seemed just as far as ever out of reach.

Here was a puzzle. Jo's comrades knew him well and would not have been surprised to see him in a sudden rage attempt to shoot the Stallion down. But Jo had no such mind. During that long week of following he had watched the horse all day at speed and never once had he seen him gallop.

The horseman's adoration of a noble horse had grown and

grown, till now he would as soon have thought of shooting his best mount as firing on that splendid beast.

Jo even asked himself whether he would take the handsome sum that was offered for the prize. Such an animal would be a fortune in himself to sire a race of pacers for the track.

But the prize was still at large – the time had come to finish up the hunt. Jo's finest mount was caught. She was a mare of Eastern blood, but raised on the plains. She never would have come into Jo's possession but for a curious weakness. The loco is a poisonous weed that grows in these regions. Most stock will not touch it; but sometimes an animal tries it and becomes addicted to it. It acts somewhat like morphine, but the animal, though sane for long intervals, has always a passion for the herb and finally dies mad. A beast with the craze is said to be locoed. And Jo's best mount had a wild gleam in her eye that to an expert told the tale.

But she was swift and strong and Jo chose her for the grand finish of the chase. It would have been an easy matter now to rope the mares, but was no longer necessary. They could be separated from their black leader and driven home to the corral. But that leader still had the look of untamed strength. Jo, rejoicing in a worthy foe, went bounding forth to try the odds. The lasso was flung on the gound and trailed to take out every kink, and gathered as he rode into neatest coils across his left palm. Then putting on the spur the first time in that chase he rode straight for the Stallion a quarter of a mile beyond. Away he went, and away went Jo, each at his best, while the fagged-out mares scattered right and left and let them pass. Straight across the open plain the fresh horse went at its hardest gallop, and the Stallion, leading off, still kept his start and kept his famous swing.

It was incredible, and Jo put on more spur and shouted to his horse, which fairly flew, but shortened up the space between by not a single inch. For the Black One whirled across the flat and passed a soapweed mesa and down across a sandy treacherous plain, then over a grassy stretch where prairie dogs barked, then hid below, and on came Jo, but there to see, could he believe his eyes, the Stallion's start grown longer still, and Jo began to curse his luck, and urge and spur his horse until the poor uncertain brute got into such a state of nervous fright, her eyes began to roll, she wildly shook her head from side to side, no longer picked her ground – a badger-hole received her foot and down she went, and Jo went flying to the earth. Though badly bruised, he gained his feet and tried to mount his crazy beast. But she, poor brute, was done for, her off fore-leg hung loose.

There was but one thing to do. Jo loosed the cinch, put Lightfoot out of pain, and carried back the saddle to the camp. While the Pacer steamed away till lost to view.

This was not quite defeat, for all the mares were manageable now, and Jo and Charley drove them carefully to the 'L cross F' corral and claimed a good reward.

The cook on that trip was Bates – Mr Thomas Bates, he called himself at the post-office where he regularly went for the letters and remittance which never came. Old Tom Turkeytrack, the boys called him, from his cattlebrand, which he said was on record at Denver, and which, according to his story, was also borne by the countless beef and saddle stock on the plains of the unknown North.

When asked to join the trip as a partner, Bates made some sarcastic remarks about horses not fetching $12 a dozen, which had been literally true within the year, and he preferred to go on a very meagre salary. But no one who once saw the Pacer going had failed to catch the craze.

from WILD ANIMALS I HAVE KNOWN *1913*

Persimmon

Hon. GEORGE LAMBTON

As to the owner, it is not for me to write about King Edward. His character and life are too well known to everyone, but as a sportsman he was by far the most popular man in England, and in this respect Mr Rothschild was second only to him. It is when you get the rivalry of such men and horses that racing deserves the title of 'The Sport of Kings'.

In the spring of 1896, two horses were reported to have wintered well, and in the Craven week at Newmarket everyone was keen to see them at work. St Frusquin came out in the Column Produce Stakes, which he won easily, pleasing everybody. He was well forward in condition, while Persimmon was backward in his coat, and did not altogether satisfy the critics.

Report for once was correct, for Persimmon was struck out of the Two Thousand Guineas, the Prince taking the sound advice of Lord Marcus Beresford and Dick Marsh, that if he wanted to win the Derby he had better forego the Guineas. St Frusquin won the race in great style, beating a good horse in Love Wisely (afterwards winner of the Ascot Cup and the Jockey Club Stakes), and settled down into a good favourite for the Derby.

Meanwhile, Persimmon was doing well, and Thais, the property of the Prince of Wales, won the One Thousand Guineas, which raised the hopes of his supporters.

As I have already said, Persimmon did not please everyone in his work, and he certainly was not a taking mover in his slow paces, but one gallop I saw him do convinced me that he was a great horse. The last fortnight before the Derby the going was very hard, and both Hayhoe and Marsh were very anxious, as neither horse really liked such conditions. I think perhaps St Frusquin was the chief sufferer. But good trainers can overcome most things, and they arrived at Epsom both fit to run for their lives.

I was staying with Lord Rosebery at the Durdans, and went out in the morning to see the work. It was very hot when I got on the Downs. One of the first horses I met was Persimmon, rather irritable, the sweat running off him, and not looking in the least like a Derby winner, with Marsh, quite as hot and nearly as irritable, his hopes having sunk almost to zero. Then I met St Frusquin and Hayhoe, the horse looking beautiful, but moving a little short, and Hayhoe in a very bad temper, declaring that the course was beastly. Mr Rothschild was there, beaming as usual, but also hot and nervous. Such are the pleasures of owning and training Derby favourites.

In the paddock and parade there were only two horses that people wanted to see, but Persimmon was saddled at Sherwood's stable, not far from the start, and he took no part in the Parade (there was no rule then that horses had to go past the stands before a race), and St Frusquin was saddled in the grounds of the Durdans, adjoining the paddock.

He was a brown horse of lovely quality, on short legs, with a wonderful back and loins, and a real good game head. If you could pick a fault you might have said that he was a trifle short. Persimmon, also a horse of great quality, was exactly the opposite type. A great lengthy bay, slightly on the leg, with the most perfect shoulders, bloodlike head and neck, great quarters, and very straight hocks. The public like a horse that has been out, and in consequence of that, added to the report of Persimmon's nervous state in the morning, St Frusquin started at eleven to eight on and Persimmon at five to one against. Like Ormonde and the Bard, it was a two-horse race, St Frusquin taking up the running when fairly in the straight, followed by Persimmon. Then ensued the most exciting struggle, and a beautiful one to watch. Tommy Loates on the rails riding for all he was worth, St Frusquin gamely answering every call, and Watts patiently holding his horse together for one run. When he did call on him he gradually but surely drew up to St Frusquin, then he appeared for one moment to falter, and Watts had to balance him once more perilously near home, but in the last hundred yards he shot up and won by a neck.

I shall always think that Watts's quietness and nerve in such a critical moment was one of the greatest feats of jockeyship I ever saw. When you think what it means to a jockey to win or lose the Derby, add to that the responsibility of riding for the Prince of Wales, one can imagine Watts's feeling when he found it necessary to take that pull so close home, for if it had not come off it would have looked as if he had ridden a tame finish, and he would have come in for much criticism.

The scene after the race will remain in the memory of all who were fortunate enough to be present. The Prince walked down from the stand amid a wild tumult of excitement and enthusiasm, and went with his equerry and Marsh on to the course to lead his horse in.

The crowd broke through the cordon of police, and it was with difficulty that the Prince could get near his horse. I think in later years, when Minoru won for him as King of England, that the enthusiasm was even greater. The police were then quite unable to cope with the crowd, who patted the King on the back and shook him by the hand with cries of 'Good old Teddie'. Some distinguished foreigner who witnessed it said that nothing like this could happen outside England, which recalls to one's mind what Bismarck said to Disraeli, 'You will never have a revolution in England as long as you keep up your racing'.

from MEN AND HORSES I HAVE KNOWN *1924*

Tod Sloan

Hon. GEORGE LAMBTON

It was Sloan's misfortune to be always surrounded by a crowd of the worst class of people that go racing. Once a man gets into that set, I have hardly ever known him get out of it, even if he wants to. This was the ruin of Sloan, and eventually brought about his downfall.

He was a genius on a horse; off one, erratic and foolish. He threw away a career that was full of the greatest promise. As a jockey, in many ways he reminded me of Fred Archer. He had the same wonderful hands, and was as quick as lightning to take advantage of any opportunity that occurred in a race. Like Archer, once he had been on the back of any horse, he had an almost uncanny intuition into its peculiarities and nature.

A race I remember well was when he rode Knight of the Thistle in the Jubilee. The Knight was a great big good-looking horse, but a loose-made sort of customer, and easily unbalanced, in addition to which he was not too generous. He was owned by Lord William Beresford, who had backed him very heavily for the race, and he started favourite.

In the parade, Sloan seemed like a pea on a drum on this big horse, and, knowing that other good jockeys had found him more than a handful, I would not back him. The horse was as obstinate as a mule at the post. During the long delay it looked very much as if he would be left. In the end he got off fairly well, but all Sloan's usually quiet persuasive efforts to induce him to race properly were unavailing. He had to fall back on the whip, and in the end slammed him home by a length. When he rode back to the unsaddling enclosure, Sloan looked quite exhausted.

I had engaged him to ride a two-year-old filly of Horace Farquhar's in the next race. Bill Beresford came to me and said, 'Sloan has asked me to tell you he can't ride for you, as he is so tired'. I tried to get another jockey, but as there was a big field I found every one was engaged. So I went to Sloan and told him he must ride. With his funny American twang he replied, 'That was the meanest horse I've ever ridden. I'm tired to death, and I can't ride any more'. But I insisted and weighed him out. When he came into the paddock he lay on his back in the grass, repeating, 'It's no use; I can't ride'.

Bobette, who was a beautiful little filly, was walking about close by. Sloan, still lying on his back, asked, 'Is that my horse?' When I said, 'Yes', he was on his feet in a moment, and all his depression and lassitude disappeared. He won the race easily. Sloan was like that: when he was full of life and confidence he could do anything, but when he was down he could do nothing, and would get beaten on the best thing in the world.

from MEN AND HORSES I HAVE KNOWN *1924*

Steve Donoghue over Hurdles

FRANK ATHERTON BROWN

Steve was a generous hearted soul and much beloved by all race-goers, especially by the down-and-outs, whom he never failed to help, whether he could afford it or not. He made friends wherever he went, and it is doubtful if he ever made an enemy, unless it was himself. Generous people usually end up by becoming their own worst enemy, and Steve most certainly was generous and kind, almost to a fault.

About the nearest he ever came to making an enemy was on the second day of the November Jumping Meeting at Birmingham in 1912.

It happened this way. Steve had made a bet of £50 with Snowy Whalley, who was one of the leading flat race jockeys of that time, that he would ride a winner over hurdles before Whalley did. Neither of them had ever ridden over hurdles before. As they were both booked up with engagements to the end of the flat racing season, it was agreed that the bet should not become valid until after the final Saturday at Lingfield and Manchester. Donoghue, who was always quick off the mark, tried hard to fix up a ride on the Monday at Birmingham, but having failed to find a suitable one that day, he got a ride in the Handicap Hurdle Race on the Tuesday, as he managed to arrange with Fred Hunt to let him ride Lady Diane. This handy little brown mare, who was a perfect jumper, looked a reasonably good thing with 10 st 8 lbs, but with Steve on her, claiming the 5 lb allowance, she was as near a certainty as possible.

The secret had been well kept and no one knew that Steve had got a ride at Birmingham until he started to dress for the race. Whalley had fixed up a good ride in the Weight for Age Selling Hurdle Race at Newbury the next day, and nobody knew that either.

There were sixteen runners in Steve's race and among the jockeys who had mounts in it were Ivor Anthony, Billy Payne, Frank Morgan, 'Jack' Leader, Alf Newey and Tich Mason. Most of them welcomed Steve and thought that it would be a good joke to have him go round with them, but Tich Mason took a different view. He did not want fashionable jockeys coming off the flat to take the bread and butter out of his mouth. Tich became rather abusive while little Steve was sitting on the bench in the dressing-room pulling on his breeches and boots. Steve remained quite unmoved and assured everyone, with an amused smile on his face, that this would be his one and only appearance under National Hunt Rules, so they need not worry. But Tich was still being truculent, when the big Irishman Dick Morgan came on the scene and immediately offered to fight anybody and everybody who dared to stand in Steve's way. During this pandemonium in the dressing room the call came for the jockeys who were to ride in the next race, to go out to the paddock. So poor old Dick had to forgo his fight, and as he had no ride in this race he had to content himself by watching it from the trainers' and jockeys' stand. He probably paid a visit to Tattersalls' Ring before going up on the stand, and maybe even to the bar as well for a spot of consolation. Even in those days jockeys were not allowed to bet, but this rule had never worried Dick, and no doubt he further consoled himself by having a nice little bet on Lady Diane, who was favourite at eleven-to-eight. He may have had £110–£80 on the nod, or if credit was in short supply for him just then, £11–£8 in ready, who knows?

There were only two amateurs riding in this race. One was George Pigot-Moodie, a Greys subaltern, who was known as 'Doodie', and who afterwards commanded his regiment. He was riding a horse of his own called Bright Park, and I was the other amateur riding an old stager called Mint Tower, which was trained by Dick Payne. As Mint Tower had not much of a chance, I inwardly resolved to help Steve to win if an opportunity to do so occurred on the way round.

I already had a soft spot for the little man, though I didn't know him very well in those days. One of the reasons for this regard was that Donoghue had ridden a winner for me at Haydock Park a few months before, on a very moderate three-year-old which was being got ready for hurdling. A better reason was that no one who ever had anything to do with Steve could possibly help liking him.

When the jockeys were getting up on their horses in the paddock a snowstorm started, and by the time we got down to the post the flakes were coming down thick and fast. Soon after the start Steve settled down to a nice position on the inside with me just on his left. Lady Diane was jumping beautifully and Steve was sitting like George Duller over the hurdles. We turned into the straight with three horses in front of us, and when we landed over the second flight in the straight, it was easy to see that these three in front would not last much longer as all three jockeys were hard at it. By now there was such a blinding snowstorm that it was impossible to see the next flight of hurdles until nearly on top of it, so thinking I would soon be losing sight of Lady Diane in the snow, I called out: 'Mine's getting tired; how are you going Steve?' Steve shouted back: 'All right, how many more of these bloody things have we got to jump?' I said: 'Only two more flights, but don't be in a hurry yet.' Then almost before the words

were out of my mouth I heard one coming up from behind. After
a quick glance round I yelled: 'Look out, Steve, here's one coming
full of running.' Then I saw Doodie go by on Bright Park in hot
pursuit of Lady Diane, and the leaders. Steve and Doodie both
caught up the three leading horses approaching the last flight but
one. Lady Diane was still about a couple of lengths in front of
Bright Park when they landed, and these two now had the race to
themselves. Between the last two flights Doodie caught up Steve
and they rose at the last hurdle side by side. They both jumped
well, landing together, and then Lady Diane ran Bright Park out
of it on the flat, winning by a length. 'Jack' Leader finished third
on Independence, five lengths behind Bright Park.

On riding into the winner's unsaddling enclosure, Steve was
greeted by his wife who had made a dash to Birmingham to stop
him riding as soon as she found out what he was up to. Luckily,
she only arrived on the course just in time to cheer him home, a
winner, so instead of spoiling his little game she was the first of
many to congratulate him.

from SPORT FROM WITHIN *1952*

Brown Jack

R. C. LYLE

A little before nine o'clock on Friday morning, June 22nd 1934,
the motor horse-box was waiting at Wroughton. At nine o'clock
Brown Jack was led from his box and Mail First from his. The
sun was shining brilliantly and a high wind was blowing white
clouds across the blue sky and their dark shadows across the
green-grey slopes of the Downs. Brown Jack was on his toes.
He knew that the motor box meant something was afoot. He
looked in perfect condition. His coat shone like a mirror, his mane
and tail were darkly sleek – a credit to Alfie Garrat who had

groomed him for seven years, but had never before perhaps done his work so nicely nor found the work with brush and comb so satisfying an expression of his pent-up feelings.

Under the eye of Mrs Hastings and her daughters, of Ivor Anthony, of Harry Wilkins and Dicky his son, and with all the stable lads watching, Brown Jack and Mail First entered the motor box. Paddy Nolan, the head travelling man, was at the wheel. Alfie Garratt took his place, as so often he had done before, and amidst the good wishes of the whole yard the motor box drove away westwards. Brown Jack had left Wroughton to run in his sixty-fifth race.

At half past eleven the box arrived at Ascot. After three days of stormy weather the sun shone out to grace this great occasion, and when shortly before one o'clock the Royal Procession drove down the long wide stretch of green turf past the Stands to the Royal Enclosure, the stage was set for this last memorable and historic day of the meeting. At 1.30 pm the first race was run and won by a short head by the favourite Mediaeval Knight, ridden by Gordon Richards. That was a happy beginning, and it was followed at 2.30 pm by the spectacular race for the Britannia Stakes over the Royal Hunt Cup course of 7 furlongs and 155 yards. There was an enormous field of thirty-seven starters for this event, and few more stirring sights could be witnessed than the race, I would almost say charge, of these thirty-seven horses for the winning post; the jockeys were a rainbow stream of colour as the horses thundered up the hill past the Stands; and for the second time a well backed favourite, Guinea Gap, ridden by Dines, won by a head. Three more races followed, and then a few minutes after four o'clock all steps were turned towards the paddock, and on every side the question was being asked, or thought: Can he really do it?

There was a larger field than for some years past for the Queen Alexandra Stakes. Amongst the nine starters appeared as usual a French challenger, a five year old, Dark Dew. There was the good mare Nitsichin who had won a Cesarewitch: there was Harinaro winner of the Irish Derby of 1933: Solatium who had been expected to win the Ascot Stakes on the first day of the meeting but had failed unaccountably: and Gordon Richards riding Loosestrife, a combination that some thought might bring about

Brown Jack's downfall. And, of course, there was Mail First, come for the last time to do his honourable duty.

Ivor Anthony for the sixth successive year saddled Brown Jack in the now familiar saddling enclosure. He gave him a last look over, patted his neck, wished him luck, and handed him over to Alfie Garratt. Alfie had been a youth of twenty-one when he first led Brown Jack in the Parade Ring. He was now a man of twenty-eight, tall, slim, blue-eyed, immensely proud and immensely confident. That Brown Jack could be defeated in this his last race was unthinkable: his horse was invincible. Harry Wilkins and his son Dicky were there too, the one outwardly calm, the other irrepressibly excited, both equally sure of victory: Dicky had in his pocket as a trophy an *Evening Standard* poster bearing the three words in large red letters 'Brown Jack Today'. And perhaps more moved and more profoundly confident than anyone else was Mrs Aubrey Hastings, who had shared with Ivor Anthony since her husband's death the care of the horse in whom her husband had had such faith: for her Brown Jack had a special significance and this day a crowning greatness.

The throng who pressed, many deep, about the Parade Ring, had no fault to find with Brown Jack as Alfie led him round. Ivor Anthony had once again timed his preparation unerringly and brought him to Ascot in perfect condition. He walked round the Ring with ears pricked, knowing full well that all eyes were upon him, waiting for his friend Donoghue to come and mount him and ride him away to the start so that they could get on with the job.

Donoghue was at hand. He was talking to Sir Harold Wernher.

'Shall I put these on?' Donoghue asked, holding out a pair of spurs.

'Put on everything to-day', said Sir Harold Wernher.

But both of them knew that the spurs would not be used.

At last the time came for Donoghue to mount. A few minutes later a cheer broke out all along the Stands, as Brown Jack and Mail First, ridden by Steve Donoghue and his son Pat Donoghue, cantered down to the start. They were the last of the nine horses to make their appearance, and many friendly shouts followed them. As I watched I found it almost impossible to believe that Brown Jack was really ten years old, he went so nicely and was so obviously gay and free and full of life and youthful enjoyment.

At the beginning of the betting on the race there had seemed to be indications that Brown Jack would not on this occasion start favourite. The Ring seemed to think for a moment that the old horse had at last come to his favourite racecourse once too often; odds of 3 to 1 were offered against his chance, such odds seeming to me to savour of gross impertinence. But whatever the Ring might think the great majority of the visitors had but one idea: Brown Jack's appearance in the Paddock, in the Parade Ring, and as he cantered down to the start, must have impressed them, and they acted accordingly, with the result in the end Brown Jack, quite properly, started favourite at 6 to 4 against.

'They're off!' It was 4.34 pm – the start was four minutes late. Mail First as ever, jumped into the lead. He did his best, but there were other horses in the race who, aided and abetted by their riders, thought that it would not be fair that he should always have the honour of being pacemaker: and they also set off as fast as they could go, thinking that the old gentleman behind might crack up and cry 'enough' long before the winning post was reached. As the field came past the Stands for the first time, rather more than seven furlongs from the start, Benskin and Mail First were leading, followed by Solatium and Loosestrife. Brown Jack was running with Nitsichin several lengths behind the leaders. Quite early on the stretch of the course going down to the Swinely Bottom Loosestrife went on in front with a definite lead. Mail First had done his bit and retired gracefully. Solatium followed Loosestrife, and it seemed to some visitors just for a moment that Loosestrife might run away. On the far side of the course Brown Jack moved up, followed by the French horse, Dark Dew. Before the Straight was reached Loosestrife was in trouble and Brown Jack came on in front with Solatium, the latter running a much better race than he had done in the race for the Ascot Stakes earlier in the week.

The bell rang and Brown Jack and Solatium entered the straight well clear of any other runner. It was certain then that one of the two would win. Solatium, on the rails, hung on most gallantly to Brown Jack. Indeed, he hung on so long that the suspense to me became almost unbearable.

Solatium belongs to a great friend of mine, but how I hoped this horse would fall away beaten so as Brown Jack could win! And then slowly but surely Brown Jack and Donoghue began to draw away; at first by inches then by feet, and then, quite close to the winning post, they were clear and the race was over. Brown Jack and his friend won by two lengths from Solatium, who had run a most gallant race and had been ridden as ably as a horse could be ridden by Caldwell. Some of the runners were straggling past the winning post after Brown Jack had been pulled up and was returning to the Paddock, and Mail First received a special cheer as he went by long after his friend.

I have never seen a sight anywhere, and especially never at Ascot, as I was privileged to see when Brown Jack went past the winning post. Eminently respectable old ladies in the Royal Enclosure gathered up their skirts with such dignity as they could command in their excitement, to make the best of their way as quickly as they could command towards the place where Brown Jack and Donoghue would return after the race. Hats were raised in the air in every enclosure and there were cheers from all parts of the course. Such a scene could only be witnessed in this country, and it has never in my time been witnessed here in such intensity. The unsaddling enclosure to which Brown Jack was returning for the sixth time after winning this race was surrounded many times deep. Crowds were waiting round the gateway leading from the course to the Enclosure. Police made a lane for the triumphant pair, Brown Jack and Donoghue. The trainer, Ivor Anthony, as shy and as bashful as ever, had already gone into the unsaddling enclosure where he was standing stroking his chin and trying to look unconcerned: he had been too nervous to watch the race, and had sat alone under the trees in the paddock until the great roar of the cheering told him all was well.

And then at last Brown Jack came in. He looked to the left and to the right as he walked through the lane from the course to his own enclosure. His ears were pricked and he knew full well what was happening and what had happened. He was being patted on both sides from head to tail as he made his progress. 'Half his tail was pulled out', Sir Harold Wernher told me afterwards. And then when he got to the gateway of his own enclosure he stood still. Donoghue tried to persuade him to go in, but he would not move. His ears were pricked and he was most certainly watching the people still pouring into the Paddock to see his return. He would not disappoint them. When he thought that all had arrived he walked in quietly and received the congratulations of his owner, his owner's wife, and his trainer. Donoghue, in some wonderful way, wormed his way through the people to the weighing room, and after that came the end.

As I have recorded before, I have never seen anything like it at all before on a racecourse. I hope that I shall see it again but I doubt whether in my time, or in anyone else's time, a horse will win this historic race for six years in succession. After the excitement had subsided the King sent for Sir Harold Wernher and congratulated him on the success of his wonderful horse.

To Solatium, Brown Jack had conceded 8 lbs and 6 years, and to Dark Dew, who was third, six lengths behind the second, 2 lbs and 5 years. After the race Donoghue came up to Ivor Anthony and confided to him that coming into the straight he had lost his whip. He would not have used it, of course, but he had been anxious, for he knew, no one knew better, how his old friend was inclined to ease off when he thought the race was won, and he knew other jockeys knew this and might take advantage of their knowledge. Donoghue would have felt safer had he had his whip to flourish in case of threatened danger. But, as it happened, Brown Jack had sized up the situation and ran his hardest all up the Straight to the finish.

And so Brown Jack achieved his amazing record. For seven years in succession he and Donoghue had come to Ascot and returned victorious. For six years in succession they had won the race for the Queen Alexandra Stakes, the longest race under Jockey Club Rules in this country.

from BROWN JACK *1934*

Kichizō

Corporal ASHIHEI HINO

October 28, 1937.
Aboard the [Censored] Maru.

Dear Brother:

Again today, there is the blue sky and the blue water. And here I am writing this while lying on the upper deck of the same boat. I wish this were being written at the front, but not yet. All I can tell you is about the soldiers, lolling about the boat, the pine groves and the winding, peaceful line of the Japanese coast. What will be our fate? Nobody knows. The speculation about our point of disembarkation is still going on. Rumours that we are bound for Manchukuo are gaining strength. . . .

This sort of life, while it is bad for the men because it is too easy, is even worse for the war horses, down in the hatch. They have been stabled below decks, in a dark and unhealthy hole. Sometimes, you can see them, clear down in the hold, standing patiently in the darkness. Some have not survived so well. They have lost weight. Their ribs are showing and they look sickly.

They have the best in food and water. Actually, they get better care than the men. Does it surprise you to know that, in war, a horse may be much more valuable than a man? For example, the horses get all the water they need. On the other hand, the supply of water for the men is limited, barely enough for washing, let alone the daily bath to which we are accustomed.

From that standpoint, the horses are much better off than we are. But the poor creatures have no opportunity for exercising, breathing fresh air, and feeling the sunlight. They are growing weaker. With my own eyes, I have seen a number of them collapse.

I never looked at a war horse, without thinking of poor Yoshida Uhei, who lives on the hillside, at the back of our town. In my memory, they are always together, just as they were before the war ever came. It is impossible to disassociate one from the other.

Perhaps you do not remember Uhei. He was a carter. He had a wagon, with which he did hauling jobs. His horse, Kichizō, drew it.

In all my life, I have never known such affection between man and animal. Kichizō was a big, fine chestnut, with great, wide shoulders and chest, and a coat like velvet. It used to shimmer in the sun and you could see the muscles rippling underneath the skin. Uhei cared for Kichizō like a mother with a baby.

I suppose this can be explained, at least in part, by the fact that Uhei had no children. He was already past forty, but his wife had never conceived. Undoubtedly, Uhei long ago gave up hope of having a child. So all his affection turned towards Kichizō, the horse. You have heard fathers brag about their sons? In a way, he did the same thing about Kichizō. 'What strength!' he would say, 'and yet how gentle he can be. He's a dear fellow, that Kichizō, even though he is so big and strong.'

Then the war came. It came clear down to our little town, into nooks and corners of the country, taking men and horses. Kichizō was commandeered by the army.

When he heard the news, Uhei was speechless with surprise for a while. I remember it very well. 'The army needs your horse, Uhei,' someone told him. 'It is for the nation.' Uhei looked at the speaker with dumb disbelief in his face. His eyes were frozen, uncomprehending. 'Don't worry,' they told him, 'Kichizō will be all right. He isn't a cavalry horse. He won't be in any danger. They'll use him behind the lines, to pull wagons. It won't be anything different than what he does here. And the army takes good care of its horses. They're very important. Don't you worry about him.'

Uhei turned away without speaking and began to run towards his home. He broke into a dead run, like a crazy man, and we saw him disappear behind the bend in the road. 'He'll be all right,' someone said, 'after all, it's only a horse.'

That same afternoon, Uhei came back to town. He looked different then. He was smiling and his eyes were shining, and he swaggered around the streets. 'Have you heard the news?' he kept saying, 'Kichizō, my horse, is going to the war. They need big strong fellows for the army, so of course Kichizō was the first horse they thought about. They know what they're doing, those fellows. They know a real horse when they see one.'

He went to the flagmaker and ordered a long banner, exactly like the ones people have when a soldier is called to the war.

'Congratulations to Kichizō on his entry into the army,' this banner said, in large, vivid characters. Uhei posted a long pole in front of his house, high on the hillside, and attached this banner. It streamed out in the wind, where everyone could see. Uhei was bursting with pride. As soon as the banner was up, he took Kichizō out from the field and pointed up to where it floated gracefully above the house. 'You see that, Kichizō,' he said. "That's for you. You're a hero. You've brought honour to this village.'

Meanwhile, Uhei's wife, O-shin, was carrying this human symbolism even further. She bought a huge piece of cloth and began preparing a 'thousand-stitches belt' for the horse.*

This cloth that O-shin bought was big enough to cover four or five men. When she stood in the street, asking passers-by to sew a stitch, they all laughed, but they did it. She had a needle that she borrowed from a matmaker to do such a big piece of work. When the stitches were all in, she herself worked all through one night, finishing the belt. It was very difficult, with such a big needle, but she finished it.

They put the good-luck belt around Kichizō's middle, just as though he were a soldier. At the same time, Uhei visited a number of different shrines in the neighbourhood and bought lucky articles. O-shin sewed them into the belt.

And finally, he gave a farewell party and invited all the neighbours. Uhei was not a rich man and he couldn't afford it. If he had any savings, they were all spent that night. I was among those he invited. I took, as a gift, a bottle of wine.

Most of the guests were already there, in Uhei's neat little house, by the time I arrived. They were in good humour, laughing and drinking. Uhei was excited and bustling around, seeing to everything. His eyes were glistening. 'Yes, it's rare to

---

* The 'thousand-stitches belt' is a talisman, with red threads sewn by well-wishers for a Japanese soldier when he leaves for the front. It is supposed to protect him from wounds.

find such a wonderful horse,' he said. 'You seldom find a horse with so much spirit and intelligence and at the same time so strong and vigorous. Oh, he'll show them! I'm so happy. Have a drink! Have many cups of wine for this happy occasion!'

There were tears rolling down his cheeks as he spoke and the bitter salt mingled with the wine he was drinking. Everyone was making a noise, laughing and talking and roaring jokes. O-shin kept hustling in and out of the kitchen, bringing hot food and warming the wine. She was a plain little thing, drab, I used to think. But that night, smiling and exuberant, she seemed transformed and almost beautiful.

When the party was at its height, Uhei suddenly jumped up from the table and ran outside. We heard the heavy clomp-clomp of a horse, walking through the front yard. And then, through an open window, Kichizō's long graceful neck came in. His head stretched all the way to the banquet table. He looked at us gravely; I again had the feeling that he knew all about this occasion, and knew it was for him, and what it meant.

Uhei ran into the room again and threw his arms around the horse's neck, and gave him boiled lobster and some octopus, and poured the ceremonial wine into his mouth. 'To Kichizō,' he cried. 'Dear, brave Kichizō!' We all stood and drank and roared 'Banzai' three times. It must have seemed a little silly and sentimental. Yet, Uhei had inoculated us all with something of the love he had for that horse and it seemed natural enough to us.

In the later afternoon of the next day, I saw Uhei at Hospital Hill, returning from the army station. He had delivered Kichizō to them. I spoke to him, but he seemed not to recognise me, nor to have heard my voice, for he walked on a few paces. Then he turned and acknowledged the greeting in a distant, absent-minded sort of way. He looked haggard and sickly, as though he had lost his strength, and he left me hurriedly. All he said was 'Kichizō has gone'.

Later, someone told me how he brought the horse to the station. It was a terribly warm day. So Uhei took his own grass hat, cut two holes in the side for Kichizō's ears, and put it on the horse's head. Poor Kichizō, that heavy 'thousand-stitches belt' must have been very warm and uncomfortable in such weather. Besides, Uhei had decorated him with national flags, so that he looked like some sacred animal on the way to dedication at a shrine. I suppose he felt just that way about him.

O-shin accompanied them, holding the reins, as they walked to the station. It was a curious and sad little trio, the man and woman with that great sleek horse in its strange attire, walking slowly down the hillside, through the village and up the other side. Everyone watched silently. No one laughed.

At the army station, a good many other horses were already gathered together in the yard. They had been examined by the army veterinarians before being accepted. Now they were merely waiting to be taken away on the train. No one knew just when it would come.

O-shin left immediately, but Uhei stayed and stayed beside Kichizō, patting his hip and running his fingers through his mane. At first, the soldiers laughed, just as the people in the village had done. But they soon saw how Uhei felt about his horse and then they told him, kindly, 'Don't cry, Uncle. It's a great promotion for your horse, isn't it? He's going to serve the nation now, instead of pulling a cart around the village. That's something, isn't it? Well, then, cheer up. Besides, he'll get better care in the army than you could ever give him. Don't you worry. He's going to be all right.' So they tried to console Uhei. Nevertheless, he stayed until dark.

Early the next day, he was back at the army station, fussing over Kichizō. Of course, there was nothing to be done. The army grooms had already cared for and fed and watered the horses, but the poor man wanted to see for himself. He clucked around Kichizō like a hen with its chicks. Not that day, nor for several days afterwards, did the train come to take the horses away.

It was quite a distance from Uhei's house to the army station, but he came every day, faithfully. He came early and stayed until dark.

At last the fatal day came. All the horses were loaded on the train and taken to the harbour, where they went aboard the transports. Uhei went along. He went as far as they would let him and then the grooms again told him not to worry, and promised they would take good care of Kichizō. He bowed, eyes brimming with tears. He bowed and bowed, and could only mumble, 'Thanks, thanks, very much'.

As the boat moved out of the harbour, he ran up to a bridge overlooking the water. It was high above the water and he stayed there until the very smoke from the steamer had vanished beneath the horizon. He waved his flag and shouted, 'Kichizō,' until he was hardly able to speak. And he kept his eyes riveted on the spot where the ship had disappeared.

from HORSES IN JAPAN *1964*

Mississippi

JOHN HISLOP

Full of optimism, I now saw myself taking the first real step forward in the attainment of my ambition: riding a winner under National Hunt Rules. Mississippi was entered in a hunters' chase on Easter Monday, at the West Norfolk Hunt meeting, and I was hopeful that he would win. What was more, I had been offered (and immediately accepted) another ride the same day in a hurdle race, on a horse called Jacobite, trained at Balsham, by Gerry Laurence, who thought him sure to win. If I were to ride two winners in a day, as seemed more than possible, I really would be on the way to success.

'Don't you go galloping him any more with they racehorses, Mister John, you leave 'un to me. He's as fit as can be and only wants keeping fresh and happy,' Piper said to me that evening.

'I should do as he suggests. The little man worships the horse and knows what he's about; besides, he barely weighs eight stone,' Victor advised. Piper was, in fact, working on the general principle of Victor's own methods: getting a horse thoroughly fit, but not letting him become stale.

Thus, in his preparation for this race, Piper rode Mississippi himself, not taking him on the Heath, but walking and jogging him about the side-roads and hack-cantering round a ploughed and harrowed field sitting down in the saddle, and riding him on a long rein, the horse crackling his nostrils, as some do, obviously enjoying the change of work and training-ground. One of Piper's

favourite fields lay beside the far end of Waterhall, and I occasionally caught a glimpse of him and Mississippi when the string
worked on that part of the Heath, and thought that Mississippi
looked more beautiful than ever.

When the day came, Piper set off with Mississippi in the horse-
box. Victor used to let me borrow one of his paddock-sheets, a
running bridle, and exercise-saddle and a weight-cloth, as I did
not have much tack of my own. The Clarehaven paddock-sheets
were of a particularly attractive pattern, fawn, with a thin over-
check of dark blue and yellow, edged in these two colours. And
when he appeared in the paddock, Mississippi looked as distinguished as any runner at Ascot.

It seemed a good omen when View Label, who had finished
third behind us at the Suffolk point-to-point, won the second race.
From the start, I felt that this auspicious sign was going to bring
me my third victory in succession, for I found Mississippi going
better than ever. Though the fences were bigger than those to
which we had been accustomed, he jumped them superbly.
Neither of us had ever been over a water-jump before, but it
proved no difficulty: a fleeting glimpse of water below us, and it
was past. With three fences to go I had moved up immediately
behind the leaders, Mississippi going so well that I felt he was
bound to win. He rose at the last fence but one, a length behind
the two horses in front, who were racing neck and neck just to
our left. The right-hand one hit the fence hard and crumpled up
on landing. I remember seeing him roll over in front of us while
we were in mid-air – and nothing more. When I recovered consciousness the last race was being run; ironically, it was won by
Jacobite. I was in the ambulance tent, which faintly resembled a
casualty clearing station in war. There were three or four injured
riders laid out on the ground beside me, and from behind a
screen in the corner came the sounds of someone in great pain –
I discovered afterwards that it was some unfortunate woman in
the throes of unexpected childbirth. The Cimmerian state of half-
consciousness, the dim light of the tent and the cries of the woman
in travail gave me the impression of being in Purgatory itself.
This disturbing illusion was dispelled by Piper's familiar and
reassuring voice:

'How d'you feel, now, Mister John?'

'All right, thanks, Piper, a bit muzzy. What happened?'

'You fell over the horse in front. Demm'd bad luck it was, too; you were sure to have won.'

'What about the horse? Is he all right?'

Before Piper opened his mouth I knew that something dreadful had happened. I felt it in his quiet, sympathetic manner and his slight, but perceptible hesitation before answering the question.

'You mustn't take it bad, Mister John, but the old fellow's gone – broke 'is neck. It warn't your fault, just pure bad luck.' And he patted my arm gently, as he might have done a child with a broken toy. But Mississippi had been far more than a toy to me. He was my first horse, my friend and tutor, my companion in many pleasant hours, hacking, hunting and racing, and he had given me my first winner as an owner-rider. I was as fond as I was proud of him, had got to know his ways, and he mine, so that we understood each other well; and I had looked forward to sharing with him further joys and triumphs in the future.

The Turf is as searching a test of a man's character as it is of the qualities of a racehorse. On the one hand it holds out glittering prizes, in the other bitter disappointments. Few can go through a racing career untouched by either of these influences. In my misery I could not stop the tears starting in my eyes, or quell the sobs which rose within my throat.

from FAR FROM A GENTLEMAN *1954*

Jumping for Joy

PAT SMYTHE

Monday dawns and I rise at six-thirty. I am staying with a friend not far from central London – but jumping often starts at nine o'clock and I must reach White City by eight in order to look around the course, learn my order of jumping and, probably, write four or five postcards over a cup of tea. Long before entering the ring to compete, I must 'ride in' the horses to make them supple and receptive, for the excitement of coming to London and settling is unsettling – even for a horse. Then, some five horses before our own turn, we are called to the inner collecting ring, where we walk about on the peat surface, pretending to be very cool and confident. When our number comes up, Paul quickly cleans the peat from the horse's studs, and then into the ring we ride. We have, we hope, memorized the direction, order, and nature of eighteen or twenty fences. And so to the jumps.

After a brilliant – or, as the case may be, awful, indifferent, disastrous, or merely infuriating – round, we come from the ring and go to be weighed like any jockey of the race track; if we have done well, we wait for the jump off against the other competitors who pass the early stages, or for the finals, or maybe march to the centre of the ring to receive a rosette if we're lucky. Then the horse cools off and goes back to the temporary stable. But at White City's international shows there are morning, afternoon and evening sessions; with two or three horses you may be jumping from nine in the morning until eleven at night – and I frequently am. An official party may follow and I get to bed at two, rise at seven, reach the White City by eight-thirty and start a new day in the show ring; there is not much time for day dreaming.

As for the horses, the qualities of character which must be fostered all the time are their courage, confidence, and calmness. Once a horse has reached international status, the courage is there for all to see; but calmness and confidence are things that must be nurtured. A horse will jump calmly if it is not over-anxious or frightened, or lacking confidence in the rider; and, of course, a naturally excitable animal, like Prince Hal, needs a great quantity of schooling and obedience training, until he knows that jumping is all in the day's work. Hal and Tosca absorbed the lesson long ago, but not without struggle and anxiety.

Good show jumpers, like good athletes, love jumping, and those with the rare brave qualities that lead to the top of their world, usually have a temperament to go with it all. For me, one of the most profitable and fascinating experiences has been to live alongside the strikingly different characters of Hal and Tosca, and to observe the processes through which one – Tosca – has found her element jumping in the open air, and the other – Hal –

reaches his highest peaks on the courses of the indoor arena.

Why is Prince Hal an indoor character, and Tosca an outdoor girl? It is a question of their different veins of boldness. Hal, the excitable thoroughbred, has tremendous natural impulsion and an almost libertine boldness. He demands freedom and the right to assume complete control. But these he must not be allowed, and thus a valuable paradox is created; difficult to control, hemmed in by the limited spaces and the solid walls of the indoor ring, Hal acquires a sense of discipline – without losing his natural daring. His boldness soars. And so, indoors – the bolder the horse, the better he jumps. Tosca, on the other hand, is ultra-careful, hates touching a fence, and on the indoor course often becomes over-anxious – thus losing her 'joie de vivre'. In the open air, however, Tosca usually offers me her total obedience, and so marshals herself that I can take her with deadly accuracy to all her fences.

One of my chief difficulties at Miserden is that I do not own a single square foot of land, and must therefore rely for my paddock facilities upon local farmers and the landlord. Few people have fields to spare, even for renting, and I am unable to construct the track, jumping lane, ditches, and water jumps which would be invaluable for training and practice. Photographers and journalists, visiting me at Miserden, have usually said, 'Now I'd like to see your paddock and jumps'. Then they walk alongside while I ride the horse to a pleasant stone-walled field behind the village, and are shocked by the sight of my collection of old pine poles, resting on tar barrels or oil drums. Some suspect that I possess a finely-equipped dream of a paddock hidden round the corner. I do. But it remains a dream. . . .

Finality's swan song was played in that Horse of the Year Show; this was her night if ever she knew one – the night of the Fred Foster test competition. The night of my duel with Colonel Harry Llewellyn, of Final's duel with the magnificent Foxhunter. The night when television cameras helped to bring the fascination and thrills of show jumping into millions of homes where show jumping was no more than a name, where several thousand enthusiasts for the sport were created inside a single hour.

Llewellyn and Foxhunter had been going exceptionally well,

and at one stage it seemed certain, so smooth and pure was Foxhunter's display, that the victory would be theirs. Finality, nevertheless, was equally inspired, and as the tension grew, and the crowds became more hushed with suppressed excitement, I realized that she was truly in the mood that makes for faultless jumping. Higher and higher went the fences. Foxhunter cleared them all; but so did Finality. Higher still; and still they went on brilliantly. Jump off followed jump off, and I wondered how and when it would end. The roof of my mouth became dry, I longed for a drink, licked the damp from my upper lip, felt certain my lipstick was smeared, and knew that my nose was shining. I glanced across at Harry Llewellyn, who smiled, set his jaw, and rode into the last stages of the battle.

The final jump off included a high wall with a pole on top, and I made our approach confidently but with extra care. Finality was so small that spectators on the far side of the fence could not even see her coming, and their first glimpse of her was at the moment of our take off. She jumped – high and well, but a fraction too low to clear the pole, which toppled lightly into the dirt. Four faults, and the great Foxhunter also had four faults. So, after an hour's jumping, the contest was called off and the result declared a tie. We were equal firsts with no less than Llewellyn himself – and his Foxhunter. I remembered my first sight of the Colonel in action at a White City show where I had been an unhappy schoolgirl spectator; it seemed like a lifetime ago; it was, in fact, just four years.

from JUMP FOR JOY *1952*

Olympic Gold Medal

DORIAN WILLIAMS

Foxhunter came in as the best known and most popular show jumper in the world. Harry Llewellyn had planned and trained for this moment; with no less determination and devotion, in fact, then Mike Ansell himself. He would scarcely have been human had he not 'tensed up' on entering that great arena. Yet I do not believe that it was nerves, either of horse or rider, that accounted for the *débâcle* that followed: at least not directly. The fact is that Foxhunter was too fresh: he was insufficiently 'ridden-in', had been taken over too few schooling fences. Anxious that Foxhunter, for this great course – two rounds, each well over half a mile – should possess his maximum energy, Harry Llewellyn had felt justified in reducing the preliminaries to a minimum.

Any personal anxiety Llewellyn himself may have been feeling was increased as soon as he rode in the arena, for Foxhunter started peeking, looking at and shying at the fences as though he had never seen such things before. This boded ill for the concentration so necessary with a course such as this. At the parallel doubles Foxhunter faulted. This unbalanced him slightly and he met the 5 foot 3 inch wall so completely wrong that he all but stopped. However, like Maguire at the White City in 1945, he made a tremendous jump from a stand, taking a brick out of the wall, but getting to the other side. Worse than the fault, however, he completely unseated his rider. Llewellyn was hanging round Foxhunter's neck, virtually upside down. Foxhunter was still moving and it seemed that at any moment he must lose Harry Llewellyn and perhaps gallop out of the arena, thus eliminating the whole team. As the seconds ticked by while Harry, resolutely refusing to capitulate, struggled back into the saddle, the British contingent watched white-faced and appalled. But struggle back he did – an astonishing feat by itself, as the film sequence testifies – and got Foxhunter going again. Three faults for a refusal had been added to his score due to his circling before the next fence, which came at a slight angle, and as, in his urgency to make up time, Harry Llewellyn rushed this next fence he added yet another four faults, though he finished the course without further incident, the water followed by the gate being taken easily. By this time Foxhunter had sobered up. Indeed the great old horse himself must have been greatly shocked by an experience such as this, the like of which, one can factually say, he had not suffered for years. This alone must have had a steadying effect on the old boy; to say nothing of the message that passed to him from his greatly disconcerted rider.

To add insult to injury, when his round had finished a further

1¾ faults were added for exceeding the time allowance as was only to be expected, giving him a total of 16¾, appreciably worse than either of the other riders in the team: and more humiliating still, to place him, at the end of the first round, thirty-sixth out of forty-eight. Britain's total score was now 32¾ and we could rate no better than sixth to USA, Portugal, Argentina, Chile and France. Obviously we were now out of the hunt, a great disappointment to those who had hoped and planned for so much. But there was still something to hold our interest and fan our hopes. No one in the first round had gone clear. Nizefela had only four faults, so he could yet win the individual. That, of course, would be triumphant; though it was as a team we had been so anxious to succeed.

There were some three hours before the afternoon session started at three-fifteen, and they were full of every conceivable emotion. There were those who were hopeful, those who were angry, those who were despondent. Disappointments, tentative celebrations, arguments, post-mortems: all the atmosphere, in fact, of an Olympic. And then, with the crowd now at capacity, it all started again. And how quickly the whole picture changed: how quickly hopes were dashed: how quickly dreams revived.

'Do your best,' said Mike Ansell. 'That is all. Do your very best.'

Aherlow did even better than his best and Duggie Stewart more than justified the belief that had been placed in him when he was selected for the team. He had but one fence down, four faults. By the time the first horse for each team had completed its second round, Portugal and Argentina had jumped themselves right out of it. But Britain had crept up to third place. Chile had gone into the lead and those who had backed a South American victory were already cheering them home.

Then thanks to a magnificent round by Nizefela, the end of the second leg suddenly saw Britain with more than a fighting chance for the gold medal itself. Nizefela cannot have done many greater rounds than this one. Meeting every fence right, he never looked like faulting, though checked suddenly after the water to negotiate accurately the big wall, he made such a jump that poor Wilf White found himself short of an iron. But he was over and home, and together with most British supporters – and many others – he expected to hear announced the clear round that would have given him the individual gold medal. At the water-jump, however, there were two judges on the ground and, with dismay, the flag of one of the judges was seen to be raised. Four faults. The water was 16 feet, at the end of which there was a tape. A certain amount of overflow water flooded a few inches beyond the tape. To make a splash by landing in the overflow water did not matter as long as the tape was cleared. The question was whether or not Nizefela had one foot behind the tape. Unfortunately the edge of the water had been raked over before an objection, or at least a query, to the one judge's decision could be made. Four faults. But Britain could still win.

All now depended on Foxhunter, who had so surprised and disgraced himself in the morning. Was his first round too bad to be true? Was he in some strange way off-colour? Was his rider over-anxious? Had the morning's experience upset him or steadied him? All these thoughts had been racing through everyone's taut and exhausted mind for over four hours, and not until nearly six o'clock could the question be answered.

By the time Foxhunter jumped, about fifth from the end, with no one of danger to follow, Britain had a lead of 5 points – one of the Chileans, too, had collected time-faults. Leaving time out of it, this meant that for Britain to win a gold medal, Foxhunter must not have more than four faults – one fence down. Two mistakes and we would fall behind Chile. More than three of these great Olympic fences down, and we would not even be third.

In the interval between the two rounds, Foxhunter and his rider had rested – and relaxed. Like most great commanders Llewellyn had the knack of shutting out the problems of the moment and relaxing completely. In addition to which the strain of the morning's experience had considerably exhausted him; so much perhaps that sleep was almost inevitable. An hour before he was due to jump he started riding Foxhunter in, popping him over fences and warming him up. By the time his turn came Foxhunter was properly settled, sensible. But his rider knew, too, just what was now expected of him. Harry Llewellyn is the sort of character to rise to an occasion and this he now did.

Safely over the treble: safely over the bogy parallels and the red wall: safely over the water. Two fences to go. Clear at the gate.

And Britain had won. Clear at the last and Foxhunter had done the only completely clear round out of nearly a hundred.

Everyone went mad, and not only the British spectators. Foxhunter was the favourite, and in many countries besides England it was appreciated that this great horse with his cavalier partner had made show jumping a sport of enormous and financially advantageous popular appeal. Crowds had flocked to see him in Paris, Lucerne, Rome, the States even. Now, super horse that he was, he had turned disaster into glory and from the humble position of 6th, by team work at its best, Britain had climbed to the very pinnacle. Cheers! Cheers! Cheers! – and perhaps a few tears. This for some was a moment of poignant emotion.

from CLEAR ROUND *1957*

European Horse Trials, Windsor – 1955

SHEILA WILLCOX

Competitors set off on the Speed and Endurance Test at five-minute intervals; as Chips and I started on the long, lonely ride, I was filled with an unswerving determination to finish the course – come what may – especially now that it had come to my ears that odds-on were being offered against Chips completing the day's course. We had never attempted to ride over a steeple-chase course beforehand, so I had no idea how Chips would respond to it, but he galloped round the two-and-a-quarter mile circuit without incurring penalties, and even managed to record a few bonus points. As we flashed through the Steeplechase finishing posts, to set off on the second Roads and Tracks, one of the spectators shouted to me that Chips's girth had come undone, and I looked down to see his safety girth flapping loose against his flanks. I had to stop and readjust it, and then we were off again at a trot and canter for the next six-mile phase.

We came to the starting posts for the cross-country. This was to be the real test, with those thirty-odd solid, fixed obstacles ahead of us, and as we galloped into the first fence I was threatening Chips with extinction were he to dare repeat his Stowell form. At the seventh fence, a giant tree-trunk, I lost my whip in the effort of getting over, but there was no time to retrieve it, and on we had to go. We sailed over enormous parallel birch poles with a deep ditch between them, and then ran into our first trouble at the Culvert fence, where one had to jump down a drop of four feet into water, cross the culvert and leap up three and a half feet to get out. Chips's eyes nearly jumped out of his head at the sight of this atrocity, and he hovered on the brink, taking a step backwards before jumping in; this constitutes a refusal. Then we went on until we caught up one of the Italian team who had set off five minutes ahead of me. He had obviously run into a good deal of trouble, and his horse was exhausted. At that time I didn't have the experience then that I have now, so I held back waiting for him to go on, whereas, in actual fact I should have pressed on.

As it was, Chips lost all his impulsion, and when I decided we could hold back no longer, we had to jump one of the most difficult fences on the course, the fearsome Sand Quarry. In the ordinary way it would have been terrifying for us, but after the mix-up with the Italian, it was even worse, and Chips came to a stop at the rails which stood at the top of the Quarry. It was a wicked jump and had already caused great grief even to the most experienced horses and riders. On our second attempt we managed it; we had to slither down the quarry side to the bottom, then negotiate the two timber-faced steps up the other side, and finally leap over the single fixed pole erected on the far edge of the top and step into space. Five feet down we hit solid ground again, and then were off towards the next fence, over which Chips soared easily. Out of the corner of my eye I noticed a still shape lying to the right of the obstacle's landing side. Later I learnt that this had been the horse which had fallen at the fence, to incur fatal injuries.

Our third refusal was due to bad luck, really, for we met a simple pile of cordwood absolutely on the wrong stride, and it was impossible to jump from right underneath the fence. Chips did make a half-hearted effort at getting over, but succeeded only in trapping one of his front legs in the wire that bound the logs in place. Someone rushed to the rescue, and quickly disentangled the leg, no doubt expecting Chips to struggle frantically in panic. He was quite unmoved, however, and while he was being freed, he stood on his three legs and calmly surveyed the scene taking the opportunity to recover his breath. With four legs on the ground again, we turned for another try; and this time flew over the cordwood, and pressed on towards the end of the course.

As we approached the Irish Bank, five feet high, with a three-foot-six ditch on the take-off side, a violent hail-storm scattered the crowds. Chips and I struggled on, up and over the Bank, and away to the water-jump. The hail pelted into our eyes as we galloped straight into its fury, and I could not even see the water. Luckily my sense of direction must have been good that day for we arrived at the right fence, and then turned homewards with the storm at our back. We leapt the last few obstacles, and started off on the Run-In, finishing our first gruelling Speed and Endurance Test a few minutes later. When at last I was able to get off Chips and 'weigh-in' I had collected so much moisture from the hailstones that I weighed five pounds more than at the start of the day. I was absolutely soaked to the skin and was walking in boots half-filled with icy cold water; my mother became concerned lest I catch cold wandering about in such a state. . . .

I shot back to the hotel six miles away for a quick bath and change, while Chips returned at a more sedate pace in his horse-box. When I went out to see how he was after his efforts, I saw that one of his knees was beginning to swell slightly as a result of a bang he must have had somewhere on the course; apart from that, he seemed none the worse, and after Jean had rubbed him down, fed him and bandaged his legs, we were able to leave him for the night and go into the hotel again.

Early next morning Jean was out walking Chips round the yard in an effort to wear off his understandable stiffness before the veterinary examination at ten o'clock. We were now standing thirteenth, an improvement of one place from the dressage tests, and had only to jump round the show-fences in the afternoon to complete the Three-Day Trials. Chips was passed by the vets, and in due time we appeared in the parade of competitors still remaining in the event; taking our turn we cantered into the ring alone and went round the show jumps. We had one fence down, and our position remained unaltered, so Chips and I filed into the ring again with the other prize-winners to receive our award. There were fifteen awards, and as we stood in the line I realized that apart from Mrs Boon with Neptune, and myself, all the rest of the places were taken by the male riders, and all except one were members of the different teams. It meant that Chips had really surpassed himself, for he stood above thirteen team riders and their horses, not to mention our own British individuals. I felt I had reason to be proud of him, having so neatly confounded the critics, and now I looked forward to the autumn season, when with this experience I could prepare for the Trials even more thoroughly, knowing what was wanted, and take part in the events with a far greater confidence in our ability.

from THREE DAYS RUNNING *1958*

Hyperion

CLIVE GRAHAM

Visitors from all over the world – Australia, New Zealand, America and even Japan – have called at Lord Derby's Woodlands Stud situated off the Snailwell Road near Newmarket to pay their respects to Hyperion during this past year [1954].

They found there no decrepit old veteran, but a lively and active stud-horse, whose alertness belies his twenty-four years.

He will prance and rear and roll with the supple vigour of a horse less than half his age. Jim Courtney, his attendant, let him show off some of his tricks to us when we visited him one day in August.

And then, at a gentle word of command, he stood stock still, arched his neck and cocked his ears to pose for his photograph.

'He wouldn't know how to do anything wrong!' exclaimed Michael Ryan who served his apprenticeship at Mentmore and now runs the Woodlands Stud for Lord Derby under the direction of Lt-Col Adrian Scrope.

The sleek and shining coat testified to Hyperion's well-being, and Mr Ryan added that in all the time Hyperion has been at stud since his retirement from racing in 1934, he had never had a day's serious illness.

Exercise – and plenty of it – is probably the secret. During the mating season, he has one-and-a-half hours' walking, morning and afternoon.

He is turned out, in his own private paddock, for three to four hours each day. 'We take mercy on him when there's a shower,' says Jim Courtney. 'The old horse hates the feel of the rain on him.'

He will come to hand, without being called. When three hours are past, he drifts towards the paddock-gate. The scent and promise of a carrot are enough to make him submit quietly to the fixing of head-collar and leading-rein.

Sugar does not mean much to him: nor apples, either. The gift of a carrot, though, will rate you among his valued friends.

At this time of writing, twenty-one years have elapsed since Hyperion dispelled the theory that horses with four white feet were soft and useless. With Tommy Weston in the saddle, he danced away with the Derby and won the St Leger with equal ease.

He changed from George Lambton's training to that of Colledge Leader at the end of his three-year-old career. The slipping stifle joint which had been a continual source of worry to George Lambton provided deep anxiety to his new trainer. Although his objective was the Ascot Gold Cup, he was not given the necessary tough preparation, and the hard trained Felicitation was able to make all the running.

Hyperion 'blew up' before the straight was reached. 'I picked up my whip and showed it to him,' recalls Tommy Weston, who dearly loved the little colt, 'but I just could *not* bring myself to use it on him. It would have done no good, anyway.'

Hyperion was beaten again in a two-horse race at Newmarket, largely by the guile of Harry Wragg on Lord Rosebery's Caithness.

That was his last race, so he went to stud with his racing reputation slightly tarnished.

As a stallion though, he became an immediate success. Heliopolis, for long a leading sire in America, was one of his first good sons. He has now [1954] sired nearly 250 individual winners, and his classic winners include Owen Tudor, Sun Stream, Sun Chariot, Godiva, Sun Castle and Hycilla.

Khaled and Alibhai (sire of 1954 Kentucky Derby winner, Determine) have added lustre to his name in the United States, where Citation, first horse ever to win a million dollars in stakes, focused attention on the progeny of Hyperion mares.

He is now limited to 25 mares. During the past season, twenty-two of these were tested and found to be in foal. One of the few failures was Mrs 'Elizabeth Arden' Graham's champion American filly, Rose Jet. Mrs Graham had her transported from Kentucky by air to Newmarket in 1953. The first mating proved successful and she had running by her side in the paddocks a filly foal who looked the image of her sire.

If the war had not intervened, his record at stud would be even more impressive, but there is no stud book anywhere in the world which does not include a son or daughter of his in their files. He has become famous from Sydney to Buenos Aires, and in Aureole he has sired, in this country, a son worthy to carry on his line.

from GREAT HORSES OF THE YEAR 1954–1955 *1954*

Wilhelmina Henrietta

LORINER

Wilhelmina Henrietta. I remember smiling to myself the first time I saw the name. It seemed to me both pretty and comic. I have a godchild called Jemima Jane: pretty and comic in the same way. Perhaps it was for this reason that I followed Wilhelmina Henrietta's future from the first: both when she ran on the flat and when she ran over hurdles. It soon became apparent that she had a heart as impressive as her name.

Doubtless it was the obvious existence of this great heart, in addition to her other racing qualities, to say nothing of her breeding, that influenced her connections in their decision to retire her to stud, at the comparatively early age of six.

In fact she was by Chamier out of Thebaine. It would have

been intriguing to know what horse had been chosen as her first mate: even more intriguing to have seen her first progeny, and to have heard what name would have been chosen for it.

But that, of course, is not to be. Wilhelmina Henrietta will never have a foal; never be mated. She will never now be more than a name, briefly reported in the sporting columns of the Press over a period of two or three years; briefly lamented in the columns agog with the glamour and the giants of Cheltenham; and then forgotten.

A few, like me, will remember her pretty, comic name. A few, like me, will have won a bit on her from time to time. A few, like me, will have gone specially to see her run at Sandown, where she won the Bass-Worthington: many more will have admired her courage when she finished fourth, close behind Magic Court, Another Flash, and Kirriemuir himself, in last year's [1964] Champion Hurdle.

Many, too, will have hoped, like me, that despite the firm going, which she never liked, she would disport herself creditably in the Champion Hurdle this year. That she did, and more, will not be appreciated by very many, satiated in the glory and the triumphs of the greatest National Hunt week of the year: the utter demolition of Ben Stack by Dunkirk, the unforgettable hat-trick by Baulking Green, Arkle's devastating Gold Cup, gallant Scottish Memories.

But she did. Wilhelmina Henrietta ran the race of her life – and death – when she notched up this 'also ran' in the Champion Hurdle of 1965.

It had been announced that it was to be her last race before being retired to stud. The going was against her; but her heart was as big as ever. She was running for her life; and she gave her all.

Approaching the very last fence – the last fence, the last furlong of her career – she stopped. She broke a blood vessel, and, her great heart overtaxed, she died.

I have never, to my knowledge, met the owner of Wilhelmina Henrietta, Mrs L. W. Ritchie, nor her trainer, M. Bolton. Certainly I have never met the lad, or possibly the girl, who did her. But my heart goes out to them all. At 3.30 on Wednesday afternoon at Cheltenham each of them, and many others connected with Wilhelmina Henrietta, and others, like myself, unconnected interested parties, had high hopes, full hearts, and a yearning ambition that some six minutes later Wilhelmina Henrietta might have crowned her distinguished career with a fairy-tale climax.

Instead a horse box drove home empty: a box, perhaps the most special box of the yard, waited in vain.

'Also ran.' But for a few Cheltenham 1965 will not be remembered for Kirriemuir, Arkle, Dunkirk, Baulking Green, Scottish Memories: it will be remembered for the last race of Wilhelmina Henrietta.

It is, perhaps, unfortunate to dwell on something so sad, when Cheltenham generally was so splendid. The world and his wife were there – our world, anyway. It was friends, friends, old friends, acquaintances; 'Come and have a drink' 'So-and-so's a cert' 'What sort of a season are you having?' 'Doesn't the course look marvellous?' 'Come and have a drink'.

I cannot remember a better Cheltenham. Racing of Classic proportions; wonderful fields; cold but agreeably spring-like weather; a great challenge to the Irish by the home team; Dave Dick reminding us that he is one of the greatest – what a race he rode on Exhibit A! – superb organization, and in one way or another, everything that is best in National Hunt racing.

And incidentally, on the one day I watched, quite exceptional television coverage. I really do not know the moral of this: so superbly presented one felt that one could not be possibly better off even if actually there; and yet it made one long to be there.

But despite all the wonders and excitements of Cheltenham, racing is still something concerning horses and people; and regrettably one horse – in fact, more than one horse – is dead, and for some there is a sense of bereavement.

These things happen. It is inevitable. How well I remember as a child – or rather in my teens, when one is expected to display on occasion adult qualities – a very favourite horse of mine – about 15 hands, the promotion from pony to horse – breaking its leg.

I just could not bring myself to see it destroyed – by the farmer on whose land the accident occurred. Cowardly, I know, and squeamish, but it is not a pleasant experience. There is something grotesque, obscene almost, about a dead horse.

So often a human being in the repose of death looks serene, more so in fact than in life. It is not so with a horse. Lying on its side, its vaulted rib-cage distended, destroys the wonderful symmetry and elegance so exquisitely boasted by a living horse.

It is death at its worst; a sad sight, even if it's only some derelict animal that has been sent to the knackers. Nor is death by the humane killer – humane as it may be – particularly edifying. I, for one, rejoice to know that the veterinary service has been successfully experimenting with alternative methods.

As I say, these things happen. Horses are killed; horses have to be destroyed; foals are born dead. But it's all, nevertheless, sad: doubly so when a horse is in the prime of life.

To the multitude, maybe, it is just a name that will appear in the list of runners no more. But to a few its loss will be something extremely tragically personal, and it is right that one should remember for a moment those who suffer such losses, even at a moment when there are also such glories, such triumphs, such titanic feats to be remembered.

Arkle, Baulking Green, Kirriemuir came home in triumph to their stables. Wilhelmina Henrietta did not come home at all: but her name is inscribed in the roll of achievement on the English race-course. She provided, gallantly and consistently, her share of excitement, allied with pluck and courage, such as is the very life-blood of National Hunt racing: to say nothing of a name pretty and comic.

Thank you dear Wilhelmina Henrietta: and goodbye.

from HORSE AND HOUND *20–3–1965*

Arkle for President

DEREK MALCOLM

The capacity of sporting journalists to wax lyrical in face of the exceptional is only matched by the speed with which they run out of adjectives in doing so. In the case of an outwardly placid bay gelding called Arkle, the point of no return was reached long ago. What more can one do when his winning a race had already been described thus: 'I am not ashamed to say that tears coursed unhindered down my cheeks as this great and lovely creature, looking for all the world like an emperor striding into his kingdom (*sic*) progressed with unconcerned imperiousness past the winning post, with his humble subjects puffing shamefacedly up the hill behind him.'

There's certain to be an unholy sound of blubbing when he finally comes unstuck, for the racing public, its scant imagination caught in a way unheard of since Charlie Smirke made a very rude sign as he passed the enclosures on a long-priced winner, wears its heart quite as much on its sleeve where Arkle is concerned.

At Cheltenham, a hard-faced member of the racing sisterhood was heard to observe as Arkle looked unflinchingly past her: 'Oh, what a darling. I could cuddle him to death.' Even bookies have been known to doff their bowlers to him. No horse could do more for racing than that.

[On December 27, 1965] the Irish champion, whose owner, Anne, Duchess of Westminster, would scoff at an offer of £250,000, did it again at Kempton Park by loping away with the King George the Sixth Stakes despite the brave, ill-fated challenge of Dunkirk. He has now won 24 of 30 races, over £60,000 in prize money (a UK steeplechase record) and still has two or three years of his prime left. That's quite a bargain for a horse that went for £1,150 in a Dublin auction five years ago.

You cannot bet on him in the normal sense because the price is now prohibitive; but what you can do is to lend £100 to your bookmaker for 15 minutes and expect a margin of profit on the deal a good bit higher than bank rate. . . .

He is undoubtedly the fastest three-miler in the history of racing, and only Golden Miller can compete with him for the accolade of the greatest 'chaser of all time. True, some will never call him the supreme champion because he will never win a Grand National. The reason is simple. He is considered too valuable to enter. That is the real measure of his success to date.

'The Miller' won the National under top weight at a time when the fences offered appalling hazards. He also won the Gold Cup five times running. Next March, barring accidents, will be Arkle's third. A meeting between the two is something to dream about. Most think Arkle would have won.

He is not an absurdly good-looking horse, though his carriage is noticeably proud. Nor is he exceptionally well-bred – his dam has consistently failed to produce other good winners at stud. But he clearly loves racing and his general intelligence on the course is obvious. Watch him in the paddock and there's no gainsaying the pricked ears, the inquisitive eyes and the interest he takes in everything around him.

When he gets out on to the course he gallops with his head held astonishingly high and his deep-chested power is such that it takes all the strength of Pat Taaffe, his regular rider, to hold him back over the first few fences. His jumping is safe and clean, but no more than that. Plenty of others have been known to clear obstacles with more panache. His stamina is good (it has to be because he automatically runs with top weight), but not unshakable. It could well be that the Grand National ($4\frac{1}{2}$ miles) is too long for him.

What gains him his victories is purely and simply his powers of acceleration. These are so great that should he be put in the Cesarewitch, the long distance flat race, he would have a sporting chance of winning it – an unheard-of feat for a steeplechaser. Even Mill House, the English champion, a perfect jumper with tremendous strength, has shown time and again that he cannot, in spite of a generous weight allowance from the handicapper, cope with his rival's sheer speed.

'The b— went past me as if I were a double-decker bus,' one rider remarked sourly after his mount, no slouch, had received the full Arkle treatment near the finish: 'He'd have won with the whole Taaffe family on his back.' 'There wasn't anything I could do,' said another hard-bitten professional, 'I'll swear he was laughing as he passed.' Such anthropomorphic comments are the sort of thing only a legendary animal encourages.

And a living legend Arkle certainly is. They say in Ireland that with-it tourists would as soon visit Tom Dreaper's stable at Greenouge as kiss the blarney stone. Tales of how Arkle swigs Guinness twice a day and allows noisy children to sit on him in perfect safety circulate daily to the newspapers. The chap who scrawled 'Arkle for President' on a Dublin wall was probably perfectly serious.

If he was an 'entire', in the racing world's delicate parlance, he would certainly have multiplied exceedingly during his retirement, and at enormous expense. But, alas, he is not – and who-ever was responsible must be kicking himself from here to Tip-perary. There'll only be one Arkle. Perhaps, for the sake of one's adjectives, it's just as well.

from THE GUARDIAN *28–12–1965*

The Master's Voice

ALWIN SCHOCKEMÖHLE

I've no objection if boys today say that I am their idol. At first, a boy admires his father. Then he looks elsewhere for his heroes. When my life became more and more concerned with horses, I too had my heroes, of course. But here one must make a distinction. One person was to be admired, but one tried to model oneself on someone else. As a boy I admired Winkler and Thiedemann, but I wanted to be able to ride like Raimondo d'Inzeo. In one respect that still holds good today. My feelings when I watch him ride are quite different from those I have towards other horsemen.

I have been tremendously influenced by the Italian master, not only in the arena, but most of all in schooling and training. Naturally I have also adopted various details from other riders and adapted them for my own purposes, but most of them come from Raimondo d'Inzeo. However, the decisive factor was that I didn't confine myself to observing him at competitions. A rider's real work takes place at home – and this is probably true for much more than riding. At horse shows, only the result of your labour is visible, and not how your success was arrived at. But that is the really interesting and useful part of it.

And then one day the truth dawns on you that you can't simply adopt something blindly – because it won't fit in with other things, and because what is good for one person isn't necessarily right for another, not by a long chalk. There exists a certain class, a certain standard. After that, you must put it all together for yourself and establish a style of your own. Style – all it means is putting your personal stamp on all you have learnt.

Riders in specific countries often have adopted their style to the kind of horse that is available. Our heavy halfbreeds need a lot of control, that is why West German riders usually do everything themselves. Their style is much more dominant than, for example, the style of the Americans, who often ride Thoroughbreds. If I had grown up in America, my style would be completely different.

A man like Harvey Smith goes from one extreme to the other. One day he will be riding a horse with a double bridle, the next day he suddenly uses a totally different bit. There is no system. I try to work as much as possible in one particular way. For years I have only used an ordinary bridoon; only when riding Warwick do I need a gag. The difference between Harvey and myself is enormous. I have to bend a horse completely to my will; I must thoroughly train it and make it obey me before I will bring him out. Harvey does not need so much time; he even takes bad horses with him to competitions, and what is more he even wins with them!

That is because physically he is so strong, he can bend a horse shoe with his bare hands. He can do things that others cannot. Which is not to say that he only uses force, for his best horses often go very lightly; but still force takes an important place in Harvey's style of riding. Style depends a lot on the build of the rider. All top riders are built differently, therefore all their styles differ.

Raimondo d'Inzeo is the best rider in the world. I want to get where he is. With him everything is of the highest standard. In dressage, his horses have style; it is pure joy to observe them; he controls them beautifully, and they win competitions. But there is one drawback: for years he has not had enough horses and so he has been forced to make them perform too much. That is why he rode old Bellevue for so long even when he had to be kept upright by artificial means.

I especially admire him in his elegance achieved by adapting his concentration and harmony to that of the horse. With his brother Piero d'Inzeo, style often takes precedence over effectiveness and Piero's horses often throw their heads high before taking an obstacle. He never corrects them and that is why his horses often make unnecessary mistakes. Over the years Raimondo has always been better than Piero in the big competitions.

After Raimondo I think that Nelson Pessoa and Caroline Bradley are very good, at the moment. Nelson's first generation of horses developed without any trouble and he did it all his way. That was the time of Huipil and Gran Geste. Lately he has had to work hard with his young horses. With Nelson and Caroline it looks as if the horses arrive completely naturally at the correct point of take-off before an obstacle.

Of course they ride with the same control as I demand from my horses, but with them it all flows so well! The whole trick is to bring the horse at the right speed to the correct point of take-off. The speed varies with different obstacles. At a width jump one has to have a higher speed than at a height jump. Riders with West German style, like me, often make sharper commands to change their speed or to prepare for take-off.

from ALWIN SCHOCKEMÖHLE *1977*

The Legend of Skittles

H. L. GIBSON

In a book, *Rum Ones to Follow*, by a Melton Rough Rider, published in 1934, I read as follows about a lady whose nickname was 'Skittles': 'See that fence? I once saw a lady jump it. They called her Skittles. I never knew her proper name. She were not what you'd call a 'lady', but she was a fine rider, went like smoke, and was very quiet and well-spoken. A merry lass she was, and as pretty as a peach. Open-handed lady she was; did a wonderful lot of kindness to the poor. One day she had a fall, and her skirt got left hung up on the saddle. Real murderous things they wore then, long and heavy, not mere aprons, as they are now, and underneath they wore white frillies. There was a lot of chaff among the gentlemen as to who should go to her rescue. They all asks for a married man.'

The author was writing about the Fernie country, and the period seems to have been about 1865, when Mr Tailby was Master.

In a book about Wilfred Scawen Blunt, by Edith Finch, published in 1938, quite a lot of information is given about 'Skittles' as well as her portrait. Her name was Catherine Walters, and she was born in 1839. She was one of the most renowned demi-mondaines of the late nineteenth century, and her bright chestnut hair, delicate, clear-cut features, slender figure and sensitive hands made her very charming. In early life she was in Paris, and later in England. Her receptions in South Street, Park Lane, were frequented by the then Prince of Wales and others famous in the public life of England. Even Gladstone came alone to take tea with her, having sent her beforehand 12 lb of Russian tea.

In public she was to be seen roller-skating in the fashionable rinks of London and Tunbridge Wells, driving the ponies of her phaeton in Hyde Park, or riding in Rotten Row a horse that no one else could ride and which had finished second in the Grand National. She was interested in modern art, knew something about music and liked serious reading, even on religious subjects. Her letters, although illiterate and nearly illegible, were highly entertaining. Even those who ceased to be her lovers remained her devoted friends. Of the German Kaiser she wrote in November, 1914: 'I knew him so well when he was Crown Prince. He gave me his photograph and a jewelled sunshade. The latter I have sold for the Red Cross. He was most charming to me, and went cracked about my riding. He looked well on horseback, and had a handsome face.'

In later life she was known as Mrs Bailey. She died on 4 August 1920, and was buried in the churchyard of the Franciscan monastery at Crawley, and the grave-stone is lettered 'C.W.B.'.

17 January 1941
from NINETY YEARS OF HORSE AND HOUND *1977*

Death of Fred Archer

AUDAX

The one absorbing topic in Turf circles this week has been the melancholy death of Fred Archer, and never have I noted more signs of genuine grief than when it transpired at Albert Gate on Monday afternoon that he had passed away by his own hand whilst under the influence of delirium. So much has been written on the subject that I will not fill our pages with a lengthened account of his career, but briefly express my own sorrow for the death of the brightest ornament of his profession and one who made many real friends by his undeviating truthfulness, his modesty under adulation which might have turned weaker heads and his gentlemanly bearing in every relation of life.

As a jockey I never saw his superior, and I have seen James Robinson, Sam Chifney, Frank Butler, Sam Rogers, Alfred Day, Custance, Tom French, Tom Aldcroft and the immortal George Fordham show their brilliant skill in the pigskin. Many of these may have shown as grand horsemanship in special instances, but as an all-round jockey Fred Archer has had no equal, in my opinion. One main secret of his success was his undeviating attention to business, always seeing that his weight was right, his horse properly saddled and that he reached the post in good time. The starters will miss him, as he set a bright example of submission to those in authority, never attempting to take advantage until the flag was dropped; yet so skilful was he, and so keenly did he watch the starter's movements, that he knew when to go, and won scores of races by his judgement at the starting-post. In the actual race, too, how different was his riding to that of the many headless horsemen that call themselves jockeys, and I pause to think how many races I have seen him snatch out of the fire, and drop a tear of unfeigned sorrow to think I shall never see his brilliant horsemanship again.

Born at Cheltenham in 1857, when eleven years old he won a steeplechase at Bangor on a noted pony, Maid of Kent, and two years later on, in 1870, he won a Nursery at Chesterfield on Athol

Daisy. In 1872 he won the Cesarewitch on Salvanos for poor Joe Radcliffe, who has since joined the great majority, and from the moment that, in 1874, he won the Two Thousand Guineas for Lord Falmouth on Atlantic his name has been a household word, as he won that race four times, the One Thousand twice, and he can claim five Derbies, four Oaks, and the St Leger six times, and I learn from a contemporary that he has had in England 8,084 mounts, and ridden 2,748 winners, whilst he has won the City and Suburban five times, the Great Metropolitan once, Woodcote Stakes six times, Lincolnshire Handicap once, Northamptonshire Stakes once, Cesarewitch twice, Clearwell Stakes eight times, Middle Park Plate thrice, Dewhurst Plate five times, Ascot Stakes once, Prince of Wales's Stakes (Ascot) three times, Royal Hunt Cup twice, Alexandra Plate twice, Great Ebor Handicap twice, Great Yorkshire Stakes once, Northumberland Plate once, Stewards' (Goodwood) twice, Great Yorkshire Handicap once, Champagne Stakes seven times, Portland Plate twice, Doncaster Cup once, Liverpool Autumn Cup thrice and Manchester Cup once.

Whilst dwelling on poor Fred's career, it is not too much to say that his success in life is in no small degree owing to the kindness of Lord Falmouth and his good friend and relative, Mr Matthew Dawson. Singularly enough, his first great success in the classic races was in the ever-popular magpie jacket of Lord Falmouth, and it was the last he wore to victory, when he won on Blanchland the last race of the Houghton Friday. Would to heavens that, like the jockeys of old, he had wound up the year on that Houghton afternoon, as the cold, treacherous air of the Southdowns no doubt aggravated what would only too probably have proved a fatal illness. What hope there may have been was cut short, alas! by a fit of frenzy that has caused deep grief amongst racing men of every grade; for, from the first gentleman in the land to the mildest punter at the street corner, his name was respected as the emblem of manliness and integrity.

I fear that poor Fred Archer only adds another to the list of those whose lives have been shortened by excessive wasting – at least, I can call to mind that Tom French, another of the best type of horsemen, wrecked his brilliant career by excessive wasting to ride in France. Men, however wealthy, will run extraordinary risks to gratify their ambition in winning races, and Archer pinched himself cruelly to ride St Mirin for the Cambridgeshire, as he fully thought he could win on him; whilst last week one of the richest commoners in England faced the starter in a silk jacket, minus his shirt, to save half a pound, when riding at a country meeting, in spite of the advice of his friends, who begged him to put on a thick flannel and declare the extra weight.

I do not on this account desire a higher scale of weights, as there is no necessity for those who cannot get down to a certain standard to sport silk, and there are plenty of lads anxious to ride intermediate weights. Now that there is 'No Best' left in the riding world, owners need require no one to make special exertions on their account, and the almost superhuman excellence of one bright star will not confound the most careful calculations of handicappers; although I would not have it understood that I consider that many of the existing jockeys do not ride quite up to the average of the present or past years.

13 November 1886
from NINETY YEARS OF HORSE AND HOUND *1977*

Leopard

COLONEL SIR MICHAEL ANSELL

A troop horse, Teddy, was possibly the best show jumper I had: never unplaced at Nice in 1939, and jumping two clear rounds in the Nations Cup. But when War came and Teddy went to Palestine with the Yorkshire Hussars, while I went to France in a rather useless light tank, I was glad of this. War is no place for horses.

However, without question, the most unique horse was Leopard, a chestnut spotted grey and black, bought by our veterinary surgeon at York, Adam Hodgkins, who 'saw him trekking behind a tinker's cart looking awful!' Bought him for £20. So this miserable-looking horse paraded on the square with a couple of dozen others: it was customary for the Sergeant-Major's advice to be taken into account, and he naturally preferred a horse that was easy to feed, that would look well. But I took no chances, and begged my Squadron Leader 'How' Wiley to make the dejected chestnut first pick, which he did, saying 'you take him and keep him in your stable'.

Leopard was the most extraordinary horse, standing 16·2, almost perfect in conformation, and although he took time to build up he proved easy to train and would do anything asked. A supreme hunter, he won many hunter trials and point-to-points. Superb on parade, so very proud, and in the Trick Ride he would do anything without a bridle. I could go for a hack or take a ride of recruits bridleless, and yet the next day in some race over fences in a snaffle bit he would take a real hold.

Three years in succession he won me the bronze medal, at the Royal Military Tournament, both at 'Dummy Thrusting' and 'All Arms' – when the rider uses sword, lance and revolver.

He won show jumping, and on one particular occasion I had to 'jump-off' against Lady Wright, who was surprised to see me come into the ring without a bridle, and equally surprised when Leopard won and accepted his rosette lying down. He without a bridle because he jumped the better if I couldn't interfere with him.

Once in 1934 I had to make a major decision. The King with Queen Mary and the Princess Royal were coming to review the troops at Aldershot, and His Majesty had expressed a wish to see a display of our Trick Ride horses. This would be on a Wednesday and unfortunately I'd entered Leopard for a race at Hawthorne Hill the Saturday before. Dare I risk that when I'd be jumping such things as swords, without a bridle, a few days later? I took the chance because I thought I could win at Hawthorne Hill and had complete confidence in Leopard. And I should have won that race – it was my own fault that I was second – but on Wednesday I left it to Leopard, without a bridle, and there were no mistakes then.

In February 1935 at Colchester, I was giving Leopard a canter before going to Tweeseldown to race, when he suddenly dropped and died instantly from a clot of blood near the heart. I removed the saddle and wept. Not only a great horse, but human in friendship, and he was only ten years old.

When I married in 1936 I had some sixty silver cups melted down, and these were made into a model of that superb horse; and so Leopard stands permanently on my dining-room table.

from SOLDIER ON *1973*

So Long in the Saddle

DORIAN WILLIAMS

No one in any way associated with the Horse of the Year Show – until 1975 – could ever be in any doubt as to who was in the saddle. Colonel Sir Michael Picton Ansell towered over the whole Show both in physique and in authority. Though he always denied it, his was in fact a benevolent dictatorship; when on occasions it was something less than benevolent, then as a rule there was justification for what could be described as autocratic behaviour.

Michael Ansell was born in 1905. His father, a regular cavalry officer, was killed, leading his regiment, the 5th Dragoon Guards, in September 1914. My father, Colonel V. D. S. Williams, his equitation officer, became his guardian. Mike never had any desire to be anything but a soldier. In 1923 he joined the Inniskillings, which a year earlier had amalgamated with the 5th Dragoon Guards. He quickly made his mark in every sphere: he represented his regiment at polo, and later his country; he was a very successful point-to-point rider, he became his regiment's equitation officer, he represented the army in show jumping, winning his fair share of prizes in international competition; and he produced the famous trick ride which achieved great fame between the wars. Especially popular was the jumping section when, led by Mike Ansell on his legendary horse Leopard, they jumped about everything that could be jumped, without stirrups or reins, including a line of swords.

In the late 'twenties he was selected for a course at the Cavalry School at Weedon. As Weedon was only a few miles from our home at Towcester for that year he almost lived in our house. It was a memorable part of my childhood. When Mike was around life was always exciting: or, as he would say, fun. He revelled in leg-pulls, teasing, practical jokes and hoaxes. There was an almost non-stop banter between him and my father, and frequent horse-play. Looking back, those ten months seem to have been months of non-stop laughter.

At that time my father was Master of the Grafton, one of the packs with which the officers at Weedon hunted. There were few better men across country than Mike Ansell that season, even though it was a vintage era. As my father used to say, for the Master to keep in front in those days was no mean task, for there were some of the finest horsemen in the country at Weedon, led by the instructors which included Arthur Brooke, Jock Campbell, 'Bede' Cameron, 'Friz' Fowler: all well known in the annals of the cavalry.

By the mid-thirties Ansell had made a very considerable reputation for himself. In 1940 he was given command of the Lothian and Border Yeomanry – at thirty-four the youngest commanding officer in the army. Being ambitious he was naturally delighted, though sad to leave the Inniskillings, which he had always hoped to command. His contemporaries at the time speak of him with admiration, respect and, of course, affection; though many were aware of the ruthless streak in him, and realized even then that if Mike really wanted something, practically nothing would stop him. His determination, always, was to win.

There is a story told of how when the Colonel came round to inspect the recruits' ride he was greatly impressed by those in Captain Ansell's squadron. His brother officers were not altogether amused when they learnt that he had substituted experienced riders for the recruits! In his book, *Soldier On*, he tells how when he learned that under new regulations shortly to come into being no officer under thirty-five could be promoted to the rank of major, even to fill a vacancy, he persuaded a fellow officer who was leaving to send in his papers a month early, for which he paid him a month's major's pay. He thus got early promotion: as he says in the book, a 'very good deal'. Certainly, but it showed him to be an opportunist, always ready to seize a chance, having had the foresight to be ready for it.

In 1936 he had married Victoria Fuller and with the birth of his elder son, Nicholas, in 1937 and his unusually successful career with its exceptional promise, the world appeared to be at his feet. But in 1939 war broke out. At St Valery a few months later he received wounds that were to alter his whole life.

For many months he was 'missing'. Then when in hospital in Paris he persuaded a visiting Irish priest to get in touch with Dan Corry, a doyen of the Irish show jumpers and now frequently a judge at the Horse of the Year Show, and ask him to let Victoria know that he was alive. Eventually he was repatriated after a long spell in a German prisoner of war camp, time not entirely wasted as he spent much of it planning the revival of show jumping in Britain. He still retained a little sight in the corner of one eye, 'guiding vision'. It was made clear to him that if he lived a quiet and sedentary life his limited sight need not for many years deteriorate: but if he lived a 'normal' life it would go.

Inevitably, of course it did go. It happened at the time when the *Daily Mirror* was putting on a Cavalcade of Sport at the White City. There had been a rehearsal the evening before, after which I had had dinner with Mike at the Cavalry Club. When I collected him next morning he said, 'I think I've had it. I couldn't find my razor this morning.'

Months attending St Dunstan's had prepared him for this, so that for most people Mike's transition from limited sight to blindness was virtually undiscernible. Even today many who have been intimately associated with him for years find it easy to forget that he is blind. They hold out a hand, expecting him to take it; they pass the salt to him across the table, expecting him to know where it is; they assume that he knows who it is that has entered the room. Frequently, in fact, he does, because he recognizes a voice instantly, even though he may not know the person very well. Often – deliberately, it seems – he uses the words 'see' and 'look': 'I see you're wearing a new dress.' 'Don't the flowers look marvellous?' Like so many blind people he has a remarkable memory and has only to be shown the geography of a room, or indeed a house, once for him to be able to find his way around: though there is no doubt that in recent years his reluctance to hold the

Royal International anywhere other than at Wembley was because he knew Wembley so well: he was not prepared to 'learn' a new environment.

Mike frankly admits that on occasions he has turned blindness to an advantage, to get something he wants, to achieve something through sympathy. On one occasion, he even told me that if, miraculously, he learned that his sight could be restored he would reject it. His whole life, he said, was now orientated towards being blind: sight, all that it entailed in so big a change to his way of living, would only be confusing and disillusioning after so long. Once again, in his extraordinary manner and thanks to his remarkable fortitude, he has managed to make a virtue out of a necessity. A few years ago after I had survived a serious illness he wrote to me, 'Remember fortitude is so much greater than courage.' This, of course, is what he has himself proved.

With his customary resilience, once home again he sought out some kind of creative activity. Flowers had always been his second love and so he decided, with his wife Victoria, to start a flower market garden – which has, incidentally, been a very considerable success – at Bideford in Devon. This, probably, would have been his full-time job had he not been persuaded to stand for the chairmanship of the B.S.J.A. In December 1944 he was elected by one vote. What a crucial vote that one turned out to be.

In September 1945 he organized, at the White City, the very successful Victory Championship at which he was able to put much of his prisoner of war camp thinking into practice. In 1947 when the International Horse Show was revived, also at the White City, my father as chairman asked him to be responsible for the organization of all the jumping events. In 1950 he became show manager, having a year earlier launched the Horse of the Year Show.

For twenty-five years, therefore, he has dominated the two major or 'official' shows. In addition to this he was for over twenty years chairman of the B.S.J.A. and for nearly as long chairman of the B.H.S., having previously been honorary director. In 1972 he became chairman/president of the British Equestrian Federation, retiring in April 1976.

For anyone, let alone a blind man, this has surely been an unusually full and rewarding life. Yet is a man of Mike Ansell's character ever wholly rewarded, entirely satisfied? It is a curious trait in the personality of men of ambition, even the greatest, to feel that they have not achieved quite all that they should have. There are endless examples in history of men who have attained the highest office, yet have died disappointed. Recently in the diaries of Lord Reith, father of the B.B.C., it is evident that although he achieved an eminence that most would feel as great as any one man could expect, he felt frustrated not to have reached even the greater heights.

When in the New Year's Honours of 1968, Mike received a knighthood, many believed that he would then retire, or at least allow himself gradually to be relieved of some of his work. He was nearly sixty-five; he had been running the two shows for twenty years; he had held for a considerable time the highest offices in the horse world; in addition he was, at that time, suffering considerably from back trouble. He had certainly earned an easier life. But, in fact, he appeared to attack the 1968 Show with more than usual vigour, as if to make it quite clear that he had no intention of giving up, or perhaps to prove to himself that he was not going to be beaten either by his bad back or increasing tiredness: once again he had to win.

It was noticeable, too, that he paid even more attention to detail, delegated even less. One example from many: a presentation was to be made by the Pony Club to a children's charity. General Vivian Street was to receive the presentation at the foot of the royal box. Some twenty children were to ride in, each carrying a bag of money. At the morning conference I was detailed to organize this and a rehearsal was to be held after the afternoon performance at 5.30 p.m. As the performance ended early and all the children were ready by about 5.20 p.m. I went ahead with the rehearsal. The ring was to be in darkness; suddenly the twenty young riders, all in their coloured shirts, were to explode into the arena as the lights blazed on, gallop round and draw up in a posse before the royal box, throwing their bags on to the floor.

We had just finished the rehearsal when Mike Ansell was led into the ring. He came across to where the children were congregated and started to address them, telling them what to do and so on. After a few moments I interrupted, telling him that I had arranged it all, that it was all over. He was obviously not pleased.

Why had we started before 5.30 p.m.? I explained. What exactly
had been organized? I told him. Had I not added that Colonel
Guy Cubitt, chairman of the Pony Club, was there and had
approved it all I believe he would have insisted on taking charge
himself and re-rehearsing. He would never abdicate complete
responsibility.

He would argue – perhaps with some justification – that a great
leader leaves nothing to chance: yet it has also been said that too
great attention to detail can be a weakness in a leader. In the case
of Mike Ansell it was, quite simply, that he saw his attention to
detail as part of his image. It is his philosophy that it is to the
benefit of any group or body or organization, if there is only one
personality at its head, only one person surrounded by an aura. If
a structure is to be formidable and effective the driving force must
emanate from just one person. Was this not the case with Churchill
and Monty? Mike Ansell did not consciously suppress those
efforts of others which might gain them kudos, increase their
stature: rather, as Lord Hailsham once said of Edward Heath, he
was like a massive oak that by nature allows little to grow underneath it. That this was an entirely subconscious attitude there can
be no doubt. Privately he was often lavish with his praise: there
are few senior stewards who have not experienced evidence of his
gratitude.

He was hurt and surprised, and therefore angry, when I suggested after the twenty-first Horse of the Year Show that it would
have been a gesture much appreciated if he had in some way
singled out and rewarded others who had been associated with the
Show for the whole twenty-one years, as he had: invite their
wives into the royal box one evening, give them a table in the
restaurant or ask them to present a trophy. That he had not
thought along these lines was not deliberate: it just had not
occurred to him that such a gesture was necessary. He was, deep
down, immensely grateful for the help that he had received from
these senior lieutenants, but he knew that their contribution was
only contingent upon his.

On one occasion a visitor was heard by a senior steward to
remark to Mike that he must have a wonderful team of helpers.
His reply, instinctively, was that it was a wonderful team 'because
they bloody well do as I tell them'. The senior steward was

annoyed until he appreciated that this was Mike, the essential character of the man. He genuinely saw his stewards' efforts as reflections of his overall design: and he was right. Every department reflected his planning, his thinking, his inspiration.

At the dinner to celebrate his knighthood, in proposing his health I reminded the distinguished gathering that we had all enjoyed the experience of coming to him with some idea which he had immediately rejected, only to produce a few weeks later as his own! I was, of course, pulling his leg and no one laughed louder than Mike, except perhaps Prince Philip. But the germ of truth in my joke had been appreciated by all present who recognized his occasional tendency to take credit to himself, rather than allow it to others, but a characteristic that few resented.

Surprisingly, he has, on occasions, shown himself to be extremely sensitive to criticism, especially from the press. More than once, when a correspondent has been critical in his or her paper, instead of ignoring the matter as his closest associates have advised, he has retaliated: first by referring to the matter in scathing terms at the morning conference, then by summoning the offender and giving him or her a sharp, sometimes bitter rebuke. It has to be admitted, however, that once he has relieved himself of his anger he has behaved towards the offender with charm and generosity. Once he attempted, unsuccessfully, to persuade an editor to dismiss the equestrian correspondent. On another occasion he went out of his way to attack a correspondent in front of other people at a reception, because he had taken offence at a headline, which, of course, was not the correspondent's responsibility. He would have been surprised if he had known that he had offended the correspondent in question. He had not meant to hurt, just to get his own back, to achieve the last word.

'You're not here to think,' became a joke phrase among stewards for several years after a senior steward had been reprimanded for giving what was, in Mike's opinion, wrong advice to one of the displays:

'I'm sorry, sir, I only thought . . .'

'You're not here to think.'

'No, sir, and I'm not just here to be a yes man.'

Which, of course, Mike Ansell appreciated, and respected.

Why, then, these flaws in a character that has so easily and convincingly won universal admiration and respect? Let it first be said that the great man who has no flaws does not exist and never has. The portrait of a man, at least in words, that is anything less than 'warts and all' is false. The very greatest are human, and humans are subject to the frailties of nature.

Having said that, it does seem that in a surprising number of great men there is a hidden, almost inexplicable lack of confidence in themselves. Why this should be so is difficult to understand. It is as though, despite the apparent success of their lives, they feel that they have not achieved all that they might have done. Something has eluded them: so they must press on, continue to prove themselves to themselves, and to the world, whatever the cost: there is ample evidence of this, even in Napoleon.

At the end of his autobiography, Mike Ansell writes: 'Many would say that I've had more than a glimpse of fame and glory: but the iron fulcrum has turned my fate another way and complete happiness eludes me.' Fate has certainly dealt him cruel blows, but perhaps there is more to it than that – it is not just a matter of his personal happiness. Subconsciously, he must be aware that were it not for his disability he might have become chief of the general staff, the highest position in the Army. He must feel, too, that with his proven drive, ability, clear thinking and personality, he could have been a captain of industry, in the £40,000-a-year bracket; he could have been at the top of almost any profession that he chose. Somewhere in his make-up, therefore, it is almost inevitable that there is a sense of frustration. In settling for the horse world – or having had it thrust upon him in 1944 – he accepted a great challenge. It must be accepted as of no less importance than any other of the worlds that he might have conquered but for his disability. It was a challenge that he had to win: 'We've damn well got to win' – how often one has heard him say that.

And he has won: but to win this particular battle it has been essential for him to dominate. On occasions his domination may, unintentionally, have hurt or offended; but it has seldom been resented because everyone in the horse world has appreciated that at its head was a man with the stature to have been head of almost any organization in the country. We have been proud of this, particularly, perhaps, those of us concerned with the Horse of the

Year Show, for it is this Show more than anything else that has popularized the horse with the general public.

In 1954 Mike Ansell asked Ronald Duncan to write that famous tribute to the horse, 'Where in this Wide World?', which has perhaps become more identified with the Horse of the Year Show than anything else. In 1975 I suggested to Ronald Duncan that he might write a tribute to Mike Ansell for inclusion in this book. To my delight he agreed.

> Taller than his shadow: a man
>   who is patient with servants,
>   impatient only with his friends;
>   we like him for his virtues,
>   love him for his faults. A man
>   who knows the difference between fortitude
>   and courage; discipline
>   and obedience. Who
>   to a rude age brings a consistent gentleness.
>   His perceptive hands sign kindness
>   on flank, girth or flower.
>   He, grateful for our sight; we for his vision.
>   There is a bright candle burning in his mind.
> They say he is blind.

Blind, yes: but he 'saw' the Horse of the Year Show.

from HORSE OF THE YEAR *1976*

PART IV

Great Races

There was the course, stand, rail and pen,
Peopled with seventy thousand men;
Seventy thousand faces staring,
Carriages parked, a brass band blaring;
Over the stands the flags in billows
Bent their poles like the wands of willows.
All men there seemed trying to bawl,
Yet a few great voices topped them all:
'I back the Field! I back the Field!'

John Masefield

Mrs Thornton's Match

THOMAS BROWN

The lady of the late distinguished Colonel Thornton appears to have been equally attached to the sports of the field with her husband; and the extraordinary contest which took place between Mrs Thornton and Mr Flint, in 1804, not only stands recorded on the annals of the turf, as one of the most remarkable occurrences which ever took place in the sporting world, but also a lasting monument of female intrepidity. It arose out of the following circumstances.

A great intimacy subsisted between the families of Colonel Thornton and Mr Flint, arising from their being brother-in-laws, as the ladies were sisters, so that Mr Flint was a frequent visitor at Thornville Royal.

In the course of one of their equestrian excursions in Thornville park, Mrs Thornton and Mr Flint were conversing on the qualities of their respective favourite horses. With the spirit and keenness which generally exists on such occasions, they differed widely in their opinions, and an occasional spurt took place to try the mettle of their steeds; when Old Vingarillo, under the skilful management of his fair rider, distanced his adversary at every attempt; which so nettled Mr Flint, that he challenged the fair equestrian to ride against him on a future day. This challenge was immediately accepted by Colonel Thornton, on the part of his lady; and it was fixed, by the respective parties, that the race should be run on the last day of the York August Meeting, 1804. This singular match was announced by the following notice:

> A match for five hundred guineas, and one thousand guineas bye – four miles – between Colonel Thornton's Vingarillo, and Mr Flint's br. h. Thornville, by Volunteer. Mrs Thornton's to ride her weight against Mr Flint's.

On Saturday the 25th of August, this race was decided, and the following account of it appeared in the *York Herald*:

'Never did we witness such an assemblage of people as were

drawn together on the above occasion – one hundred thousand at least. Nearly ten times the number appeared on Knavesmire than did on the day when Bay Malton ran, or when Eclipse went over the course, leaving the two best horses of the day a mile and a half behind. Indeed, expectation was raised to the highest pitch, from the novelty of the match. Thousands from every part of the country thronged to the ground. In order to keep the course as clear as possible, several additional people were employed, and much to the credit of the 6th Light Dragoons, a party of them were also on the ground, on horseback, for the like purpose, and which unquestionably were the means of many lives being saved.

'About four o'clock, Mrs Thornton appeared on the ground, full of spirit, her horse led by Colonel Thornton, and followed by Mr Baker, and Mr H. Bonyton; afterwards appeared Mr Flint. They started a little past four o'clock. The lady took the lead, for upwards of three miles, in a most capital style. Her horse, however, had much the shorter stroke of the two. When within a mile of being home, Mr Flint pushed forward, and got the lead, which he kept. Mrs Thornton used every exertion; but finding it impossible to win the race, she drew up, in a sportsmanlike style, within about two distances.

'At the commencement of the running, bets were five and six on the lady: in running the three first miles, seven to four and two to one in her favour. Indeed, the oldest sportsmen on the stand thought she must have won. In running the last mile, the odds were in favour of Mr Flint.

'Never, surely, did a woman ride in better style. It was difficult to say whether her horsemanship, her dress, or her beauty, were most admired – the tout ensemble was unique.

'Mrs Thornton's dress was a leopard-coloured body, with blue sleeves, the vest buff, and blue cap. Mr Flint rode in white. The race was run in nine minutes and fifty-nine seconds.

'Thus ended the most interesting race ever run upon Knavesmire. No words can express the disappointment felt at the defeat of Mrs Thornton. The spirit she displayed, and the good humour with which she bore her loss, greatly diminished the joy of many of the winners. From the very superior style in which she performed her exercising gallop of four miles on Wednesday, betting was greatly in her favour; for the accident which happened, in

consequence of her saddle-girths having slackened, and the saddle turning round, was not attended with the slightest accident to her person, nor did it in the least damp her courage; while her horsemanship, and her close seated riding, astonished the beholders, and inspired a general confidence in her success.

'Not less than £200,000 were pending upon Mrs Thornton's match; perhaps more, if we include the bets in every part of the country; and there was no part, we believe, in which there were not some.

'It is but justice to observe, that if the lady had been better mounted, she could not possibly have failed of success. Indeed, she laboured under every possible disadvantage; notwithstanding which, and the ungallant conduct of Mr Flint, she flew along the course with an astonishing swiftness, conscious of her own superior skill, and would ultimately have outstripped her adversary, but for the accident which took place.'

from BROWN'S ANECDOTES OF HORSES *1830*

The Derby Day

THE SPORTING MAGAZINE

Wednesday. This was the day 'big with the fate of thousands', and never did the month of May give birth to a more lovely morning than the one that ushered in this memorable day. The town of Epsom was 'uncomfortably full', lodgings being at a very great premium. Towards eleven o'clock carriages of all descriptions came pouring in, and shortly a Ring was formed for the betting men to exercise their judgment at the eleventh hour. Marshal Soult had risen most rapidly in the odds, and at the commencement of the betting he unquestionably was 'Premier'. The confident smile that sat upon that excellent judge of racing, Isaac Day, was anything but pleasing to the betters against Coronation. Some idle reports were put into circulation by a 'dishonest few', to the effect that Van Amburgh would not start, and the rumor caused considerable excitement among the 'lion-tamer's' admirers. There were also some strange tales told about certain parties bearing up strongly against Coronation to the last day; and, as one or two of the *suspected* have the character of being very hard to stop, a certain degree of caution was absolutely necessary: however Isaac Day proved too good a general, and crushed their 'golden hopes', and left them to gnash their teeth in anger and disappointment.

By half-past one a very extensive Ring was formed on the Hill, and the speculators were certainly far more numerous than on any previous occasion. Now that Coronation 'had passed a quiet night', and was 'much better *than might have been expected*', he gradually rose to be the *crack* favorite; and finally few were bold enough to bet more than 5 to 2 against him. In the pages of THE SPORTING MAGAZINE almost every month may be found the high opinion I entertained of this colt's merits, and those who have been fortunate enough to be guided by the remarks must be considerable gainers. – But to the Starting Post where *twenty-nine* horses and Jockeys are preparing to start. Since the St Leger race in Memnon's year (1825) we never saw such a Field for either of the great Stakes. The result –

The DERBY Stakes of 50 sovs each, h. ft, for three-year-olds:–
colts, 8st 7lb; fillies, 8st 2lb. – The owner of the second horse
to receive 100 sovs out of the Stakes, and the winner to pay
100 sovs towards the expenses of additional police-officers. –
Last Mile and a Half. – One hundred and fifty-four subs.

Mr Rawlinson's Coronation, by Sir Hercules (Connelly)
. . . . 1

Lord Westminster's Van Amburgh, by Pantaloon (Holmes)
. . . . 2

Not placed:– Lord Albemarle's Ralph, by Dr Syntax
(John Day); Lord Westminster's Marshal Soult, by Velocipede
(Scott); Mr Vansittart's Galaor, by Muley Moloch (Heseltine);
Lord Lichfield's Belgrade, by Belshazzar (Wakefield); Lord
Jersey's Joachim, by Glaucus (E. Edwards); Mr Dixon's
Knightsbridge, by Bran (Buckle); Duke of Rutland's Sir Hans,
by Physician (W. Boyce); Colonel Peel's Chameleon, by Camel
(N. Stagg); Mr Greville's Palaemon, by Glaucus (Flatman);
Colonel Wyndham's Monsieur Le Sage, by Nonsense (W.
Day); Mr Thornhill's E.O., by Emilius (Pettit); Mr Thornhill's
Eringo, by Emilius (Hornsby); Mr Combe's The Nob, by
Glaucus (Bartley); Mr Copeland's Mustapha Muley, by Muley
(Marlow); Sir G. Heathcote's Mongolian, by Glaucus (Chapple);
Mr Saddler's Protection, by Defence (Rogers); Lord Exeter's
Cesarewitch, by Rockingham (Darling); Mr Wimbush's
Finchley, by Glaucus (W. Cotton); Lord Orford's Arundel,
by Reveller (Samm Mann); Captain Ridge's c. by Coelebs, dam
by Young Woodpecker (Callaway); Mr Rush's c. by Plenipo
out of Obelisk's dam (Robinson); Mr Buckley's Gilbert, by
Muley (M. Jones); Captain Williamson's St Croix, by Glaucus
(Macdonald); Colonel Craufurd's Ermengardis, by Langar
(Templeman); Mr E. Griffiths's Hereford, by Sir Hercules
(Whitehouse); Mr Batson's Potentia, by Plenipo (Sly); and
Mr J. Negus's Negus Portstoken, by Divan (A. Perren).

The following were the odds as nearly as I could possibly
obtain them at the opening of the Ring; the intense excitement
manifested, and the numerous *hedging* bets made, rendered it a
matter of great difficulty to get at the exact prices:– 5 to 2 against

Coronation, 9 to 2 against Ralph, 7 to 4 against Marshal Soult (taken freely), 10 to 1 against Belgrade, 10 to 1 against Van Amburgh, 13 to 1 against Galaor (taken), 25 to 1 against Sir Hans, 35 to 1 against Potentia, 50 to 1 against E.O., 50 to 1 against Mustapha Muley (taken), 50 to 1 against Cesarewitch, and longer odds against any other.

Although the race was fixed by the Stewards to 'come off' at half-past two, it was nearly four o'clock before the actual start took place; the unusual number of horses made it a matter of great difficulty for the starter to get them off upon anything like equal terms. At last, after four or five false starts, the whole lot got off in good style, Ralph, Chameleon, Coronation, Potentia, Joachim, Belgrade, and Arundel being in the best situations after going about two hundred yards. At the Mile Post Chameleon made a grand attempt to lead the van, in which he succeeded, and carried the lot to the Turn, where 'honest John' increased the pace amazingly so much that before Ralph had reached the Road he was dead beat, as were all the Field save and except Coronation, Van Amburgh, Mustapha Muley, Arundel, E.O., and Belgrade. After crossing the Road it was clear enough how the grand event would end, for Coronation was pulling double, and Holmes (who rode exceedingly well) was evidently nursing Van Amburgh for a desperate chance, which was indeed desperate, for, after getting clear of the dip, Connelly let Coronation go, and he won in a common canter by four or five lengths. To prove how easily the race was won, I will just mention the fact of being on the Hill near the Betting Ring in a carriage, close to which Mr Tattersall's also drew up to see the race. Immediately upon the run in, Mr T. with his glass decided the event to the astonishment of Mr Justice, myself, and many others, by saying 'Coronation in a canter – Van Amburgh second'. Mr Rawlinson is said to have won £8,000, and Mr Isaac Day considerably more than that sum. Mr W. Hicks is also a good Winner. Value of the Stakes £4,275. The losers are the great betting men, including most of what are termed the 'play men', and I feel pretty certain that on the settling day we shall have a 'heavy sessions'. Coronation is engaged at Ascot, and also in the St Leger at Doncaster. Every one, even the losers, heartily congratulated Connelly upon his grand victory. He certainly rode upon the safe system, 'not to give a chance away'.

Most of the leading Gentry left the course immediately after the Derby race.

from THE SPORTING MAGAZINE *1841*

The First National

CON O'LEARY

The first Grand National starts two hours late, for it is nearly three o'clock before all the seventeen jockeys have been weighed-out by the clerk of the scales in the weighing-house. There has been time for Lottery to come in from 9 to 1 to 5 to 1, and displace as favourite the Irish pair Rust and Daxon, who start respectively at 7 and 8 to 1. But all human eternities have an end, and at last those who have been diligently watching the line of horses and their gaily-coloured riders forming and reforming at the angle of the course in front of the stables, no distance beyond the stone-wall and the grand stand, cry with throats of brass and lungs of leather: 'They're off!'

The coldly disgruntled who say it will be another false start are not listened to, for there is no doubt that Lord Sefton has lowered his starter's flag, and as there is nobody who can shout like the Irish, as great Dr Cahill has been telling Liverpool, everybody knows that Tom Ferguson has taken Daxon out in front and they have gone like the hop of a ball over the railed hawthorn

before others have got up a gallop. But what are the Irish shouting about? There are four miles to go, with fifteen jumps on the
first circuit and fourteen on the second, and now Captain Becher
is coming up with Conrad, and the ploughland is knocking some
of the shine out of Daxon's gallop – no, the race is not won yet –
not by a long chalk. Now they come to the railed fence with the
six-foot brook, and Daxon hits the top such a crack that it will
sound for a hundred years but you can put your faith in God and
an Irish hunter, and that part is true of Daxon, at that brook
anyhow. While Daxon works an equine miracle in springing to
safety, with the elegance of a performing horse at the end of a
circus trick, Conrad has been too close for comfort, and Becher
takes his best tumble into the brook. But Ferguson and Daxon
have no advantage in ingenuity on the son of the old leather
breeches. A moment ago it might have been Daxon's brook, but
now, and for ever until the last National chaser is forgotten, it is
'Becher's Brook'.

The captain felt the wind of Lottery's heels, and Rust, The Nun,
Dictator, and Charity, were leading the others when he dived for
safety into the deepest part of the brook, keeping down in his
watery shelter until all danger of a brain-smashing cavalcade had
gone with the leaping hoofs. But you know that the captain was
not one who in self-pity would stay down, though uncommonly
soaked in that christening of the Brook. It was not of fame or
self that he was thinking as he pursued his horse and, catching up
with him leaped into the saddle, looking, we may suppose to
labourers attired in smocks and corduroys in the fields, like a
merman on the kelpie. The others having been delayed by plough
and a deep wheat field, he caught up with them, and he was
among the leaders at the next brook. But though Conrad was a
great horse among the great, the contending pick of the country's
chasers, and Jem Mason himself had ridden him in one of the St
Albans Steeplechases, he was too exhausted or unstrung to cope
with that awkward rail and brook after the sharp turn by the canal.
It was no great fault that he crashed into the rail and slithered into
the water, for many horses since that time who had escaped un-
scathed at Becher's have failed at Valentine's Brook because of
that ugly turn, being unable to gather themselves from one fence
to the next. Ninety years afterwards that fence before the brook

was made virtually innocuous, as the crowded ordeal at the canal turn was judged to be too severe on the horses.

Now Conrad, picking himself out of the brook, takes care that the amphibious captain does not catch up with him again. The seeming phenomenon of riderless horses continuing to race is then a people's sight novel enough to be reported, and the early accounts, which leave so much to the imagination, will sometimes mention where these loose but game fellows come at the finish, if they keep going so long. Minus the weight and guidance of their jockeys they are a picturesque nuisance, though with some merit as a jumping performance, if in laziness they are apt to machicolate their fences. But when a horse goes on, the blame is not invariably his for leaving his jockey in the ditch.

Charity, who was supposed to be as familiar with stone as a bricklayer, because of her Gloucestershire training, was the only horse to fall at the stone-wall opposite the stand – perhaps it didn't seem a stone-wall to Charity, being less than five feet high. Meanwhile Rust had got trapped in a lane, the exit from which was closed by members of the crowd who did not want him to win, and Mr William McDonough's temper and blarney were equally ineffective in moving the gateholders to clear the way. Lottery raced up to Daxon on the second round, with Dictator, True Blue, Paulina, and The Nun (who had been judged too fat in the paddock), going well enough to keep their backers vacillating between hope and fear. Dictator came down heavily at the first brook, and now jockey Carlin was up again, but the revival there was even shorter-lived than that of Becher and Conrad, for at the next fence Dictator fell dead. Thus passed the first martyr to Aintree, his saddle on his back, a St Albans worthy going till his last wind in the colours of Mr Oswell. Now Daxon, too, was down, and when The Nun failed to get the second brook after the puzzle of the canal turn it was seen that 'Black Tom' Olliver on Seventy Four, a dashing but too unlucky horse, had gone past Pioneer and Railroad and was catching up on True Blue and Mr Theobald's mare Paulina.

And now in a last call on *Jorrocks's Jaunts and Jollies* we can say: 'Now all is tremor: silence stands breathless with expectation – all eyes are riveted – the horses come within descrying distance – "beautiful" three close together, two behind'.

But in the first Grand National there is one other horse in the finish, and he is coming away to win on his own. Lottery is the word and Jem Mason is the man. It was said that they understood each other perfectly. Now is the fruitful fortune of all Jem's careful and rather stern tutoring of Elmore's performing horse, with the finishing gallops by trainer Dockery for a spell on Epsom Down. Do not be jealous of Epsom's part in Lottery, Jem, or disdain to wipe your fashionable boots on the Down, for no story of the Derby will gain more admiration than that of the finish of the first Grand National, when Lottery carried you thirty feet, forelegs to hind, in that record leap over the last of the three hurdles before the run-in. He won in a common canter, though not showing clean hoofs, after the ordeal of the plough-land, to Seventy-Four and Paulina, True Blue and Railroad and Pioneer. All the others fell except Rust, who, as the irrepressible punsters of the time must have said, was rusticated in the lane.

from GRAND NATIONAL *1945*

The Ascot Cup

Hon. F. LAWLEY

Which is the most important race in the world? Tradition and courtesy would probably vote in favour of 'The Epsom Derby'; although it is notorious that within the last few years half-a-dozen 'prizes' – the word is rapidly becoming more fashionable than its old-time analogue, 'stakes' – have sprung up, which that most cogent of persuaders, *argumentum ad crumenam* – that is to say, an appeal to the pocket – would dispose some owners of racehorses greatly to prefer to the 'blue riband of the Turf'. Fifty years ago, however, there is little doubt that the Ascot Cup was regarded (and especially in the North of England) as conferring greater distinction upon its winner than the Epsom Derby or the Doncaster St Leger. For instance, the Ascot Cup was won in 1842 by Mr Orde's gallant old mare Beeswing, ridden by Cart-

wright, and beating Mr Combe's The Nov, who was second,
Mr Pettit's St Francis, third, Mr Kirby's Lanercost (who was
poisoned), and Mr Thornhill's Eringo. Odds of 6 to 5 were laid
on Lanercost; 7 to 1 against Beeswing. The scene witnessed on
that occasion at Newcastle-on-Tyne, where Mr Orde lived, was
never paralleled on the banks of that grimy stream, in the neighbourhood of which George Stephenson – the greatest benefactor
that the human race has known since the days of James Watt –
first saw the light. On the arrival at 'Carbonopolis' of the
Edinburgh mail, bearing the glad tidings that 't'auld meer' had
won, 'it might have been imagined', wrote the late Rev. George
Bigge, 'that the population – more particularly that portion of it
which ascended to the upper regions from the depths of many a
dark coal-pit – had gone mad. In the midst of the frantic enthusiasm, which exceeded the emotional display called forth a few
years before by the crowning victory of Waterloo, the joy-bells
suddenly burst forth with clangorous volume from the oldest
steeple in Newcastle, so that women rushed forth from their
homes, shop-girls from behind their counters, and many a
comely lass from the factory in which she toiled, to enquire what
on earth had happened. "T'auld meer's woon t'Coop! t'auld
meer's woon t'Coop!" There was no need to tell even the young
children in that sporting hive of industry that "t'auld meer"
meant Beeswing, and that "t'Coop" meant "the Ascot Cup".'

It is not generally known that during the seventeenth century
the custom of ringing church bells to celebrate the victory of a
racehorse was universally prevalent.

In an entertaining book published in 1890, and called *Curiosities
of the Church* by William Andrews, FRHS, of Hull, several instances of this strange exhibition of local feeling in honour of a
successful racehorse are recorded. Among other cases, it is
mentioned that in the parish register of St Edmund's Church, at
Salisbury, the following entry appears:– 'A.D. 1646. For ringing
in the race-day, that the Earle of Pembroke, his horse, did winne
the Cuppe – five shillings and eightpence.'

To which Mr William Andrews adds:– 'Ringing Church bells
when horses won races was not confined to Salisbury. In olden
days the practice was common in many parts of the country.'

The race was founded in 1807, and according to Sir Joseph

Hawley, owed its origin to Lord George Cavendish (great-grand-father of the present Duke of Devonshire) and to Squire Thornhill of Riddlesworth. In its early years it suffered, like every other Turf interest of that day, from the deadly struggle with Napoleon, which held this country in thrall from the outbreak of the French Revolution in 1793, until the fall, in 1815, of the most command-ing military genius that the world has seen since Julius Caesar. The storm did not cease, however, until many additional years had flown. There are few men now living who can remember the tremendous commercial and financial panic of 1825, of which the effects were sensibly felt down to the end of George IV's reign in June, 1830. Then, with the dawn of a less gloomy era, and with a king whose good nature exceeded his discretion, the whole *mise en scène* changed. The new order of things was inaugurated on the Turf by Sir Mark Wood, who had sold his pocket borough of Gatton, in Surrey, to the father of the present Lord Oxen-bridge for a fancy price, because it placed two seats in the House of Commons at the disposal of the owner of that stately white mansion on the hill near Reigate – seats, however, which appeared shortly afterwards in Schedule A of the Reform Bill of 1832, and were by it abolished for ever. Sir Mark Wood opened the ball well by winning three Ascot Cups in succession – that of 1830 with Lucetta, that of 1831 with Cetus, and that of 1832 with Camarine – all of them ridden by Jem Robinson, some of whose finest efforts were made at Ascot. In the last of the three races, Camarine, aged four, ran a dead-heat with Mr W. Chifney's Rowton, aged six, who was ridden by Sam Chifney. It was a common saying at that time that Jem Robinson always won the second race, when a dead-heat had taken place; and the victory he had gained at Epsom in 1828 on the Duke of Rutland's Cad-land, against Bill Scott on Mr Petre's The Colonel, was repeated at Ascot in 1832, when he triumphed on Camarine over Sam Chifney and Rowton. Nevertheless, the spell was broken eighteen years later, when, after a dead-heat for the Doncaster St Leger between Voltigeur and Russborough, Job Marson (who ought to have won easily the first time), the second time of asking got the better of the Irish colt and of Jem Robinson.

We come in 1834, 1835, 1836, and 1837, to three of the best Ascot Cup winners that ever galloped – in 1834 to Lord Chesterfield's Glaucus, aged four, ridden by Bill Scott; in 1835 to Lord Jersey's Glencoe, aged four, ridden by Jem Robinson; and in 1836 and 1837 to the Marquis of Westminster's Touchstone, in 1836, aged five, ridden by John B. Day, and in 1837 aged six by Bill Scott. Sir Joseph Hawley used often to quote 1836 as the best year that he had ever read of; for he did not join the English Turf until six years later than 1836, in which latter year he resided at Florence, and was engaged in running a few English platers against Prince Poniatowski's Italian 'cracks'. The lucky Baronet's opinion was that Rockingham, who in 1836 was sixth, Touchstone, who was fifth, and Bay Middleton, Gladiator, Venison, and Slane, who finished first, second, third, and fourth for the Derby of that year, were the most prepotent and epoch-making sires of the nineteenth century. From Rockingham came Miss Twickenham, the dam of Teddington, whose sire was Orlando, a son of Touchstone. To Bay Middleton he was indebted for his two famous mares, Aphrodite and Kalipyge; another of his Derby winners, Musjid, was a son of Newminster, who was, again, a son of Touchstone; and from Mendicant, a daughter of Touchstone, he obtained a long list of winners in Beadsman, Blue Gown, Pero Gomez, and Green Sleeve. Turning away from Sir Joseph's own stud, we have the Derby form of 1836 established by the sons of its heroes – viz., The Flying Dutchman, son of Bay Middleton; Sweetmeat, son of Gladiator; Alarm, son of Venison; and Sting, son of Slane. Let it not be forgotten that better stayers than The Flying Dutchman, Sweetmeat and Alarm were never stripped upon an English racecourse.

The year 1838 introduces us to the unusual spectacle of the Ascot Cup being won by a three-year-old – Lord George Bentinck's Grey Momus, who was ridden in a weak field by the still living William Day. Mr Pettit's St Francis – a great favourite with Admiral Rous – made his mark for the same race in 1840, with Sam Chifney on his back, the last appearance of that great master of equitation upon the Royal Heath, where so many of his earlier triumphs had been won. Our next experience is the victory of Mr Ramsay's Lanercost, aged six, in 1841, when Noble, a North-country jockey was in the saddle, who, in 'The Druid's' words, 'cut his races out of the horses he bestrode with whip and spur'. But the date is rapidly approaching which sets its seal for all time upon the Ascot Cup as one of the most conspicuous and important races of the world, as was evidenced by its being selected as the medium for the grandfather of the present Emperor of Russia to make, through it, a votive offering of good-will to the English nation, and to Her Majesty, who had entertained him with princely hospitality at Windsor Castle in 1844.

The first race for the Emperor's Gold Cup was run at Ascot on June 15th, 1845, and ended – such is the irony of that 'glorious uncertainty' which makes so many rich men poor, and so many poor men rich – in the victory of the only starter to whom no backer thought of trusting a single shilling.

ASCOT HEATH RACES
Thursday, June 15th, 1845

A Piece of Plate, value 500 sovs, the gift of His Majesty the Emperor of All the Russias, added to a Sweepstakes of 20 sovs each; three-year-olds, 6 st 10 lb; four, 8 st 5 lb; five 9 st; six and aged, 9 st 3 lb. Mares and geldings allowed 3 lb. To start at the Cup Post, and go once round and in; about 2½ miles; 26 subs.

Lord Albemarle's The Emperor by Defence, 4 years . . . . (Whitehouse)	1
Mr Irwin's Faugh-a-Ballagh, 4 years . . . . (H. Bell)	2
Mr Salvin's Alice Hawthorne, 4 years . . . (Robinson)	3
Lord G. Bentinck's Cowl, 3 years . . . . . . (Abdale)	4

Betting: 7 to 4 on Faugh-a-Ballagh (offered currently); 5 to 2 agt Alice Hawthorne; 6 to 1 agt Cowl; 10 to 1 (nominal) agt The Emperor.

The race was won by Whitehouse's judicious riding. Faugh-a-Ballagh, whom his trainer and owner regarded as one of the greatest horses ever seen, made tremendous running until the brick-kiln turn was reached, when Robinson on Alice Hawthorne, went up and raced with him desperately for half-a-mile, coming round the last turn with a strong lead. In this way they ran to the distance; The Emperor lying a length behind the second horse, who resumed the lead when the mare died away. The two cracks, however, had cut each other's throats, and the despised Emperor took the lead about a hundred yards from home, and went in an easy winner by two lengths. The Emperor was trained by William Edwards, George IV's last trainer. All who were present, except the backers of the two cracks, felt the appropriateness of the winner's name.

from THE SPORTING LIFE *1897*

'Snowstorm' Derby

HENRY BLYTH

The morning of Derby day, 22 May 1867, dawned grey and bitterly cold. As the day wore on, biting winds, sleet and finally flurries of snow swept across Epsom Downs. The huge crowds which normally flocked to the course from London were reduced to a trickle, and *The Times*, in its subsequent report of the scene, referred to the inclement weather 'which froze the general current gaiety of the holiday-makers'. There was a forest of umbrellas on the course and in the stands, and the racegoers slapped their hands for warmth as they watched the horses parading in the paddock.

Henry Chaplin arrived in the Prince of Wales's party, but he was soon forced to leave it in order to continue his now desperate search for a jockey for Hermit. Harry Hastings arrived debonair and smiling with Florence, who was muffled up against the cold in furs and looked drawn and tired.

Harry had his colt, Uncas, in the race, but Uncas had done little to justify any support. Danebury were behind Vauban to a man. The Duke of Beaufort's colt held an outstanding chance, and Harry Hastings had gone for a big win over him. With Fordham riding, and Harry in the mood to bet on this Danebury 'pot', the Ring were in an ungenerous mood, offering Vauban at no more than 6 to 4. Hermit was being laid at 66 to 1 and even at 100 to 1. Uncas was at double this price. The only runners being seriously backed to beat Vauban were The Palmer, Van Amburgh, The Rake and Marksman – Mr Merry's purchase at the Blenkiron sale.

Hermit himself was led down the course by Old Bloss, who was comforting him as best he could. Because of the supposed need to keep him cool, he was without any covering at all, although it seemed hardly possible that he could be in any danger of becoming over-heated in the miserable conditions which prevailed. He looked lifeless and utterly dejected. His coat was staring with cold, and his tail was tucked in between his legs. He walked slowly and heavily, and there seemed no life in him.

Meanwhile the search for a jockey continued. The official race-card had no jockey's name against that of Hermit, and it seemed unlikely that any rider of experience would be found at this late hour, when all the top jockeys had been booked. Finally it was Lord Coventry who suggested to Henry Chaplin that he might do worse than employ Johnny Daley, who had often ridden in the Coventry colours. He was only twenty, a Newmarket lad and the son of a trainer, and had ridden his first winner at the age of ten, when he weighed only 3 stone 10 lb. He had been popular enough as a lightweight, and had won the Goodwood Stakes and the Stewards' Cup, but no other race of any importance. His weight had increased as he grew up, and he had lost favour with most of his former owners. In short, he was not a 'fashionable' jockey; but he was honest and intelligent, and could be relied upon to obey orders.

Chaplin and Machell were in no position to be selective. They ascertained that Daley was available and booked him on the spot. Captain Machell led him to a corner of the paddock and instructed him on the tactics he was to pursue. Hermit, he emphasized, had fine finishing speed and abundant stamina. Daley was therefore to wait with him approaching Tattenham Corner, but to keep in touch with the leaders. Once into the straight, Daley was to come with one long, sustained run on the outside to overhaul the leaders – if he could. Hermit was to be handled gently and was not to be punished unduly; and if he showed any sign of breaking a blood vessel he was to be pulled up at once. He had courage and would give of his best without being driven.

The terms on which Daley was to ride were simple and generous. Machell himself would give him £300 if he finished in the first three, and a further £3,000 if he won. To this Chaplin would add £6,000 in the event of victory. Daley listened and nodded his head, but said nothing. He could scarcely believe his ears.

He had arrived at Epsom on that Wednesday morning with but little hope of finding a mount at all, let alone one in the Derby itself. Indeed he had been booked for only one ride during the whole of the three-day meeting, and that was on Baron Rothschild's filly, Hippia, who had only an outside chance in the Oaks on the Friday. Until this moment his financial hopes for the meeting had amounted to, at most, a few guineas. And now he found himself, shortly before three o'clock on this bitter afternoon, in a position in which he might enrich himself for life.

His introduction to Hermit was the first obstacle to be met and this was successfully overcome. The colt had shown a readiness in trials to give of his best for a stable lad, but had demonstrated a growing aversion to the strong handling of Custance. Now Johnny Daley, far quieter and less forceful in personality, was able to strike up an immediate sympathy and understanding with the horse.

Not that Hermit was in any condition to show anger or resentment. He shivered miserably in the biting wind, his tail was tucked even more firmly between his legs, his head hung down and he presented a picture of misery. Old Bloss walked him slowly round and round, comforting him as though he were a sick child. An observer of this scene was heard to remark that Hermit would not fetch £15 at a fair.

The Downs were sparsely covered with shivering spectators, sheltering for the most part under umbrellas, the stands were only half-filled and there were only a few people standing round the ring as the runners were paraded before the race. Henry Chaplin watched in company with the Prince, Captain Machell and Sir Frederick Johnstone. Harry Hastings stood not far away, while Uncas was saddled and then mounted by Salter. His stable companion, Vauban, as is the custom with Derby favourites, was surrounded by a little group of acolytes led by John Day and what *The Times* referred to as several 'Danebury *attachés*'. George Fordham, who was to ride him, stood watching these preparations, outwardly calm but inwardly nervous and apprehensive. The last Derby favourite which he had ridden had been Lord Clifden, and he had run a poorly judged race then and been beaten by a neck. They were still saying that he was not a Derby jockey. Now was the chance to prove them wrong. He, too, was shivering with cold, and he felt sick and ill. He could have wished that it had been a brighter day.

They saddled 'poor Hermit', as he was now being referred to, in a corner of the paddock where a thorn bush offered some slight shelter from the biting wind. He trembled as he was mounted, and plodded slowly and miserably forward to join the rest of the field as they threaded their way out on to the course. Gone was his old swagger – gone, too, all suggestion of *argutus*.

Henry Custance sat resignedly astride The Rake. He had been assured that the colt was only lazy and would give a good account of himself once the race was reaching its climax, but he reserved his opinion. He was *not* impressed by his mount's chances. But at least these chances were infinitely better than those of his former ride, 'poor Hermit'.

As Henry Chaplin and Captain Machell passed through the Ring on their way back to the Stands, they were joined by Harry Hastings, who had come to make a final bet on the Danebury 'pot', Vauban. Henry Chaplin paused for a moment to speak to him.

'I think Hermit still has a chance, Harry,' he said. 'You can easily cover your bet with me by taking the odds which they are offering now.'

Harry Hastings gave his old, disarming, half-condescending smile.

'Thank you, Henry—but I will not trouble. I fancy that Vauban is the only one that need be seriously considered.'

He moved away to join his Marchioness in the stand. Chaplin and Machell watched him go. A bookmaker standing close to them touched his cap.

'Do you fancy 1,000 to 15 against Hermit, Squire?'

Henry Chaplin nodded and accepted the bet. It was an act of defiance – not one of confidence. Captain Machell followed suit. He took £3,000 to £45.

Snow and sleet were still blowing across the Downs as the riders assembled at the start to hear the customary lecture given to them by the starter, Mr McGeorge. They were to come into line quietly, he warned them, and without jostling, and not to anticipate the dropping of his flag. They were not to argue, swear or shout abuse.

Even so, there were ten false starts, Hardcastle on Master Butterfly, Payne on Fitz-Ivan, and John Grimshaw on Marksman, each lost his temper, ignored Mr McGeorge's instructions and tried to anticipate the dropping of the flag. They were sternly admonished, and another attempt was made. Meanwhile, D'Estournel stubbornly refused to come into line. There were a few derisive catcalls from the crowd, but the cold froze their normal powers of invective.

In the stand, Henry Chaplin watched Mr McGeorge's efforts in company with the Prince of Wales. Harry Hastings surveyed them with an air of bored indifference from his private box, and gave orders for the opening of yet another case of champagne. Florence shivered in the cold and pulled her furs about her. She prayed that it might soon be over.

At his eleventh attempt, Mr McGeorge was satisfied with the start, and the field – all except for D'Estournel – streamed away up the hill towards Tattenham Corner, whilst the starting bell in the stand clanged out mournfully to announce that the eighty-eighth renewal of the Derby Stakes was now in the process of being decided. Harry Hastings paused in the act of sipping his champagne, but showed no outside sign of excitement. Henry Chaplin became tense and strained. Captain Machell focused his glasses on the runners and watched their progress across the sky-line.

The crucial moment in any Derby is that at which the field rounds Tattenham Corner. A horse must hold a good position at this point if he is to have a reasonable chance of winning. Ideally, he should be in the first half-dozen. To be in the rear is generally fatal.

Now, as they rounded the famous corner, it was seen that Fordham was in the lead on the favourite, Vauban. With him were Wild Moor, Marksman and Julius. Behind these leaders were The Rake, Van Amburgh, Corporal, The Palmer and Hermit. The remainder were already trailing.

Into the straight they came and the stands and the winning post were in sight. Vauban was still in the lead, but a groan went up when it was seen that Fordham was feeling for his whip.

Vauban was joined by Marksman and Van Amburgh, and he faltered as they drew level with him.

With a furlong to go, Grimshaw forced Marksman into the lead. Van Amburgh was done with now and dropped back, but Vauban struggled on.

It was then that Daley, obeying his instructions to the letter, brought Hermit with a long run on the outside. Vauban, he realized, had hit the front too soon and was visibly tiring; but Marksman was still full of running. Now John Grimshaw on Marksman was watching Fordham closely. He knew only too well how Fordham loved to 'kid' his opponents and to keep something up his sleeve for a last sudden burst of speed on the post. Grimshaw saw Fordham falter and drop back, but he still watched for that sudden burst. And on his right, and unnoticed, Daley was bringing Hermit up to challenge.

Now, at last, the chestnut threw off his misery. He forgot the cold in his bones and the fear in his heart that there might be another sudden rush of blood in his nostrils. Racehorses are sensitive to the mood of a great occasion, and now the cheering, and the waving of hats and umbrellas, galvanized him into life. He was being brought from behind, and that is a great challenge. He lengthened his stride, as do all great horses when they are under pressure, and power surged back into his weakened body and forced him forward. His jockey was not driving him mercilessly but was yet conveying to him the desperate need for one final, magnificent effort. A tired horse tends to swerve as he struggles forward. Hermit was tired, but he ran on straight and true. It was the moment in which he sought for greatness and found it.

In its last hundred yards the Epsom course slopes sharply upwards to the winning post. It is this final rise which can break the heart of a horse that has given of his best and is nearing exhaustion. But the great Derby winners of the turf have breasted this final slope with resolution, refusing to give in. They find within themselves a hidden strength to carry them forward.

Hermit found it now. He passed Vauban and reached Marksman's quarters, but the winning post was almost upon them. Daley, still cool and quiet, asked him for the final, supreme effort, and he gave it unflinchingly. In the last few strides they were locked together; but in the final stride Hermit was in front.

The judge gave his verdict. Hermit – by a neck. Marksman second. Vauban third.

There was a moment of stunned incomprehension in the crowd. In his box, Harry Hastings lowered his glasses and went pale, but his usual smile remained on his face. Then he turned to his wife.

'Hermit has run a great race. I must go and see him unsaddled.'

She said nothing. There was nothing to say.

In the royal box, the Prince and his friends were laughing and shouting and thumping Henry Chaplin on the back. Captain Machell was smiling, his hands trembling a little with excitement. But Henry Chaplin remained mute and incomprehending. He had never really convinced himself that Hermit could win. It had been in his mind no more than a dream. He could not now believe that the dream had materialized. He had won an immense fortune; and he had done more than that. He had found immortality on the turf.

By the unsaddling enclosure, Old Bloss wiped the tears from his eyes, and his simple, honest face was red with emotion. For eighteen long months he had watched devotedly over the chestnut colt, had slept in the stable with him, groomed him, fondled him and talked to him. Now the long months of strain and worry were over. His child had repaid him in full. The name of Hermit would never be forgotten.

Henry Chaplin led Hermit from the course into the little unsaddling enclosure, still too bewildered to speak. Daley slipped the saddle from Hermit's back, and Hermit stood steaming and exhausted, his body played out with fearful effort, the cold already beginning to numb his bones. He shivered and hung his head.

Then the ranks of the crowd of top-hatted watchers were broken, and Harry Hastings pushed forward and came forward to pat Hermit on his sweat-flaked neck. He turned to Henry Chaplin.

'A great horse,' he said. 'A truly great horse.'

A few minutes later Harry Hastings was seen to leave the course with his wife and a party of friends. They were bound for a dinner party in Richmond, and no one, watching Harry at this moment, would have believed that he had been almost beggared by Hermit's success. He was laughing and talking with the utmost gaiety – even speaking of Hermit's victory with enthusiasm. He took no thought for the morrow – or for the settling day that was to come.

from THE POCKET VENUS *1966*

The Race Round the Houses

RALEIGH TREVELYAN

Of all Italian towns Siena is the one that preserves most perfectly its early Renaissance character. When the Palio takes place, each year on 2nd July and 16th August, one feels closer still to the days of Leonardo and Machiavelli – despite the immense crowds of tourists that jostle through the narrow streets.

What is the Palio? Briefly, it is a race on horseback, the riders representing ten of the seventeen *contrade* or districts of the city. The course is round the fabulous main square, shaped like a scallop shell and overlooked by ancient ochre-coloured palaces. Before the race there is a procession: knights in armour, drummers, standard-bearers in vivid fifteenth century costume, crimson-draped chargers wearing hoods with holes cut for eyes and ears – all this before a wildly excited mob, crammed in the centre of the square, and bulging from specially erected wooden stands, and every balcony and terrace.

The first Palio (so called from the Latin for the painted silk banner presented to the winning *contrada*) was run in 1482, to celebrate the return of the 'reformer citizens' to the government. This set a precedent for regular junketings, often in the guise of tournaments, bull-baitings, or buffalo fights, until in 1659 the horse-race was established as a yearly event – twice yearly after 1701, wars and such like excepted. Since then the whole life of Siena has become focused on these two dates in the summer months. Outsiders are baffled by the complicated series of alliances, intrigues and bribes that gather momentum once competitors have 'drawn' their horses. 'It costs a million lire to win the

Palio', someone told me quite seriously. Much apparently turns on who should give way to whom at the start of the race – the course being so irregular with steep and sharp, not to say dangerous curves. One is kept guessing right until the last minute, even after the horses have been taken to be blessed, each in the church of its own *contrada*, a couple of hours before the Palio begins.

The seventeen *contrade* are mostly called after animals and birds – Giraffe, Unicorn, Eagle, Panther, Owl – even Caterpillar and Snail. Others are called after inanimate objects, such as Shell, Wave or Tower. When I went to Siena for the July 1953 Palio, the 534th in its history, I found myself very much involved with the fortunes of the *contrada* called Selva, which literally means Forest, although its emblem is a rhinoceros standing in front of an oak tree.

On this occasion the Selva had drawn the best horse – a remarkably handsome grey mare. At all the trials it had come in first or second, and what was more, its rider was to be the dare-devil Ivan, known of course as 'The Terrible'. Everyone was confident and tremendously elated, the Selva not having won since 1919, due to somewhat sinister circumstances.

In 1919 the favourite horse had been that of the Panther. Just before the race, however, its rider had been stabbed, whether fatally or not history does not seem to relate. As a means of revenge or merely to assuage her disappointment, the wife of the unfortunate man – called Bubbulo – brought down a curse on the winning *contrada*, which happened to be the Selva. For thirty-five years, she swore, it would never win again. 1953 was the thirty-fourth year. Would the curse of Bubbulo's wife be broken a year too soon? Prospects seemed decidedly hopeful, at least judging by the atmosphere at a banquet given by the Selva on the night preceding the Palio.

This banquet was held in a hall, built like a crypt into the hill-side under the church of the Assumption, where our horse was to be blessed the following day. We sat at long trestle tables under elaborate paper festoons painted with the Selva's colours, orange and green. Chianti flowed copiously and the noise was uproarious. We toasted Ivan; we toasted our Captain, actually a woman, a scion of the old Sienese family of Chigi; we toasted the priest, who to everyone's delight had changed the buttons on his soutane for orange and green badges. Groups of youths, wearing rhinoceros masks, at intervals came prancing into the room, yelling out a special Selva 'signature tune', whilst the rest of us joined in the choruses at the top of our voices. The party went on until after midnight and finished off in the illuminated square itself.

Partly as a result of these festivities I had made up my mind not to get up early to watch the last trial race. Sleep, however, was utterly impossible after dawn, with church bells pealing and children blowing tin trumpets in the streets below. The continual throbbing of the drums sounded almost ominous, as if rousing the populace for some great public execution, instead of a day of pageantry and traditional celebration.

Nevertheless, I kept to my decision and gave the trial race a miss. Having been warned to arrive early at the church of the Assumption if I wanted a good seat at the blessing of the Selva's horse, I went down to the church soon after lunch. It was only then that I heard the disastrous news: our mare had been lamed at the trial race, and several old women were volubly accusing the Goose. Tempers rose with the temperature, and when more than an hour had passed without even the arrival of the priest, we had all grown exceedingly restless on our wooden benches. The church of the Assumption was only very small, in the shape of a Latin cross, and apart from a terra-cotta Madonna ascribed to Donatello, there was little else to occupy the attention. It was a relief for me at any rate when the young English governess who looked after the Captain's children came into the church. She was able to tell me that what had really happened to the Selva's horse was that one of its own shoes had cut into its hind fetlock, so deeply as to put the animal quite out of action. As a staunch Selva supporter of some years' standing, she was both distressed and agitated. 'They're treating the cut with cold compresses,' she hissed. 'Just the wrong thing to do!' At that moment the priest arrived at the church and she hurried on to join the guests of honour inside the altar rails – the Captain's family, a number of black-robed ecclesiastics, and one Franciscan monk in dark glasses.

But there was another long period of waiting still to follow.

The vestry door kept opening and shutting, and through it came bursts of chatter from the various Selva representatives who were dressing up in their Renaissance finery for the procession before the race. Sometimes we caught glimpses of orange and green or flashes of polished armour. After several false alarms the crowd by the entrance eventually drew back to make way for our extremely bewildered-looking grey mare, which was led in by a middle-aged gentleman in a bobbed auburn wig, an orange doublet and green tights.

Alas, there was no doubt of the animal's plight. Its near hind fetlock was bandaged and it could barely hobble into the church.

The priest came forward and, with two fingers raised, began the blessing. This produced an unexpected reaction from the horse, to which the congregation responded with unconcealed delight; a shovel and brush were hurriedly found, and the service continued without further hitch. A few prayers were said, and the limping horse was dragged out again to where its escorts were forming up for the march down to the square.

Now the drums of the Selva began to roll. At the same time the two standard-bearers – self-conscious in their white tunics emblazoned with rhinoceroses and oak trees, their long white sleeves, and their orange and green hose – twirled the huge flags, tossed them skywards, and caught them on the downward flight. Standing stiffly to one side was a knight in full armour, with a helmet shaped like the head of a rhinoceros. Some of them, one felt, might almost have stepped straight from a Signorelli fresco, although there were others, it must be admitted, who with their ill-fitting Nordic wigs over black eyes and swarthy skins might have belonged to some down-at-heel repertory company.

As they marched off, so the rest of us, too, hurried through the narrow streets towards the square. Hopes of victory had been dashed, but for the time being we had forgotten our disappointment in the scramble to gain our seats before the procession started.

The ancient bell of the Mangia – 'not a tower, but a flight', as Baedeker records in one of his more lyrical moods – tolled out in mournful single beats, whilst the crowds packed into the square. There must have been at least 50,000 people. From our balcony, hung with purple and gold embroidered brocades, the scene was like a vast shifting kaleidoscope. Then, with the fading of the sun, everything – the overloaded loggias, the miraculous crenellated palaces, the marble fountain, the distant dome of the Cathedral – became tinged with coral. Several balloons were let loose, floating high out of sight into the evening air. Occasionally the supporters of this or that *contrada* would break out into their own particular sing-song refrain, such as we had heard the evening before under the church of the Assumption.

At last, with the explosion of a mortar, the procession began. First came the trumpeters, then a group of worthies privileged to ride on the crimson-hooded chargers. Next came more notabilities of Siena, on foot and dressed in suitably decorous Renaissance garb. Finally the contingents of each of the seventeen *contrade*, though only ten were to take part in the race: maroon for the Tower, with alternating white and sky-blue squares; green, blood-red and yellow for the Dragon; white for the Porcupine, with black, dark blue and red stripes; yellow and turquoise for the Tortoise; and of course orange and green for our own Selva, its colours mounted on a background of white.

I tried, unprofitably perhaps, to make comparisons with the Coronation procession, and concluded that the main difference was in the *speed* of progress. No whisking past of Queens of Tonga this time; there was ample opportunity to study every bewigged Romeo in the closest detail. At each corner of the square the contingents would halt and their standard-bearers would go through the routine of flag twirling and tossing, to the drummers' frantic accompaniment. If the standard-bearer managed to catch his flag on its return to earth, there were prolonged and appreciative cheers from the crowd; if he failed, there were dismal boos.

As the end of the procession approached, I found to my surprise that I had been joined on the balcony by the English governess. She still looked anxious, but as usual was informed with the latest news.

'They've given that wretched animal a shot of cocaine.'

'Good heavens,' I exclaimed, 'they're not going to make the Selva horse run to-day?'

She replied indignantly:

'Even if it had only *two* legs left, they'd send it in to race.'

Down in the square the painted banner – the Palio itself for the victorious *contrada* – had been trundled by in its garlanded chariot, drawn by four weary white oxen, and the course was being swept and cleared. All the members of the procession, looking like some exotic herbaceous border, had settled themselves in special seats below the Mangia tower. A few breathless minutes followed, until amid tumultuous roars from the crowd the horses of the ten competitors came frisking into the square. I could easily recognise the grey mare of the Selva; she appeared to be perfectly fit and quite as lively as the others.

Many of the more sensitive inhabitants of Siena refuse to watch the race. Admittedly the cobbles of the square are covered with a moderately thick layer of sand, but the angles of some of the corners, especially that of S. Martino (which was directly below our balcony) make it a most hair-raising event to watch. A year without a casualty is rare, and generally at least one horse has to be shot.

The jockeys ride bareback, wearing special metal crash-helmets. It is a case of no holds barred, for they are free to lash out at one another with their rawhide whips. Falls being frequent, it is quite in order for a riderless horse to win – provided it keeps the plume on its head.

The mortar exploded again and, at long last, they were off. The immense bellow from the crowd kept on unabated all during that breakneck dash three times round the square. From where I was sitting it was impossible to see who had gained best place at the all-important start. I soon made out, however, that the Shell was in the lead, followed by – I could scarcely believe my eyes – the Selva! The Tortoise was third and the Tower fourth.

By the fateful S. Martino both the Tortoise and the Tower had almost caught up level with the Shell. At once the Shell's rider seemed to lose his head and came hurtling off as he charged straight into the padded wall of the corner. In a flash he was up and belabouring furiously his now stationary horse (small wonder it refused to budge, it had to be destroyed within the hour). But this did not last for long. Again, in a matter of seconds, he was bowled over and trampled mercilessly underfoot by the Selva and others as they rounded the corner.

The Tower fell at S. Martino in the second round. Soon after-wards it was the turn of the Selva, and Ivan the Terrible was thrown. Perhaps the cocaine was wearing off, or perhaps it was working too well. Anyhow, the Selva's grey mare immediately lost interest in the race, even though its orange plume was perfectly intact.

Aesop would have appreciated the result; it was the Tortoise which won the 534th Palio, for the 44th time.

Palios had already begun to seem all too remote when about two months later I happened to be walking down Albemarle Street and ran into the governess. She had just come back from Siena, she told me, where she had stayed on to attend the August Palio.

'It was marvellous,' she cried enthusiastically. 'The best I've ever seen.'

This time, apparently, the Selva had not drawn the grey mare, but it had gone to the Selva's hated rival, the Goose.

'You couldn't imagine anything more thrilling,' the governess went on. 'We all thought the Goose was going to win, but our horse kept catching up until it was well in the lead on the final lap. Then, at the corner of S. Martino, Ivan fell off. It was terrible; the priest fainted and nearly tumbled from the balcony. But – to our amazement – our horse somehow kept going and finished before the others. Luckily the plume was still on its head . . . We had won! The Goose was third.'

So the curse of Bubbulo's wife *had* come to an end a year too soon. Or was it just a case of those odd million lire?

from THE HORSEMAN'S YEAR *1955*

An Amateur at Aintree – I

Brigadier 'MONKEY' BLACKER

Back in England, it was hard at first to take an interest in theoretical soldiering after so much practical experience. It soon became apparent, however, that unless I took the theory, and the `examinations which went with it, seriously, I should very soon drop out of the race and end up as an elderly and unpromoted officer posted to some unattractive and boring part of the world. This prospect by no means fitted in with my plans . . . .

I have thus lived, in varying degrees of intensity, a kind of double life ever since. The soldiering side has necessarily been my main preoccupation, with the other side, whatever it may have been, fitted into any gaps which appeared in the military edifice. Balancing these two lives has sometimes been a precarious business but there is nothing wrong with that.

My first 'second life' was lived in the world of steeple-chasing. This was natural, for I had ridden in many point-to-points in those far-off days before the war, and in a few steeplechases. Perry Harding, one of the best amateur jockeys ever to ride, had been my Commanding Officer for four of the war years, and his stories of pre-war racing experiences had made me determined to try to emulate him.

I was not going to waste time paddling about in the shallows of point-to-point racing and I proceeded to jump in at the deep end as an amateur steeplechase jockey. Fortunately, I had saved up my pay during the war for just this moment and was able to buy a steeplechaser of my own. I thus avoided the alternative of letting it be known that there was no horse, however bad its jumping or unpleasant its habits, that I would not ride; a starting-point which was perfectly feasible though distinctly hazardous to life and limb.

When you know comparatively little about a new enterprise, it is best to put yourself in the hands of an expert. I had the luck, and for once the good sense, to place myself in the hands of Alec Kilpatrick, who trains at Collingbourne Ducis in Wiltshire. It was Alec who bought my first steeplechaser for me, who trained the horse, advised me, guided my footsteps and generally played the part of candid friend. My new purchase was a little horse called September Air. He knew not much more about the game than I did, but his form was quite promising and he was a good if rather light-hearted jumper.

Our first venture together was at Nottingham, and, not un-expectedly, I fell off – though not before we had every prospect of otherwise finishing in the first three. Highly delighted, I rode him again at Fontwell Park, and this time we were fourth. Then came the big freeze of 1947 and racing closed down till March. The thaw came only just in time for the Grand National Meeting.

I was determined to ride in the Grand National one day but this year, naturally, I was not entered, nor indeed was my horse qualified to run. There was, however, an opportunity of riding round part of the course, in one of the lesser steeplechases at the meeting, and this chance I seized. Since this was only our third race together (and, owing to the frost, the second one had been some two months earlier) this enterprise was foolhardy in the extreme – but ignorance is bliss.

Those whose experience of National Hunt fences has been restricted to a distant view from the stands, or to television, may perhaps have a false idea of their size. The width of each fence and its slope tend to make it look smaller than it really is. In fact, regulations permit no fence to be lower than four feet six inches except the water jump, which has to be twelve feet wide. These are normal fences, and Aintree is far from normal. The average height there is four feet ten inches and some are five feet; all are extremely solid; many, particularly Becher's Brook, have disconcerting drops on the landing side; and in those days the fences were very upright. While inspecting this course before your first ride at Aintree, it is hard to keep the conversation going in the lighthearted and cheerful style desirable for the occasion.

On that chilly and fogbound afternoon in March, sixteen jockeys, of whom I was one, rode forth to contest the Stanley Chase, over one circuit of the National course. Cantering down to the start, I remember thinking how unkind it was that on my first appearance at Aintree the fog should make the already formidable fences look double their real size. But, once we started, the ordeal did not seem so bad as I feared; the first two obstacles were surmounted successfully, and we turned away down the long line of fences leading to Becher's, swallowed up, as far as the stands were concerned, by the fog.

But now the race really became quite exciting. As the cavalcade encountered each fence, it was as if a covey of partridges was passing over a line of accurate guns; a proportion would plunge violently to the rear whilst the survivors streamed anxiously on. The company was dwindling considerably and, filled with an altogether premature optimism, I advanced confidently upon the fence before Becher's. Perhaps I had communicated my misplaced optimism to September Air, for at this point he underestimated the height of the fence by a considerable margin and paid the inevitable penalty.

We hit the ground hard; it had seemed a long drop. My horse got up and galloped senselessly off into the fog. I rose, somewhat crestfallen and rather sore. Loose horses were circling round in the gloom; I could dimly see a solitary rider (later found to be Anthony Mildmay) vainly trying to make his horse jump the big open ditch further on. Otherwise, the race seemed to have passed out of view. Discontentedly I began to search for my whip.

I took some minutes to find it and had just begun my trudge back when my attention was attracted by a hail. There was my horse, held captive by a spectator whom I recognised as one of the lesser-known professional jockeys, and whom for the purposes of this narrative we will call H.C. Before I could thank him for saving me a long walk, he burst out: 'Well, come on, don't you want to win?' I gaped at him. He continued, 'Everyone else is down – jump on and finish the course and the race is yours!'

I suppose I should have rushed enthusiastically to my horse and bounded into the saddle, all agog. My true reactions were, I regret to say, far otherwise. No prospect has ever seemed more repugnant; I recoiled. I was cold and rather stiff. Almost five minutes had elapsed since I had fallen. It was absurd to think that not one of the sixteen runners had finished. How could anyone tell in this fog, anyhow? And yet . . . 'Is my horse all right?' I asked weakly. 'Absolutely,' came the implacable reply. I fell silent, pondering on the dilemma with which I now saw I was confronted. On the one side was the prospect of a solo turn in cold blood over eleven Aintree fences, an ordeal which might well turn out to be quite pointless in the end, and which was made all the starker by the knowledge that my first fence would be Becher's Brook itself. On the other – well, suppose no one else *had* finished! What a fool one would feel, and look! I gazed frantically round. Anthony Mildmay, still striving, was the only competitor visible. Silently, and quite unfairly, I cursed H.C.

A crowd of spectators had, meanwhile, gathered round and

were showing signs of joining in the debate. In general, they supported H.C.; their manner was strongly reminiscent of a boxing crowd which, from the safe recesses of a hall, urges the smaller man to 'go in and fight'. I could delay my decision no longer – I gave in. Assuming an entirely bogus nonchalance, I mounted, turned my horse round and urged it rather forlornly in the general direction of Becher's Brook.

It says a great deal for September Air's courage that he judged it without demur. As we rose in the air, however, I saw that below me, on the landing side, was a crowd of spectators gazing with morbid satisfaction at the corpse of a horse stretched out upon the ground. I swooped upon them with a loud yell; they shrieked hideously in reply but scattered with such resolution that all survived my descent. Pursued by faint cries of indignation and dismay, I sped onwards, my courage rising. Over the Canal turn we sailed, and on over Valentine's and the big open ditch – over, in fact, Anthony Mildmay's horse, which had by this time descended into it. On we went; spectators, who by this time were walking about examining the fences, gaped to see this wild and muddy apparition careering round the course in what, as far as they knew, was the interval between races.

We turned into the straight, jumped the last two fences and passed the winning-post. The stands were almost deserted, but here and there knots of spectators turned to look and some raised a rather stupefied cheer. H.C., beside himself with excitement, met me and led me in triumph to the winner's enclosure, into which we penetrated without opposition, its normal guardians having gone to watch the preliminaries to the next race. Soon, however, they realized that something unusual was occurring and sped back to their posts, scandalized, and bearing with them disillusion. Apparently the enclosure had been occupied some ten minutes previously by the real winner; Tim Molony, then at the start of his career, had done much the same as I had, but rather earlier. He had fallen at the last fence, had scrambled on again and finished alone. Nobody could deny, however, that I was second, and I moved down to the humbler berth.

H.C. then vanished in search of the Press, to make sure, he said, that his part in the affair received due recognition. Meanwhile, I looked in vain for my connections – my wife, my trainer, the 'lads', all usually immediately available to take my horse and submit their criticisms of my performance. Where were they? I was indignant. Eventually news of them arrived; after gazing for several anxious minutes into the fog, they had decided that I was not going to reappear; and bearing brandy, rugs, hot water-bottles and humane killers, they had quitted the stands and had sallied vaguely but valiantly forth into the gloom.

At last they returned. Amid a flood of explanations one fact, however, stood out pleasantly clear; I had won a stake of £200. We accordingly repaired to the bar to drink wine.

Next day I was back on duty at the military establishment in southern England in which I had found a niche after the disappearance of the 23rd Hussars. Here were the high armoured and technical experts, upon whose breakfast tables *Sporting Life* found no place. Here, surely, a merciful oblivion would reign. I was wrong. As I entered the ante-room of the Mess I became aware that I was the object of very general interest. Then, to my horror, I discovered what H.C. had done; the sporting column of almost every paper recounted with relish and with some detail my antics of the day before, as seen through H.C.'s eyes.

Attracted by the buzz of conversation, the high officers rose and rested their sober gaze upon the headlines. The *Daily Mail*, I remember, had JOCKEY, TEN MINUTES LATE, THOUGHT HE'D WON. As the great ones read, their expressions became puzzled and noncommittal – was this affair creditable or discreditable; could it be classified as a good show or a bad show? It was a difficult question; there must be no hasty or ill-considered judgment. Said one: 'This account reads, "I persuaded the rider to remount".' Their expressions darkened: had there perhaps been a want of courage? The verdict hung in the balance; all was in suspense. At last, however, the clouds rolled back; the sun shone; I was acquitted. 'Good show!' they said, 'Good show!' and, shaking their heads, they went back to their offices, to their blueprints and their diagrams. All *so* much easier to understand.

from A SOLDIER IN THE SADDLE *1957*

An Amateur at Aintree – II

CHRISTOPHER COLLINS

At 4 am on Friday, March 19, I got up in London and drove to Durham. Mr Stephenson showed me Mr Jones. He was big and his black coat was beginning to come through. Thirty seconds after being legged up I decided to buy him. He was all I admired in a horse. But when we got to the gallops I couldn't really manage him. I got hold of his head too tight. He hung inwards when we cantered round and then more or less ran away. I got off and watched Kit Stobbs galloping him – he moved magnificently. I got on again undecided. I thought it over as we rode back. I worked out that he must be all right in a race. There would be plenty of horses in the National in front to stop him running away. I made up my mind to buy him subject to his being passed sound by the Vet.

I concluded the deal and drove back South. I was apprehensive. I thought perhaps I was being over ambitious. My proper place was in the Old Berkeley Members race (in which I finished last the next day).

The Vet rang just before I went off to the point-to-point. Mr Jones was sound. I was nervous about my rides that afternoon. The prospect of Aintree the following Saturday was terrifying.

I had arranged to go up to Durham on Sunday morning to school Mr Jones over Sedgefield race course, but Mr Stephenson rang me at 5.30 am to say that there was too much snow. We postponed everything to Monday. On Sunday I rode out at home. I took an anti-hunger pill and didn't eat a lot. I had weighed 11 stone 8 lbs stripped at the point-to-point. Mr Jones had 11 stone 2 lbs and I didn't want to ride on my lightest saddle. I drove up to Durham that evening.

The next day the weather was still bad so Mr Jones and some other horses went to a field near the sea to gallop $2\frac{1}{2}$ miles. He went well and I got on much better with him. On Tuesday I schooled him twice over three fences. He jumped safely and well.

I drove down to Doncaster and rode in a Hurdle Race. I drove on home. I had missed lunch and had a little soup for dinner.

On Wednesday I drove to London. I then took the train to Plumpton and rode Surely Shaken in a Novice Chase – we finished third. I did not eat a lot that day.

On Thursday I rode to work at a trainer's. I watched Aintree on television; the jumps did not look small. I then drove North in a sweat suit. The next morning, Friday, Mr Jones had his final pipe-opener: He went about 3 furlongs, uphill, twice. I was getting on quite well with him now. We then drove to Liverpool. We arrived and I saw the fences for the first time. I gave lunch a miss and set off to walk the course. I felt a bit white – people told me afterwards I looked ghastly. I walked on round; I didn't really mind what I saw. The fences were big but I could almost look forward to jumping them. The angle of Becher's was tricky, but the drop not as bad as it had grown in my mind. For years I had fed myself on Aintree literature. The descriptive powers of the writers and my own timidity had built up the fences into shadowy monsters quite different from normal Steeplechase fences. After passing the last I caught up someone I knew; I said that I had not found it as bad as all that. He told me to wait until I saw the Chair. I looked forward towards a dark green bungalow which rose out of a moat. It got larger and larger as I approached; it seemed bigger than it really was as the wings were hardly higher than the fence, and unlike the others it did not stretch the whole way across the course. I foolishly went up and looked into the ditch. I stood on the guard rail and gazed down into a chasm. I had to remind myself that Mr Jones had already jumped it twice. I then walked on to the water where Mr Jones had fallen in the 1963 National. After the Chair it did not look big.

After racing we went to our hotel. I had planned to have a Turkish bath but gave up the idea. I was feeling a bit weak. I went off to meet the rest of the family and one or two people I knew at the Airport. They brought up a new whip; I had left my old one in the train coming back from Plumpton. The *Evening Standard* said that Mr Jones was the best outsider.

While I was waiting I thought over my plans for the race; I had been thinking a lot during the week.

I had asked Mr Stephenson if he had any specific instructions. He said that in such a large field he wouldn't give any, but that I was best away from the middle as everyone wanted it. Also he thought Becher's was best jumped on the outside. Walking round I noticed that the drop at Becher's was much more severe on the inside than on the outside. My plan for evolving tactics was that the first walk round on the Friday was merely for looking at the ground and the approach to the fences. I would make my final plan on my second walk round on the day of the race.

I had a bit of dinner on Friday night. I watched television and then went to bed. I read for a bit. I was reading a biography of Lloyd George at the time, but I substituted this with *Sanders of the River* which I had bought at the Airport bookstall. When I stopped reading I did not immediately go into a sound, dreamless sleep.

Mr Jones was coming to Liverpool on the day of the race to avoid the cough. There was, therefore, no early morning pipe-opener to ride. I had a leisurely breakfast with all the papers. I thought I had better have a bit to eat to keep up my strength. After breakfast I had a very hot bath with $3\frac{1}{2}$ lbs of Epsom Salts in it to make me sweat. I then put on a lot of clothes – sweat-shirt, long underpants, 3 jerseys, etc. We drove to the course with the heater full on. I took off a bit of weight on the way.

I kept all the extra clothes on and took my saddle and kit to the Changing Room. We had decided that I should not ride on my 2 lb saddle but on a larger 4 lb one. I then set off on my second walk round the course. There was a lot of wind; it dried up my energy and breath. Walking courses always makes me tired and nervous. I was at work on my plan. I saw some people I knew. This time I made a detour round the Chair and looked at the run in instead. By the time I got round my plan was formed. I would start towards the outside – I would keep there till after Becher's – I would then come across to the middle – I would try and lie close enough so as to be in the first 15 or 20.

When I got back it was too early to change. I hung around a bit. Someone advised me to have a good bet on Salmon Spray in the first to take my mind off the National. I followed this advice. I then went to change. There was not a lot of room. I changed slowly and deliberately. I then went to see Salmon Spray win the first. Between the first and second races I fitted the elastic girths on to my saddle and was weighed on the trial scales. I was going to be over. There was nothing I could take off. I joined the queue to be weighed out – I was 3 lbs over. When I had been passed I left the saddle in the Weighing Room and went back into the Changing Room. I had a glucose tablet and then went to watch the second race. I came back to the Changing Room. I had another glucose tablet. I got my crash helmet and whip ready. I sat down to rest. A jockey made us laugh. I could feel the tension seeping out of me. Lord Sefton came in and told us to keep straight until Becher's and not to go too fast. We were then called out. The valet tied on my cap. I went out with the others. It was windy. My silks were blown about and did not keep me warm. I stood in the paddock. Mr Jones had not come in. He came in, looking calm and magnificent. We were told to mount. I was given a leg up. We left the paddock, and then walked round and round getting into order for the parade. We were led past the stands. I asked myself if with a free choice I would like to swop places with Kit Stobbs who was leading Mr Jones. I took a second or two to say no. By the Silver Ring we turned round and cantered to the start. I went down fairly slowly. I did not want to be run away with. We got to the start.

We walked round for a long time. Someone asked how long there was to go. Eventually we were told to line up. I stood about three-quarters of the way to the outside. I noticed The Rip away on my right. Time was next to me. Mr Jones stood quietly – a bit too quietly as when the tapes went up he wasn't too fast into his stride.

Going over the Melling Road I got boxed in and the tan came flying into my face. I decided we must see the first fence. I steered Mr Jones out and gave him a good view of it. As we swept up to it I sat down and kicked him in. He took off at my third kick and soared over it. He was a long time coming down. Then we were away and everything was all right. The second is small. The third is much bigger – it is an open ditch. The fence rises out of the bottom of it like a great green wall. Mr Jones jumped it, and the next two, beautifully. We then came to Becher's. The fence is normal looking but all you can see of the outside as you approach is the wall at the end of the course curving round towards the Canal Turn. I jumped it towards the outside as planned. Mr Jones met it right. We floated down and landed with a slight thud and then were away. After the next there was a loose horse just in front. It was the Canal Turn. I pulled inside the loose horse thinking he wouldn't want to take the turn as tightly as us. Luckily he jumped away, straight on, and we were all right. There was a lot of noise from the crowd at the Canal Turn. The leaders were quite a long way ahead of us. I was not as close up as I had planned. Mr Jones was set in a rhythm and I did not like to disturb it at this stage. Valentine's was big, but nothing to Mr Jones. Soon we were galloping across the Anchor Bridge and down towards the last two for the first time. At the first of these I saw a loose horse run right across the field; it was a terrifying sight. I was glad to be back where I was. Next the Chair. This was the fence that had frightened me when I walked round. Mr Jones made nothing of it, he took off near the guard rail and jumped it easily. We then came to the water. He met this wrong and put in an extra stride, but we got over safely.

As we turned away on the second circuit I was a bit dissatisfied with my position. I began to nudge Mr Jones. On the way to Becher's we steadily made up ground. Horses seemed to be falling all the time but we passed them safely. One fell very close beside me and I nearly jumped on a jockey. As we came to Becher's Kapeno was not far ahead; he ran sideways down the fence and did not reappear. Mr Jones met it right and we parachuted down as before – just on the outside of where Kapeno had gone. As we landed Kapeno got up and cannoned into us. He knocked us sideways. Luckily Mr Jones got back into his stride and went on. At the Canal Turn there was a huge roar from the crowd. As we jumped it and went away towards Valentine's I heard one voice out of it shouting 'Go on, Chris'. Mr Jones was now going really well. At Valentine's he stood back and put in a tremendous jump. He put his nose practically on the ground to balance himself when he landed. He was beginning to wear down the horses in front of him. I saw The Rip's colours and also Vultrix. As we galloped over the bridge with two to go I thought I'd got so far I didn't want to fall now. I was kicking him on as hard as I could. When we came to the last there were only three in front. Mr Jones was going so well he went into the last as if it was a hurdle, but it took him a bit longer to land. I knew we would beat one of those in front. We made ground on the third horse and passed him as we came past the Chair on the racecourse proper. The noise was fantastic. When we passed the winning post I pulled up. Mr Jones was still full of running and I myself was not as exhausted as I had expected.

We were led in towards the unsaddling enclosure behind Jay Trump and Freddie. There were hundreds of people about. I was conscious mostly of what a tremendous ride I had had. I didn't fully absorb that we were third.

I was thrilled with Mr Jones. He had gone better and better the further we went. The sensation of jumping those fences on him was quite different from anything I had ever experienced before. Except for the water he met every fence bang right in his stride. Sometimes he took off quite close and made little of the fence. At others he stood back and threw tremendous leaps; when this happened he put his head down towards the ground to balance himself on landing. What was so different from normal steeplechase fences was the time it took to land. There was a noticeable gap between the summit of the fence and the actual moment of touching down. There was time to enjoy the movement of jumping itself. In an ordinary race things happen too fast for this.

Mr Jones was a great horse and he had won a lot of good races, but I think with this performance he reached the peak of his ability. He was absolutely right on the day. Earlier in the week he had blown a bit after his gallop. Now, prepared to run the race of his life, he carried with precisioned expertise someone, who really had no real right to be in the race, round the 4½ miles and 30 fences which constitute the Grand National.

from THE HORSEMAN'S YEAR *1966*

Devon Loch's National, 1956

DICK FRANCIS

Even though the start was a good one, and there were, at twenty-nine, far fewer runners than usual, four horses came down at the first fence.

M'as-Tu-Vu went off in front, and Devon Loch jumped the first two in the middle of the field. But I soon found that he was not going to go slowly for the first mile, for he was striding out comfortably, and his leap at each fence gained him lengths. I have never ridden another horse like him. He cleared the formidable Aintree fences as easily as if they had been hurdles. He put himself right before every one of them, and he was so intelligent at the job that all I had to do was to ride him quietly and let him jump without fussing him.

Usually the National is more of a worry than a pleasure to anyone riding in it: Devon Loch made it a delight. Usually one is kicking one's horse along and taking risks to keep one's place: Devon Loch was going so easily that he had time to think what he was doing.

Over Becher's we went, round the Canal Turn, and over Valentine's, and two fences later had our only anxious moment. Domata, ridden by Derek Ancil, was just ahead of us on the inside, and as he came up to the open ditch he dived at it, and I could see he was going to fall. As he landed he rolled over on to the patch of ground where Devon Loch would have landed, but the great horse literally changed his direction in mid-air, sidestepped the sprawling Domata, and raced on without hesitation.

From then on I had the sort of run one dreams about. Horses which fell did so at a convenient distance, loose horses did not bother us, and Devon Loch's jumping got better and better. He cleared the Chair fence and the water jump in front of the stands, and we went out into the country again lying sixth or seventh in a fairly closely bunched field. M'as-Tu-Vu was just behind us then, but three fences later he miscalculated the open ditch, and went no further.

During the next mile Devon Loch was gradually passing horse after horse by out-jumping them, and as we approached the Canal Turn we were lying second. Armorial III was in front, but Devon Loch was going so splendidly that there was no need for us to hurry.

Never before in the National had I held back a horse and said, 'Steady, boy'. Never had I felt such power in reserve, such confidence in my mount, such calm in my mind.

Armorial III fell at the fence after Valentine's, and Eagle

Lodge took his place, but Devon Loch went past him a fence later, and, with three to jump, he put his nose in front. Amazingly, I was still holding Devon Loch back, and when I saw beside me that E.S.B., Ontray and Gentle Moya were being ridden hard, I was sure we were going to win.

Twenty yards from the last fence I could see that Devon Loch was meeting it perfectly, and he jumped it as stylishly as if it had been the first of thirty, instead of the last.

Well, I had my moment.

I know what it is like to win the National, even though I did not do it, and nothing that happened afterwards had clouded the memory of the seconds when Devon Loch went on to win. One might adapt an old saying to sum up my feelings exactly. Better to have won and lost, than never to have won at all.

An appalling minute after Devon Loch had fallen, I stood forlornly on the course looking for my whip. I had thrown it away from me in anger and anguish at the cruelty of fate; and now felt rather foolish having to pick it up again.

Devon Loch was being led back to his stable, and the stragglers of the race were trotting in, and I took my time over finding the whip, knowing that when I did I would have to face the long walk back to the weighing-room and the turned faces, the curious eyes, the unmanning sympathy of the huge crowd. I wanted very much to be alone for a few minutes to get my breath back, and as if he had read my thoughts an ambulance driver came to my rescue.

'Hop in, mate,' he said, jerking his thumb at the ambulance.

So I hopped in, and he drove down through the people in the paddock and stopped at the first-aid room, so that I could go straight from there into the weighing-room without having to push my way through the dense crowd round the main door, and I was very grateful to him.

While I was slowly dressing and tying my tie Mr Cazalet came into the changing-room.

'Dick,' he said, 'come along up to the Royal box. They want to see you.'

We walked across and up the stairs together. Losing the National like that was as disappointing to him as to anybody, and in some ways worse, for twenty years before he had seen

Davy Jones break a rein and run out at the last fence with the race in his pocket, and such dreadful luck should not happen to any trainer twice.

It was quiet in the Royal box. It was as if the affectionate cheers for Devon Loch which had died a long time ago in a million throats all over Britain had cast a shadow of silence. There was, after all, very little to be said. Their Majesties tried to comfort me, and said what a beautiful race Devon Loch had run; and in my turn I tried to say how desperately sorry I was that we had not managed to cover those last vital fifty yards.

Her Majesty the Queen Mother said resignedly, 'That's racing, I suppose.' But she and the Queen were obviously sorrowful and upset by what had happened.

Mr Cazalet came down again with me from the Royal box, and we went over to the stables to see Devon Loch. He was munching some hay and being groomed, and apart from looking like a horse which has just had a hard race, there was nothing the matter with him. His intelligent head lifted as we went into his box, and I patted him while Mr Cazalet ran his hand down his legs to see if there was any heat or swelling in them, but they were cool and firm.

I stood close to Devon Loch and leaned my head against his neck. We were both tired. 'Oh, Devon Loch,' I was saying in my mind, 'Devon Loch, what happened?' If only he could have answered.

Mr Cazalet came back to the weighing-room with me and with a few sad words, we parted. Still a bit dazed and very unhappy, I collected Mary, and we drove with Father and my uncle back along the road we had travelled with such hope in the morning, to Douglas's house at Bangor-on-Dee. We hardly spoke a word the whole way.

The little house was full of children, ours and Douglas's, who were too young to understand what the lost race meant to us, and who met us with blunt and penetrating candour.

'The man on the wireless said Devon Loch sat down. Jolly silly sort of thing to do, wasn't it?'

'It's a pity you didn't win, Uncle Dick. I had a shilling on you and now I've lost it, and the stable lads say their beer money's gone down the drain too.'

'Never mind, I expect you'll win a race next week.'

'Was the Queen cross, Daddy?'

And the youngest, just three, said nothing, but after he had seen the pictures of Devon Loch's spread-eagled fall in the next day's newspapers, I found him playing behind the sofa, running and falling flat on his tummy and saying, 'I'm Devon Loch. Down I go, bump.'

All evening the telephone rang, and Douglas answered it. Mary and I went for a walk. There was a gentle wind blowing clouds slowly across the moon, and we walked along the country road towards the racecourse. Somewhere not far ahead in the shifting moonlight lay the rails and the now deserted fences of the course where I had ridden my first race and my first winner, where so much that was good had begun for me, and where I came now needing solace.

We reached a place where the River Dee runs close to the road, and we stood beside a tree there, looking down into the black sliding water.

'Do you feel like jumping in?' said Mary.

'It looks a bit too wet,' I said, 'and cold.'

The load of the day lifted suddenly and we laughed, yet nothing could for long ease our thoughts, and as we walked back in the wind and into our quiet room our sadness was still with us. Miserable and silent, we went to bed, but we could not sleep. To ourselves and to each other we were saying again and again, 'Why, why, why did it have to happen?' It still seemed unbelievable that it should have done so.

We went back to Berkshire the next day, and during the week which followed hundreds of letters arrived, many of them from strangers and from people who never go racing, and all kind and sympathetic. I had expected at least a few from cranks accusing me of driving my mount on to his knees from exhaustion, but I was pleased to find that the 'cruelty to horses at Aintree' brigade had not written a single abusive letter.

Four days after the National Her Majesty the Queen Mother went down to Fairlawne to see Devon Loch, and I went too, to ride him in the park, and to school Her Majesty's other horses. Devon Loch was looking very fit and well, and gave us no clue to the cause of his collapse, and as his Royal owner patted him I was sure she must have been wishing, as I had done, that he could tell us what had struck him down.

Her Majesty said she would like to see me again to talk about the race, and later sent a message asking me to go to Windsor.

She received me in a sunny room overlooking the mile-long, tree-bordered drive which stretches away into Windsor Great Park, and within the quiet solid walls of the Castle we talked of the excitement and the heartache that we had shared at Liverpool.

Before I went Her Majesty gave me a cheque and a silver cigarette box as a memento of the race that was so nearly won. It is a lovely box, and I am deeply honoured by the inscription on its lid. It means so much to me that I keep it safely in its case (and in the bank when I am away, burglars please note), and it will always hold more memories than cigarettes.

Over the finish of the 1956 Grand National there still hangs a gigantic question mark.

Much has been written, much discussed, many theories aired, many ideas exploded, but from all the fantastic explanations offered in a rush of journalistic blood to the head immediately after the race, four main possibilities emerge.

First, did Devon Loch have a heart attack? It has been suggested that when he is hard pressed a fault appears in his pumping arrangements, and lack of oxygen in his lungs and head makes him falter and stop. After some races he has panted deeply and longer than one would expect, but this is normal with any horse when it is not fully fit, and after the National, when if this theory is correct one would expect to see him gasping for air, he did not blow unduly.

This theory also takes it for granted that Devon Loch was at the end of his strength when he collapsed. I cannot believe it. He was not going like a tired horse, rolling and staggering with effort, and I have ridden a lot of tired horses, so I know the feel of them. He had jumped the last fence powerfully, and was almost sprinting away along the run-in: he had had an extraordinarily easy race all the way round, and was not having to fight hard in a close finish; and if he had completed the course he would have broken the time record for the race.

A seizure severe enough to stop him drastically in mid-stride would also, I think, have killed him. Yet five minutes later he was walking away as if nothing had happened. I have seen several horses have bad heart attacks when they were racing: they stagger for a few strides before they fall, and they go down dead. Devon Loch did not stagger, and he recovered within minutes.

One cannot entirely rule out a constitutional weakness of heart, but to me it does not seem at all probable.

The second explanation seems to be the one most widely believed, and I am emphatically convinced it is not the true one.

'A ghost jump,' said newspapers and newsreels in chorus. 'He tried to jump the water jump which he saw out of the corner of his eye.'

They printed strips of pictures and slow motion bits of film to prove it, and they did a good job on even the racing world, which is half persuaded to believe them rather than me.

The facts offered by the press to support their idea seem reasonable at first glance. Devon Loch had had a hard race, they said, and when he saw the wing of the water jump on his left he was too tired to realize that the jump itself was not in front of him, so being a game-to-the-end horse he tried to take off in a last second reaction to the half sight of the wing on the edge of his vision.

Also, said the press, he pricked his ears as a horse does before he is going to jump, and a horse does not prick his ears for nothing, especially after a long race. It seems to me that if a horse has enough time and energy to prick its ears it also has time and enough command of its senses to see what is or what is not in front of it.

The press published pictures of Devon Loch with his hind feet on the ground and his forelegs in the air. See him jump, they said. But if a horse is galloping at thirty miles an hour and his hind legs abruptly stop and drop, it is easy to see that the sudden heavy drag behind will throw the forelegs into the air like a see-saw. His former momentum was enough after that to throw him forward through the air to land on his belly, and this is what has been interpreted as an attempt to jump.

A lot was made of the fact that the horse collapsed by the wing of the water jump. In fact, if he had been going to jump the water jump, Devon Loch would have taken another stride before he did so; no horse of such experience would attempt to jump the water from outside the wings, for he would know he could not do it.

The real answer to the ghost-jumpites is Devon Loch himself. He is a horse of extreme intelligence. He is an outstandingly brilliant jumper. He was not noticeably tired and he was not being hard pressed. It is completely inconceivable that such a horse in such circumstances should have made such a shattering mistake. After all, he was used to passing the wings of jumps beside him. A hundred and fifty yards back he had passed the wing of the Chair fence without a flicker of emotion, and on other courses and in the park at home he was well accustomed to galloping along beside fences and hurdles without attempting to jump them.

Because I was on the horse and not watching I am sure that the ghost jump theory is wrong. When a horse is going to jump he gathers the muscles of his hindquarters and tucks his legs under him for the spring. However hurried he was no horse would attempt to jump without doing it, and if he were very tired he would be more likely to run straight into a fence and fall over it, than to start to take off with his weight in the wrong place. I have ridden horses over more than forty thousand fences in racing alone, not counting hunting and show jumping, and never has a horse intending to jump failed to gather himself together to take off. The feeling is absolutely unmistakable. Devon Loch did not try to jump.

The third theory is that Devon Loch suffered a sudden and severe muscular spasm in his hindquarters, and the jolt it gave him at the speed he was going was enough to throw him down.

In the actual second of his fall, I thought he had broken a hind leg, for he collapsed from the back, but when I found that he was unhurt, cramp seemed the only solution.

Very little is known about the physiology of cramp, and the cause of the lightning spasm known as stitch in humans is a complete mystery. Ordinary cramp in athletes usually comes on after the end of a great physical effort, and is thought to be due to an excess of lactic acid in the muscles; in horses it is called 'setfast' and often lasts for six or seven hours. Obviously Devon Loch did not suffer from any prolonged cramp, for he was walking normally within two minutes of his fall, but a violent spasm equivalent to stitch seems a reasonable possibility.

If this sort of thing were at all common there would of course be no mystery, but veterinary opinion seems to be that it is so rare as to be almost unknown. On the other hand, soon after the race a retired huntsman told me that he used to ride a mare which did the same thing. She collapsed twice without warning in the hunting field while galloping, and once trotting along a road; and after that he felt that she was more of a risk than a pleasure, and she was pensioned off.

Sudden cramp seems to be the most sensible, down-to-earth answer to the problem, but it does not explain why Devon Loch pricked his ears before he fell.

There is a fourth possibility. At first it may seem a fanciful and extravagant one, almost as alarming as the 'ghost jump'.

Devon Loch was galloping easily, he pricked his ears, and he fell for no visible reason in a peculiar way not seen before or since on a racecourse. If this was the only fall of its kind it is worth asking whether on this one occasion there was anything else which had never happened before. There was. It was the only time that a reigning Sovereign had been at Liverpool cheering home a Royal winner of the Grand National.

Could there possibly be any connection of cause and effect in these two unique events? Sad and ironic though it may be, it is conceivable that it was simply and solely because he belonged to the Queen Mother that Devon Loch fell where and how he did.

From the last fence onwards the cheers which greeted us were tremendous and growing louder with every yard we went, and although I knew the reason for them, they may have been puzzling and confusing to my mount, who could not know that his owner was a Queen.

In order to hear better what was going on he would make a horse's instinctive movement to do so, and into those newly pricked and sensitive ears fell a wave of sound of shattering intensity. The noise that to me was uplifting and magnificent may have been exceedingly frightening to Devon Loch. He may have tried to throw himself backwards away from it; he may have reacted to it in the same convulsive way as a human being jumps at a sudden loud noise, and a severe nervous jerk at such a stage in the race could certainly have been enough to smash the rhythm of his stride and bring him down.

The cheering was incredible. Everyone on the stands was yelling, and Raymond Glendenning's wireless commentary though he was shouting into a microphone at the top of his voice, could scarcely be heard above the happy din going on about him. I have never in my life heard such a noise. It rolled and lapped around us, buffeting and glorious, the enthusiastic expression of love for the Royal Family and delight in seeing the Royal horse win. The tremendous noise was growing in volume with every second, and was being almost funnelled down from the stands on to the course. The weather records show that there was a light breeze blowing that day from behind the stands, and this must have carried the huge sound with it.

I remember how startled I was when I first heard the cheers for M'as-Tu-Vu at Lingfield, and they were a whisper compared with the enveloping roar at Liverpool; so I think one must seriously consider whether Devon Loch may not have been struck down by joy.

Heart failure, ghost jump, cramp, and a shock wave of sound may still not include the real cause of Devon Loch's fall, and in this tantalising mystery there is no Sherlock Holmes to unravel its elementariness on the last page. What happened to Devon Loch is Devon Loch's secret, and I doubt if he even remembers it now.

But what would happen, I wonder, if we took him to Aintree and galloped him again along the straight to the winning post. Would he notice when he came to the fatal place? Would he stop and back away from it with any show of distress, or even fall there again, or would he, as I certainly believe he would, gallop on without faltering past the water jump and past the unattained winning post? Would he hear the echo of the roar which met him there so long ago?

Devon Loch, a noble and courageous horse, will not be forgotten in racing history. Fifty years from now, about National time, newspaper articles will mention his tragedy as a curious event in a distant past. Octogenarians will sigh, 'I was there. . . .' The old photographs will be pulled out, and one's grandsons will wonder at the horse's sprawled legs, and perhaps smile at the old-fashioned clothes of the crowd.

And my fate? I know already.

I heard one man say to another, a little while ago, 'Who did you say that was? Dick Francis? Oh, yes, he's the man who didn't win the National.'

What an epitaph!

from THE SPORT OF QUEENS *1957*

Moments of Glory which turned to Nightmare

JOHN LAWRENCE

There are 494 yards between the last fence and the winning post in the Grand National at Aintree – and, for about 480 of them, I was, last Saturday afternoon, the happiest man in the world. But the last battle is the only one to count – and for that, for those final, ghastly 14 yards, Carrickbeg and I had nothing left. So there, in a split second, the dream of glory became a nightmare and Pat Buckley swept past on Mr P. B. Raymond's Ayala to win the great steeplechase.

The pair of them won it fair and square because, together, with certain defeat staring them between the eyes, they had the courage and endurance to go on fighting what was an apparently hopeless battle.

A horse with slightly less bottomless stamina than Ayala, or a man slightly less strong, fit and determined than Buckley, would never have been able to seize the chance when it came.

At the time – at that bitter moment when Ayala's head appeared at my knee – I wished them both at the bottom of the deep, blue sea. Now, with admiration and only a little envy, I salute them for winning, deservedly, a truly wonderful race – a race, I think, as thrilling and spectacular as any Grand National since the war.

But besides the winner there was another hero. At the age of seven, in only his second season as a 'chaser, Carrickbeg had out-jumped and out-galloped 46 older, more experienced horses for nearly four and a half miles.

Steady as the rock of Gibraltar from the first fence to the last, he was never for one single moment in danger of falling and, until his last reserves gave out ten strides before the end, he had answered my every call with cheerful and unhesitating obedience.

Unless he gives it me, I never expect to have a better ride at Aintree or anywhere else, and for those nine and a half unforgettable minutes I offer him my heartfelt thanks.

They had begun as, with the long, nerve-racking preliminaries over at last, Mr Alec Marsh got the huge field off to a perfect start.

A bitter, biting wind had greeted us as we left the weighing-room, and, by the time we turned in front of the stands to canter down, my spirits, for once, were at their lowest ebb.

Carrickbeg restored them slightly – striding out like a lion on the way to the post – but the last moments before a National will never be anything but a dreadful, goldfish-bowl ordeal and only when the first few fences are safely crossed can you forget how much is at stake and settle down to enjoy the greatest thrill the sport of steeplechasing has to offer.

After our dismal experience at Cheltenham, those first few fences were, for Carrickbeg and me, especially important. But if he felt the same misgivings as his rider, Carrickbeg concealed them well. He measured the first to an inch, and, even more encouraging, hit the top of the open ditch quite hard – and somehow made it feel no stiffer than a soft French hurdle.

As expected, Out and About (10 st 7 lbs) had led from the start, but Josh Gifford held him well and the pace they set was nothing extraordinary. As the red and white flag fluttered its awe-inspiring warning over Becher's Brook, Jonjo (10 st 6 lbs), French Lawyer (10 st 6 lbs), Forty Secrets (10 st 7 lbs), Chavara (10 st 2 lbs) and Dandy Tim (10 st 6 lbs) were in the leading group – and Carrickbeg (10 st 3 lbs) sailed over like a bird not far behind to land far out and beyond the ditch and gallop on without a check.

Good Gracious (10 st 7 lbs) fell at Becher's. Magic Tricks (10 st) had gone at the first, Look Happy (10 st) at the second,

Merganser (10 st 4 lbs) and Wingless (10 st 3 lbs) at the third and Solonace (10 st) somewhere thereabouts. But for most, as we swung round the Canal Turn, the fences were setting no great problems.

I personally had not seen one fallen until Connie II (10 st) ploughed through the tenth beside me, but the sickening crash she made was a violent reminder that this is still Aintree, where to take one liberty too many can mean a sudden end to all your hopes.

Ayala (10 st), never far from the leaders, had, in fact, taken one at the Canal – carving a huge chunk from the fence, but failing completely to disturb his own or Pat Buckley's equilibrium. I watched, with admiration, their recovery – and little knew how dear it was to cost me by and by.

On the long run back towards the stands, loose horses began to be a problem. Merganser, riderless, was a serious thorn in Josh Gifford's flesh, constantly unsettling Out and About and making him pull harder than ever, and, as we galloped towards the Chair – never an enjoyable moment – Wingless, dodging gaily about in front of Carrickbeg, made the towering cliff of the great fence an even less welcoming prospect than usual.

But all was well and now, with the water safely crossed, I found myself, for the first time ever, in a position from which the National had to be considered as a race – not merely as a struggle for survival. And the next 100 yards – swinging out into the country – were, in a way, more exciting than any in the whole four and a half miles.

There, deciding that the moment had come to get a bit closer, I picked Carrickbeg up for the first time – and the effortless power with which he surged towards the leaders suddenly brought home the unbelievable truth that we were in the race with a real chance.

At Becher's the second time, in nine Grand Nationals out of ten, the shape of the finish can already be seen.

And so it was now, for although Out and About was still in front together with Loyal Tan, French Lawyer and Dandy Tim, Ayala was close behind them, Springbok (10 st 12 lbs) was improving steadily and, as Carrickbeg landed over the Brook, the leaders were not ten lengths ahead of us.

At the fence after Becher's Loyal Tan and Dandy Tim dropped

out exhausted and by the Canal there were (although I certainly did not realize it at the time) only six left in the race with a real chance. They were Out and About, now disputing the lead with French Lawyer, Hawa's Song (10 st), Springbok, Ayala and Carrickbeg.

This list may be wronging some who were, in fact, still close enough to win at the Canal, but the fact is that from Valentine's on I saw only five horses.

And now it was a race in deadly earnest – no longer time to look about or manoeuvre for a clean run – but kick and push and get ground where you can.

The four fences from Valentine's to Anchor Bridge were as exciting as any I ever jumped – and at one of them, the fourth from home, the dice rolled fractionally against Carrickbeg for the first and only time in the whole race.

Understandably, having led almost all the way, Out and About was tiring now and, as French Lawyer went on, he crashed low through the fence and fell.

Perhaps three lengths behind, confronted with a gaping hole, and a cloud of flying twigs Carrickbeg hesitated for a split second, failed to take off when I asked, scrambled through the gap – and had then to swerve to pass his fallen rival.

These things happen so fast – and are so quickly driven from one's mind by what comes after – that it is all too easy to exaggerate their importance.

The newsreel film does not, unfortunately, show the incident in full, but it does, I think, prove that whereas Carrickbeg was bang with the leaders five from home, one fence later, after Out and About's fall, he had definitely lost at least a couple of lengths. Whatever the truth I do not offer it as an excuse. Such things happen in all Grand Nationals and the winner is the one who best overcomes them.

Probably, in any case, I should have given Carrickbeg a better chance to recover before asking him to go and win. But, passing Anchor Bridge, with second last in sight, I saw Gerry Scott go for his whip on Springbok, saw the favourite stagger sideways, beaten – and, with Carrickbeg strong under me, it seemed that the time had come.

Until you have tried to ride a finish up it no one, I think, can fully appreciate just how long and wearisome the run-in at Aintree can be after four miles and 30 fences.

In the back of my mind now, as I sent Carrickbeg past Ayala and Springbok to join Hawa's Song at the second last there was the foolish fear that something with a better turn of speed – Owen's Sedge, for instance – would come from behind and beat us all.

In fact, of course, what I should have feared was the dreadful strain put upon any horse who, after jumping for four miles, finds himself in front with neither fence nor company to help him up that final desperate, staring straight.

Next time, perhaps, I shall know better, but now, as Carrickbeg swept gallantly over the last with Ayala at his quarters it still seemed possible. His stride had still not faltered and, straightening round the elbow half-way home with the roar of the crowd rising to a crescendo in our ears, the only feeling I remember was one of wild, incredulous hope that the dream first dreamt on a nursery rocking horse long ago was really coming true.

Until this moment, sustained by my horse's strength and by the heat of battle, I had felt no real physical strain; but now, all at once, the cold, clammy hand of exhaustion closed its grip on my thighs and arms.

Even to swing the whip had become an effort and the only thing that kept me going was the unbroken rhythm of Carrickbeg's heroic head, nodding in time with his stride. And, suddenly, even that was gone.

With a hundred yards to go and still no sound of pursuit, the prize seemed within our grasp. Eighty, seventy, sixty perhaps – and then it happened. In the space of a single stride I felt the last ounce of Carrickbeg's energy drain away and my own with it. One moment we were a living working combination, the next, a struggling, beaten pair. There was still hope – but not for long.

As we passed Ayala before the second last, Carrickbeg had, to Pat Buckley himself, looked the winner bar a fall. 'Go on, John', he found the breath and good nature to say, but saying it, did not for one second relax his efforts. He had been riding hard for longer than I but, with the strength and determination of youth, managed to keep Ayala in the race.

Half-way up the run-in, still two lengths behind, it must have looked as hopeless to him as it did to, I believe, the stands. But he never gave up and, as Carrickbeg began to falter, pulled Ayala out for a final desperate effort.

The gallant chestnut cannot, I think, have quickened much if at all; but the depths of his stamina were as yet unplumbed, and so abrupt and complete was Carrickbeg's collapse that in half a dozen strides the gap was closed and the race over.

To my dying day I shall never forget the sight of Ayala's head beside my knee. Two heartbeats later he was half a length in front and, although I dropped my hands before the post, I can honestly promise any aggrieved supporter that it made not one yard of difference.

A wonderful race had been gallantly won and, though perhaps it is not for me to say it, almost equally gallantly lost. . . .

from HORSE AND HOUND *6-4-1963*

Mandarin Day

JOHN LAWRENCE

From Agincourt to D-Day, France, I suppose, has been the scene of more brave deeds by Englishmen than any other country in the world. Mostly, of course, they were inspired by the horrid waste of war, but sport in its less serious tragic way can also lift a man to heights of daring and achievement, and as Fred Winter and Mandarin came back last Sunday after winning the Grand Steeplechase de Paris (1962), I like to think that the ghosts of long-dead English horsemen rode beside them, glad and proud to know that the flag for which they fought and died still flies, even in this sad, dull and mechanical age.

To win at all would have been a famous victory – to win as Winter and Mandarin did was an heroic triumph over odds so steep that no normal man or horse could have been blamed for giving up long before the end.

None of this, of course, could even be guessed at, as, in the atmosphere of a Turkish bath, the fourteen runners swept gaily past the stands for the first of three intricate, twisting circuits.

So far as one could see in the friendly but chaotic tangle that serves Auteuil for a parade ring, the French horses were not a wildly impressive sight. Nor, to someone who had never seen him before, would Mandarin have been, but to the large band of English supporters the sheen on his coat, the hard muscles writhing over his quarters, and the way he pulled 'Mush' Foster round the paddock all told their own encouraging tale.

Sure enough, after flicking neat and fast over the preliminary hurdle jumped on the way to the start, Mandarin was soon up-sides in front and passed the stands pulling, as usual, like a train. He has always been a 'heavy-headed' ride with precious little feeling in his mouth – and always runs in a rubber-covered snaffle to save his lips and jaws.

At the beginning of last season a brand-new bridle was bought – and Mandarin had worn it only half a dozen times, including both his victories in the Hennessey and Cheltenham Gold Cups. But the trouble with rubber bits is that a fault or wear can develop unseen in the steel chain – and this, no doubt, is what had happened now.

After the first, sharp, left-hand bend the Grand Steeple course comes back towards the stands, and there, going to the fourth, a soft but staring privet fence the best part of six feet high, the bit snapped clean in the middle, inside Mandarin's mouth. I remember thinking at the time 'he got a little close to that one', but for another full circuit none of us in the stands realized the dreadful truth.

In fact, of course, Fred Winter now had no contact whatsoever with the horse's mouth or head. The reins, kept together by the Irish martingale (or 'rings') were still round Mandarin's neck – and they, together with the thin neck-strap of the breast-girth, were Winter's only hand hold.

To visualize the full impossibility of the situation you must

remember first that when a racehorse, particularly a hard-pulling
'chaser, is galloping on the bit, much of the jockey's weight is
normally balanced, through the reins, against that of the horse's
head and forehand. Now, for both Fred Winter and Mandarin,
this vital counterbalance was gone completely. The man, with
no means of steering but his weight, had to rely entirely on grip
and balance – the horse, used to steady pressure on his mouth,
had to jump twenty-one strange and formidable obstacles with
his head completely free – a natural state admittedly, but one to
which Mandarin is wholly unaccustomed.

Small wonder then that at the huge 'Rivière de la Tribune' –
the water in front of the stands – he fiddled awkwardly, landing
only inches clear of the bank and disaster. Thereafter, save for
another nasty moment at the same fence next time round, the
little horse jumped unbelievably well – Fred Winter, sitting still
or driving on as the need arose, matched his every move with
the sympathetic rhythm that is nine-tenths of horsemanship.

But the fences, needless to say, were only half the problem.
Walking the course that morning with Winter, Dave Dick and
Joe Lammin, Fulke Walwyn's head lad, we had all wondered
afresh at the many turns and countless opportunities for losing
your way. The Grand Steeple is, roughly, two figures of eight in
opposite directions and one whole circuit outside both. There
are at least four bends through 180 degrees, and to negotiate
them all as Winter and Mandarin did, without bit or bridle, was,
quite literally, miraculous.

The answer lies, of course, in many things – in the matchless
strength of Winter's legs, in Mandarin's own good sense – and
in the absolute determination of them both never to give up
while there was one shot, however forlorn, left on the board.

It is also, I think, only fair to give some credit – and our thanks
– to the French jockeys, several of whom could, had they pleased,
have taken advantage of the disaster and, without much risk to
themselves, got rid of the bigger danger. Instead, at least one –
Daumas on Taillefer – and probably several others, actually did
their best to help, proving gloriously that the comradeship of
dangers shared can, in some sports at least, count far more than
international rivalry.

Throughout the race, save for a moment on the last bend,

Mandarin was up in the first four – and, as he jumped the Rivière for the last time, the full horror of his situation dawned upon us in the stands.

From that moment on, the nerve-racking suspense, the wild impossible hope, plunging to black despair and back again, were like nothing I have ever known on a racecourse – or for that matter anywhere else.

Mandarin cleared with ease the tricky post and rails at which he hesitated fatally three years ago – and came to the junction of the courses close fourth – close enough to lift the hearts of those who knew his and Winter's invincible finishing power.

But now disaster almost struck. Before the last right-handed turn a large bush must be passed on the left – but can with equal ease be passed on the right. Mandarin, on the inside, with no rail to guide him, could not know until the last moment which way to go. For a few heart-stopping strides he hesitated, Winter threw all his strength and weight into one last desperate swerve – and somehow they were safe.

But priceless lengths had been lost and now, round the final bend, with only two obstacles to jump, Mandarin was only fifth, some six or seven lengths behind the leader.

On the turn, of course, Winter could hardly ride at all, but then, facing the Bullfinch, in a straight line for home at last it was a different matter. From the stands we saw the familiar crouching drive of the shoulders, and Mandarin, responding as he always has and always will, thrust out his gallant head and went for the Bullfinch like a tank facing tissue paper.

None will ever know what the little horse felt or thought between those last two fences. I have always believed he knows just what it means to win – and now none will ever convince me otherwise. In a hundred desperate yards he passed three horses as if they were walking, and, as he landed in front on the long run-in, my eyes, I am not ashamed to say, were half-blind with tears.

But it was not over yet. Mandarin was deadly tired, and Winter, the reins gathered useless in his left hand, could do nothing to hold him together. He could only push and drive – and how he drove. Even so, inch by inch, Lumino, the only French horse able to accelerate, crept nearer and nearer.

In the final desperate strides, not knowing the angle, not one of us could really tell who had won. Fred Winter thought he had got up, but he could not speak, so for several ghastly moments we had to sweat it out. But then, there it was – number one in the frame – and as Mandarin came back, mobbed as no film star has ever been, head down, dog-tired, sweating – but surely happy – a cheer went up such as I have never heard on any racecourse.

from HORSE AND HOUND *23–6–1962*

Red Rum's Record

IVOR HERBERT

The ground on 31 March 1973 was exactly as Red Rum loves it: firm. Brian Fletcher had warmed up with a 4th in the first race the BP Shield Handicap Hurdle. Don McCain was relieved to see him safe round and home.

Thirty-eight runners paraded for the Grand National. It was worth £25,486 and, three minutes late at 3.18 p.m., the field leapt forward on the start of a journey of 4 miles and 856 yards which only seventeen would complete. The firmness of the ground wrongly suggested a fast pace. The jockeys had received their customary half-heard cautionary warning against going a mad gallop early on. No one, in fact, believed that records were about to be broken.

Nothing accelerated steeplechasing's soaring popularity more than its television coverage by the cool and competent B.B.C. Its leading racing commentator Peter O'Sullevan is a legend in his lifetime. A victorious owner himself on the highest level both on the flat and under N.H. Rules, he knows the game from the muck-yard up to its rich and noble patrons. His commentaries set a standard so far unequalled. And he begins:

They're off. And Rouge Autumn starts fast on the inside, with Sunny Lad and Go-Pontinental moving up on the outside with Beggar's Way, then comes Black Secret with General Symons on his outside and Richeleau and Glenkiln. Crisp has gone right up there with Sunny Lad on the inside, then comes Hurricane Rock, then Mill Door over on the far side with Endless Folly, Beggar's Way and Black Secret, and with Rouge Autumn disputing it, they come to the first.

John Hanmer takes up the commentary:

Black Secret over in the lead. There's a faller – Richeleau has gone at the first – and as they go towards the second, Grey Sombrero on the outside along with Ashville, then Glenkiln, then comes Black Secret, General Symons then Highland Seal . . . Over the ditch and Grey Sombrero over first. There's a faller at that one – Ashville fell.

Then shrewd Julian Wilson, beady-eyed, the intense and furrowed-brow'd skilled television interviewer, takes up the racing tale:

And spread right across the course with Grey Sombrero the leader over that one, from Endless Folly in the centre, Black Secret towards the outside, Highland Seal just scrambled over that one. Crisp is right up there on the inside, as they race down towards the fifth. As they race down towards Bechers, it's the grey, Grey Sombrero, racing wide of the field, the clear leader from Crisp in second, Black Secret third. At Bechers – Grey Sombrero over – and just clears it – from Crisp in second, Black Secret third, Endless Folly fourth, Sunny Lad five, Rouge Autumn is sixth and Beggar's Way is a faller at Bechers. Over the next, with Crisp now the leader from Grey Sombrero, then Black Secret and Endless Folly . . . they come towards the Canal Turn. Nereo has been pulled up and Crisp is the leader from Grey Sombrero, Black Secret, Endless Folly . . . then comes Spanish Steps. Highland Seal has been pulled up as they jump the next. Crisp over it from Grey Sombrero, Black Secret. . . .

John Hanmer resumes from his vantage point:

As they go towards the next fence it's Crisp the clear leader from Grey Sombrero, Endless Folly, Black Secret, then comes Great Noise, Sunny Lad, then Rouge Autumn, then comes Tarquin Bid, behind Tarquin Bid is Red Rum, then Spanish

Steps, then Hurricane Rock and Glenkiln as they go across the Melling Road.

We pick up Peter O'Sullevan again as they turn on to the race-course.

Crisp, well clear, over from Grey Sombrero who jumps it second, Endless Folly jumps it third, then Great Noise fourth, five Black Secret, six is Rouge Autumn, seven is Spanish Steps and eight Tarquin Bid and nine is Red Rum and ten, on the inside, is Sunny Lad as they come to the next. Crisp over in the lead and clear . . . Red Rum well in there [he was 12th] and then comes Glenkiln. . . . Coming to the Chair now – this is one of the biggest. Crisp, his ears pricked, jumps it beautifully in the lead – he just pecked a little bit, but got away with it. Grey Sombrero's gone at that one. Grey Sombrero's a faller, Glenkiln's a faller –

Beryl McCain was staring from the top of the stand. 'I saw Red Rum on the wide outside all the way round. I saw Crisp. Then I saw poor Glen fall. We'd all got soft spots for him, 'cos he's a super and very kind horse. He fell at the Chair and I saw him struggle. He couldn't get up. His leg was stuck in the bottom of the fence. Canharis jumped over after him and clouted him on the back of the head. He got up. He was dazed. He jumped the water and fell in and the whole of his back legs were covered with water. And he pulled himself out and they caught him by the stables. I hadn't watched Red Rum. And by the time Glen was out of the water, they'd jumped the first fence second time round and Crisp was still in the lead, but Red Rum was second!'

'Ginger' McCain was delighted to see Brian Fletcher really riding Red Rum along over the Chair and then the water. They improved five or six places very rapidly.

Thus away over the Melling Road with the giant Crisp loping along in front, turning the enormous fences into hurdles, seeming as if he was cantering ahead of a pack of galloping ponies.

Fletcher says: 'From the third fence on the second circuit, from the ditch, I was chasing this horse in front of me. I didn't know what it was. I couldn't tell it was Crisp.'

John Hanmer calls the remnants as they thunder past him:

Crisp at the ditch, the nineteenth, he stood right back, he jumped it well, he's right out in front still of Red Rum, second, Rouge Autumn is third, Spanish Steps fourth, Tarquin Bid is fifth, Great Noise is sixth, then Endless Folly and Black Secret.

Julian Wilson's admiration of great Crisp sends his voice sailing :

And Richard Pitman over that one on Crisp and what a fantastic ride he's having! I can't remember a horse so far ahead in the Grand National at this stage! Jumping that second was Red Rum, then Spanish Steps on the outside of Rouge Autumn. Great Noise made a mistake there, but coming to the next . . . Crisp is over that one, safely over the one before Bechers from Red Rum . . . Crisp comes on his own to Bechers Brook for the second time, Crisp the top weight. Richard Pitman over it in tremendous style and he's about twenty lengths clear from Red Rum in second place, behind comes Spanish Steps, then Hurricane Rock. Crisp is over the twenty-third already, and racing down to the Canal Turn, as Red Rum jumps the twenty-third in second. . . . Crisp jumps the Canal Turn clear. He's still twenty lengths clear from Red Rum in second.

'I just thought at the Canal Turn,' says Ginger McCain, 'that we'd be second and how unlucky we were to meet Crisp. . . .'

'Seeing the race afterwards,' reflects little Brian Fletcher, 'I've often said to myself that if I'd ever said "I'm going to be second", if I'd ever dropped my hands or eased off Red Rum for one moment, then I would have been second.'

Fletcher did not ease. Red Rum did not falter. Fletcher drew his whip at Anchor Bridge. He hit Red Rum twice, thrice, four times. The bay horse quickened. 'Knowing the horse would stay and jump,' says Fletcher, 'and had only 10 st 5 lb on his back, I never accepted he'd be second.'

John Hanmer saw the move, but Crisp was still, as Julian Wilson had shouted, a long way ahead of Red Rum. Hanmer called quickly,

Crisp has got three to jump, he's well clear of Red Rum, who's made a bit of ground. Spanish Steps is third, Hurricane

Rock is fourth. Over the third from home, Crisp over safely. Red Rum in second place, then Spanish Steps, Hurricane Rock just passing Spanish Steps. . . . As they go across the Melling Road, with two to jump, it's Crisp with Red Rum in second place making ground, but a very long gap after that to Hurricane Rock, Spanish Steps and Rouge Autumn. . . .

Peter O'Sullevan takes up the saga of the slowly shrinking lead, Crisp conceding one stone nine pounds to his pursuer.

It's Crisp in the lead from Red Rum, but Red Rum still making ground on him! Brian Fletcher on Red Rum chasing Dick Pitman on Crisp. Crisp still well clear with two fences left to jump in the 1973 Grand National and this great Australian 'chaser, Crisp, with twelve stone on his back and ten stone five on the back of Red Rum, who's chasing him and they look to have it absolutely to themselves. At the second last . . . Crisp is over. And clear of Red Rum who's jumping it a long way back. In third place is Spanish Steps then Hurricane Rock and Rouge Autumn and L'Escargot. But coming to the final fence in the 'National now . . . and it's Crisp still going in great style with twelve stone on his back. He jumps it well. Red Rum is about fifteen lengths behind him as he jumps it. Dick Pitman coming to the elbow now in the 'National. He's got two hundred and fifty yards to run. But Crisp is just wandering off the true line now. He's beginning to lose concentration. He's been out there on his own for so long. And Red Rum is making ground on him. Still as they come to the line, it's a furlong to run now, two hundred yards now for Crisp, and Red Rum still closing on him, and Crisp is getting very tired, and Red Rum is pounding after him and Red Rum is the one who finishes the strongest. He's going to get up! Red Rum is going to win the 'National! At the line Red Rum has just snatched it from Crisp! And Red Rum is the winner! And Crisp is second and L'Escargot is just coming up to be third. . . .

Red Rum had smashed the generally accepted Grand National record time set up by Golden Miller in 1934. (In some record books Reynoldstown carrying 11 st 4 lb in 1935 – the first year of his double – is credited with 9 mins 20·2 secs compared with The

Miller's 9 mins 20·4 secs carrying 12 st 2 lb.) Red Rum's time, an incredible half-a-minute quicker than the average time, was 9 mins 1·9 secs – a speed over the thirty biggest obstacles in Britain of nearly 29 m.p.h.

from RED RUM *1974*

The Pardubice

CHRISTOPHER COLLINS

In June 1973 I flew out to Prague to inspect the Pardubice course, to put into perspective the more fearsome descriptions of it, and to decide which horse to take. I was whisked out to Pardubice in a black government car with Babanek, the Director General of Racing, and an interpreter, and spent the day trudging round the course under a boiling sun which later gave way to sticky rain.

I was genuinely horrified by the Taxis fence – a straight-up, 5 ft (1·5 m) high and 5 ft thick with a 16 ft 6 in (5 m) ditch on landing. To begin with I thought I had been shown it as a joke and that it was in fact a sort of giant boundary between different sections of the course. After being assured that horses did clear it, I saw that it was jumpable at racing pace if everything went right. I didn't much like the big waters, and the amount of waving corn which by October would give way to plough would ensure that the whole affair would be a gigantic test of stamina. Having got so far I decided that I had better have a go and that Stephen's Society was the horse for the job. He was a seven-year-old, a great quality bulldozer who so far had failed to win a race, but was a brilliant hunter.

Not much went right with his preparation. He came in from the field coughing and then got beaten in his two preparatory runs, blowing heavily after both. It took from dawn on the Monday until 10 p.m. on the Wednesday for him to reach Pardubice, stopping overnight at pre-arranged places under the care of Charlie, my driver, and Sue, who normally looked after my event horses.

His appearance excited great interest when I took him out on to the course for a few practice jumps on the Friday morning. Unfortunately he rather dented our image by promptly refusing at a small island bank in the middle of a field. He was a little difficult at Fence 3, a small water, which I took him over backwards and forwards several times, but jumped some hedges extremely well. Afterwards the consensus was that he was lacking in elegance for a racehorse, his arrival three days before the race in contrast to the Russians' three weeks was casual, and that my three-pound saddle was ridiculous for the Pardubice.

I spent that afternoon walking the course, charting where the plough was lightest and evaluating the best places to take the fences. That evening we attended a veterinary lecture, which, as it was delivered in Czech, was of limited benefit to me. However, it was followed by some films of previous Pardubices which were of real value. Up to then I had rather fancied the idea of jumping Taxis, the fourth fence, in front on the left where it was the lowest. In order to avoid the risk of getting brought down one would have to get there first, but they seemed to go off at such a pace that it looked as if this would not be possible for Stephen. I therefore decided I must have an alternative. Plan A would be to jump off in front. Plan B would be to let them go, and jump the big part of Taxis on the right, where I would be more likely to get a free passage.

The next morning I gave Stephen a good gallop and jumped some more fences. He blew but there was nothing more to be done. The rest of the morning was occupied by the jockeys' briefing, again in Czech, which meant rather less to me than the others. In the afternoon I walked the course again meticulously. At 7 p.m. sharp the Chefs d'Equipe's dinner took place. As the sole British representative I was invited. The hierarchy started with the Russian trainer on the right of Babanek and worked its way down via West Germans, Bulgars and Czechs to myself at the bottom of the table. I pecked as sparingly as possible at the fare. I was worried about my weight.

The next day at the course there was a festive atmosphere. Streamers streamed, trumpets blared, whistles blew and there were many thousands of people. I was worried about Stephen's fitness, Taxis and the opposition and could not see us doing well. The trip was a reconnaissance and afterwards I would know if it was worth returning another year to try to win.

Finally the preliminaries were disposed of and we were away in the race. The early pace was terrific and far too much for Stephen. I adopted Plan B. As we swung into Taxis most of the field made left for the easier end of it. I kept Stephen hard right and gave him a real shake-up fifty yards away. He went on towards the fence and took off close to it, not throwing much of a leap. 'Christ, we're going in the ditch!' I thought and leaned so far back I practically touched his quarters with the back of my head. In fact he touched lightly down, weaved his way through the odd faller and made nothing of the Irish bank and the next two fences. Then came a hiccup. At the In and Out we were carried out by a loose horse. I rejoined the race at least fifty lengths to the bad. Incredibly, without me hurrying him, after another mile and a half or so Stephen had made this up. We got over the waters, a horse fell at the next and we were third with a mile-and-a-half to go. We bided our time and a Czech horse kicked on. We survived the remaining difficult fences and came on to the racecourse for the last time, second and full of running. At the second last we jumped past the leader, galloped into the straight in front, cleared the last, a simple hurdle, and held on to win by eight lengths.

There was great ceremonial to winning. Six-foot rosettes were presented, the Union Jack hoisted, God Save the Queen played and we jockeys presented to the high officials. Later Stephen was asked to print his foot on to a racecard to give his autograph and I to make over my colours to the hippological museum.

from CROSS COUNTRY RIDING *1977*

PART V

Horse and Hound

Of all the creatures that God made at the Creation, there is none (except man) more excellent, or so much to be respected as a Horse: For in disposition and qualitie he is but little inferiour to Man (excepting theire difference): in strength hee may be compared to a huge Elephant, for boldnes to the Lyon, for swiftness to the Roe or Hinde, in smelling hee resembles the Hound, for toughnesse hee excelleth the slow toyling Oxe, for love hee checkes the Spaniell and for understanding hee may oppose himselfe against the Serpent; but for beauty hee is a blacke Swanne amongst all that Species: and further for the use of man, not onely for pleasure, but also for necessity and profit, there is none to be compared to him. For he is as delightfull a Creature to behold as any, and then, if a man will travaile upon pleasure abroad, how can hee bee more delightfully and easily carryed then upon a faire, comely, and well going Horse? And also for necessitie, if a man be upon earnest affayres or hazard of life, for to travaile a great journey in a little time, what Creature is so fit to performe it as a Horse, both for toughnesse and speede? And further, for Oeconomicall affayres, what Creature is so fit to performe both for Plow and portage as a Horse? And lastly, for profit (I pray you), what greater profit can come to a man then a race of good Mares and a right Stallion doth bring.

And further, he hath given the Horse such naturall affection and love to the Hounds, that he doth seem to swallow the earth for the desire of their noyse, nay hee is so chary of his feet (if he be thrust amongst them through his riders ignorance,) that hee will make a false steppe rather than treade on any of them: and also hee is of such puissant strength, courage, and swiftnesse, that he will carry his Maister through the deepe and toylesome earths, and brocken swaches, for contentment in his solace.

M. Baret (1618)

John Peel

THE SPORTING MAGAZINE

On March 27th, 1818, the Caldbeck pack of hounds belonging to Mr John Peel, innkeeper, unkennelled a fine old fox in Denton Side, parish of Sebergham, and immediately on gaining the brow of the forest he directed his steps for the mountains, passing near to the village of Caldbeck. Reynard's subtlety was soon apparent. He sprang upon the top of a high parapet wall, and ran along its whole length, notwithstanding that the hounds were in full chase. On arriving at the foot of Brag Fell, from the great depth of the snow Mr Peel and two other horsemen were obliged to dismount, and were here joined by several expert pedestrians. Mr Peel's acquaintance with the mountains directed him to a well-known shelter for animals, named Iron Crag. They found that the chase [*sic*] had been there, but was prevented from taking the ground by the snow, which lay in large masses. Reynard then took an easternly direction, passing over High Pike, Carrick, and thence visited the different high mountains in that direction, each of which, no doubt, from the cause before mentioned, he found to afford no place of shelter. He was then found to be aiming west again, passing over Saddleback, and approaching Skiddaw. Here the pedestrians came in touch with him, but notwithstanding Mr Peel's knowledge of the district, and his able management of the pack, all exertion was unavailing; for the hounds were found upon Skiddaw, returning from the chase after a pursuit of more than eight hours, during which time it is supposed that they ran at least fifty miles.

from THE SPORTING MAGAZINE *1840*

The Huntsman

PETER BECKFORD

I will endeavour to describe what a good huntsman should be.
He should be young, strong, active, bold, and enterprising; fond
of the diversion, and indefatigable in the pursuit of it: he should
be sensible and good-tempered; he ought also to be sober; he
should be exact, civil, and cleanly; he should be a good horseman
and a good groom: his voice should be strong and clear; and he
should have an eye so quick, as to perceive which of his hounds
carries the scent when all are running; and should have so excellent an ear, as always to distinguish the foremost hounds when
he does not see them: he should be quiet, patient, and without
conceit. Such are the excellences which constitute a good huntsman: he should not, however be too fond of displaying them till
necessity calls them forth: he should let his hounds alone whilst
they can hunt, and he should have genius to assist them when they
cannot.

I have always thought a huntsman a happy man: his office is
pleasing, and at the same time flattering: we pay him for that
which diverts him, and he is enriched by his greatest pleasure;
nor is a general, after a victory, more proud than is a huntsman
who returns with his fox's head.

from THOUGHTS ON HUNTING *1781*

A Huntsman's Place

THOMAS SMITH

That a huntsman should be a bold rider is proved by every check
the hounds come to when he is away; for even when he is present
he will have enough to do to prevent over-riding; but unless he
can ride at head, and see the very spot on which they throw up,
he will be puzzled to know who of those up to apply to, and must

often use his own judgment: in short, the greatest use he can be of, when a good scent, is to prevent men doing mischief: therefore he must have nerve to ride well up, and equal to any man in the kingdom; for, unless he can be forward enough to look men in the face, and request them to hold hard, he may ride behind and call after them till he is hoarse, and they will not turn their heads – probably believing that jealousy alone is the cause, and they go the faster for it: but if he is in his place, none but a madman would do mischief if requested to pull up: even the hard riders from the Universities – that is, if they can stop their horses – will do so.

If a huntsman feels obliged to speak to those who over-ride hounds, it should be *at* them rather than *to* them, thus: 'Hold hard; pray, black horse, hold hard', etc. Few men like to be attacked by name, even when they have done mischief; nor does a huntsman feel comfortable if he has been led to speak sharply in the heat of the chase; for, on second thoughts, he will recollect that it was owing to that ardor which he most likes to see that led them on. A story is told of a good old sportsman who was often annoyed by some men for not acting as he thought right in the field, and the only method he had of correcting them was by taking an opportunity, when the whipper-in was also committing the same fault, of heartily cursing *him* in their presence, finishing with 'I *may* d—n *you*!'

from THE DIARY OF A HUNTSMAN *1840*

The MFH and the Hunting Parson

ANTHONY TROLLOPE

I – THE MFH

Five hundred pounds a day is about the sum which a master should demand for hunting an average country – that is, so many five hundred pounds a year as he may hunt in days in the week. If four days a week be required of him, two thousand a year will be little enough. But as a rule, I think masters are generally supposed to charge only for the advertised days, and to give the bye-days out of their own pocket. Nor must it be thought that the money so subscribed will leave the master free of expense. As I have said before, he should be a rich man. Whatever be the subscription paid to him, he must go beyond it – very much beyond it – or there will grow up against him a feeling that he is mean, and that feeling will rob him of all his comfort. Hunting men in England wish to pay for their own amusement; but they desire that more shall be spent than they pay. And in this there is a rough justice – that roughness of justice which pervades our English institutions. To a master of hounds is given a place of great influence, and into his hands is confided an authority of the possession which among his fellow-sportsmen is very pleasant to him. For this he is expected to pay and he does pay for it. A Lord Mayor is, I take it, much in the same category. He has his salary as Lord Mayor, but if he do not spend more than that on his office he becomes a byword for stinginess among Lord Mayors. To be Lord Mayor is his whistle, and he pays for it.

For myself, if I found myself called upon to pay for one whistle or another, I would sooner be a master of hounds than a Lord Mayor. The power is certainly more perfect, and the situation, I think, more splendid. The master of hounds has no aldermen, no common council, no liverymen. As long as he fairly performs his part of the compact, he is altogether without control. He is not unlike the captain of a man-of-war; but, unlike the captain of a man-of-war, he carries no sailing orders. He is free to go where he lists, and is hardly expected to tell anyone whither he goeth. He is enveloped in mystery which, to the young, adds greatly to his grandeur; and he is one of those who in spite of the democratic tenderness of the age, may still be said to go about as a king among men. No one contradicts him. No one speaks evil of him to his face; and men tremble when they have whispered anything of some half-drawn covert, of some unstopped earth, some fox that should not have escaped, and, looking round, see that the master is within earshot. He is flattered, too, if that be of any avail to him. How he is flattered! What may be done in this way to Lord Mayors by common councilmen who like Mansion-House crumbs, I do not know; but kennel crumbs must be very sweet to a large class of sportsmen. Indeed, they are so sweet that almost every man will condescend to flatter the master of hounds. And ladies too – all the pretty girls delight to be spoken to by the master! He needs no introduction, but is free to sip all the sweets that come. Who will not kiss the toe of his boots, or refuse to be blessed by the sunshine of his smile?

But there are heavy duties, deep responsibilities, and much true heart-felt anxiety to stand as make-weight against all these sweets. The master of hounds, even though he take no part in the actual work of hunting his own pack, has always his hands full of work. He is always learning, and always called upon to act on his own knowledge suddenly. A Lord Mayor may sit at the Mansion House, I think, without knowing much of the law. He may do so without discovery of his ignorance. But the master of hounds who does not know his business would take a paper longer than this, and the present writer by no means considers himself equal to such a task. But it is multifarious, and demands a special intellect for itself. The master should have an eye like an eagle's, an ear like a thief's, and a heart like a dog's that can be either soft or ruthless as occasion may require. How he should love his foxes, and with what pertinacity he should kill them! How he should rejoice when his skill has assisted in giving the choice of men of his hunt a run that they can remember for six years! And how heavy should be his heart within him when he trudges home with them, weary after a blank day, to the misery of which his incompetency has, perhaps, contributed! A master of hounds should be an anxious man; so anxious that that privilege of talking to pretty girls should be of little service to him.

II – THE HUNTING PARSON

For myself I own that I like the hunting parson. I generally find him to be about the most pleasant man in the field, with the most to say for himself, whether the talk be of hunting, politics, of literature, or of the country. He is never a hunting man unalloyed, unadulterated, and unmixed – a class of man which is perhaps of all classes the most tedious and heavy in hand. The tallow-chandler who can talk only of candles, or the barrister who can talk only of his briefs, is very bad; but the hunting man who can only talk of his runs is, I think, worse even than the unadulterated tallow-chandler, or the barrister unmixed. Let me pause for a moment here to beg young sportsmen not to fall into this terrible mistake. Such bores in the field are, alas, too common; but the hunting parson never sins after that fashion. Though a keen sportsman, he is something else besides a sportsman, and for that reason, if for no other, is always a welcome addition to the crowd.

But still I confess that the hunting parson seems to have made a mistake. He is kicking against the pricks, and running counter to that section of the world which should be his section. He is making himself to stink in the nostrils of his bishop, and is becoming a stumbling block, and a rock of offence to his brethren. It is bootless for him to argue, as I have here argued, that his amusement is in itself innocent, and that some open-air recreation is necessary to him. Grant him that the bishops and old ladies are wrong and that he is right in principle, and still he will not be justified. Whatever may be our walk of life, no man can walk well who does not walk with the esteem of his fellows. Now those little walks by the covert sides – those pleasant little walks of which I am writing – are not, unfortunately, held to be estimable, or good for themselves, by English clergymen in general.

The Man Who Hunts and Never Jumps

ANTHONY TROLLOPE

The British public who do not hunt believe too much in the jumping of those who do. It is thought by many among the laity that the hunting man is always in the air, making clear flights over five-barred gates, six foot walls, and double posts and rails – none of which would the average hunting man any more think of riding than he would at a small house. We used to hear much of the Galway Blazers, and it was supposed that in County Galway a stiff built wall six feet high was the sort of thing that you customarily met from field to field when hunting in that comfortable country. Such little impediments were the ordinary food of a real Blazer, who was supposed to add another foot of stonework and a sod of turf when desirous of making himself conspicuous in his moments of splendid ambition. Twenty years ago I rode in Galway now and then, and I found six foot walls all shorn of their glory, and that men whose necks were of any value to themselves were very anxious to have some preliminary knowledge of the nature of the fabric – whether for instance it might be solid or built of loose stones – before they trusted themselves to encounter a wall of four feet and a half. And here, in England, history, that nursing mother of fiction, has given hunting men honours which they have never fairly earned. The traditional five-barred gate is, as a rule, used by hunting men as it was intended to be used by the world at large; that is to say, they open it; and the double posts and rails which look so very pretty in sporting pictures, are thought to be very ugly things whenever an idea of riding at them presents itself. It is well that mothers should know – mothers full of fear of their boys who are beginning – that the necessary jumping of the hunting field is not after all of so very tremendous a nature; and it may be well also to explain to them and to others that many men hunt with great satisfaction to themselves who never by any chance commit themselves to the peril of a jump, either big or little.

And there is much excellent good sense in the mode of riding adopted by such gentlemen. Some men ride for hunting, some for jumping, and some for exercise – some no doubt, for all three of these things. Given a man with a desire for the latter, no taste for the second, and some partiality for the first, and he cannot do better than ride in the manner I am describing. He may be sure that he will not find himself alone; and he may be sure also that he will incur none of the ridicule which the non-hunting man is disposed to think must be attached to such a pursuit. But the man who hunts and never jumps – who deliberately makes up his mind that he will amuse himself after a fashion – must always remember his resolve, and be true to the conduct which he has laid down for himself. He must not jump at all. He must not jump a little, when some spurt or spirit may move him, or he will infallibly find himself in trouble. There was an old Duke of Beaufort who was a keen and practical sportsman, a master of hounds and a known Nimrod on the face of the earth; but he was a man who hunted and never jumped. His experience was perfect, and he was always true to resolution. Nothing ever tempted him to cross the smallest fence. He used to say of his neighbour, who was not so constant, 'Jones is an ass. Look at him now. There he is, and he can't get out. Jones doesn't like jumping, but he jumps a little, and I see him pounded one day. I never jump at all, and I'm always free to go where I like.' The Duke was certainly right, and Jones was certainly wrong. To get into a field, and then to have no way of getting out, is very uncomfortable. As long as you are on the road you have a way open before you to every spot on the world's surface – open, or capable of being opened; or even if incapable of being opened, not positively detrimental to you as long as you are on the right side. But that feeling of a prison under the open air is very terrible, and is rendered almost agonizing by the prisoner's consciousness that his position is the result of his own imprudent temerity – of an audacity which falls short of any efficacious purpose. When hounds are running, the hunting man should always, at any rate, be able to ride on – to ride in some direction, even though it be in the wrong direction. He can then flatter himself that he is riding wide and making a line for himself. But to be entrapped into a field without any power of getting out of it; to see the red backs of the forward men becoming smaller and smaller in the distance, till the last speck disappears over some hedge; to see the fence before you and know that it is too much for you; to ride round and round in an agony of despair which is by no means mute, and at last to give sixpence to some boy to conduct you back into the road; that is wretched – that is real unhappiness. I am, therefore, very persistent in my advice to the man who purposes to hunt without jumping. Let him not jump at all. To jump, but only jump a little, is fatal. Let him think of Jones.

The man who hunts and doesn't jump, presuming him not to be a duke or any man as greatly established as a Nimrod, in the hunting world, generally comes out in a black coat and a hat, so that he may not be specially conspicuous in his deviations from the line of running. He began his hunting probably in the search of exercise, but has gradually come to add a peculiar amusement to that pursuit; and of a certain phase of hunting he at last learns more than most of those who ride closest to hounds. He becomes wonderfully skilful in surmising the line which a fox may probably take, and in keeping himself upon the roads parallel to the ruck of the horsemen. He is studious of the wind, and knows to a point of the compass whence it is blowing. He is intimately conversant with every covert in the country; and, beyond this, is acquainted with every earth in which foxes have had their nurseries, or are likely to locate them. He remembers the drains on the different farms in which the hunted animal may possibly take refuge, and has a memory for rabbit holes. His eye becomes accustomed to distinguish the form of a moving horseman over half a dozen fields; and let him see but a cap of any leading man, and he will know which way to turn himself. His knowledge of the country is correct to marvel. While the man who rides straight is altogether ignorant of his whereabouts and will not even distinguish the woods through which he has ridden scores of times, the man who rides and never jumps always knows where he is with utmost accuracy. Where parish is divided from parish and farm from farm, has been a study to him; and he has learned the purpose of bearing every lane. He is never thrown out, and knows the nearest way from every point to point. If there be a line of gates across from [one] road to another he will use them, but he will commit himself to a line of gates on the land of no farmer who uses padlocks.

As he trots along the road, occasionally breaking into a gallop when he perceives from some sign known to him that the hunt is turning from him, he is generally accompanied by two or three unfortunates who have lost their way and have straggled from the hounds; and to them he is a guide, a philosopher, and a friend. He is good natured for the moment, and patronizes the lost ones. He informs them that they are at last in the right way, and consoles them by assurances that they have lost nothing. 'The fox broke, you know, from the sharp corner of Grandby-Wood,' he says; – 'the only spot that the crowd had left for him. I saw him come out, standing on the bridge by the road. Then he ran up-wind as far as Green's barn.' 'Of course he did,' says one of the unfortunates who thinks he remembers something of a barn in the early part of the performance. 'I was with the first three or four as far as that.' 'There were twenty men before the hounds there,' says our man of the road, who is not without a grain of sarcasm, and can use it when on strong ground. 'Well, he turned there and ran back very near the corner; but he was headed by a sheep dog, luckily, and went to the left across the brook.' 'Ah, that's where I lost them,' says one of the unfortunates. 'I was with them miles beyond that,' says another. 'There were five or six men rode the brook,' continues our philosopher. Who names the four or five, not mentioning the unfortunate who had spoken last as having been among the number. 'Well; then he went across by Ashby Grange, and tried the drain at the back of the farmyard, but Bootle had stopped it. A fox got in there one day last March, and Bootle always stops it since. So he had to go on, and he crossed the turnpike close by Ashby Church. I saw him cross, and the hounds were then five full minutes behind him. He went through Frolic Wood, but he didn't hang a minute, and right up the pastures to Morley Hill.' 'That's where I was thrown out,' says the unfortunate who had boasted before, and who is still disposed to boast a little. But our philosopher assures him that he has not in truth been near Morley Hall; and when the unfortunate one makes an attempt to argue, puts him down thoroughly. 'All I can say is, you couldn't have been there and be here too at this moment. Morley Hall is a mile and a half to our right, and now they're coming round to the Linney. He'll go into the little wood there, and as there isn't so much as a nutshell open for him, they'll kill him there. It'll have been a tidy little thing, but not very fast. I've hardly been out of a trot yet, but we may as well move on now.' Then he breaks into a canter by the side of the road, while the unfortunates, who have been rolling among the heavy ploughed ground in the early part of the day, make vain efforts to ride by his side. They keep him, however, in sight and are comforted; for he is a man with a character, and knows what he is about. He will never be utterly lost, as long as they can remain in his company, they will not be subjected to that dreadful feeling of absolute failure which comes upon an inexperienced sportsman when he finds himself quite alone, and does not know which way to turn himself.

A man will not learn to ride after this fashion in a day, nor yet in a year. Of all fashions of hunting it requires, perhaps, the most patience, the keenest observation, the strongest memory, and the greatest efforts of intellect. But the power, when achieved, has its triumph; it has its respect, and it has its admirers. Our friend, while he was guiding the unfortunates on the road, knew his position, and rode for a while as though he were a chief of men.

He was the chief of men there. He was doing what he knew how to do, and was not failing. He had made no boasts which stern facts would afterwards disprove. And when he rode up slowly to the woodside, having from a distance heard the huntsman's whoop that told him of the fox's fate, he found that he had been right in every particular. No one at that moment knows the line they have all ridden as well as he knows it. But now, among the crowd, when men are turning their horse's heads to the wind, and loud questions are being asked, and false answers are being given, and the ambitious men are congratulating themselves on their deeds, he sits by listening in sardonic silence. 'Twelve miles of ground!' he says to himself, repeating the words of some valiant youngster; 'If it's eight, I'll eat it.' And then when he hears – for he is all ear and eye – when he hears a slight boast from one of the unfortunate's companions, a first small blast of the trumpet which will become loud anon if it be not checked, he smiles inwardly, and moralizes on the weakness of human nature. But the man who never jumps is not usually of a benevolent nature, and it is almost certain that he will make a little story against the boaster.

Such is the amusement of the man who rides and never jumps. Attached to every hunt there will always be one or two such men. Their evidence is generally reliable; their knowledge of the country is not doubted; they seldom come to any severe trouble; and have usually made for themselves a very wide circle of hunting acquaintances by whom they are quietly respected. But I think that men regard them as they do the chaplain on board a man-of-war, or as they would regard a herald on a field of battle. When men are assembled for fighting, the man who notoriously does not fight must feel himself to be somewhat lower than his brethren around him, and must be so esteemed by others.

the foregoing pieces by Trollope all appeared originally in the Pall Mall Gazette. Reprinted in
HUNTING SKETCHES *1865*

Vintage Years

GEORGE OSBALDESTON

In a former part of this narrative I promised my readers to furnish them with an account of the many incidents, accidents, etc., which happened to me during my hunting the Quorn country and also Northamptonshire; and the cause of my selling the hounds, all of which I bred myself, to Sir B[ellingham] Graham; which pledge I will now redeem as far as my treacherous memory will permit. I must, in the first place, state that during the thirty-five years I was Master I hunted the hounds myself; and in consequence could not keep the field in such order as otherwise I might have done. It is a most difficult thing to control a field; in many instances I have been obliged in self-defence to stop the hounds; but this produced a good effect only for a few weeks, and in the end was perfectly useless.

A very large field, perhaps 300, was out one day in the neighbourhood of Billesdon Coplow, where we found; and the fox after running three-quarters of a mile went to ground in a drain in a very large grass field near Quenby Hall. Having before had a taste of their disorderly proceedings I foresaw what was likely to happen, and cautioned the field most particularly not to ride after the fox; for if they did I should stop the hounds immediately. They promised to let the hounds get fairly away, and we proceeded to get the fox out. Within a quarter of an hour we bolted him; and as soon as he was on his legs the whole crowd galloped after him, and did not pull up until he was lost to sight. I and my two whippers-in were standing about 200 yards from the drain, and when the field broke away after the fox we could not prevent the hounds from following, with the result that the pack got mingled with the 300 horsemen, never saw the fox, nor, of course, hunted him a yard.

They ran in this manner for nearly half a mile, when Reynard escaped the view of the field; and all, horsemen and hounds, came to a check. I arrived with the hunt servants at this juncture and at once ordered them to turn the hounds. I blew my horn and trotted away towards the kennels, at the same time telling those who followed us that I was keeping my word, as they would find I always should do. Perhaps never in the annals of fox-hunting has so wild and unsportsmanlike a proceeding been witnessed; it was an everlasting disgrace to the field of that day. How any gentlemen calling themselves sportsmen could be guilty of such conduct I cannot imagine, particularly after pledging their word to me, as they had done, not to behave as they did. That the green-eyed monster got the better of their reason is the best excuse that can be urged in their defence.

Another instance of such conduct occurred which obliged me to have recourse to the same disagreeable expedient, but it was not of the same character, being a declaration of defiance of the Master's authority. We found in the neighbourhood of Rolleston, and came away with a tremendous scent. Leaving Quenby Hall to the left, the fox ran straight for Ashby Pastures. About a mile before you reach the Pastures there is a brook at the end of a very large grass field; the hounds had never come to a check up to this point, and had run so hard that out of a very large field only Lord Plymouth, Mr Blunt, and myself were with them, the rest being completely beaten. We had to jump a low rail into the field before mentioned; and one hound, from what cause I don't know, separated from the pack and [I] was in the act of taking it to join the rest when Mr Blunt rode over him. I had only just before particularly warned him against doing this, telling him if he did so I should stop hounds. In the very act of doing it he cried 'D— the hounds!' and snapping his fingers at me, added, 'You can't stop them!'

I answered that I would soon show him whether I could or not, and galloping as fast as my horse could go, headed them just before they reached the brook and stopped them. Lord Plymouth came up and entreated me to let them hunt the fox, as he must die soon, and this was the most glorious run he had ever seen in his life and over the best country. I told him I was always as good as my word, and reminded him of the specimen of this I gave when the field rode after the fox near Quenby Hall. I said it certainly distressed me exceedingly to act as I did, but to be defied and have my authority flouted, by one of the most reckless of my field, was sufficient reason to take such strong measures. It is right to say that when we met next day, in the

Harborough country, Blunt came up to me and made a most ample apology. We were always very good friends both before and after this unfortunate occurrence. Men get excited in the heat of a good thing with hounds.

Blunt used to come and shoot with me in Yorkshire. He was a very good shot, but could not walk, being lame from a wound in the ankle; but he rode well to hounds. He was a very gentlemanly man and very amusing. He married when he was about forty and lived in Sussex till his death, which occurred a few years after his marriage.

I forgot to mention the name of the horse I was riding that day I stopped hounds near the brook; it was Assheton. The only reason why I do so is that he was the very best I ever possessed or heard of. He was a bay without white, about 15.1½, the most perfect model I ever saw; he had all the appearance of being thoroughbred, but I could never trace his pedigree. Mr Cracroft, who lived and hunted in the Spilsby country in Lincolnshire, was the first person who hunted him. Mr Assheton Smith hunted the Lincolnshire at that time. They had a most tremendous day, changing foxes, until only Mr Smith and Mr Cracroft remained when hounds were stopped. Mr Smith completely tired two horses, but Assheton was not even then beaten, and I believe Mr Cracroft assisted Mr Smith in stopping the hounds. His fame soon spread and was not long in reaching Leicestershire. The Rev. John Empson, who lived about five miles from Melton, went into Lincolnshire and bought the horse. Mr Empson was a most ardent admirer of Mr Thomas Assheton Smith – it almost amounted to an infatuation; and in compliment to him he christened the horse Assheton. Mr Empson rode well on a very quiet, perfect hunter, but Assheton frightened him because he pulled and was determined to go. He sold him to me for £130 or £140.

I had a very excellent whipper-in by the name of Burton, who afterwards hunted the hounds when Lord Southampton had the Quorn country [1827–31]. He was a good rider and lighter than me; he rode Assheton two seasons and I think I rode him three; and during the five seasons he never gave either of us a fall. In consequence of a most serious accident which obliged me to resign the Quorn for two seasons, I hunted part of Suffolk

[1822-3] not above ten miles from Newmarket for one season. We had a most extraordinary run in that plough country, a run never excelled in any. Hounds ran one hour and 35 minutes without the shadow of a check, and ran into the fox in the middle of a field. Nobody was with them for the last 20 minutes but Burton on Assheton, and he told me the horse was not tired at all.

On my return to the Quorn, which took place the following season [1823-4], I determined to ride Assheton myself. I communicated my intention to Burton, but he endeavoured to dissuade me from it, saying he was too wild and random a horse to suit me. I told him that he had ridden the horse for two years and had never had a fall with him, and I should certainly try the experiment. I did so; and at the end of the run I smilingly said to Burton: 'You will never ride him again while you live with me except when I am not out with the hounds'.

Soon after this we met at Houghton-on-the-Hill, found in the neighbourhood and had a pretty good run for one hour and 20 minutes. It was not a fast one, but sufficiently so to take a good deal of the steel out of some of the nags. Sir Harry Goodricke and Mr Holyoake amongst a large field were out, and they came up and asked me to draw the Coplow. I told them there was a rattling fox there, and as it did not appear to be a real scenting day it was a pity to disturb the covert as we could not expect to vanquish so formidable an enemy. However, I was so pressed by them that I yielded, and we found my friend. We had the bitch pack out, and they went away over Newton Hills, pointing for Tilton Wood at first; then they bore to the left and never checked till they ran the fox to ground in Ranksborough Gorse in Lord Lonsdale's country near Oakham.

I rode Assheton all day. Up to the time we marked to ground all were beaten but Assheton and the second horses ridden by Sir H. Goodricke and Mr Holyoake. When hounds marked to ground a fresh fox went away, and the body of the pack went after him, a few couples only remaining at the earth. The run was 40 minutes, but the severity of the pace and the country beat all but the three horses above mentioned. We followed the pack for four or five miles, and knowing that it was a fresh fox and we had not a chance of killing him I determined to stop the hounds as soon as I could. Luckily they came to a check at the end of that distance, and I actually stopped them on Assheton; and though perhaps few foxhunters will believe me, I declare he was not beaten even then! Sir Harry Goodricke's and Mr Holyoake's second horses were not so fresh as mine.

I took the hounds home to Quorn afterwards, 21 miles; we were obliged to pass through Melton, and there I got some gruel for Assheton, and some capital refreshment for myself.

That run from the Coplow was often discussed in Melton; it was allowed to be the best thing they had seen, taking the pace and the severity of the country and the beauty of it into consideration; and perhaps if you picked the cream of Leicestershire you could not have surpassed it.

J. E. Ferneley, a great animal and portrait painter, resided at Melton, and he painted a picture for me in commemoration of Assheton's performance on that day. In it there are also portraits of many of the most celebrated riders of that time, and portraits also of all the hounds which composed the pack on the occasion.

Mr Holyoake had a beautiful thoroughbred grey horse, for which he asked £800 or £1,000; it was equal to 14 stone, and being considered quite the best horse in Leicestershire, his owner was open to run him against any other in England over the country. Assheton's extraordinary powers of endurance were reviewed, and Holyoake, jealous perhaps of the praise bestowed on him, said he believed he had a better horse for a light weight, though not capable of carrying a man of any size, referring to Baronet, the grey I have named. I said I would run a horse against Baronet for a thousand, ten miles over the country, carrying 12 stone each. He answered that he did not call 12 stone a high weight, and I then offered to make the match at 13 stone each; but he declined.

I had another horse which I bought of Mason, who was then a dealer at Stilton (the father of the present steeple-chase rider). He called him Shamrock, but how he was bred I don't know. He was nearly as good as Assheton, but I don't think would have gone so long – I never saw one that could – but as I never rode him on a day when my mount was severely tried it is impossible to be certain. He was a beautiful chestnut, about 15.2½, a most perfect snaffle-bridle horse. No man ever possessed a more perfect hunter. I remember jumping him over a fence on the other side of which was a cross-ditch. Seeing that he most likely must fall, Shamrock opened his fore-legs so wide that he bestrode it. Not many horses would have had the sense or presence of mind to thus save themselves.

When I commenced hunting the Quorn country I did so without any subscription, and continued to do so for a few years; then, finding the expense amounted to more than I could afford, I applied for a subscription, which I obtained – I may be pardoned for mentioning that I saved the country perhaps £500 per annum by hunting the hounds myself. Mr Assheton Smith and other Masters had received a subscription also.

One of the greatest difficulties to be contended with in the Quorn country (other than the Meltonian practice of riding over the hounds and heading foxes!) was the behaviour of the stocking-makers and weavers, who used to assemble in crowds at the covert-side. It seemed impossible to keep them together in the right place in order to let the fox go away. At first we could not manage them at all; we tried persuasion and kind words, without any success. Then we tried force; but being totally unsupported by any of the Meltonians that method also failed. At last we had recourse to bribery; we used to give every village two sovereigns a year for drink, and this plan had a far better effect, though on occasions the people were still unruly.

Another exceedingly vexatious habit these people had was their Sunday pastime of collecting terriers and curs to hunt our coverts. I frequently sent my two whippers-in, accompanied by local persons who knew the intruders, to warn them that hunting with dogs on Sunday was an offence punishable by fine, and they might even get into prison. This served to deter a good many, and after a time only a few of the more hardened spirits attempted it. Some bad feeling remained, however, and in the end resulted in a fight between myself, one of my whippers-in and a little man who lived in the neighbourhood on the one side, and the stocking-makers on the other; and the fight ended in a general row. We came off victorious, but it was a wonder we were not nearly killed.

The affair occurred in a village called Sileby, which was full of stocking-makers, and only three miles from Quorn. We met annually on the first Monday in November at Kirby Gate, which is two miles or a little more from Melton Mowbray, the celebrated resort of the wild Meltonian, and on the turnpike road to Leicester. We used always to draw Cream Lodge Gorse, near Ashby Pastures, a famous covert; we only cub-hunted the coverts in the open country once, and then only those which we knew held a litter of foxes.

It was the case here; a large field was out, and very wild and unruly; also the foxes were young: these untried circumstances destroyed all chance of a run and we had very little sport. I almost always took the hounds home myself, and I did so in this instance. Of course, I was very much annoyed at the day's doings and not in a very amiable temper.

As we frequently ran the foxes to ground in drains, almost every field in Leicestershire being hollow-drained, we always took a terrier with us and left him shut up in some place as conveniently situated for the coverts we intended to draw as we could judge. This precaution was necessary because some of the mad-headed Meltonians would certainly have ridden over the little unfortunate animal if he had run with the hounds. On this occasion I had sent my second whipper-in for the terrier, the place where we had left him being some distance out of our road to Quorn; in consequence, my only companions were my first whipper-in, Stevens, and the little man I have mentioned – I forget his name. Sileby was in our road home; and soon after we entered the village two men with a sort of bulldog came out of a public house and began kicking and striking the hounds. They lamed one or two of them. I immediately said: 'What right have you to kick the hounds. I'll give you something you won't like if you repeat that game!' One of them answered with abuse, saying he would knock me off my horse. I had a hunting whip made of cane, the butt not at all heavy, only sufficient to open a gate, which was fortunate, as the sequel will show. The man came round to me, took hold of my bridle and seized my leg, meaning to pull me off. I allowed him to do so because I thus had a better purchase to stand up and hit him over the head. Notwithstanding my whip was rather light, I hit him so hard two or three times that I cut his hat open and his head bled a good deal. Finding that he had the worst of it and could not get me off he bolted.

Whilst the fellow was attacking me his companion attacked Stevens, wrenched his whip away, and holding it with both hands struck at Stevens' head. He missed his mark but knocked one of the horses' eyes clean out, so that nothing remained but the empty socket. Had my whip been furnished with a knob as heavy as Stevens' I might have killed my antagonist; Stevens' would knock off any padlock. As soon as the poor horse lost his eye he began neighing and plunging to such an extent that his assailant bolted after his friend. We immediately gave chase, and saw the two run into another public house. By this time 40 or 50 stocking-makers had collected and began abusing us. Stevens jumped off his horse, and giving it to the little man to hold, rushed into the public house after the two, meaning to find out who they were.

My horse was rather shy and seemed afraid of the people, but after a touch of the spurs he would have gone at anything. One or two of the blackguards talked of attacking me, and one came too close. I rode at him and knocked him end over end. While these encounters were going on the hounds were sitting looking at us; but no further attempt was made to ill-use them. I have often thought since that we were very lucky to have come off as well as we did; had the whole mob joined in the attack upon us we might have been killed.

As soon as Stevens, having failed in his errand, came out of the public house, I addressed the crowd in nearly the following words: 'I rather think you have mistaken me for one of my whippers-in. I am the Master of the Hounds, and you must know that I live at Quorn. If any two of you will come to Quorn to-morrow morning about eleven o'clock, and will identify the two ruffians who assaulted us, and will swear to them, I will give you five pounds.' (The mistake might easily arise as I wore a cap.)

I did not expect any of them would come, but two men made their appearance next morning and told me who the fellows were. I consulted a gentleman by the name of Craddock, a solicitor who hunted constantly with us, and also collected the subscriptions and paid the rents of the coverts and expenses of earth-stopping; but we did not agree as to the best mode of proceeding against our assailants. I was for endeavouring to obtain redress for the damage done to the horse; he was for prosecuting them for a violent assault; and considering his judgment better than mine I gave way. The men were arrested and tried at Quarter Sessions; the two informants kept their word to me and swore to the prisoners' identity; and on conviction each was sentenced to six months' imprisonment and hard labour. This had a good effect which lasted for a considerable time. One of the men convicted was a carpenter and a desperate character who was afterwards transported for attempting the life of a constable in the execution of his duty.

Near the close of my career in Leicestershire we had another row of a different kind. It happened in the Harborough country, and our opponents were very much of the same character as the Sileby stocking-makers. We had had only a short burst of about a quarter of an hour when the fox went to ground in Hallaton Bottoms; as we did not know where to find another fox, and the one which had gone to ground could not have been tired, we determined to get him out, particularly as the drain was only a short one. About twenty stocking-makers and similar people collected and assisted the second whipper-in to get the fox out; and after 20 minutes' work they bagged him, having a sack in their possession. We turned him down and gave him two fields start, but I think he must have been hurt in the process of getting him out of the drain, for he could not run and hounds ran into him in less than a mile.

The terrier we put into the drain had remained there, and my whipper-in hearing him at bay, thought there must be another fox; so, having killed the one we went back. Before we reached the spot, however, we learned that it was a badger the terrier had bayed; and when we arrived the men had got him out and put him into their sack. We had some young terriers at home and wanted the badger to try them with; and as the fellows had been liberally paid for their help in getting out the fox I felt that we were entitled to claim the badger; so I asked the men to give it to my whipper-in. They refused and cursed us freely. Sebright, my first whipper-in, got off his horse and tried civil persuasion, whereupon one of the men knocked him down. That made an end of the endeavours to negociate, and determined me to have the badger. As soon as Sebright had picked himself up I called

him and the second whipper-in and told them to remount.
When they had done so I bade them keep their reins tight so
that they could not be caught hold of, and we would charge the
men in line.

The gang were moving off by this time and were about 50 yards
away. We put our horses into a gallop and were upon them before
they guessed our intention. Taken by surprise they scattered and
ran in different directions, but we knocked several of them down
before they could get away. The man who carried the badger ran
as well as he could for his load, towards a thick gorse covert,
thinking we could not follow. I had kept my eye upon him and
soon caught him up in the covert. He dropped the sack and
seized hold of my bridle. I rose in my stirrups and hit him on
the hands with the butt end of my whip, which made him quickly
let go. Then I gave him a few hard knocks with my fist and drove
him off. The whipper-in came at my call and took the badger,
while the men from a respectable distance swore at us, saying
they would kill all the foxes and uttered other threats. The covert
belonged to the Rev. Mr Bewick, who frequently hunted with us;
he was a good friend to foxhunting, and was also a magistrate;
so I told the men I should report their threats to him.

No attempt was made to destroy the foxes; we always found
when we drew that covert as we had done before the row.

Two other incidents may be worth recording. Near Ashby
Pastures an old crusty, cross-grained farmer occupied a few fields
close to the covert. He was always grumbling, though we scarcely
ever crossed one of them once in a year. He never discarded us
and we never contemplated that he would resort to such dis-
graceful means of revenge. Cream Lodge Gorse was not above a
mile from his land; a most celebrated covert and a certain find.
He put poison in and about it, but of course, we were perfectly
ignorant of this. He knew the day we should draw it, so that the
poison could not have lost any of its power. We found as usual and
went away, but whether we had a good run or not I don't remember. However, in a few hours after reaching Quorn, my kennel
huntsman came to me in the evening and said, 'Sir, three couples
of the hounds which were out to-day are very ill indeed and I am
afraid will die'.

Of course I was very much annoyed; we applied every remedy

we could think of, but two died in a few hours after his announcement, being very much convulsed. Their appearance created suspicion and I sent for the doctor; he opened them and said they had been poisoned. By his treatment, however, we saved the others. Two more which were among the pack had not returned home, and we were certain then that they had shared the same fate. I sent one of my men to see if he could discover the lost ones in or about Cream Lodge Gorse, and he did. One was dead close to it and the other a few fields off, so I suppose the poor creature had struggled as long as it could to follow the pack.

There was a very gallant colonel who had distinguished himself in many actions as a cavalry officer and constantly hunted with my hounds. Notwithstanding the diabolical conduct of the old farmer, we had the courage to draw the covert some time afterwards again. It so happened that the colonel and I were obliged to cross one of his fields with several others. There was a flight of rails into it, and the hounds running very hard at the time, there was no time for reflection. To our great dismay and surprise we saw at some distance before we reached them old 'Cerberus' with a pitchfork in his hand and another man armed with a similar weapon standing on the opposite side of the rails, ready to receive us. The colonel said, 'Charge them in line!' which, although it appeared a most dangerous experiment, we did; and most miraculously, after knocking our two antagonists over we galloped on without receiving any injury. I have often thought since what an extraordinary escape we had.

Through the intervention of several influential farmers adjoining old 'Cerberus's' land all hatred, malice and uncharitableness ceased, and we hunted in future without any molestation.

Another remarkable occurrence happened to us in the same neighbourhood, but not in the same direction. A very sporting farmer, one of those who had assisted in the pacification of old 'Cerberus' and farmed a large tract of land, met us at a village within two miles of Ashby Pastures, the advertised place of meeting, but the name I forget. Being only four miles from Melton, and a favourite part of the country, a large field assembled. The farmer came up to me and said, 'I'be got a fox lying asleep in one of my stubble field; you are sure to find him.' I answered, 'Oh, he must be gone long before now', and he said he was sure the fox was not, as he had placed his workmen all round the field so they must see whether he was gone or not.

As the field was two miles out of our road to the covert we intended drawing we hesitated; but at last decided to go with him. Before we reached it, however, we were certain the fox was there, because the men were still watching. The farmer knowing the exact *lair*, if you may so call it, whipped him up like a hare when coursing. Unfortunately, the scent was bad and we had only a moderate run with him, but strange to say, he ran straight for the very covert we intended drawing.

from SQUIRE OSBALDESTON: HIS AUTOBIOGRAPHY
1856–62 (*first published 1926*)

Dreams of a Run with the Pytchley

G. J. WHYTE MELVILLE

We know every yard of the country, every field and every fence – though we can practise it no longer, we *think* we know every move in the game. We fancy ourselves astride of a good horse by the side of Jack Woodcock as he views the fox away from the lower corner of the gorse. What a long, wiry, tough-looking animal it is, with a white tag to that handsome brush, which, as he steals across the neighbouring pasture, he whisks in derision, as much as to say, 'Gallop away, my fine fellows! according to your wont; hurry and hustle, and jump and splutter! The harder you ride the better for me!'

'Tally-ho!' shouts our friend Jack, erect in his stirrups. 'Twang' goes Charles Payne's horn from the middle of the gorse. Already the owner of the covert is coming best pace round the corner. Trust him not to lose his start, and to make good use of it when he has got it. In twos and threes the hounds are pouring through the boundary fence; ten or twelve couple are settling to the scent; the rest, with ears erect, are flying to the cry. Now they stoop together with collected energy, and drive along over the grass in all the mute ecstasy of *pace*. A burst such as this is pastime for the gods!

It sobers our imaginary steed, our pen and ink Pegasus; he drops quietly to his bridle, a turn in our favour enables us to pull him into a trot, and to look about us. Seven or eight men are in the same field with the hounds; half a dozen stiff fences and a couple of miles of grass have shaken off the larger portion of the field, but they are even now coming through a bridle gate not far distant in the rear, and should a check unfortunately occur at this critical moment, they will be up in plenty of time to do lots of mischief still. But no; the pack is streaming on. 'Forward,' says Charles Payne, cramming his horn into its case, and gathering his horse for an 'oxer'. 'Forward!' echoes Mr Villiers, 'doubling' it neatly on his right. 'Forward!' adds Mr Cust, cracking the far rail as he swings over the obstacle in his stride. 'Line!' shouts a Meltonian at an unfortunate aspirant whose horse is swerving to the thickest place in the fence. 'Serve him right!' remarks the Meltonian to himself, landing safely in the next field, while the aspirant rolls headlong to the earth. Jack Woodcock, with an amused smile, slips quietly to the front. Three or four more men, one in a black coat, enter the field at different points; that quiet gentleman *over*, not *through* the gate. A loose horse with streaming reins gallops wildly after the chase; and the hounds with a burning scent are pointing straight for Naseby Field.

And now every man hugs his trusty hunter by the head, and spares his energies as much as possible ere he encounters the yielding soil of that classic ground. Many a tired horse has Naseby Field to answer for, from the thundering battle steeds of the Cavaliers, led by hot Prince Rupert, to the panting thoroughbreds of Jersey and Allix, and Cooke and Knightley, and the heroes of fifty years ago, who urged the mimic war over that eventful plain. Ay, down to our own time, when, although the plough has passed over its marshy surface, and draining and high farming have given secure foothold to man and beast, many a sobbing steed and dejected rider can still bear witness to the exhaustive properties of that black adhesive soil, many a dirty coat and stationary hunter rues the noble impulse that *would* follow the fleeting pack over such a country as this after a three-days' rain.

Some of them begin to hope that we may have entered the thick holding covert of Naseby Thorns, and that the conclusion of so rapid a burst may save their own and their horse's credit. But a countryman on the opposite side of the hill is holloaing as if his throat must crack. Our fox is forward still; he has not a notion of entering the covert, warmed as he is by the merry pace of the last mile or so.

'No occasion to lift them, Charles,' observed Mr Villiers, as he lends an ear to the far-off countryman, and points to the streaming pack wheeling with every turn of the scent, like pigeons on the wing.

'Couldn't get near enough if there was. Come up, horse!' mutters Charles in reply, as he bores through a black close-cut hedge, sinking up to the hocks on the taking-off side. There is no chance of a check now; and as the professed jester of the Hunt remarks, 'If he don't stop at Tally-ho, he may go on to Texas!'

The field, that enterprising body, whose self-dependence is so touchingly illustrated at every sign-post, are already somewhat hopelessly behindhand and considerably puzzled by the coincidence of two safe practicable lanes, leading equally in the direction of the line of chase. It divides accordingly into two hurrying columns, neither of which will in all probability see a hound again to-day.

So, 'on we go again', leaving 'Tally-ho Gorse' to the left, and up the hill for Hazelbeech, threading the fine old trees that tower upon its heights, and pointing ever onwards for the wide grassy vale of the Cottesbrooke, spread out like a panorama before us, shut in by wooded hills, and dotted with fine old standard trees, and smiling beauteous and peaceful in the chequered light of a February sun.

Thank Heaven! a check at last. Pegasus was beginning to want it sadly. He struck that top-rail uncommonly hard, and has dropped his hind legs in the last two consecutive ditches. There are still some half-dozen men with the hounds, but their horses look as if they had had nearly enough, we are inclined to believe one or two of the riders are beginning to wish it was over. The country for miles back is dotted with equestrians of every rank and every hue. . . . Charles Payne opines he cannot have entered the gorse with so 'warm a jacket', as he phrases it; so he holds his hounds towards the plantations on his right. Fairplay whisks her stern about her sides, and drops a note or two to her comrades as they gather to the line.

'Yo-geote, old lady!' says Charles, in the inexplicable language of a huntsman.

'She always right, that old bitch!' remarks Mr Villiers, who has just turned Olympian's head for an instant to the wind.

'Twang' goes the horn once more, and away score the hounds to 'Pursar's Hills', as if they were fresh out of the kennel, and over the wild grassy pastures below, and up the opposite rise, with untiring energy, leaving the foremost horsemen toiling a field and a half behind them, till a pause and momentary hover in the Welford Road enables Pegasus and his comrades to reach them once more.

It is labour and sorrow now, yet it is sweet and joyous pain. Still, we can hardly call that enjoyment which we wish was over; and most devoutly now do we all hope that we may soon kill this gallant fox before *he* kills our gallant horses. The best blood of Newmarket is but mortal, after all; and Pegasus by this time is going most unreservedly on his own shoulders and his rider's hands.

Down the hill between Creaton and Holywell we make a tolerable fight; but though Olympian clears the brook at the bottom, the rest of us flounder through. We have no false pride now, and do not any of us turn our noses up at gates or gaps, or other friendly egress. Everything is comparative. A country doctor on his fresh hack, meeting us at this period, opines we are going quite slow, but *we know better*; so does Pegasus, so does old Fairplay, so does the fox.

He is not travelling straight now. Up and down yonder hedgerow the pack turn like harriers, and we think we must be very near him. But see: the crows are stooping yonder over a low black object in the distance. 'Tis the hunted fox, pointing straight for the coverts of Althorpe. He will never reach them, for the hounds are now close upon his track, and they run him into the large grass field by Holmby House under the old oak tree.

Our dream is over. Hounds and horses and sportsmen are all gone home. The excitement has evaporated, and left its usual depression of spirits behind. We are left alone – all alone – under the old oak tree. What is life at best but a dream? What is happiness but a dream? – fame, honour, love, ambition? Dreams all. Bitterness is in the waking.

Let us put the clock back a couple of centuries or so, when the old oak was stately and vigorous as now, his branches as spreading, his stem as gnarled and knotted, his growth as majestic. What a lesson to us creatures of a day, in our short span of earthly existence, is instilled by the comparative duration of these vegetable giants! How they outlive us! How their 'winter of discontent', unlike our own, is annually succeeded by a spring of promise! How they spread and tower upwards into heaven, whilst we grovel upon earth. *Væ mihi!* 'twere a weary world, my masters, if there were nothing beyond. A weary world! Let us put the clock back, I say, and dream again.

from HOLMBY HOUSE *1860*

The Greatest Run I Ever Saw

ALFRED E. PEASE

Monday, 9th January 1882. – Hounds met at Ayton, where there was breakfast at the Buck. This was the most extraordinary day I ever had. I rode Queen Mab in the morning till she got an over-reach, when I changed on to Faraway, on which horse I finished the first and was there when Bob Brunton took for fox from the hounds in Hell Gill. . . . The first was a rising run, fairly fast, on the hills between Roseberry Topping and Guisborough Banks, and for forty minutes I rode Faraway up and down the hill, over the moors, and in and out of the gills before we found the second and ever-memorable fox. My brother Jack did not have a second horse, but rode his mount (a blood Irish hunter called Sligo, that cost 250 guineas, and was worth every sixpence of the money) all day, and 'let him have it' in the first run. If we had both started from scratch, he might have taken first honours; as it was, he took the second place in a numerous field, as the sequel will show. I have no doubt that the competition between us ministered to my success, for we generally rode a trifle jealous, but were always best pleased when we could share the honours.

I must for a moment depart from my diary, and say a word about Faraway. He was an Irish thoroughbred, by Fairyland, purchased at Tattersall's in 1880, from the stud of chestnuts sent up by Captain Amcotts, of the 5th Dragoon Guards. He was knocked down to me for fifty guineas. I followed him back to his box, and when I asked the groom why he had only two old shoes on, and what was wrong with the brute, he said, 'Sure, he's a grand hunter and nothing wrong wid him; but ye can't shoe him, clip him, or physic him'. Some years after I found that he had killed a blacksmith just before I bought him; he was quite capable of killing any number of that profession or any other – yet it was not temper, but fear and nerves, that made him dangerous. Fast as the wind, hard as nails, wild as a hawk, and all expressions that fitted him. His little failings were discourtesy – for he met strangers visiting his box on his hind-legs and sparred at them – and buck-jumping, at which he could beat anything I ever saw at the Wild West Show, refusing to let any-one hold his bridle or to stand still while being mounted. One great fault he had – he would not, when hounds ran, allow you to open a gate, always managing, if you did succeed in getting your hand out to reach the catch, to dive under your arm and whip round; while, if anyone opened the gate for you, he went through it like a bullet. But when once I had become familiar with his eccentricities, and abandoned all attempts to differ with his methods and manners, I found him one of the most delightful mounts I ever got across – all life, liberty and whalebone, and impossible to tire. I counted him among my most precious possessions, till after a bad fall he nearly killed me, breaking a few of my bones, and making me literally sit up and spit blood. I then yielded to the solicitations of my friends, and sold him to Mr James Darrell, who told me he had gone well in Leicestershire in other hands.

To return to my diary. After the first fox had been broken up, the brush presented to the Hon. A. Sidney, of Ingleby, the head being attached to my own saddle, we went to Highcliff, where we found the real old Caesar, a great greyhound fox. He broke over the moor at once, and we raced across to Bethel Slack. They drove down Wiley Gill, making the ravine ring again, as far as Slapewath, and then he again took the open for a short time, till he got level with Cass Rock. He then took along Guisborough Banks to where we found him, hounds running hard all the way. He now tried a change of tactics, and took a line that was to astonish all and to make most cry '*capevi*'* breaking on to Guisborough Moor. Hounds followed at a terrific pace, leaving all but the blood horses far behind. By Sleddale he turned west and crossed the great bog. My brother (who was level with, or in front of me here) and I went straight at it, our only chance of getting near the now flying pack being to take everything as it came. In we went, both together, he getting to the other side with a frantic struggle; Faraway, mad with being thus checked, rolled, plunged and kicked, so that I could not recover the reins after I had got on to my feet. After a minute's delay, that seemed an eternity, we bucketed up the hill, while below us were others in the bog, looking in vain for a crossing. When I reached the sky-line nothing could I see or hear. One moment of agonizing anxiety, and I caught a glimpse of my brother's hat, bobbing up as he rose a distant hill. As hard as I could take my horse, I made for this ever-blessed top-hat, and came up with him near the Piggeries, as he rode at the tail of the now almost silent pack, streaming in a file along the moor road. They ran as if it were a drag; it was real business. A mile like this on the straight and then a swift sure swing over the wall to the right, and they were flying over the Kildale Valley – my brother and I, in our glory, taking every wall and fence as it met us. A left turn, and in a minute we were going up the valley to the moors above Baysdale. Here were sheep pastures enclosed with hideous walls, wire on most, and all uphill. Sligo takes a line of barricaded gaps; Faraway goes slap-bang through the first gate, and then takes the timber decently and in order. Another bog, another stream, a few more fences, and then the open moor. How much longer can a horse go this pace? It is too serious a business to speak to each other as we pound down into Baysdale, the hounds getting the better of us. As we cross the enclosures by Baysdale Abbey, the one solitary ploughman in the out-of-the-world valley stops in his work to look at the rare spectacle.

* Mr John Jorrocks' Latin.

'Have you seen him?' I shout.

'Ay! a gurt greyhound fox.'

'How long since?'

'Seven minutes.'

Seven minutes, and hounds racing like this! Will they never check? – no, they never will, and some will never return to the kennel again. The Abbey is passed in one hour and twenty minutes from the find, with only one momentary check, and the mountain beyond looks impossible to negociate. I cross the stream, and begin the ascent with a few tail hounds. They have shot their bolt, and are struggling on with bloodshot eyes, dropping into my wake as I pass them.

'Come on, Jack! You must do it.'

'I can't. Look at Sligo.'

Sligo was standing rocking at the foot of the hill, with his back up and staring eye – he was completely done. Could I get up to that skyline where the last trailing hounds were disappearing? It looked desperate, but Faraway did it, and now I must give him a minute. I had dismounted the last twenty yards to pull him up the top edge of the scar. I could see about eleven couple filing a mile ahead. Absolutely nothing but range after range of barren moors was now in sight! Where was this strange fox bound for? I was astonished to find my horse still full of going, as I got on to the ridge and on to sound ground, and in a few minutes I was alongside the leading seven couple. Hounds now bore along for the Farndale head moors, and one by one the stragglers gave up the chase. Now and then one of these would pull up all at once. I saw the veteran Hermit roll into the heather, where he was found cold and dead next day. Still the leading bunch held on, and Wrangle (from the Oakley) is driving away first, followed closely by Statesman, Bajazet, Rascal and Ringwood. As they crossed a boggy slack, I strained my eyes to see this terrible fox; it was impossible he could stand up many minutes more. I felt for my knife – but the end is not to be yet. The thought uppermost in my mind is, what a wonder my horse is! Is it possible for any animal to survive this? And yet he is going strong. The moors look endless; I can see, even in the fast-deepening dusk, miles of desolation in front.

A turn to the right, and we reach the edge of the hillside above

Ingleby. Down the rocks and the cliff-side dash the now only seven couple, and once more open into cry. The pace on the moor was too great for much speaking. I cannot get down there. I make a despairing effort to cross the bog at the top – I cannot do it. The north wind is blowing a cloud of spray from the dripping bog at the edge of the cliff, and the stars are coming out. I see beyond me an abandoned workman's shanty, and my mind is made up. The door is locked; a good kick and it is open. In the inside there is just room for my horse. The ceiling is low, but so now is his head. I shut the door and run as fast as top-boots will allow along the edge of the cliff to the top of Midnight Crags. Here I hear the hounds still running some hundred of feet below me in the darkness. I labour on, till, exhausted, I sit down above the pass into Bilsdale. I can still hear them occasionally, in spite of the wind howling up the gully, and then all is still. I wait some minutes, then halloo with all my might. They have either killed or run to ground, but wherever it is, I cannot reach them.

Eventually five and a half couples came to me, and I floundered and blundered over the moor to my horse. I had not a match, so as to examine the mouths of the hounds, but, as far as I could judge, they had not killed. I could find no blood – perhaps if they had run into him they had not managed to do more than just kill. I drained my flask and led my horse down the Ingleby incline, reaching at length Ingleby village.

When I got to the inn, to my surprise, there was Bob Brunton, who, having lost all trace of us in Kildale, whither he had tracked us, had ridden on here with Richard Spink of the Bilsdale, where, night over-taking them, they had sought shelter and refreshment. Bob, on seeing me, literally hugged me, and swore I ought to be knighted. We got the hounds bedded in a barn and fed, and my horse gruelled, and then I jogged home – but sleep was banished by aching limbs, and the excitement of the day. All night I saw the whole scene enacted over again. The streaming ten couple always tearing and racing on as if for ever over valley and lonely moor. I felt my horse floundering through the bogs again; myself clambering up and down those gills under the stars – each wall and stream, gate and stile were jumped a dozen times. I could see again the straggling hounds, run out, sitting in the heather, and hear their dismal howling as they realized they were 'done' and 'lost'.

This run was an extraordinarily long one; it cannot be made less than 19 miles, and is more like 21. It was 11 miles from point of find to Ingleby Landslip; but where I think it tops the record is the pace. I believe the whole run to have occupied 1 hour and 45 minutes – 1 hour and 20 minutes to Baysdale, and 25 on to the landslip. I know that it will not be credited by most hunting men, but it must be remembered that it was mostly over open moorland, with few obstacles to check hounds, and, except the solitary ploughman in Baysdale, no sign of humanity all the way. Three hounds died of exhaustion and the other lost ones were only got back by degrees during the week following.

In connection with this run I think the following performance of Bob Brunton's worth recording. He had hunted all day, being at the meet at Ayton some miles from his home, and I found him at Ingleby at night. He remounted after he had attended to the hounds, and rode to Guisborough, say 8 miles, where he looked in at a political meeting which was being held; he rode on the same night to the kennels at Warrenby, 8 miles more, and found the huntsman sitting up disconsolate and refusing to go to bed without his hounds. He started before daybreak (3 am), and, riding the same horse, accompanied the huntsman, Will Nicoll, to Ingleby (16 miles); hence he helped to collect the lost hounds on the moor and in Bilsdale; and the following afternoon I met him, still on the same horse, now more like a gigantic greyhound than anything else, escorting the hounds back to Warrenby from Ingleby (16 miles); and when this was accomplished, he rode home to Marton (7 miles); so that if we put down 40 miles for the long hard day's hunting, we have

To the meet and two long runs, and to Ingleby	40
Ingleby to Guisborough	8
Guisborough to Warrenby	8
Warrenby to Ingleby	16
Collecting hounds	10
Ingleby to Warrenby	16
Warrenby to Marton	7
	105

a total of 105 miles, 65 of which were undoubtedly ridden after the day's hunting by Mr Brunton on the same horse that he had ridden hard (for he was among the hardest riders ever seen in Cleveland) during the longest and severest day the Cleveland hounds have had in my lifetime.

As for the horses, Faraway was at covert side again within three weeks. Sligo, with whom it appeared to be a case for an anxious hour or so, came up to time as well.

from HUNTING REMINISCENCES *1888*

The Badby Wood Run

FRANK FREEMAN
as told to Guy Paget

It was in 1911 in March. That was the year I killed 104 brace of foxes, a record for the Pytchley country. We'd met at Daventry. There had been a lot of rain the night before, but it was a fine but cold morning. It must have been about 12.15, just as I was beginning to fear Badby Wood was blank, that Ted Molyneux, who was my first whip then, holloaed a fox away by the lodge over the Banbury Road. He took the usual line out by Ryton Hill right-hand round Arbury Hill pointing for Staverton. Here a silly fellow holloaed in his face and he turned back for Badby Wood, but could not get through the crowd on the Banbury Road, so ran down beside the hedge towards Byfield where hounds checked. Mr Paget, who lived at Brixworth then, was riding a new horse he could not hold, so he jumped it out of the road on the other side, where he saw Gaylass and Garnish hit off the line down one of those Fawsley doubles.

That Garnish was the best bitch I ever had. Hunt a line on the hardest dusty road, and always in front. Gaylass was her sister by Desperate; they were both almost black with white collars, Garnish never bred anything half so good as herself, but Gaylass did. It was extraordinary how they picked the line through all that crowd on the road. I saw most of the field turn and ride up the road back to Badby Wood as I clapped my hounds over the road. They started to run like hell. The Fawsley doubles are almost unjumpable, and the hand gates delayed the field, which gave the hounds a real chance of settling down, not that they could have been interfered with much that day, they were running that hard.

They just touched Church Wood, but they never stopped for a second, and I am sure they never changed there. Beyond Preston Capes they ran over an easy country into the heart of the Grafton. They only went through a corner of Ashby Bushes. At Adstone Bottom, about a mile or so on, there were a lot of falls – even Lord Annaly had a scramble there and lost his whip – but there was no time to pick it up. Garnish and Gaylass, and a light-coloured bitch called Dimple, I could see were leading, but you could have covered the whole pack with a sheet.

Near here Mr Pat Nickalls and Mr Tweed saw the fox only about four hundred yards ahead of hounds, going straight for the railway, which was crossed by Plumpton Wood, which would be about six miles straight from Arbury Hill. It is a great big wood, half the size of Badby, but the fox ran down the middle ride most of the way. Here I saw Postcript and Fatal turn sharp to the left. I don't think we could have changed there as they never left the line for a moment. They ran on, still going very fast by Woodend, pointing for Wappenham, to the railway straight over the brook. Lord Annaly was the only one to fly it and I heard several fall in, and a lot of horses were too done to face it. I struck it lucky by a ford. There's a bit of a plough near Greens Park, but it did not seem to slow them down. Rarity, Garnish and Gaylass I noticed were still leading.

They left Weedon Bushes on the right and turned right-handed for Aswell Mill, and then turned left after crossing the stream, over some more plough, for what a Grafton gentleman told me was Crown Lands, a huge, great woodland. Just before we got there we ran into a little wood called Priest's Hay, where hounds divided. I was a bit puzzled which lot were right, but I thought I had better trust the hounds who had been leading. Molyneux and Tom Peaker, who were both up, soon stopped the others, but two foxes had gone on and hounds divided again near the allotments below Silverstone village. I at first thought my fox must have turned into Bucknells Wood and asked Mr Paget, who was close to me, to stop the lot which were running between Crown Lands and Bucknells Wood.

Mr Garrard, of Welton, went with him, and they jumped the gate which was wired up into the allotments, but my lot threw up, so I blew my horn, the first time I had used it since re-crossing the Banbury Road, to prevent those gentlemen stopping hounds. I thought all was over when, as I had hoped, the fox did not run on but turned in at the furthest corner of Bucknells Wood, a tremendous great place, bad scenting and full of foxes.

Here Lord Rosebery, Lord Dalmeny he was then, caught a glimpse of a beaten fox with a couple of hounds close behind him. He could not tell me which they were. I got the rest of the pack on to the line, and they carried it right through the wood and out on the Wappenham side. A man from the village told me the couple had hunted up to the hedge by a stream, where they had checked, and I was afraid he must have got in somewhere, which would have been a terrible disappointment to the hounds after such a hunt. I cast round to make sure and returned to the hedge, when I saw Rarity's hackles go up and she dived into the ditch and pinned him. He was a great greyhound of a fox, and had all his teeth – not at all an old fox. He went quite stiff the moment he was dead, and stood up to face the hounds. Molyneux was sure he was the same fox he viewed away from Babdy Wood.

The time was two hours and five minutes from find to kill, a fourteen mile point and about twenty-two miles as hounds ran. I think it was about half-an-hour after entering Bucknells that we killed, which shows how fast the pace had been. If Garnish and Gaylass were the hounds his Lordship saw in the wood they had never left the line for a second. Not a hound was missing.

I am sorry I cannot tell you much about the people. When one is hunting hounds one has no time or thought for anything else. I was luckily on one of the best horses I ever rode, called Starlight, who was quite fresh at the end, as were the two whips', which speaks well for Mr Gibbs, the kennel studsman. Not a single second horse arrived at the kill. They had all waited at Preston Capes.

I remember his Lordship kept the mask and gave Lady Dalmeny the brush, and Mr Tweed, Mrs Borrett, Mr Romer Williams and Captain Elmhirst got the pads. The last two came up from Wapping village just as we killed. I saw Captain Sowerby's little grey lying down in Bucknells Wood, but it recovered.

Lord Annaly ordered hounds home from here.

We had about twenty miles home, and his Lordship told us to go into the Pomfret Arms as we passed through Towcester; but Captain Elmhirst said we would have to stop at his place at Blisworth if we put in at twenty Pomfret Armses.

He rode on and had port and cake waiting for us in the road as we passed; as we were finished Lord Annaly passed us in a cab he had hired in Towcester. There were not many motors cars or telephones in those days.

Mr Tweed rode all the way home with the hounds to Brixworth, where we found some champagne and sandwiches in the feeding house, sent by one of the gentlemen who lived in the village.

I think it was the best day I ever had.

from LIFE OF FRANK FREEMAN *1948*

Will Pope's Last Hunt

DORIAN WILLIAMS

It was on April 8th, 1953, that Will Pope took hounds on for the last time. We had arranged to hold the meet at Leckhampstead, of shire-horse fame, at the home of Leslie Lester, one of Will's oldest and truest friends. It was a fine morning and crowds poured into the village from far and wide – mounted, driving, walking, cycling.

They came from the Old Berkeley, Bicester, Warwickshire, Oakley and Pytchley hunts, as well as from the Grafton – testimony to Pope's popularity and fame; and to say that hospitality flowed at Church Farm is an understatement. It overflowed. The story was told later that when Leslie Lester himself came home in the evening he found bodies of contented and over-contented farmer-pals all over the floor of his dining-room and sitting-room!

Hounds moved off at about mid-day, followed by a great

concourse, mounted and in cars; it was more like Boxing Day. Will Pope's last day had started. How one prayed that it might be a good one. Not finding in the first two draws caused anxiety, but it was not long before a fox was afoot. I could take you now to the exact spot where it got up; just as I could show you exactly where Will jumped out of the road; where he cleared his last fence; where finally, and for the last time, he blew for home. Those of us out that day knew we were present on an historic occasion, and every minute of it printed itself indelibly on our memories.

It was in the rough patch of osiers, scrub and willows on the Buckingham–Stony Stratford road, known as Hyde Lane, that we found. A fox moved at the edge of the water and a moment later Hardiman, the Oakley huntsman, saw it swimming across from the island, with only Warble, one of Pope's favourite bitches, in pursuit. Scent was good, and in no time twenty-two and a half couple had pushed their fox over the main road despite all the traffic, and across the fine strongly fenced grass enclosures to Foxcote.

Swinging right handed, Pope, on Jane, led the way over a handsome piece of timber with a wide, dry ditch in front. It stands there today and is likely to for some time, for it is not the sort of timber that is tackled on ordinary occasions. Across behind Leckhampstead, in and out of the Wicken road, over a hairy old Grafton hedge with a drop that downed half-a-dozen, surprising everyone except Will – but then he knew every blade of grass in the country – left-handed over a gate and up to Park Copse. Twenty minutes, to be compared with anything in the last quarter of a century: with the first twenty minutes of that twelve mile point from Ascote Thorns to Cockley Brakes in 1933, for instance; or the last five miles of the famous hunt from Timms' Gorse to Moreton Pinkney in 1929; or the first leg of the last hunt before the war, when a Grimscote fox was hunted at racing pace to Adstone and with the cavalry charge that followed him from the famous Weedon Equitation school. Compared with them, how very insignificant we must seem.

Interfered with by the over-zealous road followers hounds could now only hunt on more slowly to Wicken Wood, and then out to Lillingstone, where Pope decided to call it a day.

The easy, familiar notes of his battered, rimless horn wafted up to us as he blew finally for home. The company, lingering, sad, gradually departed, and we made our way towards the kennels. I rode beside Will in the midst of the bitches, the vivid spring sunset casting our exaggerated, distorted figures ahead of us.

At this moment I felt suddenly full of emotion. It was unbelievable that after a quarter of a century this was the very last time that Pope would ever ride home with his hounds, through the country that he knew so well, loved so well, that he had in fact almost made his own.

'Good old Billy Pope.' 'There goes our Will.' 'Old Will, he'll never let you down.' 'Wouldn't be the same without our Billy Pope.' The countryside adored him.

What a strange, paradoxical position a huntsman holds in the country in which he hunts. Courted like a prince, feted like a hero, yet always a servant; and servant to whoever the Committee might appoint as Master – octogenarian, grocer, drunkard.

I tried to visualize this moment from his point of view. I tried to say something, but couldn't.

Nor, for a long time, did he speak; and for two or three fields and up Roddis' lane we rode silently in the April sunset; only the squelch of our horses' strides, the jingle of their bits, the occasional crack of Joe's whip, or his call to a lagging hound.

'I hope you'll have as good an innings as I have had, sir,' he eventually volunteered. 'I started at 2s 6d a week in the hunt stables when they were at Towcester, sir. That was fifty years ago, sir. Then I was covert-lad to Mr McNeil when he took over the hounds in 1907. He paid me 2s 6d too, sir.' He chuckled.

I wanted to ask him what covert-lad was, but I could not trust myself to speak.

We rode on.

'I didn't think it enough, sir, so I packed my tin-trunk and departed overnight, sir. Went to Captain Paynter's racing stable at Grantham. There was a gentleman, sir, a real gentleman. I might still have been there hadn't it been for the war, sir. But then I came back here, sir. A good innings, sir; I've been very lucky; but, of course, things aren't what they were. When this last war broke out there were forty-five horses in the stables and over fifty couple of hounds in the kennels. Those were the days, sir. Good days, sir. And I've had good times, sir, and good Masters. Your father, sir, and Mr Guinness, and then his Lordship. Good masters, sir – knew their job.'

He made me aware of my own inadequacy and shortcomings; but at least I had been instrumental in his remaining until the end of his time, enabling him to go out on the blaze of glory he deserved.

We had reached the Paulerspury turn where our ways diverged. Shooting buds in the hedgerows and the gay, evening chatter of birds told of spring, but it was the sweet melancholy of autumn that dominated the atmosphere: and I wished intensely that it was autumn and that the season was just beginning.

For a moment we stood by the signpost, as I tried to pluck up the courage to say something. He gathered his reins.

'Just a minute, Will,' I blurted out, 'I want to ask you something.'

As though divining my request he pulled out his bent and battered old horn from his case and handed it to me.

'I would like you to have this, sir,' he said. 'It's the one I always use, always have. Lord Hillingdon gave it to me when he retired the first time, when I came here as huntsman. He had it from Lord Chesham, who was Master of the Bicester, and who gave it to his Lordship when he first took on a pack of hounds. Lord Chesham, you see, was given it by Lord Valentia, sir, who was Master of the Bicester in the seventies. He first used it at Cambridge, I believe. Must be nearly a hundred years old, sir. But I'd like you to have it. You ought to have it, sir.'

I would have liked to explain that I had been going to ask for it, but would never had entered the idea had I known its history. I only muttered that I could not take it before he reached home, because I knew he always blew as he entered the village to warn the stables and kennelman that hounds were coming in.

'That's all right, sir. We'll manage all right tonight, sir. We'll be all right, sir.'

Perhaps, unwittingly, he was sparing both himself and his staff, by denying them that final call on his horn as he rode into his kennels for the last time.

'Better get on then, sir. Good night, sir. Come on, little bitches,' and they moved down the road before the sun.

'Good night, Will,' I called after him, clutching his little horn, as a bewildered child clutches a toy, 'and thank you.'

from PENDLEY AND A PACK OF HOUNDS *1959*

The First Day

SIEGFRIED SASSOON

By all the laws of aunthood we should by now have been well on our way home. But Dixon was making a real day of it. The afternoon hunt was going to be a serious affair. There never appeared to be any doubt about that. The field was reduced to about forty riders, and the chattersome contingent seemed to have gone home. We all went into the covert and remained close together at one end. Dixon got off and tightened my girths, which had got very loose (as I ought to have noticed). A resolute-looking lady in a tall hat drew her veil down after taking a good pull at the flask which she handed back to her groom. Hard-faced men rammed their hats on to their heads and sat silently in the saddle as though, for the first time in the day, they really meant business. My heart was in my mouth, and it had good reason to be there. Lord Dumborough was keeping an intent eye on the ride which ran through the middle of the covert.

'Cut along up to the end, Charlie,' he remarked without turning his head; and a gaunt, ginger-haired man in a weather-stained scarlet coat went off up the covert in a squelchy canter.

'That's Mr Macdoggart,' said Dixon in a low voice, and my solemnity increased as the legendary figure vanished on its mysterious errand.

Meanwhile the huntsman was continuing his intermittent yaups as he moved along the other side of the wood. Suddenly his cheers of encouragement changed to a series of excited shoutings. 'Hoick-holler, hoick-holler, hoick-holler!' he yelled, and then blew his horn loudly; this was followed by an outbreak of vociferation from the hounds, and soon they were in full cry across the covert. I sat there petrified by my private feelings;

Sheila showed no symptoms of agitation; she merely cocked her ears well forward and listened.

And then, for the first time, I heard a sound which has thrilled generations of fox-hunters to their marrow. From the far side of the wood came the long shrill screech (for which it is impossible to find an adequate word) which signifies that one of the whips has viewed the fox quitting the covert. 'Gone Away' it meant. But before I had formulated the haziest notion about it, Lord Dumborough was galloping up the ride, and the rest of them were pelting after him as though nothing could stop them. As I happened to be standing well inside the wood and Sheila took the affair into her own control, I was swept along with them, and we emerged on the other side among the leaders.

I cannot claim that I felt either excitement or resolution as we bundled down a long slope of meadowland and dashed helter-skelter through an open gate at the bottom. I knew nothing at all except that I was out of breath and that the air was rushing to meet me, but as I hung on to the reins I was aware that Mr Macdoggart was immediately in front of me. My attitude was an acquiescent one. I have always been inclined to accept life in the form in which it has imposed itself upon me, and on that particular occasion no doubt, I just felt that I was 'in for it'. It did not so much as occur to me that in following Mr Macdoggart I was setting myself rather a high standard, and when he disappeared over a hedge I took it for granted that I must do the same. For a moment Sheila hesitated in her stride. (Dixon told me afterwards that I actually hit her as we approached the fence, but I couldn't remember having done so.) Then she collected herself and jumped the fence with a peculiar arching of her back. There was a considerable drop on the other side. Sheila had made no mistake, but as she landed I left the saddle and flew over her head. I had let go of the reins, but she stood stock-still while I sat on the wet ground. A few moments later Dixon popped over a gap lower down the fence and came to my assistance, and I saw the boy on the chestnut pony come after him and gallop on in a resolute but unhurrying way. I scrambled to my feet, feeling utterly ashamed.

'Whatever made you go for it like that?' asked Dixon, who was quite disconcerted.

'I saw Mr Macdoggart going over it, and I didn't like to stop,'

I stammered. By now the whole hunt had disappeared and there wasn't a sound to be heard.

'Well, I suppose we may as well go on.' He laughed as he gave me a leg up. 'Fancy you following Mr Macdoggart over the biggest place in the fence. Good thing Miss Sherston couldn't see you.'

The idea of my aunt seemed to amuse him, and he slapped his knee and chuckled as he led me onward at a deliberate pace. Secretly mortified by my failure, I did my best to simulate cheerfulness. But I couldn't forget the other boy and how ridiculous he must have thought me when he saw me rolling about on the ground. I felt as I must be covered with mud. About half an hour later we found the hunt again, but I can remember nothing more except that it was beginning to get dark and the huntsman, a middle-aged, mulberry-faced man named Jack Pitt, was blowing his horn as he sat in the middle of his hounds. The other boy was actually talking to him – a privilege I couldn't imagine myself promoted to. At that moment I almost hated him for his cocksureness.

Then, to my surprise, the Master himself actually came up and asked me how far I was from home. In my embarrassment I could only mutter that I didn't know, and Dixon interposed with 'About twelve miles, m'lord,' in his best manner.

'I hear he's quite a young thruster.' The great man glanced at me for a moment before he turned away. Not knowing what he meant, I went red in the face and thought he was making fun of me.

from MEMOIRS OF A FOX-HUNTING MAN *1930*

Gillian's Ordeal

MARIGOLD ARMITAGE

On this day, at this time, over this piece of country, Mike's theory about good scenting conditions seemed to be right. Hounds were racing, flinging, driving forward like a dappled cloud. There they went, over the bloody great ditch, leaping, falling short, splashing, scrambling out and on without pausing to shake themselves. There went old George on his neat, wise horse, jumping cleverly, not an inch too far, not a second too soon, his ears cocked. Then Gillian, gloriously leading the field, going at it wildly. I knew that in the last second before the take-off, an expression of ecstatic agony on her face, she would shut her eyes and hang tightly on to a plait of mane, leaving the reins to flap loose, and I was glad that Jane's mare knew her business. Then Tommy Dwyer, still crying encouragement to the tail hound, now streaking just behind old George, a personification of silent, bitter determination to catch up with the pack. Then it was my turn and the grey's stride never seemed to vary, only the dark water, the rushes fleeted suddenly backwards and were gone and he lowered his lean head as we met the steeply rising ground on the far side and his shoulder muscles worked like pistons beneath my knees. Now I was trying to control my wild excitement enough to think which would be the best line to take when we reached the top of the hill, where hounds were driving already over the low wall into the road. It was so long since I had hunted here I had difficulty in visualizing the country. Once across the road there would be two or three fields, part of the point-to-point course, sloping gently towards Kilgarvan. But if they got him through the big covert would he swing right or left? On which flank of the pack should I station myself? And what the hell was the wind doing? It seemed to be blowing on my heated face from all directions at once. A snorting horse came up on my right hand, Father Carrigan tucked like a jockey behind its withers on a ragged racing saddle, his eyes gleaming wildly, his spectacles crooked on his nose, his bowler on the back of his head. I sighed inwardly with relief, for Father Carrigan knew the mind of every fox in the country.

'Follow me now, Anthony,' he shouted exultantly. 'Sure, I know this felly, he wouldn't mind how many miles he'd run. If he can't go down in Kilgarvan he'll go across the bog and make for the hills.'

Here he cursed his horse startlingly as it bungled the tiny walls into and out of the road, and streaked away down the big field, half-turned in his saddle to shout advice to me still over his black-clad shoulder.

'Bear right now, Anthony. Follow me. We must jump McCarthy's Double where it's sound.'

McCarthy's Double was the biggest bank in the country. Once I had gone over it on my feet when I was a boy and it was like climbing a minor Alp. I had sprung over the deep wet ditch, alighted about a quarter way up, hauled myself by grass-tuft and root and bramble on to the wide top where there was a beaten path amongst bushes and small trees, crept nervously half-way down the far side and then jumped unsuccessfully out over the six-foot stream and failed to clear it. I had got very wet and Nanny had lectured me.

In the middle of the field, cleared and reinforced, this bank was the official double of the point-to-point course – an enormous, smooth, green hummock, tempting you to jump it and carefully wired up to prevent just such goings-on. In some other places it was unsound, but Father Carrigan would know exactly where to have it. I took a pull and looked for Gillian. She was bearing away left, the silly piece, going down into Kilgarvan with old George and Tommy Dwyer, and she would certainly get lost and left and probably bogged. I yelled despairingly at her and waved furiously and at last she saw me, hesitated, pulled round and came galloping over to me.

'Follow me, you silly woman. Follow Father Carrigan.'

We fled together down the gentle slope.

'Jump this exactly where he does. Look – there he goes.'

'*Jump this?*'

'Just leave it to the mare.'

'Oh – it's too easy.'

'Of course it is. You go first. I'll push you off the top if you stick.'

'Oh God – why did I *ever* imagine I was an outdoor girl?'

She shut her eyes.

The mare knew exactly what to do and she did it very slowly and deliberately. She looked at the ditch and decided the bottom was sound and waded slowly into it. 'No heroics for me,' her behind expressed to my horse, who was dancing with impatience. She then reared herself straight up with a wallowing noise, like a sea-monster, and arrived at the top of the bank in two heaving bounds which slightly loosened Gillian, even though she had a different plait in each hand. They disappeared from my view and there was a series of sliding sounds and then – heavy thump. I could not see them, but I knew exactly what the mare had done. She had clambered carefully half-way down, just as I had done on my feet, and had then paused waving her head and neck at the stream like an elephant testing something with its trunk and shifting her hind-legs carefully to see if she had a firm take-off, while Gillian crouched nervelessly in her saddle with popping eyes, swallowing. Then she had jumped out and over it, just far enough and no further.

'Are you out of the way?' I shouted.

A faint, wordless shriek of assent came back to me. Just as the grey started at it I was aware of Mike Harrington on his chestnut coming as if he was going into the last at Sandown and I thought, 'They'll both be killed without a doubt'. Then the grey was up and changing and over and out with a wonderful feeling of freedom and ease and effortless timing, so that for a second I saw myself on him, as Aunt Emmy did, 'tipping the double like a Punchestown horse', leading the field in the Hunt Cup – but only for a second.

Hounds were chiming away confidently down in Kilgarvan, and were obviously running hard through it. Father Carrigan had disappeared from my view but Gillian was galloping down the field in a determined manner that indicated she knew where he had gone. I set off after her, glancing uneasily back over my shoulder – for Mike was obviously going to be on the ground in a minute and supposing there was nobody else coming that way to pick him up? I wrestled unhappily with my conscience and the grey horse raked angrily at my uncertain hands and said 'For God's sake let's go'. And then Mike and his chestnut appeared behind us, apparently soaring down from the sky, and turned a complete somersault before they hit the ground.

I very much regret having to record that my sole feeling as I pulled my horse round, was one of fury. I was going to miss what looked like an excellent hunt because Mike chose to ride a crazy racehorse over a country where what was needed was a cross between a pony and a panther. As I trotted back to them the horse thrashed uncertainly to its feet, looked round vaguely, saw Gillian's mare and made off down the field at full gallop, inextricably entangled in its reins. But Mike remained on the ground. And then like an answer to prayer, something altogether too good to be true, O excellent, cosy, capable, self-sacrificing man, Dr Paddy Herlihy from Garnagarry came slipping down off the bank on Mick O'Connor's pony that drew a cart to the creamery when it wasn't hunting.

He pulled up and dismounted in sad resignation, his pug-like face puckered.

'Couldn't I see what would happen a field away? Not the thrack of a heel did the horse lay to it, only knocked back at it with his tail – was it hurdling, God help us, he thought he was at? And I to have my first hunt for a fortnight, with the 'flu that's about.'

I hovered helpfully, and he looked up at me, from where he was poking gently at Mike, and grinned.

'Get away on to them, then, you. What good that we'd both miss it? Sure, he's only winded and there's a dozen felly's about with dogs that can help me instead of confusing the hunt.'

With enormous relief and a certain amount of shame, I hustled the willing grey off down the field. At the bottom was a sticky gap jammed with thorny bushes. I jumped it and heard hounds very close and swung right through an open gateway and there were Gillian and Father Carrigan, that first-class reader of foxy minds, breathing heavily and trying to hold their shifting horses still, while fifty yards away hounds went streaming and singing across the field in front of us.

'Oh, oh,' said Gillian to me, with shining eyes, her stock under one ear and both leathers twisted where she had lost her irons over the double and jammed her feet back into them in a carefree manner.

'Didn't I tell you,' shouted Father Carrigan triumphantly, 'sharp right he turned out of Kilgarvan and he's for the hills this minute.'

'Have you seen Brigadier Harrington's horse?' I asked him.

'I have, and he wouldn't let us lay a finger on him – he's gone in to McCarthy's yearlings below – sure, McCarthy'll catch him when he'd settle.'

'Have you seen Mike?' Gillian asked me.

'I have, indeed, and the doctor from Garnagarry is with him now.'

'Oh, poor Mike – is he all right?'

'Not very.'

'Oh, Anthony, how can you be so heartless?'

'I feel like a character in Nimrod – the pace was too good to enquire. Come on, now.'

For old George had gone by, scrubbing his wise horse that wouldn't gallop unless the necessity was stark, and Tommy Dwyer had gone by with a purple, intent face and as we set off again two or three toiling figures were coming up from Kilgarvan – I looked back and thought I saw Hubert and the roan mare, Jane Harrington and a couple of unidentifiable forms behind them.

'Where's Andrew?' I shouted to Gillian as we galloped along the rutty headland with Father Carrigan, all rebounding off each other from time to time in a not very controlled manner. Her answer which seemed to contain the words 'little brute' was lost to me in the confusion that ensued at the next gap, where Father Carrigan's horse, who was slightly leading as we came to it, resolutely refused to jump a timber rail jammed across it that could not have been much more than eighteen inches high, coming to a jarring halt with a swerve that sent its rider down its shoulder. Gillian always said afterwards that she had heaved him back into the saddle by his respectable black breeches, but all I can remember is Father Carrigan pulling out of our way with a despairing cry of 'Holy God!' and sending his now willing horse scrambling over the bank, which was about twelve feet high, very narrow, extremely slippery and crowned with jagged broken tree stumps.

I reflected, as I looked back at him, on what a pity it was that his horse and Mike's could not somehow manage to combine their respective talents.

We pounded on. The banks were becoming wide, low slippery humps, with big ditches full of water – we were approaching the bog. Here we would cross it at its narrowest part – about a mile – and then if we were lucky find ourselves in an excellent part of the country; grazing grounds with big, sound banks and small walls. 'The hills' which Father Carrigan had referred to was really *a* hill – Slievemore, the big blue shoulder rising out of the plain, with the dark, shifting cloud shadows fleeting across its bulk, and the low, ragged clouds themselves lying now across its peak in banks which the freshening wind was beginning to blow away.

'See where's he's making for,' I called to Gillian.

'If only I could breathe,' was her response, the brown mare plugging determinedly on beside me, her head low, delighted with her breathless and light and unmasterful rider, and confident in her own power to get there, wherever it might be. Behind us came Father Carrigan, still bitterly lecturing his non-timber-jumper, and behind him, apparently, still no one else at all. We pulled to a walk to slide down an extremely steep, short slope, at the bottom of which we would jump a huddle of stones pretending to be a wall, and find ourselves on the bog-road.

'Are we leading the field?' gasped Gillian as we slithered down towards it.

'Pounded 'em.'

'Oh . . . *fascinating*. . . . Do I look at all like Dick Christian?'

'Not really.'

'Oh . . . I so hoped I did. . . . I've never done such a thing before.'

Hounds went fleeting like a blizzard across the bog, old George and Tommy Dwyer battering at a shameless gallop up the road after them.

'Oh,' said Gillian, as we landed together on to it, 'their poor glass legs will never stand it.'

I thought it more than probable. But there was nothing else to be done. There was goat-nibbled turf at the sides of the road, but there were deep, irregular ditches cut into it at frequent intervals, tiring and dangerous to horse and rider. Anyone who has tried to gallop a horse on a grass verge will know what a great penchant they have for the hard, high road in spite of their four glass legs and how they will bend and lurch and pull sideways towards it, refusing to look where they are going until they get their way and the unique sensation of galloping on a hard, clattering surface.

'Anyway, it's not slippery,' said Gillian hopefully, as we fled along, scattering stones, lurching in and out of ruts and making a noise like a hundred Crusaders charging in armour, 'but I couldn't feel guiltier, could you?'

Certainly I couldn't. Would the grey horse, I wondered, be lamed for life? But still the pace was too good to enquire. We must gallop or hounds would run away from us, so we galloped, guilty or not.

There was a broken-down cabin a little way on and from out of it slipped two lurchers, oblivious of shouted curses from within, to race, shrieking and nipping at the heels of old George's horse, who, endeavouring to kick back at them as it galloped, very nearly came down. Old George's scream of execration and the pistol-cracks of his and Tommy Dwyer's thongs sent them howling and cowering into the ditch, from where they launched a further attack on us, while at the same time two apparently idiot children ran gaily out under our horses' feet. Their mother, incredibly tangled-looking and quite oblivious to their fate, hung over the half-door of their home and screamed harshly, hadn't she seen the fox himself and the dogs too ahead of us and they never stropping to draw breath?

Neither did we draw breath, not then or for some time after. It was a fearful moment. I shall never know exactly what the grey horse did, but he managed somehow not to lay the thrack of a heel on those undeserving brats – presumably he knocked back at them with his tail. Gillian's mare appeared to rise straight into the air in a sort of confused *fouetté* – her feet working on nothing. Then we were past.

'I can't look back,' chattered Gillian.

I did so, with dread. The children, undismayed, were just jumping gaily under Father Carrigan's horse – who ended up wallowing in the ditch, with the lurchers in hysterics around it. Benediction flowed from the Father in an unending stream as they struggled out again. Gillian always swore that he had laid about the children with his whip, but I am ready to believe that this was artistic licence on her part, for Father Carrigan, wild though he might be in appearance and behaviour, was the soul of kindness.

Now he came clattering on again behind us, talking angrily to himself and suddenly behind him again there was an eager

hooting, and, looking back, I saw my mother remorselessly driving the groaning little green car with Richmond hanging out of
the window as if chasing gangsters in rather a bad film. On one
step clung somebody in pink (Mike? Colonel Wilbraham? The
Pytchley?) and on the other – could it be? – it surely must be
the tangled and unmaternal figure from the cabin. Around the
back wheels the indefatigable lurchers nipped and shrieked once
again, and further back, running nobly but rather hopelessly,
wreathed in smelly clouds from the exhaust came the abandoned
children. And then, far, far, far behind, just coming down on to
the road, four or six or so more conventional figures, correctly
mounted and no doubt absolutely furious.

The grey cannoned heavily off Gillian's mare.

'Oh, do, *do* look where you're going, Anthony.'

'Oh, Lord,' I said, bending on the grey's neck.

'You're ill,' said Gillian, pallidly.

'No. But I've just seen Mama and Richmond with that terrible
woman from the cabin.'

'Where? Where?'

'Not very far behind us.'

'I can't look. I daren't. If I start laughing now I'm finished.'
She stared desperately ahead with a fixed face.

We were coming off the bog. The road was ceasing to have the
appearance of a causeway and was tending to sink between
thorn-crowned banks and become a boreen. We could hear hounds
off on our left and bearing away.

'We must get out of here at the next jumpable place,' I said to
Gillian.

Then we turned a sharp, downhill corner and fell slap on to
old George and Tommy Dwyer, who were penned up facing an
enormous, enthralled horse who was drawing a cart that just
fitted the boreen. A small boy gesticulated helplessly from where
he was sitting on the near shaft.

'Back,' roared old George to him in a Jehovah voice. 'Back,
damn it, *back*!'

The boy stood up obediently and leaned heavily on the reins
with the whole weight of his meagre body. The horse opened its
mouth very wide, stuck its neck straight out and advanced towards us with an eager welcoming sound.

'Sweet Christ,' said old George hoarsely.

'Oh, *darling*,' said Gillian to me with tears in her eyes. '*Do* something. Make a hole in that.'

'That' was the high and healthy and thick growth of blackthorn that crowned the bank on our left. The bank itself was not very high, but it looked slippery and rotten and the take-off out of the boreen was appalling.

'And the grandest gate you ever saw only just down from us!' wailed Tommy Dwyer.

He backed his horse and turned and booted him into the bank. Both were game but the thorns made a quick, clean jump impossible and as the horse dwelt the bank gave way immediately under his floundering feet. For a long few seconds he thrashed like a stranded whale above us. He was going to fall but would he fall over or back into the lane? Tommy had slipped neatly off his back and was perched, like an anxious robin amongst the thorns, clutching the end of the reins. The horse gave one final desperate kick and disappeared from our view, sliding on his stomach. Tommy leapt after him into space. There was a hideous squelching sound.

'They'll be into the boggy dyke beyond for sure,' the small boy remarked conversationally.

Old George gave him a brimstone look. Suddenly the boy's face became illuminated with an idea.

'Wait while I'd run down and get the slasher for you.'

He leapt up and disappeared down the boreen. The abandoned horse and cart moved further into the fearful *mêlée*.

'Tommy, are you clear, damn you?' bawled old George.

'Wait no, wait, sir.'

There were flounderings, and urging noises and then the encouraging cry, 'Come on now, sir, but sure 'tis a grave you have to leap, 'tis a fearful place altogether.'

Old George and his horse went the same way as Tommy and his – with the difference that old George was not spry enough to nip off. They rolled together out of sight.

'He'll be killed,' said Gillian, faintly. 'Why do we like doing this?'

Crash. Flounder. Squelch. And then a slightly shaken bawl:

'Come on then, you two.'

I wrestled strongly with the cart horse.

'Listen, Gillian, don't have it. It's a bloody awful place. Give it up.'

I felt a sharp panic for her, she looked so small suddenly. Her lips folded obstinately. Apparently she was still feeling like Dick Christian. The brown mare cocked her ears and seemed to take a deep breath.

They had it, determinedly. Old George said afterwards that even at that flustering moment, with his hounds running away from him every second, with his own horse still on the ground trying to get its breath back, with the winded Tommy Dwyer's whole weight on him as he tried to put him up; even so he was struck to stone by the sight of Gillian's arrival. She came with her eyes shut. She had abandoned her reins altogether and clung tightly with both hands to the pommel of her saddle. The mare made a wonderful effort, hit the edge of the 'grave' and tipped up. She ploughed on her head for a few yards and then righted herself, blowing mud triumphantly from her nostrils, with her bridle on the ground and her rider still in the saddle.

'I declare to my God,' Tommy Dwyer was wont to say, in describing this feat afterwards, which he did very often, 'there's not a jock in the country, no not J.J. himself, would have stayed on the way Mrs Lodwick did, and the mare walking on her head the way she might be in a circus.'

But now it was my turn and the grey's. The expression 'riding for a fall' is very easily used and has a dashing ring about it – actually to do such a thing, however, arouses a feeling of sick anticipation comparable only to that experienced at the moment when the dentist's hand reaches for the drill.

We were not only going to fall, I felt, but there was also nothing to prevent the cart and horse from falling on top of us, since the horse was obviously feeling ambitious and there was no one to curb his feelings once I had gone. I belaboured him rather hopelessly with my whip until he gave way sufficiently to allow us a little room. My heart and stomach had changed places as the grey heaved himself up into the thorny gap, with everything giving way at once under his clever feet. But I need not have worried. The grey had brains and he decided instantly that, with no firm take-off, any attempt to jump the boggy dyke beyond would end in failure. Instead he dropped lightly and neatly and deliberately down into it and heaved himself out again, light and neat still, and shook himself with a noise like thunder all over old George's horse, which at once got to its feet indignantly.

'By God, that's a clever horse of Emmy's,' said old George. 'My b— just lost his head.'

He was clasping Gillian's mare's naked face delicately to his chest by nose and ear while Tommy Dwyer endeavoured to pick up her bridle, much hampered by his horse who had decided that the bridle was alive, and was refusing to go near it. I jumped off and took his horse and old George's while they restored to Gillian a measure of control and then I put them both up, and by that time I was so breathless with fright and exhaustion that I really thought I should lose the hunt yet through sheer physical inability to get up on the grey again. But Tommy Dwyer leant from his saddle and heaved nobly and I was aboard again and flying, for the grey had breathed himself nicely – there was agonizing mud in my right eye and I could not find my irons for the moment but ahead was good grass and sound banks – and behind a piteous, lonely, beseeching scream. I looked back. The cart horse stood reared up with his forefeet on the bank, imploring us to return.

We fled on, through two delicious gateways without gates.

'Where's Father Carrigan?' Gillian shouted breathlessly.

Where indeed? I had forgotten him. I looked back. Nobody. He had been close behind us coming off the bog, and it was not like Father Carrigan to lose a good start. Nor had he, for as I looked forward again, across the country that was now beginning to rise slightly as we went towards Slievemore, there was the familiar crouched dark back, slipping along at least two fields ahead of us all.

'How did he get there?'

'God knows.'

'That damned priest,' growled old George, 'he's always ahead of me, blast his Papist soul.'

Old George was well known never to have entered a church since he had left Eton, but in the presence of Roman Catholicism his Protestantism was relentless and militant. He preferred, he said, his own type of damnation.

Old George's horse was tiring now; at the next bank he misjudged his distance and nearly fell back. Gillian's mare had a slight roll in her stride as we crossed the next field. I was frankly exhausted but the grey horse was going on as light as thistledown, his ears cocked still, still reaching for each jump eagerly, and I tried to sit as quiet as possible and not hinder him, even if I could not help him. There came a wall on to a cart-track, with a stone-faced bank out of it. Old George's horse came to his knees over the wall, slithered and scuffed and heaved and stopped with his chest against the bank, his head hanging over it and his tail stretched out, quivering.

'He's beat,' said old George. 'The b—. He's old, like me.'

He ran his hand lovingly down the wet shoulder.

'Get on to them, Tommy, damn you. What the hell are you hanging about for?'

Tommy got on, with slither and slip and clatter, into a herd of young bullocks who wallowed excitedly with him down the field, ponderously playful.

'Get on, you two,' said old George. He had got off and was loosening his horse's girths, his head hidden under the saddle flap so that his voice was muffled.

He didn't want us to see his face. 'Oh, hell,' I thought, 'hell,' and got off the grey and plucked George's reins from his hand.

'Get up quick – he's a bottomless horse.'

Honour and glory for Aunt Emmy, anyway. Old George's face, taken from beneath the saddle flap, was even purpler than usual.

'I shouldn't do it to you, Anthony.'

'Don't be a fool.'

I pitched him up. My leathers were much too long – he crossed them over the pommel of the saddle and was gone, the grey jumping out big over the slight drop. Gillian looked woefully at me before she followed.

'Oh, darling, the *chivalry*. Roger need never speak about Round Tables again.'

Then she, too was gone. There was the slap and thunder of their hooves and the bawling of the bullocks. Then silence, except for the heavy panting of old George's horse. Silence? Yes, silence. I strained my ears, but I could not hear hounds. And they had only been two or three fields ahead of us. A check?

Had they over-run in this poached, bullock-foiled field? If so, there was hope for me yet. I turned the horse's head to the wind and earnestly exhorted him to breathe deeply which he did without hesitation. Then I heard Tommy Dwyer's voice not very far away raised in gentle encouragement to his hounds. Undoubtedly a check. And yet, what hope could there really be for me, since the fox was bound to be forward if he was making for Slievemore? Or had he thought up something very tricky through the bullocks? I clambered to the top of the bank and looked about me. The field directly to the right of the one which the bullocks were in, ran increasingly boggily down to a narrow stream. Had he gone to cross it, the old customer, the cunning Charles James, running first in the middle of the bullocks and then turning sharply at a right angle off his point? If so, he would now be slipping at ease along the far bank, looking for a suitable place to re-cross it and point again for the haven of Slievemore. As I cogitated and still no hound spoke, the little green car came roaring indomitably towards me and lurched to a standstill with its curious load.

'Anthony,' said my mother serenely, peering out at me. 'That's not Emmy's horse.'

'I know,' I said.

'Then where *is* Emmy's horse?'

Before I could answer there was another diversion – a clapping and flapping and thudding and a loose horse landing over the wall into our midst, wild-eyed, mud on its saddle, a leather gone and broken reins. My heart leapt up as I beheld it to be Conor Molloy's horse. It slithered up to old George's horse and blew on it in a friendly 'Thank-goodness-I've-found-someone-at-last' manner. Old George's horse laid back its ears and bit the new-comer smartly on the shoulder just to show it its place.

'You hold this one,' said my mother sweetly to Richmond, pressing the broken rein into his hand with the air of someone distributing favours to the gentlemen at a charity ball. Richmond's hand closed, nervelessly, on it. He appeared to be speechless and was obviously strongly affected, but in what way I was not quite certain.

'Have the dogs the fox ate?' enquired the careless mother from the cabin.

'They have not, then,' I answered in the idiom.

'Where are they, Anthony? Oh, I forgot, this is Colonel Bowser, he's staying with Poodle. (The Pytchley collar looked sharply defensive and fingered his stock.) And they're coming to have a drink with us tonight, that is, of course, if we can find her – or anyone – where *is* everyone, anyway?'

'All I know is that George has got Aunt Emmy's horse and he and Tommy and Gillian and Father Carrigan are over there – they seem to have checked and I think they probably over-ran it through those bullocks. I haven't seen anyone else at all, except as we came across the bog I thought perhaps I saw Jane and Poodle, a long way back.'

'Nearly everybody went to the left around Kilgarvan, that's what happened and they got thrown out and they haven't caught up yet.' She looked back over the wall. 'Here's somebody now.'

It was Caroline. The Araby little horse, black with sweat, landed neatly and jauntily beside us and tossed its head rudely at the other two. Caroline's smile was enchanting, her face creamy under mud-splashes, her velvet eyes glowing.

'Thank heaven I found somebody at last – I do hate following hoof marks. Where are they? Why have you got my father's horse, Anthony?'

Oh, noble, pure and unselfish motive thus happily turned to glorious gain! I explained.

'How *very* kind of you. Listen, I'll tell you what you can do. Change bridles and get up on Conor's horse.'

'Oh, yes, Anthony,' said my mother. 'You mustn't miss it now.' She was already divesting George's horse of its bridle. 'Just take hold of an ear, would you, Mr Kerr. That's right, he won't try and move.'

But he did. For at that very instant the ringing, the clamour, broke again on the air and the triumphant twanging of old George's horn. My thumb was in Conor's horse's mouth as it mumbled angrily at the strange and frothy bit, refusing to take it.

'Oh, hurry, hurry,' wailed Caroline, in a frenzy. 'Oh, listen to them, the darlings – hurry, hurry.'

Old George's horse, breathed and rid of the weight and highly indignant at the strange turn of affairs, twitched his ear away from Richmond, jumped the bank with a grunt and was away, the saddle slowly sliding round under his belly as he went.

'I told you to hold his ear, Mr Kerr,' said my mother, mildly.

I twisted my thumb madly in Conor's horse's mouth, jammed in the bit, pulled the bridle with an effort over his ears – it was too tight for the poor brute – and left the throat-latch dangling as Poodle's boy-friend bent to give me a leg-up; a noble lift that nearly sent me clean over the big horse – the Pytchley back, I saw as he bent, was smeared with mud from collar to skirt.

I am very glad that there exists no photograph of myself jumping that bank on Conor's horse. I think my head was somewhere near his tail as we landed and I can remember seeing my hands raised in front of me as if in prayer. Then we were scudding away after Caroline and from somewhere not so very far ahead, once again unfaltering, the glorious voices came back to us.

I have no very clear recollection of the rest of that hunt. I realized at once that I had no hope of holding Conor's horse, who seemed to be as fresh as a daisy, and was taking delighted advantage of the mild half-moon snaffle that had replaced his own twisted one. He was big and awkward, green and hot, and his jumping was slapdash, to say the least of it. No thought of refusing ever entered his head, he went gaily and gallantly into his fences with ears cocked, but with no very clear-cut idea as to what he was going to do about them. He had great panache, but all his decisions were made in mid-air. Twice he was nearly down – more times than I care to remember I was nearly off. I was riding without stirrups, since one is no good to anybody, and I was getting very tired. I gave him his head and prayed and once or twice adopted Gillian's expedient of shutting my eyes. We passed Caroline, who shouted something happily to me, we passed Father Carrigan, whose horse was reduced to a toiling jog, 'God help us, Anthony, what horse have you now?'

Half a field ahead Gillian's brown mare was doggedly cantering, rolling like the *Queen Mary* in a heavy sea, and ahead again, forcing further, jumping cleanly still, the game grey horse carried old George to his hounds.

'By God,' I thought momentarily, 'I *will* win the Hunt Cup on him.'

The land was rising ever more steeply, the wide green fields, the sound banks giving way to rough, tussocky little enclosures, patchworked by little, crumbling walls. Slievemore, enormous in the fading light, bulked silent and close above us, shutting out the pallid evening sky. We were coming on to its lower slopes. At the next wall Gillian's mare's heels waved in the air, she tipped up and crumpled amongst the tussocky grass. I landed near them.

'Oh, darling, *heavens*, what horse have you got now – did you see us fall? – do, *do*, go on, quick. I'll just wait until this poor honey gets her breath – I see Father Carrigan coming – do, *do* go on.'

Now, as I went, I saw hounds again for the first time since we had crossed the bog, driving across a low ridge above and to the left of me. They had had a view, I thought, for the high screaming for blood had come into their voices. After them the grey horse slipped like a ghost. Conor's horse lowered his head to climb, picking his way on the rocky outdrop. We came up with Tommy Dwyer limping, leading his beaten horse, almost in tears.

'Sure, don't they deserve him, if hounds ever did? But he'll get into the rocks above and then he can run the whole inside of the hill – the bloody place is hollow – who'd ever think they'd bring him to here from Drumanagh?'

'Never mind, Tommy – it must be a twelve-mile point – you've given us all something to talk about.'

But Tommy was thinking of his hounds. Conor's horse slid and slithered.

'Best get off now, sir, 'tis a dreadful place for a tired horse.'

When I did so I went to my knees. My legs seemed to be made of cotton-wool, and my feet to have no connection with the rest of me. I was not quite sure where I was putting them and I staggered along drunkenly. Away in front, abruptly, the voices died. Then they clamoured again, but singly, brokenly, mournfully, informing us of frustration and a thirst unassuaged. Old George's horn told us the same and round the spine of the ridge we came upon them, a little above us, milling and crying around the great earth in the rocks, the grey horse standing amongst them, his head drooping at last, and old George's face glowing like a lantern through the deepening dusk.

'By God, they nearly had him, the darlings, they were running right into him – ten yards more, five even and he wouldn't have made it.'

'A good fox,' I said. 'A marvellous run, George. You've made history to-day. Congratulations.'

'And only the locals up,' said old George with immense satisfaction. 'Leave him, leave him now, my darlings. Count 'em, Tommy – I think they were all on.'

'Here comes one non-local,' I said, as Gillian came plodding up towards us, trailing Jane's mare, like a tired child dragging a balloon away from a party. Behind her came Caroline and Father Carrigan, both also on foot. Father Carrigan seemed to have caught old George's horse and was leading it by the thong of his whip looped round its throat. The old horse lifted his head and whinnied in a throaty murmur when he saw hounds.

We stood around idly, enveloped in an immense tiredness and content. Old George and Tommy were murmuring endearments to their lovely hounds as they counted them and pulled thorns out of sore pads.

There was a smell of sweating horses and the evening wind, and a star was out above Slievemore. Old George put the horn to his lips for the last time and blew the long, heartrending 'Home'.

from A LONG WAY TO GO *1952*

Has Bonaparte Landed in England, Sir?

GORDON GRAND

Colonel Weatherford was to shoot the coverts west of Bagdollen, and I, the Willow Beds and Three Spires Upland, we to meet at Thatcher's Oak for luncheon.

The coverts proving generous, I shot my allotted woodcock before it was yet noon, and so walked on to Thatcher's great tree to await the Colonel.

In all this pleasant county of Dutchess there is no spot at which I would rather tarry than Thatcher's Oak, a gnarled giant standing upon a westering hill sloping to the river. Across the river, good lands of agriculture spread on and on to the horizon at Peckham's Ridge. Leaning back against the tree, my old dog Feathers stretched out beside me, I gazed appreciatively upon this stage of husbandry, its setting and its actors.

Gabriel Le Coste, the French Canadian who lives in a cabin on the marsh, passed down the river in his gray, flatbottomed boat, collecting firewood against the coming of winter. He stood in the stern, polling with leisurely, graceful strokes, towing a silvered log behind the boat. Long after he had passed, the sound of his pole striking the gravel drifted back to me.

In a field to the south, Tom Thatcher was fall-plowing, his dog companioning him from furrow to furrow. At the corner of Thatcher's house the canopied crest of an elm tree showed against the empurpled Catskills. 'A homestead signalling to other homesteads through distant elms.'

Then silver-throated bells, the bells of St Matthew's, drifted to me with muffled notes and I recalled that Tom Baget, our village cobbler, scion of an ancient line of English huntsmen, was this noon being laid to rest at St Matthew's in our Dutchess County.

Seated thus in the warm, saffron sun of that gossamer day, listening the while to the last katydid of the year and to my dog's somnolent breathing, I fell to musing upon our old cobbler and how he was forever harking back with pride to a famous forbear, McFadden Baget, the eighteenth-century English huntsman whose keen, restless spirit was said still to haunt the Pytchely Country. 'Mr. Pendleton, sir, it's God's truth, you wouldn't be abroad in the Pytchely Country of a fair night, that McFadden wouldn't limp up alongside of you, always in a hurry, always acting like he'd lost something but never telling what it was.'

As my thoughts wandered drowsily on into the annals of English shires the bells became only as faint, lingering echoes and the fragile tempo of passing grew ever slower; then for me there was no time. Thatcher's Oak and my old dog and I were of infinity.

It was then that the little man climbed over the stone wall, a limping, bandy-legged wizened little man in a huntsman's garb of an earlier fashion. He was on in years, and seemed perplexed and weary, yet gnarled and tough as huntsmen ever get. He jerked a finger to his misshapen velvet cap. 'Excuse me, sir. Have you seen a horse? I've lost my horse. He fell with me over the wall into Aylestone Park. I've been a-looking for him a long time, a long time, sir. And please, would you have heard whether Bonaparte landed in England while I've been looking for my horse? When we were drawing Frisby Gorse, His Grace said as how we had no business taking hounds out, what with Bonaparte and the French apt to land in England at any minute. You haven't heard of them landing, have you, sir? You haven't seen the signal fires?'

'No,' I answered. 'I have not heard of Bonaparte landing in England.'

'That's good, sir. That's good. His Grace said that if Boney landed, there would be no more hunting this season in old England. I'm glad he didn't land.

'It's odd, sir, where that horse got to. He was the best the Duke mounted me on – a big horse, fifteen hands and an inch he stood, by Arch Duke, winner of the Derby Stakes in ninety-nine, afore he went to Maryland in the Americas. I came down hard at the park wall, sir. The horse was very tired. I don't think I've felt so good since then. It seems as though I been a-lookin' for him, days and days, maybe longer than that. I best be movin' on now. I always think as how he may be grazing over the next hill. If you see him, sir, would you send word on to the kennels? Thank you, sir?'

'Wait! Wait a moment!' I said. 'Sit down, sit down. So you were an English huntsman, hunting hounds across the shires of England when the Emperor's fleet made ready on the coast of France. Tell me, man, what sort of day were you having when you fell? The day you watched for the signal fires. What had hounds been doing? How long had they been running?'

The little man looked at me in a dazed, lonesome way, then squatted down on the grass, adjusted his odd-looking neckcloth, and laid a broken stirrup leather beside him.

'Why, sir, we met at Wineswold Croft, the wind northwest, the weather cold. I cast my hounds in Frisby Gorse but finding it blank went on to Bradgate. On Fenway Heath hounds feathered a mite and hunted up to their fox in Goadby Burrow.

'We gave him an airing down to Barkley, then brought him

back to Keythorpe Spinney. He went away fast by Thrussington Wolds, skirting Midburn Hill and Dalby Cordle, setting his head for Walden Great Wood.

'A drover turned him on Hecking Hill. I lifted and galloped to a view-halloo. Hounds raced on for Halleck's Spinney by way of Pimpton and Sutton Edley, throwing their tongues and gaining on him.

'At Runcliff Brook His Grace came down. Lord Fenway fell on Hunger Hill. My horse turned over on Ashby Wolds. Lord Bromley went off at Breedon Thorns.

'At Tilton a shepherd gave the fox a scare, and he raced six miles for Strathern Uplands. The earths were stopped, so we turned for Grafton, swimming the river near Swinbourne Abbey. We had crossed our country and gone beyond it, hunting our fox to Belvoir Vale.

'The find at Goadby, just at noon, was four and twenty miles behind us. Of all the field but three remained, His Grace, Lady Margaret and her brother Francis.

'Then Aylestone Park rose up in front, with an ugly wall for a horse that's weary. His Grace and the rest turned left to skirt it but my hounds were running so I had to face it.

'That be all that I know, sir, of that day's sport, of the fox, or the hounds, or of those that stayed with 'em. I rode at the wall the best I knew how, but please, sir, my horse was a good bit spent. I must find my horse afore it's dark and learn did they kill in Aylestone Park.'

The little man gathered up his broken stirrup leather, touched his cap and limped slowly away on his ancient quest. I watched him until he melted into the azure-tinted horizon of the November day.

Then from out of the far-distant English gorse and fens, came a well-known voice. 'What's this you're muttering, Pendleton, about Napoleon landing in England? God bless me, man, God bless me! Wake up.'

from THE MILLBECK HOUNDS *1932*

Philippa's Foxhunt

E. Œ. SOMERVILLE AND M. ROSS

As I struggled into my boots the following morning, I felt that Sir Valentine's acid confidences on cub hunting, bestowed on me at midnight, did credit to his judgement. 'A very moderate amusement, my dear Major,' he said, in his dry little voice; 'you should stick to shooting. No one expects you to shoot before day break.'

It was six o'clock as I crept downstairs, and found Lady Knox and Miss Sally at breakfast, with two lamps on the table, and a foggy daylight oozing in from under the half raised blinds. Philippa was already in the hall, pumping up her bicycle, in a state of excitement at the prospect of her first experience of hunting that would have been more comprehensible to me had she been going to ride a strange horse, as I was. As I bolted my food I saw the horses being led past the windows, and a faint twang of a horn told that Flurry Knox and his hounds were not far off.

Miss Sally jumped up.

'If I'm not on the Cockatoo before the hounds come up, I shall never get there!' she said, hobbling out of the room in the toils of her safety habit. Her small, alert face looked very childish under her riding-hat; the lamp-light struck sparks out of her thick coil of golden-red hair: I wondered how I had ever thought her like her prim little father.

She was already on her white cob when I got to the hall door, and Flurry Knox was riding over the glistening wet grass with his hounds, while his whip, Dr Jerome Hickey, was having a stirring time with the young entry and the rabbit holes. They moved on without stopping, up a back avenue, under tall dripping trees, to a thick laurel covert, at some little distance from the house. Into this the hounds were thrown, and the usual period of fidgety inaction set in for the riders, of whom, all told, there were about half-a-dozen. Lady Knox, square and solid, on her big, confidential iron-grey, was near me, and her eyes were on me and my mount; with her rubicund face and white collar she was more than ever like a coachman.

'Sorcerer looks as if he suited you well,' she said, after a few minutes of silence, during which the hounds rustled and cracked steadily through the laurels; 'he's a little high on the leg, and so are you, you know, you show each other off.'

Sorcerer was standing like a rock, with his good-looking head in the air and his eyes fastened on the covert. His manners so far, had been those of a perfect gentleman, and were in marked contrast to those of Miss Sally's cob, who was sidling, hopping and snatching unappeasably at his bit. Philippa had disappeared from view down the avenue ahead. The fog was melting, and the sun threw long blades of light through the trees; everything was quiet, and in the distance the curtained windows of the house marked the warm response of Sir Valentine, and those of the party who shared his opinion of cubbing.

'Hark! hark to cry there!'

It was Flurry's voice, away at the other side of the covert. The rustling and brushing through the laurels became more vehement, then passed out of hearing.

'He will never leave his hounds alone,' said Lady Knox disapprovingly.

Miss Sally and the Cockatoo moved away in a series of heraldic capers towards the end of the laurel plantation, and at the same moment I saw Philippa and her bicycle shoot into view on the drive ahead of us.

'I've seen a fox!' she screamed, white with what I believe to have been personal terror, though she says it was excitement: 'it passed quite close to me!'

'What way did he go?' bellowed the voice which I recognized to be Dr Hickey's, somewhere in the deep of the laurels.

'Down the drive!' returned Philippa, with a pea-hen quality in her tones with which I was quite unacquainted.

An electrifying screech of 'Gone away!' was projected from the laurels by Dr Hickey.

'Gone away!' chanted Flurry's horn at the top of the covert.

'This is what he calls cubbing!' said Lady Knox, 'a mere farce!' but none the less she loosed her sedate monster into a canter.

Sorcerer got his hind-legs under him, and hardened his crest against the bit, as we all hustled along the drive after the flying figure of my wife. I knew very little about horses, but I realized that even with the hounds tumbling hysterically out of the covert, and the Cockatoo kicking the gravel into his face, Sorcerer comported himself with the manners of the best society. Up a road I saw Flurry Knox opening a half gate and cramming through it; in a moment we also had crammed through, and the turf of a pasture field was under our feet. Dr Hickey leaned forward and took hold of his horse; I did likewise, with the trifling difference that my horse took hold of me, and I steered for Flurry Knox with single-hearted purpose, the hounds already a field ahead, being merely an exciting and noisy accompaniment of this endeavour. A heavy stone wall was the first occurrence of note. Flurry chose a place where the top was loose, and his clumsy looking brown mare changed feet on the rattling stones like a fairy. Sorcerer came at it, tense and collected as a bow at full stretch, and sailed steeply into the air; I saw the wall far beneath me, with an unsuspected ditch on the far side, and I felt my hat following me at the full stretch of its guard as we swept over it, then, with a long slant, we descended to earth some sixteen feet from where we had left it, and I was possessor of the gratifying fact that I had achieved a good-sized 'fly', and had not perceptibly moved in my saddle. Subsequent disillusioning experience has taught me that but few horses jump like Sorcerer, so gallantly, so sympathetically, and with such supreme mastery of the subject; but none the less the enthusiasm that he imparted to me has never been extinguished, and that October morning ride revealed to me the unsuspected intoxication of fox-hunting.

Behind me I heard the scrabbling of the Cockatoo's little hoofs among the loose stones, and Lady Knox, galloping on my left, jerked a maternal chin over her shoulder to mark her daughter's progress. For my part, had there been an entire circus behind me, I was far too much occupied with ramming on my hat and trying to hold Sorcerer, to have looked round, and all my spare faculties were devoted to steering for Flurry, who had taken a right handed turn, and was at that moment surmounting a bank of uncertain and briary aspect. I surmounted it also, with the swiftness and simplicity for which the Quaker's methods of bank jumping had not prepared me, and two or three fields, traversed at the same steeple-chase pace, brought us to a road and to an abrupt check. There, suddenly, were the hounds,

scrambling in baffled silence down the road from the opposite
bank, to look for the line they had overrun, and there, amazingly,
was Philippa, engaged in excited converse with several men with
spades over their shoulders.

'Did ye see the fox, boys?' shouted Flurry, addressing the
group.

'We did! we did!' cried my wife and her friends in chorus: 'he
ran up the road!'

'We'd be badly off without Mrs Yeates!' said Flurry, as he
whirled the mare round and clattered up the road with a hustle
of hounds after him.

It occurred to me as forcibly as any mere earthly thing can
occur to those who are wrapped in the sublimities of a run, that,
for a young woman who had never before seen a fox out of a
cage at the Zoo, Philippa was taking to hunting very kindly.
Her cheeks were a most brilliant pink, her blue eyes shone.

'Oh! Sinclair!' she exclaimed, 'they say he's going for Aussolas,
and there's a road I can ride all the way!'

'Ye can, Miss! Sure we'll show you!' chorused her cortège.

Her foot was on the pedal ready to mount. Decidedly my wife
was in no need of assistance from me.

Up the road a hound gave a yelp of discovery, and flung
himself over a stile into the fields; the rest of the pack went

squealing and jostling after him, and I followed Flurry over one
of those infinitely varied erections, pleasantly termed 'gaps' in
Ireland. On this occasion the gap was made of three razor-edged
slabs of slate leaning against an iron bar, and Sorcerer conveyed
to me his knowledge of the matter by a lift of his hind quarters
that made me feel as if I were being skilfully kicked downstairs.
To what extent I looked it, I cannot say, nor providentially can
Philippa, as she had already started. I only know that undeserved
good luck restored to me my stirrup before Sorcerer got away
with me in the next field.

What followed, I am told, was a very fast fifteen minutes; for
me time was not; the empty fields rushed past uncounted, fences
came and went in a flash, while the wind sang in my ears, and the
dazzle of the early sun shone in my eyes. I saw the hounds
occasionally, sometimes pouring over a green bank, as the
charging breaker lifts and flings itself, sometimes driving across
a field, as the white tongues of foam slide racing over the sand;
and always ahead of me was Flurry Knox, going as a man goes
who knows his country, who knows his horse, and whose heart
is wholly and absolutely in the right place.

Do what I would, Sorcerer's implacable stride carried me closer
and closer to the brown mare, till, as I thundered down the slope
of a long field, I was not twenty yards behind Flurry. Sorcerer had
stiffened his neck to iron, and to slow him down was beyond me;
but I fought his head away to the right, and found myself coming
hard and steady at a stone-faced bank with broken ground in
front of it. Flurry bore away to the left, shouting something that
I did not understand. That Sorcerer shortened his stride at the
right moment was entirely due to his own judgement; standing
well away from the jump, he rose like a stag out of the tussocky
ground and as he swung my twelve stone six into the air the
obstacle revealed itself to him and me as consisting not of one
bank but of two, and between the two lay a deep and grassy lane,
half choked with furze. I have often been asked to state the width
of the bohereen, and can only reply that in my opinion it was at
least eighteen feet; Flurry Knox and Dr Hickey, who did not
jump it, say that it is not more than five. What Sorcerer did with
it I cannot say; the sensation was of towering flight with a kick
back in it, a biggish drop, and a landing on cee-springs, still on

the downhill grade. That was how one of the best horses in Ireland took one of Ireland's most ignorant riders over a very nasty place.

A sombre line of fir-wood lay ahead, rimmed with a grey wall, and in another couple of minutes we had pulled up on the Aussolas road, and were watching the hounds struggling over the wall into Aussolas demesne.

'No hurry now,' said Flurry, turning in his saddle to watch the Cockatoo jump into the road, 'he's to ground in the big earth inside. Well, Major, it's well for you that's a big-jumped horse. I thought you were a dead man a while ago when you faced him at the bohereen!'

I was disclaiming intention in the matter when Lady Knox and the others joined us.

'I thought you told me your wife was no sportswoman,' she said to me, critically scanning Sorcerer's legs for cuts the while, 'but when I saw her a minute ago, she had abandoned her bicycle and was running across country like . . .'

'Look at her now!' interrupted Miss Sally. 'Oh! – oh.' In the interval between these exclamations my incredulous eyes beheld my wife in mid-air, hand in hand with a couple of stalwart country boys, with whom she was leaping in unison from the top of a bank on to the road.

Everyone, even Dr Hickey, began to laugh; I rode back to Philippa, who was exchanging compliments and congratulations with her escorts.

'Oh, Sinclair!' she cried, 'wasn't it splendid? I saw you jumping, and everything! Where are they going now?'

'My dear girl,' I said, with marital disapproval, 'you're killing yourself. Where's your bicycle?'

'Oh, it punctured in a sort of lane, back there. It's all right; and then they' – she breathlessly waved her hand at her attendants – 'they showed me the way.'

'Begor! you proved very good, Miss!' said a grinning cavalier.

'Faith she did!' said another, polishing his shining brow with his white flannel coat-sleeve, 'she lepped like a haarse!'

'And may I ask how you propose to go home?' said I.

'I don't know and I don't care! I'm not going home!'

She cast an entirely disobedient eye at me. 'And your eye glass is hanging down your back and your tie is bulging out over your waistcoat!'

The little group of riders had begun to move away.

'We're going into Aussolas,' called out Flurry; 'come on, and make my grandmother give you some breakfast, Mrs Yeates; she always has it at eight o'clock.'

The front gates were close at hand, and we turned in under the tall beech-trees, with the unswept leaves rustling round our horse's feet, and the lovely blue of the October morning sky filling the spaces between grey branches and golden leaves. The woods rang with the voices of the hounds, enjoying an untrammelled rabbit hunt, while the Master and Whip, both on foot, strolled along unconcernedly with their bridles over their arms, making themselves agreeable to my wife, an occasional touch of Flurry's horn, or a crack of Dr Hickey's whip, just indicating to the pack that the authorities still took a friendly interest in their doings.

Down a grassy glade in the wood a party of old Mrs Knox's young horses suddenly swept into view, headed by an old mare, who, with her tail over her back, stampeded ponderously past our cavalcade, shaking and swinging her handsome old head, while her youthful friends bucked and kicked and snapped at each other round her with the ferocious humour of their kind.

'Here, Jerome, take the horn,' said Flurry to Dr Hickey: 'I'm going to see Mrs Yeates up to the house, the way these tomfools won't gallop on top of her.'

From this point it seems to me that Philippa's adventures are more worthy of record than mine, and as she has favoured me with a full account of them, I venture to think my version may be relied upon.

Mrs Knox was already at breakfast when Philippa was led, quaking, into her formidable presence. My wife's acquaintance with Mrs Knox was, so far, limited to a state visit on either side, and she found but little comfort in Flurry's assurances that his grandmother wouldn't mind if he brought all the hounds in to breakfast, coupled with the statement that she would put her eyes on sticks for the Major.

Whatever the truth of this may have been, Mrs Knox received her guest with an equanimity quite unshaken by the fact that her boots were in the fender instead of on her feet, and that a couple of shawls of varying dimensions and degrees of age did not conceal the inner presence of a magenta flannel dressing-jacket. She installed Philippa at the table and plied her with food, oblivious as to whether the needful implements with which to eat were forthcoming or no. She told Flurry where a vixen had reared her family, and she watched him ride away, with some biting comments on his mares' hocks screamed after him from the window.

The dining room at Aussolas Castle is one of the many rooms in Ireland in which Cromwell is said to have stabled his horse (and probably no one would have objected less than Mrs Knox had she been consulted in the matter). Philippa questions if the room had ever been tidied up since, and she endorses Flurry's observation that 'there wasn't a day in the year you wouldn't get feeding for a hen and chickens on the floor'. Opposite to Philippa, on a Louis Quinze chair, sat Mrs Knox's woolly dog, its suspicious little eyes peering at her out of their setting of pink lids and dirty white wool. A couple of young horses outside the windows tore at the matted creepers on the walls, or thrust their faces that were half shy, half impudent, into the room. Portly pigeons waddled to and fro on the broad window-sill, sometimes flying to perch on the picture-frames, while they kept up incessantly a hoarse and pompous cooing.

Animals and children are, as a rule, alike destructive to conversation; but Mrs Knox, when she chose, *bien entendu*, could have made herself agreeable in a Noah's ark, and Philippa has a gift of sympathetic attention that personal experience has taught me to regard with distrust as well as respect, while it has often made me realize the worldly wisdom of Kingsley's injunction:

Be good, sweet maid, and let who will be clever.

Family prayers, declaimed by Mrs Knox with alarming austerity, followed close on breakfast, Philippa and a vinegar-faced henchwoman forming the family. The prayers were long, and through the open window as they progressed came distantly a whoop or two; the declamatory tones staggered a little, and then continued at a distinctly higher rate of speed.

'Ma'am! Ma'am!' whispered a small voice at the window.

Mrs Knox made a repressive gesture and held on her way. A sudden outcry of hounds followed, and the owner of the whisper, a small boy with a face freckled like a turkey's egg, darted from the window and dragged a donkey and bath-chair into view. Philippa admits to having lost the thread of discourse, but she thinks that the 'Amen' that immediately ensued can hardly have come in its usual place. Mrs Knox shut the book abruptly, scrambled up from her knees, and said, 'They've found!'

In a surprisingly short space of time she had added to her attire her boots, a fur cape, and a garden hat, and was in the bath-chair, the small boy stimulating the donkey with the success peculiar to his class, while Philippa hung on behind.

The woods of Aussolas are hilly and extensive, and on that particular morning it seemed that they held as many foxes as hounds. In vain was the horn blown and the whips cracked, small rejoicing parties of hounds, each with a fox of its own, scoured to and fro: every labourer in the vicinity left his work, and was sedulously heading every fox with yells that would have befitted a tiger hunt, and sticks and stones when occasion served.

'Will I pull out as far as the big rosydandhrum, ma'am?' inquired the small boy; 'I seen three of the dogs go in it, and they yowling.'

'You will,' said Mrs Knox, thumping the donkey on the back with her umbrella; 'here! Jeremiah Regan! Come down out of that with that pitchfork! Do you want to kill the fox, you fool?'

'I do not, your honour, ma'am,' responded Jeremiah Regan, a tall young countryman, emerging from a bramble brake.

'Did you see him?' said Mrs Knox eagerly.

'I seen himself and his ten pups drinking below at the lake 'ere yesterday, your honour, ma'am, and he is as big as a chestnut horse!' said Jeremiah.

'Faugh! Yesterday!' snorted Mrs Knox, 'go on to the rhododendrons, Johnny!'

The party, reinforced by Jeremiah and the pitchfork, progressed at a high rate of speed along the shrubbery path, encountering en route Lady Knox, stooping on to her horse's neck under the sweeping branches of the laurels.

'Your horse is too high for my coverts, Lady Knox,' said the Lady of the Manor, with a malicious eye at Lady Knox's flushed face and dinged hat. 'I'm afraid you will be left behind like Absalom when the hounds go away!'

'As they never do anything but hunt rabbits here,' retorted her ladyship, 'I don't think that's very likely.'

Mrs Knox gave her donkey another whack and passed on.

'Rabbits, my dear!' she said scornfully to Philippa. 'That's all she knows about it. I declare it disgusts me to see a woman of that age making such a Judy of herself! Rabbits indeed!'

Down in the middle of the rhododendrons everything was quiet for a time. Philippa strained her eyes in vain to see anything of the riders; the horn blowing and the whip cracking passed on almost out of hearing. Once or twice a hound worked through the rhododendrons, glanced at the party, and hurried on, immersed in business. All at once, Johnny, the donkey boy, whispered excitedly:

'Look at he! Look at he!' and pointed to a boulder of grey rock that stood out among the dark evergreens. A big yellow cub was crouching on it; he instantly slid down into the shelter of the bushes, and the irrepressible Jeremiah, uttering a rending shriek, plunged into the thicket after him. Two or three hounds came rushing at the sound, and after this Philippa says she finds some difficulty in recalling the proper order of events: chiefly, she confesses, because of the wholly ridiculous tears of excitement that blurred her eyes.

'We ran,' she said, 'we simply tore, and the donkey galloped, and as for that old Mrs Knox, she was giving cracked screams to the hounds all the time, and they were screaming too; and then somehow we were all out of the road!'

What seems to have occurred was that three couple of hounds, Jeremiah Regan, and Mrs Knox's equipage, amongst them somehow hustled the cub out of Aussolas' demesne and up on to a hill on the farther side of the road. Jeremiah was sent back by his mistress to fetch Flurry, and the rest of the party pursued a thrilling course along the road, parallel with that of the hounds, who were hunting slowly through the gorse on the hillside.

'Upon my honour and word, Mrs Yeates, my dear, we have the hunt to ourselves!' said Mrs Knox to the panting Philippa, as they pounded along the road. 'Johnny, d'ye see the fox?'

'I do, ma'am!' shrieked Johnny, who possessed the usual

field-glass vision bestowed upon his kind. 'Look at him over-right of us on the hill above! Hi! The spotty dog have him! No, he's gone from him! Gwan out o' that!'

This to the donkey, with blows that sounded like the beating of carpets, and produced rather more dust.

They had left Aussolas some half a mile behind, when, from a strip of wood on their right, the fox suddenly slipped over the bank on to the road just ahead of them, ran up it for a few yards and whisked in at a small entrance gate, with the three couple of hounds yelling on a red-hot scent, not thirty yards behind. The bath-chair party whirled in at their heels, Philippa and the donkey considerably blown, Johnny scarlet through his freckles, but as fresh as paint, the old lady blind and deaf to all things save the chase. The hounds went raging through the shrubs beside the drive, and away down a grassy slope towards the shallow glen, in the bottom of which ran a little stream, and after them over the grass bumped the bath-chair. At the stream they turned sharply and ran up the glen towards the avenue, which crossed it by means of a rough stone viaduct.

"Pon me conscience, he's into the old culvert!' exclaimed Mrs Knox; 'there was one of my hounds choked there once, long ago! Beat on the donkey, Johnny!'

At this juncture Philippa's narrative again becomes incoherent, not to say breathless. She is, however, positive that it was some-where about here that the upset of the bath-chair occurred, but she cannot be clear as to whether she picked up the donkey or Mrs Knox, or whether she herself was picked up by Johnny while Mrs Knox picked up the donkey. From my knowledge of Mrs Knox I should say she picked herself up and no-one else. At all events, the next salient point is the palpitating moment when Mrs Knox, Johnny and Philippa, successively applying eye to the opening of the culvert by which the stream trickled under the viaduct, while five dripping hounds bayed and leaped around them, discovered by more senses than that of sight that the fox was in it, and furthermore that one of the hounds was in it too.

'There's a strong grating before him at the far end,' said Johnny, his head in at the mouth of the hole, his voice sounding as if he were talking into a jug, 'the two of them's fighting in it; they'll be choked surely!'

'Then don't stand gabbling there, you little fool, but get in and pull the hound out!' exclaimed Mrs Knox, who was balancing herself on a stone in the stream.

'I'd be in dread, ma'am,' whined Johnny.

'Balderdash!' said the implacable Mrs Knox. 'In with you!'

I understand that Philippa assisted Johnny into the culvert, and presume that it was in doing so that she acquired the two Robinson Crusoe bare footprints which decorated her jacket when I met her next.

'Have you got hold of him yet, Johnny?' cried Mrs Knox up the culvert.

'I have, ma'am, by the tail,' responded Johnny's voice, sepulchral in the depths.

'Can you stir him, Johnny,?'

'I cannot, ma'am, and the water is rising in it.'

'Well, please God they'll not open the mill-dam!' remarked Mrs Knox philosophically to Philippa, as she caught hold of Johnny's dirty ankles. 'Hold on to the tail, Johnny!'

She hauled, with, as much might be expected, no appreciable result. 'Run my dear and look for somebody, and we'll have that fox yet!'

Philippa ran, whither she knew not, pursued by fearful visions of bursting mill-dams, and maddened foxes at bay. As she sped up the avenue she heard voices, robust male voices, in a shrubbery, and made for them. Advancing along an embowered walk towards her was what she took for one wild instant to be a funeral; a second glance showed her that it was a party of clergymen of all ages, walking by twos and threes in the dappled shade of the over-arching trees. Obviously she had intruded her sacrilegious presence into a Clerical Meeting. She acknowledges that at this awe-inspiring spectacle she faltered, but the thought of Johnny, the hound and the fox, suffocating, possibly drowning together in the culvert, nerved her. She does not remember what she said or how she said it, but I fancy she must have conveyed to them the impression that old Mrs Knox was being drowned, as she immediately found herself leading a charge of the Irish Church towards the scene of the disaster.

Fate has not always used me well, but on this occasion it was mercifully decreed that I and the other members of the hunt should be privileged to arrive in time to see my wife and her rescue party precipitating themselves down the glen.

'Holy Biddy!' ejaculated Flurry, 'is she running a paper chase with all the parsons? But look! For pity's sake will you look at my grandmother and my Uncle Eustace?'

Mrs Knox and her sworn enemy, the old clergyman, whom I had met at dinner the night before, were standing, apparently in the stream, tugging at two bare legs that projected from a hole in the viaduct, and arguing at the top of their voices. The bath-chair lay on its side with the donkey grazing beside it, on the bank a stout Archdeacon was tendering advice, and the hounds danced and howled round the entire group.

'I tell you, Eliza, you had better let the Archdeacon try,' thundered Mr Hamilton.

'Then I tell you I will not!' vociferated Mrs Knox, with a tug at the end of the sentence that elicited a subterranean lament from Johnny. 'Now who was right about the second grating? I told you so twenty years ago!'

Exactly as Philippa and her rescue party arrived, the efforts of Mrs Knox and her brother-in-law triumphed. The struggling, sopping form of Johnny was slowly drawn from the hole, drenched, speechless, but clinging to the stern of a hound, who, in its turn, had its jaws fast in the hind-quarters of a limp, yellow cub.

'Oh, it's dead!' wailed Philippa. 'I did think I should have been in time to save it!'

'Well, if that doesn't beat all!' said Dr Hickey.

from Badminton Magazine reprinted in SOME EXPERIENCES
OF AN IRISH R.M. *1899*

A 'deuce of a dustin''

R. S. SURTEES

The hounds had not been long in cover ere the feathering of Trumpeter and Tuneable (both from the Badminton) satisfied our distinguished master that a fox was at home, and, getting the Baker horse by the head, he dashed into the nearest thicket of the brushwood, followed by such of the pack as had witnessed the move. 'Yooi, push 'em up,' cheered Facey, with a slight crack of his whip, and on the instant a great ruddy-coated, white throated, irate-looking dog fox dashed out of his grassy lair in full view of Trumpeter, who raised such an exclamation of joy and surprise as electrified the rest of the pack, and brought them pell-mell to the spot to share in the crash and the triumph. What a commotion was there! A pack of vigorous foxhounds, all getting a whiff of the scent by turns, each particular hound giving as it were a receipt in full for the whole. What a crash they make! and the old wood echoes and reverberates the sound with most usurious interest. Then the critics, both hostile and friendly, began cocking their ears for censure or for praise, while the unprejudiced sportsmen sat revelling in the melody, half wishing the fox would break cover, and yet half that he would stay, and have a little more taken out of him ere he fled. And sly Reynard, apparently considering the matter, and leaving the dreadful clamour behind him, thought he had better get a little farther ahead before he ventured to leave his comfortable quarters, so, running a couple of liberal rings, he so foiled the ground as to bring the clamorous hounds to their noses, and give him a much better chance of escape. And as the music sensibly lessened and some were beginning to abuse the scent and Facey was cheering on the hounds that could hold it, the twang of a horn softened through the wood, changing the whole course of the performance.

It was Daniel! The Right Honourable the Hurl of Scamperdale's Daniel! doing with his horn what he was unable to do with his husky voice, and its notes were caught and immediately drowned by the clamour that followed them.

The fox was indeed away! Well away; for he must have been a bold one to return in the face of such a yelling.

Meanwhile Daniel was on with the leading hounds, leaving Facey and Chowey to bring the rest after him. There was a rare scent, and he chuckled to himself to think they would never catch him up. So he sailed gallantly over Mapperton Meadows, taking Babington Brook in his stride. Then Romford, who had nothing but his quick ear to guide him – never having seen a yard of the country before – settled himself in his saddle, and went tearing and crashing away through the cover to where he thought he heard the last notes of the horn, while the well-informed field diverged to the right or the left, according as their former experience guided them; some thinking the fox was away for Helsope Hill, others that he was sure to go to Hurlestone Crags, and the leader of each detachment coursed over the country, so as to lead his followers to the point with as little risk to his life or limb as possible. Each party came in view just as Romford with a gallant effort, superseded Swig, who now fell back upon the mouth-extended, gaping Chowley. 'For-rard! For-rard!' was the cry, though it was scarcely possible for hounds to go faster.

Most hunts have their crack rider, a man whom they think can beat everybody; and Captain Spurrier, of Cherrymount, had long held that honourable office with the old Larkspur Hunt. Not that it is usual form to ride at the master or huntsman; but the other Mr Romford not having the same reputation of being a great horseman, the Captain thought it might be well to show him how they did things in the far-famed Doubleimupshire. But for this he would have preferred retiring into private life now on the accession of a new master, for a strong tinge of hoar-frost had shot across his once dark brown whiskers, and hardish falls had somewhat quenched the love of leaping. Still, men don't like to admit they are not so good as they have been, and persevere on, in hopes that it is only a temporary depression, from which they will speedily rally. Each time they go out they think they will just show off that day, and be done; but somehow they always think they will just have another last day, and then one more, and so on, till they get beat, and give up hunting in disgust.

Happy are they who go out to please themselves, and not to astonish others. So thought Mr Joseph Large, as, having taken the fiery edge off the chestnut in the deep holding clay rides of the cover, he gained the hard road, and resolved to stick to it as long as he could. 'Pretty thing it would be for a man of his means to break his neck after a nasty, crafty, hen-stealing fox.' So saying, he knotted his curb-rein, and letting it drop, proceeded to take his charge out of the chestnut now that he had got him subdued. He even ventured to spur him, not very severely, but just sufficient to let the horse know that he had a pair on.

With the before mentioned erroneous impression of the prow-

ess of friend Facey, Captain Spurrier hustled his horse and hardened
his heart, determined to ride as of yore; and great was his surprise
when, on clearing the cover, he saw the pusillanimous Romford,
as he thought, sailing away, taking the large bull-finchers just as
if they came in his way, without swerving either to the right or
the left.

'Spurting rider!' muttered Spurrier, grinding his teeth, adding,
'he'll change his tune before he gets to Collington Wood', for
which the hounds seemed then to be evidently pointing. So
saying, the Captain put spurs to his little thoroughbred steeplechase horse, and shot in between Facey and Daniel Swig, who
was now careering along in the wake of his master.

A great and widespread avalanche of sportsmen followed,
some by one route, some by another, the programme widening
towards its base, just like the pyramids of Egypt, or a lady's
petticoat. The ground sloped gradually to the right, giving all
those who had time to look after anything but themselves a fine
panoramic view of the chase – hounds in a cluster – Romford
close up – Spurrier hard upon him – Swig next to Spurrier, and
Chowey mixed up in a miscellaneous group of horsemen –
now a red coat leading, now a black, now a red again. The air
was bright and rarefied, and echo multiplied the music of hounds.
It was both a good seeing, a good scenting, and a good hearing
day – quite a bespeak for an opening day.

The farther they went, the more Captain Spurrier was lost in
astonishment of Mr Romford's masterly performance. He didn't
seem to care a halfpenny for anything. All he looked to was
being with hounds. Brooks, banks, walls, woods, all seemed
equally indifferent to him. 'What nonsense people talked about
Romford not being a rider,' he thought. '[He] was just about the
hardest rider he had ever seen. Little Spratt was nothing to him.'
And Spurrier inwardly congratulated himself upon not being
bound to beat Mr Romford. Such a back and such shoulders he
had never seen in conjunction with such a powerful horse.
Altogether, Spurrier pronounced Romford a very formidable
opponent. And he wondered if Romford would introduce him
to Lord Lovetin. Mrs Spurrier would like it very much, if he
would. So they sailed away over Sharperow and Strother lord-
ships, past Tasborough, leaving Thirkeld on the right and

Welbury on the left, till the ploughed lands of Portgate slackened their paces and brought the hounds to their noses.

'Hold hard!' was at length the cry, and gratefully it sounded to the ears of the forward; grateful it was, too, to those behind, who by now putting on might yet hope to get a saving view of the scene. So they hurried forward in clamorous vigour, determined to be able to say how it was up to Heatherwicke Green, at all events; and a great wave of sportsmen surged to the front ere Mr Romford, having let the hounds make their own cast, now essayed to assist them in full view of a panting but still critical field.

We are all great judges of hunting. Romford, nothing flurried, had employed a brief interval in watching the spreading and trying of the hounds, and surveying the same.

'Francis Romford,' said he to himself, 'if you were the fox, what would you do under these circumstances? You may have been headed by that noisy long-tailed team, with the man riding on stilts, or you may have been chased by that ill-conditioned cur who has a very felonious look about him; but, anyhow, I think, Francis Romford, with that range of rocky hills in front, you would get on ahead, and try to ensconce yourself amongst them.' So saying, Facey determined to make a wide cast in front, and try to recover his friend. And the perspiring field sat watching the move – if successful, to call it a good one; if not, to denounce it as the wildest cast that ever was made.

Facey didn't get his hounds together like a flock of sheep, but allowed them to spread and use their own sagacity, going at a very gentle pace, without hurrying and blustering from the whips. Two fields ahead brought him to the rapid-running eddying Fleet, now even with the banks from the effects of recent rains. It was neither jumpable nor fordable, but it was swimmable, and as such Facey took it.

He blobbed in and scrambled out. The hounds blobbed in and scrambled out.

Chowey declined.

It suddenly occurred to him the Raschild was missing.

Captain Spurrier looked at the still agitated water, and said, 'Ah! that would not have stopped me, but I've got a dose of camomile in me this morning'. He then joined the ruck, and rode by the bridge at Beltingford Burn. A hard road here favoured them, and as the field clattered along, they commented in the fragmentary ejaculations on the rashness of swimming, and the general disagreeableness of water in winter.

'He must have viewed the fox,' said Mr Tuppen, 'or he would never have risked his life in that way,' adding, 'Have known many a man drowned in that river.'

'Or is going to be a halloo!' suggested Mr Markwell, who had just joined.

'A rare 'un to ride!' observed Mr Joseph Large, proud of his protégé.

But Romford had neither viewed the fox nor heard a halloo. He was simply following his own instinct that the fox was forrard; and if he didn't find him forrard, he would have swum it back to try it again.

But fortune does favour the brave, and Facey had no occasion to give his new coat laps or Bedford cords another wetting; for, after a hearty shaking, the bustling pack again spread to pursue their sniffing investigations on the south side of the river; and at a reverse in the second hedgerow dividing a ploughed from a pasture field, the Beaufort Brilliant gave such a note of exclamation as electrified the pack, and in an instant the rickety fence cracked and bent with their weight.

'HOOP!' cheered Facey, delighted with his prowess. He didn't care a copper for his Bedford cords, nor yet for his new coat laps.

Meanwhile the hounds got away with renewed melody, renovating the roadsters, and making the country ring with their energy. The face of the landscape now changed, inclining upwards the dark frowning hills, which divided the vale from the moorlands above. The enclosures, too, got larger and larger – twenty, thirty and forty acres each – while the surface was more openly exposed, flat and expansive, with very weak hedges, and few hollows for concealment or out-of-sight running. The hounds showed to great advantage, striving and racing for the mastery. A sheet would cover them.

'Dash it! but they are a rare lot!' muttered Facey, eyeing their performances. 'And didn't cost much either,' chuckled he, thinking how he got them. 'Forrard! forrard!' cheered he, fanning the flame of ardour. So they went screeching and pressing to the front – now Prosperous leading, now Terrible. Dash it! He didn't know whether the Beaufort or the Belvoir were the best. Didn't think even Bonsman himself could beat some of the former. Monstrous lucky he was to get them.

Facey next views the fox stealing steadily over what was once Coltsfoot Common, with an attendant canopy of crows hovering over him, indicating his course. 'Yow! yow! yap!' went the bustling hounds. 'Caw! caw! caw!' went the birds. So the poor fox had a double set of pursuers.

On he went, however, steadily and perseveringly. He had beat the old Larkspur hounds twice, and did not see why he should not beat Mr Romford's. But nearer and nearer came the notes of the pack, commingling with the vociferous cawing of the black gentry above. It was hard to say which seemed the most inveterate against the unfortunate fox. Still, the many caverned rocks were close at hand, and if he could gain them, they might work for a week before they got him out. There they girded the horizon in frowning attitude, the dark interstices looking a most inviting refuge. Facey saw the difficulty. If the fox and hounds held on at the same pace the fox would inevitably gain the rocks and beat the hounds. This was not to be desired. Especially on a first day after a good run. So clapping spurs to Pull-Devil-Pull Baker, now, indeed, made into Placid Joe, he capped them on from scent to view; and, after a smart race, the Belvoir Dreadnought pulled the fox down by the brush, just as he was ascending the reef of rocks.

'WHO-HOOP!' shrieked Romford, in a voice that made the hills ring and reverberate. '*Who-hoop!*' repeated he, throwing himself from his horse, and diving into the midst of the pack, to extricate the fox from their fangs. Up he held him triumphantly, with the baying of the hounds jumping and frolicking around. 'Take my horse away now,' cried Facey to Swig, and the coast being clear Facey advanced a few steps to where a soft mossy bank seemed to invite the performance of the last obsequies of the chase. There, on the bright green cushion, he cast the nut-brown fox.

Meanwhile, the field having availed themselves of the facilities of Beltingford Bridge, were now making the air and the hard road ring with the voices and the noise of their horses' hoofs, all in a deuce of a stew lest they should lose the hounds, or not be up at the kill. They had not yet arrived at the elegant point of indifference that makes men turn their horses' heads homewards as soon as they hear the 'who-hoop!' and most satisfactorily (though none of them admitted it) Romford's death note sounded on their ears.

They had all about had enough. The gallant Captain Spurrier had lost a shoe, Mr Blanton had lost two, while Mr James Allnut and his son had lost five between them.

Mr Romford took no advantage of their circumlocution, but keeping the fox on the green bank, maintained the ardour of the pack by repeated whoops and halloos. So there was a very lively circle when the last of the field arrived. Facey and the fox in the centre, the baying hounds all around, Chowey and Swigg outside, contributing their occasional quota of noise to the scene.

'Well (puff) done!' exclaimed Mr Bullpig, mopping himself.

'Capital (gasp) run!' shouted Allnut, who had only seen half of it.

'Never saw better (puff) hounds in my life!' asserted Mr Large, who had never seen any but the Surrey.

Then all having come up, Chowey, at a signal from Facey, proceeded to divest the fox of his brush and his pads, prior to presenting the remainder to the hounds. Up then went the carcase, which was caught by a myriad of mouths as it fell. Tear him and eat him, was then the cry. And tear him and eat him they did. The master of the circle, Facey Romford, then quitted the ring, now somewhat difficult to maintain in consequence of the struggling efforts of the fox-devouring hounds, and having decorated Master Allnut's pony with the brush, and given the pads to those who would have them, proceeded to the outer ring, to hear how things were going on there.

There was a great discussion about the time and distance.

Mr Pyefinch said it was nine miles as the crow flies. Doctor Snuff, who had joined promiscuously on a cob, thought it was hardly that, but it was a good eight.

Mr Kickton thought it was more than eight. It was seven to Stewley Hill, and the rocks were two good miles beyond it.

Then they appealed to Mr Romford.

'How far should you say it is, Mr Romford?' demanded Mr Joseph Large, who thought he had come twenty at least.

'Faith, I have no notion!' replied Facey, adding, 'It was a right good fox anyway.'

'Capital!' ejaculated Mr Large, adding, 'It was almost a pity to kill him.'

'Not a bit,' retorted Facey; 'always kill 'em when you can. The more you kill the more you'll have to kill.'

The teapot-handle maker didn't understand that doctrine but took it for granted. He inwardly hoped there were not many such foxes in the country.

Then Facey, pretending that the run was nothing out of the way, remounted his horse, demanding where they should go next; whereupon they all cried, 'Content!' recommending him to go home and change, for he must be very wet, and began asking their own individual ways, for some people will live in the country all their lives, and yet never know where they are after hunting.

Then Mr Bullpig, having identified Hazelton Hill, and Mr Blanton the far-off Castlefield Clump, the respective cohorts filed off together to be further distributed as they proceeded. And Mr Romford having looked over his hounds and found them all right to a fraction, moved away in the direction of Middlethorpe Steeple, well pleased at having given the field such a stinger at starting. And he smoked his pipe, and played the flute with great glee, at Beldon Hall, that evening telling Lucy and her mamma that he had given his new friends a *'deuce of a dustin' '*.

from MR FACEY ROMFORD'S HOUNDS *1865*

Lost

R. S. SURTEES

''Ow that Scotch beggar rides!' exclaimed Mr Jorrocks, eyeing Pigg going as straight as an arrow, which exclamation brought him to his first fence at the bottom of the hill, over which both horsemen had passed without disturbing a twig. ''Old up hoss!' roared Mr Jorrocks, seizing the reins and whip with one hand and the cantrel of the saddle with the other, as Arterxerxes floundered sideways through a low fence with a little runner on the far side. ''Old up!' repeated he, as they scrambled through, looking back and saying, 'Terrible nasty place – wonders I ever got over. Should ha' been drund to a certainty if I'd got in. Wouldn't ride at it again for nothin' under knighthood – Sir John Jorrocks, Knight!' continued he, shortening his hold of his horse. 'And my ladyship Jorrocks!' added he. 'She'd be bad to 'old – shouldn't wonder if she'd be for going to Halmack's. Dash my buttons, but I wish I was off this beastly fallow', continued he; 'wonderful thing to me that the farmers can't see there'd be less trouble i' growing grass than in makin' these nasty rutty fields. 'Eavens be praised, there's a gate – and a lane, too,' saying which he was speedily in the latter, gathering his horse together, he sets off at a brisk trot in the direction he last saw the hounds going.

Terribly deep it was, and great Arterxerxes made a noise like the drawing of corks as he blobbed along through the stiff, holding clay.

Thus Mr Jorrocks proceeded for a mile or more, until he came upon a red-cloaked gipsy wench stealing sticks from a rotten fence on the left.

''Ave you see my 'ounds, ould gal?' inquired he, pulling up short.

'Bless your beautiful countenance, my cock angel!' exclaimed the woman, in astonishment at the sight of a man in scarlet with a face to match; 'bless your beautiful countenance, you're the very babe I've been looking for all this blessed day – cross my palm with a bit o' siller, and I'll tell you sich a fortin!'

'Cuss your fortin!' roared Jorrocks, sticking spurs into his horse, and grinning with rage at the idea of having pulled up to listen to such nonsense.

'I hope you'll brick your neck, ye nasty, ugly, old thief!' rejoined the gipsy, altering her tone.

''Opes I sharn't,' muttered Mr Jorrocks, trotting on to get out of hearing. Away he went, blob, blob, blobbing through the deep holding clay as before.

Presently he pulled up again with a 'Pray, my good man, 'ave you see my 'ounds – Mr Jorrocks' 'ounds, in fact?' of a labourer scouring a fence gutter. 'Don't you 'ear me man?' bellowed he, as the countryman stood staring with his hands on his spade.

'I be dull of hearin', sir,' at length drawled the man, advancing very slowly towards our master with his hand up to his ear.

'Oh, dear! oh, dear!' exclaimed Mr Jorrocks, starting off again, 'was there ever sich a misfortunate indiwidual as John Jorrocks? – 'Ark! vot's that? Pigg's 'orn! oh, dear, only a cow! Come hup, 'oss, I say, you hugly beast! – there surely never was sich a worthless beast lapped in leather as you,' giving Arterxerxes a good double thonging as he spoke. 'Oh, dear! oh, dear!' continued he, 'I wish I was well back at the Cross, with my 'ounds safe i' kennel. Vot a go is this! – Dinner at five – baked haddocks, prime piece of fore chine, Portingal Honions, and fried plum-pudding; and now, by these darkening clouds, it must be near four, and here I be's, miles and miles away – 'ounds still runnin', and adwertised for the "Beef and Carrots", on Wednesday – never will be fit to go, nor to the "Daisy" nouther.

'Pray, my good man,' inquired he of a drab-coated, big-backed farmer, on a bay cart-horse, whom he suddenly encountered at the turn of the road, ''ave you see anything of my 'ounds? Mr Jorrocks' 'ounds, in fact.'

'Yes, sir,' replied the farmer, all alive; 'they were running past Langford plantations with the fox dead beat close afore them.'

''Ow long since, my frind?' inquired Mr Jorrocks, brightening up.

'Oh, why just as long as it's taken me to come here – mebbe ten minutes or a quarter of an hour, not longer certainly. If you put on you may be in at the death yet.'

Away went the spurs, elbows and legs, elbows and legs, Arterxerxes was again impelled to canter, and our worthy master pounded along, all eyes, ears and fears.

from HANDLEY CROSS *1854*

The Hunt

ANTHONY TROLLOPE

Yes; the parson was as right as if he had been let into the fox's confidence overnight and had betrayed it in the morning. Gaylass was hardly in the gorse before she discovered the doomed brute's vicinity, and told of it to the whole canine confraternity. Away from his hiding-place he went, towards the open country, but immediately returned into the covert, for he saw a lot of boys before him, who had assembled with the object of looking at the hunt, but with the very probable effect of spoiling it; for, as much as a fox hates a dog, he fears the human race more, and will run from an urchin with a stick into the jaws of his much more fatal enemy.

'As long as them blackguards is there, a-hollowing, and a-screeching, divil a fox in all Ireland'd go out of this,' said Mick to his master.

'Ah, boys,' said Frank, riding up, 'if you want to see a hunt, will you keep back!'

'Begorra we will, yer honer,' said one.

'Faith – we wouldn't be afther spiling your honer's diversion, my lord, on no account,' said another.

'We'll be out o' this altogether, now this blessed minute,' said a third, but still there remained, each loudly endeavouring to banish the others.

At last, however, the fox saw a fair course before him, and away he went; and with very little start, for the dogs followed him out of the covert almost with a view.

And now the men settled themselves to the work, and began to strive for the pride of place, at least the younger portion of them: for in every field there are two classes of men. Those who go out to get the greatest possible quantity of riding, and those whose object is to get the least. Those who go to work their nags, and those who go to spare them. The former think that the excellence of the hunt depends on the horses; the latter, on the dogs. The former go to act, and the latter to see. And it is very generally the case that the least active part of the community know the most about the sport.

They, the less active part above alluded to, know every high-road and bye-road; they consult the wind, and calculate that a fox won't run with his nose against it; they remember this stream and this bog, and avoid them; they are often at the top of eminences, and only descend when they see which way the dogs are going; they take short cuts, and lay themselves out for narrow lanes; they dislike galloping, and eschew leaping; and yet when a hard-riding man is bringing up his two-hundred-guinea hunter, a minute or two late for the finish, covered with foam, trembling with his exertion, not a breath left in him – he'll probably find one of these steady fellows there before him, mounted on a broken-down screw, but as cool and as fresh as when he was brought out of the stable; and what is, perhaps, still more amazing, at the end of the day, when the hunt is canvassed after dinner, our dashing friend, who is in great doubt whether his thoroughbred steeplechaser will ever recover from his day's work, and who has been personally administering warm mashes and bandages before he would venture to take his own boots off, finds he does not know half as much about the hunt, or can tell half as correctly where the game went, as our quiet-going friend, whose hack will probably go out on the following morning under the car, with the mistress and children. Such a one was Parson Armstrong; and when Lord Ballindine and most of the others went away after the hounds, he coolly turned round in a different direction, crept through a broken wall into a peasant's garden, and over a dunghill, by the cabin door into a road, and then trotted along as demurely and leisurely as though he were going to bury an old woman in the next parish.

Frank was, generally speaking, as good-natured a man as is often met, but even he got excited and irritable when hunting his own pack. All masters of hounds do. Someone was always too forward, another too near the dogs, a third interfering with the servants, and a fourth making too much noise.

'Confound it, Peter,' he said, when they had gone over a field or two, and the dogs missed the scent for a moment, 'I thought at any rate you knew better than to cross the dogs that way.'

'Who crossed the dogs?' said the other. 'What nonsense you're talking: why I wasn't out of the potato field till they were nearly all at the next wall.'

'Well, it may be nonsense,' continued Frank; 'but when I see a man riding right through the hounds, and they hunting, I call that crossing them.'

'Hoicks! tally' – hollowed someone – 'there's Graceful has it again – well done, Granger! Faith, Frank, that's a good dog! if he's not first, he's always second.'

'Now, gentlemen, steady, for heaven's sake. Do let the dogs settle to their work before you're a-top of them. Upon my soul, Nicholas Brown, it's ridiculous to see you!'

'It'd be a good thing if he were half as much in a hurry to get to heaven,' said Bingham Blake.

'Thank'ee,' said Nicholas; 'go to heaven yourself. I'm well enough where I am.'

And now they were off again. In the next field the whole pack caught a view of the fox just as he was stealing out; and after him they went, with their noses well above the ground, their voices loud and clear, and in one bevy.

Away they went; the game was strong; the scent was good; the ground was soft, but not too soft; and a magnificent hunt they had; but there were some misfortunes shortly after getting away. Barry Lynch, wishing, in his ignorance, to lead and show himself off, and not knowing how – scurrying along among the dogs, and bothered at every leap, had given great offence to Lord Ballindine. But, not wishing to speak severely to a man whom he would not under any circumstances address in a friendly way, he talked at him, and endeavoured to bring him to order by blowing up others in his hearing. But this was thrown away on Barry, and he continued his career in a most disgusting manner; scrambling through gaps together with the dogs, crossing other men without the slightest reserve, annoying everyone, and evidently pluming himself on his performance. Frank's brow was getting blacker and blacker. Jerry Blake and young Brown were greatly amusing themselves at the exhibition, and every now and then gave him a word or two of encouragement, praising his mare, telling him how well he got over that last fence, and bidding him mind and keep well forward. This was all new to Barry, and he really began to feel himself in his element; – if it hadn't been for those abominable walls, he would have enjoyed himself. But this was too good to last, and before very long he made a *faux pas*, which brought down on him in a torrent the bottled-up wrath of the viscount.

They had been galloping across a large, unbroken sheepwalk, which exactly suited Barry's taste, and he had got well forward towards the hounds. Frank was behind, expostulating with Jerry Blake and the other for encouraging him, when the dogs came to a small stone wall about two feet and a half high. In this there was a broken gap, through which many of them crept. Barry also saw this happy escape from the grand difficulty of jumping, and, ignorant that if he rode the gap at all, he should let the hounds go first, made for it right among them, in spite of Frank's voice, now raised loudly to caution him. The horse the man rode knew his business better than himself, and tried to spare the dogs which were under his feet; but, in getting out, he made a slight spring, and came down on the haunches of a favourite young hound called 'Goneaway', he broke the leg close to the socket, and the poor beast most loudly told his complaint.

This was too much to be borne, and Frank rode up red with passion; and a lot of others, including the whipper, soon followed.

'He has killed the dog!' said he. 'Did you ever see such a clumsy, ignorant fool? Mr Lynch, if you'd do me the honour to stay away another day, and amuse yourself in any other way, I should be much obliged.'

'It wasn't my fault then,' said Barry.

'Do you mean to give me the lie, sir?' replied Frank.

'The dog got under the horse's feet. How was I to help it?'

There was a universal titter at this, which made Barry wish himself home again, with his brandy-bottle.

'Ah! sir,' said Frank; 'you're as fit to ride a hunt as you are to do anything else which gentlemen usually do. May I trouble you to make yourself scarce? Your horse, I see, can't carry you much further, and if you'll take my advice you'll go home, before you've ridden over yourself. Well, Martin, is the bone broken?'

Martin had got off his horse, and was kneeling down beside the poor hurt brute. 'Indeed it is, my lord, in two places. You'd better let Tony kill him; he has an awful sprain in the back, as well; he'll niver put a foot to the ground again.'

'By heavens, that's too bad! isn't it, Bingham? He was, out and out, the finest puppy we entered last year.'

'What can you expect,' said Bingham, 'when such fellows as that come into a field? He's as much business here as a cow in a drawing-room.'

'But what can we do? – one can't turn him off the land; if he chooses to come, he must.'

'Why yes,' said Bingham, 'if he will come he must. But then, if he insists on doing so, he may be horsewhipped; he may be ridden over; he may be kicked; and he may be told that he's a low, vulgar, paltry scoundrel; and, if he repeats his visits, that's the treatment he'll probably receive.'

Barry was close to both the speakers, and of course heard, and was intended to hear, every word that was said. He contented himself, however, with muttering defiances, and was seen and heard no more of that day.

The hunt was continued, and the fox was killed; but Frank and those with him saw but little more of it. However, as soon as directions were given for the death of poor Goneaway, they went on, and received a very satisfactory account of the proceedings from those who had seen the finish. As usual, the Parson was among the number, and he gave them a most detailed history, not only of the fox's proceedings during the day, but also of all the reasons which actuated the animal, in every different turn he took.

'I declare, Armstrong,' said Peter Dillon, 'I think you were a fox yourself, once! Do you remember anything about it?'

'What a run he would give!' said Jerry; 'the best pack that was ever kennelled wouldn't have a chance with him.'

'Who was that old chap,' said Nicholas Dillon, showing off his classical learning, 'who said that dead animals always became something else? – maybe it's only in the course of nature for a dead fox to become a live parson.'

'Exactly: you've hit it,' said Armstrong; 'and, in the same way, the moment the breath is out of a goose it becomes an idle squireen, and, generally speaking, a younger brother.'

from THE KELLYS AND THE O'KELLYS *1848*

Squire Western in Pursuit

HENRY FIELDING

The reader may be pleased to remember that the said squire departed from the inn in great fury, and in that fury he pursued his daughter. The ostler having informed him that she had crossed the Severn, he likewise passed that river with his equipage, and rode full speed, vowing the utmost vengeance against poor Sophia, if he should but overtake her.

He had not gone far before he arrived at a cross-way. Here he called a short council of war, in which, after hearing different opinions, he at last gave the direction of his pursuit to Fortune, and struck directly into the Worcester road.

In this road he proceeded about two miles, when he began to bemoan himself most bitterly, frequently crying out, 'What a pity is it! Sure never was so unlucky a dog as myself!' And then burst forth a volley of oaths and execrations. . . . 'Pogh! d—n the slut! I am lamenting the loss of so fine a morning for hunting. It is confounded hard to lose one of the best scenting days, in all appearance, which hath been this season, and especially after so long a frost.'

Whether Fortune, who now and then shows some compassion in her wantonest tricks, might not take pity on the squire, and, as she had determined not to let him overtake his daughter, might not resolve to make him amends some other way, I will not assert; but he had hardly uttered the words just before commemorated, and two or three oaths at their heels, when a pack of hounds began to open their melodious throats at a small distance from them, which the squire's horse and his rider both perceiving immediately pricked up their ears, and the squire crying, 'She's gone, she's gone! damn me if she is not gone!' instantly clapped spurs to the beast, who little needed it, having indeed the same inclination with his Master; and now the whole company, crossing into a corn-field, rode directly towards the hounds, with much hallooing and whooping, while the poor parson, blessing himself, brought up the rear. . . .

The hounds ran hard, as it is called, and the squire pursued over hedge and ditch, with all his usual vociferation and alacrity, and with all his usual pleasure nor did the thoughts of Sophia ever once intrude themselves to allay the satisfaction he enjoyed in the chase, and which he said was one of the finest he ever saw, and which he swore was very well worth going fifty miles for. As the squire forgot his daughter, the servants, we may easily believe, forgot their mistress; and the parson after having expressed much astonishment, in Latin, to himself, at length likewise abandoned all further thoughts of the young lady, and, jogging on at a distance behind, began to meditate a portion of doctrine for the ensuing Sunday.

The squire who owned the hounds was highly pleased with the arrival of his brother squire and sportsman; for all men approve merit in their own way, and no man was more expert in the field than Mr Western, nor did any other better know how to encourage the dogs with his voice, and to animate the hunt.

Sportsmen, in the warmth of a chase, are too much engaged to attend to any manner of ceremony, nay even to the offices of humanity; for if any of them meet with an accident by tumbling into a ditch or into a river, the rest pass on regardless, and generally leave him to his fate. During this time, therefore, the two squires, though often close to each other, interchanged not a single word. The master of the hunt, however, often saw and approved the great judgement of the stranger in drawing the dogs when they were at fault, and hence conceived a very high opinion of his understanding, as the number of his attendants inspired no small reverence to his quality. As soon, therefore, as the sport was ended by the death of the little animal, which had occasioned it, the two squires met, and in all squire-like greetings saluted each other.

The conversation was entertaining enough, and what we may perhaps relate in an appendix or on some other occasion; but as it nowise concerns this history, we cannot prevail on ourselves to give it a place here. It concluded with a second chase, and that with an invitation to dinner. This being accepted, was followed by a hearty bout of drinking, which ended in as hearty a nap on the part of Squire Western.

Our squire was by no means a match either for his host or for Parson Supple at his cups that evening; for which the violent fatigue of mind as well as body that he had undergone may very well account, without the least derogation from his honour. He was indeed, according to the vulgar phrase, whistle-drunk; for before he had swallowed the third bottle he became so entirely overpowered, that though he was not carried off to bed till long after, the parson considered him as absent; and having acquainted the other squire with all relating to Sophia, he obtained his promise of seconding those arguments which he intended to urge the next morning for Mr Western's return.

No sooner, therefore, had the good squire shaken off his evening and began to call for his morning draught, and to summon his horses in order to renew his pursuit, than Mr Supple began his dissuasives, which the host so strongly seconded, that they at last prevailed, and Mr Western agreed to return home; being principally moved by one argument, viz. that he knew not which way to go, and might probably be riding farther from his daughter instead of towards her. He then took leave of his brother sportsman, and expressing great joy that the frost had broken (which might perhaps be no small motive to his hastening home), set forwards, or rather backwards, for Somersetshire; but not before he had first despatched part of his retinue in quest of his daughter, after whom he likewise sent a volley of the most bitter execrations which he could invent.

from THE HISTORY OF TOM JONES, A FOUNDLING *1749*

Training in the Hunting Field

DAVID ITZKOWITZ

Country life became associated with the hardy virtues, as contrasted with the softer, effeminate life of the city. Though these sentiments reached their peak in the mid-nineteenth century, they have their roots in the eighteenth.

Blane had contrasted the sports of the field to the 'softer amusements of the assembly and card-table', and the French war had served to raise the prestige of robust physical activities. Foxhunting was held to be especially praiseworthy because it was believed to be excellent training for war. As James Yorke wrote to the Countess de Grey in 1802:

> I need not enlarge upon the political advantages of encouraging a sport which propagates a fine breed of horses, and prevents our young men from growing quite effeminate in Bond Street, nor upon the high reputation of the English horse abroad, which are perhaps the only cavalry that ever won whole battles against a very superior force of horse and foot. . . .

The glorification of hunting as training for war persisted unchallenged up to the First World War. Hunting was credited with producing every English victory, and even gallant defeat, from Waterloo through the Crimea and the innumerable colonial wars. 'This winter belongs to history as the terrible one spent by our Army in Crimea,' wrote Will Goodall, the Belvoir huntsman, in 1854, 'and the magnificent patience and courage with which our men bore their hardships spoke volumes for the training given them by English sports.' Fifty years later, another hunting man had similar thoughts: 'How many of that first batch of gallant yeomen who sprang to arms five years ago in the hours of their country's difficulty, and who did such splendid service for their native land in South Africa, were trained in the hunting field!'

Army officers were encouraged to hunt, though few of them needed any great encouragement, and most of them generally got long leaves during the hunting season for that purpose. Officers quartered within the boundaries of a hunt were usually welcome to follow the pack without paying a subscription because it was believed that the hunt was thereby aiding the country, as well as repaying the officers for their gallant service. When Lord Lonsdale, Master of the Quorn, was told during World War I that hunting was not necessary to the War effort he was shocked. What, he wanted to know, would officers home on leave from the front do if they could not hunt? It was totally beyond his comprehension that there could be officers in Britain's wartime army who had never hunted in their lives. No one seemed to find it odd that some of the most foremost hunting officers of the Victorian years found hunting such valuable training that when their regiments were sent to fight, they transferred to others so as not to miss the hunting.

Ironically, not only was hunting not the good training that its proponents claimed, it may even have been harmful. Though it undoubtedly inculcated reckless courage in many young officers, it taught neither prudence nor good sense; the hard riding and reckless, devil-may-care bravery that made Lord Cardigan one of the most prominent Meltonians of his day also contributed to the charge at Balaclava. Cardigan, a hero to most of the population, was an even greater hero to foxhunters, who quickly pointed out that both Cardigan and Captain Nolan were staunch foxhunters and that several packs of hounds were kept by British officers in the Crimea.

Throughout the nineteenth century hunting continued to be justified on the grounds that it was conducive to manliness. Manliness was taken to mean more than simple physical courage. It included such virtues as hardiness, temperance, coolness, and clearheadedness. It was considered as much a mental as a physical trait. Hunting was held to strengthen the mind, intellectually and morally, as well as the body. Delabere Blaine, who wrote a treatise on field sports in 1840, for example, included a chapter entitled 'The Beneficial Effects of Field Sports on the Mind'. The Rev. Charles Kingsley, Canon of Chester and Westminster, Chaplain to Queen Victoria, and Professor of Modern History at Cambridge, 1860–69, was another ardent sportsman. He advocated hunting for clergymen as much as, or even more than, laymen.

Foxhunters were also quick to seize upon the fact that, though other nations had their own forms of hunting, foxhunting existed nowhere else. It was uniquely British. They therefore treated it as being both the product and the moulder of a uniquely British character. They were proud of the fact that few foreigners seemed capable of understanding its traditions. Stories abound in sporting literature of foolish mistakes made by foreigners in the hunting field. Their point was generally not that foreigners were themselves laughable or contemptible, but that, by its very nature, hunting was incomprehensible to them. A typical example was this story told by a Berkshire foxhunter in 1851:

> I recollect once having met a foreigner at a foxhunt. The horses and dogs were in the best of spirits, the sky was everything that it ought to be, and everything looked promisingly, and augured a good day's sport: but there occurred one of those untoward accidents which it is impossible to forsee or provide against, and the fox was chopped in cover. My friend the foreigner thereupon turned to the Master of Hounds . . . and exclaimed: 'Oh, my lord Duke, I congratulate you on having killed that animal so soon, and with so little trouble!'

from PECULIAR PRIVILEGE *1977*

PART VI

The Horse in Fiction

With lightest of hands on the bridle, with lightest of
hearts in the dance,
To the gods of Adventure and Laughter he quaffed
the red wine of Romance,
Then wistfully turning the goblet he spilled the last
drops at our feet,
And left us his tales to remember and left us his
songs to repeat.

Will Ogilvie

The First Ride

GEORGE BORROW

And it came to pass that, as I was standing by the door of the barrack stable, one of the grooms came out to me, saying, 'I say, young gentleman, I wish you would give the cob a breathing this fine morning.'

'Why do you wish me to mount him?' said I, 'you know he is dangerous. I saw him fling you off his back only a few days ago.'

'Why, that's the very thing, master. I'd rather see anybody on his back than myself; he does not like me; but, to them he does, he can be as gentle as a lamb.'

'But suppose,' said I, 'that he should not like me?'

'We shall soon see that, master,' said the groom; 'and, if so be he shows temper, I will be the first to tell you to get down. But there's no fear of that; you have never angered or insulted him, and to such as you, I say again, he'll be as gentle as a lamb.'

'And how came you to insult him,' said I, 'knowing his temper as you do?'

'Merely through forgetfulness, master. I was riding him about a month ago, and having a stick in my hand, I struck him, thinking I was on another horse, or rather thinking of nothing at all. He has never forgiven me, though before that time he was the only friend I had in the world; I should like to see you on him, master.'

'I should soon be off him; I can't ride.'

'Then you are all right, master; there's no fear. Trust him for not hurting a young gentleman, an officer's son who can't ride. If you were a blackguard dragoon, indeed, with long spurs, 'twere another thing; as it is, he'll treat you as if he were the elder brother that loves you. Ride! He'll soon teach you to ride, if you leave the matter with him. He's the best riding master in all Ireland, and the gentlest.'

The cob was led forth; what a tremendous creature. I had frequently seen him before, and wondered at him; he was barely fifteen hands, but he had the girth of a metropolitan dray-horse, his head was small in comparison with his immense neck, which curved down nobly to his wide back. His chest was broad and fine, and his shoulders models of symmetry and strength; he stood well and powerfully upon his legs, which were somewhat short. In a word, he was a gallant specimen of the genuine Irish cob, a species at one time not uncommon, but at the present day nearly extinct.

'There!' said the groom, as he looked at him, half-admiringly, half-sorrowfully. 'With sixteen stone on his back, he'll trot fourteen miles in one hour; with your nine stone, some two and half more, ay, and clear a six-foot wall at the end of it.'

'I'm half afraid,' said I. 'I had rather you would ride him.'

'I'd rather so, too, if he would let me; but he remembers the blow. Now, don't be afraid, young master, he's longing to go out himself. He's been trampling with his feet these three days, and I know what that means; he'll let anybody ride him but myself, and thank them; but to me he says, "No! you struck me."'

'But,' said I, 'where's the saddle?'

'Never mind the saddle if you are ever to be a frank rider, you must begin without a saddle; besides, if he felt a saddle, he would think you don't trust him, and leave you to yourself. Now, before you mount, make his acquaintance – see there, how he kisses you and licks your face, and see how he lifts his foot, that's to shake hands. You may trust him – now you are on his back at last; mind how you hold the bridle – gently, gently! It's not four pair of hands like yours can hold him if he wishes to be off. Mind what I tell you – leave it all to him.'

Off went the cob at a slow and gentle trot, too fast and rough, however, for so inexperienced a rider. I soon felt myself sliding off, the animal perceived it too, and instantly stood stone still till I had righted myself; and now the groom came up: 'When you feel yourself going,' said he, 'don't lay hold of the mane, that's no use; mane never yet saved man from falling, no more than straw from drowning; it's his sides you must cling to with your calves and feet, till you learn to balance yourself. That's it, now abroad with you; I'll bet my comrade a pot of beer that you'll be a regular rough rider by the time you come back.'

And so it proved; I followed the directions of the groom, and the cob gave me every assistance. How easy is riding, after the first timidity is got over, to supple and youthful limbs; and there is no second fear. The creature soon found that the nerves of his rider were in proper tone. Turning his head half round he made a kind of whining noise, flung out a little foam, and set off.

In less than two hours I had made the circuit of the Devil's Mountain, and was returning along the road, bathed with perspiration, but screaming with delight; the cob laughing in his equine way, scattering foam and pebbles to the left and right, and trotting at that rate of sixteen miles an hour.

Oh, that ride! that first ride! – most truly it was an epoch in my existence; and I still look back to it with feelings of longing and regret. People may talk of first love – it is a very agreeable event, I dare say – but give me the flush, and triumph, and glorious sweat of a first ride, like mine on the mighty cob. My whole frame was shaken, it is true; and during one long week I could hardly move foot or hand; but what of that? By that one trial I had become free, as I may say, of the whole equine species. No more fatigue, no more stiffness of joints, after that first ride round the Devil's Hill on the cob.

from LAVENGRO *1851*

Malek Adel

IVAN TURGENEV

From that day forward, the main business, the main preoccupation and delight in Chertopkhanov's life, was Malek Adel. He loved him even more than Masha, grew more attached to him even than to Nedopyuskin. And what a horse he was! All fire and gunpowder – and yet with the gravity of a Boyar! Untirable, a stayer, ready to go anywhere, mild as a lamb; costing nothing to feed: if he couldn't get anything else, he would eat the ground under his feet.

He walks, and it's as if he's carrying you in his arms; he trots, and it's as if he is rocking you in a cradle; but when he gallops, not even the wind can catch him! He never loses his breath – his windpipe's too sound for that. His hooves are of steel; as for

stumbling – there's never been the slightest question of it!
Jumping a ditch or a fence means nothing to him; and what a
brain he's got! You call him, and he'll come running up, head
thrown back; you tell him to stop, and you leave him – he won't
stir; as soon as you start coming back he'll whinny faintly: 'Here
I am.' He fears nothing; in the darkest night or a snow-storm he'll
find the way; and he'll never let a stranger take hold of him, he
would tear him with his teeth! And woe betide any dog that
bothers him: he'll get a forehoof to his skull at once – ponk! and
the dog will have had its day. He's a horse with ambitions: you
can wave the whip over him, just for show – but God help you
if you touch him! Anyway, why make a long story of it: he's not
a horse, he's a treasure!

If Chertopkhanov had sat down to describe his Malek Adel –
heaven knows where he would have found the words to do so!
And how he curried him and cosseted him! Malek Adel's coat
was shot with silver – and not old silver, either, but new silver
with a dull polish on it; if you stroked him with the flat of your
hand, it was absolute velvet! Saddle, saddle-cloth, bridle – every
bit of harness was so well-fitted, well-kept, well-scrubbed – you
could just take a pencil and draw! It was Chertopkhanov himself –
who else? – who with his own hand plaited his darling's forelock,
washed his mane and tail in beer, and more than once anointed
his hooves with oil.

He would mount Malek Adel and ride out, not exactly to visit
his neighbours – he had no more connection with them than
before – but over their land, and past their seats . . . as if to say:
Admire, you fools, from afar! Then he'd hear of hunting in
progress somewhere – some rich landowner visting his outlying
properties – and at once he'd be off there, and prance about in
the distance, on the horizon, amazing all beholders with the
beauty and speed of his horse, but letting no one come near him.
On one occasion a huntsman set off after him, with all his suite
in attendance, saw that Chertopkhanov was walking away from
him, and started shouting after him with all his might, while at
full gallop: 'Hey, you, listen! Take what you like for your horse!
I won't grudge you a thousand! I'll give my wife and children for
him! Take my last penny!'

Chertopkhanov suddenly halted Malek Adel. The huntsman

dashed up to him. 'Tell me, sir,' he shouted, 'what d'you want? My own father?'

'If you were the Tsar,' said Chertopkhanov deliberately (and in all his born days he had never heard of Shakespeare), 'you could give me your whole kingdom for my horse, and even so I wouldn't take it!' He spoke, he laughed, he made Malek Adel rear up, he spun him round in mid-air, standing on nothing but his hind legs, like a toy – and gallop! He fairly streaked off across the stubble. And the huntsman (who, so the story goes, was a prince, a man of enormous wealth) threw his cap on the ground – and buried his face in it. He lay like that for a good half-hour.

It was only natural that Chertopkhanov should treasure his horse. Was it not through him that further proof had been given of his own undoubted and final superiority over all his neighbours?

from THE END OF CHERTOPKHANOV *1852*

Coaching Incidents from Dickens

I. THE DOVER ROAD

It was the Dover road that lay, on a Friday night late in November, before the first of the persons with whom this history has business. The Dover road lay, as to him, beyond the Dover mail, as it lumbered up Shooter's Hill. He walked uphill in the mire by the side of the mail, as the rest of the passengers did; not because they had the least relish for walking exercise, under the circumstances, but because the hill, and the harness, and the mud, and the mail, were all so heavy, that the horses had three times already come to a stop, besides once drawing the coach across the road, with the mutinous intent of taking it back to Blackheath. Reins and whip and coachman and guard, however, in combination, had read that article of war which forbade a purpose otherwise strongly in favour of the argument, that some brute animals are endued with Reason: and the team had capitulated and returned to their duty.

With drooping heads and tremulous tails, they mashed their

way through the thick mud, floundering and stumbling between whiles, as if they were falling to pieces at the larger joints. As often as the driver rested them and brought them to a stand, with a wary 'Wo-ho! so-ho then!' the near leader violently shook his head and everything upon it – like an unusually emphatic horse, denying that the coach could be got up the hill. Whenever the leader made this rattle, the passenger started, as a nervous passenger might, and was disturbed in mind.

There was a steaming mist in all the hollows, and it had roamed in its forlornness up the hill, like an evil spirit, seeking rest and finding none. A clammy and intensely cold mist, it made its slow way through the air in ripples that visibly followed and over-spread one another, as the waves of an unwholesome sea might do. It was dense enough to shut out everything from the light of the coach-lamps but these its own workings, and a few yards of road; and the reek of the labouring horses steamed into it, as if they had made it all.

Two other passengers, besides the one, were plodding up the hill by the side of the mail. All three were wrapped to the cheek-bones and over the ears, and wore jack-boots. Not one of the three could have said, from anything he saw, what either of the other two was like; and each was hidden under almost as many wrappers from the eyes of the mind, as from the eyes of the body, of his two companions. In those days, travellers were very shy of being confidential on a short notice, for anybody on the road might be a robber or in league with robbers. As to the latter, when every posting-house and ale-house could produce somebody in 'the Captain's' pay, ranging from the landlord to the lowest stable nondescript, it was the likeliest thing upon the cards. So the guard of the Dover mail thought to himself, that Friday night in November, one thousand seven hundred and seventy-five, lumbering up Shooter's Hill, as he stood on his own particular perch behind the mail, beating his feet, and keeping an eye and a hand on the arm-chest before him, where a loaded blunderbuss lay at the top of six or eight loaded horse-pistols, deposited on a substratum of cutlass.

The Dover mail was in its usual genial position that the guard suspected the passengers, the passengers suspected one another and the guard, they all suspected everybody else, and the coachman was sure of nothing but the horses; as to which cattle he could with a clear conscience have taken his oath on the two Testaments that they were not fit for the journey.

'Wo-ho!' said the coachman. 'So, then! One more pull and you're at the top and be damned to you, for I have had trouble enough to get you to it! – Joe!'

'Hallo!' the guard replied.

'What o'clock do you make it, Joe?'

'Ten minutes, good past eleven.'

'My blood!' ejaculated the vexed coachman, 'and not atop of Shooter's yet! Tst! Yah! Get on with you!'

The emphatic horse, cut short by the whip in a most decided negative, made a decided scramble for it, and the three horses followed suit. Once more, the Dover mail struggled on, with the jack-boots of its passengers squashing along by its side. They had stopped when the coach stopped, and they kept close company with it. If any one of the three had had the hardihood to propose to another to walk on a little ahead into the mist and darkness, he would have put himself in a fair way of getting shot instantly as a highwayman.

The last burst carried the mail to the summit of the hill. The horse stopped to breathe again, and the guard got down to skid the wheel for the descent, and open the coach-door to let the passengers in.

'Tst! Joe!' cried the coachman in a warning voice, looking down from his box.

'What do you say, Tom?'

They both listened.

'I say a horse at a canter coming up, Joe.'

'I say a horse at a gallop, Tom,' returned the guard, leaving his hold of the door, and mounting nimbly to his place. 'Gentlemen! In the king's name, all of you!'

With this hurried adjuration, he cocked his blunderbuss, and stood on the offensive.

The passenger booked by this history was on the coach-step, getting in; the two other passengers were close behind him, and about to follow. He remained on the step, half in the coach and half out of it; they remained in the road below him. They all looked from the coachman, and listened. The coachman looked back and the guard looked back, and even the emphatic leader pricked up his ears and looked back, without contradicting.

The stillness consequent on the cessation of the rumbling and labouring of the coach, added to the stillness of the night, made it very quiet indeed. The panting of the horses communicated a tremulous motion to the coach, as if it were in a state of agitation. The hearts of the passengers beat loud enough perhaps to be heard; but at any rate, the quiet pause was audibly expressive of people out of breath, and holding the breath, and having the pulses quickened by expectation.

The sound of a horse at a gallop came fast and furiously up the hill.

'So-ho!' the guard sang out, as loud as he could roar. 'Yo there! Stand! I shall fire!'

The pace was suddenly checked, and with much splashing and floundering a man's voice called from the mist, 'Is that the Dover mail?'

'Never you mind what it is?' the guard retorted. 'What are you?'

'Is that the Dover mail?'

'Why do you want to know?'

'I want a passenger, if it is.'

'What passenger?'

'Mr Jarvis Lorry.'

Our booked passenger showed in a moment that it was his name. The guard, the coachman, and the two other passengers eyed him distrustfully.

'Keep where you are,' the guard called to the voice in the mist, 'because, if I should make a mistake, it could never be set right in your lifetime. Gentleman of the name of Lorry answer straight.'

'What is the matter?' asked the passenger, then, with mildly quavering speech. 'Who wants me? Is it Jerry?'

('I don't like Jerry's voice, if it is Jerry,' growled the guard to himself. 'He's hoarser than suits me, is Jerry.')

'Yes, Mr Lorry.'

'What is the matter?'

'A despatch sent after you from over yonder. T. and Co.'

'I know this messenger, guard,' said Mr Lorry, getting down

into the road – assisted from behind more swiftly than politely by the other two passengers, who immediately scrambled into the coach, shut the door, and pulled up the window. 'He may come close; there's nothing wrong.'

'I hope there ain't, but I can't make so 'nation sure of that,' said the guard, in gruff soliloquy. 'Hallo you!'

'Well! And hallo you!' said Jerry, more hoarsely than before.

'Come on at a footpace! d'ye mind me? And if you've got holsters to that saddle of yourn, don't let me see your hand go nigh 'em. For I'm a devil at a quick mistake, and when I make one it takes the form of Lead. So now let's look at you.'

The figures of a horse and rider came slowly through the eddying mist, and came to the side of the mail, where the passenger stood. The rider stooped, and, casting up his eyes at the guard, handed the passenger a small folded paper. The rider's horse was blown, and both horse and rider were covered with mud, from the hoofs of the horse to the hat of the man.

'Guard!' said the passenger, in a tone of quiet business confidence.

The watchful guard, with his right hand at the stock of his raised blunderbuss, his left at the barrel, and his eye on the horseman, answered curtly, 'Sir.'

'There is nothing to apprehend. I belong to Tellson's Bank. You must know Tellson's Bank in London. I am going to Paris on business. A crown to drink. I may read this?'

'If so be as you're quick, sir.'

He opened it in the light of the coach-lamp on that side, and read – first to himself and then aloud: 'Wait at Dover for Mam'selle.' It's not long, you see, guard. Jerry, say that my answer was, RECALLED TO LIFE.'

Jerry started in his saddle. 'That's a Blazing strange answer, too,' said he, at his hoarsest.

'Take that message back, and they will know that I received this, as well as if I wrote. Make the best of your way. Good-night.'

from A TALE OF TWO CITIES *1859*

2. MR PICKWICK DRIVES TO DINGLEY DELL

'Bless my soul!' said Mr Pickwick, as they stood upon the pavement while the coats were being put in. 'Bless my soul! Who's to drive? I never thought of that.'

'Oh! you, of course,' said Mr Tupman.

'Of course,' said Mr Snodgrass.

'I!' exclaimed Mr Pickwick.

'Not the slightest fear, sir,' interposed the hostler. 'Warrant him quiet, sir; a hinfant in arms might drive him.'

'He don't shy, does he?' inquired Mr Pickwick.

'Shy, sir? He wouldn't shy if he was to meet a vaggin-load of monkeys with their tails burnt off.'

The last recommendation was indisputable. Mr Tupman and Mr Snodgrass got into the bin; Mr Pickwick ascended to his perch, and deposited his feet on a floor-clothed shelf, erected beneath it for that purpose.

'Now, shiny Villiam,' said the hostler to the deputy hostler, 'give the gen'l'm'n the ribbins.' "Shiny Villiam" – so called, probably, from his sleek hair and oily countenance – placed the reins in Mr Pickwick's left hand; and the upper hostler thrust a whip into his right.

'Wo-o!' cried Mr Pickwick, as the tall quadruped evinced a decided inclination to back into the coffee-room window.

'Wo-o!' echoed Mr Tupman and Mr Snodgrass from the bin.

'Only his playfulness, gen'l'm'n,' said the head hostler encouragingly. 'Jist kitch hold on him, Villiam.' The deputy restrained the animal's impetuosity, and the principal ran to assist Mr Winkle in mounting.

'T'other side, sir, if you please.'

'Blowed if the gen'l'm'n worn't a-gettin' up on the wrong side,' whispered a grinning post-boy to the inexpressibly gratified waiter.

Mr Winkle, thus instructed, climbed into his saddle, with about as much difficulty as he would have experienced in getting up the side of a first-rate man-of-war.

'All right,' replied Mr Winkle faintly.

'Let 'em go,' cried the hostler. 'Hold him in, sir,' and away went the chaise, and the saddle-horse, with Mr Pickwick on the box of one, and Mr Winkle on the back of the other, to the delight and gratification of the whole inn yard.

'What makes him go sideways?' said Mr Snodgrass in the bin, to Mr Winkle in the saddle.

'I can't imagine,' replied Mr Winkle. His horse was drifting up the street in the most mysterious manner – side first, with his head towards one side of the way, and his tail towards the other.

Mr Pickwick had no leisure to observe either this or any other particular, the whole of his faculties being concentrated in the management of the animal attached to the chaise, who displayed various peculiarities, highly interesting to a bystander, but by no means equally amusing to any one seated behind him. Besides constantly jerking his head up in a very unpleasant and uncomfortable manner, and tugging at the reins to an extent which rendered it a matter of great difficulty for Mr Pickwick to hold them, he had a singular propensity for darting suddenly every now and then to the side of the road, then stopping short, and then rushing forward for some minutes, at a speed which it was wholly impossible to control.

'What *can* he mean by this?' said Mr Snodgrass, when the horse had executed his manoeuvre for the twentieth time.

'I don't know,' replied Mr Tupman. 'It *looks* very like shying, don't it?' Mr Snodgrass was about to reply, when he was interrupted by a shout from Mr Pickwick.

'Wo-o!' said that gentleman, 'I have dropped my whip.'

'Winkle,' said Mr Snodgrass, as the equestrian came trotting up on the tall horse, with his hat over his ears, and shaking all over, as if he would shake to pieces, with the violence of the exercise, 'Pick up the whip, there's a good fellow.' Mr Winkle pulled at the bridle of the tall horse till he was black in the face; and having at length succeeded in stopping him, dismounted, handed the whip to Mr Pickwick, and grasping the reins, prepared to remount.

Now whether the tall horse, in the natural playfulness of his disposition, was desirous of having a little innocent recreation with Mr Winkle, or whether it occurred to him that he could perform the journey as much to his own satisfaction without a rider as with one, are points upon which, of course, we can arrive at no definite and distinct conclusion. By whatever motives the animal was activated, certain it is that Mr Winkle had no sooner touched the reins than he slipped them over his head, and darted backwards to their full length.

'Poor fellow,' said Mr Winkle soothingly. 'Poor fellow – good old horse.' The 'poor fellow' was proof against flattery: the more Mr Winkle tried to get nearer him, the more he sidled away; and, notwithstanding all kinds of coaxing and wheedling, there were Mr Winkle and the horse going round and round each other for ten minutes, at the end of which time each was at precisely the same distance from the other as when they first commenced – an unsatisfactory sort of thing under any circumstances, but particularly so in a lonely road, where no assistance can be procured.

'What am I to do?' shouted Mr Winkle, after the dodging had been prolonged for a considerable time. 'What am I to do? I can't get on him.'

'You had better lead him till we come to a turn-pike,' replied Mr Pickwick from the chaise.

'But he won't come!' roared Mr Winkle. 'Do come and hold him.'

Mr Pickwick was the very personation of kindness and humanity: he threw the reins on the horse's back, and having descended from his seat, carefully drew the chaise into the hedge, lest anything should come along the road, and stepped back to the assistance of his distressed companion, leaving Mr Tupman and Mr Snodgrass in the vehicle.

The horse no sooner beheld Mr Pickwick advancing towards him with the chaise whip in his hand, than he exchanged the rotary motion in which he had previously indulged, for a retrograde movement of so very determined a character, that it at once drew Mr Winkle, who was still at the end of the bridle, at a rather quicker rate than fast walking, in the direction from which they had just come. Mr Pickwick ran to his assistance, but the faster Mr Pickwick ran forward, the faster the horse ran backward. There was a great scraping of feet and kicking up of the dust; and at last Mr Winkle, his arms being nearly pulled out of their sockets, fairly let go his hold. The horse paused, stared, shook his head, turned round, and quietly trotted home to Rochester, leaving Mr Winkle and Mr Pickwick gazing on each other with countenances of blank dismay.

from THE POSTHUMOUS PAPERS OF THE
PICKWICK CLUB *1837*

The Highwayman's Mare

R. D. BLACKMORE

'Your mare,' said I, standing stoutly up, being a tall boy now; 'I never saw such a beauty, sir. Will you let me have a ride of her?'

'Think thou could'st ride her, lad? She will have no burden but mine. Thou could'st never ride her. Tut! I would be loth to kill thee.'

'Ride her!' I cried with the bravest scorn, for she looked so kind and gentle; 'there never was horse upon Exmoor foaled, but I could tackle in half an hour. Only I never ride upon saddle. Take them leathers off of her.'

He looked at me with a dry little whistle, and thrust his hands into his breeches-pockets, and so grinned that I could not stand it. And Annie laid hold of me in such a way that I was almost mad with her. And he laughed and approved her for doing so. And the worst of all was – he said nothing.

'Get away, Annie, will you? Do you think I am a fool, good sir? Only trust me with her, and I will not over-ride her.'

'For that I will go bail, my son. She is liker to over-ride thee. But the ground is soft to fall upon, after all this rain. Now come out into the yard, young man, for the sake of your mother's cabbages. And the mellow straw-bed will be softer for thee, since pride must have its fall. I am thy mother's cousin, boy, and am going up to house. Tom Faggus is my name, as everybody knows; and this is my young mare, Winnie.'

What a fool I must have been not to know it at once! Tom Faggus, the great highwayman, and his young blood-mare, the strawberry! Already her fame was noised abroad, nearly as much as her master's; and my longing to ride her grew tenfold, but fear came at the back of it. Not that I had the smallest fear of what the mare could do to me, by fair play and horse-trickery; but that the glory of sitting upon her seemed to be too great for me; especially as there were rumours abroad that she was not a mare after all, but a witch. However, she looked like a filly all over, and wonderfully beautiful, with her supple stride, and soft slope of shoulder, and glossy coat beaded with water, and prominent eyes, full of love or of fire. Whether this came from her Eastern blood of the Arabs newly imported, and whether the cream-colour, mixed with our bay, led to that bright strawberry tint, is certainly more than I can decide, being chiefly acquainted with farm-horses. And these come of any colour and form; you never can count what they will be, and are lucky to get four legs to them.

Mr Faggus gave his mare a wink, and she walked demurely after him, a bright young thing, flowing over with life, yet dropping her soul to a higher one, and led by love to anything; as the manner is of females, when they know what is best for them. Then Winnie trod lightly upon the straw, because it had soft muck under it, and her delicate feet came back again.

'Up for it still, boy, be ye?' Tom Faggus stopped and the mare stopped there; and they looked at me provokingly.

'Is she able to leap, sir? There is good take-off on this side of the brook.'

Mr Faggus laughed very quietly, turning round to Winnie, so that she might enter into it. And she, for her part, seemed to know exactly where the joke was.

'Good tumble-off, you mean, my boy. Well, there can be small harm to thee. I am akin to thy family, and know the substance of their skulls.'

'Let me get up,' said I, waxing wroth, for reasons I cannot tell you, because they are too manifold; 'take off your saddle-bag things. I will try not to squeeze her ribs in, unless she plays nonsense with me.'

Then Mr Faggus was up on his mettle, at this proud speech of mine; and John Fry was running up all the while, and Bill Dadds, and half a dozen. Tom Faggus gave one glance around, and then dropped all regard for me. The high repute of his mare was at stake, and what was my life compared to it? Through my defiance, and stupid ways, here was I in a dullo, and my legs not come to their strength yet, and my arms as limp as a herring.

Something of this occurred to him, even in his wrath with me, for he spoke very softly to the filly, who now could scarce subdue herself; but she drew in her nostrils, and breathed to his breath, and did all she could to answer him.

'Not too hard, my dear,' he said; 'let him gently down on the mixen. That will be quite enough.' Then he turned the saddle off, and I was up in a moment. She began at first so easily, and pricked her ears so lovingly, and minced about as if pleased to find so light a weight on her, that I thought she knew I could ride a little, and feared to show any capers. 'Gee wugg, Polly,' cried I, for all the men were now looking on, being then at the leaving-off-time; 'Gee-wugg, Polly, and show what thou be'est made of.' With that I plugged my heels into her, and Billy Dadds flung his hat up.

Nevertheless, she outraged not, though her eyes were frightening Annie, and John Fry took a pick to keep him safe; but she curbed to and fro, with her strong fore-arms rising, like springs ingathered, waiting and quivering grievously, and beginning to sweat about it. Then her master gave a shrill clear whistle, when her ears were bent towards him, and I felt her from beneath me gathering up like whale-bone, and her hind-legs coming under her, and I knew that I was in for it.

First she reared upright in the air, and struck me full on the nose with her comb, till I bled worse than Robin Snell made me, and then down with her fore-feet deep in the straw, and her hind-feet going to heaven. Finding me stick to her still like wax (for my mettle was up as hers was), away she flew with me, swifter than ever I went before, or since, I vow. She drove full-head at the cob-wall – 'Oh, Jack, slip off,' screamed Annie – then she turned like light, when I thought to crush her, and ground my left knee against it. 'Mux me,' I cried, for my breeches were broken, and short words went the furthest – 'If you kill me, you shall die with me.' Then she took the court-yard gate at a leap, knocking my words between my teeth, and then right over a quickset hedge, as if the sky were a breath to her; and away for the water-meadows, while I lay on her neck like a child at the breast, and wished I had never been born. Straight away, all in the front of the wind, and scattering clouds around her, all I knew of the speed we made was the frightful flash of her shoulders, and her mane like trees in a tempest. I felt the earth under us rushing away, and the air left far behind us, and my breath came and went, and I prayed to God, and was sorry to be so late of it.

All the long swift while, without power of thought, I clung to her crest and shoulders, and dug my nails into her creases, and my toes into her flank-part, and was proud of holding on so long, though sure of being beaten. Then in her fury at feeling me still, she rushed at another device for it, and leaped the wide water-trough sideways across, to and fro, till no breath was left in me. The hazel-boughs took me too hard in the face, and the tall dog-briars got hold of me, and the ache of my back was like crimping a fish; till I longed to give up, and lay thoroughly beaten, and lie there and die in the cresses. But there came a shrill whistle from up the home-hill, where the people had hurried to watch us; and the mare stopped as if with a bullet; then set off for home with the speed of a swallow, and going as smoothly and silently. I never had dreamed of such delicate motion, fluent, and graceful, and ambient, soft as the breeze flitting over the flowers, but swift as the summer lightning. I sat up again, but my strength was all spent, and no time left to recover it; and at last, as she rose at our gate like a bird, I tumbled off into the mixen.

from LORNA DOONE *1869*

The White Knight

LEWIS CARROLL

Whenever the horse stopped (which it did very often), he fell off in front; and whenever it went on again (which he generally did rather suddenly), he fell off behind. Otherwise he kept on pretty well, except that he had a habit of now and then falling off sideways; and as he generally did this on the side on which Alice was walking, she soon found that it was the best plan not to walk *quite* close to the horse.

'I'm afraid you've not had much practice in riding,' she ventured to say as she was helping him up from his fifth tumble.

The Knight looked very much surprised, and a little offended at the remark. 'What makes you say that?' he asked, as he scrambled back into the saddle, keeping hold of Alice's hair with one hand, to save himself from falling over on the other side.

'Because people don't fall off quite so often, when they've had much practice.'

'I've had plenty of practice,' the Knight said very gravely: 'plenty of practice!'

Alice could think of nothing better to say than 'Indeed?', but she said it as heartily as she could. They went on a little way in silence after this, the Knight with his eyes shut, muttering to himself, and Alice watching anxiously for the next tumble.

'The great art of riding,' the Knight suddenly began in a loud voice, waving his right arm as he spoke, 'is to keep . . .' Here the sentence ended as suddenly as it had begun, as the Knight fell heavily on top of his head exactly in the path where Alice was walking. She was quite frightened this time, and said in an anxious tone, as she picked him up, 'I hope no bones are broken?'

'None to speak of,' the Knight said, as if he didn't mind breaking two or three of them. 'The great art of riding, as I was saying, is – to keep your balance properly. Like this, you know . . .'

He let go the bridle, and stretched out both his arms to show Alice what he meant, and this time he fell flat on his back, right under the horse's feet.

'Plenty of practice!' he went on repeating, all the time that Alice was getting him on his feet again. 'Plenty of practice!'

'It's too ridiculous!' cried Alice, losing all her patience this time. 'You ought to have a wooden horse on wheels, that you ought!'

'Does that kind go smoothly?' the Knight asked in a tone of great interest, clasping his arms round the horse's neck as he spoke, just in time to save himself from tumbling off again.

'Much more smoothly than a live horse,' Alice said, with a little scream of laughter, in spite of all she could do to prevent it.

'I'll get one,' the Knight said thoughtfully to himself. 'One or two – several.'

from THROUGH THE LOOKING-GLASS
AND WHAT ALICE FOUND THERE *1872*

The Fire

ANNA SEWELL

I cannot say how long I had slept, nor what time in the night it was, but I woke up feeling very uncomfortable, though I hardly knew why. I got up: the air seemed all thick and choking. I heard Ginger coughing, and one of the other horses moved about restlessly. It was quite dark, and I could see nothing; but the stable was full of smoke, and I hardly knew how to breathe.

The trap door had been left open, and I thought that was the place from which the smoke came. I listened and heard a soft, rushing sort of noise, and a low crackling and snapping. I did not know what it was, but there was something in the sound so strange that it made me tremble all over. The other horses were now all awake; some were pulling at their halters, others were stamping.

At last I heard steps outside, and the ostler who had put up the traveller's horse burst into the stable with a lantern, and began to untie the horses, and try to lead them out; but he seemed in such a hurry, and was so frightened himself, that he frightened me still more. The first horse would not go with him; he tried the second and third, but they too would not stir. He came to me next and tried to drag me out of the stall by force; of course that was no use. He tried us all by turns and then left the stable.

No doubt we were foolish, but danger seemed to be all round; there was nobody whom we knew to trust in, and all was strange and uncertain. The fresh air that had come in through the open door made it easier to breathe, but the rushing sound overhead grew louder, and as I looked upward, through the bars of my empty rack, I saw a red light flickering on the wall. Then I heard a cry of 'Fire!' outside, and the old ostler came quietly and quickly in. He got one horse out, and went to another; but the flames were playing round the trap door, and the roaring overhead was dreadful.

The next thing I heard was James's voice, quiet and cheery, as it always was.

'Come, my beauties, it is time for us to be off, so wake up and come along.' I stood nearest the door, so he came to me first, patting me as he came in.

'Come, Beauty, on with your bridle, my boy, we'll soon be out of this smother.' It was on in no time; then he took the scarf off his neck, and tied it lightly over my eyes, and, patting and coaxing, he led me out of the stable. Safe in the yard, he slipped the scarf off my eyes, and shouted, 'Here, somebody! take this horse while I go back for the others.'

A tall, broad man stepped forward and took me, and James darted back into the stable. I set up a shrill whinny as I saw him go. Ginger told me afterwards that whinny was the best thing I could have done for her, for had she not heard me outside, she would never have had courage to come out.

There was much confusion in the yard; the horses were being got out of other stables, and the carriages and gigs were being pulled out of houses and sheds, lest the flames should spread farther. On the other side of the yard windows were thrown up, and people were shouting all sorts of things; but I kept my eye fixed on the stable door, where the smoke poured out thicker than ever, and I could see flashes of red light.

Presently I heard above all the stir and din a loud, clear voice, which I knew was master's:

'James Howard! James Howard! are you there?' There was no answer, but I heard a crash of something falling in the stable, and the next moment I gave a loud, joyful neigh, for I saw James coming through the smoke, leading Ginger with him; she was coughing violently and he was not able to speak.

'My brave lad!' said master, laying his hand on his shoulder, 'are you hurt?'

James shook his head, for he could not yet speak.

'Ay,' said the big man who held me, 'he is a brave lad, and no mistake.'

'And now,' said master, 'when you have got your breath, James, we'll get out of this place as quickly as we can.'

We were moving towards the entry when from the Market Place there came a sound of galloping feet and loud rumbling wheels.

'''Tis the fire engine! the fire engine!' shouted two or three voices. 'Stand back, make way!' and clattering and thundering over the stones two horses dashed into the yard with the heavy engine behind them. The firemen leaped to the ground; there was no need to ask where the fire was – it was torching up in a great blaze from the roof.

We got out as fast as we could into the broad quiet Market Place. The stars were shining, and except for the noise behind us, all was still. Master led the way to a large hotel on the other side, and as soon as the ostler came, he said, 'James, I must now hasten to your mistress; I trust the horses entirely to you; order whatever you think is needed,' and with that he was gone. The master did not run, but I never saw mortal man walk so fast as he did that night.

There was a dreadful sound before we got into our stalls – the shrieks of those poor horses that were left burning to death in the stable were very terrible! They made both Ginger and me feel very ill. We, however, were taken in and well done by.

The next morning the master came to see how we were and to speak to James. I did not hear much for the ostler was rubbing me down; but I could see that James looked very happy, and I thought the master was proud of him.

Our mistress had been so much alarmed in the night, that the journey was put off till the afternoon; so James had the morning on hand, and went first to the inn to see about our harness and the carriage, and then to hear more about the fire. When he came back, we heard him tell the ostler about it.

At first no one could guess how the fire had been caused; but at last a man said he saw Dick Towler go into the stable with a pipe in his mouth, and when he came out he had not one, and went to the tap for another. Then the under-ostler said he had asked Dick to go up the ladder to get down some hay, but told him to lay down his pipe first. Dick denied taking the pipe with him, but no one believed him.

I remember our John Manly's rule, never to allow a pipe in the stable, and thought it ought to be the rule everywhere.

James said the roof and floor had all fallen in, and that only the black walls were standing. The two poor horses that could not be got out were buried under the burnt rafters and tiles.

from BLACK BEAUTY *1877*

The Brogue

'SAKI'

The hunting season had come to an end, and the Mullets had not succeeded in selling the Brogue. There had been a kind of tradition in the family for the past three or four years, a sort of fatalistic hope, that the Brogue would find a purchaser before the hunting was over; but seasons came and went without anything happening to justify such ill-founded optimism. The animal had been named Berserker in the earlier stages of its career; it had been re-christened the Brogue later on, in recognition of the fact that, once acquired, it was extremely difficult to get rid of. The unkinder wits of the neighbourhood had been known to suggest that the first letter of its name was superfluous. The Brogue had been variously described in sale catalogues as a light-weight hunter, a lady's hack, and, more simply, but still with a touch of imagination, as a useful brown gelding standing 15.1. Toby Mullet had ridden him for four seasons with the West Wessex; you can ride almost any sort of horse with the West Wessex as long as it is an animal that knows the country.

The Brogue knew the country intimately, having personally created most of the gaps that were to be met with in banks and hedges for many miles round. His manners and characteristics were not ideal in the hunting field, but he was probably rather safer to ride to hounds than he was as a hack on country roads. According to the Mullet family, he was not really road-shy, but there were one or two objects of dislike that brought on sudden attacks of what Toby called swerving sickness. Motors and cycles he treated with tolerant disregard, but pigs, wheel-barrows, piles of stones by the roadside, perambulators in a village street, gates painted too aggressively white, and sometimes, but not always, the newer kind of beehives, turned him aside from his tracks in vivid imitation of the zigzag course of forked lightning. If a pheasant rose noisily from the other side of a hedgerow the Brogue would spring into the air at the same moment, but this may have been due to a desire to be companionable. The Mullet family contradicted the widely prevalent report that the horse was a confirmed crib-biter.

It was about the third week in May that Mrs Mullet, relict of the late Sylvester Mullet, and mother of Toby and a bunch of daughters, assailed Clovis Sangrail on the outskirts of the village with a breathless catalogue of local happenings.

'You know our new neighbour, Mr Penricarde?' she vociferated; 'awfully rich, owns tin mines in Cornwall, middle-aged and rather quiet. He's taken the Red House on a long lease and spent a lot of money on alterations and improvements. Well, Toby's sold him the Brogue!'

Clovis spent a moment or two in assimilating the astonishing news; then he broke out into unstinted congratulation. If he had belonged to a more emotional race he would probably have kissed Mrs Mullet.

'How wonderful lucky to have pulled it off at last! Now you can buy a decent animal. I've always said that Toby was clever. Ever so many congratulations.'

'Don't congratulate me. It's the most unfortunate thing that could have happened!' said Mrs Mullet dramatically.

Clovis stared at her in amazement.

'Mr Penricarde,' said Mrs Mullet, sinking her voice to what she imagined to be an impressive whisper, though it rather resembled a hoarse, excited squeak, 'Mr Penricarde has just begun to pay attentions to Jessie. Slight at first, but now unmistakable. I was a fool not to have seen it sooner. Yesterday, at the Rectory garden party, he asked her what her favourite flowers were, and she told him carnations, and today a whole stack of carnations has arrived, clove and malmaison and lovely dark red ones, regular exhibition blooms, and a box of chocolates that he must have got on purpose from London. And he's asked her to go round the links with him tomorrow. And now, just at this critical moment, Toby has sold him that animal. It's a calamity!'

'But you've been trying to get the horse off your hands for years,' said Clovis.

'I've got a houseful of daughters,' said Mrs Mullet, 'and I've been trying – well, not to get them off my hands, of course, but a husband or two wouldn't be amiss among the lot of them; there are six of them, you know.'

'I don't know,' said Clovis, 'I've never counted, but I expect you're right as to the number; mothers generally know these things.'

'And now,' continued Mrs Mullet, in her tragic whisper, 'when there's a rich husband-in-prospect imminent on the horizon Toby goes and sells him that miserable animal. It will probably kill any affection he might have felt towards any member of our family. What is to be done? We can't very well ask to have the horse back; you see, we praised it up like anything when we thought there was a chance of his buying it, and said it was just the animal to suit him.'

'Couldn't you steal it out of his stable and send it to grass at some farm miles away?' suggested Clovis; 'write "Votes for Women" on the stable door, and the thing would pass for a Suffragette outrage. No one who knew the horse could possibly suspect you of wanting to get it back again.'

'Every newspaper in the country would ring with the affair,' said Mrs Mullet; 'can't you imagine the headline, "Valuable Hunter Stolen by Suffragettes"? The police would scour the countryside till they found the animal.'

'Well, Jessie must try and get it back from Penricarde on the plea that it's an old favourite. She can say it was only sold because the stable had to be pulled down under the terms of an old re-pairing lease, and that now it has been arranged that the stable is to stand for a couple of years longer.'

'It sounds a queer proceeding to ask for a horse back when you've just sold him,' said Mrs Mullet, 'but something must be done, and done at once. The man is not used to horses, and I believe I told him it was as quiet as a lamb. After all, lambs go kicking and twisting about as if they were demented, don't they?'

'The lamb has an entirely unmerited character for sedateness,' agreed Clovis.

Jessie came back from the golf links next day in a state of mingled elation and concern.

'It's all right about the proposal,' she announced; 'he came out with it at the sixth hole. I said I must have time to think it over. I accepted him at the seventh.'

'My dear,' said her mother, 'I think a little more maidenly

reserve and hesitation would have been advisable, as you've
known him so short a time. You might have waited till the ninth
hole.'

'The seventh is a very long hole,' said Jessie; 'besides, the
tension was putting us both off our game. By the time we'd got
to the ninth hole we'd settled lots of things. The honeymoon is
to be spent in Corsica, with perhaps a flying visit to Naples if we
feel like it, and a week in London to wind up with. Two of his
nieces are to be asked to be bridesmaids, so with our lot there
will be seven, which is rather a lucky number. You are to wear
your pearl grey with any amount of Honiton lace jabbed into it.
By the way, he's coming over this evening to ask your consent to
the whole affair. So far all's well, but about the Brogue it's a
different matter. I told him the legend about the stable, and how
keen we were about buying the horse back, but he seems equally
keen on keeping it. He said he must have horse exercise now that
he's living in the country, and he's going to start riding tomorrow. He's ridden a few times in the Row on an animal that
was accustomed to carry octogenarians and people undergoing
rest cures, and that's about all his experience in the saddle – oh,
and he rode a pony once in Norfolk when he was fifteen and the
pony twenty-four; and tomorrow he's going to ride the Brogue!
I shall be a widow before I'm married, and I do so want to see
what Corsica's like; it looks so silly on the map.'

Clovis was sent for in haste, and the developments of the
situation put before him.

'Nobody can ride that animal with any safety,' said Mrs Mullet,
'except Toby, and he knows by long experience what it is going
to shy at, and manages to swerve at the same time.'

'I did hint to Mr Penricarde – to Vincent, I should say – that
the Brogue didn't like white gates,' said Jessie.

'White gates!' exclaimed Mrs Mullet; 'did you mention what
effect a pig has on him? He'll have to go past Lockyer's farm to
get to the high road, and there's sure to be a pig or two grunting
about in the lane.'

'He's taken rather a dislike to turkeys lately,' said Toby.

'It's obvious that Penricarde mustn't be allowed to go out on
that animal,' said Clovis, 'at least not till Jessie has married him,
and tired of him. I tell you what: ask him to a picnic tomorrow,

starting at an early hour; he's not the sort to go out for a ride before breakfast. The day after I'll get the rector to drive him over to Crowleigh before lunch, to see the new cottage hospital they're building there. The Brogue will be standing idle in the stable and Toby can offer to exercise it; then it can pick up a stone or something of the sort and go conveniently lame. If you hurry on the wedding a bit the lameness fiction can be kept up till the ceremony is safely over.'

Mrs Mullet belonged to an emotional race, and she kissed Clovis.

It was nobody's fault that the rain came down in torrents the next morning, making a picnic a fantastic impossibility. It was also nobody's fault, but sheer ill-luck, that the weather cleared up sufficiently in the afternoon to tempt Mr Penricarde to make his first essay with the Brogue. They did not get as far as the pigs at Lockyer's farm; the rectory gate was painted a dull unobtrusive green, but it had been white a year or two ago, and the Brogue never forgot that he had been in the habit of making a violent curtsey, a back-pedal, and a swerve at this particular point of the road. Subsequently, there being no further call on his services, he broke his way into the rectory orchard, where he found a hen turkey in a coop; later visitors to the orchard found the coop almost intact, but very little left of the turkey.

Mr Penricarde, a little stunned and shaken, and suffering from a bruised knee and some minor damages, good-naturedly ascribed the accident to his own inexperience with horses and country roads, and allowed Jessie to nurse him back into complete recovery and golf-fitness within something less than a week.

In the list of wedding presents which the local newspaper published a fortnight or so later appeared the following item:

'Brown saddle-horse, "The Brogue", bridegroom's gift to bride.'

'Which shows,' said Toby Mullet, 'that he knew nothing.'

'Or else,' said Clovis, 'that he has a very pleasing wit.'

from BEASTS AND SUPER-BEASTS *1914*

The Maltese Cat

RUDYARD KIPLING

They had good reason to be proud, and better reason to be afraid, all twelve of them; for, though they had fought their way, game by game, up the teams entered for the polo tournament, they were meeting the Archangels that afternoon in the final match; and the Archangels' men were playing with half-a-dozen ponies apiece. As the game was divided into six quarters of eight minutes each, that meant a fresh pony after every halt. The Skidars' team, even supposing there were no accidents, could only supply one pony for every other change; and two to one is heavy odds. Again, as Shiraz, the grey Syrian, pointed out, they were meeting the pink and pick of the polo ponies of Upper India; ponies that had cost from a thousand rupees each, while they themselves were a cheap lot gathered, often from country carts, by their masters who belonged to a poor but honest native infantry regiment.

'Money means pace and weight,' said Shiraz, rubbing his black silk nose dolefully along his neat-fitting boot, 'and by the maxims of the game as I know it—'

'Ah, but we aren't playing the maxims,' said the Maltese Cat. 'We're playing the game, and we've the great advantage of knowing the game. Just think a stride, Shiraz. We've pulled up from bottom to second place in two weeks against all those fellows on the ground here; and that's because we play with our heads as well as with our feet.'

'It makes me feel undersized and unhappy all the same,' said Kittiwynk, a mouse-coloured mare with a red browband and the cleanest pair of legs that ever an aged pony owned. 'They're twice our size, these others.'

Kittiwynk looked at the gathering and sighed. The hard, dusty Umballa polo-ground was lined with thousands of soldiers, black and white, not counting hundreds and hundreds of carriages, and drags, and dog-carts, and ladies with brilliant-coloured parasols, and officers in uniform and out of it, and crowds of natives behind them; and orderlies on camels who had halted to watch the game, instead of carrying letters up and down the station, and native horse-dealers running about on thin-eared Biluchi mares, looking for a chance to sell a few first-class polo ponies. Then there were the ponies of thirty teams that had entered for the Upper India Free-for-All, Cup – nearly every pony of worth and dignity from Mhow to Peshawar, from Allahabad to Multan; prize ponies, Arabs, Syrian, Barb, country bred, Deccanee, Waziri, and Kabul ponies of every colour and shape and temper that you could imagine. Some of them were in mat-roofed stables close to the polo-ground, but most were under saddle while their masters, who had been defeated in the earlier games, trotted in and out and told each other exactly how the game should be played.

It was a glorious sight, and the come-and-go of the little quick hoofs, and the incessant salutations of ponies that had met before on other polo-grounds or racecourses, were enough to drive a four-footed thing wild.

But the Skidars' team were careful not to know their neighbours, though half the ponies on the ground were anxious to scrape acquaintance with the little fellows that had come from the North, and, so far, had swept the board.

'Let's see,' said a soft, golden-coloured Arab, who had been playing very badly the day before, to the Maltese Cat, 'didn't we meet in Abdul Rahman's stable in Bombay four seasons ago? I won the Paikpattan Cup next season you may remember.'

'Not me,' said the Maltese Cat politely. 'I was at Malta then, pulling a vegetable cart. I don't race. I play the game.'

'O-oh!' said the Arab, cocking his tail and swaggering off.

'Keep yourselves to yourselves,' said the Maltese Cat to his companions. 'We don't want to rub noses with all those goose-rumped half-breeds of Upper India. When we've won this cup they'll give their shoes to know us.'

'*We* shan't win the cup,' said Shiraz. 'How do you feel?'

'Stale as last night's feed when a musk-rat has run over it,' said Polaris, a rather heavy-shouldered grey, and the rest of the team agreed with him.

'The sooner you forget that the better,' said the Maltese Cat cheerfully. 'They've finished tiffin in the big tent. We shall be wanted now. If your saddles are not comfy kick. If your bits aren't easy, rear, and let the *saises* know whether your boots are tight.'

Each pony had his *sais*, his groom, who lived and ate and slept with the pony, and had betted a great deal more than he could afford on the result of the game. There was no chance of anything going wrong, and, to make sure, each *sais* was shampooing the legs of his pony to the last minute. Behind the *saises* sat as many of the Skidars' regiment as had leave to attend the match – about half the native officers, and a hundred or two dark black-bearded men with the regimental pipers nervously fingering the big be-ribboned bagpipes. The Skidars were what they call a Pioneer regiment; and the bagpipes made the national music of half the men. The native officers held bundles of polo-sticks, long cane-handled mallets, and as the grand stand filled after lunch they arranged themselves by ones and twos at different points round the ground, so that if a stick were broken the player would not have far to ride for a new one. An impatient British cavalry band struck up 'If you want to know the time, ask a p'leeceman!' and the two umpires in light dust-coats danced out on two little excited ponies. The four players of the Archangels' team followed, and the sight of their beautiful mounts made Shiraz groan again.

'Wait till we know,' said the Maltese Cat. 'Two of 'em are playing in blinkers, and that means they can't see to get out of the way of their own side, or they *may* shy at the umpires' ponies. They've *all* got white web reins that are sure to stretch or slip!'

'And,' said Kittiwynk, dancing to take the stiffness out of her, 'they carry their whips in their hands instead of on their wrists. Hah!'

'True enough. No man can manage his stick and his reins, and his whip that way,' said the Maltese Cat. 'I've fallen over every square yard of the Malta ground, and *I* ought to know.' He quivered his little flea-bitten withers just to show how satisfied he felt; but his heart was not so light. Ever since he had drifted into India on a troopship, taken, with an old rifle, as part payment for a racing debt, the Maltese Cat had played and preached polo to the Skidars' Team on the Skidars' stony polo-ground. Now a polo-pony is like a poet. If he is born with a love for the game he can be made. The Maltese Cat knew that bamboos grew solely in order that polo-balls might be turned from their roots, that grain was given to ponies to keep them in hard condition, and that ponies were shod to prevent them slipping on a turn. But, besides all these things, he knew every trick and device of the finest game of the world, and for two seasons he had been teaching the others all he knew or guessed.

'Remember,' he said for the hundredth time as the riders came up, 'we *must* play together, and you *must* play with your heads. Whatever happens follow the ball. Who goes out first?'

Kittiwynk, Shiraz, Polaris and a short high little bay fellow with tremendous hocks and no withers worth speaking of (he was called Corks) were being girthed up, and the soldiers in the background stared with all their eyes.

'I want you men to keep quiet,' said Lutyens, the captain of the team, 'and especially *not* to blow your pipes.'

'Not if we win, Captain Sahib?' asked a piper.

'If we win, you can do what you please,' said Lutyens, with a smile, as he slipped the loop of his stick over his wrist, and wheeled to canter to his place. The Archangels' ponies were a little bit above themselves on account of the many-coloured crowd so close to the ground. Their riders were excellent players, but they were a team of crack players instead of a crack team; and that made all the difference in the world. They honestly meant to play together, but it is very hard for four men, each the best of the team he is picked from, to remember that in polo no brilliancy of hitting or riding makes up for playing alone. Their captain shouted his orders to them by name, and it is a curious thing that if you call his name aloud in public after an Englishman you make him hot and fretty. Lutyens said nothing to his men because it had all been said before. He pulled up Shiraz, for he was playing 'back', to guard the goal. Powell on Polaris was half-back, and Macnamara and Hughes on Corks and Kittiwynk were forwards. The tough bamboo-root ball was put into the middle of the ground one hundred and fifty yards from the ends, and Hughes crossed sticks, heads-up, with the captain of the Archangels, who saw fit to play forward, and that is a place from which you cannot easily control the team. The little click as the cane-shafts met was heard all over the ground, and then Hughes made some sort of quick wrist-stroke that just dribbled the ball a few yards. Kittiwynk knew that stroke of old, and

followed as a cat follows a mouse. While the captain of the
Archangels was wrenching his pony round Hughes struck with
all his strength, and next instant Kittiwynk was away, Corks
followed close behind her, their little feet pattering like rain-
drops on glass.

'Pull out to the left,' said Kittiwynk between her teeth. 'It's
coming our way, Corks!'

The back and half-back of the Archangels were tearing down
on her just as she was within reach of the ball. Hughes leaned
forward with a loose rein, and cut it away to the left almost
under Kittiwynk's feet, and it hopped and skipped off to Corks,
who saw that, if he were not quick, it would run beyond the
boundaries. That long bouncing drive gave the Archangels time to
wheel and send three men across the ground to head off Corks.
Kittiwynk stayed where she was, for she knew the game. Corks
was on the ball half a fraction of a second before the others came
up, and Macnamara, with a back-handed stroke, sent it back
across the ground to Hughes, who saw the way clear to the
Archangels' goal, and smacked the ball in before anyone quite
knew what happened.

'That's luck,' said Corks, as they changed ends. 'A goal in
three minutes for three hits and no riding to speak of.'

'Don't know,' said Polaris. 'We've made 'em angry too soon.
Shouldn't wonder if they try to rush us off our feet next time.'

'Keep the ball hanging then,' said Shiraz. 'That wears out every
pony that isn't used to it.'

Next time there was no easy galloping across the ground. All
the Archangels closed up as one man, but there they stayed,
for Corks, Kittiwynk, and Polaris were somewhere on the top
of the ball, marking time among the rattling sticks, while Shiraz
circled about outside, waiting for a chance.

'*We* can do this all day,' said Polaris, ramming his quarters into
the side of another pony. 'Where do you think you're shoving to?'

'I'll – I'll be driven in an *ekka* if I know,' was the gasping reply,
'and I'd give a week's feed to get my blinkers off. I can't see
anything.'

'The dust is rather bad. Whew! That was one for my off hock.
Where's the ball, Corks?'

'Under my tail. At least a man's looking for it there. This is beautiful. They can't use their sticks, and it's driving 'em wild. Give old blinkers a push and he'll go over!'

'Here, don't touch me! I can't see. I'll – I'll back out, I think,' said the pony in blinkers, who knew that if you can't see all round your head you cannot prop yourself against a shock.

Corks was watching the ball where it lay in the dust close to his near fore with Macnamara's shortened stick tap-tapping it from time to time. Kittiwynk was edging her way out of the scrimmage, whisking her stump of a tail with nervous excitement.

'Ho! They've got it,' she snorted. 'Let me out!' and she galloped like a rifle-bullet just behind a tall lanky pony of the Archangels, whose rider was swinging up his stick for a stroke.

'Not today, thank you,' said Hughes, as the blow slid off his raised stick, and Kittiwynk laid her shoulder to the tall pony's quarters, and shoved him aside just as Lutyens on Shiraz sent the ball back where it had come from, and the tall pony went skating and slipping away to the left. Kittiwynk, seeing that Polaris had joined Corks in the chase for the ball up the ground, dropped into Polaris's place, and then time was called.

The Skidars' ponies wasted no time in kicking or fuming. They knew each minute's rest meant so much gain, and trotted off to the rails and their *saises*, who began to scrape and blanket and rub them at once.

'Whew!' said Corks, stiffening up to get all the tickle out of the big vulcanite scraper. 'If we were playing pony for pony we'd bend those Archangels double in half an hour. But they'll bring out fresh ones and fresh ones, and fresh ones after that – you see.'

'Who cares?' said Polaris. 'We've drawn first blood. Is my hock swelling?'

'Looks puffy,' said Corks. 'You must have had rather a swipe. Don't let it stiffen. You'll be wanted again in half an hour.'

'What's the game like?' said the Maltese Cat.

'Ground's like your shoe, except where they've put too much water on it,' said Kittiwynk. 'Then it's slippery. Don't play in the centre. There's a bog there. I don't know how their next four are going to behave but we kept the ball hanging and made 'em lather for nothing. Who goes out? Two Arabs and a couple of countrybreds! That's bad. What a comfort it is to wash your mouth out!'

Kitty was talking with a neck of a leather covered soda-water bottle between her teeth and trying to look over her withers at the same time. This gave her a very coquettish air.

'What's bad?' said Gray Dawn, giving to the girth and admiring his well-set shoulders.

'You Arabs can't gallop fast enough to keep yourselves warm – that's what Kitty means,' said Polaris, limping to show that his hock needed attention. 'Are you playing "back", Gray Dawn?'

'Looks like it,' said Gray Dawn, as Lutyens swung himself up. Powell mounted the Rabbit, a plain bay countrybred much like Corks, but with mulish ears. Macnamara took Faiz Ullah, a handy short-backed little red Arab with a long tail, and Hughes mounted Benami, an old and sullen brown beast, who stood over in front more than a polo pony should.

'Benami looks like business,' said Shiraz. 'How's your temper, Ben?' The old campaigner hobbled off without answering, and the Maltese Cat looked at the new Archangel ponies prancing about on the ground. They were four beautiful blacks, and they saddled big enough and strong enough to eat the Skidars' team and gallop away with the meal inside them.

'Blinkers again,' said the Maltese Cat. 'Good enough!'

'They're chargers – cavalry chargers!' said Kittiwynk indignantly. '*They'll* never see thirteen three again.'

'They've all been fairly measured and they've all got their certificates,' said the Maltese Cat, 'or they wouldn't be here. We must take things as they come along, and keep our eyes on the ball.'

The game began, but this time the Skidars were penned to their own end of the ground, and the watching ponies did not approve of that.

'Faiz Ullah is shirking, as usual,' said Polaris, with a scornful grunt.

'Faiz Ullah is eating whip,' said Corks. They could hear the leather-thonged polo quirt lacing the little fellow's well-rounded barrel. Then the Rabbit's shrill neigh came across the ground. 'I can't do all the work,' he cried.

'Play the game, don't talk,' the Maltese Cat whickered; and all the ponies wriggled with excitement, and the soldiers and the grooms gripped the railings and shouted. A black pony with blinkers had singled out old Benami, and was interfering with him in every possible way. They could see Benami shaking his head up and down and flapping his underlip.

'There'll be a fall in a minute,' said Polaris. 'Benami is getting stuffy.'

The game flickered up and down between goal-post and goal-post, and the black ponies were getting more confident as they felt they had the legs of the others. The ball was hit out of a little scrimmage, and Benami and the Rabbit followed it; Faiz Ullah only too glad to be quiet for an instant.

The blinkered black pony came up like a hawk, with two of his own side behind him, and Benami's eye glittered as he raced. The question was which pony should make way for the other; each rider was perfectly willing to risk a fall in a good cause. The black who had been driven nearly crazy by his blinkers trusted to his weight and his temper; but Benami knew how to apply his weight and how to keep his temper. They met, and there was a cloud of dust. The black was lying on his side with all the breath knocked out of his body. The Rabbit was a hundred yards up the ground with the ball, and Benami was sitting down. He had slid nearly ten yards, but he had had his revenge, and sat cracking his nostrils till the black pony rose.

'That's what you get for interfering. Do you want any more?' said Benami, and he plunged into the game. Nothing was done because Faiz Ullah would not gallop, though Macnamara beat him whenever he could spare a second. The fall of the black pony had impressed his companions tremendously, and so the Archangels could not profit by Faiz Ullah's bad behaviour.

But as the Maltese Cat said, when time was called and the four came back blowing and dripping, Faiz Ullah ought to have been kicked all round Umballa. If he did not behave better next time, the Maltese Cat promised to pull out his Arab tail by the root and eat it.

There was no time to talk, for the third four were ordered out.

The third quarter of a game is generally the hottest, for each side thinks that the others must be pumped; and most of the winning play in a game is made about that time.

Lutyens took over the Maltese Cat with a pat and a hug, for Lutyens valued him more than anything else in the world. Powell had Shikast, a little grey rat with no pedigree and no manners outside polo; Macnamara mounted Bamboo, the largest of the team, and Hughes took Who's Who, *alias* The Animal. He was supposed to have Australian blood in his veins, but he looked like a clothes horse, and you could whack him on the legs with an iron crow-bar without hurting him.

They went out to meet the very flower of the Archangel's team, and when Who's Who saw their elegantly booted legs and their beautiful satiny skins he grinned a grin through his light, well-worn bridle.

'My word!' said Who's Who. 'We must give 'em a little foot-ball. Those gentlemen need a rubbing down.'

'No biting,' said the Maltese Cat warningly, for once or twice in his career Who's Who had been known to forget himself in that way.

'Who said anything about biting? I'm not playing tiddlywinks. I'm playing the game.'

The Archangels came down like a wolf on the fold, for they were tired of football and they wanted polo. They got it more and more. Just after the game began, Lutyens hit a ball that was coming towards him rapidly, and it rose in the air, as a ball some-times will, with the whirr of a frightened partridge. Shikast heard, but could not see it for the minute though he looked every-where and up into the air as the Maltese Cat had taught him. When he saw it ahead and over head, he went forward with Powell as fast as he could put foot to ground. It was then that Powell, a quiet and level-headed man as a rule, became inspired and played a stroke that sometimes comes off successfully on a quiet afternoon of long practice. He took his stick in both hands, and standing up in his stirrups, swiped at the ball in the air, Munipore fashion. There was one second of paralysed astonish-ment and then from all four sides of the ground went up a yell of applause and delight as the ball flew true (you could see the amazed Archangels ducking in their saddles to get out of the line of flight, and looking at it with open mouths), and the regimental pipes of the Skidars squealed from the railings as long as the piper had breath.

Shikast heard the stroke; but he heard the head of the stick fly off at the same time. Nine hundred and ninety-nine ponies out of a thousand would have gone tearing on after the ball with a useless player pulling at their heads, but Powell knew him, and he knew Powell; and the instant he felt Powell's right leg shift a trifle on the saddle-flap he headed to the boundary, where a native officer was frantically waving a new stick. Before the shouts had ended Powell was armed again.

Once before in his life the Maltese Cat had heard that very same stroke played off his own back, and had profited by the confusion it made. This time he acted on experience, and leaving Bamboo to guard the goal in case of accidents, came through the others like a flash, head and tail low, Lutyens standing up to ease him – swept on and on before the other side knew what was the matter, and nearly pitched on his head between the Archangels' goal-post as Lutyens tipped the ball in after a straight scurry of a hundred and fifty yards. If there was one thing more than another upon which the Maltese Cat prided himself it was on this quick, streaking kind of run half across the ground. He did not believe in taking balls round the field unless you were clearly over-matched. After this they gave the Archangels five minutes' football, and an expensive fast pony hates football because it rumples his temper.

Who's Who showed himself even better than Polaris at this game. He did not permit any wriggling away, but bored joyfully into the scrimmage as if he had his nose in a feed-box, and were looking for something nice. Little Shikast jumped on the ball the minute it got clear, and every time an Archangel pony followed it he found Shikast standing over it asking what was the matter.

'If we can live through this quarter,' said the Maltese Cat, 'I shan't care. Don't take it out of yourselves. Let them do the lathering.'

So the ponies, as their riders explained afterwards, 'shut up'. The Archangels kept them tied fast in front of their goal, but it cost the Archangels' ponies all that was left of their tempers; and ponies began to kick, and men began to repeat compliments, and they chopped at the legs of Who's Who, and he set his teeth and stayed where he was, and the dust stood up like a tree over the scrimmage till that hot quarter ended.

They found the ponies very excited, and confident when they went to their *saises*; and the Maltese Cat had to warn them that the worst of the game was coming.

THE MALTESE CAT 455

'Now *we* are all going in for the second time,' said he, 'and *they* are trotting out fresh ponies. You'll think you can gallop, but you'll find you can't; and then you'll be sorry.'

'But two goals to nothing is a halter-long lead,' said Kittiwynk prancing.

'How long does it take to get a goal?' the Maltese Cat answered. 'For pity's sake, don't run away with the notion that the game is half-won just because we happen to be in luck now. They'll ride you into the grandstand if they can; you must *not* give 'em a chance. Follow the ball.'

'Football, as usual?' said Polaris. 'My hock's half as big as a nose-bag.'

'Don't let them have a look at the ball if you can help it. Now leave me alone. I must get all the rest I can before the last quarter.'

He hung down his head and let all his muscles go slack; Shikast, Bamboo, and Who's Who copying his example.

'Better not watch the game,' he said. 'We aren't playing, and we shall only take it out of ourselves if we grow anxious. Look at the ground and pretend it's fly-time.'

They did their best, but it was hard advice to follow. The hoofs were drumming and the sticks were rattling all up and down the ground, and yells of applause from the English troops told that the Archangels were pressing the Skidars hard. The native soldiers behind the ponies groaned and grunted, and said things in undertones, and presently they heard a long-drawn shout and a clatter of hurrahs!

'One to the Archangels,' said Shikast, without raising his head. 'Time's nearly up. Oh, my sire and dam!'

'Faiz Ullah,' said the Maltese Cat, 'if you don't play to the last nail in your shoes this time, I'll kick you on the ground before all the other ponies.'

'I'll do my best when the time comes,' said the little Arab sturdily.

The *saises* looked at each other gravely as they rubbed their ponies' legs. This was the first time when long purses began to tell, and everybody knew it. Kittiwynk and the others came back with the sweat dripping over their hoofs and their tails telling sad stories.

'They're better than we are,' said Shiraz. 'I knew how it would be.'

'Shut your big head,' said the Maltese Cat; 'we've one goal to the good yet.'

'Yes, but it's two Arabs and two countrybreds to play now,' said Corks. 'Faiz Ullah, remember!' He spoke in a biting voice.

As Lutyens mounted Gray Dawn he looked at his men, and they did not look pretty. They were covered with dust and sweat in streaks. Their yellow boots were almost black, their wrists were red and lumpy, and their eyes seemed two inches deep in their heads, but the expression in the eyes was satisfactory.

'Did you take anything at tiffin?' said Lutyens, and the team shook their heads. They were too dry to talk.

'All right. The Archangels did. They are worse pumped than we are.'

'They've got the better ponies,' said Powell. 'I shan't be sorry when this business is over.'

That fifth quarter was a sad one in every way. Faiz Ullah played like a little red demon; and the Rabbit seemed to be everywhere at once, and Benami rode straight at anything and everything that came in his way, while the umpires on their ponies wheeled like gulls outside the shifting game. But the Archangels had the better mounts – they had kept their racers till late in the game – and never allowed the Skidars to play football. They hit the ball up and down the width of the ground till Benami and the rest were outpaced. Then they went forward, and time and again Lutyens and Gray Dawn were just, and only just, able to send the ball away with a long splitting back-hander. Gray Dawn forgot that he was an Arab; and turned from gray to blue as he galloped. Indeed, he forgot too well, for he did not keep his eyes on the ground as an Arab should, but stuck out his nose and scuttled for the dear honour of the game. They had watered the ground once or twice between the quarters, and a careless water-man had emptied the last of his skinful all in one place near the Skidars' goal. It was close to the end of play, and for the tenth time Gray Dawn was bolting after the ball when his near hind foot slipped on the greasy mud and he rolled over and over, pitching Lutyens just clear of the goalpost; and the triumphant Archangels made their goal. Then time was called – two goals all; but Lutyens had to be helped up, and Gray Dawn rose with his near hind leg strained somewhere.

'What's the damage?' said Powell, his arm round Lutyens.

'Collar-bone, of course,' said Lutyens between his teeth. It was the third time he had broken it in two years, and it hurt him.

Powell and the others whistled. 'Game's up,' said Hughes.

'Hold on. We've five good minutes yet, and it isn't my right hand,' said Lutyens. 'We'll stick it out.'

'I say,' said the captain of the Archangels, trotting up. 'Are you hurt, Lutyens? We'll wait if you care to put in a substitute. I wish – I mean – the fact is, you fellows deserve this game if any team does. Wish we could give you a man or some of our ponies – or something.'

'You're awfully good, but we'll play it to a finish, I think.'

The captain of the Archangels stared for a little. 'That's not half bad,' he said, and went back to his own side, while Lutyens borrowed a scarf from one of his native officers and made a sling of it. Then an Archangel galloped up with a big bath-sponge and advised Lutyens to put it under his arm-pit to ease his shoulder, and between them they tied up his left arm scientifically, and one of the native officers leaped forward with four long glasses that fizzed and bubbled.

The team looked piteously at Lutyens, and he nodded. It was the last quarter, and nothing would matter after that. They drank out the dark golden drink, and wiped their moustaches, and things looked more hopeful.

The Maltese Cat had put his nose into the front of Lutyens' shirt, and was trying to say how sorry he was.

'He knows,' said Lutyens, proudly. 'The beggar knows. I've played him without a bridle before now – for fun.'

'It's no fun now,' said Powell. 'But we haven't a decent substitute.'

'No,' said Lutyens. 'It's the last quarter, and we've got to make our goal and win. I'll trust the Cat.'

'If you fall this time you'll suffer a little,' said Macnamara.

'I'll trust the Cat,' said Lutyens.

'You hear that?' said the Maltese Cat proudly to the others. 'It's worth while playing polo for ten years to have that said of you. Now then, my sons, come along. We'll kick up a little bit, just to show the Archangels *this* team haven't suffered.'

And, sure enough, as they went on to the ground the Maltese

Cat, after satisfying himself that Lutyens was home in the saddle, kicked out three or four times, and Lutyens laughed. The reins were caught up anyhow in the tips of his strapped hand, and he never pretended to rely on them. He knew the Cat would answer to the least pressure of the leg, and by way of showing off – for his shoulder hurt him very much – he bent the little fellow in a close figure-of-eight in and out between the goal-posts. There was a roar from the native officers and men, who dearly loved a piece of *dugabashi* (horse-trick work), as they called it, and the pipes very quietly and scornfully droned out the first bars of a common bazaar-tune called 'Freshly Fresh and Newly New,' just as a warning to the other regiments that the Skidars were fit. All the natives laughed.

'And now,' said the Cat, as they took their place, 'remember that this is the last quarter, and follow the ball!'

'Don't need to be told', said Who's Who.

'Let me go on. All those people on all four sides will begin to crowd in – just as they did at Malta. You'll hear people calling out, and moving forward and being pushed back, and that is going to make the Archangel ponies very unhappy. But if a ball is struck to the boundary, you go after it, and let the people get out of your way. I went over the pole of a four-in-hand once, and picked a game out of the dust by it. Back me up when I run, and follow the ball.'

There was a sort of an all-round sound of sympathy and wonder as the last quarter opened, and then there began exactly what the Maltese Cat had foreseen. People crowded in close to the boundaries, and the Archangels' ponies kept looking sideways at the narrowing space. If you know how a man feels to be cramped at tennis – not because he wants to run out of the court, but because he likes to know that he can at a pinch – you will guess how ponies must feel when they are playing in a box of human beings.

'I'll bend some of those men if I can get away,' said Who's Who, as he rocketed behind the ball; and Bamboo nodded without speaking. They were playing the last ounce in them, and the Maltese Cat had left the goal undefended to join them. Lutyens gave him every order that he could to bring him back, but this was the first time in his career that the little wise gray had ever played polo on his own responsibility, and he was going to make the most of it.

'What are you doing here?' said Hughes, as the Cat crossed in front of him and rode off an Archangel.

'The Cat's in charge – mind the goal!' shouted Lutyens, and bowing forward hit the ball full, and followed on, forcing the Archangels towards their own goal.

'No football,' said the Cat. 'Keep the ball by the boundaries and cramp 'em. Play open order and drive 'em to the boundaries.'

Across and across the ground in big diagonals flew the ball, and whenever it came to a flying rush and a stroke close to the boundaries the Archangel ponies moved stiffly. They did not care to go headlong at a wall of men and carriages, though if the ground had been open they could have turned on a sixpence.

'Wriggle her up the sides,' said the Cat. 'Keep her close to the crowd. They hate the carriages. Shikast, keep her up this side.'

Shikast with Powell lay left and right behind the uneasy scuffle of an open scrimmage, and every time the ball was hit away Shikast galloped on it at such an angle that Powell was forced to hit it towards the boundary; and when the crowd had been driven away from that side, Lutyens would send the ball over to the other, and Shikast would slide desperately after it till his friends came down to help. It was billiards, and no football, this time – billiards in a corner pocket; and the cues were not well chalked.

'If they get us out in the middle of the ground they'll walk away from us. Dribble her along the sides,' cried the Cat.

So they dribbled all along the boundary, where a pony could not come on their right-hand side; and the Archangels were furious, and the umpires had to neglect the game to shout at the people to get back, and several blundering mounted policemen tried to restore order, all close to the scrimmage, and the nerves of the Archangels' ponies stretched and broke like cobwebs.

Five or six times an Archangel hit the ball up into the middle of the ground, and each time the watchful Shikast gave Powell his chance to send it back, and after each return, when the dust had settled, men could see that the Skidars had gained a few yards.

Every now and again there were shouts of 'Side! Off side!' from the spectators; but the teams were too busy to care, and the umpires had all they could do to keep their maddened ponies clear of the scuffle.

At last Lutyens missed a short easy stroke, and the Skidars had to fly back helter-skelter to protect their own goal, Shikast leading. Powell stopped the ball with a backhander when it was not fifty yards from the goal-posts, and Shikast spun round with a wrench that nearly hoisted Powell out of his saddle.

'Now's our last chance,' said the Cat, wheeling like a cockchafer on a pin. 'We've got to ride it out. Come along.'

Lutyens felt the little chap take a deep breath and, as it were, crouch under his rider. The ball was hopping towards the right-hand boundary, an Archangel riding for it with both spurs and a whip; but neither spur nor whip would make his pony stretch himself as he neared the crowd. The Maltese Cat glided under his very nose, picking up his hind legs sharp, for there was not a foot to spare between his quarters and the other pony's bit. It was as neat an exhibition as fancy figure-skating. Lutyens hit with all the strength he had left, but the stick slipped a little in his hand, and the ball flew off to the left instead of keeping close to the boundary. Who's Who was far across the ground, thinking hard as he galloped. He repeated, stride for stride, the Cat's manoeuvres with another Archangel pony, nipping the ball away from under his bridle, and clearing his opponent by half a fraction of an inch, for Who's Who was clumsy behind. Then he drove away towards the right as the Maltese Cat came up from the left; and Bamboo held a middle course exactly between them. The three were making a sort of Government-broad-arrow-shaped attack; and there was only the Archangels' back to guard the goal; but immediately behind them were three Archangels racing all they knew, and mixed up with them was Powell, sending Shikast along on what he felt was their last hope. It takes a very good man to stand up to the rush of seven crazy ponies in the last quarters of a cup game, when men are riding with their necks for sale, and the ponies are delirious. The Archangels' back missed his stroke, and pulled aside just in time to let the rush go by. Bamboo and Who's Who shortened stride to give the Maltese Cat room, and Lutyens got the goal with a clean, smooth, smacking stroke that was heard all over the field. But there was no stopping the ponies. They poured through the goal-posts in

one mixed mob, winners and losers together, for the pace had
been terrific. The Maltese Cat knew by experience what would
happen, and, to save Lutyens, turned to the right with one last
effort that strained a back-sinew beyond hope of repair. As he
did so he heard the right-hand goal-post crack as a pony cannoned
into it – crack, splinter, and fall like a mast. It had been sawed
three parts through in case of accidents, but it upset the pony
nevertheless, and he blundered into another, who blundered into
the left-hand post, and then there was confusion and dust and
wood. Bamboo was lying on the ground, seeing stars; an Archangel pony rolled beside him, breathless and angry; Shikast had
sat down dog-fashion to avoid falling over the others, and was
sliding along on his little bobtail in a cloud of dust; and Powell
was sitting on the ground, hammering with his stick and trying
to cheer. All the others were shouting at the top of what was left
of their voices, and the men who had been spilt were shouting
too. As soon as the people saw no one was hurt, ten thousand
native and English shouted and clapped and yelled, and before
any one could stop them the pipers of the Skidars broke on to
the ground, with all the native officers and men behind them,
and marched up and down, playing a wild northern tune called
'Zakhme Bagān', and through the insolent blaring of the pipes
and the high-pitched native yells you could hear the Archangels'
band hammering, 'For they are all jolly good fellows', and then
reproachfully to the losing team, 'Ooh, Kafoozalum! Kafoozalum!
Kafoozalum!'

Besides all these things and many more there was a Com-
mander-in-Chief and an Inspector-General of Cavalry, and the
Principal veterinary officer in all India, standing on the top of a
regimental coach, yelling like school-boys; and brigadiers and
colonels and commissioners, and hundreds of pretty ladies
joined the chorus. But the Maltese Cat stood with his head down,
wondering how many legs were left to him; and Lutyens watched
the men and ponies pick themselves out of the wreck of the two
goal-posts, and he patted the Cat very tenderly.

'I say,' said the captain of the Archangels, spitting a pebble out
of his mouth, 'will you take three thousand for that pony – as
he stands?'

'No, thank you. I've an idea he's saved my life,' said Lutyens, getting off and lying down at full length. Both teams were on the ground too, waving their boots in the air, and coughing and drawing deep breaths, as the *saises* ran up to take away the ponies, and an officious water-carrier sprinkled the players with dirty water till they sat up.

'My Aunt!' said Powell, rubbing his back and looking at the stumps of the goal-posts, 'that was a game!'

They played it over again, every stroke of it, that night at the big dinner, when the Free-for-All Cup was filled and passed down the table, and emptied and filled again, and everybody made most eloquent speeches. About two in the morning, when there might have been some singing, a wise little, plain little, gray little head looked in through the open door.

'Hurrah! Bring him in,' said the Archangels; and his *sais*, who was very happy indeed, patted the Maltese Cat on the flank, and he limped in to the blaze of light and the glittering uniforms, looking for Lutyens. He was used to messes, and men's bed-rooms, and places where ponies are not usually encouraged, and in his youth had jumped on and off a mess-table for a bet. So he behaved himself very politely, and ate bread dipped in salt, and was petted all round the table, moving gingerly; and they drank his health, because he had done more to win the Cup than any man or horse on the ground.

That was glory and honour enough for the rest of his days, and the Maltese Cat did not complain much when his veterinary surgeon said that he would be no good for polo any more. When Lutyens married, his wife did not allow him to play, so he was forced to be an umpire; and his pony on these occasions was a flea-bitten gray with a neat polo-tail, lame all round, but desperately quick on his feet, and, as everybody knew, Past Pluperfect Prestissimo Player of the Game.

from THE DAY'S WORK *1898*

The Rocking-Horse Winner

D. H. LAWRENCE

There was a woman who was beautiful, who started with all the advantages, yet she had no luck. She married for love, and the love turned to dust. She had bonny children, yet she felt they had been thrust upon her, and she could not love them. They looked at her coldly, as if they were finding fault with her. And hurriedly she felt she must cover up some fault in herself. Yet what it was that she must cover up she never knew. Nevertheless, when her children were present, she always felt the centre of her heart go hard. This troubled her, and in her manner she was all the more gentle and anxious for her children, as if she loved them very much. Only she herself knew that at the centre of her heart was a hard little place that could not feel love, no, not for anybody. Everybody else said of her: 'She is such a good mother. She adores her children.' Only she herself, and her children themselves, knew it was not so. They read it in each other's eyes.

There were a boy and two little girls. They lived in a pleasant house, with a garden, and they had discreet servants, and felt themselves superior to anyone in the neighbourhood.

Although they lived in style, they felt always an anxiety in the house. There was never enough money. The mother had a small income, and the father had a small income, but not nearly enough for the social position which they had to keep up. The father went into town to some office. But though he had good prospects, these prospects never materialized. There was always the grinding sense of the shortage of money, though the style was always kept up.

At last the mother said: 'I will see if I can't make something.' But she did not know where to begin. She racked her brains, and tried this thing and the other, but could not find anything successful. The failure made deep lines come into her face. Her children were growing up, they would have to go to school. There must be more money, there must be more money. The father, who was always very handsome and expensive in his tastes, seemed as if he never *would* be able to do anything worth doing. And the mother, who had a great belief in herself, did not succeed any better, and her tastes were just as expensive.

And so the house came to be haunted by the unspoken phrase: *There must be more money! There must be more money!* The children could hear it all the time, though nobody said it aloud. They heard it at Christmas when the expensive and splendid toys filled the nursery. Behind the shining modern rocking-horse, behind the smart doll's house, a voice would start whispering: 'There *must* be more money! There *must* be more money!' And the children would stop playing, to listen for a moment. They would look into each other's eyes, to see if they had all heard. And each one saw in the eyes of the other two that they too had heard. 'There *must* be more money! There *must* be more money!'

It came whispering from the springs of the still-swaying rocking-horse, and even the horse, bending his wooden champing head, heard it. The big doll, sitting so pink and smirking in her new pram, could hear it quite plainly, and seemed to be smirking all the more self-consciously because of it. The foolish puppy, too, that took the place of the teddy-bear, he was looking so extraordinarily foolish for no other reason but that he heard the secret whisper all over the house: 'There *must* be more money!'

Yet nobody ever said it aloud. The whisper was everywhere, and therefore no one spoke it. Just as no one ever says: 'We are breathing!' in spite of the fact that breath is coming and going all the time.

'Mother,' said the boy Paul one day, 'why don't we keep a car of our own? Why do we always use uncle's, or else a taxi?'

'Because we're the poor members of the family,' said the mother.

'But why *are* we, mother?'

'Well – I suppose,' she said slowly and bitterly, 'it's because your father had no luck.'

The boy was silent for some time.

'Is luck money, mother?' he asked, rather timidly.

'No, Paul. Not quite. It's what causes you to have money.'

'Oh!' said Paul vaguely. 'I thought when Uncle Oscar said *filthy lucker*, it meant money.'

'*Filthy lucre* does mean money,' said the mother. 'But it's lucre not luck.'

'Oh!' said the boy. 'Then what is luck, mother?'

'It's what causes you to have money. If you're lucky you have money. That's why it's better to be born lucky than rich. If you're rich, you may lose your money. But if you're lucky, you will always get more money.'

'Oh! Will you? And is father not lucky?'

'Very unlucky, I should say,' she said bitterly.

The boy watched her with unsure eyes.

'Why?' he asked.

'I don't know. Nobody ever knows why one person is lucky and another unlucky.'

'Don't they? Nobody at all? Does *nobody* know?'

'Perhaps God. But He never tells.'

'He ought to, then. And aren't you lucky either, mother?'

'I can't be, if I married an unlucky husband.'

'But by yourself, aren't you?'

'I used to think I was, before I married. Now I think I am very unlucky indeed.'

'Why?'

'Well – never mind! Perhaps I'm not really,' she said.

The child looked at her to see if she meant it. But he saw, by the lines of her mouth, that she was only trying to hide something from him.

'Well, anyhow,' he said stoutly, 'I'm a lucky person.'

'Why?' said his mother, with a sudden laugh.

He stared at her. He didn't even know why he had said it.

'God told me,' he asserted, brazening it out.

'I hope He did, dear!' she said, again with a laugh, but rather bitter.

'He did, mother!'

'Excellent!' said the mother, using one of her husband's exclamations.

The boy saw she did not believe him; or rather, that she paid no attention to his assertion. This angered him somewhere, and made him want to compel her attention.

He went off by himself, vaguely, in a childish way, seeking for the clue to 'luck'. Absorbed, taking no heed of other people, he went about with a sort of stealth, seeking inwardly for luck. He wanted luck, he wanted it. When the two girls were playing dolls in the nursery, he would sit on his big rocking-horse, charging madly into space, with a frenzy that made the little girls peer at him uneasily. Wildly the horse careered, the waving dark hair of the boy tossed, his eyes had a strange glare in them. The little girls dared not speak to him.

When he had ridden to the end of his mad little journey, he climbed down and stood in front of his rocking-horse, staring fixedly into its lowered face. Its red mouth was slightly open, its big eye was wide and glassy-bright.

'Now!' he would silently command the snorting steed. 'Now, take me to where there is luck! Now take me!'

And he would slash the horse on the neck with the little whip he had asked Uncle Oscar for. He *knew* the horse could take him to where there was luck, if only he forced it. So he would mount again and start on his furious ride, hoping at last to get there. He knew he could get there.

'You'll break your horse, Paul!' said the nurse.

'He's always riding like that! I wish he'd leave off!' said his elder sister Joan.

But he only glared down on them in silence. Nurse gave him up. She could make nothing of him. Anyhow, he was growing beyond her.

One day his mother and his Uncle Oscar came in when he was on one of his furious rides. He did not speak to them.

'Hallo, you young jockey! Riding a winner?' said his uncle.

'Aren't you growing too big for a rocking-horse? You're not a very little boy any longer, you know,' said his mother.

But Paul only gave a blue glare from his big, rather close set eyes. He would speak to nobody when he was in full tilt. His mother watched him with an anxious expression on her face.

At last he suddenly stopped forcing his horse into the mechanical gallop and slid down.

'Well, I got there!' he announced fiercely, his blue eyes still flaring, and his sturdy long legs straddling apart.

'Where did you get to?' asked his mother.

'Where I wanted to go,' he flared back at her.

'That's right, son!' said Uncle Oscar. 'Don't you stop till you get there. What's the horse's name?'

'He doesn't have a name,' said the boy.

'Gets on without all right?' asked the uncle.

'Well he has different names. He was called Sansovino last week.'

'Sansovino, eh? Won the Ascot. How did you know this name?'

'He always talks about horse-races with Bassett,' said Joan.

The uncle was delighted to find that his small nephew was posted with all the racing news. Bassett, the young gardener, who had been wounded in the left foot in the war and had got his present job through Oscar Cresswell, whose batman he had been, was a perfect blade of the 'turf'. He lived in the racing events, and the small boy lived with him.

Oscar Cresswell got it all from Bassett.

'Master Paul comes and asks me, so I can't do more than tell him, sir,' said Bassett, his face terribly serious, as if he were speaking of religious matters.

'And does he ever put anything on a horse he fancies?'

'Well – I don't want to give him away – he's a young sport, a fine sport, sir. Would you mind asking him himself? He sort of takes a pleasure in it, and perhaps he'd feel I was giving him away, sir, if you don't mind.'

Bassett was serious as a church.

The uncle went back to his nephew and took him off for a ride in the car.

'Say, Paul, old man, do you ever put anything on a horse?' the uncle asked.

The boy watched the handsome man closely.

'Why, do you think I oughtn't to?' he parried.

'Not a bit of it! I thought perhaps you might give me a tip for the Lincoln.'

The car sped on into the country, going down to Uncle Oscar's place in Hampshire.

'Honour bright?' said the nephew.

'Honour bright, son!' said the uncle.

'Well then, Daffodil.'

'Daffodil! I doubt it, sonny. What about Mirza?'

'I only know the winner,' said the boy. 'That's Daffodil.'

'Daffodil, eh?'

There was a pause. Daffodil was an obscure horse comparatively.

'Uncle!'

'Yes, son?'

'You won't let it go any further, will you? I promised Bassett.'

'Bassett be damned, old man! What's he got to do with it?'

'We're partners. We've been partners from the first. Uncle, he lent me my first five shillings, which I lost. I promised him, honour bright, it was only between me and him; only you gave me that ten-shilling note I started winning with, so I thought you were lucky. You won't let it go any further, will you?'

The boy gazed at his uncle from those big, hot, blue eyes, set rather close together. The uncle stirred and laughed uneasily.

'Right you are, son! I'll keep your tip private. Daffodil, eh? How much are you putting on him?'

'All except twenty pounds,' said the boy. 'I keep that in reserve.'

The uncle thought it a good joke.

'You keep twenty pounds in reserve, do you, you young romancer? What are you betting then?'

'I'm betting three hundred,' said the boy gravely. 'But it's between you and me, Uncle Oscar! Honour bright?'

The uncle burst into a roar of laughter.

'It's between you and me all right, you young Nat Gould,' he said, laughing. 'But where's your three hundred?'

'Bassett keeps it for me. We're partners.'

'You are, are you! And what is Bassett putting on Daffodil?'

'He won't go quite as high as I do, I expect. Perhaps he'll go a hundred and fifty.'

'What, pennies?' laughed the uncle.

'Pounds,' said the child, with a surprised look at his uncle. 'Bassett keeps a bigger reserve than I do.'

Between wonder and amusement Uncle Oscar was silent. He pursued the matter no further, but he determined to take his nephew with him to the Lincoln races.

'Now, son,' he said, 'I'm putting twenty on Mirza, and I'll put five on for you on any horse you fancy. What's your pick?'

'Daffodil, uncle.'

'No, not the fiver on Daffodil!'

'I should if it was my own fiver,' said the child.

'Good! Good! Right you are! A fiver for me and a fiver for you on Daffodil.'

The child had never been to a race-meeting before, and his eyes were blue fire. He pursed his mouth tight and watched. A Frenchman just in front had put his money on Lancelot. Wild with excitement, he flayed his arms up and down, yelling '*Lancelot! Lancelot!*' in his French accent.

Daffodil came in first, Lancelot second, Mirza third. The child, flushed and with eyes blazing, was curiously serene. His uncle brought him four five-pound notes, four to one.

'What am I to do with these?' he cried, waving them before the boy's eyes.

'I suppose we'll talk to Bassett,' said the boy. 'I expect I have fifteen hundred now; and twenty in reserve; and this twenty.'

His uncle studied him for some moments.

'Look here, son!' he said. 'You're not serious about Bassett and that fifteen hundred, are you?'

'Yes, I am. But it's between you and me, uncle. Honour bright?'

'Honour bright all right, son! But I must talk to Bassett.'

'If you'd like to be a partner, uncle, with Bassett and me, we could all be partners. Only, you'd have to promise, honour bright, uncle, not to let it go beyond us three. Bassett and I are lucky, and you must be lucky, because it was your ten shillings I started winning with . . .'

Uncle Oscar took both Bassett and Paul into Richmond Park for an afternoon, and there they talked.

'It's like this, you see, sir,' Bassett said. 'Master Paul would get me talking about racing events, spinning yarns, you know, sir. And he was always keen on knowing if I'd made or if I'd lost. It's about a year since, now, that I put five shillings on Blush of Dawn for him: and we lost. Then the luck changed with that ten shillings he had from you: that we put on Singhalese. And since that time, it's been pretty steady, all things considering. What do you say, Master Paul?'

'We're all right when we're sure,' said Paul. 'It's when we're not quite sure that we go down.'

'Oh, but we're careful then,' said Bassett.

'But when are you *sure*?' smiled Uncle Oscar.

'It's Master Paul, sir,' said Bassett in a secret, religious voice.

'It's as if he had it from heaven. Like Daffodil, now, for the Lincoln. That was as sure as eggs.'

'Did you put anything on Daffodil?' asked Oscar Cresswell.

'Yes, sir, I made my bit.'

'And my nephew?'

Bassett was obstinately silent, looking at Paul.

'I made twelve hundred, didn't I, Bassett? I told uncle I was putting three hundred on Daffodil.'

'That's right,' said Bassett nodding.

'But where's the money?' asked the uncle.

'I keep it safe locked up, sir. Master Paul he can have it any minute he likes to ask for it.'

'What, fifteen hundred pounds?'

'And twenty! And *forty*, that is, with the twenty he made on the course.'

'It's amazing!' said the uncle.

'If Master Paul offers you to be partners, sir, I would, if I were you: if you'll excuse me,' said Bassett.

Oscar Cresswell thought about it.

'I'll see the money,' he said.

They drove home again, and sure enough, Bassett came round to the garden-house with fifteen hundred pounds in notes. The twenty pounds reserve was left with Joe Glee, in the Turf Commission deposit.

'You see it's all right, uncle, when I'm *sure*! Then we go strong, for all we're worth. Don't we, Bassett?'

'We do that, Master Paul.'

'And when are you sure?' said the uncle, laughing.

'Oh, well, sometimes I'm *absolutely* sure, like about Daffodil,' said the boy; 'and sometimes I have an idea; and sometimes I haven't even an idea, have I, Bassett? Then we're careful, because we mostly go down.'

'You do, do you! And when you're sure, like about Daffodil, what makes you sure, sonny?'

'Oh, well, I don't know,' said the boy uneasily. 'I'm sure, you know, uncle; that's all.'

'It's as if he had it from heaven, sir,' Bassett reiterated.

'I should say so!' said the uncle.

But he became a partner. And when the Leger was coming on

Paul was 'sure' about Lively Spark, which was a quite incon-
siderable horse, Bassett went for five hundred, and Oscar Cresswell two hundred. Lively Spark came in first, and the betting
had been ten to one against him. Paul had made ten thousand.

'You see,' he said, 'I was absolutely sure of him.'

Even Oscar Cresswell had cleared two thousand.

'Look here, son,' he said, 'this sort of thing makes me nervous.'

'It needn't, uncle! Perhaps I shan't be sure again for a long
time.'

'But what are you going to do with your money?' asked the
uncle.

'Of course,' said the boy, 'I started it for mother. She said she
had no luck, because father is unlucky, so I thought if I was lucky,
it might stop whispering.'

'What might stop whispering.'

'Our house. I *hate* our house for whispering.'

'What does it whisper?'

'Why – why' – the boy fidgeted – 'why, I don't know. But it's
always short of money, you know, uncle.'

'I know it, son, I know it.'

'You know people send mother writs, don't you, uncle?'

'I'm afraid I do,' said the uncle.

'And then the house whispers, like people laughing at you
behind your back. It's awful, that is! I thought if I was lucky –'

'You might stop it,' added the uncle.

The boy watched him with big blue eyes, that had an uncanny
cold fire in them, and he said never a word.

'Well, then!' said the uncle. 'What are we doing?'

'I shouldn't like mother to know I was lucky,' said the boy.

'Why not, son?'

'She'd stop me.'

'I don't think she would.'

'Oh!' – and the boy writhed in an odd way – 'I *don't* want her
to know, uncle.'

'All right, son! We'll manage it without her knowing.'

They managed it very easily. Paul, at the other's suggestion,
handed over five thousand pounds to his uncle, who deposited it
with the family lawyer, who was then to inform Paul's mother
that a relative had put five thousand pounds into his hands,

which sum was to be paid out a thousand pounds at a time, on the mother's birthday, for the next five years.

'So she'll have a birthday present of a thousand pounds for five successive years,' said Uncle Oscar. 'I hope it won't make it all the harder for her later.'

Paul's mother had her birthday in November. The house had been 'whispering' worse than ever lately, and, even in spite of his luck, Paul could not bear up against it. He was very anxious to see the effect of the birthday letter, telling his mother about the thousand pounds.

When there were no visitors, Paul now took his meals with his parents, as he was beyond the nursery control. His mother went into town nearly every day. She had discovered that she had an odd knack of sketching furs and dress materials, so she worked secretly in the studio of a friend who was the chief 'artist' for the leading drapers. She drew the figures of ladies in furs and ladies in silk and sequins for the newspaper advertisements. This young woman artist earned several thousand pounds a year, but Paul's mother only made several hundreds, and she was again dissatisfied. She so wanted to be first in something, and she did not succeed, even in making sketches for drapery advertisements.

She was down to breakfast on the morning of her birthday. Paul watched her face as she read her letters. He knew the lawyer's letter. As his mother read it, her face hardened and became more expressionless. Then a cold determined look came on her mouth. She hid the letter under the pile of others, and said not a word about it.

'Didn't you have anything nice in the post for your birthday, mother?' said Paul.

'Quite moderately nice,' she said, her voice cold and absent.

She went away to town without saying more.

But in the afternoon Uncle Oscar appeared. He said Paul's mother had had a long interview with the lawyer, asking if the whole five thousand could not be advanced at once, as she was in debt.

'What do you think, uncle?' said the boy.

'I leave it to you, son.'

'Oh, let her have it, then! We can get some more with the other,' said the boy.

'A bird in the hand is worth two in the bush, laddie!' said Uncle Oscar.

'But I'm sure to *know* for the Grand National; or the Lincolnshire; or else the Derby. I'm sure to know for *one* of them,' said Paul.

So Uncle Oscar signed the agreement, and Paul's mother touched the whole five thousand. Then something very curious happened. The voices in the house suddenly went mad, like a chorus of frogs on a spring evening. There were certain new furnishings, and Paul had a tutor. He was *really* going to Eton, his father's school, in the following autumn. There were flowers in the winter, and a blossoming of the luxury Paul's mother had been used to. And yet the voices in the house, behind the sprays of mimosa and almond-blossom, and from under the piles of iridescent cushions, simply trilled and screamed in a sort of ecstasy: 'There *must* be more money! Oh-h-h; there *must* be more money. Oh, now, now-w! Now-w-w – there *must* be more money! – More than ever! More than ever!'

It frightened Paul terribly. He studied away at his Latin and Greek with his tutor. But his intense hours were spent with Bassett. The Grand National had gone by; he had not 'known', and had lost a hundred pounds. Summer was at hand. He was in agony for the Lincoln. But even for the Lincoln he didn't 'know', and he lost fifty pounds. He became wild-eyed and strange, as if something were going to explode in him.

'Let it alone, son! Don't you bother about it!' urged Uncle Oscar. But it was as if the boy couldn't really hear what his uncle was saying.

'I've got to know for the Derby. I've got to know for the Derby!' the child reiterated, his big blue eyes blazing with a sort of madness.

His mother noticed how overwrought he was.

'You'd better go to the seaside. Wouldn't you like to go now to the seaside, instead of waiting? I think you'd better,' she said, looking down at him anxiously, her heart curiously heavy because of him.

But the child lifted his uncanny blue eyes.

'I couldn't possibly go before the Derby, mother!' he said. 'I couldn't possibly!'

'Why not?' she said, her voice becoming heavy when she was opposed. 'Why not? You can still go from the seaside to see the Derby with your Uncle Oscar, if that's what you wish. No need for you to wait here. Besides, I think you care too much about these races. It's a bad sign. My family has been a gambling family, and you won't know till you grow up how much damage it has done. But it has done damage. I shall have to send Bassett away, and ask Uncle Oscar not to talk racing to you, unless you promise to be reasonable about it: go away to the seaside and forget it. You're all nerves!'

'I'll do what you like, mother, so long as you don't send me away till after the Derby,' the boy said.

'Send you away from where? Just from this house?'

'Yes,' he said, gazing at her.

'Why, you curious child, what makes you care about this house so much suddenly? I never knew you loved it.'

He gazed at her without speaking. He had a secret within a secret, something he had not divulged, even to Bassett or to his Uncle Oscar.

But his mother, after standing undecided and a little bit sullen for some moments, said:

'Very well, then! Don't go to the seaside till after the Derby, if you don't wish it. But promise me you won't think so much about horse-racing, and *events*, as you call them!'

'Oh, no,' said the boy casually. 'I won't think much about them, mother. You needn't worry. I wouldn't worry, mother, if I were you.'

'If you were me and I were you,' said his mother, 'I wonder what we *should* do!'

'But you know you needn't worry mother, don't you?' the boy repeated.

'I should be awfully glad to know it,' she said wearily.

'Oh, well, you *can*, you know. I mean, you *ought* to know you needn't worry,' he insisted.

'Ought I? Then I'll see about it,' she said.

Paul's secret of secrets was his wooden horse, that which had no name. Since he was emancipated from a nurse and a nursery-governess, he had had his rocking-horse removed to his own bedroom at the top of the house.

'Surely you're too big for a rocking-horse!' his mother had remonstrated.

'Well, you see, mother, till I can have a *real* horse, I like to have *some* sort of animal about,' had been his quaint answer.

'Do you feel he keeps you company?' she laughed.

'Oh yes! He's very good, he always keeps me company, when I'm there,' said Paul.

So the horse, rather shabby, stood in an arrested prance in the boy's bedroom.

The Derby was drawing near, and the boy grew more and more tense. He hardly heard what was spoken to him, he was very frail, and his eyes were really uncanny. His mother had sudden strange seizures of uneasiness about him. Sometimes, for half an hour, she would feel a sudden anxiety about him that was almost anguish. She wanted to rush to him at once, and know that he was safe.

Two nights before the Derby, she was at a big party in town, when one of her rushes of anxiety about her boy, her first-born, gripped her heart till she could hardly speak. She fought with the feeling, might and main, for she believed in common sense. But it was too strong. She had to leave the dance and go downstairs to telephone to the country. The children's nursery-governess was terribly surprised and startled at being rung up in the night.

'Are the children all right, Miss Wilmot?'

'Oh yes, they are quite all right.'

'Master Paul? Is he all right?'

'He went to bed as right as a trivet. Shall I run up and look at him?'

'No,' said Paul's mother reluctantly. 'No! Don't trouble. It's all right. Don't sit up. We shall be home fairly soon.' She did not want her son's privacy intruded upon.

'Very good,' said the governess.

It was about one o'clock when Paul's mother and father drove up to their house. All was still. Paul's mother went to her room and slipped off her white fur cloak. She had told her maid not to wait up for her. She heard her husband downstairs, mixing a whisky and soda.

And then, because of the strange anxiety at her heart, she stole upstairs to her son's bedroom. Noiselessly she went along the upper corridor. Was there a faint noise? What was it?

She stood, with arrested muscles, outside his door listening. There was a strange, heavy, and yet not loud noise. Her heart stood still. It was a soundless noise, yet rushing and powerful. Something huge, in violent, hushed motion. What was it? What in God's name was it? She ought to know. She felt that she knew the noise. She knew what it was.

Yet she could not place it. She couldn't say what it was. And on and on it went, like a madness.

Softly, frozen with anxiety and fear, she turned the door-handle.

The room was dark. Yet in the space near the window, she heard and saw something plunging to and fro. She gazed in fear and amazement.

Then suddenly she switched on the light, and saw her son, in his green pyjamas, madly surging on the rocking-horse. The blaze of light suddenly lit him up, as he urged the wooden horse, and lit her up, as she stood, blonde, in her dress of pale green and crystal, in the doorway.

'Paul!' she cried. 'Whatever are you doing?'

'It's Malabar!' he screamed in a powerful, strange voice. 'It's Malabar!'

His eyes blazed at her for one strange and senseless second, as he ceased urging his wooden horse. Then he fell with a crash to the ground, and she, all her tormented motherhood flooding upon her, rushed to gather him up.

But he was unconscious, and unconscious he remained, with some brain-fever. He talked and tossed, and his mother sat stonily by his side.

'Malabar! It's Malabar! Bassett, Bassett, I *know*! It's Malabar!'

So the child cried, trying to get up and urge the rocking-horse that gave him inspiration.

'What does he mean by Malabar?' asked the heart-frozen mother.

'I don't know,' said the father stonily.

'What does he mean by Malabar?' she asked her brother Oscar.

'It's one of the horses running for the Derby,' was the answer.

And, in spite of himself, Oscar Cresswell spoke to Bassett, and himself put a thousand on Malabar: at fourteen to one.

The third day of the illness was critical: they were waiting for a change. The boy, with his rather long, curly hair, was tossing ceaselessly on the pillow. He neither slept nor regained consciousness, and his eyes were like blue stones. His mother sat, feeling her heart had gone, turned actually into a stone.

In the evening, Oscar Cresswell did not come, but Bassett sent a message, saying could he come up for one moment, just one moment? Paul's mother was very angry at the intrusion, but on second thoughts she agreed. The boy was the same. Perhaps Bassett might bring him to consciousness.

The gardener, a shortish fellow with a little brown moustache and sharp little brown eyes, tiptoed into the room, touched his imaginary cap to Paul's mother, and stole to the bedside, staring with glittering, smallish eyes at the tossing dying child.

'Master Paul!' he whispered. 'Master Paul! Malabar came in first all right, a clean win. I did as you told me. You've made over seventy thousand pounds, you have; you've got over eighty thousand. Malabar came in all right, Master Paul.'

'Malabar! Malabar! Did I say Malabar, mother? Did I say Malabar? Do you think I'm lucky, mother? I knew Malabar, didn't I? Over eighty thousand pounds! I knew, didn't I know I knew? Malabar came in all right. If I ride my horse till I'm sure, then I tell you, Bassett, you can go as high as you like. Did you go for all you were worth, Bassett?'

'I went a thousand on it, Master Paul.'

'I never told you, mother, that if I can ride my horse, and *get there*, then I'm absolutely sure, – oh, absolutely! Mother, did I ever tell you? I *am* lucky!'

'No you never did,' said his mother.

But the boy died in the night.

And even as he lay dead, his mother heard her brother's voice saying to her: 'My God, Hester, you're eighty-odd thousand to the good, and a poor devil of a son to the bad. But, poor devil, poor devil, he's best gone out of a life where he rides his rocking-horse to find a winner.'

printed in THE TALES OF D. H. LAWRENCE *1934*

St Mawr

D. H. LAWRENCE

Was it true St Mawr was evil? She would never forget him writhing and lunging on the ground, nor his awful face when he reared up. But then that noble look of his: surely he was not mean? Whereas all evil had an inner meanness, mean! Was he mean! Was he meanly treacherous? Did he know he could kill, and meanly wait his opportunity?

She was afraid. And if this were true, then he *should* be shot. Perhaps he ought to be shot.

This thought haunted her. Was there something mean and treacherous in St Mawr's spirit, the vulgar evil? If so, then have him shot. At moments, an anger would rise in her, as she thought of his frenzied rearing, and his mad, hideous writhing on the ground, and in the heat of her anger she would want to hurry down to her mother's house and have the creature shot at once. It would be a satisfaction, and a vindication of human rights. Because after all, Rico was so considerate of the brutal horse. But not a spark of consideration did the stallion have for Rico. No, it was the slavish malevolence of a domesticated creature that kept cropping up in St Mawr. The slave, taking his slavish vengeance, then dropping back into subservience.

All the slaves of this world, accumulating their preparations for slavish vengeance, and then, when they have taken it, ready to drop back into servility. Freedom! Most slaves can't be freed, no matter how you let them loose. Like domestic animals, they are, in the long run, more afraid of freedom than of masters: and freed by some generous master, they will at last crawl back to some mean boss, who will have no scruples about kicking them. Because, for them, far better kicks and servility than the hard, lonely responsibility of real freedom.

The wild animal is at every moment intensely self-disciplined, poised in the tension of self-defence, self-preservation, and self-assertion. The moments of relaxation are rare and most carefully chosen. Even sleep is watchful, guarded, unrelaxing, the wild courage pitched one degree higher than the wild fear. Courage, the wild thing's courage to maintain itself alone and living in the midst of a diverse universe.

Did St Mawr have this courage?

And did Rico?

Ah, Rico! He was one of mankind's myriad conspirators, who conspire to live in absolute physical safety, whilst willing the minor disintegration of all positive living.

But St Mawr? Was it the natural wild thing in him which caused these disasters? Or was it the slave, asserting himself for vengeance?

If the latter, let him be shot. It would be a great satisfaction, to see him dead.

But if the former –

When she could leave Rico with the nurse, she motored down to her mother for a couple of days. Rico lay in bed at the farm.

Everything seemed curiously changed. There was a new silence about the place, a new coolness. Summer had passed with several thunderstorms, and the blue, cool touch of autumn was about the house. Dahlias and perennial yellow sunflowers were out, the yellow of ending summer, the red coals of early autumn. First mauve tips of Michaelmas daisies were showing. Something suddenly carried her away to the great bare spaces of Texas, the blue sky, the flat, burnt earth, the miles of sunflowers. Another sky, another silence, towards the setting sun.

And suddenly, she craved again for the more absolute silence of America. English stillness was so soft, like an inaudible murmur of voices, of presences. But the silence in the empty spaces of America was still unutterable, almost cruel.

St Mawr was in a small field by himself: she could not bear that he should always be in a stable. Slowly she went through the gate towards him. And he stood there looking at her, the bright bay creature.

She could tell he was feeling somewhat subdued, after his late escapade. He was aware of the general human condemnation: the human damning. But something obstinate and uncanny in him made him not relent.

'Hello! St Mawr!' she said, as she drew near, and he stood watching her, his ears pricked, his big eyes glancing sideways at her.

But he moved away when she wanted to touch him.

'Don't trouble,' she said. 'I don't want to catch you or do anything to you.'

He stood still, listening to the sound of her voice, and giving quick, small glances at her. His underlip trembled. But he did not blink. His eyes remained wide and unrelenting. There was a curious malicious obstinacy in him which roused her anger.

'I don't want to touch you,' she said. 'I only want to look at you, and even you can't prevent that.'

She stood gazing hard at him, wanting to know, to settle the question of his meanness or his spirit. A thing with a brave spirit is not mean.

He was uneasy as she watched him. He pretended to hear something, the mares two fields away, and he lifted his head and neighed. She knew the powerful, splendid sound so well: like bells made of living membrane. And he looked so noble again, with his head tilted up, listening, and his male eyes looking proudly over the distance, eagerly.

But it was all a bluff.

He knew, and became silent again. And as he stood there a few yards away from her, his head lifted and wary, his body full of power and tension, his face slightly averted from her, she felt a great animal sadness come from him. A strange animal atmosphere of sadness, that was vague and disseminated through the air, and made her feel as though she breathed grief. She breathed it into her breast, as if it were a great sigh down the ages, that passed into her breast. And she felt a great woe: the woe of human unworthiness. The race of men judged in the consciousness of the animals they have subdued, and there found unworthy, ignoble.

Ignoble men, unworthy of the animals they have subjugated, bred the woe in the spirit of their creatures. St Mawr, that bright horse, one of the kings of creation in the order below man, it had been a fulfilment for him to serve the brave, reckless, perhaps cruel men of the past, who had a flickering, rising flame of nobility in them. To serve that flame of mysterious further nobility. Nothing matters, but that strange flame, of inborn nobility that obliges men to be brave, and onward plunging. And the horse will bear him on.

But now where is the flame of dangerous, forward-pressing nobility in men? Dead, dead, guttering out in a stink of self-sacrifice whose feeble light is a light of exhaustion and *laissez-faire*.

And the horse, is he to go on carrying man forward into this? – this gutter?

No! Man wisely invents motor-cars and other machines, automobile and locomotive. The horse is superannuated, for man.

But alas, man is even more superannuated, for the horse.

Dimly in a woman's muse, Lou realized this, as she breathed the horse's sadness, his accumulated vague woe from the generations of latter-day ignobility. And a grief and a sympathy flooded her, for the horse. She realized now how his sadness recoiled into these frenzies of obstinacy and malevolence. Underneath it all was grief, an unconscious, vague, pervading animal grief, which perhaps only Lewis understood, because he felt the same. The grief of the generous creature which sees all ends turning to the morass of ignoble living.

She did not want to say any more to the horse: she did not want to look at him any more. The grief flooded her soul, that made her want to be alone. She knew now what it all amounted to. She knew that the horse, born to serve nobly, had waited in vain for someone noble to serve. His spirit knew that nobility had gone out of men. And this left him high and dry, in a sort of despair.

from ST MAWR *1925*

Velvet Up

ENID BAGNOLD

At the post the twenty horses were swaying like the sea. Forward
. . . No good! Back again. Forward . . . No good! Back again.

The line formed . . . and rebroke. Waves of the sea. Drawing
a breath . . . breaking. Velvet fifth from the rail, between a bay
and a brown. The Starter had long finished his instructions.
Nothing more was said aloud, but low oaths flew, the cursing
and grumbling flashed like a storm. An eye glanced at her with a
look of hate. The breaking of movement was too close to movement to be borne. It was like water clinging to the tilted rim of the
glass, like the sound of the dreaded explosion after the great shell
has fallen. The will to surge forward overlaid by something
delicate and terrible and strong, human obedience at bursting-
point, but not broken. Horses' eyes gleamed openly, men's eyes
set like chips of steel. Rough man, checked in violence, barely
master of himself, barely master of his horse. The Piebald
ominously quiet, and nothing coming from him . . . up went the
tape.

The green Course poured in a river before her as she lay forward, and with the plunge of movement sat in the stream.

'Black slugs . . .' said Mi, cursing under his breath, running,
dodging, suffocated with the crowd. It was the one thing he
had overlooked, that the crowd was too dense to allow him to
reach Becher's in the time. Away up above him was the truckline,
his once-glorious free seat, separated from him by a fence. 'God's
liver,' he mumbled, his throat gone cold, and stumbled into an
old fool in a mackintosh. 'Are they off?' he yelled at the heavy
crowd as he ran, but no one bothered with him.

He was cursed if he was heeded at all. He ran, gauging his
position by the cranes on the embankment. Velvet coming over
Becher's in a minute and he not there to see her. 'They're off!'
All around him a sea of throats offered up the gasp.

He was opposite Becher's but could see nothing: the crowd
thirty deep between him and the Course. All around fell the

terrible silence of expectancy. Mi stood like a rock. If he could
not see then he must use his ears, hear. Enclosed in the dense,
silent, dripping pack he heard the thunder coming. It roared up
on the wet turf like the single approach of a multiple-footed
animal. There were stifled exclamations, grunts, thuds. Something
in the air flashed and descended. The first over Becher's! A roar
went up from the crowd, then silence. The things flashing in the
air were indistinguishable. The tip of a cap exposed for the
briefest of seconds. The race went by like an express train, and
was gone. Could Velvet be alive in that?

Sweat ran off Mi's forehead and into his eyes. But it was not
sweat that turned the air grey and blotted out the faces before
him. The ground on all sides seemed to be smoking. An extraordinary mist, like a low prairie fire, was formed in the air. It had
dwelt heavily all day behind the Canal, but the whole of the
Course had remained clear till now. And now, before you could
turn to look at your neighbour, his face was gone. The mist blew
in shreds, drifted, left the crowd clear again but hid the whole of
the Canal Corner, fences, stand and horses.

There was a struggle going on at Becher's; a horse had fallen
and was being got out with ropes. Mi's legs turned to water and
he asked his neighbour gruffly, 'Who's fallen?' But the neighbour,
straining to the tip of his toes, and glued to his glasses, was deaf
as lead.

Suddenly Mi lashed round him in a frenzy. 'Who's fallen, I
say? Who's hurt?'

'Steady on,' said a little man whom he had prodded in the
stomach.

'Who's fallen?' said Mi desperately. 'I gotta brother in this . . .'

'It's his brother!' said the crowd all around him. 'Let him
through.'

Mi was pushed and pummelled to the front and remained
embedded two from the front line. The horse that had fallen
was a black horse, its neck unnaturally stretched by the ropes that
were hauling it from the ditch.

There was a shout and a horse, not riderless, but ridden by a
tugging, cursing man, came galloping back through the curling
fumes of the mist, rolled its wild eye at the wrong side of Becher's
and disappeared away out of the Course. An uproar began along

the fringes of the crowd and rolled back to where Mi stood. Two
more horses came back out of the mist, one riderless. The shades
of others could be discerned in the fog. Curses rapped out from
the unseen mouths.

'What's happened at the Canal Turn? What's wrong down at
the Turn?'

'The whole field!' shouted a man. The crowd took it up.

'The field's out. The whole field's come back. There's no race!'
It was unearthly. Something a hundred yards down there in the
fog had risen up and destroyed the greatest steeplechase in the
world.

Nineteen horses had streamed down to the Canal Turn, and
suddenly, there across the Course, at the boundary of the fog,
four horses appeared beyond Valentine's, and among them,
fourth, was The Piebald.

'Yer little lovely, yer little lovely!' yelled Mi, wringing his
hands and hitting his knees. 'It's her, it's him, it's me brother!'

No one took any notice. The scene immediately before them
occupied all the attention. Horses that had fallen galloped by
riderless, stirrups flying from their saddles, jockeys returned on
foot, covered with mud, limping, holding their sides, some
running slowly and miserably over the soggy course, trying to
catch and sort the horses.

'It's "Yellow Messenger",' said a jockey savagely, who had
just seized his horse. 'Stuck on the fence down there and kicking
hell.' And he mounted.

'And wouldn't they jump over him?' called a girl shrilly.

'They didn't wanter hurt the por thing, lady,' said the jockey,
grinning through his mud, and rode off.

'Whole lot piled up and refused,' said a man who came up the
line. 'Get the Course clear now, quick!'

'They're coming again!' yelled Mi, watching the galloping
four. 'Get the Course clear! They'll be coming!'

They were out of his vision now, stuck down under Becher's
high fence as he was. Once past Becher's on the second round
would he have time to extricate himself and get back to the post
before they were home? He stood indecisively and a minute went
by. The Course in front of him was clear. Horses and men had
melted. The hush of anticipation began to fall. 'They're on the

tan again,' said a single voice. Mi flashed to a decision. He could
not afford the minutes to be at Becher's. He must get back for the
finish and it would take him all his time. He backed and plunged
and ducked, got cursed afresh. The thunder was coming again
as he reached the road and turned to face the far-off Stands. This
time he could see nothing at all, not even a cap in the air. 'What's
leading? What's leading?'

'Big Brown. Tantibus, Tantibus. Tantibus leading.'

'Where's The Piebald?'

'See that! Leonora coming up . . .'

They were deaf to his frantic questions. He could not wait but
ran. The mist was ahead of him again, driving in frills and wafting
sedgily about. Could Velvet have survived Becher's twice? In
any case no good wondering. He couldn't get at her to help her.
If she fell he would find her more quickly at the hospital door.
Better that than struggle through the crowd and be forbidden
the now empty Course.

Then a yell. 'There's one down!'

'It's the Yank mare!'

The horse ambulance was trundling back with Yellow Messenger from the Canal Turn. Mi leapt for a second on to the
turning hub of the wheel, and saw in a flash, across the momentarily mist-clear course, the pride of Baltimore in the mud underneath Valentine's. The Piebald was lying third. The wheel turned
and he could see no more. Five fences from the finish; he would
not allow himself to hope, but ran and ran. How far away the
Stands in the gaps of the mist as he pushed, gasping, through the
people. Would she fall now? What had he done, bringing her up
here? But would she fall now? He ran and ran.

'They're coming on to the Racecourse . . . coming on to the
Racecourse . . .'

'How many?'

'Rain, rain, can't see a thing.'

'How many?'

Down sank the fog again, as a puff of wind blew and gathered
it together. There was a steady roaring from the Stands, then
silence, then a hub-bub. No one could see the telegraph.

Mi running, gasped, 'Who's won?'

But everyone was asking the same question. Men were running, pushing, running, just as he. He came up to the gates of Melling Road, crossed the road on the fringe of the tan, and suddenly, out of the mist, The Piebald galloped riderless, lolloping unsteadily along, reins hanging, stirrups dangling. Mi burst through on to the Course, his heart wrung.

'Get back there!' shouted a policeman. 'Loose horse!'

'Hullo, Old Pie there!' shouted Mi. The animal, soaked, panting, spent, staggered and slipped and drew up.

'What've you done with 'er?' asked Mi, weeping, and bent down to lift the hoof back through the rein. 'You let 'er down, Pie? What in God's sake?' He led the horse down the Course, running, his breath catching, his heart thumping, tears and rain on his face.

Two men came towards him out of the mist.

'You got him?' shouted one. 'Good fer you. Gimme!'

'You want him?' said Mi, in a stupor, giving up the rein.

'Raised an objection. Want him for the enclosure. Chap come queer.'

'Chap did? What chap?'

'This here's the winner! Where you bin all day, Percy?'

'Foggy,' said Mi. 'Very foggy. Oh my God!'

'Taken him round to the hospital.'

'Stretcher, was it?'

'Jus' gone through where all those people are . . .'

The doctor had got back from his tour of the Course in his ambulance. Two riders had already been brought in and the nurse had prepared them in readiness for his examination. Now the winner himself coming in on a stretcher. Busy thirty minutes ahead.

'Could you come here a minute?' said the Sister, at his side a few minutes later.

She whispered to him quietly. He slapped his rain-coated cheek and went to the bed by the door. 'Put your screens round.' She planted them. 'Constable,' he said, poking his head out of the door, 'get one of the Stewards here, will you.' (The roar of the crowd came in at the door.) 'One of the Stewards! Quick's you can. Here, I'll let you in this side door. You can get through.' The crowd seethed, seizing upon every sign.

Mi crouched by the door without daring to ask after his child.

He heard the doctor call. He saw the Steward go in. 'Anyway,' he thought, 'they've found out at once. They would. What's it matter if she's all right? She's won, the little beggar, the little beggar. Oh my God!'

from NATIONAL VELVET *1935*

The Horse Fair

DAPHNE DU MAURIER

This was a gay and happy world to Mary. The town was set on the bosom of a hill, with a castle framed in the centre, like a tale from old history. There were trees clustered here, and sloping fields, and water gleamed in the valley below. The moors were remote; they stretched away out of sight behind the town, and were forgotten. Launceston had reality; those people were alive. Christmas came into its own again in the town and had a place amongst the cobbled streets, the laughing jostling crowd, and the watery sun struggled from his hiding-place behind the grey-banked clouds to join festivity. Mary wore the handkerchief Jem had given her. She even unbent so far as to permit him to tie the ends under her chin. They had stabled the pony and jingle at the tip of the town, and now Jem pushed his way through the crowd, leading his two stolen horses, Mary following at his heels. He led the way with confidence, making straight for the main square, where the whole of Launceston gathered, and the booths and tents of the Christmas fair stood end to end. There was a place roped off from the fair for the buying and selling of live-stock, and the ring was surrounded by farmers and countrymen, gentlemen too, and dealers from Devon and beyond. Mary's heart beat faster as they approached the ring; supposing there was someone from North Hill here, or a farmer from a neigh-bouring village, surely they would recognize the horses? Jem wore his hat at the back of his head, and he whistled. He looked back at her once and winked his eye. The crowd parted and made way for him. Mary stood on the outskirts, behind a fat market-woman with a basket, and she saw Jem take his place amongst a group of men with ponies, bending as he did so to a flare to light his pipe. He looked cool and unperturbed. Presently a flashy-looking fellow with a square hat and cream breeches thrust his way through the crowd and crossed over to the horses. His voice was loud and important, and he kept hitting his boot with a crop, and then pointing to the ponies. From his tone, and his air of authority Mary judged him to be a dealer. Soon he was joined by a little lynx-eyed man in a black coat, who now and again jogged his elbow and whispered in his ear.

Mary saw him stare hard at the black pony that had belonged to Squire Bassat; he went up to him, and bent down and felt his legs. Then he whispered something in the ear of the loud-voiced man. Mary watched him nervously.

'Where did you get this pony?' said the dealer, tapping Jem on the shoulder. 'He was never bred on the moors, not with that head and shoulders.'

'He was foaled at Callington four years ago,' said Jem carelessly, his pipe in the corner of his mouth. 'I bought him as a yearling from old Tim Bray; you remember Tim? He sold up last year and went into Dorset. Tim always told me I'd get my money back on this pony. The dam was Irish bred, and won prizes up-country. Have a look at him, won't you? But he's not going cheap, I'll tell you that.'

He puffed at his pipe, while the two men went over the pony carefully. The time seemed endless before they straightened themselves and stood back. 'Had any trouble with his skin?' said the lynx-eyed man. 'It feels very coarse on the surface, and sharp like bristles. There's a taint about him, too, I don't like. You haven't been doping him have you?'

'There's nothing ailing with that pony,' replied Jem. 'The other one, there, he fell away to nothing in the summer, but I've brought him back all right. I'd do better to keep him till the spring now, I believe, but he's costing me money. No, this black pony here, you can't fault him. I'll be frank with you over one thing, and it's only fair to admit it. Old Tim Bray never knew the mare was in foal – he was in Plymouth at the time, and his boy was looking after her – and when he found out he gave the boy a thrashing, but of course it was too late. He had to make the best of a bad job. It's my opinion the sire was grey; look at the short grey hair there, close to the skin – that's grey, isn't it? Tim just missed a good bargain with this pony. Look at those shoulders; there's breeding for you. I tell you what, I'll take eighteen guineas for him.' The lynx-eyed man shook his head, but the dealer hesitated.

'Make it fifteen and we might do business,' he suggested.

'No, eighteen guineas is my sum, and not a penny less,' said Jem.

The two men consulted together and appeared to disagree. Mary heard the word 'fake', and Jem shot a glance at her over the heads of the crowd. A little murmur rose from the group of men beside him. Once more the lynx-eyed man bent and touched the legs of the black pony. 'I'd advise another opinion on this pony,' he said. 'I'm not satisfied about him myself. Where's your mark?'

Jem showed him the narrow slit in the ear and the man examined it closely.

'You're a sharp customer, aren't you?' said Jem. 'Anyone would think I'd stolen the horse. Anything wrong with the mark?'

'No, apparently not. But it's a good thing for you that Tim Bray has gone to Dorset. He'd never own this pony, whatever you like to say. I wouldn't touch him, Stevens, if I were you. You'll find yourself in trouble. Come away, man.'

The loud-voiced dealer looked regretfully at the black pony.

'He's a good-looker,' he said. 'I don't care who bred him, or if his sire was piebald. What makes you so particular, Will?'

Once more the lynx-eyed man plucked at his sleeve and whispered in his ear. The dealer listened, and pulled a face, and then he nodded. 'All right,' he said aloud; 'I've no doubt that you're right. You've got an eye for trouble, haven't you? Perhaps we're better out of it. You can keep your pony,' he added to Jem. 'My partner doesn't fancy him. Take my advice and come down on your price. If you have him for long on your hands you'll be sorry.' And he elbowed his way through the crowd with the lynx-eyed man beside him, and they disappeared in the direction of the White Hart. Mary breathed a sigh of relief when she saw the last of them. She could make nothing of Jem's expression; his lips were framed in the inevitable whistle. People came and went; the shaggy moorland ponies were sold for two or three pounds apiece, and their late owners departed satisfied. No one came near the black pony again. He was looked at askance by the crowd. At a quarter to four Jem sold the other horse for six pounds to a cheerful, honest-looking farmer, after a long and very good-humoured argument. The farmer declared he would give five pounds, and Jem stuck out for seven. After twenty minutes' riotous bargaining the sum of six pounds was agreed, and the farmer rode off on the back of his purchase with a grin from ear to ear. Mary began to flag on her feet. Twilight gathered in the market square and the lamps were lit. The town wore an air of mystery. She was thinking of returning to the jingle when she heard a woman's voice behind her, and a high affected laugh. She turned and saw the blue cloak and the plumed hat of the woman who had stepped from the coach earlier in the afternoon. 'Oh, look, James,' she was saying. 'Did you ever see such a delicious pony in your life? He holds his head just like poor Beauty did. The likeness would be quite striking, only this animal of course is black, and has nothing of Beauty's breeding. What a nuisance Roger isn't here. I can't disturb him from his meeting. What do you think of him, James?'

Her companion put up his eyeglass and stared. 'Damn it, Maria,' he drawled, 'I don't know a thing about horses. The pony you lost was a grey wasn't it? This thing is ebony, positively ebony, my dear. Do you want to buy him?'

The woman gave a little trill of laughter. 'It would be such a good Christmas present for the children,' she said. 'They've plagued poor Roger ever since Beauty disappeared. Ask the price, James, will you?'

The man strutted forward. 'Here, my good fellow,' he called to Jem, 'do you want to sell that black pony of yours?'

Jem shook his head. 'He's promised to a friend,' he said. 'I wouldn't like to go back on my word. Besides, this pony wouldn't carry you. He's been ridden by children.'

'Oh, really. Oh, I see. Oh, thank you. Maria, this fellow says the pony is not for sale.'

'Is he sure? What a shame. I'd set my heart on him. I'll pay him his price tell him. Ask him again, James.'

Once more the man put up his glass and drawled, 'Look here, my man, this lady has taken a fancy to your pony. She has just lost one, and she wants to replace him. Her children will be most disappointed if they hear about it. Damn your friend, you know. He must wait. What is your price?'

'Twenty-five guineas,' said Jem promptly. 'At least, that's what my friend was going to pay. I'm not anxious to sell him.'

The lady in the plumed hat swept into the ring. 'I'll give you thirty for him,' she said. 'I'm Mrs Bassat from North Hill, and I want the pony as a Christmas present for my children. Please don't be obstinate. I have half the sum here in my purse, and this gentleman will give you the rest. Mr Bassat is in Launceston now and I want the pony to be a surprise to him as well as to my children. My groom shall fetch the pony immediately, and ride him to North Hill before Mr Bassat leaves the town. Here's the money.'

Jem swept off his hat and bowed low. 'Thank you, madam,' he said. 'I hope Mr Bassat will be pleased with your bargain. You will find the pony exceedingly safe with children.'

'Oh, I'm certain he will be delighted. Of course the pony is nothing like the one we had stolen. Beauty was a thoroughbred, and worth a great deal of money. This little animal is handsome enough, and will please the children. Come along, James; it's getting quite dark, and I'm chilled to the bone.'

She made her way from the ring towards the coach that waited in the square. The tall footman leapt forward to open the door. 'I've just bought a pony for Master Robert and Master Henry,' she said. 'Will you find Richards and tell him he's to ride it back home? I want it to be a surprise to the squire.' She stepped into the coach, her petticoats fluttering behind her, followed by her companion with the monocle.

Jem looked hastily over his shoulder, and tapped a lad who stood behind him on the arm. 'Here,' he said, 'would you like a five-shilling piece?' The lad nodded, his mouth agape. 'Hang on to this will you? I've just had word that my wife has given birth to twins and her life is in danger. I haven't a moment to lose. Here, take the bridle. A happy Christmas to you.'

And he was off in a moment, walking hard across the square, his hands thrust deep in his breeches pocket. Mary followed, a discreet ten paces behind. Her face was scarlet and she kept her eyes on the ground. The laughter bubbled up inside her and she hid her mouth in her shawl. She was near to collapsing when they reached the farther side of the square, out of sight of the coach and the group of people, and she stood with her hand to her side catching her breath. Jem waited for her, his face as grave as a judge.

'Jem Merlyn, you deserve to be hanged,' she said, when she had recovered herself. 'To stand there as you did in the market square and sell that stolen pony back to Mrs Bassat herself! You have the cheek of the Devil, and the hairs on my head have gone grey from watching you.'

He threw back his head and laughed, and she could not resist him. Their laughter echoed in the street until people turned to look at them, and they too caught the infection, and smiled, and broke into laughter; and Launceston itself seemed to rock in merriment as peal after peal of gaiety echoed in the street, mingling with the bustle and clatter of the fair; and with it all there was shouting, and calling, and a song from somewhere. The torches and the flares cast strange lights on the faces of people, and there was colour, and shadow, and the hum of voices, and a ripple of excitement in the air.

from JAMAICA INN *1936*

Old Em's Kentucky Home

DAMON RUNYON

The grounds and the house itself all look as if they can stand a little attention and there is not a soul in sight and it is rather a dismal scene in every respect. The gate is closed, so I get down off the truck and open it and Itchky drives the truck in and right up to the front door of the house under a sort of porch with white pillars.

Now the truck makes a terrible racket and this racket seems to stir up a number of coloured parties who appear from around in back of the house, along with a large white guy. This large guy is wearing corduroy pants and laced boots and a black moustache and he is also carrying a double-barreled shotgun and he speaks to Itchky in a fierce tone of voice as follows:

'Pigface,' he says, 'get out of here. Get out of here before you are hurt. What do you mean by driving in here with a load of dog meat such as this, anyway?'

He points a finger at old Em who has her head up and is snuffling the air and gazing about her with great interest, and right away Itchky climbs down off the seat of the truck and removes his derby and places it on the ground and takes off his coat and starts rolling up his sleeves.

'It is the last straw,' Itchky Ironhat says. 'I will first make this big ash can eat that cannon he is lugging and then I will beat his skull in. Nobody can refer to Emaleen as dog meat and live.'

Now the front door of the house opens and out comes a thin character in a soiled white linen suit and at first he seems to be quite an old character as he has long white hair but when he gets closer I can see that he is not so very old at that, but he is very seedy-looking and his eyes have a loose expression. I can also see from the way the large guy and the coloured parties step back this is a character who packs some weight around here. His voice is low and hard as he speaks to Itchky Ironhat and says:

'What is this?' he says. 'What name do I just hear you pronounce?'

'Emaleen,' Itchky says. 'It is the name of my race mare which you see before you. She is the greatest race mare in the world. The turf records say she is bred right here at this place and I bring her down here to see her old home, and everybody insults her. So this is Southern hospitality?' Itchky says.

The new character steps up to the truck and looks at old Em for quite a spell and all the time he is shaking his head and his lips are moving as if he is talking to himself, and finally he says to the large guy:

'Unload her,' he says. 'Unload her and take good care of her, Dobkins. I suppose you will have to send to one of the neighbours for some feed. Come in, gentlemen,' he says to Itchky and me and he holds the front door of the house open. 'My name is Salsbury,' he says. 'I am the owner of Tucky Farms and I apologise for my foreman's behaviour but he is only following orders.'

As we go into the house I can see that it is a very large house and I can also see that it must once be a very grand house because of the way it is furnished, but everything seems to be as run-down inside as it does outside and I can see that what this house needs is a good cleaning and straightening out.

In the meantime, Mr Salsbury keeps asking Itchky Ironhat questions about old Em and when he hears how long Itchky has her and what he thinks of her and all this and that, he starts wiping his eyes with a handkerchief as if the story makes him very sad, especially the part about why Itchky brings her to the Bluegrass.

Finally Mr Salsbury leads us into a large room that seems to be a library and at one end of this room there is a painting taller than I am of a very beautiful Judy in a white dress and this is the only thing in the house that seems to be kept dusted up a little and Mr Salsbury points at the painting and says:

'My wife, Emaleen, gentlemen. I name the horse you bring here after her long ago, because it is the first foal of her favourite mare and the first foal of a stallion I import from France.'

'By Christofer, out of Love Always,' Itchky Ironhat says.

'Yes,' Mr Salsbury says. 'In those days, Tucky Farms is one of the great breeding and racing establishments of the Bluegrass. In those days, too, my wife is known far and wide for her fondness for horses and her kindness to them. She is the head of the humane society in Kentucky and the Emaleen Salsbury annual award of a thousand dollars for the kindest deed brought to the attention of the society each year is famous.

'One night,' Mr Salsbury continues, 'there is a fire in the barns and my wife gets out of bed and before anyone can stop her she rushes into the flames trying to save her beautiful mare, Love Always. They both perish, and,' he says, 'with them perishes the greatest happiness ever given a mortal on this earth.'

By this time, Itchky Ironhat and I are feeling very sad indeed, and in fact all the creases in Itchky's face are full of tears as Mr Salsbury goes on to state that the only horses on the place that are saved are a few yearlings running in the pastures. He sends them all with a shipment a neighbour is taking to Saratoga to be disposed of there for whatever they will bring.

'Your mare Emaleen is one of those,' he says. 'I forget all about her at the time. Indeed,' he says, 'I forget everything but my unhappiness. I feel I never wish to see or hear of a horse again as long as I live and I withdraw myself completely from the world and all my former activities. But,' he says, 'your bringing the mare here awakens old fond memories and your story of how you cherish her makes me realize that this is exactly what my wife Emaleen will wish me to do. I see where I sadly neglect my duty to her memory. Why,' he says, 'I never even keep up the Emaleen Salsbury award.'

Now he insists that we must remain there a while as his guests and Itchky Ironhat agrees, although I point out that it will be more sensible for us to move on to Louisville and get into action as quickly as possible because we are now practically out of funds. But Itchky takes a look at old Em and he says she is enjoying herself so much running around her old home and devouring grass that it will be a sin and a shame to take her away before it is absolutely necessary.

After a couple of days, I tell Itchky that I think absolutely necessary arrives, but Itchky says Mr Salsbury now wishes to give a dinner in honour of old Em and he will not think of denying her this pleasure. And for the next week the house is overrun with coloured parties, male and female, cleaning up the house and painting and cooking and dusting and I do not know what all else, and furthermore I hear there is a great to-do all through the Bluegrass country when the invitations to the dinner start going around, because this is the first time in over a dozen years that Mr Salsbury has any truck whatever with his neighbours.

On the night of the dinner, one of the male coloured parties tells me that he never before sees such a gathering of the high-toned citizens of the Bluegrass as are assembled in the big dining hall at a horseshoe-shaped table with an orchestra going and with flowers and flags and racing colours all around and about. In fact, the coloured party says it is just like the old days at Tucky Farms when Mr Salsbury's wife is alive, although he says he does not remember ever seeing such a character sitting alongside Mr Salsbury at the table as Itchky Ironhat.

To tell the truth, Itchky Ironhat seems to puzzle all the guests no little and it is plain to be seen that they are wondering who he is and why he is present, though Itchky is sharpened up with a fresh shave and has on a clean shirt and of course he is not wearing his derby hat. Personally, I am rather proud of Itchky's appearance, but I can see that he seems to be overplaying his knife a little, especially against the mashed potatoes.

Mr Salsbury is dressed in a white dinner jacket and his eyes are quiet and his hair is trimmed and his manner is most genteel in every way and when the guests are seated he gets to his feet and attracts their attention by tapping on a wineglass with a spoon. Then he speaks to them as follows:

'Friends and neighbours,' he says. 'I know you are all surprised at being invited here, but you may be more surprised when you learn the reason. As most of you are aware, I am as one dead for years. Now I live again. I am going to restore Tucky Farms to all its old turf glory in breeding and racing, and,' he says, 'I am going to re-establish the Emaleen Salsbury award, with which you are familiar, and carry on again in every way as I am now certain my late beloved wife will wish.'

Then he tells them the story of old Em and how Itchky Ironhat cares for her and loves her all these years and how he brings her to the Bluegrass just to see her old home, but of course he does not tell them that Itchky also plans to later drop her in a race at Churchill Downs, as it seems Itchky never mentions the matter to him.

Anyway, Mr Salsbury says that the return of old Em awakens him as if from a bad dream and he can suddenly see how he is not doing right with respect to his wife's memory and while he is talking a tall old guy who is sitting next to me, and who turns out to be nobody but the guy who directs Tucky Farms, says to me like this:

'It is a miracle,' he says. 'I am his personal physician and I give him up long ago as a hopeless victim of melancholia. In fact, I am always expecting to hear of him dismissing himself from this world entirely. Well,' the old guy says, 'I always say medical science is not everything.'

'My first step toward restoring Tucky Farms,' Mr Salsbury goes on, 'is to purchase the old mare Emaleen from Mr Itchky Ironhat here for the sum of three thousand dollars, which we agree upon this evening as a fair price. I will retire her of course for the rest of her days, which I hope will be many.'

With this he whips out a cheque and hands it to Itchky and

naturally I am somewhat surprised at the sum mentioned because I figure if old Em is worth three G's War Admiral must be worth a million. However, I am also greatly pleased because I can see where Itchky and I will have a nice taw for the races at Churchill Downs without having to bother about old Em winning one.

'Now,' Mr Salsbury says, 'for our guest of honour.'

Then two big doors at one end of the banquet hall open wide and there seems to be a little confusion outside and a snorting and a stamping as if a herd of wild horses is coming in and all of a sudden who appears in the doorway with her mane and tail braided with ribbons and her coat all slicked up but old Em and who is leading her in but the large guy who insults her and also Itchky on our arrival at Tucky Farms.

The guests begin applauding and the orchestra plays My Old Kentucky Home and it is a pleasant scene to be sure, but old Em seems quite unhappy about something as the large guy pulls her into the hollow of the horsehoe-shaped table, and the next thing anybody knows, Itchky Ironhat climbs over the table, knocking glasses and dishes every which way and flattens the large guy with a neat left hook, in the presence of the best people of the Blue-grass country.

Naturally, this incident causes some comment and many of the guests are slightly shocked and there is considerable criticism of Itchky Ironhat for his lack of table manners. But then it is agreed by one and all present that Itchky is undoubtedly entitled to the Emaleen Salsbury kindness to horses award when I explain that what irks him is the fact that the large guy leads old Em in with a twitch on her lip.

Well, this is about all there is to the story, except that Itchky and I go over to Louisville the next day and remain there awaiting the Kentucky Derby and we have a wonderful time, to be sure, except that we do not seem to be able to win any bets on the horse races at Churchill Downs.

from RUNYON À LA CARTE *1946*

Sugar for the Horse

H. E. BATES

My Uncle Silas had a little mare named Jenny, warm, brown and
smooth-coated, with a cream arrow on her forehead and flecks of
cream on three of her feet. She was a very knowing, friendly
creature and she could take sugar off the top of your head. 'Go
anywhere and do anything,' my Uncle Silas would say. 'Only
got to give her the word. Goo bed wi' me.'

'Upstairs?' I said.

'Upstairs, downstairs,' my Uncle Silas said. 'Anywhere. Where
you like. I recollect –'

'Start some more tales,' my grandmother would say. 'Go on.
Stuff the child's head with rubbish. Keep on. Some day he'll
know the difference between the truth and what he hears from
you.'

'Is the truth,' Silas said. 'She come to bed with me arter the
1897 Jubilee. Over at Kimbolton. I oughta know. There was me
and Tig Flawn and Queenie White –'

'That's been a minute,' my grandmother said. She was very
small and tart and dry and disbelieving. 'How old's Jenny now?
Forty?'

'Well, she's gittin' on,' Silas said. 'I recollect that day Queenie
had a big hat on. We got the hat off her and put it on Jenny and
she come up to bed with me just like a lamb.'

'Who was Queenie White?' I said. 'Did she come to bed with
you too?'

'I'm only tellin' on you about the horse,' my Uncle Silas said.
'Queenie was afore your time.'

'Pity she wasn't before yours,' my grandmother said.

'Ah, but she wadn't. 'Course,' he said to me, 'I could tell you
a lot about her. Only you wanted to know about the horse. Well,
she come to bed in no house of mine.'

Some time later my Uncle Silas came down to Nenweald Fair,
on the second Sunday in August, about the time the corn was
cut and the first dewberries were ripe for gathering, with Jenny
in a little black trap with yellow wheels and a spray of ash-leaves

498

on her head to keep the flies away. There was always a wonderful dinner for Nenweald Fair and Silas always kept it waiting. There was always roast beef and Yorkshire pudding and horseradish sauce and chicken to choose from, and little kidney beans and new potatoes and butter, and yellow plum pie and cream with sugar on pastry. There were jugs of beer on the sideboard by the clock with the picture of Philadelphia. The batter of the York- shire pudding was as buttery and soft as custard and all over the house there was a wonderful smell of beef burnt at the edges by fire.

But my Uncle Silas was always late and my grandfather, an indulgent, mild-mannered man unaccustomed to revelry and things of that sort, was always full of excuses for him.

'Very like busted a belly-band coming down Longleys Hill or summat,' he would say.

'Start carving,' my grandmother would say. 'I'm having no dinner of mine spoilt for Silas or anybody else.'

'Hold hard a minute. Give him a chance.'

'The meat's on the table,' she would say, 'and if he's not here that's his lookout,' and she would plant the meat before my grandfather and it would sizzle in its gravy.

It was my Uncle Silas's custom, and my grandmother knew it and knew it only too well, not only to arrive late for that dinner but never to arrive alone. He had a habit of arriving with strange men with names like Tig Flawn and Fiddler Bollard and Slob Johnson and Tupman Jarvis. That day he arrived, about two o'clock, when most of the meat had gone and the last of the yellow plums were cooling in the dish, with a man named Ponto Pack. I always wanted him to arrive with Queenie White and see what my grandmother thought of that, but he never did and I was always rather disappointed. Whenever he did arrive my grandmother always looked as if she could hit him over the head with the pastry-board, or some other suitable instrument, and that day, when I looked out of the window and saw Silas and the man Ponto, like some gigantic blond sow, falling out of the trap, I felt the carving knife would hardly have been too much.

'Let 'em all come!' my Uncle Silas roared and gave prodigious beery winks from a bloodshot eye that was like a fire in a field of poppies.

'You're late,' my grandmother said. 'Get your dinner and stop shouting as if you were in Yardley Open Fields.'

'Got hung up,' Silas said. 'Belly-band broke.'

My grandmother gave my grandfather such a killing and merciless look that he went out at once to give Jenny a rub down and a drink of water, and Ponto made strange strangled noises with whole potatoes, and said, for the first of several times:

'Onaccountable. Most onaccountable.'

He was such a large man, bulging flesh as tight as bladdered lard into his suit of green-faded Sunday black, that when the rest of us had left the table it still seemed full. His eyes, pink-edged, beery, almost colourless, were uncannily like the eyes of a blond and farrowing sow. He had nothing to say all day but:

'Onaccountable, George,' or 'Onaccountable, Silas. Most onaccountable.'

In the afternoon it was very hot and everyone, including Silas, went to sleep in the front parlour or under the laurel trees, and I played giving Jenny lumps of sugar off the top of my head in the little paddock at the back of the house. I was giving her the seventh or eighth lump of sugar and wondering whether she ever did go to bed with my Uncle Silas or whether it was just another story, when my grandmother rapped on the window and said:

'Come you in out of that sun. You'll never stay awake tonight without you get some rest.'

She must have known what was coming. About half-past six my Uncle Silas and my grandfather and Ponto Pack had another jug of beer in the shade of the laurel trees and my Uncle Silas, wet-lipped, bloodshot eye wickedly cocked, began to talk about 'gittin' the belly-band mended while we think on it'. It did not seem to me to be a thing that wanted thinking on at all, and I do not think my grandmother thought so either. She had put on her grey silk dress with the parma violet stitching at the collar and her little high hat with Michaelmas daisies on the brim, and it was time now to be thinking of 'walking up street'. To walk up street on the Sunday of Nenweald Fair was a gentle, ponderous, respectable, long-winded custom, and it was something about which neither my Uncle Silas, my grandfather nor Ponto Pack seemed, I thought, very enthusiastic.

'You goo steady on up,' Silas said. 'We'll come on arter we git the belly-band mended.'

'If everything was as right as that belly-band nobody would hurt much,' she said.

'It's too 'nation hot yit for traipsing about,' Silas said.

'Onaccountable hot,' Ponto said. 'Most onaccountable.'

Ten minutes later the trap went jigging past us up the street, my Uncle Silas wearing his black-and-white deer-stalker sideways on, so that the peaks stuck out like ears, and Ponto, bowler hat perched on the top of his head like a cannon ball, looking more than ever like some pink-eyed performing pig. My grandfather pretended not to see us and my grandmother said:

'What one doesn't think of, the other will. The great fool things.'

We seemed to take longer than ever that sultry evening to make the tour under the chestnut trees about the crowded market-place. I always got very bored with the gossiping Sunday-starched crowd of bowler hats and parasols and I kept thinking how nice it would be if my Uncle Silas were to come back with Jenny and I could do my trick of giving her sugar, in full view of everybody, off the top of my head. But Silas never came and by ten o'clock I was yawning and my grandmother had even stopped saying darkly, whenever there was something nice to listen to, 'Little pigs have got big ears', as if I hadn't the vaguest idea of what she meant by that.

I went to bed with a piece of cold Yorkshire pudding to eat and fell asleep with it in my hands. It is hard to say now what time I woke up, but what woke me was like the thunder of one crazy dream colliding with another somewhere at the foot of the stairs. The piece of cold Yorkshire pudding was like a frog crawling on my pillow, and I remember wanting to shriek about it just at the moment I heard my Uncle Silas roaring in the front passage:

'Git up, old gal! Git up there! Pull up, old gal!'

A terrifying sound as of madly-beaten carpets greeted me at the top of the stairs. It was my grandmother beating Ponto Pack across the backside with what I thought was the stick we used for stirring pig-swill. She could not get at my Uncle Silas because Silas was leading Jenny up the stairs; and she could not get at my grandfather because he was lying like a sack of oats on Jenny's back. Ponto was pushing Jenny with his round black backside sticking out like a tight balloon and my Uncle Silas kept bawling:

'Git underneath on her, Ponto. You ain't underneath on her.'

Every time Ponto seemed about to git underneath on her my grandmother hit him again with the swill-stick. I thought he did not seem to mind very much. He laughed every time my grandmother hit him and then pushed himself harder than ever against Jenny's hindquarters and called with pig-like fruitiness to my Uncle Silas, tugging at the bridle on the stairs:

'Can't budge the old gal, Silas. Most aggravatin' onaccountable.'

'Get that mare out of my house, you drunken idiots!' my grandmother shrieked.

'Gotta git George to bed fust,' Silas said. 'Must git George to bed.'

'Get that horse off my stair-carpet!'

'Gotta git George to bed. Good gal!' Silas said. 'Come on now, good gal. Tchck, tchck! Up, mare! That's a good gal.'

By this time my Uncle Silas had succeeded in tugging Jenny a quarter of the way upstairs when suddenly, down below, sharp and sickening above the pandemonium of voices, there was a crack like a breaking bone. Ponto Pack roared, 'Silas, she's hittin' me on the coconut!' and at the same moment Jenny had something like hysterics, whinnying terribly, and fell down on her front kees on the stairs. My Uncle Silas yelled, 'Why th' Hanover don't you git underneath on her? She'll be down atop on y'!' and for a moment I thought she was. She gave a great lurch backwards and my grandfather let out a groan. My grandmother hit Ponto another crack on the head with the swill-stick and suddenly the whole essence of the situation became, to me at any rate, splendidly clear. My Uncle Silas and Ponto were trying to get my grandfather to bed and my grandmother, in her obstinate way, was trying to stop them.

I remembered in that moment the cold Yorkshire pudding. I fetched it from my bedroom and went half-way down the stairs and held it out to Jenny, most coaxingly, in the flat of my hand.

Whether she thought, at that moment, that I in my white nightshirt was some kind of newly-woken ghost or whether she decided she had had enough of the whole affair, I never knew. Ponto had hardly time to bawl out from the bottom of the stairs,

'It's most onaccountable, Silas. I can't budge her!' and my Uncle Silas from the top of the stairs, 'Hold hard, Pont. The old gal's knockin' off for a mite of pudden!' when my grandmother, aiming another crack at Ponto's head, hit the mare in her fury a blow above the tail.

The frenzy of her hysterical ascent up three steps of stairs and then backwards down the whole flight was something I shall not forget. My grandfather fell off the mare and the mare fell sideways on him, and then my Uncle Silas fell on the mare. The three of them fell on my grandmother and my grandmother fell on Ponto Pack. My Uncle Silas yelled, 'Let 'em all come!' and my grandmother hit Ponto twenty or thirty blows on the top of the head with the swill-stick. My grandfather fell off the horse's back and landed with a terrible crash on the umbrella-stand, and the portrait of Gladstone fell down in the hall. The cold Yorkshire pudding fell down the stairs and I fell after it. My aunt came in the front door with a policeman, and Ponto yelled, 'It's onaccountable, Silas, most onaccountable!' just as the mare broke free and charged the sideboard in the front room.

My Uncle Silas sat on the bottom of the stairs and laughed his head off, and I began to cry because I was sorry for Jenny and thought it was the end of the world.

from SUGAR FOR THE HORSE *1957*

Agony and Ecstasy

DICK FRANCIS

I watched the starter's hand. He had a habit of stretching his finger just before he pulled the lever to let the tapes up, and I had no intention of letting anyone get away before me and cut me out of the position I had acquired on the rails.

The starter stretched his fingers. I kicked Template's flanks. He was moving quite fast when we went under the rising tapes, with me lying flat along his withers to avoid being swept off, like other riders who had jumped the start too effectively in the past.

The tapes whistled over my head and we were away, securely on the rails and on the inside curve for at least the next two miles.

The first three fences were the worst, as far as my comfort was concerned. By the time we had jumped the fourth – the water – I had felt the thinly healed crusts on my back tear open, had thought my arms and shoulders would split apart with the strain of controlling Template's eagerness, had found just how much my wrists and hands had to stand from the tug of the reins.

My chief feeling, as we landed over the water, was one of relief. It was all bearable; I could contain it and ignore it, and get on with the job.

The pattern of the race was simple from my point of view, because from start to finish I saw only three other horses, Emerald and the two lightly-weighted animals whom I had allowed to go on and set the pace. The jockeys of this pair, racing ahead of me nose for nose, consistently left a two-foot gap between themselves and the rails, and I reckoned that if they were still there by the time we reached the second last fence in the straight, they would veer slightly towards the stands, as horses usually do at Ascot, and widen the gap enough for me to get through.

My main task until then was keeping Emerald from cutting across to the rails in front of me and being able to take the opening instead of Template. I left just too little room between me and the front pair for Emerald to get in, forcing the mare to race all the way on my outside. It didn't matter that she was two or three feet in front: I could see her better there, and Template was too clever a jumper to be brought down by the half-length trick – riding into a fence half a length in front of an opponent, causing him to take off at the same moment as oneself and land on top of the fence instead of safely on the ground the other side.

With the order unchanged we completed the whole of the first circuit and swept out to the country again. Template jumped the four fences down to Swinley Bottom so brilliantly that I kept finding myself crowding the tails of the pacemakers as we landed, and had to ease him back on the flat each time to avoid taking the lead too soon, and yet not ease him so much that Emerald could squeeze into the space between us.

From time to time I caught a glimpse of the grimness on Emerald's jockey's face. He knew perfectly well what I was doing to him, and if I hadn't beaten him to the rails and made a flying start, he would have done the same to me. Perhaps I had Kemp-Lore to thank that he hadn't even tried, I thought fleetingly; if the bonfire Kemp-Lore had made of my reputation had led the Irishman to misjudge what I would do, so much the better.

For another half-mile the two horses in front kept going splendidly, but one of the jockeys picked up his whip at the third last fence, and the other was already busy with his hands. They were dead ducks, and because of that they swung a little wide going round the last bend into the straight. The Irishman must have had his usual bend tactics too fixed in his mind, for he chose that exact moment to go to the front. It was not a good occasion for that manoeuvre. I saw him spurt forward from beside me and accelerate, but he had to go round on the outside of the two front horses who were themselves swinging wide, and he was wasting lengths in the process. The mare carried seven pounds less weight than Template, and on that bend she lost the advantage they should have given her.

After the bend, tackling the straight for the last time, with the second last fence just ahead, Emerald was in the lead on the outside, then the two tiring horses, then me.

There was a three foot gap then between the innermost pacemaker and the rails. I squeezed Template. He pricked his ears and bunched his colossal muscles and thrust himself forward into the narrow opening. He took off at the second last fence half a length behind and landed a length in front of the tiring horse, jumping so close to him on one side and to the wings on the other that I heard the other jockey cry out in surprise as I passed.

One of Template's great advantages was his speed away from a fence. With no check in his stride he sped smoothly on still hugging the rails, with Emerald only a length in front on our left. I urged him a fraction forward to prevent the mare from swinging over to the rails and blocking me at the last fence. She needed two lengths' lead to do it safely, and I had no intention of letting her have it.

The utter joy of riding Template lay in the feeling of immense power which he generated. There was no need to make the best of things, on his back; to fiddle and scramble, and hope for others to blunder, and find nothing to spare for a finish. He had enough reserve strength for his jockey to be able to carve up the race as he wished, and there was nothing in racing, I thought, more ecstatic than that.

I knew, as we galloped towards the last fence, that Template would beat Emerald if he jumped it in anything like his usual style. She was a length ahead and showing no sign of flagging, but I was still holding Template on a tight rein. Ten yards from the fence, I let him go. I kicked his flanks and squeezed with the calves of my legs and he went over the birch like an angel, smooth, surging, the nearest to flying one can get.

He gained nearly half a length on the mare, but she didn't give up easily. I sat down and rode Template for my life, and he stretched himself into his flat-looking stride. He came level with Emerald half-way along the run in. She hung on grimly for a short distance, but Template would have none of it. He floated past her with an incredible increase of speed, and he won, in the end, by two clear lengths.

There are times beyond words, and that was one of them. I patted Template's sweating neck over and over. I could have kissed him. I would have given him anything. How does one thank a horse? How could one ever repay him, in terms he would understand, for giving one such a victory?

from NERVE *1957*

The Birth of a Legend

SUSAN CHITTY

The first edition of *Black Beauty* was a modest enough affair. It was about the size of a pre-war Everyman and contained only one illustration, a crude woodcut of Reuben Smith's accident. It was bound in red, blue or green cloth. A rustic trellis in black flanked each side of the cover and up each climbed a golden oat plant. The title Black Beauty was written in specially cut capitals graded to diminish in the centre of each letter. Below this was a gilt horse's head looking to the right. This edition, which retailed for '2/- in cloth boards, 2/6 in extra board, gilt edges', has now become very rare indeed. Even the British Museum does not possess it, no doubt because life in the nursery is not conducive to survival in books. Norwich Library, however, possesses two copies, one of them having been formerly in the possession of the three Miss Wrights. It bears the following inscription in Anna's hand:

> To my dear Aunts
> E.M. and E. Wright
> from their loving and
> grateful neice
> the Author Jan. 1878

On the cover of a much commoner early edition the horse's head looks to the left instead of the right. Many people who possess this one (described as 'Variant C' by John Carter, the binding expert) are under the impression that it was published simultaneously with the first edition, but this is by no means certain. Both editions carried advertisements for the complete works of Mary Sewell at the end.

The immediate public reaction to the publication of *Black Beauty* was silence. Jarrolds gloomy prognostications about the book's chances of success seemed justified. Their town traveller, having made his rounds of the London booksellers, could report a subscription of only one hundred copies for the entire trade. Anna bought several copies and gave them away to her friends and relations for Christmas. The one she gave to her cousin Lucy, containing a letter in her hand, still exists. Several appreciative letters were printed in Mrs Bayly's book, including one from Philip regretting that a horse who had suffered so much in this life could not be granted a share in the next. Another cousin wrote:

> I am so delighted, so proud of my cousin, that I can never thank you enough for my Christmas present. Read it! – I should think I did. Do you remember, when you and Philip were children, how you used to have Christmas Day for your 'very own' – choose your own amusements, your own pudding? Just such a Christmas Day did I promise myself, with your capital book for my special delection. I could not quite carry out my

wishes, for J.A. had to be invited to dinner – but directly he was
gone, I petted Black Beauty and enjoyed myself.

I do like the book exceedingly, it is so good; and, forgive me,
so unladylike that but for 'Anna Sewell' on the title-page, and a
certain gentle kindliness all through the story, no one, I think,
would believe it to be written by a lady. Where you have
obtained your stable mindedness I can't imagine, but that you
fully understand your business is a fact. I like your grooms, only
I am afraid you had the pick of some exceptional ones. Manly,
James and even little Joe Green are just the jockeys for me.
Would they could be counted by thousands!

The story of poor Black Beauty and Ginger is most touching,
and the different characters of the horses admirably carried out.
The only fault I find in the translation is making Ginger exclaim
'Thank Heaven!' that being, as I suppose, a place not dreamt of
in Equine philosophy; but were I to tell you of all I admire, I
should not get this letter posted tonight. The best bit of writing
according to my ideas, is the drive through the City – that is
really wonderful. Are you sure you have never stood on the
steps of an omnibus to collect passengers and watch the traffic?

A letter that Anna appreciated more than all these, however,
was not received from a relative. It was written by a Mrs Toynbee
on behalf of Edward Fordham Flower. Mr Flower was the author
of several pamphlets on the humane treatment of horses and was
considered an expert on harness. The letter ran as follows:

January 29, 1878

Captain Toynbee and I went yesterday afternoon to see our
friends the Flowers, in Hyde Park Gardens, and found Mr
Flower in a complete state of enthusiasm over *Black Beauty*. 'It
is written by a veterinary surgeon,' he exclaimed; 'by a coachman, by a groom; there is not a mistake in the whole of it; not
one thing I wish altered, except that the cabman should have
taken that half-crown. I shall show Mr Bright the passage about
horses in war. I must make the lady's acquaintance; she must
come to London sometimes – she is my Araminta!' (Do you
remember Miss Edgeworth's *Araminta, or the Unknown Friend*?)

He particularly wished me to say that he would like to write himself, but writing is troublesome to him, from the weakness of his hand. Are we right in supposing that the book is written (translated, by-the-by) by your daughter? Is it being actively circulated? That was a point Mr Flower was very anxious about . . . Will you forgive so many questions, but Mr Flower could talk of nothing else. Now and then, when the conversation strayed to the war, or anything else, he would exclaim, 'How could a lady know so much horses?'

Mary Sewell wrote the following letter to Mr Flower on Anna's behalf.

I should have thanked you for your most welcome letter the day it came, but an infirm household and an invalid friend staying with us, obliged my pen to be quiet.

Your letter was indeed a great encouragement both to me and Anna. It was the first of the kind that had come to hand, and was accordingly treasured. Many letters followed, but when I took yours to Anna, I said I was come to put her crown on. I assure you it was a triumphant moment. She had ventured to send a copy of her book to Mr Flower, but had thought, if he noticed it at all, it would be chiefly to point out inaccuracies. But when his entire approbation came, it brought indeed a full measure of gladness and confidence. If he would add to his kindness by writing a few lines expressive of his commendation, he would be giving it a standing beyond what anyone else could do.

We are expecting every day the proofs of the School Edition; we have both a great desire that it should become a reading-book in Boys' Schools. This also was the sanguine hope of the publisher, but his sudden death, just before its publication, has deprived it of his energetic aid.

Perhaps Mr Flower obliged by writing the few lines of commendation requested and perhaps Mary Sewell brought these to the notice of Jarrold. Certainly at this point the publishers began to exert themselves on the book's behalf. By advertising, by lobbying editors, by galvanising the trade through their local travellers, Jarrolds got the book moving at last. The reviews, carefully preserved by Mary, began to roll in. They were laudatory enough to satisfy the vainest author. The publisher's selection is given below.

We are prepared to say of this story, that the readers are few who, having commenced the book, will fail to read its every page – or who, having reached the last page, will not regret that they cannot again read it with the first freshness of interest.

Isle of Wight Advertiser

The more often we have turned over the leaves of *Black Beauty*, the greater has been our delight.

Its circulation amongst boys will do a world of good.

Hand and Heart

Wherever children are, whether boys or girls, there this should be.

School Guardian

Black Beauty will be a favourite with the boys.

Schoolmaster

We do not know what could teach kindness to horses better than this story.

Christian World

We have rarely read a book with so much genuine pleasure as this. The narrative is managed with no little skill, and is full of variety and interest.

Eastern Daily Press

We are glad to see that it has already reached a fourth edition, and we hope it will be extensively circulated among owners and users of horses.

Mark Lane Express

If the Society for the Prevention of Cruelty to Animals had published the Autobiography of Black Beauty we should have said it had published its best work.

Hand and Heart

from THE WOMAN WHO WROTE BLACK BEAUTY *1971*

Lebedyan

IVAN TURGENEV

At the furthest corner of the road I noticed a big sheet of paper stuck to the gates of a little grey house. At the head of it was an ink drawing of a horse with a trumpet-shaped tail and an interminable neck, and under the horse's hooves were the following words, written in an old-fashioned hand:

> For sale, horses of various breeds, brought to Lebedyan fair from the well-known steppe-country stud of Anastasei Ivanich Chornobai, landowner of Tambov. Horses of excellent antecedents, fully broken and nice-mannered. Purchasers kindly ask for Anastasei Ivanich himself, or, in his absence, for his coachman Nazar Kubyshkin. Gentlemen customers, pray do an old man the honour of a visit!

I halted. I thought I would have a look at the horses of the well-known steppe-country breeder, Mr Chornobai. I tried to go through the gate, but, contrary to the usual practice, found it locked. I knocked.

'Who's there? . . . A customer?' squealed a woman's voice.

'Yes.'

'Coming, sir, coming.'

The gate opened. I saw a peasant woman of about fifty, bareheaded, in shoes and with a sheepskin thrown loosely on.

'Please, kind sir, come in, and I'll go and tell Anastasei Ivanich at once . . . Nazar, hey, Nazar.'

'What?' muttered a septuagenarian voice from the stable.

'Get the horses ready; a customer has come.'

The old woman ran into the house.

'A customer, a customer,' muttered Nazar, by way of answer to her. 'I haven't washed their tails yet.'

Oh, Arcadia! I thought.

'Good day, sir, and welcome,' said a pleasant, slow, fruity voice behind my back. I looked round; in front of me, in a long-skirted blue overcoat, stood an old man of middle height, with white hair, a friendly smile and beautiful blue eyes.

'Horses? Please, sir, please. . . . But wouldn't you like to come and take tea with me first?'

I thanked him and declined.

'Well, as you please. You must forgive me, sir: you see, I am old-fashioned.' Mr Chornobai spoke unhurriedly and with a broad country accent. 'Everything is simple and straightforward with me. Nazar, hey, Nazar,' he added, drawingly, and without raising his voice.

Nazar, a little, wrinkled old chap with the nose of a hawk and a triangular beard, appeared on the stable threshold.

'What sort of horses do you want, sir?' continued Mr Chornobai.

'Not too dear, well-broken, for carriage-work.'

'Certainly, I have some like that, certainly. . . . Nazar, show the gentleman the grey gelding, you know, the one at the end, and the bay with the bald spot – no, the other bay, the one by Krasotka, you know?'

Nazar turned into the stable.

'Just bring them out on the halter,' Mr Chornobai shouted after him. 'My ways, sir,' he continued, looking straight at me with his clear, mild eyes, 'are not those of the dealers – devil take them! They go in for all sorts of ginger, salt, bran. God forgive them, anyway! . . . But with me, be pleased to note, everything is open-handed and above board.'

The horses were brought out. I didn't like them.

'Well, take them back,' said Anastasei Ivanich. 'Show us some more.'

They showed us some more. Eventually I chose one of the cheaper ones. We began to bargain. Mr Chornobai remained cool, spoke so judiciously, with such dignity, that I could not fail to 'honour the old man': I paid a deposit.

'Well now,' said Anastasei Ivanich, 'allow me, in the old-fashioned way, to hand the horse over to you from coat-tail to coat-tail. . . . You'll be grateful to me. . . . He's as fresh as a nut . . . unspoiled. Straight from the steppes! He'll go in every kind of harness.'

He crossed himself, took his coat-skirt in his hand, grasped the halter, and handed the horse over to me.

'He's yours now, and good luck to you. You still won't take tea?'

'No, thank you very much indeed: I must go home.'

'As you please. . . . Shall my coachman lead the horse after you now?'

'Yes, now, if he will.'

'Certainly, my dear sir, certainly. . . . Vasily, hey, Vasily, go with the gentleman; lead the horse and take the money. Well, good-bye, sir, and God bless you.'

'Good-bye, Anastasei Ivanich.'

The horse was led home for me. The very next day he proved broken-winded and lame. I tried putting him in harness: he backed away, and when I struck him with the whip, he balked, bucked and lay down. I at once set off to see Mr Chornobai. I asked if he was at home.

'Yes.'

'How is this!' I said. 'Why, you've sold me a broken-winded horse.'

'Broken-winded? . . . Heaven preserve us.'

'And lame into the bargain, and a jibber as well.'

'Lame? I don't know, your coachman must certainly have hurt him somehow . . . but I, before God. . . .'

'Really, Anastasei Ivanich, you ought to take him back.'

'No, sir, no, I'm sorry; once he's out of my yard, the deal is done. You should have been good enough to look at him first.'

I understood what I was up against, submitted to my fate, laughed and went off. Luckily I hadn't paid too dear for my lesson.

from A SPORTSMAN'S NOTEBOOK *1950*

War Cloud

ERNEST HEMINGWAY

I guess looking at it, my old man was cut out for a fat guy, one of those regular little roly guys you see around, but he sure never got that way, except a little towards the last, and then it wasn't his fault, he was riding over the jumps only and he could afford to carry plenty of weight then. I remember the way he'd pull on a rubber shirt over a couple of jerseys and a big sweat shirt over that, and get me to run with him in the forenoon in the hot sun. He'd have, maybe, taken a trial trip with one of Razzo's skins early in the morning after just getting in from Torino at four o'clock in the morning and beating it out to the stables in a cab and then with the dew all over everything and the sun just starting to get going, I'd help him pull off his boots and he'd get into a pair of sneakers and all those sweaters and we'd start out.

'Come on, kid,' he'd say, stepping up and down on his toes in front of the jocks' dressing-room, 'let's get moving.'

Then we'd start off jogging around the infield once, maybe, with him ahead, running nice, and then turn out the gate and along one of those roads with all the trees along both sides of them that run out from San Siro. I'd go ahead of him when we hit the road and I could run pretty stout and I'd look around and he'd be jogging easy just behind me and after a little while I'd look around again and he'd begun to sweat. Sweating heavy and he'd just be dogging it along with his eyes on my back, but when he'd catch me looking at him he'd grin and say, 'Sweating plenty?' When my old man grinned, nobody could help but grin too. We'd keep right on running out towards the mountains and then my old man would yell, 'Hey, Joe!' and I'd look back and he'd be sitting under a tree with a towel he'd had around his waist wrapped around his neck.

I'd come back and sit down beside him and he'd pull a rope out of his pocket and start skipping rope out in the sun with the sweat pouring off his face and him skipping rope out in the white dust with the rope going cloppetty, cloppetty, clop, clop, clop, and the sun hotter, and him working harder up and down a patch of the road. Say, it was a treat to see my old man skip rope, too. He could whirr it fast or lop it slow and fancy. Say, you ought to have seen wops look at us sometimes, when they'd come by, going into town walking along with big white steers hauling the cart. They sure looked as though they thought the old man was nuts. He'd start the rope whirring till they'd stop dead still and watch him, then give the steers a cluck and a poke with the goad and get going again.

When I'd sit watching him working out in the hot sun I sure felt fond of him. He sure was fun and he done his work so hard and he'd finish up with a regular whirring that'd drive the sweat out on his face like water and then sling the rope at the tree and come over and sit down with me and lean back against the tree with the towel and a sweater wrapped around his neck.

'Sure is hell keeping it down, Joe,' he'd say and lean back and shut his eyes and breathe long and deep, 'it ain't like when you're a kid.' Then he'd get up before he started to cool and we'd jog along back to the stables. That's the way it was keeping down to weight. He worried all the time. Most jocks can just about ride off all they want to. A jock loses about a kilo every time he rides, but my old man was sort of dried out and he couldn't keep down his kilos without all that running.

I remember once at San Siro, Regoli, a little wop, that was riding for Buzoni, came out across the paddock going to the bar for something cool; and flicking his boots with his whip, after he'd just weighed in and my old man had just weighed in too, and came out with the saddle under his arm looking red-faced and tired and too big for his silks and he stood there looking at young Regoli standing up to the outdoors bar, cool and kid-looking, and I says, 'What's the matter, Dad?' 'cause I thought maybe Regoli had bumped him or something and he just looked at Regoli and said, 'Oh, to hell with it,' and went on to the dressing-room.

Well, it would have been all right, maybe, if we'd stayed in Milan and ridden at Milan and Torino, 'cause if there ever were any easy courses, it's those two, 'Pianola, Joe', my old man said when he dismounted in the winning stall after what the wops thought was a hell of a steeplechase. I asked him once. 'This course rides itself. It's the pace you're going at, that makes riding the jumps dangerous, Joe. We ain't going any pace here, and they ain't any really bad jumps either. But it's the pace always – not the jumps that makes the trouble.'

San Siro was the swellest course I'd ever seen, but the old man said it was a dog's life. Going back and forth between Mirafiore and San Siro and riding just about every day in the week with a train ride every other night.

I was nuts about the horses, too. There's something about it, when they come out and go up the track to the post. Sort of dancy and tight looking with the jock keeping a tight hold on them and maybe easing off a little and letting them run a little going up. Then once they were at the barrier it got me worse than anything. Especially at San Siro with that big green infield and the mountains way off and the fat wop starter with his big whip and the jocks fiddling them around and then the barrier snapping up and that bell going off and them all getting off in a bunch and then commencing to string out. You know the way a bunch of skins gets off. If you're up in the stand with a pair of glasses all you see is them plunging off and then the bell goes off and it seems like it rings for a thousand years and then they come sweeping round the turn. There wasn't ever anything like it for me.

But my old man said one day, in the dressing-room, when he was getting into his street clothes, 'None of these things are horses, Joe. They'd kill that bunch of skates for their hides and hoofs up at Paris.' That was the day he'd won the Premio Commercio with Lantorna, shooting her out of the field the last hundred metres like pulling a cork out of a bottle.

It was right after the Premio Commercio that we pulled out and left Italy. My old man and Holbrook and a fat wop in a straw hat that kept wiping his face with a handkerchief were having an argument at a table in the Galleria. They were all talking French and the two of them were after my old man about something. Finally he didn't say anything any more but just sat there and looked at Holbrook, and the two of them kept after him, first one talking and then the other, and the fat wop always butting in on Holbrook.

'You go out and buy me a *Sportsman*, will you, Joe?' my old man said, and handed me a couple of soldi without looking away from Holbrook.

So I went out of the Galleria and walked over to in front of the

Scala and bought a paper, and came back and stood a little way away because I didn't want to butt in and my old man was sitting back in his chair looking down at the coffee and fooling with a spoon and Holbrook and the big wop were standing and the big wop was wiping his face and shaking his head. And I came up and my old man acted just as though the two of them weren't standing there and said, 'Want an ice, Joe?' Holbrook looked down at my old man and said slow and careful, 'You son of a bitch,' and he and the fat wop went out through the tables.

My old man sat there and sort of smiled at me, but his face was white and he looked sick as hell and I was scared and felt sick inside because I knew something had happened and I didn't see how anybody could call my old man a son of a bitch, and get away with it. My old man opened up the *Sportsman* and studied the handicaps for a while and then he said, 'You got to take a lot of things in this world, Joe.' And three days later we left Milan for good on the Turin train for Paris, after an auction sale out in front of Turner's stables of everything we couldn't get into a trunk and a suitcase.

We got into Paris early in the morning in a long, dirty station the old man told me was the Gare de Lyon. Paris was an awful big town after Milan. Seems like in Milan everybody is going somewhere and all the trams run somewhere and there ain't any sort of mix-up, but Paris is all balled up and they never do straighten it out. I got to like it, though, part of it, anyway, and say, it's got the best racecourses in the world. Seems as though that were the thing that keeps it all going and about the only thing you can figure on is that every day the buses will be going out to whatever track they're running at, going right out through everything to the track. I never really got to know Paris well, because I just came in about once or twice a week with the old man from Maisons and he always sat at the Café de la Paix on the Opéra side with the rest of the gang from Maisons and I guess that's one of the busiest parts of the town. But, say, it is funny that a big town like Paris wouldn't have a Galleria, isn't it?

Well, we went out to live at Maisons-Lafitte, where just about everybody lives except the gang at Chantilly, with a Mrs Meyers that runs a boarding house. Maisons is about the swellest place to live I've ever seen in all my life. The town ain't so much, but there's a lake and a swell forest that we used to go off bumming in all day, a couple of us kids, and my old man made me a sling shot and we got a lot of things with it, but the best one was a magpie. Young Dick Atkinson shot a rabbit with it one day and we put it under a tree and were all sitting around and Dick had some cigarettes and all of a sudden the rabbit jumped up and beat into the brush and we chased it, but we couldn't find it. Gee, we had fun at Maisons. Mrs Meyers used to give me lunch in the morning and I'd be gone all day. I learned to talk French quick. It's an easy language.

As soon as we got to Maisons, my old man wrote to Milan for his licence and he was pretty worried till it came. He used to sit around the Café de Paris in Maisons with the gang; there were lots of guys he'd known when he rode up at Paris, before the war, lived at Maisons, and there's a lot of time to sit around because the work around a racing stable, for the jocks, that is, is all cleaned up by nine o'clock in the morning. They take the first batch of skins out to gallop them at 5.30 in the morning and they work the second lot at 8 o'clock. That means getting up early all right and going to bed early, too. If a jock's riding for somebody too, he can't go boozing around because the trainer always has an eye on him if he's a kid and if he ain't a kid he's always got an eye on himself. So mostly if a jock ain't working he sits around the Café de Paris with the gang and they can all sit around about two or three hours in front of some drink like a vermouth and seltz and they talk and tell stories and shoot pool and it's sort of like a club or the Galleria in Milan. Only it ain't really like the Galleria because there everybody is going by all the time and there's everybody around the tables.

Well, my old man got his licence all right. They sent it through to him without a word and he rode a couple of times. Amiens, up country and that sort of thing, but he didn't seem to get any engagements. Everybody liked him and whenever I'd come in to the café in the forenoon I'd find somebody drinking with him because my old man wasn't tight like most of these jockeys that have got the first dollar they made riding at the World's Fair in St Louis in nineteen ought four. That's what my old man would say when he'd kid George Burns. But it seemed like everybody steered clear of giving my old man any mounts.

We went out to wherever they were running every day with the

car from Maisons and that was the most fun of all. I was glad when
the horses came back from Deauville and the summer. Even
though it meant no more bumming in the woods, 'cause then we'd
ride to Enghein or Tremblay or St Cloud and watch them from
the trainers' and jockeys' stand. I sure learned about racing from
going out with that gang and the fun of it was going every
day.

I remember once out at St Cloud. It was a big two-hundred-
thousand-franc race with seven entries and War Cloud a big
favourite. I went around to the paddock to see the horses with my
old man and you never saw such horses. This War Cloud is a great
big yellow horse that looks like just nothing but run. I never saw
such a horse. He was being led around the paddock with his head
down and when he went by me I felt all hollow inside he was so
beautiful. There never was such a wonderful, lean, running-built
horse. And he went around the paddock putting his feet just so
and quiet and careful and moving easy like he knew just what he
had to do and not jerking and standing up on his legs and getting
wild-eyed like you see these selling platers with a shot of dope in
them. The crowd was so thick I couldn't see him again except just
his legs going by and some yellow and my old man started out
through the crowd and I followed him over to the jocks' dressing-
room back in the trees and there was a big crowd around there,
too, but the man at the door in a derby nodded to my old man and
we got in and everybody was sitting around and getting dressed
and pulling shirts over their heads and pulling boots on and it all
smelled hot and sweaty and linimenty and outside was the crowd
looking in.

The old man went over and sat down beside George Gardner
that was getting into his pants and said, 'What's the dope,
George?' just in an ordinary tone of voice 'cause there ain't any
use him feeling around because George either can tell him or he
can't tell him.

'He won't win,' George says very low, leaning over and button-
ing the bottoms of his pants.

'Who will?' my old man says, leaning over close so nobody can
hear.

'Foxless,' George says, 'and if he does, save me a couple of
tickets.'

My old man says something in a regular voice to George and George says, 'Don't ever bet on anything, I tell you,' kidding like, and we beat it out and through all the crowd that was looking in over to the 100 franc mutuel machine. But I knew something big was up because George is War Cloud's jockey. On the way he gets one of the yellow odds-sheets with the starting prices on and War Cloud is only paying 5 for 10, Cefisidote is next at 3 to 1 and fifth down the list this Foxless is 8 to 1. My old man bets five thousand on Foxless to win and puts on a thousand to place and we went around back of the grandstand to go up the stairs and get a place to watch the race.

We were jammed in tight and first a man in a long coat with a grey tall hat and a whip folded up in his hand came out and then one after another the horses, with the jocks up and a stable-boy holding the bridle on each side and walking along, followed the old guy. That big yellow horse War Cloud came first. He didn't look so big when you first looked at him until you saw the length of his legs and the whole way he's built and the way he moves. Gosh, I never saw such a horse. George Gardner was riding him and they moved along slow, back of the old guy in the grey tall hat that walked along like he was the ringmaster in a circus. Back of War Cloud, moving along smooth and yellow in the sun, was a good-looking black with a nice head with Tommy Archibald riding him; and after the black was a string of five more horses all moving along slow in a procession past the grandstand and the pesage. My old man said the black was Foxless and I took a good look at him and he was a nice-looking horse, all right, but nothing like War Cloud.

Everybody cheered War Cloud when he went by and he sure was one swell-looking horse. The procession of them went around on the other side past the pelouse and then back up to the near end of the course and the circus master had the stable-boys turn them loose one after another so they could gallop by the stands on their way up to the post and let everybody have a good look at them. They weren't at the post hardly any time at all when the gong started and you could see them way off across the infield all in a bunch starting on the first swing like a lot of little toy horses. I was watching them through the glasses and War Cloud was running well back, with one of the bays making the pace. They swept down and around and come pounding past and War Cloud was way back when they passed us and this Foxless horse in front and going smooth. Gee, it's awful when they go by you and then you have to watch them go farther away and get smaller and smaller and then all bunched up on the turns and then come around towards you into the stretch and you feel like swearing and god-damning worse and worse. Finally they made the last turn and came into the straightaway with the Foxless horse way out in front. Everybody was looking funny and saying 'War Cloud' in a sort of sick way and them pounding nearer down the stretch, and then something come out of the pack right into my glasses like a horse-headed yellow streak and everybody began to yell 'War Cloud' as though they were crazy. War Cloud came on faster than I'd ever seen anything in my life and pulled up on Foxless that was going fast as any black horse could go with the jock flogging hell out of him with the gad and they were right dead neck and neck for a second but War Cloud seemed about twice as fast with those great jumps and that head out – but it was while they were neck and neck that they passed the winning post and when the numbers went up in the slots the first one was 2 and that meant Foxless had won.

I felt all trembly and funny inside, and then we were all jammed in with the people going downstairs to stand in front of the board where they'd post what Foxless paid. Honest, watching the race I'd forgotten how much my old man had bet on Foxless. I'd wanted War Cloud to win so damned bad. But now it was all over it was swell to know we had a winner.

'Wasn't it a swell race, Dad?' I said to him.

He looked at me sort of funny with his derby on the back of his head. 'George Gardner's a swell jockey, all right,' he said. 'It sure took a great jockey to keep that War Cloud horse from winning.'

Of course I knew it was funny all the time. But my old man saying that right out like that sure took the kick all out of it for me and I didn't get the real kick back again ever, even when they posted the numbers up on the board and the bell rang to pay off and we saw that Foxless paid 67·50 for 10. All round people were saying, 'Poor War Cloud! Poor War Cloud!' And I thought, I wish I were a jockey and could have rode him instead of that son of a bitch. And that was funny, thinking of George Gardner as a son of a bitch because I'd always liked him and besides he'd given us the winner, but I guess that's what he is, all right.

from THE FIRST FORTY-NINE STORIES *1939*

PART VII

The Horse in Verse

My song is of the Horsemen, the centaurs of all time
Who stole for us the freedom of colts of every clime!
Who wore the spurs of mastery, who held the reins of pride,
Who left the world a heritage of sons to rule and ride!

Will H. Ogilvie

Hast thou given the horse strength?

Hast thou given the horse strength? hast thou clothed his neck
with thunder?

Canst thou make him afraid as a grasshopper? the glory of his
nostrils *is* terrible.

He paweth in the valley, and rejoiceth in *his* strength: he goeth
on to meet the armed men.

He mocketh at fear, and is not affrighted; neither turneth he
back from the sword.

The quiver rattleth against him, the glittering spear and the
shield.

He swalloweth the ground with fierceness and rage: neither
believeth he that *it is* the sound of the trumpet.

He saith among the trumpets, Ha, ha; and he smelleth the battle
afar off, the thunder of the captains, and the shouting.

The Book of Job

The Welsh Cob

He is a son of 'Du o Brydyn',
He would win the race in any fair field;
His mother was daughter to the stallion of
Anglesey which carried eight people.
They are descendants to Du'r Morodedd
And I know he is one of them.
He is nephew to the Myngwyn Ial.
In Powys no fetter could hold him.
He is of the stock of Ffwg Warin's stallion,
And that stock grinds its fodder small
with its strong jaws.
He is a stallion of the highest pedigree
in Anglesey.
From the line of Taleolin.

Guto'r Glyn c. 1445 – 75

Horsemen of Muscovy

[Part of letter in verse written from Moscow by George Turbervile, a member of Queen Elizabeth's embassy to Ivan the Terrible, 1568.]

'Almost the meanest man in all this country rides,
The woman eke, against our use, her trotting horse bestrides.*

· · ·

The richest use to ride
From place to place, his servant runs and follows by his side.
The Cossack bears his felt† to force away the rain.
Their bridles are not very brave, their saddles are but plain.
No bits but snaffles, all, of birch their saddles be,
Much fashioned like the Scottish seats, broad flaps to keep the
  knee
From sweating of the horse, the panels larger farre
And broader be than ours. They use short stirrups for the
  warre.
For when the Russie is pursued by cruel foe,
He rides away, and suddenly betakes him to his boe
And bends me but about, in saddle as he sits,
And therewithal amidst his race his following foe he hits. . . .

· · ·

They seldom use to shoe their horse, unless they ride
In post upon the frozen floude, then, cause they shall not slide
He sets a slender calkin, and so he rides his way.‡
The horses of the country go good fourscore versts a day,
And all without the spurre: once pricke them, and they skippe
But go not forward on their way: the Russie hath his whippe
To rappe him on the ribs, for though all booted he
Yet shall you not a pair of spurres in all this countrey see.'

George Turbervile

---

* Riding astride by women had not been practised for 200 years, and was not to become common again for another 150. Owing to the imperfections of the Elizabethan side-saddle, ladies never rode trotting horses, only amblers.
† Waterproof coat, not hat.
‡ These special shoes for ice were also used in Scandinavia, where the frozen rivers served as winter roads.

Adonis' Courser

But, lo, from forth a copse that neighbours by,
A breeding jennet, lusty, young, and proud,
Adonis' trampling courser doth espy,
And forth she rushes, snorts and neighs aloud:
    The strong-neck'd steed, being tied unto a tree,
    Breaketh his rein, and to her straight goes he.

Imperiously he leaps, he neighs, he bounds,
And now his woven girths he breaks asunder;
The bearing earth with his hard hoof he wounds,
Whose hollow womb resounds like heaven's thunder;
    The iron bit he crusheth 'tween his teeth,
    Controlling what he was controlled with.

His ears up-prick'd; his braided hanging mane
Upon his compass'd crest now stand on end;
His nostrils drink the air, and forth again,
As from a furnace, vapours doth he send:
    His eye, which scornfully glisters like fire,
    Shows his hot courage and his high desire.

Sometimes he trots, as if he told the steps,
With gentle majesty and modest pride;
Anon he rears upright, curvets and leaps,
As who should say, 'Lo! thus my strength is tried;
    And this I do to captivate the eye
    Of the fair breeder that is standing by'.

What recketh he his rider's angry stir,
His flattering 'Holla' or his 'Stand, I say'?
What cares he now for curb or pricking spur?
For rich caparisons or trapping gay?
    He sees his love, and nothing else he sees,
    Nor nothing else with his proud sight agrees.

Look, when a painter would surpass the life,
In limning out a well-proportion'd steed,
His art with nature's workmanship at strife,
As if the dead the living should exceed;
    So did this horse excel a common one,
    In shape, in courage, colour, pace and bone.

Round-hoof'd, short-jointed, fetlocks shag and long,
Broad breast, full eye, small head, and nostril wide,
High crest, short ears, straight legs and passing strong,
Thin mane, thick tail, broad buttock, tender hide:
    Look, what a horse should have he did not lack,
    Save a proud rider on so proud a back.

Sometimes he scuds farr off, and there he stares;
Anon he starts at stirring of a feather;
To bid the wind a base he now prepares,
And whe'r he run or fly they know not whether;
    For through his mane and tail the high wind sings,
    Fanning the hairs, who wave like feath'erd wings.

He looks upon his love, and neighs unto her;
She answers him as if she knew his mind:
Being proud, as females are, to see him woo her,
She puts on outward strangeness, seems unkind;
    Spurns at his love and scorns the heat he feels,
    Beating his kind embracements with her heels.

Then, like a melancholy malcontent,
He vails his tail that, like a falling plume,
Cool shadow to his melting buttock lent:
He stamps, and bites the poor flies in his fume.
    His love, perceiving how he is enraged
    Grew kinder, and his fury was assuaged.

William Shakespeare
from 'Venus and Adonis'

The Billesden Coplow Run

With the wind at north-east, forbiddingly keen,
The Coplow of Billesden ne'er witness'd, I ween,
Two hundred such horses and men at a burst,
All determined to ride – each resolved to be first.
But to get a good start over-eager and jealous,
Two-thirds, at the least, of these very fine fellows
So crowded, and hustled, and jostled, and cross'd,
That they rode the wrong way, and at starting were lost.
    In spite of th' unpromising state of the weather,
A way broke the fox, and the hounds close together.
A burst up to Tilton so brilliantly ran,
Was scarce ever seen in the mem'ry of man.
What hounds guided scent, or which led the way,
Your bard – to their names quite a stranger – can't say;
Though their names had he known, he's free to confess,
His horse could not show him at such a death-pace.
Villiers, Cholmondeley, and Forester made such sharp play,
Not omitting Germaine, never seen till to-day:
Had you judged of these four by the trim of their pace,
At Bibury you'd thought they'd been riding a race.
But these hounds with a scent, how they dash and they fling,
To o'er-ride them is quite the impossible thing;
Disdaining to hang in the wood, through he raced,
And the open for Skeffington gallantly faced;
Where he headed and foil'd, his first point he forsook,
And merrily led them a dance o'er the brook.
Passed Galby and Norton, Great Stretton and Small,
Right onward still sweeping to old Stretton Hall;
Where two minutes check served to show at one ken
The extent of the havoc 'mongst horses and men.
Such sighing, such sobbing, such trotting, such walking;
Such reeling, such halting, of fences such baulking;
Such a smoke in the gaps, such comparing of notes;
Such quizzing each other's daub'd breeches and coats:
Here a man walk'd afoot who his horse had half kill'd,
There you met with a steed who his rider had spill'd:

In short, such dilemmas, such scrapes, such distress,
One fox ne'er occasion'd, the knowing confessed.
But, alas! the dilemmas had scarcely began,
On for Wigston and Ayleston too resolute he ran,
Where a few of the stoutest now slackened and panted,
And many were seen irretrievably planted.
The high road to Leicester the scoundrel then cross'd,
As Tell-tale and Beaufremont found to their cost;
And Villiers esteem'd it a serious bore,
That no longer could Shuttlecock fly as before;
Even Joe Miller's spirit of fun was so broke,
That he ceased to consider the run as a joke.
Then streaming away, o'er the river he splash'd, –
Germaine clost at hand, off the bank Melon dash'd.
Why the Dun prov'd so stout, in a scamper so wild?
Till now he had only been rode by a Child.
After him plunged Joe Miller with Musters so slim,
Who twice sank, and nearly paid dear for his whim,
Not reflecting that all water Melons must swim.
Well soused by their dip, on they brush'd o'er the bottom,
With liquor on board, enough to besot them,
But the villain no longer at all at a loss,
Stretch'd away like a d—l for Enderby Gorse:
Where meeting with many a brother and cousin,
Who knew how to dance a good hay in the furzen;
Jack Raven at length coming up on a hack,
That a farmer had lent him, whipp'd off the game pack.
Running sulky, old Loadstone the stream would not swim,
No longer sport proving a magnet to him,
   Of mistakes and mishaps, and what each man befell,
Would muse could with justice poetical tell!
Bob Grosvenor on Plush though determined to ride –
Lost at first a good start, and was soon set aside;
Though he charged hill and dale, not to lose this rare chase,
On velvet, Plush could not get a footing alas!
   To Tilton sail'd bravely Sir Wheeler O'Cuff,
Where neglecting to hurry, to keep a good luff,
To leeward he drifts – how provoking a case!
And was forced, though reluctant, to give up the chase.

As making his way to the pack's not his forte,
Sir Lawley, as usual, lost half of the sport.
But then the profess'd philosophical creed,
That 'all's for the best', – of Master Candide,
If not comfort Sir R., reconcile may at least;
For, with this supposition, his sport is the best.

Orby Hunter, who seem'd to be hunting his fate,
Got falls, to the tune of not fewer than eight.
Basan's king, upon Glimpse, sadly out of condition,
Pull'd up, to avoid of being tired the suspicion.
Og did right so to yield; for he very soon found,
His worst had he done, he'd have scarce glimpsed a hound.
Charles Meynell, who lay very well with the hounds,
Till of Stretton he nearly arrived at the bounds,
Now discovered that Waggoner's rather would creep,
Than exert his great prowess in taking a leap;
But when crossing the turnpike, he read 'Put on here',
'Twas enough to make any one bluster and swear.
The Waggoner feeling the familiar road,
Was resolved not to quit it; so stock still he stood.
Yet prithee, dear Charles! why rash vows make,
Thy leave of old Billesden to finally take?
Since from Legg's Hill, for instance, or perhaps Melton Spinney,
If they go a good pace, you are beat for a guinea!
'Tis money, they say, makes the mare to go kind;
The proverb has vouch'd for this time out of mind;
But though of this truth you admit the full force,
It may not hold so good of every horse.
If it did, Ellis Charles need not bustle and hug,
By name, not by nature, his favourite Slug.
Yet Slug as he his – the whole of the chase
Charles ne'er could have seen, had he gone at snail's pace.
Old Gradus, whose fretting and fuming at first
Disqualify strangely for such a tight burst,
Ere to Tilton arrived, ceased to pull and to crave,
And though freshish at Stretton, he stepp'd a *pas grave*!
Where, in turning him over a cramp kind of place,
He overturn'd George, whom he threw on his face;

And on foot to walk home it had sure been his fate,
But that soon he was caught, and tied up to a gate.

   Near Wigston occurr'd a most singular joke,
Captain Miller averr'd that his leg he had broke, –
And bemoan'd, in most piteous expressions, how hard,
By so cruel a fracture, to have his sport marr'd.
In quizzing his friends he felt little remorse,
To finesse the complete doing up of his horse.
Had he told a long story of losing a shoe,
Or of laming his horse, he very well knew
That the Leicester creed out this truism worms,
'Lost shoe and dead beat are synonymous terms'.
So a horse must here learn, whatever he does,
To die game – as at Tyburn – and 'die in his shoes'.
   Bethel Cox, and TOM SMITH, Messieurs Bennet and Hawke,
Their nags all contrived to reduce to a walk.
   Maynard's Lord, who detests competition and strife,
As well in the chase as in social life,
Than whom nobody harder has rode in his time,
But to crane here and there now thinks it no crime,
That he beat some crack riders most fairly may crow,
For he lived to the end, though he scarely knows how.

   With snaffle and martingale held in the rear,
His horse's mouth open half up to his ear;
Mr Wardle, who threaten'd great things over night,
Beyond Stretton was left in most terrible plight.
Too lean to be press'd, yet egg'd on by compulsion,
No wonder his nag tumbled into convulsion.
Ah! had he but lost a fore shoe, or fell lame,
'Twould only his sport have curtail'd, not his fame.
   Loraine, – than whom no one his game plays more safe,
Who the last to the first prefers seeing by half, –
What with nicking and keeping a constant look out,
Every turn of the scent surely turn'd to account.
The wonderful pluck of his horse surprised some,
But he knew they were making point blank for his home.

'Short home' to be brought we all should desire,
Could we manage the trick like the Enderby Squire.

Wild Shelley, at starting all ears and all eyes,
Who to get a good start all experiment tries,
Yet contrived it so ill, as to throw out poor Gypsy,
Whom he rattled along as if he'd been tipsy,
To catch them again; but, though famous for speed,
She never could touch them, much less get a lead,
So disharten'd, disjoined, and beat, home he swings,
Not much unlike a fiddler hung upon strings.

An H.H. who in Leicester had never been,
So of course such a tickler ne'er could have seen,
Just to see them throw off, on a raw horse mounted,
Who a hound had ne'er seen, nor a fence had confronted.
But they found in such style, and went off at such score,
That he could not resist the attempt to see more;
So with scrambling and dashing, and one rattling fall,
He saw all the fun, up to Stretton's white Hall.
There they anchor'd, in plight not a little distressing –
The horse being raw, he of course got a dressing.
  That wonderful mare of Vanneck's, who till now
By no chance ever tired, was taken in tow:
And what's worse, she gave Van such a devilish jog
In the face with her head, plunging out of a bog,
That with eye black as ink, or as Edward's famed Prince,
Half blind has been and quite deaf ever since.
But let that not mortify thee, Shacabac;
She was only blown, and came home a rare hack.

There Craven too stopp'd, whose misfortune, not fault,
His mare unaccountably vex'd with string-halt;
And when she had ceased thus spasmodic to prance,
Her mouth 'gan to twitch with St Vitus's dance.
  But how shall described be the fate of Rose Price,
Whose favourite white gelding convey'd him so nice
Through thick and through thin, that he vow'd and protested
No money should part them, as long as life lasted?

But the pace that effected which money could not:
For to part, and in death, was their no distant lot.
In a fatal blind ditch Carlo Khan's powers fail'd,
Where no lancet or laudanum either avail'd.
More care of a horse than he took, could take no man,
He'd more straw than would serve a lying-in woman.
Still he died! – yet just how, as nobody knows,
It may truly be said, he died 'under the Rose'.
At the death of poor Khan, Melton feels such remorse,
That they've christen'd that ditch, 'The Vale of White Horse'.

   Thus ended a chase, which for distance and speed
It's fellow we never have heard of or read.
Every species of ground ev'ry horse does not suit,
What's a good country hunter may here prove a brute;
And, unless for all sorts of strange fences prepared
A man and his horse are sure to be scared.
This variety gives constant life to the chase;
But as Forester says – 'Sir, what KILLS, is the PACE'.
In most other countries they boast of their breed,
For carrying at times, such a beautiful head;
But these hounds to carry a head cannot fail,
And constantly too, for, by George – there's no tail.
   Talk of horses and hounds, and the system of kennel,
Give me Leicestershire nags, and the hounds of OLD MEYNELL!

Robert Lowth
[an edited version (1850) of
the original 'Billesden Coplow' (1800)]

How They Brought the Good News
from Ghent to Aix

I sprang to the stirrup, and Joris, and he;
I galloped, Dirck galloped, we galloped all three;
'Good speed!' cried the watch, as the gate-bolts undrew;
'Speed!' echoed the wall to us galloping through;
Behind shut the postern, the lights sank to rest,
And into the midnight we galloped abreast.

Not a word to each other; we kept the great pace
Neck by neck, stride by stride, never changing our place;
I turned in my saddle and made its girths tight,
Then shortened each stirrup, and set the pique right,
Rebuckled the cheek-strap, chained slacker the bit,
Nor galloped less steadily Roland a whit.

'Twas moonset at starting; but while we drew near
Lokeren, the cocks crew and twilight dawned clear;
At Boom, a great yellow star came out to see;
At Düffeld, 'twas morning as plain as could be;
And from Mecheln church-steeple we heard the half-chime,
So Joris broke silence with, 'Yet there is time!'

At Aerschot, up leaped of a sudden the sun,
And against him the cattle stood black every one,
To stare thro' the mist at us galloping past,
And I saw my stout galloper Roland at last,
With resolute shoulders, each butting away,
The haze, as some bluff river headland its spray.

And his low head and crest, just one sharp ear bent back
For my voice, and the other pricked out on his track;
And one eye's black intelligence, – ever that glance
O'er its white edge at me, his own master, askance!
And the thick heavy spume-flakes which aye and anon
His fierce lips shook upwards in galloping on.

By Hasselt, Dirck groaned; and cried Joris, 'Stay spur!
Your Roos galloped bravely, the fault's not in her,
We'll remember at Aix' – for one heard the quick wheeze
Of her chest, saw the stretched neck and staggering knees,
And sunk tail, and horrible heave of the flank,
As down on her haunches she shuddered and sank.

So we were left galloping, Joris and I,
Past Looz and past Tongres, no cloud in the sky;
The broad sun above laughed a pitiless laugh,
'Neath our feet broke the brittle bright stubble like chaff;

Till over by Dalhem a dome-spire sprang white,
And 'Gallop,' gasped Joris, 'for Aix is in sight!'

'How they'll greet us!' – and all in a moment his roan
Rolled neck and croup over, lay dead as a stone;
And there was my Roland to bear the whole weight
Of the news which alone could save Aix from her fate,
With his nostrils like pits full of blood to the brim,
And with circles of red for his eye-sockets' rim.

Then I cast loose my buffcoat, each holster let fall,
Shook off both my jack-boots, let go belt and all,
Stood up in the stirrup, leaned, patted his ear,
Called my Roland his pet-name, my horse without peer;
Clapped my hands, laughed and sang, any noise, bad or
   good,
Till at length into Aix Roland galloped and stood.

And all I remember is, friends flocking round
As I sat with his head 'twixt my knees on the ground;
And no voice but was praising this Roland of mine,
As I poured down his throat our last measure of wine,
Which (the burgesses voted by common consent)
Was not more than his due who brought good news from
   Ghent.

                                        Robert Browning

The Leap of Roushan Beg

Mounted on Kyrat strong and fleet,
His chestnut steed with four white feet,
Roushan Beg, called Kurroglou,
Son of the road and bandit chief,
Seeking refuge and relief,
Up the mountain pathway flew.

Such was Kyrat's wondrous speed,
Never yet could any steed
Reach the dust-cloud in his course.
More than maiden, more than wife,
More than gold and next to life
Roushan the Robber loved his horse.

In the land that lies beyond
Erzeroum and Trebizond,
Garden-girt his fortress stood;
Plundered Khan, or caravan
Journeying north from Koordistan,
Gave him wealth and wine and food.

Seven hundred and fourscore
Men at arms his livery wore,
Did his bidding night and day;
Now, through regions all unknown,
He was wandering, lost, alone,
Seeking without guide his way.

Suddenly the pathway ends,
Sheer the precipice descends,
Loud the torrent roars unseen;
Thirty feet from side to side
Yawns the chasm; on air must ride
He who crosses this ravine.

Following close in his pursuit,
At the precipice's foot
Reyhan the Arab of Orfah
Halted with his hundred men,
Shouting upward from the glen,
'La Illàh illa Allàh!'

Gently Roushan Beg caressed
Kyrat's forehead, neck and breast;
Kissed him upon both his eyes,

Sang to him in his wild way,
As upon the topmost spray
Sings a bird before it flies.

'O my Kyrat, O my steed,
Round and slender as a reed,
Carry me this peril through!
Satin housings shall be thine,
Shoes of gold, O Kyrat mine,
O thou soul of Kurroglou!

Soft thy skin as silken skein,
Soft as woman's hair thy mane,
Tender are thine eyes and true;
All thy hoofs like ivory shine,
Polished bright; O life of mine,
Leap, and rescue Kurroglou!'

Kyrat, then, the strong and fleet,
Drew together his four white feet;
Paused a moment on the verge,
Measured with his eye the space,
And into the air's embrace
Leaped as leaps the ocean surge.

As the ocean surge o'er sand
Bears a swimmer safe to land,
Kyrat safe his rider bore;
Rattling down the deep abyss
Fragments of the precipice
Rolled like pebbles on the shore.

Roushan's tasselled cap of red
Trembled not upon his head,
Careless sat he and upright;
Neither hand nor bridle shook,
Nor his head he turned to look,
As he galloped out of sight.

Flash of harness in the air,
Seen a moment like the glare
Of a sword drawn from its sheath;
Thus the phantom horseman passed,
And the shadow that he cast
Leaped the cataract underneath.

Reyhan the Arab held his breath
While this vision of life and death
Passed above him. 'Allahu!'
Cried he, 'In all Koordistan
Lives there not so brave a man
As this Robber Kurroglou!'

Jack C. Christie

The Find

Yon sound's neither sheep-bell nor bark,
They're running – they're running, Go hark.
The sport may be lost by a moment's delay;
So whip up the puppies and scurry away.
Dash down through the clover by dingle and dell,
There's a gate at the bottom, I know it full well;
And they're running – they're running,
Go hark.

They're running – they're running, Go hark,
One fence and we're out of the park;
Sit down in your saddles and race at the brook,
Then smash at the bullfinch; no time for a look;
Leave cravens and skirters to dangle behind;
He's away for the moors in the teeth of the wind,
And they're running – they're running, Go hark,
Go hark.

They're running – they're running, Go hark.
Let them run on and run till it's dark.
Well with them we are, and well with them we'll be,
While there's wind in our horses and daylight to see;
Then shog along homeward, chat over the fight,
And hear in our dreams the sweet music all night,
Of – they're running – they're running, Go hark.

Charles Kingsley

The Sporting Parson

Think you the chase unfits him for the Church?
Attend him there, and you will find his tones
Such as become the place; nay, you may search
Through many counties from cathedral thrones,
And lofty stalls where solemn prebends perch,
To parish aisles which are not cells of drones,
But echo the sweet sound of psalm and prayer,
And you will hear no voice more earnest there.

H. S. Stokes

'The Clipper That Stands in the Stall at the Top'

Go strip him, lad! Now, sir, I think you'll declare
   Such a picture you never set eyes on before.
He was bought in at Tatt's for three hundred I swear,
   And he's worth all the money to look at, and more;
For the pick of the basket, the show of the shop,
Is the Clipper that stands in the stall at the top.

In the records of racing, I read their career,
   There were none of the sort but could gallop and stay,
At Newmarket his sire was the best of his year,

And the Yorkshiremen boast of his dam to this day;
But never a likelier foal did she drop,
Than this Clipper that stands in the stall at the top.

A head like a snake, and a skin like a mouse,
 An eye like a woman, bright, gentle, and brown,
With loins and a back that would carry a house,
 And quarters to lift him smack over a town!
What's a leap to the rest, is to him but a hop,
This Clipper that stands in the stall at the top.

When the country is deepest, I give you my word,
 'Tis a pride and a pleasure to put him along,
O'er fallow and pasture he sweeps like a bird,
 And there's nothing too wide, nor too high, nor too strong;
For the ploughs cannot choke, nor the fences can crop,
This Clipper that stands in the stall at the top.

Last Monday we ran for an hour in the Vale,
 Not a bullfinch was trimmed, of a gap not a sign!
All the ditches were double, each fence had a rail;
 And the farmers had locked every gate in the line,
So I gave him the office, and over them – Pop!
Went the Clipper that stands in the stall at the top.

I'd lead of them all when we came to the brook,
 A big one – a bumper – and up to your chin.
As he threw it behind him, I turned for a look,
 There were eight of us had it, and seven got in!
Then he shook his lean head when he heard them go plop!
This Clipper that stands in the stall at the top.

Ere we got to the finish, I counted but few,
 And never a coat without dirt, but my own.
To the good horse I rode, all the credit was due,
 When the others were tiring, he scarcely was blown;
For the best of the pace is unable to stop
The Clipper that stands in the stall at the top.

You may put on his clothes – every sportsman, they say,
   In his lifetime has one that outrivals the rest,
So the pearl of *my* casket I've shown you today,
   The gentlest, the gamest – the boldest, the best –
And I never will part, by a sale or a swop,
With my Clipper that stands in the stall at the top!

                          G. J. Whyte Melville

The Old Grey Mare

Oh! once I believed in a woman's kiss,
   I had faith in a flattering tongue;
For lip to lip was a promise of bliss,
   When lips were smooth and young.
But now the beard is grey on my cheek,
   And the top of my head gets bare;
So little I speak, like an Arab sheik,
   But put my trust in my mare.

For loving looks grow hard and cold,
   Fair heads are turned away,
When the fruit has been gathered – The tale been told,
   And the dog has had his day;
But chance and change 'tis folly to rue,
   And say I, the devil may care!
Nor grey nor blue are so bonny and true,
   As the bright brown eye of my mare.

With the fair wide heaven above outspread
   The fair wide plain to meet,
With the lark and his carol high over my head,
   And the bustling pack at my feet, –
I feel no fetter, I know no bounds,
   I am free as a bird in the air;
While the covert resounds, in a chorus of hounds,
   Right under the nose of my mare.

We are in for a gallop – away, away!
  I told them my beauty could fly;
And we'll lead them a dance ere they catch us to-day,
  For we mean it, my lass and I!
She skims the fences, she scours the plain,
  Like a creature winged, I swear,
With snort and strain, on the yielding rein;
  For I'm bound to humour my mare.

Away! away! they've been running to kill,
  With never a check from the find;
Away! away! we are close to them still,
  And the field are furlongs behind!
They can hardly deny they were out of the game,
  Lost half the 'fun of the fair',
Though the envious blame and the jealous exclaim,
  'How that old fool buckets his mare!'

Who-oop! they have him – they're round him; how
  They worry and tear when he's down!
'Twas a stout hill-fox when they found him, now
  'Tis a hundred tatters of brown!
And the riders arriving as best they can,
  In panting plight declare,
That 'First in the van was the old grey man,
  Who stands by his old grey mare'.

G. J. Whyte Melville

By Flood and Field

I remember the lowering wintry morn,
And the mist on the Cotswold hills,
When I once heard the blast of the huntsman's horn,
Not far from the seven rills. . . .

I remember how merry a start we got,
When the red fox broke from the gorse,

In a country so deep, with a scent so hot,
That the hound could outpace the horse;
I remember how few in the front rank showed,
How endless appeared the tail,
On the brown hill-side, where we cross'd the road
And headed towards the vale.
The dark brown steed on the left was there,
On the right was a dappled grey,
And between the pair on a chestnut mare
The duffer who writes this lay. . . .

The right-hand man to the left-hand said,
As down in the vale we went,
'Harden your heart like a millstone, Ned,
And set your face as flint;
Solid and tall is the rasping wall
That stretches before us yonder;
You must have it at speed or not at all,
'Twere better to halt than to ponder,
For the stream runs wide on the take-off side,
And washes the clay bank under;
Here goes for a pull, tis a madman's ride,
And a broken neck if you blunder.'

No word in reply his comrade spoke,
Nor waver'd nor once looked round,
But I saw him shorten his horse's stroke
As we splashed through the marshy ground;
I remember the laugh that all the while
On his quiet features played. . . .

I remember one thrust he gave to his hat,
And two to the flanks of the brown,
And still as a statue of old he sat,
And he shot to the front, hands down;
I remember the snort and the stag-like bound,
Of the steed six lengths to the fore,
And the laugh of the rider while, landing sound,
He turn'd in his saddle and glanced around;

I remember – But little more,
Save a bird's eye gleam of the dashing stream,
A jarring thud on the wall,
A shock and the blank of a nightmare's dream –
I was down with a crashing fall.

Adam Lindsay Gordon

How We Beat the Favourite

'Aye, squire,' said Stevens, 'they back him at evens;
The race is all over bar shouting, they say;
The Clown ought to beat her; Dick Neville is sweeter
Than ever – he swears he can win all the way.

'A gentleman rider – well, I'm an outsider,
But if he's a gent, who the mischief's a jock?
Your swells mostly blunder, Dick rides for the plunder,
He rides, too, like thunder – he sits like a rock.

'He calls "hunted fairly" a horse that has barely
Been stripped for a trot within sight of the hounds,
A horse that a Warwick beat Birdlime and Yorick,
And gave Abdelkader at Aintree nine pounds.

'They say we have no test to warrant a protest;
Dick rides for a lord and stands in with a steward;
The light of their faces they show him – his case is
Prejudged and his verdict already secured.

'But none can outlast her; and few travel faster,
She strides in her work clean away from The Drag;
You hold her and sit her, she couldn't be fitter,
Whenever you hit her she'll spring like a stag.

'And perhaps the green jacket, at odds though they back it,
May fall, or there's no knowing what may turn up.
The mare is quite ready, sit still and ride steady,
Keep cool; and I think you may just win the cup.'

Dark-brown with tan muzzle, just stripped for the tussle,
Stood Iseult, arching her neck to the curb,
A lean head and fiery, strong quarters and wiry,
A loin rather light, but a shoulder superb.

Some parting injunction, bestowed with great unction,
I tried to recall, but forgot like a dunce,
When Reginald Murray, full tilt on White Surrey,
Came down in a hurry, to start us at once.

'Keep back in the yellow! Come up on Othello!
Hold hard on the chestnut! Turn round on The Drag!
Keep back there on Spartan! Back, you, sir, in tartan!
So, steady there, easy,' and down went the flag.

We started, and Ker made strong running on Mermaid,
Through furrows that led to the first stake-and-bound;
The crack, half extended, looked bloodlike and splendid,
Held wide on the right where the headland was sound.

I pulled hard to baffle her rush with the snaffle,
Before her two-thirds of the field got away,
All through the wet pasture where floods of last year
Still loitered, they clotted my crimson with clay.

The fourth fence, a wattle, floored Monk and Bluebottle;
The Drag came to grief at the blackthorn and ditch,
The rails toppled over Redoubt and Red Rover,
The lane stopped Lycurgus and Leicestershire Witch.

She passed like an arrow Kildare and Cocksparrow,
And Mantrap and Mermaid refused the stone wall;
And Giles on the Grayling came down at the paling,
And I was left sailing in front of them all.

I took them a burster, nor eased her nor nursed her
Until the Black Bullfinch led into the plough;
Her flanks mud-bespattered, a weak rail she shattered –
My cap was knocked off by the hazel-tree bough.

Then crashed a low binder, and then close behind her
The sward to the strokes of the favourite shook;
His rush roused her mettle, yet ever so little
She shortened her stride as we raced at the brook.

She rose when I hit her, I saw the stream glitter,
A wide scarlet nostril flashed close to my knee;
Between sky and water The Clown came and caught her,
The space that he cleared was a caution to see.

And forcing the running, discarding all cunning,
A length to the front went the rider in green;
A long strip of stubble, and then the big double,
Two stiff flights of rails with a quickset between.

She raced at the rasper, I felt my knees grasp her,
I found my hands give to her strain on the bit;
She rose when The Clown did – our silks as we bounded
Brushed lightly, our stirrups clashed loud as we lit.

A rise steeply sloping, a fence with stone coping,
The last – we diverged round the base of the hill;
His path was the nearer, his leap was the clearer,
I flogged up the straight, and he led sitting still.

She came to his quarter, and on still I brought her,
And up to his girth, to his breastplate she drew;
A short prayer from Neville just reach'd me, 'The Devil,'
He muttered – locked level the hurdles we flew.

A hum of hoarse cheering, a dense crowd careering,
All sights seen obscurely, all shouts vaguely heard:
'The green wins!' 'The crimson!' The multitude swims on,
And figures are blended and features are blurred.

'The horse is her master!' 'The green forges past her!'
'The Clown will outlast her!' 'The Clown wins!' 'The Clown!'
The white railing races with all the white faces,
The chestnut outpaces, outstretches the brown.

On still past the gateway she strains in the straightway,
Still struggles The Clown by a short neck at most;
He swerves, the green scourges; the stand rocks and surges,
And flashes, and verges, and flits the white post.

Aye! so end the tussle – I knew the tan muzzle
Was first, though the ring-men were yelling 'Dead heat!'
A nose I could swear by, but Clarke said, 'The mare by
A short head.' And that's how the favourite was beat.

Adam Lindsay Gordon

The Stallion

Beside the dusty road he steps at ease;
    His great head bending to the stallion-bar,
Now lifted, now flung downward to his knees,
    Tossing the forelock from his forehead star;
Champing the while his heavy bit in pride
And flecking foam upon his flank and side.

Save for his roller striped in white and blue
    He bears no harness on his mighty back;
For all the splendour of his bone and thew
    He travels burdenless along the track,
Yet shall he give a hundred hefty sons
The strength to carry what his kingship shuns.

The pheasants rustling on the roadside bank,
    The pigeons swinging out in sudden chase,
Break not his broad shoes' rhythmic clank
    Nor set him swerving from his measured pace.
He knows the road and all its hidden fears,
His the staid calm that comes with conquering years.

He snatches at the clover as he goes,
  Clinking the bit-chain as he gathers toll;
He sniffs the speedwell, through wide nostrils blows,
  And but for chain and bar would kneel and roll.
His eyes alone reveal in smouldering fire
Pride held in leash, reined Lust and curbed Desire.

Will H. Ogilvie

The Stable Path

The last red rose on the arch has faded,
  The border has mourned for its last white
    flower;
The dahlias droop where the frost has raided,
  The grass is wet with an autumn shower;

Dull are the paths with their leaf-strewn gravel,
  Cold is the wind as it wanders by,
Still there's a path that a man can travel
  Happy at heart though the roses die.

The path to the stable! – Though summer be
    ended,
  Though down through the garden no bird be
    astir,
This path has new melodies tunefully blended –
  The flick of a whip with the clink of a spur!

So – on through the yew-trees where shadows strike
    chiller,
  Across the paved courtyard, at last to the stall
Where, pawing in eagerness, chained on the pillar
  Stands, champing his bit-bars, the Pearl of them
    All!

Will H. Ogilvie

Somewhere in England

Somewhere in England are horses out grazing,
Nibbling the grass by the side of a stream,
Pausing, perhaps, to stand tranquilly gazing
Over the fields, in a midsummer's dream.

Do their thoughts turn to some days of last season,
When these same fields they went sailing across?
Do they remember that bank with the trees on,
Where some one took an imperial toss?

Do they look back with delight or displeasure
To those stern efforts to live with the pack?
Would they prefer these enforced days of leisure
To the ride out and the long homeward hack?

They who have galloped the country so gamely,
Squandered their strength through the mud and the
    mire,
Can't be contented to settle down tamely
Here, with the sheep, and to all they aspire.

See how they cock their ears forward so keenly,
When, in the distance, a motor-horn sounds;
See them trot up to a gateway serenely,
Eagerly looking for huntsman and hounds.

Well do they know that this respite from labours
Is in the way of a much-needed rest;
Just a few weeks with the flocks as their neighbours,
Then, the brave battle to live with the best.

Idly they wander the broad pastures over,
Swishing long tails at the heat and the flies,
Brushing knee-deep through the vetch and the
    clover –
Kings of the grass-lands they hold as their prize.

Edric G. Roberts

Horses on the Camargue

In the grey wastes of dread,
The haunt of shattered gulls where nothing moves
But in a shroud of silence like the dead,
I heard a sudden harmony of hooves,
And, turning, saw afar
A hundred snowy horses unconfined,
The silver runaways of Neptune's car
Racing, spray-curled, like waves before the wind.
Sons of the Mistral, fleet
As him with those strong gusts they love to flee,
Who shod the flying thunders on their feet
And plumed them with the snortings of the sea;
Theirs is no earthly breed
Who only haunt the verges of the earth
And only on the sea's salt herbage feed –
Surely the great white breakers gave them birth.
For when for years a slave,
A horse of the Camargue, in alien lands,
Should catch some far-off fragrance of the wave
Carried far inland from his native sands,
Many have told the tale
Of how in fury, foaming at the rein,
He hurls his rider; and with lifted tail,
With coal red eyes, and cataracting mane,
Heading his course for home,
Though sixty leagues before him sweep,
Will never rest until he breathes the foam
And hears the native thunder of the deep.
But when the great gusts rise
And lash their anger on these arid coasts,
When the scared gulls career with mournful cries
And whirl across the waste like driven ghosts:
When hail and fire converge,
The only souls to which they strike no pain
Are the white-crested fillies of the surge
And the white horses of the windy plain.
Then in their strength and pride

The stallions of the wilderness rejoice;
They feel their Master's trident in their side,
And high and shrill they answer to his voice.
With white tails smoking free,
Long streaming manes, and arching necks, they show
Their kinship to their sisters of the sea –
And forward hurl their thunderbolts of snow.
Still out of hardship bred,
Spirits of power and beauty and delight
Have ever on such frugal pastures fed
And loved to course with tempests through the night.

Roy Campbell

Tarquin's Ride

Tarquinius does not wait
For his servant to wake,
Or his groom to saddle;
He snatches a bridle

And forcing the iron bit
Through the beast's bared white teeth,
Runs him out of the stable,
Mounts without curb or saddle

The stallion's short straight back,
And with heel and with knees
Clicks his tongue, flicks his whip,
Throws the brute into mad gallop.

Impetuous the powered flanks,
And reckless the rider;
Now the Prince and Arab steed
Bend as one for both are speed.

Hear the hoofs punish the earth!
Muscles strain, tendons taut,
Tail held high, head thrust back,
All's compact, nothing's slack.

See, the horse takes the bit
Between his teeth, now no rein
Can impede or stop him,
Yet the Prince still whips him.

Now who rides? Who's ridden?
Tarquinius, the stallion?
Or the beast, Tarquinius?
In both blood furious

With desire impetuous
Burns for its quietus;
With speed flame through sweat and dust
The arrow flies straight as lust.

But here they cannot cross.
Turn back, Tarquinius;
Do not tempt the Tiber:
Try to swim this river!

Stallion rears, hoofs paw the stars,
The Prince desires, so he dares!
Now stallion and rider
Wake the sleep of water

Disturbing its cool dream
With hot flank and shoulder.
Tarquinius knows no fear!
He is across! He's heading here!
Lucretia!

Ronald Duncan
from 'The Rape of Lucretia'

The Huntsman's Thanksgiving

The huntsman woke to the Christmas bells:
His back was stiff, but his mind was bright:
The presents surrounding the tree downstairs
Told, he knew, of that Christmas night

When God, to set the world aright,
Had given his infant son.

The huntsman knew that the Christmas bells
Were calling people to celebrate
A mystery that for a simple man
Was never easy to contemplate.
So the huntsman thought that today he should
Thank God for the things he understood:
His family, home, his fireside chair;
His terriers that followed him everywhere;
His health, his strength, his humour, and
His little garden and bit of land:
The winter landscape, the country sounds,
The cry of his own beloved hounds,
The view of a fox as it leaves the gorse,
Between his legs his most trusted horse:
The sight of a hundred scarlet coats,
The touch of his horn with its silver notes,
The use of his voice that God had given
To ring through the woods and echo to heaven –
　　　　　Harkaway forard! Harkaway on!
For these he'd thank God till his day was done,
As well for the birth of the infant son.

Dorian Williams

The Gent From London Way

A sportin' death! My word it was!
An' taken in a sportin' way.
Mind you, I wasn't there to see;
I only tell you what they say.

They found that day at Shillinglee
An' ran 'im down to Chillinghurst;
The fox was goin' straight and free
For ninety minutes at the burst.

SIR ARTHUR CONAN DOYLE

They 'ad a check at Ebernoe
An' made a cast across the Down,
Until they got a view 'ullo
An' chased 'im up to Kindford town.

From Kindford 'e run Brander way,
An' took 'em over 'alf the weald.
If you 'ave tried the Sussex clay,
You'll guess it weeded out the field.

Until at last I don't suppose
As 'alf a dozen at the most,
Came safe to where the grassland goes
Switchbackin' southwards to the coast.

Young Captain 'Eadley 'e was there,
An' Jim the whip an' Percy Day;
The Purcells an' Sir Charles Adair,
An' this 'ere gent from London way.

For 'e 'ad gone amazing fine,
Two 'undred pounds between 'is knees;
Eight stone 'e was, an' rode at nine,
As light an' limber as you please.

'E was a stranger to the 'unt,
There weren't a person as 'e knew there;
But 'e could ride, that London gent –
'E sat 'is mare as if 'e grew there.

They seed the 'ounds upon the scent,
But found a fence across their track,
An' 'ad to fly it, else it meant
A turnin' an' a 'arking back.

'E was the foremost at the fence,
And as 'is mare just cleared the rail
'E turned to them that rode be'ind,
For three was at 'is very tail.

' 'Ware 'oles!' says 'e, an' with the word,
Still sittin' easy on 'is mare,
Down, down 'e went, an' down an' down,
Into the quarry yawnin' there.

Some say it was two 'undred foot,
the bottom lay as black as ink.
I guess they 'ad some ugly dreams
Who reined their 'orses on the brink.

'E'd only time for that one cry;
' 'Ware 'oles!' says 'e, an' saves all three.
There may be better deaths to die,
But that one's good enough for me.

For, mind you, 'twas a sportin' end,
Upon a right good sportin' day;
They think a deal of 'im down 'ere,
That gent that came from London way.

Sir Arthur Conan Doyle

The Parade

Out at the gate to cheers and banter
They paced in pride to begin their canter.
Muscatel with the big white star,
The roan Red Ember, and Kubbadar,
Kubbadar with his teeth bared yellow
At the Dakkanese, his stable-fellow.
Then Forward-Ho, then a chestnut weed,
Skysail, slight, with a turn of speed.
The neat Gavotte under black and coral,
Then the Mutineer, Lord Leybourne's sorrel,
Natuna mincing, Syringa sidling,
Stormalong fighting to break his bridling,
Thunderbolt dancing with raw nerves quick,
Trying a savage at Bitter Dick.

The Ranger (winner three years before),
Now old, but ready for one try more;
Hadrian; Thankful; the stable-cronies,
Peterkinooks and Dear Adonis;
The flashing Rocket, with taking action;
Exception, backed by the Tencombe faction;
Old Sir Francis and young King Tony,
And gaunt Path Finder with great hips bony.

At this, Charles rode through the open gate
Into the course to try his fate.
He heard a roar from a moving crowd;
Right Royal kindled and cried aloud.
There was the course, stand, rail and pen,
Peopled with seventy thousand men;
Seventy thousand faces staring,
Carriages parked, a brass band blaring:
Over the stand the flags in billows
Bent their poles like the wands of willows.
All men there seemed trying to bawl,
Yet a few great voices topped them all:
'I back the Field! I back the Field!'

Right Royal trembled with pride and squealed.

Charles Cothill smiled with relief to find
This roaring crowd to his horse's mind.
He passed the stand where his lady stood,
His nerves were tense to the multitude;
His blood beat hard and his eyes grew dim
As he knew that some were cheering him.
Then, as he turned, at his pace's end
There came a roar as when floods descend.
All down the Straight from the crowded stands
Came the yells of voices and clap of hands,
For with the bright bay beauty that shone like flame
The favourite horse, Sir Lopez, came.
His beautiful hips and splendid shoulders

And power of stride moved all beholders,
Moved non-betters to try to bet
On that favourite horse not beaten yet.
With glory of power and speed he strode
To a sea of cheering that moved and flowed
And followed and heaped and burst like storm
From the joy of men in the perfect form.

John Masefield

Envoi

To the Horse

Where in this wide world can man find
nobility without pride, friendship without
envy or beauty without vanity? Here, where
grace is laced with muscle and strength by
gentleness confined.

He serves without servility, he has fought
without enmity. There is nothing so powerful,
nothing less violent; there is nothing so
quick, nothing more patient.

England's Past has been borne on his back.
All our history is his industry. We are
his heirs, he our inheritance.
Ladies and Gentlemen – The Horse!

Ronald Duncan

Specially written for the Horse of the Year Show 1954

Acknowledgements

Index of Authors

Acknowledgements

Acknowledgements and thanks are due to the following authors
and publishers for the use of copyright material:

To Blaisdell Publishing Company for 'The Origin of the Horse' and 'The Horse Culture
amongst the American Indians', reprinted by permission of the publisher from *The
Great Plains* by the late Walter Prescott Webb (Waltham, Massachusetts, Blaisdell
Publishing Company, a Division of Ginn and Company, 1931), pp. 56-7 and 60-8

To Claassen Verlag GmbH for 'Tarpán – A Mongolian Legend' translated by
Daphne Machin Goodall from *Tarpán* by José Antonio Benton (Hamburg, 1962)

To Nymphenburger Verlagsbandlung GmbH for 'The Legend of the Odd-Coloured
Horses' ('Die Legende von den gescheckten Pferden') translated by Daphne Machin
Goodall from *Hufschlag Erkland* by Ilse Mirus (München, 1960)

To *Sankt Georg Zeitschrift für Pferdesport und Pferdezucht* (Book 5, Düsseldorf, March 1,
1965) for 'Genghis Khan's Dispatch Service' ('Dschingis-Khan verfugte über einen
hervorragenden Nachrichten-Dienst!') by the late Kurt von Knobelsdorff, and
(Book 6, Düsseldorf, March 15, 1964) 'Kincsem – the Wonder Mare' (Kinscem
die Wunderstute') by Philipp Alles, both translated by Daphne Machin Goodall

To Miss Daphne Machin Goodall and J. M. Dent & Sons Ltd for 'Hanoverian
Times' from *The Foals of Epona* by A. A. Dent and Daphne Machin Goodall (Galley
Press, 1962)

To Hammond, Hammond & Co. Ltd for 'The Mustang – Wild and Free' from *The
Mustangs* by J. Frank Dobie (1954)

To Mrs Stella A. Walker and Country Life Ltd for 'Marengo and Copenhagen'
and 'Eclipse' from *Horses of Renown* (1954); also to Country Life Ltd for 'The
Horse's Nature and Mentality' from *Equitation* by Henry Wynmalen (1930); and for
'The Make-up of a Racehorse' by R. C. Kidd, 'The Legend of Skittles' by H. L.
Gibson, and 'Death of Fred Archer' by Audax, from *Ninety Years of Horse and Hound*
(1977); and to Country Life Ltd and Walter Parrish for 'The Pardubice' from
Cross Country Riding by Chris Collins (1977)

To Eyre & Spottiswoode (Publishers) Ltd for 'The Last Great Cavalry Charge'
from *The River War* by the late Sir Winston Churchill (Longmans, 1899; 3rd ed.,
Eyre & Spottiswoode, 1933); and to The Hon. Mrs Lambton and Eyre & Spottiswoode for 'Persimmon' and 'Tod Sloan' from *Men and Horses I Have Known* by the
late Hon. George Lambton (Thornton Butterworth, 1924)

To Hodder & Stoughton Ltd for 'Warrior's Great Adventure' from *My Horse
Warrior* by Lord Mottistone (1926); and for 'The Birth of a Legend' from *The
Woman Who Wrote Black Beauty* by Susan Chitty (1971)

To Mrs Barbara W. Tuchman and Hamish Hamilton Ltd, and the Macmillan Co.,
New York, for 'The English Gentleman and His Horse' from *The Proud Tower* (1966)

To Verlag der Arche Peter Schifferli for 'The Salutation' translated by Daphne
Machin Goodall from *Der Letzte Rittmeister* by Werner Bergengruen (Zürich, 1955)

To Mr Maurice Morgan and J. A. Allen & Co. Ltd for the translations 'Hints for
the Rider' and 'In the Saddle' from *On Horsemanship* (1962) by Xenophon (365 BC);
and to Mr R. S. Summerhays and J. A. Allen & Co. Ltd for 'Hard to Catch' from
The Problem Horse (1949); also to J. A. Allen & Co. Ltd for 'Kichizō' by Corporal

Ashihei Hino from *Horses in Japan* by Vivienne Kenrick (1964); and to Messrs R. M. Williams of South Australia and J. A. Allen & Co. Ltd for 'The Stallion' and 'The Stable Path' from *Saddle for a Throne* by Will H. Ogilvie (Constable, 1922)

To Mr Jack Leach and Victor Gollancz Ltd for 'Buying a Horse' from *Sods I Have Cut on the Turf* (1961)

To William Heinemann Ltd for 'The Psychology of the Horse' from *Hints on Horsemanship* by Lt-Col M. F. MacTaggart (1919); and 'Velvet Up' from *National Velvet* by Enid Bagnold (1935)

To Seeley, Service & Co. Ltd for 'A Horse in Training' from *Modern Horsemanship* by Colonel Paul Rodzianko (1930)

To Colonel W. E. Lyon for 'The Long and Short of It' from *The Horseman's Year 1948* (Collins)

To Hutchinson Publishing Group Ltd for 'Bitting and Collection' from *Breaking and Riding* by James Fillis (Hurst & Blackett, 1902); and for 'Steve Donoghue over Hurdles' from *Sport from Within* by Frank Atherton Brown (1952)

To William Collins Sons & Co. Ltd for 'Dressage v. Uhlanage' by John Paget, and 'An Amateur at Aintree – II by Christopher Collins, both from *The Horseman's Year 1966*; for 'European Horse Trials, Windsor – 1955' from *Three Days Running* by Sheila Willcox (1958); for 'The Race Round the Houses' from 'The Palio of Siena' by Raleigh Trevelyan (*The Horseman's Year 1955*); and for 'Horse Coping' from *Drawn from Life* by John Skeaping (1977)

To Kaye and Ward Ltd for 'Horse Faces' from *The Language of the Horse* by Michael Schafer (1974)

To Christy & Moore Ltd for 'The Pacing Mustang' from *Wild Animals I Have Known* by Ernest Thompson Seton (David Nutt, 1913)

To Putnam & Co. Ltd for 'Brown Jack' from *Brown Jack* by R. C. Lyle (1934)

To Brigadier 'Monkey' Blacker for 'An Amateur at Aintree' – I from *A Soldier in the Saddle* (Burke, 1957)

To Mr John Hislop and Michael Joseph Ltd for 'Mississippi' from *Far From a Gentleman* (1954); and to Mr Dick Francis and Michael Joseph Ltd for 'Devon Loch's National' from *The Sport of Queens* (1957) and 'Agony and Ecstasy' from *Nerve* (1957)

To Miss Pat Smythe for 'Jumping for Joy' from *Jump for Joy* (Cassell, 1952)

To Mr Clive Graham and MacGibbon & Kee Ltd for 'Hyperion' from *Great Horses of the Year 1954–1955* by Baron and Clive Graham (1954)

To the Editor of *Horse and Hound* for 'Wilhelmina Henrietta' by Loriner (March 20, 1965); and for 'Moments of Glory which turned to Nightmare' (April 6, 1963) and 'Mandarin Day' (June 23, 1962) both by Mr John Lawrence

To the Editor of *The Guardian* for 'Arkle for President' by Derek Malcolm (December 28, 1965)

To Angus & Robertson Ltd for 'The Master's Voice' from *Alwin Schockemöhle* by Alwin Schockemöhle (1977)

To Peter Davies Ltd for 'Leopard' from *Soldier On* by Col. Sir Michael Ansell (1973)

To David & Charles Ltd for 'So Long in the Saddle' from *Horse of the Year* by Dorian Williams (1976)

To Barrie & Rockliff for 'The First National' from *Grand National* by Con O'Leary (1945)

To Mr Henry Blyth and Weidenfeld & Nicholson Ltd for 'Snowstorm Derby' from *The Pocket Venus* (1966)

To David Higham Associates for 'Red Rum's Record' from *Red Rum* by Ivor Herbert (William Luscombe, 1974)

To The Bodley Head Ltd for 'Vintage Years' from *Squire Osbaldeston: His Autobiography 1856-62* (first published 1926); and for 'The Brogue' from *Beasts and Superbeasts* by 'Saki' (1914)

To Edgar Backus for 'The Badby Wood Run' by Frank Freeman from *Life of Frank Freeman* by Guy Paget (1948)

To Faber & Faber Ltd for 'The First Day' from *Memoirs of a Fox-Hunting Man* by Siegfried Sassoon (1930); and for 'Gillian's Ordeal' from *A Long Way to Go* by Marigold Armitage (1952)

To Mr Gordon Grand, jr and Miss Grand for 'Has Bonaparte Landed in England, Sir?' from *The Millbeck Hounds* by the late Gordon Grand (New York, Charles Scribner's Sons, 1932)

To John Farquharson Ltd for 'Phillippa's Foxhunt' from *Some Experiences of an Irish R.M.* by E. Œ. Somerville and M. Ross (Longmans, 1899)

To Harvester Press for 'Training in the Hunting Field' from *Peculiar Privilege* by David Itzkowitz (1977)

To The Cresset Press for 'Malek Adel' from 'The End of Chertopkhanov' (1852) by Ivan Turgenev from *A Sportsman's Notebook* translated by Charles and Natasha Hepburn (Cresset Library, 1950)

To Mrs George Bambridge and Macmillan & Co. Ltd, and the Macmillan Co. of Canada Ltd, for 'The Maltese Cat' from *The Day's Work* by Rudyard Kipling (1898)

To Laurence Pollinger Ltd and the Estate of the late Mrs Frieda Lawrence for 'The Rocking-Horse Winner' from *The Complete Short Stories of D. H. Lawrence* (Heinemann, 1955); and for the extract from 'St Mawr' from *The Short Novels of D. H. Lawrence* (Heinemann, 1956)

To Miss Daphne du Maurier for 'The Horse Fair' from *Jamaica Inn* (Gollancz, 1936)

To Mr Damon Runyon, jr and J. B. Lippincott Co. for 'Old Em's Kentucky Home' from *Runyon à la Carte* by the late Damon Runyon (Constable, 1946)

To Mr H. E. Bates for 'Sugar for the Horse' from *Sugar for the Horse* (Michael Joseph, 1957)

To Barrie & Jenkins Ltd for 'Lebedyan' from *A Sportsman's Notebook* by Ivan Turgenev (1950)

To Jonathan Cape for 'War Cloud' from *The First Forty-Nine Stories* by Ernest Hemingway (1939)

'Hast thou given the horse strength?' from The Book of Job (AV, Job 39, vv. 19-25) is reprinted by permission (H.M. Printers)

To Major Edric G. Roberts and Constable & Co. Ltd for verses from 'Somewhere in England' (1929)

To the Estate of the late Roy Campbell for 'Horses on the Camargue' from *Adamastor* (Faber, 1930)

To Mr Ronald Duncan for 'Tarquin's Ride' from *The Rape of Lucretia* (Faber, 1953); and for 'Envoi – To the Horse' (1954)

To John Murray Ltd for 'The Gent from London Way' by Sir Arthur Conan Doyle from *Hunting Lays and Hunting Ways* (1924)

To the Society of Authors for 'The Parade' by John Masefield from *Right Royal* (1920)

Finally the Editor would like to thank his own publishers Hodder & Stoughton Ltd for 'Olympic Gold Medal' from *Clear Round* (1957); and for 'Will Pope's Last Hunt' from *Pendley and a Pack of Hounds* (1959)

Index of Authors